T0380794

Pro Spring Boot 3 with Kotlin

In-Depth Guide to Best Practices for Cloud-Native and Microservices Development

Third Edition

Peter Späth
Felipe Gutierrez

Apress®

Pro Spring Boot 3 with Kotlin: In-Depth Guide to Best Practices for Cloud-Native and Microservices Development, Third Edition

Peter Späth
Leipzig, Sachsen, Germany

Felipe Gutierrez
Albuquerque, NM, USA

ISBN-13 (pbk): 979-8-8688-1130-2
https://doi.org/10.1007/979-8-8688-1131-9

ISBN-13 (electronic): 979-8-8688-1131-9

Managing Director, Apress Media LLC: Welmoed Spahr
Acquisitions Editor: Melissa Duffy
Desk Editor: Laura Berendson
Editorial Project Manager: Gryffin Winkler
Copy Editor: Kezia Endsley

Cover designed by eStudioCalamar

Cover image designed by Image by esiuL from Pixabay

Distributed to the book trade worldwide by Springer Science+Business Media New York, 1 New York Plaza, Suite 4600, New York, NY 10004-1562, USA. Phone 1-800-SPRINGER, fax (201) 348-4505, e-mail orders-ny@springer-sbm.com, or visit www.springeronline.com. Apress Media, LLC is a California LLC and the sole member (owner) is Springer Science + Business Media Finance Inc (SSBM Finance Inc). SSBM Finance Inc is a **Delaware** corporation.

For information on translations, please e-mail booktranslations@springernature.com; for reprint, paperback, or audio rights, please e-mail bookpermissions@springernature.com.

Apress titles may be purchased in bulk for academic, corporate, or promotional use. eBook versions and licenses are also available for most titles. For more information, reference our Print and eBook Bulk Sales web page at http://www.apress.com/bulk-sales.

Any source code or other supplementary material referenced by the author in this book is available to readers on GitHub. For more detailed information, please visit https://www.apress.com/gp/services/source-code.

If disposing of this product, please recycle the paper

To Alina

Table of Contents

About the Authors

Felipe Gutierrez is a senior platform architect at VMware, the creators of Spring Boot and Spring Framework, where he serves as a senior consultant with the Spring team. He has more than 25 years of IT experience, during which time he developed programs for companies in multiple vertical industries such as government, retail, healthcare, education, and banking. He also develops in Kotlin, Groovy, RabbitMQ, and other technologies. He has also consulted for companies such as Nokia, Apple, Redbox, and Qualcomm, among others. He received his bachelor's and master's degrees in computer science from Instituto Tecnologico y de Estudios Superiores de Monterrey, Campus Ciudad de Mexico.

Peter Späth graduated in 2002 as a physicist and soon afterward became an IT consultant, mainly for Java-related projects. In 2016, he decided to concentrate on writing books on various aspects, but with the main focus on software development. With two books about graphics and sound processing, three books on Android app development, and several books on Java, Kotlin, Jakarta EE, and Spring development, Peter continues his effort in writing software development-related literature.

About the Technical Reviewer

 **Massimo Nardone** has more than 27 years of experience in security, web/mobile development, and cloud and IT architecture. His true IT passions are security and Android. He has been programming and teaching others how to program with Android, Perl, PHP, Java, VB, Python, C/C++, and MySQL for more than 27 years. He holds a master's in computing science from the University of Salerno, Italy. He has worked as a chief information security officer (CISO), software engineer, chief security architect, security executive, OT/IoT/IIoT security leader, and architect for many years.

Introduction

This book is a transcription to the Kotlin language. Genuine Kotlin programming techniques have been used extensively and the code has been tested thoroughly. This way, even though the Kotlin constructs are not explained in great detail, you learn about Kotlin's expressiveness, learn how to use Kotlin for Spring Boot development, and improve your Kotlin and Spring programming skills, all at the same time.

PART I

Introduction

CHAPTER 1

Spring Boot Quick Start

Felipe Gutierrez[a*]

ᵃ 4109 Rillcrest Grove Way Fuquay Varina, NC 27526-3562, Albuquerque, NM, USA

Project: Users App

The project that you are going to learn how to build, named Users App, will expose a simple CRUD (create, read, update, and delete) API over the web. Here are the requirements for this Users App project:

- A user must have a name and an email address.

- A map is used to hold the information, using the email address as the key.

- It exposes an API that uses CRUD over the web.

Initial Setup

To start with Spring Boot, you need to have the following installed:

- *Java:* You can install, for example, OpenJDK (`https://jdk.java.net/archive/`) or Eclipse Temurin (`https://adoptium.net/temurin/releases/`).

  - If you are UNIX user, you can use SDKMAN! (`https://sdkman.io/`), which works for Linux and macOS.

  - If you are Windows user, you can use Chocolatey (`https://choco-latey.org/`).

© Peter Späth, Felipe Gutierrez 2025
P. Späth and F. Gutierrez, *Pro Spring Boot 3 with Kotlin*, https://doi.org/10.1007/979-8-8688-1131-9_1

- *An integrated development environment (IDE):* As a suggestion, you can use Microsoft Visual Studio Code (https://code.visualstudio.com/download), the Community edition of IntelliJ IDEA from JetBrains (https://www.jetbrains.com/idea/download/), or Spring Tools (https://spring.io/tools).

- *The curl or http command:* For http, you can install HTTPie (https://httpie.io/). Both commands are demonstrated later in this chapter.

- *The jq command:* You can install it using the instructions at https://stedolan.github.io/jq/.

Start @ start.spring.io

start.spring.io is the official web-based tool for generating Spring Boot projects. It provides a user-friendly interface to quickly set up a new Spring Boot project with your desired dependencies and configurations. Here are some of its key features and benefits:

- *Streamlined project creation:* Eliminates the need to manually configure a project structure and dependencies.

- *Curated dependencies:* Offers a selection of common libraries and frameworks to easily add to your project.

- *Customization:* Allows you to choose the build tool (Maven or Gradle), language (Java, Kotlin, or Groovy), and Spring Boot version.

- *Downloadable project:* Generates a ZIP file containing the configured project ready to be imported into your IDE.

- *Spring Boot integration:* Leverages Spring Boot's auto-configuration and convention-over-configuration principles for rapid development.

Open a browser and go to https://start.spring.io. You should see the Spring Initializr home page, as shown in Figure 1-1.

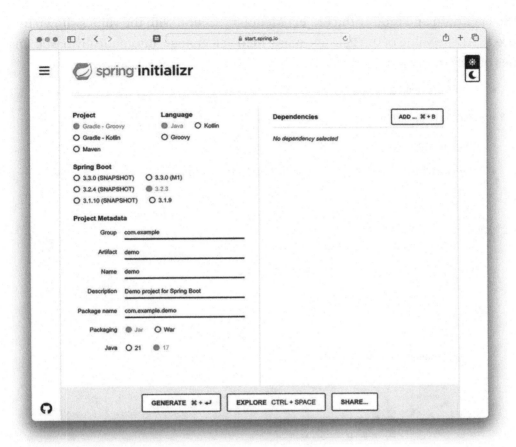

Figure 1-1. *Spring Initializr home page*

The home page includes radio buttons to select Project, Language, and Spring Boot. Project metadata includes group, artifact, name, description, package name, packaging, and Java version. Three buttons (Generate, Explore, and Share) are provided at the bottom.

Notice that by default the Spring Initializr uses Gradle—Groovy as the project builder, Java as the programming language, JAR for packaging, Java 17, and Spring Boot 3 (at the time of this writing, Spring Boot 3.2.3).

Select Kotlin and modify the Project Metadata section with the values shown in Figure 1-2. (The value of the Package name field will change automatically based on the values of the Group and Artifact fields.)

- Group: `com.apress`

- Artifact: `users`

- Name: `users`

- Dependencies: Spring Web (click Add to find it)

Figure 1-2. *Spring Initializr: Users App project*

Figure 1-2 shows all the necessary information to create the Users App project. Click the Generate button to archive the project and save it to your computer. Then, unzip it and import it to your favorite IDE. (I am using IntelliJ IDEA Community Edition, so that is what you see in the figures in this book.)

Note   You can download or fork the source code from the Apress GitHub site.

When you open the project in your IDE, you should see the project structure shown in Figure 1-3.

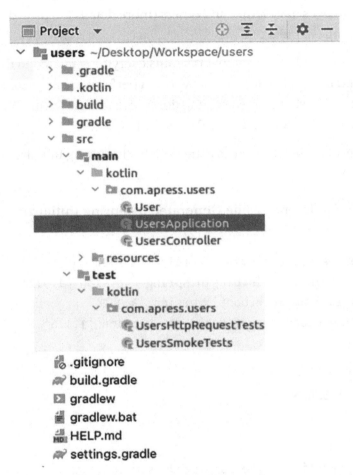

Figure 1-3. *Users App project structure*

Figure 1-3 shows the following three folders in the project structure:

- src/main/kotlin: This folder contains all the source code. By default, the Spring Initializr creates the UsersApplication.kt file. This has the main entry point where the application will start.

- `src/main/resources`: This folder contains one of the most important files, `application.properties`, which is used to modify configuration. We will use this file repeatedly throughout the book; for now, just note that it's located in this folder. This folder also contains subfolders that normally hold assets such as HTML pages, images, JavaScript, and others (more details are provided in upcoming chapters).

- `src/test/kotlin`: This folder contains everything related to the unit and integration testing that you can perform to ensure that your project does what you expect it to do. By default, the Spring Initializr creates the `UsersApplicationTests.kt` file.

Listing 1-1 shows some of the files generated by the Spring Initializr, starting with the `build.gradle` file.

Listing 1-1. The build.gradle File Generated by Spring Initializr

```
plugins {
    id 'org.jetbrains.kotlin.jvm' version '1.9.24'
    id 'org.jetbrains.kotlin.plugin.spring' version '1.9.24'
    id 'org.springframework.boot' version '3.3.2'
    id 'io.spring.dependency-management' version '1.1.6'
}

group = 'com.apress'
version = '0.0.1-SNAPSHOT'

java {
    toolchain {
        languageVersion = JavaLanguageVersion.of(17)
    }
}

repositories {
    mavenCentral()
}
```

```
dependencies {
    implementation 'org.springframework.boot:spring-boot-starter'
    implementation 'org.jetbrains.kotlin:kotlin-reflect'
    testImplementation 'org.springframework.boot:spring-boot-starter-test'
    testImplementation 'org.jetbrains.kotlin:kotlin-test-junit5'
    testRuntimeOnly 'org.junit.platform:junit-platform-launcher'
}

kotlin {
    compilerOptions {
        freeCompilerArgs.addAll '-Xjsr305=strict'
    }
}

tasks.named('test') {
    useJUnitPlatform()
}
```

The build.gradle file is important because it contains all the details about your project, some attributes, and the dependencies that will be used to generate everything you need, from compiling the code to creating an executable JAR for the Java virtual machine (JVM). This file first declares the plugins you are going to use and the dependencies repository (in this case, Maven Central, the milestone, and snapshot). It then declares the dependencies (in this case, spring-boot-starter-web and spring-boot-starter-test; one for the web application and one for the unit/integration tests, respectively). Don't worry about these dependencies for now; we discuss them in detail in the following chapters.

With the build.gradle file also come a few wrappers (gradlew for UNIX users and gradlew.bat for Windows users). These wrappers will bring the Gradle engine without any prior installation of such builder. You will be using these files when you run the application.

Before you continue to learn about the files generated by the Spring Initializr, modify the build.gradle file, as shown in Listing 1-2. This is described in more detail next.

Listing 1-2. Modified build.gradle File

```
//...
dependencies {
    // ... previous dependencies
    implementation 'org.webjars:bootstrap:5.2.3'
}
//...
test {
    testLogging {
        events "passed", "skipped", "failed"
        showExceptions true
        exceptionFormat "full"
        showCauses true
        showStackTraces true
        showStandardStreams = false
    }
}
```

First, add the bootstrap dependency. It will help you create a nice style for a home page; we are going to use bootstrap (https://getbootstrap.com/). At the time of this writing, the version is 5.2.3, but you should choose the latest version in the maven repository. Then, add the test section, which tells Gradle to show the keywords passed, skipped, or failed when running a test. If you set showStandardStreams to true, you can use System.out.println statements in the tests.

Next, open the UsersApplication.kt file generated by the Spring Initializr and view its contents, shown in Listing 1-3.

Listing 1-3. src/main/kotlin/com/apress/users/UsersApplication.kt

```
package com.apress.users

import org.springframework.boot.autoconfigure.SpringBootApplication
import org.springframework.boot.runApplication

@SpringBootApplication
class UsersApplication
```

```kotlin
fun main(args: Array<String>) {
    runApplication<DemoApplication>(*args)
}
```

UsersApplication.kt is the main file for this project because it contains the main(args: Array<String>) method that is necessary to run any Kotlin application. As shown in Listing 1-3, it uses the @SpringBootApplication annotation.

Next, add a new class that will hold the user information. Create the User.kt file in the src/main/kotlin/com/apress/users folder with the content shown in Listing 1-4.

Listing 1-4. src/main/kotlin/com/apress/users/User.kt

```kotlin
package com.apress.users

data class User(var email: String? = null, var name: String? = null)
```

As Listing 1-4 shows, the User.kt class has two fields/properties—Email and Name.

Next, add another class that will expose the API and manage the CRUD for your users. In the same folder, src/main/kotlin/com/apress/users, create the UsersController.kt file with the content shown in Listing 1-5.

Listing 1-5. src/main/kotlin/com/apress/users/UsersController.kt

```kotlin
package com.apress.users

import org.springframework.web.bind.annotation.*

@RestController
@RequestMapping("/users")
class UsersController {
    private val users = mutableMapOf(
        "ximena@email.com" to User("ximena@email.com", "Ximena"),
        "norma@email.com" to User("norma@email.com", "Norma")
    )

    @get:GetMapping
    val all: Collection<User>
        get() = users.values

    @GetMapping("/{email}")
    fun findUserByEmail(@PathVariable email: String): User? {
```

```kotlin
        return users[email]
    }

    @PostMapping
    fun save(@RequestBody user: User): User {
        users[user.email!!] = user
        return user
    }

    @DeleteMapping("/{email}")
    fun deleteByEmail(@PathVariable email: String) {
        users.remove(email)
    }
}
```

The UsersController.kt class will expose the API. This class is marked with the @RestController annotation, which tells Spring Boot that this class is responsible for accepting any incoming requests. It's also marked with @RequestMapping("/users"), which tells Spring Boot that it will have a /users endpoint for every request made with any of the HTTP methods (GET, POST, PUT, DELETE, PATCH, etc.). This class also has some methods that are marked with special annotations (such as @GetMapping, @PostMapping, and @DeleteMapping), which tell Spring Boot that those methods will be executed once a request is made.

This class also has a map that is being initialized with some users. That covers one of the requirements.

Consider the following endpoints:

- /users: This will handle the read part of CRUD. The access property that will be exposed is get. This accessor is executed when an HTTP GET request is made. This endpoint is also used when an HTTP POST request is made (can be taken as the create and update parts of CRUD). The save(@RequestBody user:User) method will be executed and it will add or update a user based on the user's email address. Note that the argument of this method has an annotation, @RequestBody, meaning that for every POST request, Spring Boot will convert the data sent over into the class type, in this case the User class. The data sent is in JSON format by default, unless you modify the HTTP header Content-Type and inform Spring Boot about that change.

- /users/{email}: This will also be your read, but it will look for an email in the map. The method that's executed is findUserByEmail (@PathVariable email:String), which will return the user found. This method also is called when an HTTP GET request is made. This endpoint is also used by the deleteByEmail(@PathVariable email:String) method when an HTTP DELETE request is made. This will remove the user from the map. This method contains the @PathVariable annotation, which will translate the path that matches the name, in this case {email} match, with the String email parameter. This means that when there is a request—either the GET or DELETE such as /users/ximena@email.com for example—it will execute any of these methods (depending on the HTTP method request) and it will assign ximena@email.com to the email variable.

Next, let's create a landing page that will open when you run this project. For this purpose, add an index.html file to the src/main/resources/static folder with the content shown in Listing 1-6.

Listing 1-6. The src/main/resources/static/index.html File

```
<!DOCTYPE html>
<html lang="en">
<head>
    <meta charset="UTF-8">
    <link rel="stylesheet" type="text/css"
        href="webjars/bootstrap/5.2.3/css/bootstrap.min.css">
    <title>Welcome - Users App</title>
</head>
<body class="d-flex h-100 text-center">
<div class="cover-container d-flex w-100 h-100 p-3 mx-auto flex-column">
    <header class="mb-auto">
        <div>
            <h3 class="float-md-start mb-0">Users</h3>
        </div>
    </header>
    <main class="px-3">
        <h1>Simple Users Rest Application</h1>
```

```
        <p class="lead">This is a simple Users app where you can access any
        information from a user</p>
        <p class="lead">
            <a href="/users">Get All Users</a>
        </p>
    </main>
    <footer class="mt-auto text-black-50">
        <p>Powered by Spring Boot 3</p>
    </footer>
</div>
</body>
</html>
```

As you can see, we are using bootstrap (https://getbootstrap.com/) to style this home page. We are passing the path for the CSS that begins with webjars. There is a convention to this, but we are going to talk about it later. For now, you can take this as a recipe. If you want to use any webjars tech, such as jQuery or any other, you must provide the path starting with webjars.

You now have everything in place for the Users App project that you need to run a web API using Spring Boot. The next section looks at how to test the application to make sure that it performs as expected.

Testing the Users App Project

Let's test the code using the testing framework that Spring Boot provides. In the src/test/kotlin folder structure, open the UserApplicationTests.kt file. Listing 1-7 shows its content.

Listing 1-7. The src/test/kotlin/com/apress/users/UsersApplicationTests.kt File

```
package com.apress.users
import org.junit.jupiter.api.Test
import org.springframework.boot.test.context.SpringBootTest

@SpringBootTest
class UsersApplicationTests {
```

```
@Test
fun contextLoads() {
}
}
```

Note in Listing 1-7 that UserApplicationTests.kt uses the @SpringBootTest annotation, which prepares your environment for executing any unit or integration testing. For every test that you want to conduct, you only need to use the @Test annotation for the method that you want to use to execute that test.

Next, replace all the code in UserApplicationTests.kt with the content shown in Listing 1-8.

Listing 1-8. The Modified src/test/kotlin/com/apress/users/ UsersApplicationTests.kt File

```
package com.apress.users

import org.assertj.core.api.Assertions
import org.junit.jupiter.api.Test
import org.springframework.beans.factory.annotation.Autowired
import org.springframework.beans.factory.annotation.Value
import org.springframework.boot.test.context.SpringBootTest
import org.springframework.boot.test.web.client.TestRestTemplate

@SpringBootTest(webEnvironment = SpringBootTest.WebEnvironment.RANDOM_PORT)
class UsersApplicationTests {
    @Value("\${local.server.port}")
    private val port = 0
    private val BASE_URL = "http://localhost:"
    private val USERS_PATH = "/users"

    @Autowired
    private val restTemplate: TestRestTemplate? = null
    @Test
    @Throws(Exception::class)
    fun indexPageShouldReturnHeaderOneContent() {
        Assertions.assertThat(
            restTemplate!!.getForObject(
```

```kotlin
                BASE_URL + port,
                String::class.java
            )
        ).contains("Simple Users Rest Application")
    }

    @Test
    @Throws(Exception::class)
    fun usersEndPointShouldReturnCollectionWithTwoUsers() {
        val response: Collection<User> =
            restTemplate!!.getForObject(BASE_URL + port + USERS_PATH,
                Collection::class.java) as Collection<User>
        Assertions.assertThat(response.size).isEqualTo(2)
    }

    @Test
    @Throws(Exception::class)
    fun userEndPointPostNewUserShouldReturnUser() {
        val user = User("dummy@email.com", "Dummy")
        val response = restTemplate!!.postForObject(BASE_URL + port +
        USERS_PATH,
                    user, User::class.java)
        Assertions.assertThat(response).isNotNull()
        Assertions.assertThat(response.email).isEqualTo(user.email)
        val users: Collection<User> =
            restTemplate.getForObject(BASE_URL + port + USERS_PATH,
                    Collection::class.java) as Collection<User>
        Assertions.assertThat(users.size).isGreaterThanOrEqualTo(2)
    }

    @Test
    @Throws(Exception::class)
    fun userEndPointDeleteUserShouldReturnVoid() {
        restTemplate!!.delete("$BASE_URL$port$USERS_PATH/norma@email.com")
        val users: Collection<User> =
            restTemplate.getForObject(BASE_URL + port + USERS_PATH,
                    Collection::class.java) as Collection<User>
```

```kotlin
        Assertions.assertThat(users.size).isLessThanOrEqualTo(2)
    }

    @Test
    @Throws(Exception::class)
    fun userEndPointFindUserShouldReturnUser() {
        val user = restTemplate!!.getForObject(
                "$BASE_URL$port$USERS_PATH/ximena@email.com",
                User::class.java)
        Assertions.assertThat(user).isNotNull()
        Assertions.assertThat(user.email).isEqualTo("ximena@email.com")
    }
}
```

The following list explains the code in the revised UsersApplicationTest.kt file:

- @SpringBootTest: To create a test for Spring Boot, you need to annotate your class with this annotation. This annotation accepts multiple parameters, one of which is the webEnvironment, which randomly assigns a port to Tomcat when the test runs. Clearly you can see that this is an integration test.

- @Value: This annotation injects the port number into the port variable by using the local.server.port property that is set by the webEnvironment parameter declaration from the @SpringBootTest annotation. This enables you to avoid any port collision.

- @Autowired: This annotation is also used to inject a new instance of a class, in this case the TestRestTemplate type class, which allows you to execute any remote request to an external web API. In this case, we are using it in every test method.

- @Test: This annotation marks a method to be a test case where you can do any assertions—from doing a request for getting a list of users, to posting or deleting user data. Spring Boot comes with some libraries to conduct unit and integration tests and to execute assertions. In this case, we are using the AssertJ library for every test method.

- `TestRestTemplate`: This class provides several methods that are convenient for executing any HTTP method requests. These methods include `.getForObject` or `.postForObject`. They wire everything up where behind the scenes and do the right conversion type to get the objects you need, in this case the User instance.

Chapter 8 is dedicated to unit and integration testing. It discusses every detail and describes what else you can do with the Spring Boot Testing Framework.

Running the UserApplicationTests Class

Now you can run the tests. If you are using an IDE, you should be able to right-click the `UsersApplicationTests.kt` file and click the Run option. If you are running IntelliJ IDEA, you should see a window similar to the one shown in Figure 1-4.

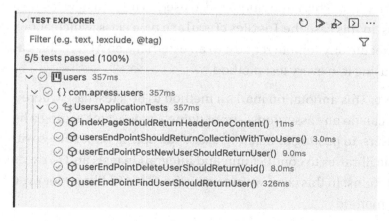

Figure 1-4. IntelliJ IDEA tests

If you have imported the project into Visual Studio Code (a.k.a. VS Code), you can run the test in the Test Explorer, which will produce a result similar to that shown in Figure 1-5.

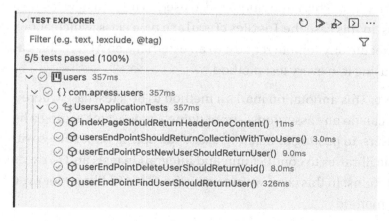

Figure 1-5. Microsoft VS Code Test Explorer

You can also execute the tests from the command line using the `gradlew` wrapper and expect the same results:

```
./gradlew test
UsersApplicationTests > userEndPointFindUserShouldReturnUser() PASSED
UsersApplicationTests > userEndPointDeleteUserShouldReturnVoid() PASSED
UsersApplicationTests > indexPageShouldReturnHeaderOneContent() PASSED
UsersApplicationTests > userEndPointPostNewUserShouldReturnUser() PASSED
UsersApplicationTests >
usersEndPointShouldReturnCollectionWithTwoUsers() PASSED
BUILD SUCCESSFUL in 3s
4 actionable tasks: 1 executed, 3 up-to-date
```

Now that your tests have passed, it's time to run the Users App project.

Running the Users App Project

To run the Users App project, you can use the IDE to which you imported the project by right-clicking the `UsersApplication.kt` file. Alternatively, you can run the project from the command line by using the following command:

```
./gradlew bootRun
> Task :bootRun

  .   ____          _            __ _ _
 /\\ / ___'_ __ _ _(_)_ __  __ _ \ \ \ \
( ( )\___ | '_ | '_| | '_ \/ _` | \ \ \ \
 \\/  ___)| |_)| | | | | || (_| |  ) ) ) )
  '  |____| .__|_| |_|_| |_\__, | / / / /
 =========|_|==============|___/=/_/_/_/
 :: Spring Boot ::        (v3.1.0)
INFO 66966 - [main] com.apress.users.UsersApplication        : Starting
UsersApplication using Java 17.0.5 ....
INFO 66966 - [main] com.apress.users.UsersApplication        : No active
profile set, falling back to 1 default profile: "default"
INFO 66966 - [main] o.s.b.w.embedded.tomcat.TomcatWebServer  : Tomcat
initialized with port(s): 8080 (http)
```

```
INFO 66966 - [main] o.a.c.core.StandardService              : Starting
service [Tomcat]
INFO 66966 - [main] o.a.c.core.StandardEngine               : Starting
Servlet engine: [Apache Tomcat/10.1.7]
INFO 66966 - [main] o.a.c.c.C.[Tomcat].[localhost].      : Initializing
Spring embedded WebApplicationContext
INFO 66966 - [main] w.s.c.ServletWebServerApplicationContext : Root
WebApplicationContext: initialization completed in 390 ms
INFO 66966 - [main] o.s.b.a.w.s.WelcomePageHandlerMapping    : Adding
welcome page: class path resource [static/index.html]
INFO 66966 - [main] o.s.b.w.embedded.tomcat.TomcatWebServer  : Tomcat
started on port(s): 8080 (http) with context path ''
INFO 66966 - [main] com.apress.users.UsersApplication       : Started
UsersApplication in 0.706 seconds (process running for 0.856)
```

Now open a browser and go to localhost:8080 to see the home page, as shown in Figure 1-6.

Figure 1-6. *The http://localhost:8080: home page*

Click the Get All Users link to see the response of the /users endpoint, as shown in Figure 1-7.

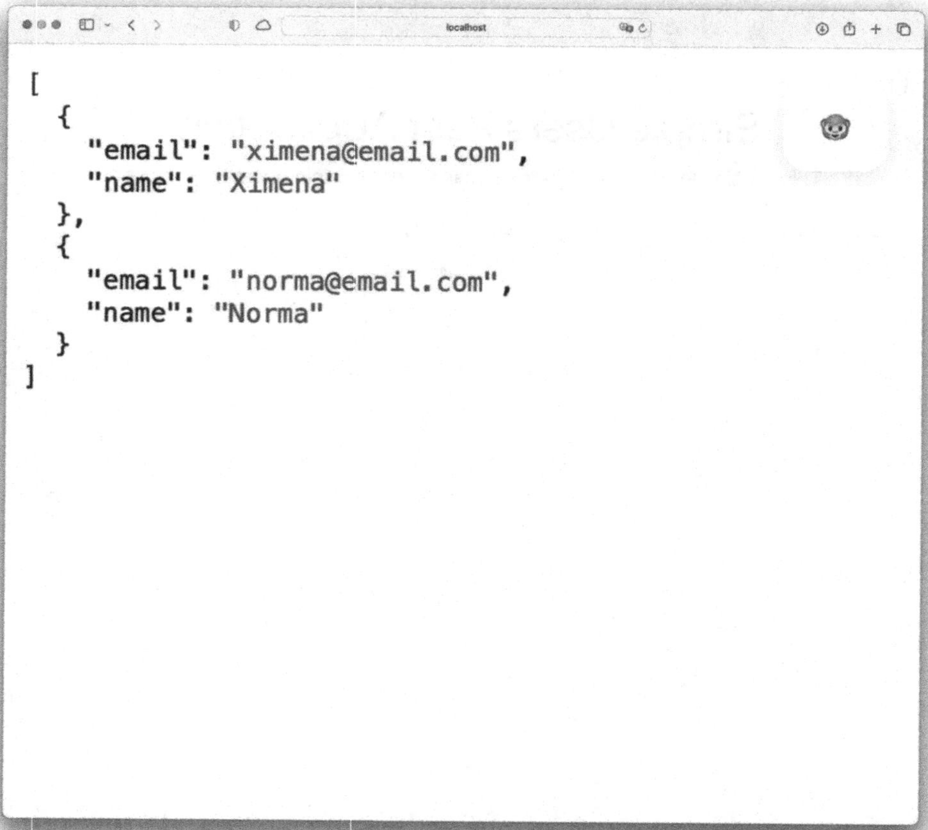

Figure 1-7. *The http://localhost:8080/users: /users endpoint*

Spring Boot responds using JSON by default (as described further in the following chapters).

You can interact with the Users App (list, add, update, or remove users) by using the command line and executing the instructions in the following list. To do so, you need to have the `curl` or `http` command and the `jq` command (as indicated earlier in this chapter).

- Listing users with the `curl` command:

```
curl -XGET -s http://localhost:8080/users | jq .
[
  {
    "email": "ximena@email.com",
```

```
        "name": "Ximena"
    },
    {
        "email": "norma@email.com",
        "name": "Norma"
    }
]
```

- Listing users with the http command:

```
http :8080/users
HTTP/1.1 200
Connection: keep-alive
Content-Type: application/json
Date: Tue, 11 Apr 2023 18:44:11 GMT
Keep-Alive: timeout=60
Transfer-Encoding: chunked
[
    {
        "email": "ximena@email.com",
        "name": "Ximena"
    },
    {
        "email": "norma@email.com",
        "name": "Norma"
    }
]
```

- Adding a new user with the curl command:

```
curl -XPOST -s -H "Content-Type: application/json" -d
'{"email":"nayely@email.com","name":"Nayely"}' http://
localhost:8080/users | jq .
{
  "email": "nayely@email.com",
  "name": "Nayely"
}
```

- Adding a new user with the http command:

```
http :8080/users email=laura@email.com name=Laura
HTTP/1.1 200
Connection: keep-alive
Content-Type: application/json
Date: Tue, 11 Apr 2023 18:48:20 GMT
Keep-Alive: timeout=60
Transfer-Encoding: chunked
{
    "email": "laura@email.com",
    "name": "Laura"
}
```

- Finding a user with the curl command:

```
curl -XGET -s http://localhost:8080/users/ximena@email.com | jq .
{
  "email": "ximena@email.com",
  "name": "Ximena"
}
```

- Finding a user with the http command:

```
http :8080/users/ximena@email.com
HTTP/1.1 200
Connection: keep-alive
Content-Disposition: inline;filename=f.txt
Content-Type: application/json
Date: Tue, 11 Apr 2023 18:50:52 GMT
Keep-Alive: timeout=60
Transfer-Encoding: chunked
{
    "email": "ximena@email.com",
    "name": "Ximena"
}
```

- Deleting a user with the `curl` command:

```
curl -XDELETE http://localhost:8080/users/ximena@email.com
```

- Deleting a user with the `http` command:

```
http DELETE :8080/users/laura@email.com
HTTP/1.1 200
Connection: keep-alive
Content-Length: 0
Date: Tue, 11 Apr 2023 18:53:02 GMT
Keep-Alive: timeout=60
```

Congratulations! This was a quick start for creating a well-defined application in Spring Boot that just runs.

Why Spring Boot?

Spring Boot is an opinionated runtime that enables you to create amazing, enterprise-grade applications faster and with ease. It gets all the best practices of the Spring Framework and uses defaults to configure everything on your behalf.

Even though we are talking about Spring Boot, it is important to understand what the Spring Framework is and why it is so important for Spring Boot. The Spring Framework has the following guiding principles (quoted verbatim from `https://docs.spring.io/spring-framework/reference/overview.html`):

- *Provide choice at every level:* Spring lets you defer design decisions as late as possible. For example, you can switch persistence providers through configuration without changing your code. The same is true for many other infrastructure concerns and integration with third-party APIs.

- *Accommodate diverse perspectives:* Spring embraces flexibility and is not opinionated about how things should be done. It supports a wide range of application needs with different perspectives.

- *Maintain strong backward compatibility:* Spring's evolution has been carefully managed to force few breaking changes between versions. Spring supports a carefully chosen range of JDK versions and third-party libraries to facilitate maintenance of applications and libraries that depend on Spring.

- *Care about API design:* The Spring team puts a lot of thought and time into making APIs that are intuitive and that hold up across many versions and many years.

- *Set high standards for code quality:* The Spring Framework puts a strong emphasis on meaningful, current, and accurate javadoc. It is one of very few projects that can claim clean code structure with no circular dependencies between packages.

The Spring Framework implements several design patterns, such as Dependency of Injection and Inversion of Control, Factories, Abstract Factories, Strategies, Singletons, Templates, MVC, and many more.

One of the main features of the Spring Framework is that it allows you to work with plain old Java objects (POJOs), making your apps easy to extend without any dependency; in other words, the Spring Framework is not invasive.

As depicted in Figure 1-8, to create an application using only the Spring Framework, you need your classes (Java, Groovy, Kotlin), some configuration that tells the Spring Framework how to wire every class (which are called Spring Beans) to set the Spring Context, and have your application ready.

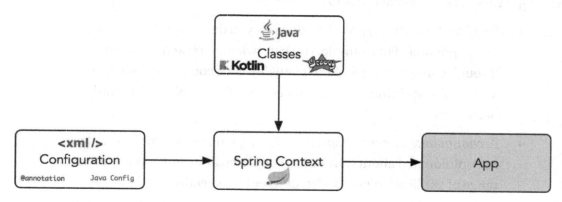

Figure 1-8. *Spring Framework: Spring Context*

This process of configuration can sometimes be challenging if you have many classes and you want to use features such as web MVC, security, or persistence.

Suppose that your application requires some web and persistence features; you must tell the Spring Framework (with configuration: XML, Annotations, or JavaConfig classes) about your `TransactionManager`, an `EntityManagerFactory`, a `DataSource`, a `ResourceViewResolver` (for your web views), a `MessageConverter` (for your web responses, based on the `Content-Type`), a `ResourceHandlerRegistry`, and some other extra configuration...yes, that's a lot of configuration, but it keeps your code clean and easy to maintain.

Then, why Spring Boot? The biggest advantage of using Spring Boot is that it is based on the Spring Framework, making it enterprise-ready with all the best practices applied. And because Spring Boot is opinionated, it will configure everything for you, resulting in (sometimes) zero configuration. How does it do it? You learn how in the next chapter.

Still questioning why to use Spring Boot or what can you do with it? Here's a sampling of what Spring Boot is suitable for:

- Cloud-native applications that follow the 12-factor app developed by the Heroku engineering team (see `https://12factor.net`)

- Native images with the new Ahead Of Time (AOT) and GraalVM support.

- Better productivity by reducing time of development and deployment.

- Enterprise, production-ready Spring applications.

- Nonfunctional requirements, such as the Spring Boot Actuator (a module that provides metrics with the new platform-agnostic Micrometer [`https://micrometer.io`], health checks, and management) and embedded containers for running web applications (Tomcat, Netty, Undertow, Jetty, etc.).

- Microservices, which create scalable, highly available, and robust applications. Spring Boot allows developers to focus only on business logic, leaving the heavy lifting to the Spring Framework.

Spring Boot Features

The following list provides a brief introduction to several of the many Spring Boot features that we describe in more depth in the following chapters:

- The `SpringApplication` class provides a convenient way to initiate a Spring application. As you saw earlier in this chapter, in a Kotlin Spring Boot application, the `main` method executes this singleton class.

- Spring Boot allows you to create applications without requiring any XML configuration. Spring Boot doesn't generate any code.

- Spring Boot provides a fluent builder API through the `SpringApplicationBuilder` singleton class, which allows you to create hierarchies with multiple application contexts. This feature is more related to the Spring Framework and how it works internally. We explain this feature in more detail in the following chapters, but if you are new to Spring and Spring Boot, at this point you only need to know that you can extend Spring Boot to get more control over your applications.

- Spring Boot offers more ways to configure the Spring application events and listeners.

- As an "opinionated" technology (as previously mentioned), Spring Boot attempts to create the right type of application, either as a web application (by embedded a Tomcat, Netty, Undertow, or Jetty container) or as a single application.

- The Spring Boot `org.springframework.boot.ApplicationArguments` interface allows you to access any application argument. This is a useful feature when you try to run your application with parameters.

- Spring Boot allows you to execute code after the application has started. You only need to implement the `CommandLineRunner` interface and provide the implementation of the `run(String ...args)` method. For example, this feature enables you to initialize records in a database during the start, or check if particular services are running before your application executes.

- Spring Boot enables you to externalize configurations by using the `application.properties` or `application.yml` files.

- Spring Boot allows you to add administration-related features, normally through JMX, by enabling the `spring.application.admin.enabled` property in the `application.properties` or `application.yml` files.

- Spring Boot offers *profiles*, which help your application run in different environments.

- Spring Boot allows you to configure and use logging in a very simple way.

- Spring Boot provides a simple way to configure and manage your dependencies by using starter poms. In other words, if you are going to create a web application, you only need to include the `spring-boot-start-web` dependency in your Maven `pom.xml` or `build.gradle` file.

- Spring Boot provides out-of-the-box nonfunctional requirements by using the Spring Boot Actuator together with the new Micrometer platform-agnostic framework that allows you to instrument your apps.

- Spring Boot provides `@Enable<feature>` annotations that help you to include, configure, and use technologies such as databases (SQL and NoSQL), Caching, Scheduling, Messaging, Spring Integration, Batch, Cloud, and more.

The new Spring Framework 6 includes a lot of improvements and new features—such as support for Java 17, Jakarta EE 9+, Servlet 6, JPA 3.1, Tomcat 10.x, and AOT transformations—the latter enables first-class support for GraalVM native images with Spring Boot 3 and an HTTP interface client, among other improvements.

Summary

In this chapter you learned how easy it is to set up a Spring Boot project by creating a simple web API project that shows the user's email address and name, using a `Map` as an in-memory solution.

You learned that you can include HTML pages in the `src/main/resources/static` folder and they can be rendered by Spring Boot. You also learned that, to expose a web API, you need to use an annotation that is a marker for the class that will have methods that will be executed when there is a request for a particular endpoint. You learned that using the `@RestController`, `@RequestMapping`, `@GetMapping`, `@PostMapping`, and `@DeleteMapping` mark the class and methods for every HTTP method request, which in this case correlate with the CRUD (Create, Read, Update and Delete).

You learned how testing works with Spring Boot by creating an integration test that uses some classes to execute requests to your application. You saw some of the assertations that are declared in each method to test the CRUD.

The most important part of this chapter showed how easy is to create a Spring Boot application with ease and understand the basics.

Chapter 2 explores all the main features that make Spring Boot an awesome technology for creating enterprise-ready applications with ease.

CHAPTER 2

Spring Boot Internals

Felipe Gutierrez[a*]

[a] 4109 Rillcrest Grove Way Fuquay Varina, NC 27526-3562, Albuquerque, NM, USA

Requirements to Create a Spring Boot App

Creating a Spring Boot application requires the following:

- A dependency management tool that allows you to use any dependency and verify, compile, test, and build your application with ease. Popular dependency management tools that support Spring Boot (through plugins) include Apache Maven (`https://maven.apache.org/`), Gradle (`https://gradle.org/`), and Apache Ant (`https://ant.apache.org/`). This book uses Gradle as the default dependency management tool.

- A *starter*, which is a convenient set of dependency descriptors that comes with what you need depending on the technology used. A starter brings a curated set of libraries to your application, and the good part is that you don't need to worry about the version (no more dependency madness). The Spring Boot team established a naming convention that is very useful: `spring-boot-starter` as the prefix, followed by the name of the technology to use. For example, if you need a web application, the starter to use is `spring-bootstarter-web`. If you need data JPA, it will be `spring-boot-start-data-jpa`. The minimum for a Spring Boot app is the `spring-boot-starter` dependency, which brings `spring-core`, `spring-beans`, `spring-context`, `spring-aop`, `spring-test`, and many other libraries.

© Peter Späth, Felipe Gutierrez 2025
P. Späth and F. Gutierrez, *Pro Spring Boot 3 with Kotlin*, https://doi.org/10.1007/979-8-8688-1131-9_2

- A structure in which you can define your classes, your tests, and any other assets or properties for your application. The following is the default structure of any Kotlin application:

```
demo
 src
  +- main
      +- kotlin
          +- com
              +- example
                  +- demo
                      +- <other-structure>
                      +- DemoApplication.kt
          +- resources
              +- application.properties
  +- test
      +- kotlin
          +- com
              +- example
                  +- demo
                      +- DemoApplicationTests.kt
```

You can create any package structure, but just make sure that your main app (DemoApplication.kt in this example) is at the top level of your main structure.

- Usage of the @SpringBootApplication annotation. This tells Spring Boot to auto-configure everything on your behalf using some defaults. More details on this annotation are provided in the following sections.

- Execution of the SpringApplication.run(<config>, <args>) method. This will boot your application and, together with the @SpringBootApplication annotation, will wire everything up for your application. The first parameter is the Configuration class, which provides any other configuration, and the subsequent parameter or parameters (if any) are the arguments (if any) passed in the command line when running the application. Here's an example:

```
@SpringBootApplication
class DemoApplication {
    companion object {
        @JvmStatic
        fun main(args:Array<String>) {
    SpringApplication.run(DemoApplication::class.java, *args)
  }
}
```

Of course, you normally don't need do this manually, because you have the Spring Initializr to do it for you. As you learned in Chapter 1, this web tool enables you to create the project quickly by choosing what you need, including the dependency management tool, the dependencies (`spring-boot-starter-<tech>`), the structure, and the main class with the annotation and the execution of the application. You can create and run the project in a matter of minutes, and it works!

Project: My Retro App

Before going into the internals of Spring Boot, this section introduces the main project: My Retro App. This project and the Users App project are referenced throughout the book. In each chapter, you see how to add to both projects' features that correspond to the chapter topic, so that by the end of the book, you will have a complete solution.

The My Retro App project is all about retrospection: review past events, share thoughts, synthesize group ideas, discuss what is important, commit and take any action to a better process in the future. This simple app has three primary components: Retro Board, Card, and Card Type. The following are the main requirements and features of this project:

- Retro Board, which contains the following:

  - UID, a unique identification

  - Name (the name of the Retro Board)

  - Multiple cards grouped by the card type (Happy, Meh, and Sad)

- Card, which includes a comment box in which users can express their ideas based on the Card Type.

- Card Type:

  - *Happy card*: All the positive thoughts, actions, or events

  - *Meh card*: Ideas that are questionable or thoughts that probably don't mean anything or don't need much attention

  - *Sad card*: Ideas that the user does not agree with, or any event that was bad or should not be happening

- Expose a web API and a UI

- UI requirements:

  - Login/Logout option.

  - Admin and User roles.

  - Admin can manage Users and multiple Retro boards.

  - A Retro Board that displays three columns (HAPPY, MEH, SAD) in which users can add cards.

  - A User is assigned to a Retro Board.

  - A User can add any Card to the right column.

Figure 2-1 shows the basic classes.

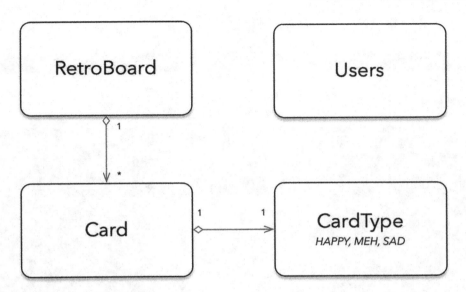

Figure 2-1. *Basic classes for the My Retro App project*

Figure 2-2 shows the UI of the My Retro App that you'll be building throughout this book.

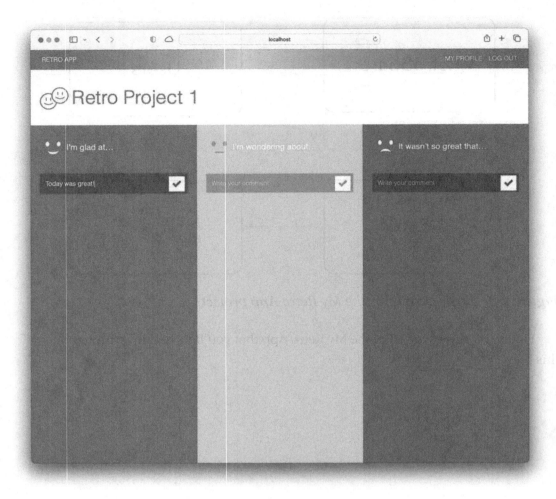

Figure 2-2. *The final My Retro App project UI*

To start this project with the Spring Initializr, open a browser and go to `https://start.spring.io`. Use the following configuration, as shown in Figure 2-3:

- Project: Gradle – Groovy

- Language: Kotlin

- Spring Boot: 3.2.3

- Project Metadata:
  - Group: `com.apress`
  - Artifact: `myretro`
  - Name: `myretro`
  - Packaging: JAR
  - Java: 17

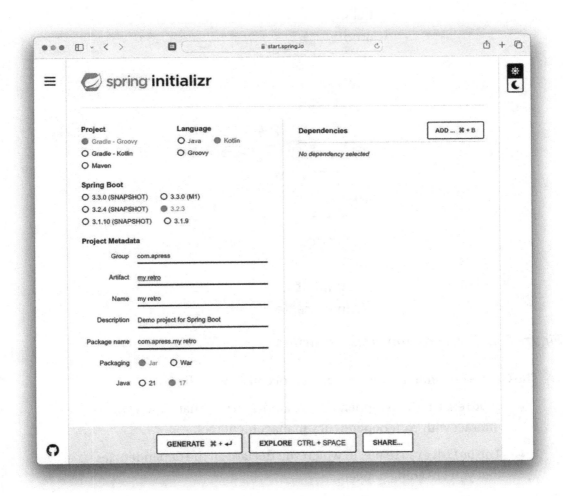

Figure 2-3. *Spring Initializr: My Retro App project configuration*

As you can see in Figure 2-3, no dependencies have been selected yet. You are going to be adding the features and technologies in the following sections and chapters. Click Generate to download the myretro.zip file, and then import it into your favorite IDE. Figure 2-4 shows the structure that was generated by the Spring Initializr.

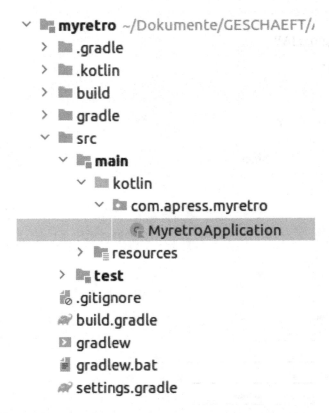

Figure 2-4. *My Retro App project structure*

The Gradle dependency management tool comes with the following:

- gradlew, Gradle Wrapper, a command-line tool that allows you to interact with your dependency management tool.

- The build.gradle file, in which you declare all the dependencies that you are going to need.

- settings.gradle, to add more configuration to it.

- The .gradle/ folder, which comes with some JARs already (meaning that you don't need to install Gradle; this is a light version that downloads all the necessary files).

Open the build.gradle file to see what's in it. See Listing 2-1.

Listing 2-1. The build.gradle File

```
plugins {
    id 'org.jetbrains.kotlin.jvm' version '1.9.24'
    id 'org.jetbrains.kotlin.plugin.spring' version '1.9.24'
    id 'org.springframework.boot' version '3.3.2'
    id 'io.spring.dependency-management' version '1.1.6'
}

group = 'com.apress'
version = '0.0.1-SNAPSHOT'

java {
    toolchain {
        languageVersion = JavaLanguageVersion.of(17)
    }
}

repositories {
    mavenCentral()
}

dependencies {
    implementation 'org.springframework.boot:spring-boot-starter'
    implementation 'org.jetbrains.kotlin:kotlin-reflect'
    testImplementation 'org.springframework.boot:spring-boot-starter-test'
    testImplementation 'org.jetbrains.kotlin:kotlin-test-junit5'
    testRuntimeOnly 'org.junit.platform:junit-platform-launcher'
}

kotlin {
    compilerOptions {
        freeCompilerArgs.addAll '-Xjsr305=strict'
    }
}
```

```
tasks.named('test') {
    useJUnitPlatform()
}
```

As described in Chapter 1, in the `build.gradle` file, you declare the plugins, app information (group, version, and compatibility), where to search (repository), and the dependencies to download. Looking at the `dependencies` section in Listing 2-1, it declares the `spring-boot-starter` and `spring-boot-starter-test` starters that will bring all related dependencies for the Spring Framework, Spring Boot, Testing, and other useful libraries. You are almost set and ready for the next part. Let's analyze the main application.

Auto-Configuration

One of the main features of Spring Boot is auto-configuration. Recall from Chapter 1 that if you want to create a Spring app using just the Spring Framework, you need to supply not only your classes but also how you want them to interact, any dependencies, and some extra configuration depending on the type of application.

Spring Boot helps with all the configuration via auto-configuration. Spring Boot favors Java/Kotlin-based configuration, which means that it looks for any class that is marked with the `@Configuration` annotation and any dependencies that are in your application (in your classpath). The `@Configuration` annotation triggers logic (during the lifecycle of the Spring Boot app) to find any `@Bean` declaration (creating the famous Spring Beans) that can help the Spring Boot app know what you need.

Within the My Retro App, open the `MyretroApplication.kt` class, as shown in Listing 2-2.

Listing 2-2. The src/main/kotlin/com/apress/myretro/ MyretroApplication.kt File

```
package com.apress.myretro

import org.springframework.boot.SpringApplication
import org.springframework.boot.autoconfigure.SpringBootApplication

@SpringBootApplication
class MyretroApplication {
```

```
    companion object {
        @JvmStatic
        fun main(args: Array<String>) {
            SpringApplication.run(MyretroApplication::class.java, *args)
            Thread.sleep(Long.MAX_VALUE)
        }
    }
}
```

When the `MyretroApplication.kt` class is executed by the `SpringApplication.run` call, it triggers the auto-configuration feature. This call needs the configuration class that has any `@Configuration` annotation and the arguments (which are passed in the command line when executing the program). You might wonder why we are passing the `MyretroApplication.class` if this class doesn't have a `@Configuration` annotation, right?

Behind the scenes, the `@SpringBootApplication` interface annotation is declared, as shown in Listing 2-3.

Listing 2-3. org.springframework.boot.autoconfigure. SpringBootApplication.java

```
@Target(ElementType.TYPE)
@Retention(RetentionPolicy.RUNTIME)
@Documented
@Inherited
@SpringBootConfiguration
@EnableAutoConfiguration
@ComponentScan(excludeFilters = { @Filter(type = FilterType.CUSTOM, classes
= TypeExcludeFilter.class),
        @Filter(type = FilterType.CUSTOM, classes =
        AutoConfigurationExcludeFilter.class) })
public @interface SpringBootApplication {
  //... some other declarations
}
```

The important parts of Listing 2-3 are as follows:

> @SpringBootConfiguration: This annotation is just an alias for
> the @Configuration annotation, which will search for any @Bean
> (Spring Bean) declarations that you have in your class. In this case,
> you don't have any declarations yet. Listing 2-4 shows what the
> SpringBootConfiguration annotation look like.

Listing 2-4. org.springframework.boot.SpringBootConfiguration.java

```
@Target(ElementType.TYPE)
@Retention(RetentionPolicy.RUNTIME)
@Documented
@Configuration
@Indexed
public @interface SpringBootConfiguration {
    // ... some other declarations
}
```

Practically, you can create your own custom annotation and extend its functionality.

- @EnableAutoConfiguration: This annotation triggers even
  more functionality because it reads the META-INF/spring/org.
  springframework.boot.autoconfigure.AutoConfiguration.
  imports file and executes every class that has the AutoConfiguration
  name at the end of the class name (this is just a naming convention)
  to identify any defaults and set everything up so that you don't
  have to. This file is part of spring-boot-starter and belongs to the
  spring-boot-autoconfigure.jar dependency. See Listing 2-5.

Listing 2-5. META-INF/spring/org.springframework.boot.autoconfigure.
AutoConfiguration.imports

```
//...
org.springframework.boot.autoconfigure.data.jdbc.
JdbcRepositoriesAutoConfiguration
org.springframework.boot.autoconfigure.data.jpa.
JpaRepositoriesAutoConfiguration
org.springframework.boot.autoconfigure.data.ldap.
LdapRepositoriesAutoConfiguration
org.springframework.boot.autoconfigure.data.mongo.
MongoDataAutoConfiguration
org.springframework.boot.autoconfigure.data.mongo.
MongoReactiveDataAutoConfiguration
org.springframework.boot.autoconfigure.data.mongo.
MongoReactiveRepositoriesAutoConfiguration
org.springframework.boot.autoconfigure.data.mongo.
MongoRepositoriesAutoConfiguration
org.springframework.boot.autoconfigure.data.neo4j.
Neo4jDataAutoConfiguration
org.springframework.boot.autoconfigure.data.neo4j.
Neo4jReactiveDataAutoConfiguration
org.springframework.boot.autoconfigure.data.neo4j.
Neo4jReactiveRepositoriesAutoConfiguration
org.springframework.boot.autoconfigure.data.neo4j.
Neo4jRepositoriesAutoConfiguration
org.springframework.boot.autoconfigure.data.r2dbc.
R2dbcDataAutoConfiguration
org
//...
```

Around 146 AutoConfiguration classes inspect which dependencies you have
declared, either in your classes or as dependencies, and then auto-configure your app
so that you don't have to. For example, if you add the Data JPA and two drivers (H2 and
PostgreSQL), the Spring Boot auto-configuration mechanism will go to the JDBC and
JPA AutoConfiguration classes and auto-configure your transaction manager, manager

factory, and `DataSource`. `DataSource` now requires some extra settings, including the URL of the database, the database name, the password, and the dialect, so how will it be configured if you have two drivers declared? That's when the defaults (opinions) kick in. If you don't have any properties that set all the values previously mentioned, it will default to use the H2 that can be set as the in-memory database, with some default values such as `username: sa` and `password (empty)` and the url: `jdbc:h2:mem:<guid-database-name>`. This means that your application will work out-of-the-box without any configuration at all. Amazing!

- `@ComponentScan`: This annotation will help search for a specific package base (if you have multiple package base name) or any other external library that must be recognized as Spring Bean (looking for `@Bean` declarations). For example, if you have a package with the path `com.mycompany` and `com.other.company`, you can use the `base Packages` parameter and set `basePackages={ "com.mycompany", "com.other.company"}`. (There are some best practices for this, but we go into them later.)

@EnableAutoConfiguration, @Enable<Technology>, and @Conditional* Annotations

Spring Boot is highly customizable, meaning that you can disable some of the `AutoConfiguration` classes. This allows you to have even more control over how you configure your application. Although the process of `AutoConfiguration` is fast (it doesn't affect performance at all because it occurs when your application is booting up), sometimes you don't need some of the defaults.

@EnableAutoConfiguration

As you know, the `@SpringBootApplication` annotation inherits from the `@EnableAutoConfiguration` annotation, which has two parameters that can be used to disable some of the defaults, as shown in Listing 2-6.

Listing 2-6. org.springframework.boot.autoconfigure.EnableAuto
Configuration.java

```
@Target(ElementType.TYPE)
@Retention(RetentionPolicy.RUNTIME)
@Documented
@Inherited
@AutoConfigurationPackage
@Import(AutoConfigurationImportSelector.class)
public @interface EnableAutoConfiguration {
    String ENABLED_OVERRIDE_PROPERTY = "spring.boot.
    enableautoconfiguration";
    Class<?>[] exclude() default {};
    String[] excludeName() default {};
}
```

As described in the previous section, the @EnableAutoConfiguration annotation triggers the AutoConfiguration classes to configure your application based on the dependencies that your application uses. This annotation also brings the exclude and excludeName parameters that can be used to avoid any other defaults (AutoConfiguration).

For example, if you have a Spring Boot Web MVC application and you want to do the configuration manually, you can add the following to the @SpringBootApplication annotation:

```
@SpringBootApplication(exclude = arrayOf(WebMvcAutoConfiguration::class))
```

@Enable<Technology>

If you are working only with the Spring Framework, you can use the auto-configuration feature for your apps. Every Spring technology has an @Enable<Technology> annotation that auto-configures some class so that you don't have to. For example, if you have the spring-rabbit dependency, this library brings the @EnableRabbit annotation that will trigger auto-configuration, such as adding the default message converters, adding a simple listener, and so forth. And, of course, if you are using Spring Boot with spring-boot-starter-amqp, you don't need to use the @EnableRabbit annotation. The AutoConfiguration will do that for you by configuring all the beans necessary to connect to Rabbit using the defaults (host, port, username, and password).

@Conditional*

In almost every AutoConfiguration class, you will find that the @Conditional*
annotation helps configure the necessary beans for the application. For example,
the WebMvcAutoConfiguration class has @ConditionalOnClass({ Servlet.class,
DispatcherServlet.class, WebMvcConfigurer.class }), which means that the Web
MVC auto-configuration logic will execute only if these classes are being used (in the
classpath) in your application (the My Retro App project). In the My Retro App project,
we are not using any web dependency, so the WebMvcAutoConfiguration will fail the
@ConditionalOnWebApplication and the @ConditionalOnClass because there is no
Servlet.class, or DispatcherServlet.class, or any other dependency declared in
the build.gradle file. Is there any way to see how this works? Yes, you can run the
application just like it is with the following parameter: --debug.

If you are using the IntelliJ, you can run the application and add the --debug
parameter as "Program arguments". See Figure 2-5.

Figure 2-5. *IntelliJ IDEA configuration to pass the --debug argument to the
launch process*

If you are using VS Code, you need to add the "args": "--debug" key to the launch.json file. See Figure 2-6.

```
{} launch.json  ×

.vscode > {} launch.json > ...
    1    {
    2         "version": "0.2.0",
    3         "configurations": [
    4             {
    5                 "type": "java",
    6                 "name": "MyretroApplication",
    7                 "request": "launch",
    8                 "mainClass": "com.apress.myretro.MyretroApplication",
    9                 "projectName": "myretro",
   10                 "args": "--debug"
   11             }
   12         ]
   13    }
```

Figure 2-6. *VS Code configuration to pass the --debug argument to the launch process*

Alternatively, you can run the application using the command line. In the root of the project, execute the following command:

```
./gradlew bootRun -args="--debug"
```

Whichever way you choose to run the application, you will see the same output:

```
...
...
WebMvcAutoConfiguration:
      Did not match:
         - @ConditionalOnClass did not find required class 'jakarta.
         servlet.Servlet' (OnClassCondition)
...
...
```

In this case, WebMvcAutoConfiguration did not match the criteria; the AutoConfiguration class did not find the Servlet.class by using the @ConditionalOnClass annotation. Additional @Conditional* annotations will be covered in other chapters, but for now you simply need to know that this annotation is used to set (or not set) some of the opinionated defaults for your Spring Boot apps.

If you add @SpringBootApplication(exclude = arrayOf(WebMvcAutoConfiguration ::class)) to the application and rerun it, you will see something different:

```
...
Exclusions:
-----------
    org.springframework.boot.autoconfigure.web.servlet.WebMvcAutoCon
    figuration
...
```

The Exclusions section shows that the WebMvcAutoConfiguration class was not executed.

So, auto-configuration involves no magic after all! Spring Boot uses the power of auto-configuration to create everything you need for your application so you don't have to, making this a faster way to create amazing apps with ease and with little effort.

Spring Boot Features

Let's explore some of the Spring Boot features by using the My Retro App project. If you look at the main class, you will find the SpringApplication.run method. This can be instantiated in a different way to take advantage of other features. Take a look at Listing 2-7.

Listing 2-7. src/main/kotlin/com/apress/myretro/MyretroApplication.kt

```
package com.apress.myretro
import org.springframework.boot.SpringApplication
import org.springframework.boot.autoconfigure.SpringBootApplication

@SpringBootApplication
class MyretroApplication {
    companion object {
```

```
@JvmStatic
fun main(args:Array<String>) {
    val sa = SpringApplication(MyretroApplication::class.java)
    // Spring Application features ...
    sa.run(*args)
    }
  }
}
```

Listing 2-7 shows a small modification from Listing 2-2. Here, we are not using the run(...args) method call. If you view the options the SpringApplication class offers (using the code-completion feature of your IDE by typing the instance variable sa.), you will see a list similar to the (partial) list shown in Figure 2-7.

ⓜ getInitializers()	Set<ApplicationContextInitializer<?>>
ⓜ getListeners()	Set<ApplicationListener<?>>
ⓜ getMainApplicationClass()	Class<?>
ⓜ getResourceLoader()	ResourceLoader
ⓜ getSources()	Set<String>
ⓜ getWebApplicationType()	WebApplicationType
ⓜ setAddCommandLineProperties(boolean addCommandLineProperties)	void
ⓜ setAddConversionService(boolean addConversionService)	void
ⓜ setAdditionalProfiles(String... profiles)	void
ⓜ setAllowBeanDefinitionOverriding(boolean allowBeanDefinitionOverriding)	void
ⓜ setAllowCircularReferences(boolean allowCircularReferences)	void
ⓜ setApplicationContextFactory(ApplicationContextFactory applicationContex…	void
ⓜ setBanner(Banner banner)	void
ⓜ setBannerMode(Mode bannerMode)	void
ⓜ setBeanNameGenerator(BeanNameGenerator beanNameGenerator)	void
ⓜ setDefaultProperties(Properties defaultProperties)	void
ⓜ setDefaultProperties(Map<String, Object> defaultProperties)	void
ⓜ setEnvironment(ConfigurableEnvironment environment)	void
ⓜ setEnvironmentPrefix(String environmentPrefix)	void
ⓜ setHeadless(boolean headless)	void
ⓜ setInitializers(Collection<? extends ApplicationContextInitializer<?>> i…	void
ⓜ setLazyInitialization(boolean lazyInitialization)	void
ⓜ setListeners(Collection<? extends ApplicationListener<?>> listeners)	void
ⓜ setLogStartupInfo(boolean logStartupInfo)	void
ⓜ setMainApplicationClass(Class<?> mainApplicationClass)	void
ⓜ setRegisterShutdownHook(boolean registerShutdownHook)	void
ⓜ setResourceLoader(ResourceLoader resourceLoader)	void
ⓜ setSources(Set<String> sources)	void
ⓜ setWebApplicationType(WebApplicationType webApplicationType)	void

Press ↵ to insert, → to replace Next Tip

Figure 2-7. *SpringApplication class*

Figure 2-7 shows you the code completion for the SpringApplication instance variable. The following sections introduce some of the most common features you can add to your Spring Boot application.

Custom Banner

When you start your application, a banner is displayed. The default is the ASCII art of Spring Boot. See Figure 2-8.

```
  .   ____          _            __ _ _
 /\\ / ___'_ __ _ _(_)_ __  __ _ \ \ \ \
( ( )\___ | '_ | '_| | '_ \/ _` | \ \ \ \
 \\/  ___)| |_)| | | | | || (_| |  ) ) ) )
  '  |____| .__|_| |_|_| |_\__, | / / / /
 =========|_|==============|___/=/_/_/_/
 :: Spring Boot ::        (v3.1.0         )

2023-04-26T07:29:33.556-04:00  INFO 27679 --- [      main] com.apress.myretro.MyretroApplication    :
2023-04-26T07:29:33.558-04:00  INFO 27679 --- [      main] com.apress.myretro.MyretroApplication    :
2023-04-26T07:29:33.880-04:00  WARN 27679 --- [      main] ocalVariableTableParameterNameDiscoverer :
2023-04-26T07:29:33.892-04:00  INFO 27679 --- [      main] com.apress.myretro.MyretroApplication    :

BUILD SUCCESSFUL in 1s
3 actionable tasks: 1 executed, 2 up-to-date
```

Figure 2-8. *Spring Boot banner*

Within the SpringApplication class, you can add a custom banner in different ways. You can do it programmatically, as shown in Listing 2-8.

Listing 2-8. src/main/kotlin/com/apress/myretro/MyretroApplication.kt

```kotlin
package com.apress.myretro
import org.springframework.boot.SpringApplication
import org.springframework.boot.autoconfigure.SpringBootApplication

@SpringBootApplication
class MyretroApplication {
    companion object {
        @JvmStatic
        fun main(args:Array<String>) {
            val sa = SpringApplication(MyretroApplication::class.java)
            // Spring Application features ...
```

```
sa.banner = object : Banner {
    override fun printBanner(environment: Environment?,
                            sourceClass: Class<*>?, out:
                            PrintStream?) {
        out!!.println(
            "\n\n\tThis is my custom Banner!\n\n".
            uppercase(Locale.getDefault()))
    }
}
sa.run(*args)
    }
  }
}
```

Listing 2-8 shows the implementation of a custom banner by using the `.banner = ...` setter. If you run this program, you will see something like Figure 2-9.

```
THIS IS MY CUSTOM BANNER!


2023-04-26T07:40:14.949-04:00  INFO 30030 --- [       main] com.apress.myretro.MyretroApplication        :
2023-04-26T07:40:14.950-04:00  INFO 30030 --- [       main] com.apress.myretro.MyretroApplication        :
2023-04-26T07:40:15.283-04:00  WARN 30030 --- [       main] ocalVariableTableParameterNameDiscoverer :
2023-04-26T07:40:15.295-04:00  INFO 30030 --- [       main] com.apress.myretro.MyretroApplication        :


BUILD SUCCESSFUL in 1s
```

Figure 2-9. *Custom banner*

Another way that you can create a custom banner is by using ASCII art. Websites that can generate this art for you. For example, go to `https://www.patorjk.com`, scroll down the page, click the Text to ASCII Art Generator link, and type **My Retro**. Figure 2-10 shows the results of selecting different fonts for the text.

Figure 2-10. *Example Text to ASCII Art Generator output (https://www. patorjk.com)*

You can browse, try various fonts, and select the one you like. Click the Select & Copy button. Then you need to create a banner.txt file in the src/main/resources directory and paste the ASCII art. Figure 2-11 shows the banner.txt file and the ASCII art.

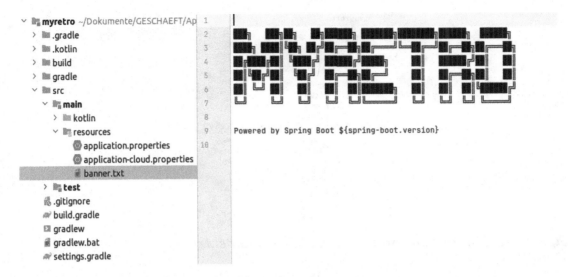

Figure 2-11. *src/main/resources/banner.txt*

Also note in Figure 2-11 that we added the `${spring-boot.version}` caption in the My Retro App. This is one of the global properties that are set at runtime, and it will display the Spring Boot version that's used. If you run the My Retro App, you should see the same result shown in Figure 2-12.

Figure 2-12. *Custom banner*

By default, Spring Boot locates the `banner.txt` file in the `resources` folder, but you can specify another location or extension. For example, you can create the `src/main/resources/META-INF` folder and add the `banner.txt` file. See Figure 2-13.

Figure 2-13. *src/main/resources/META-INF/banner.txt*

To make this work, you need to use the `spring.banner.location` property. If you want to use your IDE, you need to figure out how to override the Spring Boot configuration properties. If you are using IntelliJ IDEA, choose Edit Configurations ➤ Modify Options, locate the Override Configuration Properties section, and add `spring.banner.location` and `classpath:/META-INF/banner.txt`, as shown in Figure 2-14.

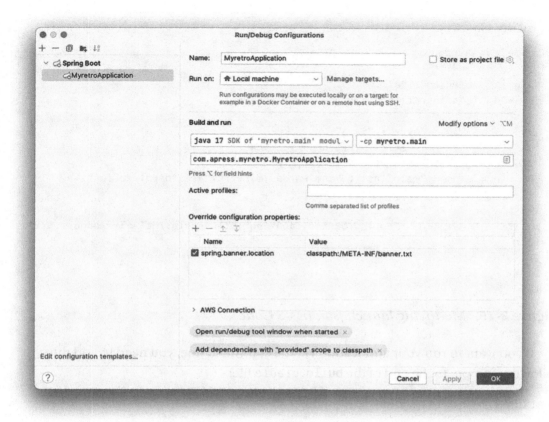

Figure 2-14. *Overriding configuration properties in IntelliJ IDEA*

If you are using VS Code, you need to modify launch.json and add the env key with the spring.banner.location and classpath:/META-INF/banner.txt values. See Figure 2-15.

```
{} launch.json  ×

.vscode > {} launch.json > ...
   1  ∨ {
   2          "version": "0.2.0",
   3  ∨       "configurations": [
   4  ∨          {
   5                  "type": "java",
   6                  "name": "MyretroApplication",
   7                  "request": "launch",
   8                  "mainClass": "com.apress.myretro.MyretroApplication",
   9                  "projectName": "myretro",
  10  ∨              "env": {
  11                      "spring.banner.location":"classpath:/META-INF/banner.txt"
  12                  }
  13              }
  14          ]
  15      }
```

Figure 2-15. *Modifying launch.json in VS Code*

If you want to run your application via the command line, you need to add the following snippet to the end of the build.gradle file:

```
bootRun {
    systemProperties = System.properties
}
```

Then you can execute the following command and expect the same result shown earlier in Figure 2-12:

./gradlew bootRun **-Dspring.banner.location=classpath:/META-INF/banner.txt**

As you can see, there are many ways to configure these features. If you don't need the banner at all, you can use the setBanner(Mode) method call, as shown in Listing 2-9.

Listing 2-9. src/main/kotlin/com/apress/myretro/MyretroApplication.kt

```
package com.apress.myretro
import org.springframework.boot.SpringApplication
import org.springframework.boot.autoconfigure.SpringBootApplication
import org.springframework.boot.Banner
```

```kotlin
@SpringBootApplication
class MyretroApplication {
    companion object {
        @JvmStatic
        fun main(args:Array<String>) {
            val sa = SpringApplication(MyretroApplication::class.java)
            // Spring Application features ...

            sa.bannerMode = Banner.Mode.OFF
            sa.run(*args)
        }
    }
}
```

SpringApplicationBuilder

Spring Boot offers a Fluent Builder API that allows you to configure your application. The API brings ApplicationContext (from the Spring Framework), making your app even more customizable. Listing 2-10 shows the SpringApplicationBuilder class, in which you can customize the startup.

Listing 2-10. src/main/kotlin/com/apress/myretro/MyretroApplication.kt

```kotlin
package com.apress.myretro
import org.slf4j.Logger
import org.slf4j.LoggerFactory
import org.springframework.boot.Banner
import org.springframework.boot.SpringApplication
import org.springframework.boot.WebApplicationType
import org.springframework.boot.autoconfigure.SpringBootApplication
import org.springframework.boot.builder.SpringApplicationBuilder
import org.springframework.context.ApplicationEvent
import org.springframework.context.ApplicationListener
import org.springframework.core.env.ConfigurableEnvironment
import org.springframework.core.env.Environment
import java.io.PrintStream
```

```kotlin
@SpringBootApplication
class MyretroApplication {
    companion object {
        var log: Logger = LoggerFactory.getLogger(MyretroApplication::
        class.java)

        @JvmStatic
        fun main(args: Array<String>) {
            SpringApplicationBuilder()
                .sources(MyretroApplication::class.java)
                .logStartupInfo(false)
                .bannerMode(Banner.Mode.OFF)
                .lazyInitialization(true)
                .web(WebApplicationType.NONE)
                .profiles("cloud")
                .listeners(ApplicationListener<ApplicationEvent> {
                  event: ApplicationEvent ->
                    MyretroApplication.log.info(
                        "Event: {}",
                        event.javaClass.getCanonicalName()
                    )
                })
                .run(*args)
        }
    }
}
```

Let's analyze the code shown in Listing 2-10:

- `.sources(Class<?>...)`: This method is where you add all the necessary configuration classes and components of your application. Remember, these classes need to be marked as `@Configuration` or as one of the other Spring-related markers such as `@Component`, `@Service`, `@Repository`, and so on.

- `.logStartup(boolean)`: This method prints out to console all the logging information about the startup. It accepts a `boolean`, so if you set it to `false`, you won't see anything (or only your own logging, if any).

- `.bannerMode(Mode)`: This method accepts a `Mode` for showing the banner. The possible values are `Banner.Mode.OFF` (disable printing of the banner), `Banner.Mode.CONSOLE` (print the banner to `System.out`), and `Banner.Mode.LOG` (print the banner to the log file).

- `.lazyInitialization(boolean)`: This method accepts a `boolean`, which by default is set to `false`, but if set to `true`, then the bean creation will not happen until the bean is needed.

- `.web(WebApplicationType)`: This method defines the type of web application. The possible values are `WebApplicationType.NONE` (instructs that the application should not run as a web application and should not start an embedded web server), `WebApplicationType.SERVLET` (means that the application should run as a servlet-based web app and start an embedded servlet web server. This will be true if you have the `spring-boot-starter-web` starter as a dependency/classpath), and `WebApplicationType.REACTIVE` (means that the application should run as a reactive web application and should start an embedded reactive web server, and you need the `spring-boot-starter-webflux` starter as a dependency/classpath).

- `.profiles(String...)`: This method lists Spring profiles that you can use. When running the application, you should see the output `The following 1 profile is active: "cloud"`. (The final section of this chapter discusses application profiles in detail.)

- `.listeners(ApplicationListener<?>...)`: This method enables you to define Spring Events. In this case (in My Retro App), you are listening to all implementations of the `ApplicationListener` interface, so if you run the application, you should have output like the following:

```
Event: o.s.boot.context.event.ApplicationPreparedEvent
Event: o.s.context.event.ContextRefreshedEvent
Event: o.s.boot.context.event.ApplicationStartedEvent
Event: o.s.boot.availability.AvailabilityChangeEvent
Event: o.s.boot.context.event.ApplicationReadyEvent
Event: o.s.boot.availability.AvailabilityChangeEvent
Event: o.s.context.event.ContextClosedEvent
```

- run(String...): This method enables you to pass any argument, as you saw earlier in this chapter. In fact, you can add the following to the args if you are still using the META-INF/banner.txt and the banner mode is set to Banner.Mode.Console:

```
.run("--spring.banner.location=classpath:/META-INF/banner.txt");
```

Application Arguments

In any Java/Kotlin application, you can pass useful arguments to your main class, and Spring Boot will help you access those arguments by providing the ApplicationArguments interface. Let's see how to use it.

Create a new class named MyRetroConfiguration under the myretro package. See Listing 2-11.

Listing 2-11. src/main/kotlin/com/apress/myretro/MyRetroConfiguration.kt

```
package com.apress.myretro
import org.slf4j.Logger
import org.slf4j.LoggerFactory
import org.springframework.boot.ApplicationArguments
import org.springframework.context.annotation.Configuration

@Configuration
class MyRetroConfiguration(arguments: ApplicationArguments) {
    var log: Logger = LoggerFactory.getLogger(MyretroApplication::
    class.java)

    init {
        log.info("Option Args: {}", arguments.optionNames)
```

```
      log.info("Option Arg Values: {}", arguments.getOptionValues
      ("option"))
      log.info("Non Option: {}", arguments.nonOptionArgs)
   }
}
```

In the `MyRetroConfiguration` class, we are going to use and pass the following arguments:

```
--enable --remote --option=value1 --option=value2 update upgrade
```

You can use your IDE (IntelliJ IDEA or VS Code) to add the preceding arguments (as you already learned). If you are using the command line, you can use

```
./gradlew bootRun --args="--enable --remote --option=value1 --option=value2 update upgrade"
```

When you execute the application, the logs of the `MyRetroConfiguration` class should be printed out:

```
Option Args: [enable, remote, option]
Option Arg Values: [value1, value2]
Option: [update, upgrade]
```

Let's analyze the code in Listing 2-11 and look at the result:

- `@Configuration`: Auto-configuration will recognize this annotation, evaluate it, and identify (in this case) that it has a constructor that uses the `ApplicationArguments` interface as a parameter. This will be injected automatically by the Spring app lifecycle. In this case, it will also pass the `args` declared by the `.run(*args)` method call in the main class. The `ApplicationArguments` interface has different methods that can help identify all the arguments if there are options with values or not (denoted by `--` and the `=` with their values) and just parameters known as non-option arguments.

- `*.optionNames`. This accessor will get all the options denoted by `--<argument name>`. In this example, they are `enable`, `remote`, and `option`.

- getOptionValues(String). This method accepts the argument name that has one or more values, denoted by --<argument-name>=<value>. In this example, we are looking for the argument named option and its values, and the result is value1 and value2 (because it repeats more than once).

- *.nonOptionArgs. This accessor gets all the arguments that are not denoted by -- (that is, only regular arguments). In this example, they are update and upgrade.

Executable JAR

This feature is more related to the Spring Boot plugin of whatever dependency management tool you chose (e.g., Maven or Gradle). Again, this book uses Gradle. To create an executable JAR in the build/libs directory, run the following command:

```
./gradlew build
```

Then, you can run it with this command:

```
java -jar build/libs/myretro-0.0.1-SNAPSHOT.jar
```

If you want to pass some parameters/arguments to your JAR, you can execute the following command:

```
java -jar build/libs/myretro-0.0.1-SNAPSHOT.jar --enable --remote
--option=value1 --option=value2 update upgrade
```

You should get the same result as before.

ApplicationRunner, CommandLineRunner, and ApplicationReadyEvent

Developers must start a process or run certain logic before their application is ready to accept any request or any other interaction. Spring Boot has several interfaces and events that enable developers to execute code before the application is ready. You can add the code shown in Listing 2-12 to the MyRetroConfiguration class.

Listing 2-12. src/main/kotlin/com/apress/myretro/MyRetroConfiguration.kt

```kotlin
package com.apress.myretro
import com.apress.myretro.MyretroApplication
import org.slf4j.LoggerFactory
import org.springframework.boot.ApplicationArguments
import org.springframework.boot.ApplicationRunner
import org.springframework.boot.CommandLineRunner
import org.springframework.boot.context.event.ApplicationReadyEvent
import org.springframework.context.ApplicationListener
import org.springframework.context.annotation.Bean
import org.springframework.context.annotation.Configuration

@Configuration
class MyRetroConfiguration {
    var log = LoggerFactory.getLogger(MyretroApplication::class.java)
    @Bean
    fun commandLineRunner(): CommandLineRunner {
        return CommandLineRunner { args: Array<String?> ->
            log.info(
                "[CLR] Args: {}",
                args.contentToString()
            )
        }
    }

    @Bean
    fun applicationRunner(): ApplicationRunner {
        return ApplicationRunner { args: ApplicationArguments ->
            log.info("[AR] Option Args: {}", args.optionNames)
            log.info("[AR] Option Arg Values: {}", args.getOptionValues
            ("option"))
            log.info("[AR] Non Option: {}", args.nonOptionArgs)
        }
    }
```

```
@Bean
fun applicationReadyEventApplicationListener():
        ApplicationListener<ApplicationReadyEvent> {
    return ApplicationListener { event: ApplicationReadyEvent? ->
        log.info("[AL] Im ready to interact...") }
    }
}
```

As you can see, we have eliminated the constructor, which is not needed because the ApplicationRunner interface brings the application arguments. Note that there are now methods that are marked with the @Bean annotation that Spring Boot auto-configuration will use to create the necessary Spring Beans. Let's review the code:

- CommandLineRunner: This interface implementation will be called after Spring and Spring Boot wires everything up. This is a functional interface that has a callback (run method) that accepts the arguments passed to the application. In this case, the result is every single argument.

- ApplicationRunner: This interface implementation will be called before the CommandLineRunner interface implementation. This is a functional interface that has a callback (run method) that has ApplicationArguments as a parameter, making it a good candidate if you want to use the arguments.

- ApplicationListener<ApplicationReadyEvent>: This event will be called when the Spring Boot app has finished wiring everything up and is ready to interact. So, this event will be the last to be called.

If you run your application as before (with the same arguments), you should have the following output:

```
...
[AR] Option Args: [enable, remote, option]
[AR] Option Arg Values: [value1, value2]
[AR] Non Option: [update, upgrade]
[CLR] Args: [--enable, --remote, --option=value1, --option=value2, update,
upgrade]
[AL] Im ready to interact...
...
```

Note that the `ApplicationRunner` is called first, then the `CommandLineRunner`, and lastly the `ApplicationReadyEvent`. You can have multiple `CommandLineRunner` classes that implement the `run` method, and they must be marked as `@Component` and, if needed, listed in order is required, then you can use the `@Order` annotation (with the `Ordered` enum as a parameter depending of the precedence).

Application Configuration

Sometimes it is necessary to have very specific access to a remote server, or have credentials to connect to a remote server, or even sensitive data that you need to store in a database. You can hard-code all this information (credentials, remote IPs, and sensitive data), but this is not a best practice because this info can change in a snap and you're probably going to end up doing something bad if you're trying to redeploy your app with bad consequences, such as connecting to the wrong server for example.

Spring Boot uses `application.properties` or `application.yaml` to externalize the configuration you need, and Spring Boot also uses these files to override some of the defaults (due to the auto-configuration and `conditionals`) in your application. You will see how to change several of these defaults throughout this book, but for now let's talk about how you can create your own properties and use them.

My Retro App and Users App Project Integration

To see how to use external configuration, let's resume our journey with the two projects— My Retro App and Users App. Although we haven't yet discussed how the projects will be integrated later in this book, at some point the My Retro App will need to reach out to the Users App to authenticate and authorize users who want to use the My Retro App. So, in this case, it's necessary to have the server, port, and other useful information.

In the My Retro App, open the `application.properties` file and add the content shown in Listing 2-13.

Listing 2-13. src/main/resources/application.properties

```
# Users Properties
users.server=127.0.0.1
users.port=8081
users.username=admin
users.password=aW3sOm3
```

Listing 2-13 shows some of the properties you are going to need for the My Retro App project. Next, open the MyRetroConfiguration class and replace the content with the code shown in Listing 2-14.

Listing 2-14. src/main/kotlin/com/apress/myretro/MyRetroConfiguration.kt

```kotlin
package com.apress.myretro
import org.slf4j.LoggerFactory
import org.springframework.beans.factory.annotation.Value
import org.springframework.boot.context.event.ApplicationReadyEvent
import org.springframework.context.ApplicationListener
import org.springframework.context.annotation.Bean
import org.springframework.context.annotation.Configuration

@Configuration
class MyRetroConfiguration {
    var log = LoggerFactory.getLogger(MyRetroConfiguration::class.java)

    @Value("\${users.server}")
    var server: String? = null

    @Value("\${users.port}")
    var port: Int? = null

    @Value("\${users.username}")
    var username: String? = null

    @Value("\${users.password}")
    var password: String? = null

    @Bean
    fun init(): ApplicationListener<ApplicationReadyEvent> {
        return ApplicationListener { event: ApplicationReadyEvent? ->
            log.info(
                "\nThe users service properties are:\n" +
                    "- Server: {}\n- Port: {}\n- Username: {}\n-
                    Password: {}",
                server,
                port,
```

```
            username,
            password
        )
    }
  }
}
```

Listing 2-14 shows the updated `MyRetroConfiguration` class. Let's analyze it:

- `@Value("${property-name}")`: This is a new annotation that collects the value of the property specified between " and using the SpEL (Spring Expression Language) that start with $ and the property name between {}. During the Spring app lifecycle (gathering information and creating the beans), it will search for any `@Value` annotation and attempt to look for it in the default file: `application.properties` or `application.yaml`. For example, we declared an Int port variable and annotated it with `@Value("${users.port}")`, so it will get the value 8081 and be assigned to the port variable when this class get instantiated.

- `ApplicationListener`: This interface will execute the `init` method when the `ApplicationReadyEvent` is fired (meaning that the app is ready to interact with other logic).

If you run the application, you should see something similar to the following output:

```
The users service properties are:
- Server: 127.0.0.1
- Port: 8081
- Username: admin
- Password: aW3s0m3
```

What will happen if you have more than four properties? You could add more variables and mark them with `@Value`, but that can get messy quickly. Spring Boot offers a better solution in such cases, described next.

Configuration Properties

Spring Boot offers a simple solution for multiple and more complex properties. It defines a class marker @ConfigurationProperties annotation, which binds the fields of the class to the properties defined externally (in this case, to the application.properties).

Create a new class, called MyRetroProperties, in the src/main/kotlin/com/apress/myretro folder with the content shown in Listing 2-15.

Listing 2-15. src/main/kotlin/com/apress/myretro/MyRetroProperties.kt

```kotlin
package com.apress.myretro.config

import org.springframework.boot.context.properties.ConfigurationProperties

@ConfigurationProperties(prefix = "service")
class MyRetroProperties {
    val users: Users? = null
}

class Users {
    var server: String? = null
    var port: Int? = null
    var username: String? = null
    var password: String? = null
}
```

Listing 2-15 shows the MyRetroProperties class that, thanks to the @ConfigurationProperties, will bind the properties found in application.properties (or application.yaml) to every field in this class. Notice that this class is just a POJO (plain old Java object, Kotlin variant). The idea is to have the same name for every field so that they match. To tell Spring Boot that this class is a ConfigurationProperties class, you need to provide a hint by either marking the class as @Component or using the @EnableConfigurationProperties annotation in a Configuration class. Listing 2-16 shows the modified MyRetroConfiguration class.

Listing 2-16. src/main/kotlin/com/apress/myretro/MyRetroConfiguration.kt

```kotlin
package com.apress.myretro

import org.slf4j.Logger
import org.slf4j.LoggerFactory
import org.springframework.boot.context.event.ApplicationReadyEvent
import org.springframework.boot.context.properties.
EnableConfigurationProperties
import org.springframework.context.ApplicationListener
import org.springframework.context.annotation.Bean
import org.springframework.context.annotation.Configuration

@EnableConfigurationProperties(MyRetroProperties::class)
@Configuration
class MyRetroConfiguration {
    var log: Logger = LoggerFactory.getLogger(MyRetroConfiguration::c
    lass.java)
    @Bean
    fun init(myRetroProperties: MyRetroProperties):
            ApplicationListener<ApplicationReadyEvent> {
        return ApplicationListener<ApplicationReadyEvent> {
            event: ApplicationReadyEvent? ->
                log.info(
                    "\nThe users service properties are:\n" +
                    "- Server: {}\n- Port: {}\n- Username: {}\n- Password: {}",
                    myRetroProperties.users!!.server,
                    myRetroProperties.users.port,
                    myRetroProperties.users.username,
                    myRetroProperties.users.password
                )
        }
    }
}
```

In the modified MyRetroConfiguration class, we are using the @EnableCon
figurationProperties annotation that accepts an array of ConfigurationProperties
marked classes. Also, note that the init method now has a MyRetroProperties
parameter. This class (MyRetroConfiguration.class) will be automatically injected
by Spring (because it's marked using the @Bean annotation). In this way you can access
these properties like any other regular class with its getters.

What happens if you have multiple services (not only Users)? It would be nice to
identify them as services, right? Meaning that you can add a prefix to the configuration
properties class. For example:

```
@ConfigurationProperties(prefix="service")
class MyRetroProperties(var users:Users)
```

The prefix parameter will use the service.* properties binding match on what you
have in your properties files. This means that application.properties should be like this:

```
service.users.server=127.0.0.1
service.users.port=8081
service.users.username=admin
service.users.password=aW3sOm3
```

If you run the application, you should get the same result.

Relaxed Binding

I previously mentioned that the properties must match the name of the field in the class,
right? Well, Spring Boot offers a relaxed binding approach. It provides some relaxed rules
for binding Environment properties to classes marked with @ConfigurationProperties.
If you have a field name that is camel case too long, you can use camel case, underscore,
kebab case, or uppercase format. Consider the following example:

```
private var hostNameServer:String
```

You can use the following notation:

- Camel case: hostNameServer

- Kebab case: host-name-server

- Underscore: host_name_server

- Uppercase: HOST_NAME_SERVER

Configuration Precedence

Another benefit of using externalized configuration is that you can use different variants to define your properties. You can use environment variables, Java system properties, JDNI, servlet content, config parameters, command-line parameters, and much more. But what happens if you have defined the same properties in all these mechanisms? Well, the good part is that Spring Boot has some precedences that can be applied when running your application.

The following list shows the precedence that will take place when running your application and the binding process for your properties:

- Default properties (specified by setting `SpringApplication.setDefaultProperties`).

- `@PropertySource` annotations on your `@Configuration` classes. Note that such property sources are not added to the environment until the application context is being refreshed. This is too late to configure certain properties such as `logging.*` and `spring.main.*`, which are read before the refresh begins.

- Config data (such as `application.properties` files).

- A `RandomValuePropertySource` that has properties only in `random.*`.

- OS environment variables.

- Java System properties (`System.getProperties()`).

- JNDI attributes from `java:comp/env`.

- `ServletContext` init parameters.

- `ServletConfig` init parameters.

- Properties from `SPRING_APPLICATION_JSON` (inline `JSON` embedded in an environment variable or system property).

- Command-line arguments.

- `properties` attribute on your tests (available on `@SpringBootTest` and the test annotations for testing a particular slice of your application).

- @TestPropertySource annotations on your tests.

- Devtools global settings properties in the $HOME/.config/spring-boot directory when devtools is active.

Using the application.properties, you have the following precedence:

- Application properties packaged inside your JAR (application.properties and YAML variants)

- Profile-specific application properties packaged inside your JAR (application-{profile}.properties and YAML variants)

- Application properties outside of your packaged JAR (application.properties and YAML variants)

- Profile-specific application properties outside of your packaged JAR (application-{profile}.properties and YAML variants)

Of course, there are many options for using external configuration, and you can even establish where to read such a file with a location, using the following property/ argument: --spring.config.location=<location>. The most important point here it to look at the precedence. To sum up this section, if you have a JAR that contains application.properties, and where you have run your app has another file (with the same name), it will override what you have, or any environment variable as well will be overriding the properties from the JAR app.

Changing Defaults

As you know, Spring Boot uses defaults to configure your application, but sometimes these defaults are not necessarily what your application needs. One of the many Spring Boot features is the ability to change these defaults. You already saw that you can exclude some of the auto-configuration by using the exclude=arrayOf() parameter in the @SpringBootApplication annotation. But there is also a way to specify how you want those defaults to change.

There is a significant list of application properties that you can access at https:// docs.spring.io/spring-boot/docs/current/reference/html/application-properties.html. For example, if you want to override the default port, 8080, you can do so by using the server.port=8082 property.

The following command achieves the same result:

```
java -jar build/libs/myretro-0.0.1-SNAPSHOT.jar --server.port=8082
SERVER_POST=8082  java -jar build/libs/myretro-0.0.1-SNAPSHOT.jar
java -Dspring.application.json='{"server.port":8082}' -jar build/libs/
myretro-0.0.1-SNAPSHOT.jar
```

Application Profiles

Spring Boot can handle profiles as well, meaning that you not only can use your custom properties or override defaults, but also use profiles for creating beans. The following chapters cover the Spring Profile as well.

As you saw earlier, you can create application-<profile>.properties (or YAML files). This is handy when you have multiple environments and want to keep track of each of them with different values. To use these features, it is necessary to activate the profile by using SpringApplicationBuilder.profiles (as you saw earlier) or by using the spring.profiles.active=<profiles> property.

For example, you can create an additional application-cloud.properties file in the resources folder with other values:

```
service.users.server=cloud.server.com
service.users.port=1089
service.users.username=root
service.users.password=Sup3RaW3sOm3
```

If you run the application by passing this property (either at the command line or in your favorite IDE):

```
--spring.profiles.active="cloud"
```

You should see only the application-cloud.properties file's values.

Using a YAML format can simplify the properties by having only one file. For example, an application.yaml file can look like this:

```
service:
  users:
    server: 127.0.0.1
    port: 8081
    username: admin
```

```
      password: aW3s0m3
---
spring:
  config:
    activate:
      on-profile: cloud
service:
  users:
    server: cloud.server.com
    port: 1089
    username: root
    password: Sup3RaW3s0m3
```

One of the important declarations here is the `spring.config.activate.on-profile` property. It specifies the section divided by three dash characters. This section will be activated only when the `cloud` profile is called. If there is no `on-profile`, it will be the `default` profile set.

Summary

This chapter covered a lot of features, focusing on the most important, or what most developers use. You learned about the internals of Spring Boot and discovered that Spring Boot uses the auto-configuration feature to set defaults that incorporate the best practices for your application. You also learned that Spring Boot, through the auto-configuration feature, will check out the dependencies or classpath your application is using and decide which defaults to apply. All of this is thanks not only to the auto-configuration classes but also to the `@Conditional*` annotations that filter what your app needs, removing a lot of configuration that normally you would need to do if you were creating just Spring apps.

This chapter also showed you that you can customize your Spring Boot app by using the `SpringApplication` class or the `SpringApplicationBuilder` fluent API. You also discovered how to use arguments in your application and how to set up and use `application.properties` and even filter them by using `profiles`.

Chapter 3 explains how to use web apps with Spring Boot and how to create web end points using the My Retro App and Users App projects.

CHAPTER 3

Spring Boot Web Development

Felipe Gutierrez[a*]

[a] 4109 Rillcrest Grove Way Fuquay Varina, NC 27526-3562, Albuquerque, NM, USA

Spring MVC

The Spring MVC technology has been around since the Spring Framework was created, including the MVC (Model View Controller) pattern for web applications, not only for the backend but for the frontend as well. It uses HTML template engines to create views (Views/JSP pages) that can access objects (Models) from the backend (Controllers) and use them.

Creating a Spring Boot web application means including the `spring-boot-starter-web` dependency, which brings all the Spring MVC dependencies, such as `spring-web`, `spring-web-mvc`, an embedded application server (which can run immediately, so there's no need to deploy it externally), and much more. By default, it will use a web server (Apache `Tomcat`).

One of the main classes for the Spring MVC is the `DispatcherServlet` servlet class. This servlet implements a `front-controller` pattern, which provides all the request processing and delegation of responsibilities to the components (classes marked with `@Controller` or `@RestController` annotations).

In a regular Spring web app, it is necessary to declare the `DispatcherServlet` class (in a `web.xml` file) and add a configuration (by declaring a context XML file). This allows the discovery of components that serve for the request mappings (for HTTP methods such as `GET`, `POST`, `PUT`, `DELETE`, `PATCH`, etc.), view resolution, exception handling, and much more.

75

The Spring MVC provides several ways to register components that serve the HTTP request mappings (through XML, JavaConfig, or annotations). It includes the @Controller and @RestController annotations.

Normally, with the @Controller annotation (a class marker annotation), your class methods must return a Model object or the name View interface to be rendered. If you want to respond with another object (such as JSON, XML, etc.), you must add the @ResponseBody annotation to your methods as well. This will set up everything you need for your content negotiation during the request/response scenario. If you use the @RestController annotation, you no longer need the @ResponseBody annotation, because Spring Boot will default to JSON as the content resolver. In other words, if you need to create a RESTful API, you need to use @RestController in your class.

As previously mentioned, the @Controller and @RestController annotations are markers for classes that register components to serve all the HTTP requests, and all the methods that will serve the request should be marked with @GetMapping (for an HTTP GET request), @PostMapping (for an HTTP POST request), @PutMapping, @DeleteMapping, or one of the many other annotations. There is one annotation, @RequestMapping, that can be configured for multiple request scenarios at once (this annotation can be used as a class marker as well).

Spring Boot MVC Auto-Configuration

With Spring Boot, you don't need anything from the previous section, because when your application runs, the auto-configuration feature will set up all the defaults. Here's what auto-configuration is doing behind the scenes:

- *Static content support*: This means that you can add static content, such as HTML, JavaScript, CSS, media, and so forth, in a directory named /static (by default) or /public, /resources, or /META-INF/ resources, which should be in your classpath or in your current directory. Spring Boot picks it up the static content and serves it upon request. You can change this easily by modifying the spring.mvc. static-path-pattern or spring.web.resources.static-locations property. One of the cool features with Spring Boot and web applications is that if you create an index.html file, Spring Boot serves it automatically without registering any other bean or the need for extra configuration.

- `HttpMessageConverters`: If you are using a regular Spring MVC application and you want to get a JSON response, you need to create the necessary configuration (XML or JavaConfig) for the `HttpMessageConverters` bean. Spring Boot adds this support by default, so you don't have to. This means you get the JSON format by default (due to the Jackson libraries that the `spring-boot-starter-web` starter provides as dependencies). If Spring Boot auto-configuration finds that you have the Jackson XML extension in your classpath, it aggregates an XML `HttpMessageConverter` to the converters, meaning that your application can serve based on your `content-type` request, either `application/JSON` or `application/XML`.

- *JSON serializers and deserializers*: If you want to have more control over the serialization/deserialization to/from JSON, Spring Boot provides an easy way to create your own by extending from `JsonSerializer<T>` and/or `JsonDeserializer<T>` and annotating your class with the `@JsonComponent` so that it can be registered for use. Another feature of Spring Boot is the Jackson support; by default, Spring Boot serializes the date fields as `2024-05-01T23:31:38.141+0000`, but you can change this default behavior by changing the `spring.jackson.date-format=yyyy-MM-dd` property. You can apply any date format pattern; the previous value generates the output `2024-05-01`.

- *Path matching and content negotiation*: One of the Spring MVC application features is the ability to respond to any suffix to represent the `content-type` response and its content negotiation. If you have something like `/api/retros.json` or `/api/retros.pdf`, the `content-type` is set to `application/json` and `application/pdf`. The response is in JSON format or a PDF file, respectively. In other words, Spring MVC performs `.*` suffix pattern matching, such as `/ api/ retros.*`. Spring Boot disables this by default. If you prefer, you can either enable it or manually add a parameter by using the `spring.mvc.contentnegotiation.favor-parameter=true` property (`false` by default). You can do something like `/api/retros?format=xml` (`format` is the default parameter name, but you can change it using `spring.mvc.contentnegotiation.parameter-name=myparam`). This triggers the `content-type` to `application/xml`.

- *Error handling*: Spring Boot uses /error mapping to create a white labeled page to show all the global errors. You can change the behavior by creating your own custom pages. You need to create your custom HTML page in the src/main/resources/public/error/ location, so you can create 500.html or 404.html pages, for example. If you are creating a RESTful application, Spring Boot responds as JSON format. Spring Boot also supports Spring MVC to handle errors when you are using @ControllerAdvice or @ExceptionHandler annotations. You can register custom ErrorPages by implementing ErrorPageRegistrar and declaring it as a Spring Bean.

- *Template engine support*: Spring Boot supports Apache FreeMarker, Groovy Templates, Thymeleaf, and Mustache. When you include the spring- boot-starter-<template engine> dependency, Spring Boot will auto-configure all the beans to enable all the view resolvers and file handlers. By default, Spring Boot looks at the src/main/resources/templates/ path. This can be overridden by using the spring.<template-engine>.prefix property.

The next sections review some of these features using the book's two main projects.

My Retro App Project

In Chapter 2, you learned how to create the basic My Retro App configuration, with no behavior or any other class, just some properties to demonstrate a few Spring Boot features. In this section, you complete that project by adding dependencies, more classes, and, of course, a REST API.

Let's start by adding some dependencies to the project. Open the build.gradle file and replace the content with the code in Listing 3-1.

Listing 3-1. The build.gradle File

```
import org.jetbrains.kotlin.gradle.tasks.KotlinCompile
plugins {
    id 'java'
    id 'org.springframework.boot' version '3.2.3'
    id 'io.spring.dependency-management' version '1.1.4'
```

```
    id 'org.jetbrains.kotlin.jvm' version '2.0.20-RC'
    id "org.jetbrains.kotlin.plugin.spring" version "2.0.20-RC"
    // <- simplifies spring proxying
}

group = 'com.apress'
version = '0.0.1-SNAPSHOT'
sourceCompatibility = '17'

repositories {
    mavenCentral()
    maven { url 'https://repo.spring.io/milestone' }
    maven { url 'https://repo.spring.io/snapshot' }
}

dependencies {
    implementation 'org.springframework.boot:spring-boot-starter-web'
    implementation 'org.springframework.boot:spring-boot-starter-
    validation'
    implementation 'org.springframework.boot:spring-boot-starter-aop:'
    implementation "org.jetbrains.kotlin:kotlin-stdlib-jdk8"
    implementation "org.jetbrains.kotlin:kotlin-reflect"

    implementation 'org.slf4j:slf4j-api:2.0.15'

    // Properties
    annotationProcessor "org.springframework.boot:spring-boot-
    configuration-processor"

    // Web
    implementation 'org.webjars:bootstrap:5.2.3'

    testImplementation 'org.springframework.boot:spring-boot-starter-test'
}

tasks.named('test') {
    useJUnitPlatform()
}
```

```
test {
    testLogging {
        events "passed", "skipped", "failed"
        showExceptions true
        exceptionFormat "full"
        showCauses true
        showStackTraces true
        showStandardStreams = false
    }
}

//     kotlin {
//         jvmToolchain(17)
//     }
tasks.withType(KotlinCompile) {
    kotlinOptions {
        freeCompilerArgs = ['-Xjsr305=strict']
        jvmTarget = '17'
    }
}
```

Let's review this new build.gradle file:

- spring-boot-starter-web: This dependency brings all the necessary JARs to My Retro App. It brings the spring-web, spring-webmvc, tomcat, Jackson (for JSON manipulation) modules, and much more. This starter enables you to use the web annotations (@RestController, @GetMapping, and many more) that are necessary to create a web application. And, of course, everything will be auto-configured for you.

- spring-boot-starter-validation: This dependency brings the jakarta-validation JARs, which help you validate that you are sending and creating the objects you need for the domain—the RetroBoard and Card classes (discussed later in this section).

- `spring-boot-starter-aop`: This dependency brings JARs to use *aspect-oriented programming (AOP)*, which is what Spring uses to perform some of the amazing logic, behavior, and auto-configuration to make your applications run smoothly. AOP will help you remove some of the code scattering and code tangling, so that your code looks readable and understandable.

- `spring-boot-starter-configuration-processor`: This dependency adds features such as preprocessing the custom properties (used in the previous chapter) and adding hints for IDEs that have *IntelliSense* and thus know the meaning of the property you are setting up.

- `bootstrap`: This dependency brings the CSS and JavaScript files from the Bootstrap Project (`https://getbootstrap.com/`) and adds them as resources to the `webjars/resource` folder. Although you are not going to build a frontend with Spring (because you are going to use JavaScript), this will make the front page look nice.

- `test > testLogging`: These declarations help with all the logging when you are executing the `test` task from the command line. It will give you more information about each individual test. This was added in previous chapters.

Adding Dependencies

When Spring Boot starts, auto-configuration will review all the dependencies in `build.gradle` and configure and wire up everything for you so that your web app is ready to use.

So far, the My Retro App project has the directory and package structure shown in Figure 3-1. This structure was sufficient to demonstrate the features discussed earlier.

Figure 3-1. *Original directory/package structure*

Now you are going to learn how to transform the project by using the directory/
package structure shown in Figure 3-2.

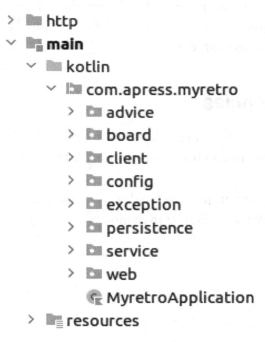

Figure 3-2. *Updated directory/package structure*

This section examines every package in detail and discusses all the classes that we are going to create. Let's start with the domain/model classes. Recall from Chapter 2 that you have two main classes—RetroBoard and Card—and one enum—CardType.

So, let's create these classes and enum in the board package, beginning with RetroBoard. Listing 3-2 shows the RetroBoard class.

Listing 3-2. src/main/kotlin/com/apress/myretro/board/RetroBoard.kt

```kotlin
package com.apress.myretro.board

import jakarta.validation.constraints.NotBlank
import jakarta.validation.constraints.NotNull
import java.util.*

data class RetroBoard(
    var id: UUID? = null,
    @get:NotNull
    @get:NotBlank(message = "A name must be provided")
    val name: String? = null,
    var cards: List<Card> = mutableListOf()
)
```

The RetroBoard class has three fields: a UUID (for the user ID), a String (for the name), and a List (for the Cards). Remember that the RetroBoard can have from 0 to N Cards. RetroBoard also has the following annotations:

- @NotNull: This annotation, part of the Jakarta project, allows you to mark a field as requiring a value (i.e., it can't have a null value).

- @NotBlank: This annotation, also part of the Jakarta project, allows you to mark a field for further processing to check that it is not empty (i.e., it needs to have a value). You can add a message explaining why the field cannot be blank or null.

Listing 3-3 shows the Card class.

Listing 3-3. src/main/kotlin/com/apress/myretro/board/Card.kt

```
package com.apress.myretro.board

import jakarta.validation.constraints.NotBlank
import jakarta.validation.constraints.NotNull
import java.util.*

data class Card(
    var id: UUID? = null,
    @get:NotBlank(message = "A comment must be provided always")
    @get:NotNull
    val comment:  String? = null,
    @get:NotNull(message = "A CardType HAPPYIMEHISAD must be provided")
    val cardType:  CardType? = null
)
```

Again, `Card` is a very simple class with three fields. It has a relationship of type `CardType` that is marked to indicate that this field must not be `null`.

Listing 3-4 shows `CardType`, an enum that provides three elements: HAPPY, MEH, and SAD.

Listing 3-4. src/main/kotlin/com/apress/myretro/board/CardType.kt

```
package com.apress.myretro.board
enum class CardType {
    HAPPY,MEH,SAD
}
```

You need to hold the information about the `RetroBoard` and the `Cards` objects. In this chapter, we are going to do everything in memory. We are going to use a map that allows you to use keys for faster lookup. For example, consider the `persistence` package. We create the `Repository` interface (see Listing 3-5) and the `RetroBoardRepository` that implements the `Repository` interface (see Listing 3-6).

Listing 3-5. src/main/kotlin/com/apress/myretro/persistence/Repository.kt

```kotlin
package com.apress.myretro.persistence

interface Repository<D, ID> {
    fun save(domain: D): D
    fun findById(id: ID): D
    fun findAll(): Iterable<D>
    fun delete(id: ID)
}
```

As Listing 3-5 shows, the `Repository` interface has generic placeholders so that you can use the actual domain/model and the type as the primary key.

Listing 3-6 shows the `RetroBoardRepository` class that implements the `Repository` interface.

Listing 3-6. src/main/kotlin/com/apress/myretro/persistence/
RetroBoardRepository.kt

```kotlin
package com.apress.myretro.persistence

import com.apress.myretro.board.Card
import com.apress.myretro.board.CardType
import com.apress.myretro.board.RetroBoard
import org.springframework.stereotype.Component
import java.util.*

@Component
class RetroBoardRepository : Repository<RetroBoard, UUID> {
    private val retroBoardMap = mutableMapOf(
        UUID.fromString("9DC9B71B-A07E-418B-B972-40225449AFF2") to
        RetroBoard(id=UUID.fromString("9DC9B71B-A07E-418B-
        B972-40225449AFF2"),
            name = "Spring Boot 3.0 Meeting",
            cards = listOf(
                Card(
                    id = UUID.fromString("BB2A80A5-A0F5-4180-
                    A6DC-80C84BC014C9"),
                    comment = "Happy to meet the team",
```

```kotlin
                    cardType = CardType.HAPPY),
                Card(
                    id = UUID.fromString("011EF086-7645-4534-9512-
                    B9BC4CCFB688"),
                    comment = "New projects",
                    cardType = CardType.HAPPY),
                Card(
                    id = UUID.fromString("775A3905-D6BE-49AB-A3C4-
                    EBE287B51539"),
                    comment = "When to meet again??",
                    cardType = CardType.MEH),
                Card(
                    id = UUID.fromString("896C093D-1C50-49A3-A58A-
                    6F1008789632"),
                    comment = "We need more time to finish",
                    cardType = CardType.SAD)
            )
        )
    )

    override fun save(domain: RetroBoard): RetroBoard {
        domain.id = domain.id ?: UUID.randomUUID()
        retroBoardMap[domain.id] = domain
        return domain
    }

    override fun findById(uuid: UUID): RetroBoard = retroBoardMap[uuid]!!

    override fun findAll(): Iterable<RetroBoard> = retroBoardMap.values

    override fun delete(uuid: UUID) {
        retroBoardMap.remove(uuid)
    }
}
```

The RetroBoardRepository class has a marker, the @Repository annotation, which is essential when the application starts, because it will be injected in the service that you will create later in this section. The retroBoardMap will act as in-memory persistence.

The My Retro App project will include a nice way to show any errors that occur when a RetroBoard or a Card is not found or when the validation you set already (using @NotNull and @NotBlank) is triggered.

Now we create the exception package and add the RetroBoardNotFoundException, CardNotFoundException, and RetroBoardResponseEntityExceptionHandler classes. First, Listing 3-7 shows the RetroBoardNotFoundException class.

Listing 3-7. src/main/kotlin/com/apress/myretro/exception/
RetroBoardNotFoundException.kt

```kotlin
package com.apress.myretro.exception

class RetroBoardNotFoundException : RuntimeException {
    constructor() : super("RetroBoard Not Found")
    constructor(message: String?) :
        super(String.format("RetroBoard Not Found: {}", message))
    constructor(message: String?, cause: Throwable?) :
        super(String.format("RetroBoard Not Found: {}", message), cause)
}
```

The RetroBoardNotFoundException class extends the RunTimeException and has some fixed messages for easy handling. An instance of this class will be thrown when you try to search for a RetroBoard with a UUID that doesn't exist.

Listing 3-8 shows the CardNotFoundException class, which will be thrown when a Card within the RetroBoard is not found.

Listing 3-8. src/main/kotlin/com/apress/myretro/exception/
CardNotFoundException.kt

```kotlin
package com.apress.myretro.exception

class CardNotFoundException : RuntimeException {
    constructor() : super("Card Not Found")
    constructor(message: String?) : super(String.format("Card Not Found:
    {}", message))
    constructor(message: String?, cause: Throwable?) :
        super(String.format("Card Not Found: {}", message), cause)
}
```

87

Listing 3-9 shows the RetroBoardResponseEntityExceptionHandler class, which extends from the ResponseEntityExceptionHandler class, meaning that when it finds an error, it will know how to handle it and how to create the *response* for the requester.

Listing 3-9. src/main/kotlin/com/apress/myretro/exception/
RetroBoardResponseEntityException.kt

```
package com.apress.myretro.exception

import org.springframework.http.HttpHeaders
import org.springframework.http.HttpStatus
import org.springframework.http.ResponseEntity
import org.springframework.web.bind.annotation.ControllerAdvice
import org.springframework.web.bind.annotation.ExceptionHandler
import org.springframework.web.context.request.WebRequest
import org.springframework.web.servlet.mvc.method.annotation.
    ResponseEntityExceptionHandler
import java.time.LocalDateTime
import java.time.format.DateTimeFormatter

@ControllerAdvice
class RetroBoardResponseEntityExceptionHandler :
ResponseEntityExceptionHandler() {
    @ExceptionHandler(value =
            [CardNotFoundException::class, RetroBoardNotFoundException
            ::class])
    protected fun handleNotFound(
        ex: RuntimeException, request: WebRequest?
    ): ResponseEntity<Any>? {
        val response: Map<String, Any> = mapOf(
            "msg" to "There is an error",
            "code" to HttpStatus.NOT_FOUND.value(),
            "time" to LocalDateTime.now().
                format(DateTimeFormatter.ofPattern("yyyy-mm-dd HH:mm:ss")),
            "errors" to mapOf(
                "msg" to ex.message
            )
```

```
        )
    return handleExceptionInternal(
        ex, response,
        HttpHeaders(), HttpStatus.NOT_FOUND, request!!
    )
    }
}
```

The following list explains the RetroBoardResponseEntityExceptionHandler class:

- @ControllerAdvice: This annotation uses AOP to implement the *Around Advice* (this means that it will intercept all the method calls defined in the controller and execute them inside a try and catch, and if there is any exception, the handleNotFound method will be called; here is where you add you own logic to handle the error). This annotation is registered to catch errors thrown during runtime. It declares a method that is marked with the @ExceptionHandler annotation.

- @ExceptionHandler: This annotation catches any exception declared as part of the parameter value. In this case, it executes the handleNotFound method when a RetroBoardNotFoundException or CardNotFoundException is thrown.

- ResponseEntity<T>: This annotation extends from an HttpEntity class that represents an HTTP request or response entity, consisting of headers and body. As you can see in Listing 3-9, we are creating a Map, which will be translated by default as a JSON content-type.

- handleExceptionInternal: This method belongs to the extended class, and it will prepare all the common handling and will create the ResponseEntity.

As you can see, the RetroBoardResponseEntityExceptionHandler class provides a special way to handle web errors that occur during the process of looking for a RetroBoard or Card object, or even at the beginning of the request or response.

Next, create the service package and add the RetroBoardService class to it, as shown in Listing 3-10.

Listing 3-10. src/main/kotlin/com/apress/myretro/service/
RetroBoardService.kt

```kotlin
package com.apress.myretro.service

import com.apress.myretro.board.Card
import com.apress.myretro.board.RetroBoard
import com.apress.myretro.exception.CardNotFoundException
import com.apress.myretro.persistence.Repository
import org.springframework.beans.factory.annotation.Autowired
import org.springframework.stereotype.Service
import java.util.*

@Service
class RetroBoardService {
    @Autowired
    lateinit var repository: Repository<RetroBoard, UUID>

    fun save(domain: RetroBoard): RetroBoard? {
        //if (domain.cards == null) domain.cards = mutableListOf<Card>()
        return repository.save(domain)
    }

    fun findById(uuid: UUID): RetroBoard = repository.findById(uuid)

    fun findAll(): Iterable<RetroBoard> = repository.findAll()

    fun delete(uuid: UUID) {
        repository.delete(uuid)
    }

    fun findAllCardsFromRetroBoard(uuid: UUID): Iterable<Card> =
        findById(uuid).cards.asIterable()

    fun addCardToRetroBoard(uuid: UUID, card: Card): Card {
        card.id = card.id ?: UUID.randomUUID()
        val retroBoard: RetroBoard = findById(uuid)
        retroBoard.cards = retroBoard.cards.toMutableList().apply { add(card) }
        return card
    }
```

```
fun findCardByUUIDFromRetroBoard(uuid: UUID, uuidCard: UUID?): Card =
    findById(uuid).cards.filter {
        c -> c.id == uuidCard }.firstOrNull()?:throw
        CardNotFoundException()

fun removeCardFromRetroBoard(uuid: UUID, cardUUID: UUID) {
    val retroBoard: RetroBoard = findById(uuid)
    val cardList: MutableList<Card> = retroBoard.cards.toMutableList()
    cardList.removeIf { card: Card -> card.id!! == cardUUID }
    retroBoard.cards = cardList
    }
}
```

The RetroBoardService class will help you drive all the business logic you need for the application. Let's analyze this class:

- For the repository field, we are using the Repository<D,ID> interface, so the Spring Framework will inject the implementation of this interface by looking at all the Spring Beans registered. We registered this bean in Listing 3-6 using the @Respository annotation, meaning that the RetroBoardRepository implementation will be injected and have access to the in-memory persistence. This capability to use or swap different implementations and still use the same code is one of the features that makes the Spring Framework awesome.

- @Service: This annotation is another stereotype that marks the class as a Spring Bean so that it can be injected or used somewhere in your code. In this case, we will be using this service in the web controller.

Now, before continuing with the other classes in the My Retro App, review the RetroBoardService code (see Listing 3-10) again and look for the findById(UUID) method. Note that we call the repository.findById(UUID) method. If you take a look at Listing 3-6, the function by virtue of the !!-operator will throw a NullPointerException if it cannot find the repository. So, how can you handle this and translate it into a Not Found exception? We are going to use AOP for this. Also notice in the RetroBoardService code that findById is called in several other methods, and you can implement simple logic to catch the error, handle it, or throw the exception. Using this idea, we would be scattering and tangling the code all over the place, and we don't want to do that. The next section provides the solution.

AOP to the Rescue

Aspect-oriented programming (AOP) can help you treat this concern in a separate class, make the logic more readable, and avoid code scattering and tangling.

Now create the advice package and the RetroBoardAdvice class. See Listing 3-11.

Listing 3-11. src/main/kotlin/com/apress/myretro/advice/RetroBoardAdvice.kt

```kotlin
package com.apress.myretro.advice

import com.apress.myretro.board.RetroBoard
import com.apress.myretro.exception.RetroBoardNotFoundException
import org.aspectj.lang.ProceedingJoinPoint
import org.aspectj.lang.annotation.Around
import org.aspectj.lang.annotation.Aspect
import org.slf4j.LoggerFactory
import org.springframework.stereotype.Component
import java.util.*

@Component
@Aspect
class RetroBoardAdvice {
    @Around("execution(* com.apress.myretro.persistence.
    RetroBoardRepository.
            findById(java.util.UUID))")
    @Throws(
        Throwable::class
    )
    fun checkFindRetroBoard(proceedingJoinPoint: Proceeding
    JoinPoint): Any {
        LOG.info("[ADVICE] {}", proceedingJoinPoint.signature.name)
        try {
            return proceedingJoinPoint.proceed(
                arrayOf<Any>(
                    UUID.fromString(proceedingJoinPoint.args[0].toString())
                ))
        }catch (e:NullPointerException) {
```

```
        throw RetroBoardNotFoundException()
    }
}

companion object {
    val LOG = LoggerFactory.getLogger(RetroBoardAdvice::class.java)
}
}
```

The following list breaks down the RetroBoardAdvice class:

- @Component: This annotation is a marker that tells the Spring
  Framework to register it as a Spring Bean and use it when needed.

- @Aspect: This annotation is a marker for a class and it tells the
  Spring Framework that the class has an *Aspect* that will contain an
  Advice (Before, After, Around, AfterReturn, AfterThrowing) that
  will be intercepting a particular method depending on the matcher
  declaration. Behind the scenes, Spring creates proxies for these
  classes and applies everything related to AOP.

- @Around: This annotation is one of the many annotations to create an
  Advice. In this case, it will intercept the call (based on the execution
  declaration that matches the method) before it gets executed, create
  an instance of the ProceedingJoinPoint, execute the method you
  marked with this annotation, and execute your logic. Then, you can
  execute the actual call, do some more logic, and return the result.
  Related annotations include the @Before advice, which will execute
  your method logic before the actual call happens, the @After advice,
  which will execute your method logic after the call, and the
  @AfterReturning advice, which will execute the logic when
  after a successful call and allows to investigate the result.

- execution: This is the key to the advice. This keyword needs pattern
  matching to identify the method to be advised, in AspectJ/Java
  notation. In this case, we are looking for every method with any
  return type (*) and looking for that specific method in the com.
  apress.myretro.repository.RetroBoardRepository.findById that
  has as a parameter that matches the UUID. In this case, this is very

straightforward, but you could have an expression like this: `* com.apress.*..*.find*(*)`. This means finding any class that is between the package `apress` and up and any class that has the `find` prefix for the method that accepts any number of parameters, no matter the type.

- `ProceedingJoinPoint`: This is an interface, and its implementation knows how to get the object that is being advised (`RetroBoardRepository.findById`). It has the actual object, and you can call the parameter that will execute it, get the result, and return it. You can manipulate the result or even the parameters that you are sending. Only the `Around Advice` must have this `ProceedingJoinPoint`.

So, when you tell the service to look for a `RetroBoard` instance (saved in-memory), it will intercept the call (*advice/around*) to the `RetroBoardRepository` and will execute the `checkFindRetroBoard` method. It will gather all the information from the `ProcedingJoinPoint` and check for a `NullPointerException`. If it occurs, it will throw the `RetroBoardNotFoundException` and will return the result otherwise.

With this `Advice`, we are isolating our concern about a check, avoiding any repetition of code (tangling and scattering), and making our code more understandable and cleaner.

This is just a small example of the power of the AOP paradigm. You can use your own custom annotation and advice on methods. For example, you can create a `@Cache` annotation and use the `Around Advice` for every method that uses that annotation.

Tip   If you want to know more about AOP, we recommend *Pro Spring 6* (Apress, 2023) or the Spring documentation, where you can find a very good explanation of what advice types are and what else you can do with them (`https://docs.spring.io/spring-framework/docs/current/reference/html/core.html#aop`).

Now it's time to do some web logic!

Spring Web Annotated Controllers

Spring MVC provides annotation-based programming and includes two useful annotations—@Controller and @RestController. These annotations are used for request mappings, request input, exception handling, and much more.

The @Controller annotation is used with the Model and ModelAndView classes and the View interface. When they are used together, you have access to Session attributes and to objects that you can use in your HTML pages. With this functionality, you need to return the name of the view, and Spring Web will handle the resolution and the rendering of the HTML page. Consider the following snippet:

```
// more ...
@Controller
class MyRetroBoardController {
    private lateinit
    var retroBoardService:RetroBoardService
    @GetMapping("/retros")
    fun handle(model:Model):String {
        model.addAttribute("retros",
                            retroBoardService.findAll())
        return "listRetros"
    }
    // more ...
}
```

The preceding snippet marks MyRetroBoardController as a *web controller* (using the @Controller annotation). When you access the "/retros" endpoint, it will create the necessary Model class to which you can add an attribute (in this case, the retros attribute with the value of all the retros), then return the name of the HTML page (listRetros, which lives in src/main/resources/templates/listRetros.html) that will do the rendering and use the retros data within the page. The Spring Web will know how to resolve the location of the page and how to render it using a template engine. If you need to respond with a particular value (different from the View), you need to add the @ResponseBody annotation to the return type (declared in the method) so that the Spring Web will use the HTTP message converter and respond properly.

The @RestController annotation is another class marker (this is a compose annotation from @Controller) and will write directly to the response body (so there is no need for the @ResponseBody annotation). We use this annotation throughout the book, because we use Spring Boot much more for the backend.

The Spring Web technology also includes the @RequestMapping annotation, which can be a marker for a class or a method because it is useful for mapping requests to controllers. One of the benefits of @RequestMapping is that it brings access to request parameters, headers, and media types. @RequestMapping can be used for every method, but sometimes you can use shortcuts: @GetMapping, @PostMapping, @PutMapping, @DeleteMapping, and many others. These shortcuts are described following their appearance in Listing 3-12.

Now it's time to code the web controller. Create the web package and the RetroBoardController class, as shown in Listing 3-12.

Listing 3-12. src/main/kotlin/com/apress/myretro/web/ RetroBoardController.kt

```
package com.apress.myretro.web

import com.apress.myretro.board.Card
import com.apress.myretro.board.RetroBoard
import com.apress.myretro.service.RetroBoardService
import jakarta.validation.Valid
import org.springframework.http.HttpStatus
import org.springframework.http.ResponseEntity
import org.springframework.validation.FieldError
import org.springframework.validation.ObjectError
import org.springframework.web.bind.MethodArgumentNotValidException
import org.springframework.web.bind.annotation.*
import org.springframework.web.servlet.support.ServletUriComponentsBuilder
import org.springframework.beans.factory.annotation.Autowired
import java.io.Serializable
import java.net.URI
import java.time.LocalDateTime
import java.time.format.DateTimeFormatter
import java.util.*
```

```kotlin
@RestController
@RequestMapping("/retros")
class RetroBoardController {
    @Autowired
    private lateinit var retroBoardService: RetroBoardService

    @get:GetMapping
    val allRetroBoards: ResponseEntity<Iterable<RetroBoard>>
        get() = ResponseEntity.ok(retroBoardService.findAll())

    @PostMapping
    fun saveRetroBoard(@RequestBody retroBoard: @Valid RetroBoard):
            ResponseEntity<RetroBoard> {
        val result: RetroBoard? = retroBoardService.save(retroBoard)
        val location: URI = ServletUriComponentsBuilder
            .fromCurrentRequest()
            .path("/{uuid}")
            .buildAndExpand(result!!.id.toString())
            .toUri()
        return ResponseEntity.created(location).body<RetroBoard>(result)
    }

    @GetMapping("/{uuid}")
    fun findRetroBoardById(@PathVariable uuid: UUID): Response
    Entity<RetroBoard> {
        return ResponseEntity.ok<RetroBoard>(retroBoardService.
        findById(uuid))
    }

    @GetMapping("/{uuid}/cards")
    fun getAllCardsFromBoard(@PathVariable uuid: UUID):
            ResponseEntity<Iterable<Card>> {
        return ResponseEntity.ok(retroBoardService.findAllCardsFromRetro
        Board(uuid))
    }

    @PutMapping("/{uuid}/cards")
```

```kotlin
fun addCardToRetroBoard(@PathVariable uuid: UUID, @RequestBody card:
@Valid Card):
        ResponseEntity<Card> {
    val result: Card = retroBoardService.addCardToRetroBoard
    (uuid, card)
    val location: URI = ServletUriComponentsBuilder
        .fromCurrentRequest()
        .path("/{uuid}/cards/{uuidCard}")
        .buildAndExpand(uuid.toString(), result.id.toString())
        .toUri()
    return ResponseEntity.created(location).body<Card>(result)
}

@GetMapping("/{uuid}/cards/{uuidCard}")
fun getCardFromRetroBoard(@PathVariable uuid: UUID, @PathVariable
uuidCard: UUID?):
        ResponseEntity<Card> {
    return ResponseEntity.ok<Card>(retroBoardService.
            findCardByUUIDFromRetroBoard(uuid, uuidCard))
}

@ResponseStatus(HttpStatus.NO_CONTENT)
@DeleteMapping("/{uuid}/cards/{uuidCard}")
fun deleteCardFromRetroBoard(@PathVariable uuid: UUID,
        @PathVariable uuidCard: UUID) {
    retroBoardService.removeCardFromRetroBoard(uuid, uuidCard)
}

@ExceptionHandler(MethodArgumentNotValidException::class)
@ResponseStatus(HttpStatus.BAD_REQUEST)
fun handleValidationExceptions(ex: MethodArgumentNotValidException):
        Map<String, Any> {
    val response:MutableMap<String,Any> = mutableMapOf(
      "msg" to "There is an error",
      "code" to HttpStatus.BAD_REQUEST.value(),
      "time" to LocalDateTime.now().format(
            DateTimeFormatter.ofPattern("yyyy-MM-dd HH:mm:ss"))
```

```
    )
    val errors: MutableMap<String, String> = mutableMapOf()
    ex.bindingResult.allErrors.forEach{ error: ObjectError ->
        val fieldName: String = (error as FieldError).field
        val errorMessage: String = error.getDefaultMessage()!!
        errors[fieldName] = errorMessage
    }
    response["errors"] = errors
    return response
    }
}
```

Let's analyze the RetroBoardController class:

- Spring will *inject* the RetroBoardService bean because of the @Autowired annotation, so you have access in this controller class.

- @RestController: We are marking this class using the @RestController annotation. This annotation writes directly to the response body using all the methods declared.

- @RequestMapping: This annotation marks the class as the one that will respond to any request with the right HTTP method, and it will have the /retros endpoint as a base for any other path declared.

- @GetMapping: This annotation marks several methods that will respond with the HTTP GET method to the /retros endpoint. This is a shortcut of @RequestMapping(method = RequestMethod.GET), which has more parameters that you can use. If you look at the findRetroBoardById method, you will see that @GetMapping is using the "/{uuid}" value. This is a path variable that is mapped to URL patterns. In this case, the PathPattern allows you to use matching patterns such as the following:

  - "/retros/docu?ent.doc": Match only one character in a path.

  - "/retros/*.jpg": Match zero or more characters in a path.

  - "/retros/**": Match multiple path segments.

- "/retros/{project}/versions": Match a path segment and capture it as a variable.

- "/retros/{project:[a-z]+}/versions": Match and capture a variable with a regex.

You can have something like this in your method: @GetMapping("/{product:[a-z-]+}-{version:\\d\\.\\d\\.\\d}{ext:\\.[a-z]+}"). As you can see, you have options to declare how you want to access your endpoint, and this applies for every @RequestMapping and their shortcuts.

- ResponseEntity: This class extends from the HttpEntity (a generic) class that represents an HTTP request or response entity that brings the headers and the body. If you look around the code, you will see that the type varies. Including the ResponseEntity class is one of the common practices to use for a web app in Spring Boot or Spring Web applications. By default, Spring Boot will respond using an HTTP JSON message converter, so you can always expect a JSON response. Of course, you can override this default and respond in another format, such as XML.

- @PostMapping: This is another annotation that responds to the HTTP POST method request, sending a body (data) in the HTTP packet. This is the same as @RequestMapping(method = RequestMethod.POST). For this type of request, you normally send data, so you will probably be required to use the @RequestBody annotation.

- @RequestBody: This annotation looks at the body of the web request and tries to bind it (using the HttpMessageConverter) to the instance that is marked with this annotation. And in this controller, we have two: one for the RetroBoard and another for the Card classes. You can use validation to validate the data using the @Valid annotation.

- @Valid: This annotation marks a parameter to do a cascading validation to see if the parameter passes validation based on the constraints used, such as @NotNull, @NotEmpty, @NotBlank, and so on. All these annotations are present in the RetroBoard and Card classes and belong to the Jakarta library. Behind the scenes, this will do the validation when the web request is happening, and it will throw an exception that you can catch.

- `@PathVariable`: This annotation does the binding with the path declared in the `@RequestMapping` or the shortcuts used, like in the `findRetroBoardById` method, where the value of the `/retros/{uuid}` path is bound to the UUID instance. So, you can access it using something like this:

  GET `http://localhost:8080/retros/`**9dc9b71b-a07e-418b-b972-40225449aff2**

  `9dc9b71b-a07e-418b-b972-40225449aff2` will be set to the UUID instance variable. The name of the path (`{uuid}`) must match the name of the parameter declared in the function.

- `ServletUriComponentsBuilder`: This is a helper class that can be used to create a URI and expand to the base path with the keys and values. In this case, this class is used in the `saveRetroBoard` method, where it will create the location needed in the `Header` that will be set as part of the response with the `ResponseEntity.create(<URI>)` method call.

- `@PutMapping`: This annotation responds to the HTTP PUT method request, which normally brings an HTTP `Body` into the request. In this case, it is a combination of a particular path (with a URL pattern) and an HTTP `Body` (`@RequestBody`). See the `addCardToRetroBoard` method, which also brings some validation with the `@Valid` annotation.

- `@ResponseStatus`: This annotation is used to customize the HTTP status code returned in a response for a given controller method or exception handler. Sometimes, regardless of the operation, you can return a particular *HTTP status code*. In this case, in the `deleteCardFromRetroBoard` method, we are returning the `HttpStatus.NO_CONTENT` status (204 code).

- `@DeleteMapping`: This annotation responds to the HTTP DELETE request method. In this code, we also declare a URL path using the `@PathVariable`.

- @ExceptionHandler: This annotation is used to define methods
  that handle specific exceptions thrown during the execution of
  controller methods (or within the scope of a @ControllerAdvice
  class for global exception handling). When an exception occurs
  that matches the type declared in the @ExceptionHandler method's
  parameter, Spring MVC will invoke this method to handle the
  exception and generate an appropriate response. Sometimes, it is
  necessary to respond in a specific way to an error or exception that
  occurred in the application. By default, Spring will answer with an
  exception that the Tomcat server (embedded) will throw as "Server
  Internal error" (or any other error), without much information about
  what happened. To avoid this, you can catch these types of errors,
  such as the error that occurs when you don't have valid data (from
  the RetroBoard or Card), and explain what happened. You can
  annotate a method that can take care of that. This code includes the
  handleValidationExceptions method. The @ExceptionHandler
  has the MethodArgumentNotValidException class declared as a
  parameter, meaning that it will be triggered only when the validation
  that is happening throws this error.

- MethodArgumentNotValidException: This class is thrown
  when the @Valid cascading validation is happening. The
  handleValidationExceptions method will create the necessary
  response with any errors, and it will return a Map that will be
  converted to JSON format, which is a better way to understand what
  is happening.

You have just learned how to implement a web application with Spring Boot. Before
you continue by testing it, take another look at the RetroBoardController class. Check
out every detail.

Testing My Retro App

To test this application, let's start by testing the RetroBoardService class, which
is the core of the application. So, in the test folder, replace the contents of
MyretroApplicationTests with the code shown in Listing 3-13.

Listing 3-13. src/test/kotlin/com/apress/myretro/MyRetroApplicationTests.kt

```kotlin
package com.apress.myretro

import com.apress.myretro.board.Card
import com.apress.myretro.board.CardType
import com.apress.myretro.board.RetroBoard
import com.apress.myretro.exception.CardNotFoundException
import com.apress.myretro.exception.RetroBoardNotFoundException
import com.apress.myretro.service.RetroBoardService
import org.assertj.core.api.Assertions
import org.assertj.core.api.AssertionsForClassTypes
import org.junit.jupiter.api.Test
import org.springframework.beans.factory.annotation.Autowired
import org.springframework.boot.test.context.SpringBootTest
import java.util.*

@SpringBootTest
internal class MyretroApplicationTests {
    @Autowired
    lateinit var service: RetroBoardService

    var retroBoardUUID = UUID.fromString("9DC9B71B-A07E-418B-
B972-40225449AFF2")
    var cardUUID = UUID.fromString("BB2A80A5-A0F5-4180-A6DC-80C84BC014C9")
    var mehCardUUID = UUID.fromString("775A3905-D6BE-49AB-A3C4-
EBE287B51539")

    @Test
    fun saveRetroBoardTest() {
        val retroBoard = service.save(RetroBoard(name = "Gathering 2023"))
        Assertions.assertThat(retroBoard).isNotNull()
        Assertions.assertThat(retroBoard!!.id).isNotNull()
    }

    @Test
    fun findAllRetroBoardsTest() {
        val retroBoards = service.findAll()
```

```kotlin
        Assertions.assertThat(retroBoards).isNotNull()
        Assertions.assertThat(retroBoards).isNotEmpty()
    }

    @Test
    fun cardsRetroBoardNotFoundTest() {
        AssertionsForClassTypes.assertThatThrownBy {
                service.findAllCardsFromRetroBoard(UUID.randomUUID()) }
            .isInstanceOf(
                RetroBoardNotFoundException::class.java
            )
    }

    @Test
    fun findRetroBoardTest() {
        val retroBoard = service.findById(retroBoardUUID)
        Assertions.assertThat(retroBoard).isNotNull()
        Assertions.assertThat(retroBoard!!.name).isEqualTo("Spring Boot 3.0
        Meeting")
        Assertions.assertThat(retroBoard.id).isEqualTo(retroBoardUUID)
    }

    @Test
    fun findCardsInRetroBoardTest() {
        val retroBoard = service.findById(retroBoardUUID)
        Assertions.assertThat(retroBoard).isNotNull()
        Assertions.assertThat(retroBoard!!.cards).isNotEmpty()
    }

    @Test
    fun addCardToRetroBoardTest() {
        val card = service.addCardToRetroBoard(
            retroBoardUUID, Card(
                comment = "Amazing session",
                cardType = CardType.HAPPY)
        )
        Assertions.assertThat(card).isNotNull()
```

```kotlin
        Assertions.assertThat(card.id).isNotNull()
        val retroBoard = service.findById(retroBoardUUID)
        Assertions.assertThat(retroBoard).isNotNull()
        Assertions.assertThat(retroBoard!!.cards).isNotEmpty()
    }

    @Test
    fun findAllCardsFromRetroBoardTest() {
        val cardList = service.findAllCardsFromRetroBoard(retroBoardUUID)
        Assertions.assertThat(cardList).isNotNull()
        Assertions.assertThat((cardList as Collection<*>).size).
        isGreaterThan(3)
    }

    @Test
    fun removeCardsFromRetroBoardTest() {
        service.removeCardFromRetroBoard(retroBoardUUID, cardUUID)
        val retroBoard = service.findById(retroBoardUUID)
        Assertions.assertThat(retroBoard).isNotNull()
        Assertions.assertThat(retroBoard!!.cards).isNotEmpty()
        Assertions.assertThat(retroBoard.cards).hasSizeLessThan(4)
    }

    @Test
    fun findCardByIdInRetroBoardTest() {
        val card = service.findCardByUUIDFromRetroBoard(retroBoardUUID,
        mehCardUUID)
        Assertions.assertThat(card).isNotNull()
        Assertions.assertThat(card.id).isEqualTo(mehCardUUID)
    }

    @Test
    fun notFoundCardInRetroBoardTest() {
        AssertionsForClassTypes.assertThatThrownBy {
            service.findCardByUUIDFromRetroBoard(
                retroBoardUUID,
```

```
                UUID.randomUUID()
            )
        }.isInstanceOf( CardNotFoundException::class.java )
    }
}
```

As you can see, the MyretroApplicationTests class only tests the service. This test uses very simple assertions from the *AssertJ library*. To test whether My Retro App returns the correct exception, you can use the assertThatThrownBy method. You can run these tests either by using your IDE or by running the following command:

```
./gradlew clean test
Starting a Gradle Daemon, 2 incompatible Daemons could not be reused, use
--status for details
> Task :compileJava
> Task :test
MyretroApplicationTests > saveRetroBoardTest() PASSED
MyretroApplicationTests > findAllRetroBoardsTest() PASSED
MyretroApplicationTests > findRetroBoardTest() PASSED
MyretroApplicationTests > removeCardsFromRetroBoardTest() PASSED
MyretroApplicationTests > cardsRetroBoardNotFoundTest() PASSED
MyretroApplicationTests > notFoundCardInRetroBoardTest() PASSED
MyretroApplicationTests > findCardsInRetroBoardTest() PASSED
MyretroApplicationTests > addCardToRetroBoardTest() PASSED
MyretroApplicationTests > findCardByIdInRetroBoardTesT() PASSED
MyretroApplicationTests > findAllCardsFromRetroBoardTest() PASSED
BUILD SUCCESSFUL in 10s
5 actionable tasks: 5 executed
```

What you really want to do is test the web API, right? There are various tools that can help you to do this, such as PostMan (https://www.postman.com) and Insomnia (https://insomnia.rest), but we want to introduce you to a tool called REST Client that can help you perform HTTP requests directly. There is an open source version and a paid version, sharing the same style. The paid version is within the IntelliJ IDEA Enterprise Edition, called the REST Client. And if you are using VS Code, you must install REST Client (v0.25.x) from the Plugins tab. The author of this plugin is Huachao Mao (see Figure 3-3).

Figure 3-3. *REST Client is a VS Code plugin created by Huachao Mao*

Next, we demonstrate the use of the VS Code REST Client plugin to test the My Retro App. To follow along, download the plugin, create the src/http folder, and add the myretro.http file with the content shown in Listing 3-14.

Listing 3-14. src/http/myretro.http

```
### Get All Retro Boards
GET http://localhost:8080/retros
Content-Type: application/json
### Get Retro Board
GET http://localhost:8080/retros/9dc9b71b-a07e-418b-b972-40225449aff2
Content-Type: application/json
### Get All Cards from Retro Board
GET http://localhost:8080/retros/9dc9b71b-a07e-418b-b972-40225449aff2/cards
Content-Type: application/json
### Get Single Card from Retro Board
GET http://localhost:8080/retros/9dc9b71b-a07e-418b-b972-40225449aff2/
cards/bb2a80a5-a0f5-4180-a6dc-80c84bc014c9
Content-Type: application/json
### Create a Retro Board
POST http://localhost:8080/retros
```

```
Content-Type: application/json
{
  "name": "Spring Boot Conference"
}
### Add Card to Retro
PUT http://localhost:8080/retros/9dc9b71b-a07e-418b-b972-40225449aff2/cards
Content-Type: application/json
{
  "comment": "We are back in business",
  "cardType": "HAPPY"
}
### Delete Card from Retro
DELETE http://localhost:8080/retros/9dc9b71b-a07e-418b-b972-40225449aff2/
cards/bb2a80a5-a0f5-4180-a6dc-80c84bc014c9
Content-Type: application/json
```

Listing 3-14 shows all the necessary calls to cover the My Retro App. At the top of every call, you should have enabled a Send Request link; if you click it, you will see the response in another window. Experiment with each call.

Using this type of client is very easy. This plugin can do much more than described in this brief introduction. If you want to learn more about how to use it, visit https:// github.com/Huachao/vscode-restclient.

Users App Project

Now it's time to transform the Users App project that you saw in Chapter 1. This section shows you how to make it more functional. Figure 3-4 shows the directory structure that you will end with after completing this section.

```
v ■ src
    > ■ http
    v ■ main
        v ■ kotlin
            v ■ com.apress.users
                ☰ Repository
                ☰ User
                ☰ UserRepository
                ☰ UserRole
                ☰ UsersApplication
                ☰ UsersHandler
                ☰ UsersRoutes
```

Figure 3-4. *Users App project*

Open the build.gradle file and replace the existing content with the content shown in Listing 3-15.

Listing 3-15. The New build.gradle File

```
import org.jetbrains.kotlin.gradle.tasks.KotlinCompile
plugins {
    id 'java'
    id 'org.springframework.boot' version '3.2.3'
    id 'io.spring.dependency-management' version '1.1.4'
    id 'org.jetbrains.kotlin.jvm' version '2.0.20-RC'
    id "org.jetbrains.kotlin.plugin.spring" version "2.0.20-RC"
    // <- simplifies spring proxying
}

group = 'com.apress'
version = '0.0.1-SNAPSHOT'
sourceCompatibility = '17'

repositories {
    mavenCentral()
}
```

```
ext['jakarta-servlet.version'] = '5.0.0'

dependencies {
    //implementation 'jakarta.servlet:jakarta.servlet-api:5.0.0'
    implementation 'jakarta.platform:jakarta.jakartaee-api:10.0.0'

    implementation('org.springframework.boot:spring-boot-starter-web')
    modules {
        module("org.springframework.boot:spring-boot-starter-tomcat") {
            replacedBy("org.springframework.boot:spring-boot-
            starter-jetty",
                        "Use Jetty instead of Tomcat")
        }
    }
    implementation 'org.springframework.boot:spring-boot-starter-
    validation'
    implementation "org.jetbrains.kotlin:kotlin-stdlib-jdk8"
    implementation "org.jetbrains.kotlin:kotlin-reflect"

    // Jetty
    implementation 'org.springframework.boot:spring-boot-starter-jetty'

    // Web
    implementation 'org.webjars:bootstrap:5.2.3'

    testImplementation 'org.springframework.boot:spring-boot-starter-test'
}

tasks.named('test') {
    useJUnitPlatform()
}

test {
    testLogging {
        events "passed", "skipped", "failed"
        showExceptions true
        exceptionFormat "full"
        showCauses true
        showStackTraces true
```

```
        showStandardStreams = false
    }
}

//    kotlin {
//        jvmToolchain(17)
//    }
tasks.withType(KotlinCompile) {
    kotlinOptions {
        freeCompilerArgs = ['-Xjsr305=strict']
        jvmTarget = '17'
    }
}
```

This new build.gradle file incorporates validation.

Next, open the User class and replace its content with the code shown in Listing 3-16.

Listing 3-16. src/main/kotlin/com/apress/users/User.kt

```
package com.apress.users

import jakarta.validation.constraints.NotBlank
import jakarta.validation.constraints.Pattern

data class User(
    @get:NotBlank(message = "Email cannot be empty")
    var email:  String? = null,
    @get:NotBlank(message = "Name cannot be empty")
    var name:  String? = null,
    var gravatarUrl: String? = null,
    @get:Pattern(
        message = "Password must be at least 8 characters long and contain
        at least one number, one uppercase, one lowercase and one special
        character",
        regexp = "^(?=.*[0-9])(?=.*[a-z])(?=.*[A-Z])(?=.*[@#$%^&+=!])(?=\\
        S+$).{8,}$"
    )
```

```
    var password:  String? = null,
    var userRole: List<UserRole> = mutableListOf(),
    var active:Boolean = false
)
```

The following describes the annotations in the new User class:

- @NotBlank/@Pattern: These annotations are used when the validation starts with a web request. @NotBlank was introduced earlier. The @Pattern annotation performs a match pattern validation, and if it fails, it produces an error message.

As you can see, you are adding a few more features to this app, such as validation. Next, create the UserRole enum, the Repository interface, and the UserRepository class. Listing 3-17 shows the enum for the User roles.

Listing 3-17. src/main/kotlin/com/apress/users/UserRole.kt

```
package com.apress.users
enum class UserRole {
    USER, ADMIN, INFO
}
```

Listing 3-18 shows the Repository interface, which in fact is the same as the one in the My Retro App project (shown in Listing 3-5).

Listing 3-18. src/main/kotlin/com/apress/users/Repository.kt

```
package com.apress.users

interface Repository<D, ID> {
    fun save(domain: D): D
    fun findById(id: ID): D?
    fun findAll(): Iterable<D>
    fun deleteById(id: ID)
}
```

Listing 3-19 shows the UserRepository implementation class.

Listing 3-19. src/main/kotlin/com/apress/users/UserRepository.kt

```kotlin
package com.apress.users

import org.springframework.stereotype.Component
import java.util.*

@Component
class UserRepository : Repository<User, String> {
    private val users: MutableMap<String, User> = mutableMapOf(
        "ximena@email.com" to
            User(email = "ximena@email.com",
                name = "Ximena",
                gravatarUrl = "https://www.gravatar.com/avatar/"+
                            "23bb62a7d0ca63c9a804908e57bf6bd4?d=wavatar",
                password = "aw2s0meR!",
                userRole = listOf(UserRole.USER),
                active = true
            ),
        "norma@email.com" to
            User(name = "Norma",
                email = "norma@email.com",
                gravatarUrl = "https://www.gravatar.com/avatar/"+
                            "f07f7e553264c9710105edebe6c465e7?d=wavatar",
                password = "aw2s0meR!",
                userRole = listOf(UserRole.USER,UserRole.ADMIN),
                active = true
            )
    )

    override fun save(user: User): User {
        user.gravatarUrl = user.gravatarUrl?: "https://www.gravatar.com/
        avatar/"+
                "23bb62a7d0ca63c9a804908e57bf6bd4?d=wavatar"
        //if (user.userRole == null) user.userRole = emptyList()
        users[user.email!!] = user
        return user
    }
```

```
    override fun findById(id: String): User? = users[id]

    override fun findAll(): Iterable<User> = users.values

    override fun deleteById(id: String) {
        users.remove(id)
    }
}
```

Review the listings closely and you'll see that the updated Users App is very similar to the My Retro App, and that it now uses in-memory persistence.

Spring Web Functional Endpoints

Spring MVC provides functional programming as well to define web endpoints. Functions are used to define routes and handle requests. Every HTTP request is handled by a HandlerFunction (RouterFunction) that takes a ServerRequest and returns a ServerResponse.

These requests are routed to a RouterFunction that takes the ServerRequest and returns an optional HandlerFunction. You can consider this RouterFunction as being equivalent to the @RequestMapping annotation but with the advantage that it deals not only with data but also with behavior.

Next, add the UsersRoutes class. See Listing 3-20.

Listing 3-20. src/main/kotlin/com/apress/users/UsersRoutes.kt

```
package com.apress.users

import org.springframework.context.annotation.Bean
import org.springframework.context.annotation.Configuration
import org.springframework.http.MediaType
import org.springframework.validation.Validator
import org.springframework.validation.beanvalidation.
LocalValidatorFactoryBean
import org.springframework.web.servlet.function.*
```

```
@Configuration
class UsersRoutes {
    @Bean
    fun userRoutes(usersHandler: UsersHandler):
    RouterFunction<ServerResponse> {
        return RouterFunctions.route().nest(RequestPredicates.path("/
        users")) {
            builder: RouterFunctions.Builder ->
                builder.GET(
                    "",
                    RequestPredicates.accept(MediaType.APPLICATION_JSON)
                ) { request: ServerRequest -> usersHandler.findAll(request) }
                builder.GET(
                    "/{email}",
                    RequestPredicates.accept(MediaType.APPLICATION_JSON)
                ) { request: ServerRequest -> usersHandler.
                findUserByEmail(request) }
                builder.POST("") { request: ServerRequest -> usersHandler.
                save(request) }
                builder.DELETE("/{email}") {
                    request: ServerRequest -> usersHandler.
                    deleteByEmail(request) }
            }.build()
    }

    @Bean
    fun validator(): Validator = LocalValidatorFactoryBean()
}
```

The UsersRoutes class has the following components:

- @Configuration: Spring Boot looks for this annotation when the
  application starts; it helps to identify any possible Spring Beans,
  marked with the @Bean annotation. This class defines two beans—the
  userRoutes and the validator.

- `RouterFunction<ServerResponse>`: This is an interface that defines several methods that help to build a `RouterFunction`. The common way is to use the Fluent API that defines the `RouterFunction` interface. Note the `userRoutes(UsersHandler)` method, which is expecting the Spring Bean `UsersHandler`. For Spring to know about this bean, it must be declared (using `@Bean` or marking the class using the `@Component` annotation).

- `route()`: This is a Fluent API that defines the necessary routing depending on the endpoint defined. In this case, we are creating a common path called `/users` using the `RequestPredicates` abstract class.

- `builder`: We are using a builder (a `java.util.function.Consumer`) that allows us to define which HTTP methods will be routed to the handler, in this case to the `UsersHandler` class. Here we are declaring the `GET`, `POST`, and `DELETE` HTTP methods and defining the method that will be used from the handler.

- `@Bean`: This annotation is used to declare the Spring Beans used in the application.

- `Validator/LocalValidatorFactoryBean`: This bean validator returns a `LocalValidatorFactoryBean` class that is used when using the constraints (`@NotBlank` and `@Pattern`) in the `User` class. This is the only way to do validation using the functional way to declare web API endpoints. This validator is going to be used in the `UsersHandler` class, covered next.

Next, add the `UsersHandler` class. See Listing 3-21.

Listing 3-21. src/main/kotlin/com/apress/users/UsersHandler.kt

```
package com.apress.users

import jakarta.servlet.ServletException
import org.springframework.beans.factory.annotation.Autowired
import org.springframework.http.HttpStatus
import org.springframework.http.MediaType
import org.springframework.stereotype.Component
```

```kotlin
import org.springframework.validation.BindingResult
import org.springframework.validation.DataBinder
import org.springframework.validation.Validator
import org.springframework.web.servlet.function.ServerRequest
import org.springframework.web.servlet.function.ServerResponse
import org.springframework.web.servlet.support.ServletUriComponentsBuilder
import java.io.IOException
import java.time.LocalDateTime
import java.time.format.DateTimeFormatter

@Component
class UsersHandler {
    @Autowired
    private lateinit var userRepository: Repository<User, String>
    @Autowired
    private lateinit var validator: Validator

    fun findAll(request: ServerRequest): ServerResponse {
        return ServerResponse
            .ok()
            .contentType(MediaType.APPLICATION_JSON)
            .body(userRepository.findAll())
    }

    fun findUserByEmail(request: ServerRequest): ServerResponse {
        return ServerResponse
            .ok()
            .contentType(MediaType.APPLICATION_JSON)
            .body(userRepository.findById(request.
            pathVariable("email"))?:"{}")
    }

    @Throws(ServletException::class, IOException::class)
    fun save(request: ServerRequest): ServerResponse {
        val user = request.body(User::class.java)
        val bindingResult = validate(user)
        if (bindingResult.hasErrors()) {
            return prepareErrorResponse(bindingResult)
```

```kotlin
        }
        userRepository.save(user)
        val location = ServletUriComponentsBuilder
            .fromCurrentRequest()
            .path("/{email}")
            .buildAndExpand(user.email)
            .toUri()
        return ServerResponse.created(location).body(user)
    }

    fun deleteByEmail(request: ServerRequest): ServerResponse {
        userRepository.deleteById(request.pathVariable("email"))
        return ServerResponse.noContent().build()
    }

    private fun validate(user: User): BindingResult {
        val binder = DataBinder(user).apply {
            addValidators(this@UsersHandler.validator)
        }
        binder.validate()
        return binder.bindingResult
    }

    private fun prepareErrorResponse(bindingResult: BindingResult):
    ServerResponse {
        val response: MutableMap<String, Any> = mutableMapOf(
            "msg" to "There is an error",
            "code" to HttpStatus.BAD_REQUEST.value(),
            "time" to LocalDateTime.now().format(
                DateTimeFormatter.ofPattern("yyyy-MM-dd HH:mm:ss")),
            "errors" to bindingResult.fieldErrors.associate { fieldError ->
                fieldError.field to fieldError.defaultMessage
            }
        )
        return ServerResponse.badRequest().body(response)
    }
}
```

The UsersHandler class has the following parts:

- Spring will inject the beans that correspond to each field in question via the @Autowired annotation. One will be the UserRepository and the other one is declared in the UsersRoutes class, the validator (LocalValidationFactoryBean).

- @Component: This annotation is the marker that identifies this class as Spring Bean to be used in the web app when needed. In this case, this is the handler that will attend every web request.

- ServerRequest: This is an interface that represents a server-side HTTP request and it's being handled by a HandlerFunction. It has access to the headers and body. The save(ServerRequest) method has access to the HTTP body when using request.body(<class-type>). Behind the scenes it's using all the necessary HTTP message converters to get the right class-type (in this case, the User class).

- ServerResponse: This interface represents the server-side HTTP response, as returned by a HandlerFunction. Similar to the ResponseEntity class discussed earlier in this chapter, it can build the whole response with several helpful methods.

- BindingResult: In the save method, we are using the validate(user); this will return a BindingResult interface that invokes the validator for every constraint set in the class that is being validated. Look at the prepareErrorResponse; if the validation caught any errors, we could iterate over and prepare the message using the ServerResponse.

Testing the Users App

It's time to test the Users App. Add the UsersHttpRequestTests class to the src/main/test/kotlin/com/apress/users folder. See Listing 3-22.

Listing 3-22. src/test/kotlin/com/apress/users/UsersHttpRequestTests.kt

```kotlin
package com.apress.users

import org.assertj.core.api.Assertions
import org.junit.jupiter.api.Test
import org.springframework.beans.factory.annotation.Autowired
import org.springframework.beans.factory.annotation.Value
import org.springframework.boot.test.context.SpringBootTest
import org.springframework.boot.test.web.client.TestRestTemplate

@SpringBootTest(webEnvironment = SpringBootTest.WebEnvironment.RANDOM_PORT)
class UsersHttpRequestTests {
    @Value("\${local.server.port}")
    private val port = 0

    private val BASE_URL = "http://localhost:"
    private val USERS_PATH = "/users"

    @Autowired
    private lateinit var restTemplate: TestRestTemplate

    @Test
    @Throws(Exception::class)
    fun indexPageShouldReturnHeaderOneContent() {
        Assertions.assertThat(
            restTemplate.getForObject(
                BASE_URL + port,
                String::class.java
            )
        ).contains("Simple Users Rest Application")
    }

    @Test
    @Throws(Exception::class)
    fun usersEndPointShouldReturnCollectionWithTwoUsers() {
        val response: Collection<User> =
            restTemplate.getForObject(BASE_URL + port +
                    USERS_PATH, Collection::class.java) as Collection<User>
```

```kotlin
    Assertions.assertThat(response).isNotNull()
    Assertions.assertThat(response).isNotEmpty()
}

@Test
@Throws(Exception::class)
fun userEndPointPostNewUserShouldReturnUser() {
    val user: User = User(email = "dummy@email.com", name = "Dummy",
            password = "aw2sOm3R!")
    val response = restTemplate.postForObject(BASE_URL + port + USERS_
    PATH, user,
            User::class.java)
    Assertions.assertThat(response).isNotNull()
    Assertions.assertThat(response.email).isEqualTo(user.email)
    val users: Collection<User> =
        restTemplate.getForObject(BASE_URL + port + USERS_PATH,
                Collection::class.java) as Collection<User>
    Assertions.assertThat(users.size).isGreaterThanOrEqualTo(2)
}

@Test
@Throws(Exception::class)
fun userEndPointDeleteUserShouldReturnVoid() {
    restTemplate.delete("$BASE_URL$port$USERS_PATH/norma@email.com")
    val users: Collection<User> =
        restTemplate.getForObject(BASE_URL + port + USERS_PATH,
                Collection::class.java) as Collection<User>
    Assertions.assertThat(users.size).isLessThanOrEqualTo(2)
}

@Test
@Throws(Exception::class)
fun userEndPointFindUserShouldReturnUser() {
    val user = restTemplate.getForObject(
            "$BASE_URL$port$USERS_PATH/ximena@email.com",
            User::class.java)
    Assertions.assertThat(user).isNotNull()
```

```kotlin
        Assertions.assertThat(user.email).isEqualTo("ximena@email.com")
    }

    @Test
    @Throws(Exception::class)
    fun userEndPointPostNewUserShouldReturnBadUserResponseIfBadPasswd() {
        val user: User = User(email = "dummy@email.com", name = "Dummy",
                password = "aw2s0m")
        val response: Map<*, *> =
            restTemplate.postForObject(BASE_URL + port + USERS_PATH,
                    user, Map::class.java)
        Assertions.assertThat<Any>(response).isNotNull()
        Assertions.assertThat(response["errors"]).isNotNull()
        val errors = response["errors"] as Map<*, *>?
        Assertions.assertThat(errors!!["password"]).isNotNull()
        Assertions.assertThat(errors["password"])
            .isEqualTo("Password must be at least 8 characters long and
            contain at least one number, one uppercase, one lowercase and
            one special character")
    }
}
```

The UsersHttpRequestTests class includes the following:

- **@SpringBootTest**. This annotation sets up the integration tests that let you interact with a running web application. As you can see, it is using a webEnvironment = SpringBootTest.WebEnvironment. RANDOM_PORT parameter, which instructs Spring Boot to start the application with a real web server listening on a randomly chosen available port.

- **@Value**: This annotation is used to inject values into fields, method parameters, or constructor arguments in Spring-managed beans. It provides a convenient way to externalize configuration values and inject them directly where they are needed.

- **@Autowired**: This annotation is used to enable automatic dependency injection. It instructs Spring to resolve and inject collaborating beans into other beans, automatically wiring them together.

- TestRestTemplate: This class is a convenient alternative to the standard RestTemplate specifically designed for integration testing of RESTful web services. It provides several features that make it easier to test your application's endpoints in a controlled environment. It automatically configures an HTTP client (Apache HttpClient or OkHttp) for testing purposes, eliminating the need for manual setup. Unlike RestTemplate, which throws exceptions for 4xx and 5xx status codes, TestRestTemplate handles these errors gracefully by returning a ResponseEntity object. This allows you to easily check the response status and handle errors in your test code. It provides convenient methods for handling basic authentication (with BasicAuth) and OAuth2 authentication (with OAuth2Client).

In the last method (userEndPointPostNewUserShouldReturnBadUserResponse IfBadPasswd()), we are testing the actual response. In this case, there's no need for an exception; practically we are receiving a JSON (based on the Map interface). In other words, the Map interface can be converted to a JSON with no issues. We can also assert that the password does not comply with the constraints. If you want to see this in action using the REST Client (VS Code or IntelliJ plugin), check out the users.http file in the src/http folder.

Congratulations! You have created two awesome web applications with Spring Boot!

Note   Remember that you have access to all the source code for this book. Go to the Apress site under the book's name and click Resources/Source Code.

Spring Boot Web: Overriding Defaults

Now that you have completed the two apps, this section explores some of the defaults that you can override. The main goal with the two apps is that the My Retro App will use the Users App for authentication and authorization, plus some other features. If you want to run the two apps on the same machine, it won't be possible with the default settings, because both apps use the same port to run. But no worries—Spring Boot allows you to override this default, as described next. Spring Boot also allows you to override the default JSON date format and the default application container, as described in the subsequent sections.

Overriding Default Server Settings

By default, the embedded Tomcat server starts on port 8080, but you can easily change that by using the following property:

```
server.port=8082
```

One of the cool features of Spring is that you can apply the Spring Expression Language (SpEL) to these properties. For example, when you create an executable JAR (`./gradlew build`), you can pass parameters when running your application. You can do the following:

```
java -jar users-0.0.1-SNAPSHOT.jar --port=8082
```

and in your `application.properties` file, you have something like this:

```
server.port=${port:8082}
```

This expression means that if you pass the `--port` argument, the application takes that value for the port; if not, it's set to 8182.

Tip   This is just a small taste of what you can do with SpEL. If you want to know more, go to `https://docs.spring.io/spring/docs/current/spring-framework-reference/core.html#expressions`.

You can also change the server address, which is useful when you want to run your application using a particular IP address. For example:

```
server.address=10.0.0.7
```

You can also change the context of your application:

```
server.servlet.context-path=/contacts-app
```

And you can execute a cUrl command like this:

```
curl -I http://localhost:8080/contacts/users
```

You can have Tomcat with SSL by using the following properties:

```
server.port=8443
server.ssl.key-store=classpath:keystore.jks
server.ssl.key-store-password=secret
server.ssl.key-password=secret
```

You can manage a session by using the following properties:

```
server.servlet.session.store-dir=/tmp
server.servlet.session.persistent=true
server.servlet.session.timeout=15
server.servlet.session.cookie.name=todo-cookie.dat
server.servlet.session.cookie.path=/tmp/cookies
```

You can enable HTTP/2 support as follows (if your environment supports it):

```
server.http2.enabled=true
```

JSON Date Format

By default, the date types are exposed in the JSON response in a long format, but you can change that by providing your own pattern in the following properties:

```
spring.jackson.date-format=yyyy-MM-dd HH:mm:ss
spring.jackson.time-zone=MST7MDT
```

These properties format the date and use the time zone that you specify.

Tip   If you want to know more about the available time zone IDs, execute `java. util.TimeZone#getAvailableIDs`. If you want to know more about which properties exist, check out `https://docs.spring.io/spring-boot/docs/ current/reference/html/common-application-properties.html`.

Using a Different Application Container

By default, Spring Boot uses Tomcat (for web servlet apps) as an application container and sets up an embedded server. If you want to override this default, you can do so by modifying the Gradle `build.gradle` file, as shown in Listing 3-23.

Listing 3-23. The build.gradle File

```
...

dependencies {
    ...
    modules {
        module("org.springframework.boot:spring-boot-starter-tomcat") {
            replacedBy("org.springframework.boot:spring-boot-
            starter-jetty",
                    "Use Jetty instead of Tomcat")
        }
    }
    // Jetty
    implementation 'org.springframework.boot:spring-boot-starter-jetty'
    ...
}
...
```

Spring Boot Web Clients

This section shows you how to create a client that will connect to the Users App and obtain user information. It uses the RestTemplate class to connect externally to a service.

To create this client, you need to modify the current configuration of My Retro App. In the config package, we previously had only two classes—MyRetroConfiguration and MyRetroProperties. We need to add a third class, UsersConfiguration. In MyRetroProperties, we currently have some class declarations that allow us to bind the properties, but the problem is just the visibility, we need access to them. Figure 3-5 shows the new classes and packages for the client that the following listings will produce.

```
✓ ▶ main
  ✓ ▶ kotlin
    ✓ ▶ com.apress.myretro
      > ▶ advice
      > ▶ board
      ✓ ▶ client
          ⓒ User
          ⓒ UserRole
          ⓒ UsersClient
      ✓ ▶ config
          ⓒ MyRetroConfiguration
          ⓒ MyRetroProperties
          ⓒ UsersConfiguration
      > ▶ exception
```

Figure 3-5. *The config and client packages*

The `MyRetroConfiguration.kt`, `MyRetroProperties.kt`, and `UsersConfiguration.kt` files for the `config` package are shown in Listings 3-24, 3-25, and 3-26, respectively.

Listing 3-24. src/main/kotlin/com/apress/myretro/config/ MyRetroConfiguration.kt

```
package com.apress.myretro.config

import org.springframework.boot.context.properties.
EnableConfigurationProperties
import org.springframework.context.annotation.Configuration

@EnableConfigurationProperties(MyRetroProperties::class)
@Configuration
class MyRetroConfiguration
```

Listing 3-25. src/main/kotlin/com/apress/myretro/config/MyRetroProperties.kt

```
package com.apress.myretro.config
import org.springframework.boot.context.properties.ConfigurationProperties

@ConfigurationProperties(prefix = "service")
data class MyRetroProperties(
    var users: UsersConfiguration? = null
)
```

Listing 3-26. src/main/kotlin/com/apress/myretro/config/
UsersConfiguration.kt

```
package com.apress.myretro.config

data class UsersConfiguration(
    var server: String? = null,
    var port: Int? = null,
    var username: String? = null,
    var password: String? = null
)
```

As you can see, the only change is the visibility to add separated classes.

Next, let's look at the client package. Listings 3-27 and 3-28 show the User class and the UserRole enum. As you can see, they are the same fields, except that you don't need the password.

Listing 3-27. src/main/kotlin/com/apress/myretro/client/User.kt

```
package com.apress.myretro.client

data class User(val email: String? = null,
    val name: String? = null,
    val gravatarUrl: String? = null,
    val userRole: List<UserRole>? = null,
    val active: Boolean = false
)
```

Listing 3-28. src/main/kotlin/com/apress/myretro/client/UserRole.kt

```
package com.apress.myretro.client
enum class UserRole {
    ADMIN, USER, INFO
}
```

The important class in the client package is UsersClient, shown in Listing 3-29, which will connect remotely to the other web app (Users App).

Listing 3-29.   src/main/kotlin/com/apress/myretro/client/UsersClient.kt

```
package com.apress.myretro.client

import com.apress.myretro.config.MyRetroProperties
import org.springframework.stereotype.Component
import org.springframework.web.client.RestTemplate
import java.text.MessageFormat

@Component
class UsersClient(val USERS_URL: String = "/users",
                  val restTemplate: RestTemplate = RestTemplate(),
                  val myRetroProperties: MyRetroProperties? = null) {
    fun findUserByEmail(email: String): User? {
        val uri: String = MessageFormat.format(
            "{0}:{1}{2}/{3}",
            myRetroProperties!!.users!!.server,
            myRetroProperties!!.users!!.port.toString(),
            USERS_URL, email
        )
        return restTemplate.getForObject(uri, User::class.java)
    }
}
```

Let's analyze the UsersClient class:

- MyRetroProperties: These are the properties that define the external services. You can add them using the prefix service and the class UsersConfiguration. So, the properties will be like this (from the src/main/resources/application.yaml file):

```
service:
  users:
    server: http://localhost
    port: 8082
    username: admin
    password: aW3sOm3
```

- RestTemplate: This class uses the Template pattern, which hides all the boilerplate of creating a connection and dealing with exceptions. The RestTemplate provides several useful methods that allow you to get the objects. We use more features of this class throughout the book.

As you can see, this is very simple. Right now, we only need a method to look up the users using their emails (except for the password, for now).

Testing the Client

To test the client, create the UsersClientTest class in the test structure. See Listing 3-30.

Listing 3-30. src/test/kotlin/com/apress/myretro/UsersClientTest.kt

```kotlin
package com.apress.myretro

import com.apress.myretro.client.UsersClient
import org.assertj.core.api.Assertions
import org.junit.jupiter.api.Test
import org.springframework.beans.factory.annotation.Autowired
import org.springframework.boot.test.context.SpringBootTest
import org.springframework.boot.test.web.client.TestRestTemplate
import org.springframework.web.client.RestTemplate

// the @users:UsersApplication.kt must be running, and
// see @users:resources/application.properties
@SpringBootTest
class UsersClientTest {
    @Autowired
    lateinit var usersClient: UsersClient

    @Test
    fun findUserTest() {
        val user = usersClient.findUserByEmail("norma@email.com")
        Assertions.assertThat(user).isNotNull()
        Assertions.assertThat(user!!.name).isEqualTo("Norma")
```

```
        Assertions.assertThat(user.email).isEqualTo("norma@email.com")
    }
}
```

Listing 3-30 shows the test for the UsersClient. Of course, to run it, you need to run the Users app on port 8082.

Summary

In this chapter you learned how to create a Spring Boot web application. You learned that Spring Web and Spring Web MVC are the foundation of Spring Boot. Spring Boot uses the default settings to configure your web application, but you learned how to change those defaults.

You learned the two different methods of using Web Servlet applications: annotation based and functional based. You completed the formal structure for the two projects— Users App and My Retro App—which means that adding new features in subsequent chapters will be relatively easy.

Currently, these applications hold the data using in-memory persistence. Chapter 4 explores how to store the data on a SQL database and how Spring Boot can help you manage that data using a database engine.

CHAPTER 4

Spring Boot SQL Data Access

Felipe Gutierrez[a*]

[a] 4109 Rillcrest Grove Way Fuquay Varina, NC 27526-3562, Albuquerque, NM, USA

Spring Boot Features for SQL Databases

After you create a project in Spring Boot and add the data driver's dependencies (e.g., `org.postgresql:postgresql`), when the app starts, the Spring Boot *auto-configuration* will try to configure everything to create a `DataSource` implementation. If you are new to data development, normally you will need some information about your database: the URL (in the form `jdbc:<engine>://<server>:<port>/<database>[/|?<additio nal-parameters>]`), the *username* and *password* for the database, and sometimes the database engine *driver*. All these will be configured by Spring Boot unless you override the default values.

Another important feature is that Spring Boot uses *connection pools* that allow the application to have a better management, better concurrency, and performance when your application has persistence. By default, the *HikariCP* connection pool is selected if present; normally this happens when you use the `spring-boot-starter-jdbc` or `spring-boot-starter-data-jpa` starter as a dependency. You can change the connection pool from the default.

If you deploy your Spring Boot application to an application server, such as Tomcat, IBM WebSphere, Jetty, GlassFish, WildFly, or JBoss, among others, you can use the JNDI connection property in the `DataSource` (`spring.datasource.jndi-name`).

This chapter covers many new features for the main two applications, so let's get started with the Spring Framework Data Access.

© Peter Späth, Felipe Gutierrez 2025

P. Späth and F. Gutierrez, *Pro Spring Boot 3 with Kotlin*, https://doi.org/10.1007/979-8-8688-1131-9_4

Spring Framework Data Access

As part of its core, the Spring Framework has Data Access, which offers the following features:

- *Transaction management*: Spring provides a complete abstraction for transaction management with features such as a consistent programming model across different APIs (such as JTA, JDBC, Hibernate, and JPA), supports a declarative transaction management or annotation based (using `@Transactional`), a way to configure transaction isolation levels, and excellent integration with Spring data access abstractions.

- *Data Access Object (DAO) support*: DAO support provides a consistent way to interact with different APIs (such as JDBC, Hibernate, and JPA), so any switch between them is easy to do and maintain. Spring also supplies an exception translator that is consistent between technologies, so you don't have to worry about specific API errors. To get all the benefits of DAO support, it's necessary to use the `@Repository` annotation.

- *Data Access with JDBC*: Using Spring JDBC you will only take care of specifying the SQL statements, declare parameters and provide the values, and provide the connection parameters. You can use the `JdbcTemplate` class to take care of the boilerplate of interacting with the database, and it can provide better error interpretation. Spring JDBC provides features such as executing operations for batch processing, using the `SimpleJDBC` classes, and modeling JDBC operations as Java or Kotlin objects. It also provides embedded support and a way to initialize the `DataSource`. The easy way to start with Spring JDBC is to provide the `DataSource` (which requires the URL, username, password, and driver of your database engine), and then you can use the `JdbcTemplate` (this class requires the `DataSource`). Another important Spring JDBC feature is embedded database support (for database engines such as H2, HSQL, and Derby, among others), and you can initialize a database by providing SQL files with schema definitions and data.

- *Data Access with R2DBC*: Spring supports the implementation of reactive patterns for databases that use SQL for non-blocking scenarios. The Spring R2DBC brings the `DatabaseClient` class that is the core for control basic R2DBC processing and error handling, among other utility classes. It also brings the `ConnectionFactory` implementation for R2DBC connectivity, among other utility classes.

- *Object Relational Mapping (ORM)*: Spring's ORM supports integration with the Java Persistence API (JPA) and Hibernate, Data Access Object (DAO) implementations, and transaction strategies. One of the most popular features of this technology is the use of reverse engineering, because it can create the table relationships based on the classes without any XML mapping.

- *Object-XML mappers*: Spring supports Object-XML mapping to convert an XML document to and from an object.

As you can see, the Spring Framework Data Access is the core of several data technologies that enable developers to create enterprise-ready data applications following the consistent Spring programming model. And, of course, Spring Boot takes advantage of all of this to help developers apply the common and default practices to avoid any errors and help with development.

JDBC with Spring Boot

As previously mentioned, Spring JDBC requires you to provide the connection parameters, specify the SQL statements, declare parameters and parameter values, and do some work when you have a result set, among other settings. With Spring Boot, you are covered with some of these features, where you don't need to specify any configuration at all.

By using the `spring-boot-starter-jdbc` starter dependency, Spring's `JdbcTemplate` and `NamedParameterJdbcTemplate` are auto-configured, enabling you to use Spring JDBC directly in your classes using the constructor. There are also some `spring.jdbc.template.*` properties that you can modify when needed.

Users App: Using Spring Boot JDBC

The Users App project is currently using in-memory persistence, so now it's time to switch and use the JDBC. We recommend creating an empty project from the Spring Initializr (`https://start.spring.io`) and starting from there. After you download the project and unzip it, you can import it into your favorite IDE. If you feel comfortable modifying your existing code, that will be fine as well. Figure 4-1 shows the structure and code that you'll develop in this section.

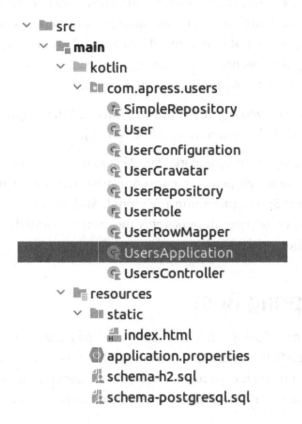

Figure 4-1. *Users App project directory structure*

As you can see, we are going to use the controller programming again.

Start by opening the `build.gradle` file and replacing the contents with the contents shown in Listing 4-1.

Listing 4-1. The build.gradle File

```
import org.jetbrains.kotlin.gradle.tasks.KotlinCompile
plugins {
    id 'org.springframework.boot' version '3.2.3'
    id 'io.spring.dependency-management' version '1.1.4'
    id 'org.jetbrains.kotlin.jvm' version '2.0.20-RC'
    id "org.jetbrains.kotlin.plugin.spring" version "2.0.20-RC"
    // <- simplifies spring proxying
}

group = 'com.apress'
version = '0.0.1-SNAPSHOT'
sourceCompatibility = '17'

repositories {
    mavenCentral()
}

dependencies {
    implementation "org.jetbrains.kotlin:kotlin-stdlib-jdk8"
    implementation "org.jetbrains.kotlin:kotlin-reflect"

    implementation 'org.springframework.boot:spring-boot-starter-web'
    implementation 'org.springframework.boot:spring-boot-starter-
    validation'

    implementation 'org.springframework.boot:spring-boot-starter-jdbc'
    runtimeOnly 'com.h2database:h2'
    runtimeOnly 'org.postgresql:postgresql'

    // Web
    implementation 'org.webjars:bootstrap:5.2.3'

    testImplementation 'org.springframework.boot:spring-boot-starter-test'
}

tasks.named('test') {
    useJUnitPlatform()
}
```

```
test {
    testLogging {
        events "passed", "skipped", "failed"
        showExceptions true
        exceptionFormat "full"
        showCauses true
        showStackTraces true
        showStandardStreams = false
    }
}

//     kotlin {
//         jvmToolchain(17)
//     }
tasks.withType(KotlinCompile) {
    kotlinOptions {
        freeCompilerArgs = ['-Xjsr305=strict']
        jvmTarget = '17'
    }
}
```

The important change to the build.gradle file (from the previous version) is that we are adding three additional dependencies: the spring-boot-starter-jdbc dependency and the h2 and postgresql drivers (which are used only at runtime). Keep in mind that we are using two drivers. If you are wondering which database driver Spring Boot will configure, h2 or postgresql, that answer is provided later in this chapter.

Next, create the SimpleRepository interface with the code shown in Listing 4-2.

Listing 4-2. src/main/kotlin/com/apress/users/SimpleRepository.kt

```
package com.apress.users

interface SimpleRepository<D, ID> {
    fun findById(id: ID): D?
    fun findAll(): Iterable<D>
```

```kotlin
    fun save(d: D): D
    fun deleteById(id: ID)
}
```

Note that the SimpleRepository interface is the same as in the previous version.

Gravatar: Identifying the User

Create the UserGravatar object as shown in Listing 4-3.

Listing 4-3. src/main/kotlin/com/apress/users/UserGravatar.kt

```kotlin
package com.apress.users

import java.security.MessageDigest

object UserGravatar {
    @OptIn(ExperimentalStdlibApi::class)
    fun getGravatarUrlFromEmail(email: String) =
        String.format("https://www.gravatar.com/avatar/%s?d=wavatar",
        md5Hex(email))

    @kotlin.ExperimentalStdlibApi
    private fun md5Hex(message: String) =
        MessageDigest.getInstance("MD5")
            .digest(message.toByteArray(charset("CP1252"))).toHexString()
}
```

The UserGravatar object is a simple utility object that enables you to add a Gravatar icon to your web application based on the user's email address.

Model: enum and record Types

Create the UserRole enum, as shown in Listing 4-4. This enum is very simple and is the same as in the previous versions.

Listing 4-4. src/main/kotlin/com/apress/users/User.kt

```kotlin
package com.apress.users
enum class UserRole {
    USER, ADMIN, INFO
}
```

The User class is similar to previous versions; see Listing 4-5.

Listing 4-5. src/main/kotlin/com/apress/users/User.kt

```kotlin
package com.apress.users

import java.util.regex.Pattern

class User(
    var id: Int? = null,
    var email: String,
    var name: String,
    var password: String,
    var active: Boolean,
    var gravatarUrl: String? = null,
    var userRole: MutableList<UserRole>? = mutableListOf()
) {
    fun withId(id: Int): User {
        return User(id, email, name, password, active, gravatarUrl,
        userRole)
    }

    init {
        var pattern = Pattern.compile(
            "^(?=.*[0-9])(?=.*[a-z])(?=.*[A-Z])(?=.*[@#$%^&+=!])(?=\\
            S+$).{8,}$")
        var matcher = pattern.matcher(password)
        require(matcher.matches()) { "Password must be at least 8
        characters "+
          "long and contain at least one number, one uppercase, one
          lowercase "+
          "and one special character" }
```

```
pattern = Pattern.compile("^[a-zA-ZO-9_!#$%&'*+/=?`{|}~^.-]+@
[a-zA-ZO-9.-]+$")
matcher = pattern.matcher(email)
require(matcher.matches()) { "Email must be a valid email
address" }
gravatarUrl = gravatarUrl?:UserGravatar.
getGravatarUrlFromEmail(email)
userRole = userRole?: mutableListOf(UserRole.INFO)
    }
}
```

JdbcTemplate and RowMapper

Create the UserRowMapper class shown in Listing 4-6.

Listing 4-6. src/main/kotlin/com/apress/users/UserRowMapper.kt

```
package com.apress.users

import org.springframework.jdbc.core.RowMapper
import java.sql.ResultSet
import java.sql.SQLException
import java.util.*
import java.util.stream.Collectors

class UserRowMapper : RowMapper<User> {
    @Throws(SQLException::class)
    override fun mapRow(rs: ResultSet, rowNum: Int): User {
        val array = rs.getArray("user_role")
        val roles = (array.array as Array<Any>).map(Any::toString).
            map{UserRole.valueOf(it)}.toMutableList()
        return User(
            id = rs.getInt("id"),
            name = rs.getString("name"),
            email = rs.getString("email"),
            password = rs.getString("password"),
            active = rs.getBoolean("active"),
```

```
            userRole = roles)
    }
}
```

The UserRowMapper class implements the RowMapper functional interface (with the mapRow(ResultSet,int) method), which is being used along with the JdbcTemplate class (introduced shortly) to map rows of java.sql.ResultSet results, one row at a time. As you can see, we are building the User object and returning it.

Next, create the UserRepository class. See Listing 4-7.

Listing 4-7. src/main/kotlin/apress/com/users/UserRepository.kt

```kotlin
package com.apress.users

import org.springframework.jdbc.core.JdbcTemplate
import org.springframework.jdbc.support.GeneratedKeyHolder
import org.springframework.jdbc.support.KeyHolder
import org.springframework.stereotype.Repository
import java.sql.Connection
import java.sql.Statement
import java.sql.Types

@Repository
class UserRepository : SimpleRepository<User, Int> {
    @Autowired
    private lateinit var jdbcTemplate: JdbcTemplate

    override fun findById(id: Int): User? {
        val sql = "SELECT * FROM users WHERE id = ?"
        val params = arrayOf<Any>(id)
        val user = jdbcTemplate.queryForObject(sql, params,
            intArrayOf(Types.INTEGER), UserRowMapper())
        return user
    }

    override fun findAll(): Iterable<User> {
        val sql = "SELECT * FROM users"
        return jdbcTemplate.query(sql, UserRowMapper())
    }
```

```kotlin
override fun save(user: User): User {
    val sql =
        "INSERT INTO users "+
        "  (name, email, password, gravatar_url,user_role,active) "+
        "VALUES (?, ?, ?, ?, ?, ?)"
    val keyHolder: KeyHolder = GeneratedKeyHolder()
    jdbcTemplate.update({ connection: Connection ->
        val array: Array<String> =
            user.userRole!!.map(UserRole::name).toTypedArray()
        connection.prepareStatement(sql, Statement.RETURN_GENERATED_
        KEYS).apply {
            setString(1, user.name)
            setString(2, user.email)
            setString(3, user.password)
            setString(4, user.gravatarUrl)
            setArray(5, connection.createArrayOf("varchar", array))
            setBoolean(6, user.active)
        }
    }, keyHolder)
    return user.withId(keyHolder.keys!!["id"] as Int)
}

override fun deleteById(id: Int) {
    val sql = "DELETE FROM users WHERE id = ?"
    jdbcTemplate.update(sql, id)
}
}
```

The UserRepository class implements the SimpleRepository interface. In this class, we are using the JdbcTemplate class. This class will be *autowired* by Spring Boot auto-configuration. Remember, this class will do the heavy lifting of the interaction with the database through JDBC calls. With JdbcTemplate, you have several ways to interact with the database:

- query: This is one of several overload methods that executes a SQL query and maps each row to a result object via RowMapper—in this case our UserRowMapper.

- queryForObject: This is one of several overload methods that query a given SQL statement to create a prepared statement from a list of arguments to bind to the query, and it maps a single result row to a result object via a RowMapper.

- update: This is one of several overload methods that issues a single SQL update operation (you can use INSERT, UPDATE, or DELETE statements) via a prepared statement, binding the given arguments.

It's worth mentioning that in the save(user:User) method, we are using the record withId method call, so we add the Id from the keyHolder (this is how we get an *auto-increment* value back). The keyHolder will be populated with different keys, and the one we want will be generated.

If you look at the JdbcTemplate documentation (https://docs.spring.io/spring-framework/docs/current/javadoc-api/org/springframework/jdbc/core/JdbcTemplate.html), you'll see that it brings implementation to methods such as queryForMap, queryForList, queryForRowSet, queryForStream, execute, batchUpdate, and many more.

Remember that the JdbcTemplate already knows how to interact with the database based on the DataSource information (URL, username, password, etc.).

Adding the Web Controller

Create the UsersController class shown in Listing 4-8.

Listing 4-8. src/main/kotlin/apress/com/users/UsersController.kt

```
package com.apress.users

import jakarta.validation.Valid
import org.springframework.http.HttpStatus
import org.springframework.http.ResponseEntity
import org.springframework.http.converter.HttpMessageNotReadableException
import org.springframework.validation.FieldError
import org.springframework.validation.ObjectError
import org.springframework.web.bind.MethodArgumentNotValidException
import org.springframework.web.bind.annotation.*
```

```kotlin
import org.springframework.web.servlet.support.ServletUriComponentsBuilder
import java.time.LocalDateTime
import java.time.format.DateTimeFormatter

@RestController
@RequestMapping("/users")
class UsersController {
    @Autowired
    private lateinit var userRepository: SimpleRepository<User, Int>

    @get:GetMapping
    val all: ResponseEntity<Iterable<User>>
        get() = ResponseEntity.ok(userRepository.findAll())

    @GetMapping("/{id}")
    fun findUserById(@PathVariable id: Int): ResponseEntity<User> =
        ResponseEntity.ofNullable(userRepository.findById(id))

    @RequestMapping(method = [RequestMethod.POST, RequestMethod.PUT])
    fun save(@RequestBody user: @Valid User): ResponseEntity<User> {
        val result = userRepository.save(user)
        val location = ServletUriComponentsBuilder
            .fromCurrentRequest()
            .path("/{id}")
            .buildAndExpand(user)
            .toUri()
        return ResponseEntity.created(location).body(
            userRepository.findById(result.id!!)
        )
    }

    @DeleteMapping("/{id}")
    @ResponseStatus(HttpStatus.NO_CONTENT)
    fun delete(@PathVariable id: Int) {
        userRepository.deleteById(id)
    }

    @ExceptionHandler(MethodArgumentNotValidException::class)
```

```
    @ResponseStatus(HttpStatus.BAD_REQUEST)
    fun handleValidationExceptions(ex: MethodArgumentNotValidException):
        Map<String, String> =
        ex.bindingResult.allErrors.associate { error: ObjectError ->
            (error as FieldError).field to (error.getDefaultMessage() ?:
            "undef")
        }.toMutableMap().apply {
            this["time"] = LocalDateTime.now().
                format(DateTimeFormatter.ISO_LOCAL_DATE_TIME)
        }

    @ExceptionHandler(HttpMessageNotReadableException::class)
    @ResponseStatus(HttpStatus.BAD_REQUEST)
    fun handleHttpMessageNotReadableException(ex:
    HttpMessageNotReadableException):
        Map<String, Any> =
        mapOf(
            "code" to HttpStatus.BAD_REQUEST.value(),
            "message" to (ex.message?:"undef"),
            "time" to LocalDateTime.now().format(DateTimeFormatter.ISO_
            LOCAL_DATE_TIME)
        )
}
```

The UsersController class should be familiar at this point. We are using annotation-based programming to create our web controller, which will respond to any of the /users endpoint requests. Note that the save method has the @Valid annotation for the User class. Actually, the validation will never trigger, because the object is constructed first, then the validation happens. What this means is that the constructor will send an error if the fields fail in the Objects.requireNonNull call or the pattern matcher logic. If the logic fails, the constructor will throw IllegalArgumentException, which will cascade to HttpMessageNotReadableException, and handleHttpMessageNotReadableException will then be called.

Adding Users when the App Is Ready

Create the UserConfiguration class shown in Listing 4-9.

Listing 4-9. src/main/kotlin/apress/com/users/UserConfiguration.kt

```kotlin
package com.apress.users

import org.springframework.boot.context.event.ApplicationReadyEvent
import org.springframework.context.ApplicationListener
import org.springframework.context.annotation.Bean
import org.springframework.context.annotation.Configuration

@Configuration
class UserConfiguration {
    @Bean
    fun init(userRepository: SimpleRepository<User, Int>):
            ApplicationListener<ApplicationReadyEvent> =
        ApplicationListener<ApplicationReadyEvent> { _:
        ApplicationReadyEvent ->
            val ximena: User = User(
                email = "ximena@email.com",
                name = "Ximena",
                password = "aw2sOmeR!",
                active = true,
                userRole = mutableListOf(UserRole.USER))
            userRepository.save(ximena)
            val norma: User = User(
                email = "norma@email.com",
                name = "Norma",
                password = "aw2sOmeR!",
                active = true,
                userRole = mutableListOf(UserRole.USER,UserRole.ADMIN))
            userRepository.save(norma)
        }
}
```

The `UserConfiguration` class is marked with the `@Configuration` annotation, which means that Spring Boot will execute any declaration of `@Value`, `@Bean`, and so on. In this case, the `@Bean` will create an `ApplicationListener<ApplicationReadyEvent>`, which means that it will be executed when the application is ready. Also, note that it has the `SimpleRepository` interface as a parameter, and right now, we have only the `UserRepository` implementation, so it will be injected here. This method creates two users and saves them into the database, but which one? `H2` or `PostgreSQL`? If there are no properties declared (driver, username, password), the auto-configuration will set up the `H2` by default. But if you provide the driver, username, and password, the auto-configuration will use those values to create the `DataSource` object to connect to the database and perform an SQL statement.

Next, open the `application.properties` file and add the code shown in Listing 4-10.

Listing 4-10. src/main/resources/application.properties

```
# If you don't have a schema.sql file in resources, but a
# schema-h2.sql file instead, uncomment this:
# spring.sql.init.platform=h2

# H2
spring.h2.console.enabled=true
# DataSource
spring.datasource.generate-unique-name=false
spring.datasource.name=test-db
```

The following are the new properties in the `application.properties` file:

- `spring.sql.init.platform`: This indicates the usage of a certain database. If this is commented out, you need a `schema.sql` file for DB initialization.

- `spring.h2.console.enable`: This property allows you to have in development the `/h2-console` endpoint that brings a small UI to manipulate in-memory databases for the H2 engine. The default is `false`, but this example enables it.

- spring.datasource.generate-unique-name: By default, Spring Boot auto-generates the name of the database, so by setting this property to false, you are stopping that logic.

- spring.datasource.name: This property names the database test-db, regardless of the database engine.

We discuss a few more properties that are important for this project later in this chapter.

Database Initialization

One of the most important features of Spring Boot when you have the spring-boot-starter-jdbc starter is that you can add SQL files that will be executed automatically if found in the classpath. They must follow a specific naming convention. In this case, the schema.sql file (for CREATE, DROP, etc., statements to manipulate the database), and a data.sql file (where you can have all the INSERT or UPDATE statements). You can have multiple schema files and even can be recognized by database engine, for example you can have schema-h2.sql and schema-postgresql.sql. The same applies to the data-{engine}.sql files. To use this feature, it is important to use the spring.sql.init.platform property and then h2, postgresql, mysql, oracle, hsqldb, and so on.

Next, create the schema.sql file shown in Listing 4-11. You don't need the data.sql file because you already created some users in the UserConfiguration class.

Listing 4-11. src/main/resources/schema.sql

```
DROP TABLE IF EXISTS USERS CASCADE;
CREATE TABLE USERS
(
    ID            INTEGER           NOT NULL AUTO_INCREMENT,
    EMAIL         VARCHAR(255)      NOT NULL UNIQUE,
    NAME          VARCHAR(100)      NOT NULL,
    GRAVATAR_URL  VARCHAR(255)      NOT NULL,
    PASSWORD      VARCHAR(255)      NOT NULL,
    USER_ROLE     VARCHAR(5) ARRAY  NOT NULL DEFAULT ARRAY ['INFO'],
    ACTIVE        BOOLEAN           NOT NULL,
    PRIMARY KEY (ID)
);
```

Listing 4-11 shows the SQL statement that will be executed when the application starts. As you can see, it is very simple.

Next, create the index.html file (this is just to render something when you go to the / endpoint). You can copy it from the other projects and put/create it in the src/main/ resources/static folder. Remember that in a web app with Spring Boot, if it finds an index.html in the static (or public/) folder, it will be rendered. Now you are ready!

Testing the Users App

As this point, you need to test the application again. Create the UsersHttpRequestTests class shown in Listing 4-12.

Listing 4-12. src/test/kotlin/apress/com/users/UsersHttpRequestTests.kt

```kotlin
package com.apress.users

import org.assertj.core.api.Assertions
import org.junit.jupiter.api.Test
import org.springframework.beans.factory.annotation.Autowired
import org.springframework.beans.factory.annotation.Value
import org.springframework.boot.test.context.SpringBootTest
import org.springframework.boot.test.web.client.TestRestTemplate

@SpringBootTest(webEnvironment = SpringBootTest.WebEnvironment.RANDOM_PORT)
class UsersHttpRequestTests {
    @Value("\${local.server.port}")
    private val port = 0

    private val BASE_URL = "http://localhost:"
    private val USERS_PATH = "/users"

    @Autowired
    private lateinit var restTemplate: TestRestTemplate

    @Test
    @Throws(Exception::class)
    fun indexPageShouldReturnHeaderOneContent() {
        Assertions.assertThat(
            restTemplate.getForObject(
```

```kotlin
            BASE_URL + port,
            String::class.java
        )
    ).contains("Simple Users Rest Application")
}

@Test
@Throws(Exception::class)
fun usersEndPointShouldReturnCollectionWithTwoUsers() {
    val response: Collection<User> =
        restTemplate.getForObject(BASE_URL + port + USERS_PATH,
            Collection::class.java) as Collection<User>
    Assertions.assertThat(response.size).isGreaterThan(1)
}

@Test
@Throws(Exception::class)
fun shouldReturnErrorWhenPostBadUserForm() {
    Assertions.assertThatThrownBy {
        val user: User = User(
            email = "bademail",
            name = "Dummy",
            active = true,
            password = "aw2s0")
    }.isInstanceOf(IllegalArgumentException::class.java)
        .hasMessageContaining("Password must be at least 8
    characters "+
                "long and contain at least one number, one
                uppercase, "+
                "one lowercase and one special character")
}

@Test
@Throws(Exception::class)
fun userEndPointPostNewUserShouldReturnUser() {
    val user: User = User(
        email = "dummy@email.com",
```

```
            name = "Dummy",
            password = "aw2sOmeR!",
            active = true,
            userRole = mutableListOf(UserRole.USER))
        val response = restTemplate.postForObject(BASE_URL + port + USERS_
    PATH, user,
            User::class.java)
        Assertions.assertThat(response).isNotNull()
        Assertions.assertThat(response.email).isEqualTo(user.email)
        val users: Collection<User> =
            restTemplate.getForObject(BASE_URL + port + USERS_PATH,
                    Collection::class.java) as Collection<User>
        Assertions.assertThat(users.size).isGreaterThanOrEqualTo(2)
    }

    @Test
    @Throws(Exception::class)
    fun userEndPointDeleteUserShouldReturnVoid() {
        restTemplate.delete("$BASE_URL$port$USERS_PATH/norma@email.com")
        val users: Collection<User> =
            restTemplate.getForObject(BASE_URL + port + USERS_PATH,
                    Collection::class.java) as Collection<User>
        Assertions.assertThat(users.size).isLessThanOrEqualTo(2)
    }

    @Test
    @Throws(Exception::class)
    fun userEndPointFindUserShouldReturnUser() {
        val user = restTemplate.getForObject("$BASE_URL$port$USERS_PATH/1",
                User::class.java)
        Assertions.assertThat(user).isNotNull()
        Assertions.assertThat(user.email).isEqualTo("ximena@email.com")
    }
}
```

Listing 4-12 shows the tests for the Users app. The only difference from previous versions is the User instance creation. Before you run the code, analyze the various tests.

When you are ready, you can run the tests either in your IDE or by executing the following command:

```
./gradlew clean test
..
UsersHttpRequestTests > userEndPointFindUserShouldReturnUser() PASSED
UsersHttpRequestTests > userEndPointDeleteUserShouldReturnVoid() PASSED
UsersHttpRequestTests > shouldRetrunErrorWhenPostBadUserForm() PASSED
UsersHttpRequestTests > indexPageShouldReturnHeaderOneContent() PASSED
UsersHttpRequestTests > userEndPointPostNewUserShouldReturnUser() PASSED
UsersHttpRequestTests >
usersEndPointShouldReturnCollectionWithTwoUsers() PASSED
..
```

But Wait... What Happened with the Tests?

These tests passed, but how? Where does the data persist? Which database engine was used when you have two drivers declared? Do you know the answer? Did you notice that we are missing something?

We are missing the connection parameters! The URL, username, password, and database driver are missing! You need to set up the DataSource with these parameters (the JdbcTemplate has the DataSource dependency, so it's necessary to declare it).

Normally, we declare these parameters in the command line, as environment variables, or in the application.properties/yaml file, and it looks something like this:

```
spring.datasource.url=jdbc:h2:mem:test-db;DB_CLOSE_DELAY=-1;DB_CLOSE_ON_
EXIT=FALSE
spring.datasource.username=sa
spring.datasource.password=
spring.datasource.driver-class-name=org.h2.Driver
```

Thanks to the magic of Spring Boot auto-configuration, you no longer need to do this. It will detect that you have two drivers but no connection parameters set, so it will use the H2 embedded driver to set up the default values and create the DataSource for the JdbcTemplate class, then execute the schema.sql script, and that's it! You have a fully functional application that is using an H2 engine in-memory database.

This database initialization (execution of the schema.sql and data.sql) happens *only* with embedded databases such as H2, HSQL, and Derby. If you want initialization regardless of the database engine you use, you need to set the spring.sql.init.mode property to always.

Note   Remember that you have access to all the source code for this book (https://github.com/felipeg48/pro-spring-boot-3rd). You can find it in the Apress site; search for the appropriate chapter https://www.apress. com/gp/services/source-code.

Running the Users App

Now you can run the application and see some of the endpoints in action. You can run it from your IDE or you can use the following command in the terminal:

```
./gradlew bootRun
```

You should see the following in the console output:

```
..
o.s.b.a.h2.H2ConsoleAutoConfiguration    : H2 console available at '/h2-
console'. Database available at 'jdbc:h2:mem:test-db'
..
```

It shows that the /h2-console endpoint is available, so open it in a browser by going to http://localhost:8080/h2-console. See Figure 4-2.

Figure 4-2. *http://localhost:8080/h2-console*

Make sure the JDBC URL field has the following value and then click the Connect button:

`jdbc:h2:mem:test-db;DB_CLOSE_DELAY=-1;DB_CLOSE_ON_EXIT=FALSE`

After you connect, you'll see the USERS table and the data, as shown in Figure 4-3.

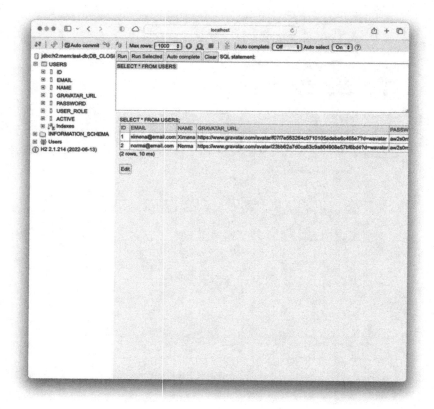

Figure 4-3. *The USERS table*

If you direct your browser to the `http://localhost:8080/users` endpoint, you should see the JSON response shown in Figure 4-4.

Figure 4-4. *http://localhost:8080/users*

Using PostgreSQL

To use PostgreSQL, we are going to use Docker Compose, as shown in Listing 4-13.

Listing 4-13. docker-compose.yaml

```
version: "3"
services:
  postgres:
    image: postgres
    restart: always
    environment:
      POSTGRES_USER: postgres
```

```
    POSTGRES_PASSWORD: postgres
    POSTGRES_DB: test-db
  ports:
    - 5432:5432
```

Using Docker Compose is the best option. You don't have to install multiple external services and can emulate a real-world scenario of using containers. Execute the following command in the terminal:

```
docker compose up
[+] Running 1/1
Container users-postgres-1  Started
```

Now you need to add a new SQL script for PostgreSQL. Create the schema-postgresql.sql script shown in Listing 4-14.

Listing 4-14. src/main/resources/schema-postgresql.sql

```
DROP TABLE IF EXISTS USERS CASCADE;
CREATE TABLE USERS
(
    ID              SERIAL          NOT NULL,
    EMAIL           VARCHAR(255)    NOT NULL UNIQUE,
    NAME            VARCHAR(100)    NOT NULL,
    GRAVATAR_URL    VARCHAR(255)    NOT NULL,
    PASSWORD        VARCHAR(255)    NOT NULL,
    USER_ROLE       VARCHAR[]       NOT NULL,
    ACTIVE          BOOLEAN         NOT NULL,
    PRIMARY KEY (ID)
);
```

Listing 4-14 shows the PostgreSQL schema version. Notice that the ID changed from AUTO_INCREMENT to SERIAL, and the USER_ROLE from ARRAY to VARCHAR[] declaration.

Next, rename the current schema.sql file to schema-h2.sql. This is very important! Open your application.properties file and replace its contents with the contents shown in Listing 4-15.

Listing 4-15. src/main/resources/application.properties

```
# H2
# spring.h2.console.enabled=true
# DataSource
spring.datasource.generate-unique-name=false
spring.datasource.name=test-db
# SQL init
spring.sql.init.mode=always
spring.sql.init.platform=postgresql
# Postgresql
spring.datasource.url=jdbc:postgresql://localhost:5432/test-db
spring.datasource.username=postgres
spring.datasource.password=postgres
spring.datasource.driver-class-name=org.postgresql.Driver
```

Let's analyze the new `application.properties` file:

- We added a comment for the `spring.h2.console.enable` property, since we don't need it anymore.

- The new `# SQL init` section has the `spring.sql.init.mode` property set to `always`, meaning that it will do the initialization of the database and will search for the `schema.sql` and `data.sql` files. However, we renamed the `schema.sql` file to `schema-h2.sql` and added the `schema-postgresql.sql`, so we need to specify which platform the app needs to use. In this case, we are using the `spring.sql.init.platform` set to `postgresql`, which means that it will execute the `schema-postgresql.sql` script.

- The new `# Postgresql` section shows all the properties required for the Postgres engine to run (with Docker Compose). All these variables could be omitted and you could use environment variables as well.

If you execute the tests from Listing 4-14 again, they should pass without any issue, and if you run your application, you should get the same result.

My Retro App: Using Spring Boot JDBC

This section shows how you can use JDBC in the My Retro App. Again, we recommend creating an empty project from the Spring Initializr (`https://start.spring.io`) and starting from there. After you download the project and unzip it, you can import it into your favorite IDE. If you feel comfortable modifying your existing code, that will be fine as well. Figure 4-5 shows the structure and code that you'll develop in this section.

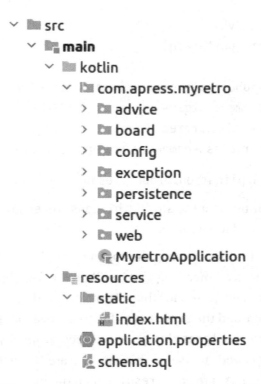

Figure 4-5. *My Retro App with JDBC project structure*

Make sure to enter com.apress in the Group field and myretro in the Artifact and Name fields. After you download the project, unzip it and import it into your favorite IDE. Open the build.gradle and replace its contents with the contents shown in Listing 4-16.

Listing 4-16. The build.gradle File

```
import org.jetbrains.kotlin.gradle.tasks.KotlinCompile
plugins {
    id 'org.springframework.boot' version '3.2.3'
    id 'io.spring.dependency-management' version '1.1.4'
    id 'org.jetbrains.kotlin.jvm' version '2.0.20-RC'
    id "org.jetbrains.kotlin.plugin.spring" version "2.0.20-RC"
    // <- simplifies spring proxying
}

group = 'com.apress'
version = '0.0.1-SNAPSHOT'
sourceCompatibility = '17'

repositories {
    mavenCentral()
}

dependencies {
    implementation "org.jetbrains.kotlin:kotlin-stdlib-jdk8"
    implementation "org.jetbrains.kotlin:kotlin-reflect"

    implementation 'org.springframework.boot:spring-boot-starter-web'
    implementation 'org.springframework.boot:spring-boot-starter-
    validation'
    implementation 'org.springframework.boot:spring-boot-starter-aop'

    implementation 'org.springframework.boot:spring-boot-starter-jdbc'

    developmentOnly 'org.springframework.boot:spring-boot-docker-compose'

    annotationProcessor 'org.springframework.boot:spring-boot-
    configuration-processor'

    runtimeOnly 'org.postgresql:postgresql'

    // Web
    implementation 'org.webjars:bootstrap:5.2.3'
```

```
    testImplementation 'org.springframework.boot:spring-boot-starter-test'
}

tasks.named('test') {
    useJUnitPlatform()
}
//    kotlin {
//        jvmToolchain(17)
//    }
tasks.withType(KotlinCompile) {
    kotlinOptions {
        freeCompilerArgs = ['-Xjsr305=strict']
        jvmTarget = '17'
    }
}
```

As you can see in Listing 4-16, we are using the `spring-boot-starter-jdbc` starter dependency, the `postgresql`, and a new `spring-boot-docker-compose` starter dependency. Note that we are not using the H2 dependency. Also note that the `spring-boot-docker-compose` dependency will be used as `developmentOnly`. We discuss what this new dependency does when we run the application. This is a new feature in Spring Boot 3.1.

Next, create the `board` package with the following domain/model classes: `CardType`, `Card`, and `RetroBoard` (see Listings 4-17, 4-18, and 4-19, respectively).

Listing 4-17. src/main/kotlin/apress/com/myretro/board/CardType.kt

```
package com.apress.myretro.board
enum class CardType {
    HAPPY,MEH,SAD
}
```

Listing 4-18. src/main/kotlin/apress/com/myretro/board/Card.kt

```
package com.apress.myretro.board

import jakarta.validation.constraints.NotBlank
import jakarta.validation.constraints.NotNull
import java.util.*
```

```kotlin
data class Card(
    var id: UUID? = null,

    @get:NotBlank(message = "A comment must always be provided")
    @get:NotNull
    var comment:  String? = null,

    @get:NotNull(message = "A CarType HAPPYIMEHISAD must be provided")
    var cardType:  CardType? = null,

    var retroBoardId: UUID? = null
)
```

Listing 4-19. src/main/kotlin/apress/com/myretro/board/RetroBoard.kt

```kotlin
package com.apress.myretro.board

import jakarta.validation.constraints.NotBlank
import java.util.*

data class RetroBoard(
    var id: UUID? = null,

    @get:NotBlank(message = "A name must be provided")
    var name: String? = null,

    var cards: MutableMap<UUID, Card> = mutableMapOf()
)
```

Note in Listing 4-19 that the cards field is now a Map type, which provides an easy way to find Card objects by UUID.

Next, create the persistence package with the SimpleRepository interface (see Listing 4-20) and the RetroBoardRowMapper and RetroBoardRepository classes (see Listings 4-21 and 4-22, respectively).

Listing 4-20. src/main/kotlin/apress/com/myretro/persistence/
SimpleRepository.kt

```kotlin
package com.apress.myretro.persistence

import java.util.*

interface SimpleRepository<D, ID> {
    fun findById(id: ID): D?
    fun findAll(): Iterable<D>
    fun save(d: D): D
    fun deleteById(id: ID)
}
```

Listing 4-21. src/main/kotlin/apress/com/myretro/persistence/
RetroBoardRowMapper.kt

```kotlin
package com.apress.myretro.persistence

import com.apress.myretro.board.Card
import com.apress.myretro.board.CardType
import com.apress.myretro.board.RetroBoard
import org.springframework.jdbc.core.RowMapper
import java.sql.ResultSet
import java.sql.SQLException
import java.util.*

class RetroBoardRowMapper : RowMapper<RetroBoard> {
    @Throws(SQLException::class)
    override fun mapRow(rs: ResultSet, rowNum: Int): RetroBoard {
        val retroBoard = RetroBoard(
            id = UUID.fromString(rs.getString("id")),
            name = rs.getString("name"))
        val cards: MutableMap<UUID, Card> = mutableMapOf()
        do {
            val card = Card(
                id = UUID.fromString(rs.getString("card_id")),
                comment = rs.getString("comment"),
```

```kotlin
                cardType = CardType.valueOf(rs.getString("card_type")),
                retroBoardId = retroBoard.id
            )
            cards[card.id!!] = card
        } while (rs.next() && retroBoard.id == UUID.fromString(rs.
getString("id")))
        retroBoard.cards = cards
        return retroBoard
    }
}
```

Listing 4-22. src/main/kotlin/apress/com/myretro/persistence/
RetroBoardRepository.kt

```kotlin
package com.apress.myretro.persistence

import com.apress.myretro.board.Card
import com.apress.myretro.board.RetroBoard
import org.springframework.beans.factory.annotation.Autowired
import org.springframework.jdbc.core.JdbcTemplate
import org.springframework.stereotype.Repository
import org.springframework.transaction.annotation.Transactional
import java.sql.Types
import java.util.*

@Repository
class RetroBoardRepository : SimpleRepository<RetroBoard, UUID> {
    @Autowired
    private lateinit var jdbcTemplate: JdbcTemplate

    override fun findById(uuid: UUID): RetroBoard? {
        val sql = """
                SELECT r.ID AS id, r.NAME, c.ID AS card_id, c.CARD_TYPE AS
                card_type,
                    c.COMMENT AS comment
                FROM RETRO_BOARD r
                LEFT JOIN CARD c ON r.ID = c.RETRO_BOARD_ID
                WHERE r.ID = ?
```

```kotlin
                """.trimIndent()
        val results: List<RetroBoard> =
            jdbcTemplate.query(sql, arrayOf<Any>(uuid),
                    intArrayOf(Types.OTHER), RetroBoardRowMapper())
        return if (results.isEmpty()) null else results[0]
    }

    override fun findAll(): Iterable<RetroBoard> {
        val sql = """
                SELECT r.ID AS id, r.NAME, c.ID AS card_id, c.CARD_TYPE,
                c.COMMENT
                FROM RETRO_BOARD r
                LEFT JOIN CARD c ON r.ID = c.RETRO_BOARD_ID
                """.trimIndent()
        return jdbcTemplate.query<RetroBoard>(sql, RetroBoardRowMapper())
    }

    @Transactional
    override fun save(retroBoard: RetroBoard): RetroBoard {
        retroBoard.id = retroBoard.id ?: UUID.randomUUID()
        val sql = "INSERT INTO RETRO_BOARD (ID, NAME) VALUES (?, ?)"
        jdbcTemplate.update(sql, retroBoard.id, retroBoard.name)
        val cards: MutableMap<UUID, Card> = retroBoard.cards.
        mapValues { me ->
            me.value.let { it.retroBoardId = retroBoard.id; saveCard(it) }
        }.toMutableMap()
        retroBoard.cards = cards
        return retroBoard
    }

    @Transactional
    override fun deleteById(uuid: UUID) {
        var sql = "DELETE FROM CARD WHERE RETRO_BOARD_ID = ?"
        jdbcTemplate.update(sql, uuid)
        sql = "DELETE FROM RETRO_BOARD WHERE ID = ?"
        jdbcTemplate.update(sql, uuid)
    }
```

```kotlin
    private fun saveCard(card: Card): Card {
        card.id = card.id ?: UUID.randomUUID()
        val sql = """INSERT INTO CARD (ID, CARD_TYPE, COMMENT, RETRO_
        BOARD_ID)
            VALUES (?, ?, ?, ?)"""
        jdbcTemplate.update(sql,
            card.id, card.cardType!!.name, card.comment, card.retroBoardId)
        return card

    }
}
```

Listings 4-20, 4-21, and 4-22 show familiar classes from the previous version of the project. Notice that we are using the @Repository annotation, which sets all the necessary DAO support, including a convenient translation from tech-specific exceptions such as SQLException. This is a more understandable way to know what's going on when errors occur.

If you look closer at the save(RetroBoard) method in Listing 4-22, you will see that it is necessary to save Card in a different statement, which means that you'll have two tables: one is the RetroBoard, and the other is the Card that must have an association with the RetroBoard. Also notice that we are using the @Transactional annotation, which is a declarative way to add transactions to your app. This annotation is based on aspect-oriented programming (AOP) and it performs the transaction flow, the begin transaction, the commit, and the rollback if necessary.

Tip   If you want to know more about transactions, consult the Spring Data Access documentation at https://docs.spring.io/spring-framework/reference/data-access/transaction/declarative/tx-decl-explained.html.

After you have thoroughly analyzed the preceding classes, create the exception package with the following classes: CardNotFoundException, RetroBoardNotFoundException, and RetroBoardResponseEntityExceptionHandler. See Listings 4-23, 4-24, and 4-25, respectively.

Listing 4-23. src/main/kotlin/apress/com/myretro/exception/
CardNotFoundException.kt

```
package com.apress.myretro.exception

class CardNotFoundException : RuntimeException {
    constructor() : super("Card Not Found")
    constructor(message: String?) : super(String.format("Card Not Found:
    {}", message))
    constructor(message: String?, cause: Throwable?) :
        super(String.format("Card Not Found: {}", message), cause)
}
```

Listing 4-24. src/main/kotlin/apress/com/myretro/exception/
RetroBoardNotFoundException.kt

```
package com.apress.myretro.exception

class RetroBoardNotFoundException : RuntimeException {
    constructor() : super("RetroBoard Not Found")
    constructor(message: String?) :
        super(String.format("RetroBoard Not Found: {}", message))
    constructor(message: String?, cause: Throwable?) :
        super(String.format("RetroBoard Not Found: {}", message), cause)
}
```

Listing 4-25. src/main/kotlin/apress/com/myretro/exception/
RetroBoardResponseEntityExceptionHanlder.kt

```
package com.apress.myretro.exception

import org.springframework.http.HttpHeaders
import org.springframework.http.HttpStatus
import org.springframework.http.ResponseEntity
import org.springframework.web.bind.annotation.ControllerAdvice
import org.springframework.web.bind.annotation.ExceptionHandler
import org.springframework.web.context.request.WebRequest
import org.springframework.web.servlet.mvc.method.annotation.
```

```kotlin
    ResponseEntityExceptionHandler
import java.time.LocalDateTime
import java.time.format.DateTimeFormatter

@ControllerAdvice
class RetroBoardResponseEntityExceptionHandler :
ResponseEntityExceptionHandler() {
    @ExceptionHandler(value =
        [CardNotFoundException::class, RetroBoardNotFoundException::class])
    protected fun handleNotFound(
        ex: RuntimeException, request: WebRequest
    ): ResponseEntity<Any>? {
        val response: Map<String, Any> = mapOf(
            "msg" to "There is an error",
            "code" to HttpStatus.NOT_FOUND.value(),
            "time" to LocalDateTime.now().format(DateTimeFormatter.
                ofPattern("yyyy-mm-dd HH:mm:ss")),
            "errors" to mapOf(
                "msg" to ex.message
            )
        )
        return handleExceptionInternal(
            ex, response,
            HttpHeaders(), HttpStatus.NOT_FOUND, request
        )
    }
}
```

The `exception` package is the same as in previous versions. Take a moment and review these classes, which are very straightforward.

Next, create the `service` package with the `RetroBoardService` class, as shown in Listing 4-26.

Listing 4-26. src/main/kotlin/apress/com/myretro/service/
RetroBoardService.kt

```kotlin
package com.apress.myretro.service

import com.apress.myretro.board.Card
import com.apress.myretro.board.RetroBoard
import com.apress.myretro.persistence.SimpleRepository
import org.springframework.beans.factory.annotation.Autowired
import org.springframework.stereotype.Service
import java.util.*

@Service
class RetroBoardService {
    @Autowired
    lateinit var retroBoardRepository: SimpleRepository<RetroBoard, UUID>

    fun save(domain: RetroBoard): RetroBoard {
        return retroBoardRepository.save(domain)
    }

    fun findById(uuid: UUID): RetroBoard? = retroBoardRepository.
    findById(uuid)

    fun findAll(): Iterable<RetroBoard> = retroBoardRepository.findAll()

    fun delete(uuid: UUID) {
        retroBoardRepository.deleteById(uuid)
    }

    fun findAllCardsFromRetroBoard(uuid: UUID): Iterable<Card> {
        return findById(uuid)!!.cards.values
    }

    fun addCardToRetroBoard(uuid: UUID, card: Card): Card {
        val retroBoard: RetroBoard = findById(uuid)!!
        card.id = card.id ?: UUID.randomUUID()
        retroBoard.cards[card.id!!] = card
        save(retroBoard)
        return card
    }
```

```kotlin
fun findCardByUUID(uuid: UUID, uuidCard: UUID): Card? {
    val retroBoard: RetroBoard = findById(uuid)!!
    return retroBoard.cards.get(uuidCard)
}

fun saveCard(uuid: UUID, card: Card): Card {
    val retroBoard: RetroBoard = findById(uuid)!!
    retroBoard.cards[card.id!!] = card
    save(retroBoard)
    return card
}

fun removeCardByUUID(uuid: UUID, cardUUID: UUID) {
    val retroBoard: RetroBoard = findById(uuid)!!
    retroBoard.cards.remove(cardUUID)
    save(retroBoard)
}
}
```

The `RetroBoardService` class now contains additional methods that interact even more with the whole application, from the `RetroBoard` and its `Cards`. This class is very straightforward. What is important to notice is that this class has the `@Service` annotation to make it a Spring Bean. This class will be injected into the web controller.

Next, create the `web` package and the `RetroBoardController` class, as shown in Listing 4-27.

Listing 4-27. src/main/kotlin/apress/com/myretro/web/ RetroBoardController.kt

```kotlin
package com.apress.myretro.web

import com.apress.myretro.board.Card
import com.apress.myretro.board.RetroBoard
import com.apress.myretro.service.RetroBoardService
import jakarta.validation.Valid
import org.springframework.http.HttpStatus
import org.springframework.http.ResponseEntity
import org.springframework.validation.FieldError
```

171

```kotlin
import org.springframework.web.bind.MethodArgumentNotValidException
import org.springframework.web.bind.annotation.*
import org.springframework.web.servlet.support.ServletUriComponentsBuilder
import java.net.URI
import java.time.LocalDateTime
import java.time.format.DateTimeFormatter
import java.util.*

@RestController
@RequestMapping("/retros")
class RetroBoardController {
    private lateinit var retroBoardService: RetroBoardService

    @get:GetMapping
    val allRetroBoards: ResponseEntity<Iterable<RetroBoard>>
        get() = ResponseEntity.ok(retroBoardService.findAll())

    @PostMapping
    fun saveRetroBoard(@RequestBody retroBoard: @Valid RetroBoard):
            ResponseEntity<RetroBoard> {
        val result: RetroBoard = retroBoardService.save(retroBoard)
        val location: URI = ServletUriComponentsBuilder
            .fromCurrentRequest()
            .path("/{uuid}")
            .buildAndExpand(result.id.toString())
            .toUri()
        return ResponseEntity.created(location).body(result)
    }

    @GetMapping("/{uuid}")
    fun findRetroBoardById(@PathVariable uuid: UUID): ResponseEntity
    <RetroBoard> =
        ResponseEntity.ok(retroBoardService.findById(uuid))

    @GetMapping("/{uuid}/cards")
    fun getAllCardsFromBoard(@PathVariable uuid: UUID):
            ResponseEntity<Iterable<Card>> =
```

```kotlin
    ResponseEntity.ok(retroBoardService.findAllCardsFromRetro
    Board(uuid))

@PutMapping("/{uuid}/cards")
fun addCardToRetroBoard(@PathVariable uuid: UUID, @RequestBody card:
@Valid Card):
        ResponseEntity<Card> {
    val result: Card = retroBoardService.addCardToRetroBoard
    (uuid, card)
    val location: URI = ServletUriComponentsBuilder
        .fromCurrentRequest()
        .path("/{uuid}/cards/{uuidCard}")
        .buildAndExpand(uuid.toString(), result.id.toString())
        .toUri()
    return ResponseEntity.created(location).body(result)
}

@GetMapping("/{uuid}/cards/{uuidCard}")
fun getCardByUUID(@PathVariable uuid: UUID, @PathVariable
uuidCard: UUID):
        ResponseEntity<Card> =
    ResponseEntity.ok(retroBoardService.findCardByUUID(uuid, uuidCard))

@PutMapping("/{uuid}/cards/{uuidCard}")
fun updateCardByUUID(
    @PathVariable uuid: UUID,
    @PathVariable uuidCard: UUID,
    @RequestBody card: Card
): ResponseEntity<Card> {
    return ResponseEntity.ok(retroBoardService.saveCard(uuid, card))
}

@ResponseStatus(HttpStatus.NO_CONTENT)
@DeleteMapping("/{uuid}/cards/{uuidCard}")
fun deleteCardFromRetroBoard(@PathVariable uuid: UUID, @PathVariable
uuidCard:
        UUID) {
```

```kotlin
        retroBoardService.removeCardByUUID(uuid, uuidCard)
    }

    @ExceptionHandler(MethodArgumentNotValidException::class)
    @ResponseStatus(HttpStatus.BAD_REQUEST)
    fun handleValidationExceptions(ex: MethodArgumentNotValidException):
            Map<String, Any> {
        val response: Map<String, Any> = mapOf(
            "msg" to "There is an error",
            "code" to HttpStatus.BAD_REQUEST.value(),
            "time" to LocalDateTime.now().format(DateTimeFormatter.
                    ofPattern("yyyy-MM-dd HH:mm:ss")),
            "errors" to ex.bindingResult.allErrors.associate { err ->
                (err as FieldError).field to (err.getDefaultMessage()?:
                "undef")
            })
        return response
    }
}
```

The RetroBoardController class will serve the /retros, /retros/{uuid}/cards endpoints. As you can see, this class hasn't changed too much from the previous version. Analyze it and then continue.

Next, create the config package and the UsersProperties, MyRetroProperties, and MyRetroConfiguration classes, as shown in Listings 4-28, 4-29, and 4-30, respectively.

Listing 4-28. src/main/kotlin/apress/com/myretro/config/UsersProperties.kt

```kotlin
package com.apress.myretro.config

data class UsersProperties(
    var server: String? = null,
    var port: Int? = null,
    var username: String? = null,
    var password: String? = null
)
```

Listing 4-29. src/main/kotlin/apress/com/myretro/config/MyRetroProperties.kt

```kotlin
package com.apress.myretro.config

import org.springframework.boot.context.properties.ConfigurationProperties

@ConfigurationProperties(prefix = "service")
data class MyRetroProperties(var users: UsersProperties? = null)
```

Listing 4-30. src/main/kotlin/apress/com/myretro/config/
MyRetroConfiguration.kt

```kotlin
package com.apress.myretro.config

import com.apress.myretro.board.Card
import com.apress.myretro.board.CardType
import com.apress.myretro.board.RetroBoard
import com.apress.myretro.service.RetroBoardService
import org.springframework.boot.context.event.ApplicationReadyEvent
import org.springframework.boot.context.properties.
EnableConfigurationProperties
import org.springframework.context.ApplicationListener
import org.springframework.context.annotation.Bean
import org.springframework.context.annotation.Configuration
import java.util.*

@EnableConfigurationProperties(MyRetroProperties::class)
@Configuration
class MyRetroConfiguration {
    @Bean
    fun ready(retroBoardService: RetroBoardService):
            ApplicationListener<ApplicationReadyEvent> {
        return ApplicationListener<ApplicationReadyEvent> {
                applicationReadyEvent: ApplicationReadyEvent? ->
            val retroBoardId = UUID.fromString("9dc9b71b-a07e-418b-
            b972-40225449aff2")
            val retroBoard: RetroBoard = RetroBoard(
                id = retroBoardId,
                name = "Spring Boot Conference",
```

```
        cards = mutableMapOf(
            UUID.fromString("bb2a80a5-a0f5-4180-a6dc-80c84bc014c9") to
            Card(id = UUID.fromString("bb2a80a5-a0f5-4180-a6dc-
            80c84bc014c9"),
                comment = "Spring Boot Rocks!", cardType =
                CardType.HAPPY),
            UUID.fromString("f9de7f11-5393-4b5b-8e9d-10eca5f50189") to
            Card(id = UUID.fromString("f9de7f11-5393-4b5b-8e9d-
            10eca5f50189"),
                comment = "Meet everyone in person",
                cardType = CardType.HAPPY),
            UUID.fromString("6cdb30d6-43f2-42b7-b0db-f3acbc53d467") to
            Card(id = UUID.fromString("6cdb30d6-43f2-42b7-b0db-
            f3acbc53d467"),
                comment = "When is the next one?", cardType =
                CardType.MEH),
            UUID.fromString("9de1f7f9-2470-4c8d-86f2-371203620fcd") to
            Card(id = UUID.fromString("9de1f7f9-2470-4c8d-86f2-
            371203620fcd"),
                comment = "Not enough time to talk to everyone",
                cardType = CardType.SAD)
        )
    )
    retroBoardService.save(retroBoard)
        }
    }
}
```

Notice in Listing 4-28 that we've renamed the UsersConfiguration.kt file from Chapter 3 to UsersProperties.kt (this makes more sense). And in Listing 4-30, we added some initial data to MyRetroConfiguration using the ApplicationListener. When the application is ready, it will execute all the code in the ready() method. In this method (ready()), we have the RetroBoardService as a parameter. This will be injected by the Spring Framework.

The previous version had an Advice, so create the advice package and the RetroBoardAdvice class, as shown in Listing 4-31.

Listing 4-31. src/main/kotlin/apress/com/myretro/advice/RetroBoardAdvice.kt

```kotlin
package com.apress.myretro.advice

import com.apress.myretro.board.RetroBoard
import com.apress.myretro.exception.RetroBoardNotFoundException
import org.aspectj.lang.ProceedingJoinPoint
import org.aspectj.lang.annotation.Around
import org.aspectj.lang.annotation.Aspect
import org.slf4j.LoggerFactory
import org.springframework.stereotype.Component
import java.util.*

@Component
@Aspect
class RetroBoardAdvice {
    @Around("""execution(* com.apress.myretro.persistence.RetroBoard
    Repository.
        findById(java.util.UUID))""")
    @Throws(
        Throwable::class
    )
    fun checkFindRetroBoard(proceedingJoinPoint: ProceedingJoinPoint): Any {
        LOG.info("[ADVICE] {}", proceedingJoinPoint.signature.name)
        try {
            return proceedingJoinPoint.proceed(
                arrayOf<Any>(
                    UUID.fromString(proceedingJoinPoint.args[0].toString())
                ))
        }catch (e:NullPointerException) {
            throw RetroBoardNotFoundException()
        }
    }

    companion object {
        val LOG = LoggerFactory.getLogger(RetroBoardAdvice::class.java)
    }
}
```

Recall that the RetroBoardAdvice class will intercept the findById and, if a NullPointerException occurs, it will throw the RetroBoardNotFoundException, which will be handled by the controller advice RetroBoardResponseEntityExceptionHandler class.

Next, open the application.properties file and add the contents shown in Listing 4-32.

Listing 4-32. src/main/resource/application.properties

```
# DataSource
spring.datasource.generate-unique-name=false
spring.datasource.name=test-db
# SQL init
spring.sql.init.mode=always
```

Listing 4-32 shows that now you are using the spring.sql.init.mode so it reads the schema.sql file. Next, create the schema.sql file, as shown in Listing 4-33.

Listing 4-33. src/main/resources/schema.sql

```
CREATE EXTENSION IF NOT EXISTS "uuid-ossp";
DROP TABLE IF EXISTS CARD CASCADE;
DROP TABLE IF EXISTS RETRO_BOARD CASCADE;
CREATE TABLE CARD
(
    ID              UUID DEFAULT uuid_generate_v4() NOT NULL,
    CARD_TYPE       VARCHAR(5)                      NOT NULL,
    COMMENT         VARCHAR(255),
    RETRO_BOARD_ID UUID,
    PRIMARY KEY (ID)
);
CREATE TABLE RETRO_BOARD
(
    ID   UUID DEFAULT uuid_generate_v4() NOT NULL,
    NAME VARCHAR(255),
    PRIMARY KEY (ID)
);
```

```
ALTER TABLE IF EXISTS CARD
    ADD CONSTRAINT RETRO_BOARD_CARD FOREIGN KEY (RETRO_BOARD_ID) REFERENCES
    RETRO_BOARD;
```

The first line of Listing 4-33 enables a function (uuid_generate_v4()) that generates the required UUID. You need two tables, one for the RetroBoard, and one for the Card, where you need to add the relationship, a one-to-many relationship.

Next, create in the root of the project a docker-compose.yaml file with the content shown in Listing 4-34.

Listing 4-34. docker-compose.yaml

```
version: "3"
services:
  postgres:
    image: postgres
    restart: always
    environment:
      POSTGRES_USER: postgres
      POSTGRES_PASSWORD: postgres
      POSTGRES_DB: test-db
    ports:
      - 5432:5432
```

As you can see, this file is the same as in the Users App. You need to use the PostgreSQL database, so you are all set.

Running the My Retro App

Now it's time to run the application. You can run it by using your IDE or using the following command:

```
./gradle bootRun
..
.s.b.d.c.l.DockerComposeLifecycleManager : Using Docker Compose file ...
..
..
```

There is new info about the docker-compose file, but what is happening? More about this later.

Open a browser (http://localhost:8080/retros) or execute a curl command in another terminal window. The following code shows the use of the jq tool (https://stedolan.github.io/jq/) to print the result of the curl command:

```
curl -s http://localhost:8080/retros | jq .
[
  {
    "id": "9dc9b71b-a07e-418b-b972-40225449aff2",
    "name": "Spring Boot Conference",
    "cards": {
      "2ca35157-63eb-4950-ac10-fc75ab828fcb": {
        "id": "2ca35157-63eb-4950-ac10-fc75ab828fcb",
        "comment": "Meet everyone in person",
        "cardType": "HAPPY",
        "retroBoardId": "9dc9b71b-a07e-418b-b972-40225449aff2"
      },
      "bb2a80a5-a0f5-4180-a6dc-80c84bc014c9": {
        "id": "bb2a80a5-a0f5-4180-a6dc-80c84bc014c9",
        "comment": "Spring Boot Rocks!",
        "cardType": "HAPPY",
        "retroBoardId": "9dc9b71b-a07e-418b-b972-40225449aff2"
      },
      "b0b993c7-83a3-4ab8-9a15-d9b160228da4": {
        "id": "b0b993c7-83a3-4ab8-9a15-d9b160228da4",
        "comment": "When is the next one?",
        "cardType": "MEH",
        "retroBoardId": "9dc9b71b-a07e-418b-b972-40225449aff2"
      },
      "394676ba-8609-4677-8ef1-420851139410": {
        "id": "394676ba-8609-4677-8ef1-420851139410",
        "comment": "Not enough time to talk to everyone",
        "cardType": "SAD",
```

```
        "retroBoardId": "9dc9b71b-a07e-418b-b972-40225449aff2"
      }
    }
  }
]
```

But Wait... What... Again?

Did you realize that we never specified the connection parameters for the DataSource? The spring-boot-docker-compose dependency auto-configured this application. It runs in the background a Docker image by executing docker compose up, and it creates the DataSource with the right parameters based on the docker-compose.yaml file. This feature is amazing! Of course, this only happens in development time. You don't need to do these extra steps to create an infrastructure anymore. We continue to use this development approach in the following chapters.

Summary

In this chapter, you discovered how Spring Framework Data Access works with Spring Boot, and how Spring Boot helps configure most of the Data Access components, such as the DataSource and the JdbcTemplate.

You learned the following ideas in this chapter:

- You need to specify SQL statements and work directly with ResultSets.

- Spring Framework Data Access brings simplified classes like JdbcTemplate to remove all the boilerplate of dealing with connections, sessions, transactions, exceptions, and much more.

- Spring Boot helps you initialize embedded database engines such as H2, HSQL, and Derby without providing any connection parameters to set up the DataSource.

- You can have multiple drivers in your dependencies, but you need to provide the connection parameter to the driver you want to connect, as well as the initialization of the database through the `schema.sql` or `data.sql`.

- A new Spring Boot 3.1 feature allows you to add a `docker-compose.yaml` file and declare a service, and by adding the `spring-boot-docker-compose` starter dependency, Spring Boot will auto-configure all the necessary parameters to set up the `DataSource` based on the environment variables declared in `docker-compose.yaml`.

Chapter 5 explores the Spring Data project and shows how Spring Boot helps configure everything.

Spring Data with Spring Boot

Felipe Gutierrez[a*]

[a] 4109 Rillcrest Grove Way Fuquay Varina, NC 27526-3562, Albuquerque, NM, USA

Spring Data

Chapter 4 introduced the features that the Spring Framework Data Access provides for creating persistent data applications. Another extension of the Spring Framework is the Spring Data technology, which offers even more features to make data persistence a breeze.

Spring Data brings the consistent way of programming model that does the heavy lifting when talking to persistence engines, from creating the connection and sessions, to mapping your classes to a tables and rows, to implementing database operations, all the way to committing or rolling back your data and showing you a better error message if something happens during any operation. Spring Data makes data access easy not only for relational and nonrelational databases but also for MapReduce frameworks (such as Apache CouchDB, Apache Hadoop, Infinispan, and Riak, among others), reactive databases, and cloud-based data services. The Spring Data project (which includes the Spring Framework Data Access as its core) is an umbrella project that contains many other subprojects, including the Spring Data JDBC, Spring Data JPA, Spring Data REST subprojects covered in this chapter.

Spring Data provides all the following features (and many more), which are discussed in this and the following chapters:

© Peter Späth, Felipe Gutierrez 2025

P. Späth and F. Gutierrez, *Pro Spring Boot 3 with Kotlin*, https://doi.org/10.1007/979-8-8688-1131-9_5

- An easy way to extend interfaces that gives you a base for CRUD actions (using the domain model and IDs, Spring Data provides the Repository<T,ID> and CrudRepository<T,ID> interfaces)

- Implementation of these interfaces with basic properties

- A query derivation based on the fields of the domain class

- Support for auditing based on events and callbacks (such as date created and last changed)

- A way to override any implementation from the interfaces

- JavaConfig support for configuration

- Experimental support for cross-store persistence, meaning that you can use the same model and multiple engines

Let's start by exploring the features that Spring Data JDBC offers to developers.

Spring Data JDBC

Spring Data JDBC provides enhanced support for JDBC-based data access, making it a simple and opinionated Object Relational Mapping (ORM) tool. Spring Data JDBC is based on the *Aggregate Root* design pattern explained in the book *Domain Driven Design* by Eric Evans (Addison-Wesley Professional, 2003). These are some of the many features that you will find in Spring Data JDBC:

- A NamingStrategy implementation based on the CrudRepository that provides a specific table structure based on your domain classes. You can override this by using annotations such as @Table and @Column, among others.

- When you have a particular SQL query to execute that is not part of the default implementation, you can use the @Query annotation, which allows you to customize your queries.

- Support for the legacy MyBatis framework.

- Support for callbacks and events.

- Support for JavaConfig classes where you configure your repositories by using the `@EnableJdbcRepositories` annotation. Normally this annotation is only used in Spring applications (the same as `@ComponentScan` in Spring Boot). If you are using Spring Boot, you don't need to use the `@EnabledJdbcRepositories` annotation, because it is activated from the auto-configuration.

- Entity state detection strategies. By default, Spring Data JDBC looks at the identifier. If it's `null` or `0`, Spring Data JDBC recognizes that the entity is new.

- Default transactionality when extending the `CrudRepository`, so there's no need to mark your interface using the `@Transactional` annotation. You can override some methods, though, and add very specific parameters to the annotation.

- Auditing with the `@CreatedBy`, `@LastModifiedBy`, `@CreatedDate`, and `@LastModifiedDate` annotations.

Spring Data JDBC with Spring Boot

When you use Spring Boot and add the `spring-boot-starter-data-jdbc` starter dependency to your application, the auto-configuration will add the `@EnableJdbcRepositories` annotation and configure everything depending on which driver you have and the properties you've set for your applications. The following sections demonstrate the Users App and My Retro App with Spring Boot and Spring Data JDBC.

Users App with Spring Boot and Spring Data JDBC

It's time to see in action the Users App with Spring Boot and Spring Data JDBC. You can start from scratch by going to the Spring Initializr (`https://start.spring.io`) and selecting a base project. In the Project Metadata section, make sure to set the Group field to `com.apress` and the Artifact and Name fields to `users`. For dependencies, add Web, Validation, JDBC, H2, and PostgreSQL. Download the project, unzip it, and import it into your favorite IDE. By the end of this section, you should have the structure shown in Figure 5-1.

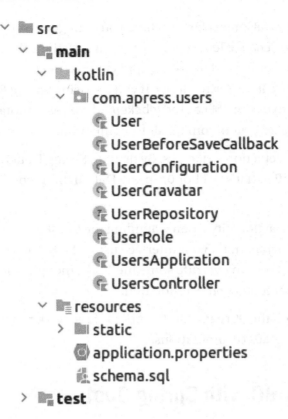

Figure 5-1. *Users App structure*

Tip   After clicking Add Dependencies in the Spring Initializr, you can easily locate each dependency from the long list of dependencies by typing its name in the field at the top of the panel.

Open the `build.gradle` file and add the `spring-boot-starter-data-jdbc` starter dependency, as shown in Listing 5-1.

Listing 5-1. The build.gradle File

```
import org.jetbrains.kotlin.gradle.tasks.KotlinCompile
plugins {
    id 'org.springframework.boot' version '3.2.3'
    id 'io.spring.dependency-management' version '1.1.4'
    id 'org.jetbrains.kotlin.jvm' version '2.0.20-RC'
```

```
    id "org.jetbrains.kotlin.plugin.spring" version "2.0.20-RC"
    // <- simplifies spring proxying
}

group = 'com.apress'
version = '0.0.1-SNAPSHOT'
sourceCompatibility = '17'

repositories {
    mavenCentral()
}

dependencies {
    implementation "org.jetbrains.kotlin:kotlin-stdlib-jdk8"
    implementation "org.jetbrains.kotlin:kotlin-reflect"

    implementation 'org.springframework.boot:spring-boot-starter-web'
    implementation 'org.springframework.boot:spring-boot-starter-
    validation'

    implementation 'org.springframework.boot:spring-boot-starter-data-jdbc'
    runtimeOnly 'com.h2database:h2'
    runtimeOnly 'org.postgresql:postgresql'

    // Web
    implementation 'org.webjars:bootstrap:5.2.3'

    testImplementation 'org.springframework.boot:spring-boot-starter-test'
}

tasks.named('test') {
    useJUnitPlatform()
}
test {
    testLogging {
        events "passed", "skipped", "failed"
        showExceptions true
        exceptionFormat "full"
        showCauses true
```

```
            showStackTraces true
            showStandardStreams = false
        }
    }

//      kotlin {
//          jvmToolchain(17)
//      }
    tasks.withType(KotlinCompile).configureEach {
        kotlinOptions {
            freeCompilerArgs = ['-Xjsr305=strict']
            jvmTarget = '17'
        }
    }
}
```

The addition of spring-boot-starter-data-jdbc will bring all the Spring Data dependencies. Note that there are two drivers—h2 (embedded in-memory) and PostgreSQL. You already know from Chapter 4 what happens when Spring Boot sees two drivers and no connection parameters.

Next, create the UserRole enum (see Listing 5-2) and the User class (see Listing 5-3).

Listing 5-2. src/main/kotlin/apress/com/users/UserRole.kt

```
package com.apress.users
enum class UserRole {
    USER, ADMIN, INFO
}
```

Listing 5-3. src/main/kotlin/apress/com/users/User.kt

```
package com.apress.users

import jakarta.validation.constraints.NotBlank
import jakarta.validation.constraints.Pattern
import org.springframework.data.annotation.Id
import org.springframework.data.relational.core.mapping.Table

@Table("USERS")
data class User(
```

```kotlin
@Id
var id: Long? = null,

@get:NotBlank(message = "Email cannot be empty")
var email:  String? = null,

@get:NotBlank(message = "Name cannot be empty")
var name: String? = null,

var gravatarUrl: String? = null,

@get:Pattern(
    message = "Password must be at least 8 characters long and contain
    at least one number, one uppercase, one lowercase and one special
    character",
    regexp = "^(?=.*[0-9])(?=.*[a-z])(?=.*[A-Z])(?=.*[@#$%^&+=!])
    (?=\\S+$).{8,}$"
)
var password: String? = null,

var userRole: MutableList<UserRole>? = null,

var active:Boolean = false
)
```

As you can see in Listing 5-2, the `UserRole` enum is the same as in previous chapters. On the other hand, Listing 5-3 shows that the `User` class is different from it was in the previous chapters. As shown next, you need to extend from the `CrudRepository<T,ID>` interface, which requests the *entity* (T) and its *identifier* (ID). With this interface, Spring Data uses a `NamingStrategy` logic that uses the name of the entity as the name of the table and the identifier as the primary/indexed key. In this example, it will be USER as the table name and `id` (type `Long`) as the primary key. But in this case, that logic would result in USER as the table name, but in Listing 5-3 we marked the class with the `@Table` annotation and passed the name USERS as a parameter, overriding the default strategy so that the name of the table will be USERS. Also, we are using the `@Id` annotation, which marks the `Long` type as the identifier, in this case our primary key in the database. An important point here is that both annotations come from the Spring Data package (`org. springframework.data.*`).

Next, create the UserRepository interface. See Listing 5-4.

Listing 5-4. src/main/kotlin/apress/com/users/UserRepository.kt

```kotlin
package com.apress.users

import org.springframework.data.jdbc.repository.query.Query
import org.springframework.data.repository.CrudRepository
import org.springframework.data.repository.query.Param

interface UserRepository : CrudRepository<User, Long> {
    fun findByEmail(email: String): User?
    fun deleteByEmail(email: String)

    // Example of a custom query
    @Query("SELECT GRAVATAR_URL FROM USERS WHERE EMAIL = :email")
    fun getGravatarByEmail(@Param("email") email: String): String?
}
```

Note that the UserRepository interface is new. Let's analyze it:

- CrudRepository: The interface extends the public interface
  CrudRepository<T, ID> and extends the Repository<T, ID> interface.
  The CrudRepository interface declares several methods:

```java
public interface CrudRepository<T, ID> extends Repository
<T, ID> {
    <S extends T> S save(S entity);
    <S extends T> Iterable<S> saveAll(Iterable<S> entities);
    Optional<T> findById(ID id);
    boolean existsById(ID id);
    Iterable<T> findAll();
    Iterable<T> findAllById(Iterable<ID> ids);
    long count();
    void deleteById(ID id);
    void delete(T entity);
    void deleteAllById(Iterable<? extends ID> ids);
    void deleteAll(Iterable<? extends T> entities);
    void deleteAll();
}
```

One of the most impressive details here is that you don't need to implement anything—Spring Data will implement everything for you, so you can use the `UserRepository` interface directly in the *service* or *controller*.

- `findBy` and `deleteBy`: We declare these methods in the `UserRepository`. Using Spring Data, we can use the naming convention to create query methods that execute queries based on the name of the field and some keywords (that you normally would use in a SQL statement). In this case, we are using the `findBy` keyword and adding the `Email` field name (`findByEmail`). With the `Email` field, Spring Data will generate the implementation to do something like this:

```
select * from users where email = ?
delete from users where email = ?
```

If you use something like `findByMyAwesomeName`, Spring Data won't do anything, because it must follow the fields declared in the entity. In other words, the fields must name-match the query methods you are creating. Additional keywords include `After`, `GreaterThan`, `Before`, `In`, `NotIn`, `Like`, `Containing`, `IsTrue`, and `IsFalse`. To see all the available keywords, go to `https://docs.spring.io/spring-data/jdbc/docs/current/reference/html/#jdbc.query-methods`. If you have an IDE with IntelliSense, you should get all the possible combinations.

Spring Data also brings a *Query Lookup Strategy* in place, so you can extend some of the default queries by using the @Query annotation that accepts a `String` (a SQL statement) as a parameter. Sometimes you will find out that the default implementation of the CRUD doesn't cover your requirements. For example, imagine that you only want to retrieve `Gravatar` from the `User`. In that case, you could declare a method in the `UserRepository` interface like the following:

```
@Query("SELECT GRAVATAR_URL FROM USERS WHERE EMAIL = :email")
    String getGravatarByEmail(@Param("email") String email);
```

It's that simple!

The `UserRepository` interface is an amazing new feature for speeding up the development process!

Next, create the `UserGravatar` and `UserConfiguration` classes. See Listings 5-5 and 5-6. Note that the `UserGravatar` class is the same as the one Chapter 4 (Listing 4-3).

Listing 5-5. src/main/kotlin/apress/com/users/UserGravatar.kt

```kotlin
package com.apress.users

import java.security.MessageDigest

object UserGravatar {
    @OptIn(ExperimentalStdlibApi::class)
    fun getGravatarUrlFromEmail(email: String) =
        String.format("https://www.gravatar.com/avatar/%s?d=wavatar",
        md5Hex(email))

    @kotlin.ExperimentalStdlibApi
    private fun md5Hex(message: String) =
        MessageDigest.getInstance("MD5")
            .digest(message.toByteArray(charset("CP1252"))).toHexString()
}
```

Listing 5-6. src/main/kotlin/apress/com/users/UserConfiguration.kt

```kotlin
package com.apress.users

import org.springframework.boot.context.event.ApplicationReadyEvent
import org.springframework.context.ApplicationListener
import org.springframework.context.annotation.Bean
import org.springframework.context.annotation.Configuration

@Configuration
class UserConfiguration {
    @Bean
    fun init(userRepository:
            UserRepository): ApplicationListener<ApplicationReadyEvent> {
        return ApplicationListener<ApplicationReadyEvent> { _:
        ApplicationReadyEvent ->
            userRepository.save(
                User(
                    email="ximena@email.com",
                    name="Ximena",
```

```
                    password="aw2sOmeR!",
                    userRole = mutableListOf(UserRole.USER),
                    active = true)
            )
            userRepository.save(
                User(
                    email="norma@email.com",
                    name="Norma",
                    password="aw2sOmeR!",
                    userRole = mutableListOf(UserRole.USER,UserRole.ADMIN),
                    active=true)
            )
        }
    }
}
```

The UserGravatar class will create the Gravatar based on the email digest.
Listing 5-6 shows the configuration. As you can see, this is the same as in the previous
chapter. The init method will be executed when the application is ready.

Note in Listing 5-6 that you are not setting the gravatarUrl field. How can you
calculate it and add it to the User entity? In Chapter 4, you used User as the data class
type and then used the init method to set the gravatarUrl field, so every time there
is a new instance, you get the Gravatar for that user. To solve this issue, you can use a
callback feature from Spring Data. You need to create the UserBeforeSaveCallback class
to implement the BeforeSaveCallback<T>; see Listing 5-7.

Listing 5-7. src/main/kotlin/apress/com/users/UserBeforeSaveCallback.kt

```
package com.apress.users

import org.springframework.data.relational.core.conversion.
MutableAggregateChange
import org.springframework.data.relational.core.mapping.event.
BeforeSaveCallback
import org.springframework.stereotype.Component
import java.util.List
```

```kotlin
@Component
class UserBeforeSaveCallback : BeforeSaveCallback<User> {
    override fun onBeforeSave(aggregate: User,
            aggregateChange: MutableAggregateChange<User>): User
    {
        aggregate.gravatarUrl =
            aggregate.gravatarUrl ?:
            UserGravatar.getGravatarUrlFromEmail(aggregate.email!!)
        aggregate.userRole =
            aggregate.userRole ?:
            mutableListOf(UserRole.INFO)
        return aggregate
    }
}
```

The UserBeforeSaveCallback class is marked as @Component so that Spring can find it and add it to the logic to execute a callback before the User entity is saved into the database. This implements the BeforeSaveCallback of type User, which allows you to implement the onBeforeSave method with User and MutableAggreateChange as parameters. You therefore have access to the entity and can add any defaults you want, in this case the gravatarUrl.

Spring Data offers more entity callbacks by process—BeforeDeleteCallback and AfterDeleteCallback for the delete process, BeforeConvertCallback, BeforeSaveCallback, and AfterSaveCallback for the save process, and AfterConvertCallback for the load process.

Next, create the UsersController class, as shown in Listing 5-8.

Listing 5-8. src/main/kotlin/apress/com/users/UsersController.kt

```kotlin
package com.apress.users

import org.springframework.beans.factory.annotation.Autowired
import org.springframework.http.HttpStatus
import org.springframework.http.ResponseEntity
import org.springframework.validation.FieldError
import org.springframework.validation.ObjectError
import org.springframework.web.bind.MethodArgumentNotValidException
import org.springframework.web.bind.annotation.*
```

```kotlin
import org.springframework.web.servlet.support.ServletUriComponentsBuilder
import java.net.URI
import java.time.LocalDateTime
import java.time.format.DateTimeFormatter

@RestController
@RequestMapping("/users")
class UsersController {
    @Autowired
    private lateinit var userRepository: UserRepository

    @get:GetMapping
    val all: ResponseEntity<Iterable<User>>
        get() = ResponseEntity.ok(userRepository.findAll())

    @GetMapping("/{email}")
    @Throws(Throwable::class)
    fun findUserByEmail(@PathVariable email: String):
    ResponseEntity<User> =
        ResponseEntity.ofNullable(userRepository.findByEmail(email))

    @RequestMapping(method = [RequestMethod.POST, RequestMethod.PUT])
    fun save(@RequestBody user: User): ResponseEntity<User> {
        userRepository.save(user)
        val location: URI = ServletUriComponentsBuilder
            .fromCurrentRequest()
            .path("/{email}")
            .buildAndExpand(user.id)
            .toUri()
        return ResponseEntity.created(location).
            body(userRepository.findByEmail(user.email!!))
    }

    @DeleteMapping("/{email}")
    @ResponseStatus(HttpStatus.NO_CONTENT)
    fun delete(@PathVariable email: String) {
        userRepository.deleteByEmail(email)
    }
```

```kotlin
//Example custom Query
@GetMapping("/gravatar/{email}")
@Throws(Throwable::class)
fun getGravatarByEmail(@PathVariable email: String):
ResponseEntity<String> =
    ResponseEntity.ok(userRepository.getGravatarByEmail(email))

@ExceptionHandler(MethodArgumentNotValidException::class)
@ResponseStatus(HttpStatus.BAD_REQUEST)
fun handleValidationExceptions(ex: MethodArgumentNotValidException):
        Map<String, String> =
    ex.bindingResult.allErrors.associate { error: ObjectError ->
        (error as FieldError).field to (error.getDefaultMessage() ?:
        "undef")
    }.toMutableMap().apply {
        this["time"] = LocalDateTime.now().
            format(DateTimeFormatter.ISO_LOCAL_DATE_TIME)
    }
}
```

As you can see, the UsersController class differs from the one in the previous chapter because you are using the findByEmail and deleteByEmail methods in the repository. The most important part is that you are using the UserRepository interface directly.

Next, open the application.properties file and use the contents shown in Listing 5-9. As you can see, it's the same as in Chapter 4.

Listing 5-9. src/main/resources/application.properties

```
spring.h2.console.enabled=true
spring.datasource.generate-unique-name=false
spring.datasource.name=test-db
```

Next, create the schema.sql file. See Listing 5-10.

Listing 5-10. src/main/resources/schema.sql

```
DROP TABLE IF EXISTS USERS CASCADE;
CREATE TABLE USERS (
    ID LONG NOT NULL AUTO_INCREMENT,
    EMAIL VARCHAR(255) NOT NULL UNIQUE,
    NAME VARCHAR(100) NOT NULL,
    GRAVATAR_URL VARCHAR(255) NOT NULL,
    PASSWORD VARCHAR(255) NOT NULL,
    USER_ROLE VARCHAR(5) ARRAY NOT NULL DEFAULT ARRAY['INFO'],
    ACTIVE BOOLEAN NOT NULL,
    PRIMARY KEY (ID));
```

The `schema.sql` file will be executed when the app starts—this is the power of Spring Boot. Remember that this happens only with embedded databases such as H2, Derby, or HSQL. Because you haven't specified any connection parameters, Spring Boot will set up H2 as the in-memory database. You are all set!

Testing the Users App

To test the Users App, create the `UsersHttpRequestTests` class in the `test` folder structure. See Listing 5-11.

Listing 5-11. src/test/kotlin/apress/com/users/UsersHttpRequestTests.kt

```kotlin
package com.apress.users

import org.assertj.core.api.Assertions
import org.junit.jupiter.api.Test
import org.springframework.beans.factory.annotation.Autowired
import org.springframework.beans.factory.annotation.Value
import org.springframework.boot.test.context.SpringBootTest
import org.springframework.boot.test.web.client.TestRestTemplate

@SpringBootTest(webEnvironment = SpringBootTest.WebEnvironment.RANDOM_PORT)
class UsersHttpRequestTests {
    @Value("\${local.server.port}")
    private val port = 0
```

```kotlin
private val BASE_URL = "http://localhost:"
private val USERS_PATH = "/users"

@Autowired
private lateinit var restTemplate: TestRestTemplate

@Test
@Throws(Exception::class)
fun indexPageShouldReturnHeaderOneContent() {
    Assertions.assertThat(
        restTemplate.getForObject(
            BASE_URL + port,
            String::class.java
        )
    ).contains("Simple Users Rest Application")
}

@Test
@Throws(Exception::class)
fun usersEndPointShouldReturnCollectionWithTwoUsers() {
    val response: Collection<User> =
        restTemplate.getForObject(BASE_URL + port + USERS_PATH,
            Collection::class.java) as Collection<User>
    Assertions.assertThat(response.size).isGreaterThanOrEqualTo(2)
}

@Test
@Throws(Exception::class)
fun userEndPointPostNewUserShouldReturnUser() {
    val user: User = User(
        email="dummy@email.com",
        name = "Dummy",
        gravatarUrl" = "https://www.gravatar.com/avatar/23bb62a7d0ca63
                        c9a804908e57bf6bd4?d=wavatar",
        password = "aw2sOmeR!",
        userRole = mutableListOf(UserRole.USER),
        active = true)
```

```kotlin
    val response = restTemplate.postForObject(BASE_URL + port + USERS_
    PATH, user,
        User::class.java)
    Assertions.assertThat(response).isNotNull()
    Assertions.assertThat(response.email).isEqualTo(user.email)
    val users: Collection<User> =
        restTemplate.getForObject(BASE_URL + port + USERS_PATH,
            Collection::class.java) as Collection<User>
    Assertions.assertThat(users.size).isGreaterThanOrEqualTo(2)
}

@Test
@Throws(Exception::class)
fun userEndPointDeleteUserShouldReturnVoid() {
    restTemplate.delete("$BASE_URL$port$USERS_PATH/norma@email.com")
    val users: Collection<User> =
        restTemplate.getForObject(BASE_URL + port + USERS_PATH,
            Collection::class.java) as Collection<User>
    Assertions.assertThat(users.size).isLessThanOrEqualTo(2)
}

@Test
@Throws(Exception::class)
fun userEndPointFindUserShouldReturnUser() {
    val user = restTemplate.getForObject(
        "$BASE_URL$port$USERS_PATH/ximena@email.com", User::class.java)
    Assertions.assertThat(user).isNotNull()
    Assertions.assertThat(user.email).isEqualTo("ximena@email.com")
}
}
```

You can run the test class in your IDE or you can use the following command:

```
./gradlew clean test
```

Running the Users App

You can run the Users App in your IDE or you can use the following command:

```
./gradlew clean bootRun
```

You can either open a browser and go to http://localhost:8080/users or execute the following curl command at the command line:

```
curl -s http://localhost:8080/users | jq .
[
  {
    "id": 1,
    "email": "ximena@email.com",
    "name": "Ximena",
    "gravatarUrl": "https://www.gravatar.com/avatar/f07f7e553264c9710105ede
be6c465e7?d=wavatar",
    "password": "aw2sOmeR!",
    "userRole": [
      "USER"
    ],
    "active": true
  },
  {
    "id": 2,
    "email": "norma@email.com",
    "name": "Norma",
    "gravatarUrl": "https://www.gravatar.com/avatar/23bb62a7d0ca63c9a80490
8e57bf6bd4?d=wavatar",
    "password": "aw2sOmeR!",
    "userRole": [
      "USER",
      "ADMIN"
    ],
    "active": true
  }
]
```

> **Note**   You can find all the source code at the Apress website: `https://www.` `apress.com/gp/services/source-code.` or `https://github.com/` `felipeg48/pro-spring-boot-3rd`

My Retro App with Spring Boot and Spring Data JDBC

As with the Users App, to configure the My Retro App with Spring Boot and Spring Data JDBC, you can start from scratch by going to the Spring Initializr (`https://` `start.spring.io`). Set the Group field to `com.apress` and the Artifact and Name fields to `myretro`. For dependencies, add Web, Validation, JDBC, and Docker Compose. Download the project, unzip it, and import it into your favorite IDE. By the end of this section, you should have the structure shown in Figure 5-2.

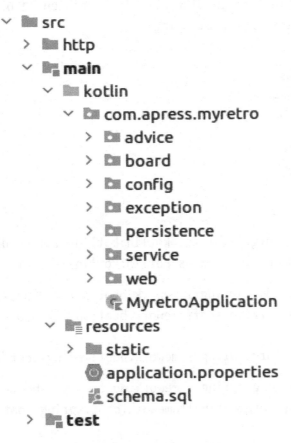

Figure 5-2. *My Retro App structure*

Note that the structure is very similar to that of the previous version (see Figure 4-5 in Chapter 4) and we are going to reuse almost the same code, so we describe only the most important changes here. If you compare the persistence package, there is only one interface! That is the power of Spring Data and Spring Boot.

Open the build.gradle file and replace its contents with the contents shown in Listing 5-12.

Listing 5-12. The build.gradle File

```
import org.jetbrains.kotlin.gradle.tasks.KotlinCompile
plugins {
    id 'org.springframework.boot' version '3.2.3'
    id 'io.spring.dependency-management' version '1.1.4'
    id 'org.jetbrains.kotlin.jvm' version '2.0.20-RC'
    id "org.jetbrains.kotlin.plugin.spring" version "2.0.20-RC"
    // <- simplifies spring proxying
}

group = 'com.apress'
version = '0.0.1-SNAPSHOT'
sourceCompatibility = '17'

repositories {
    mavenCentral()
}

dependencies {
    implementation "org.jetbrains.kotlin:kotlin-stdlib-jdk8"
    implementation "org.jetbrains.kotlin:kotlin-reflect"

    implementation 'org.springframework.boot:spring-boot-starter-web'
    implementation 'org.springframework.boot:spring-boot-starter-
    validation'
    implementation 'org.springframework.boot:spring-boot-starter-aop'

    implementation 'org.springframework.boot:spring-boot-starter-data-jdbc'
    developmentOnly 'org.springframework.boot:spring-boot-docker-compose'
```

```
annotationProcessor 'org.springframework.boot:spring-boot-
configuration-processor'

runtimeOnly 'com.h2database:h2'
runtimeOnly 'org.postgresql:postgresql'

// Web
implementation 'org.webjars:bootstrap:5.2.3'

testImplementation 'org.springframework.boot:spring-boot-starter-test'
}

tasks.named('test') {
    useJUnitPlatform()
}

//      kotlin {
//          jvmToolchain(17)
//      }
tasks.withType(KotlinCompile).configureEach {
    kotlinOptions {
        freeCompilerArgs = ['-Xjsr305=strict']
        jvmTarget = '17'
    }
}
```

Note that Listing 5-12 uses the dependencies `spring-boot-starter-data-jdbc` starter and `spring-boot-docker-compose` (as development only; remember that you need to add the connection properties if you go to production).

Note   Again, we are going to work only on the classes that changed using Spring Data JDBC. You can find the complete code by going to `https://www.apress.com/gp/services/source-code`.

Next, create/view the `board` package and create/open the `Card` and `RetroBoard` classes, as shown in Listing 5-13 and Listing 5-14, respectively.

Listing 5-13. src/main/kotlin/apress/com/myretro/board/Card.kt

```kotlin
package com.apress.myretro.board

import com.fasterxml.jackson.annotation.JsonIgnore
import jakarta.validation.constraints.NotBlank
import jakarta.validation.constraints.NotNull
import org.springframework.data.annotation.Id
import org.springframework.data.relational.core.mapping.Table
import java.util.*

@Table
data class Card(
    @Id
    var id: UUID? = null,

    @get:NotBlank
    var comment: String? = null,

    @get:NotNull
    var cardType:  CardType? = null,

    @JsonIgnore
    var retroBoardId: UUID? = null
)
```

Notice in the Card class that we are using the @Table and @Id annotations (from the Spring Data package), plus one special annotation, @JsonIgnore, which is more for the web endpoint (this annotation will not render the retroBoardId value when requested). We discuss @JsonIgnore in more detail later in the chapter.

Listing 5-14. src/main/kotlin/apress/com/myretro/board/RetroBoard.kt

```kotlin
package com.apress.myretro.board

import jakarta.validation.constraints.NotBlank
import org.springframework.data.annotation.Id
import org.springframework.data.relational.core.mapping.MappedCollection
import org.springframework.data.relational.core.mapping.Table
import java.util.*
```

```
@Table
data class RetroBoard(
    @Id
    var id: UUID? = null,

    @get:NotBlank(message = "A name must be provided")
    var name:  String? = null,

    @MappedCollection(idColumn = "retro_board_id", keyColumn = "id")
    var cards: MutableMap<UUID, Card> = mutableMapOf()
)
```

The RetroBoard class will be the entity class. Note that we are using the @Table and @Id annotations. The important code is the @MappedCollection annotation, which uses two parameters—idColumn and keyColumn. It's important to know that Spring Data JDBC has support for the following types (among others):

- enum: Get mapped to their name.

- int, flow, Integer, Float, and more: All primitive types.

- String, java.util.Date, java.time.LocalDate, java.time.LocalDateTime, java.time.LocalTime: Arrays and collections are mapped if your selected database engine has array types.

- Set, Map: This is normally good for one-to-many relationships.

If you want to see the complete list of types, go to https://docs.spring.io/spring-data/jdbc/docs/current/reference/html/#jdbc.entity-persistence.types. It's important to mention that reference is limited, and this is based on the Aggregate Root pattern. In this case, it's a one-to-many relationship. Many-to-one or many-to-many relationships need to be handled using the AggregateReference interface. This interface is a wrapper around an ID that is the reference of a different aggregate you are mapping.

Also notice in the @Table annotation that it doesn't use the name parameters (like @Table("RETROBOARD")); we are going to let the NamingStrategy logic do its job, which uses snake name convention, instead of camel case. So the RetroBoard class will be retro_board as the table name. And in the Card class, the retroBoardId field will become retro_board_id as the column for the card table.

Next, open/create the persistence package and the RetroBoardRepository interface. See Listing 5-15.

Listing 5-15. src/main/kotlin/apress/com/myretro/persistence/
RetroBoardRepository.kt

```
package com.apress.myretro.persistence

import com.apress.myretro.board.RetroBoard
import org.springframework.data.repository.CrudRepository
import java.util.*

interface RetroBoardRepository : CrudRepository<RetroBoard, UUID>
```

The `RetroBoardRepository` interface extends from the `CrudRepository` interface. Remember that this interface includes several methods (previously discussed in the "Users App with Spring Boot and Spring Data JDBC" section).

Next, open/create the `MyRetroConfiguration` class. See Listing 5-16.

Listing 5-16. src/main/kotlin/apress/com/myretro/config/
MyRetroConfiguration.kt

```
package com.apress.myretro.config

import com.apress.myretro.board.Card
import com.apress.myretro.board.CardType
import com.apress.myretro.board.RetroBoard
import com.apress.myretro.service.RetroBoardService
import org.springframework.boot.context.event.ApplicationReadyEvent
import org.springframework.boot.context.properties.
EnableConfigurationProperties
import org.springframework.context.ApplicationListener
import org.springframework.context.annotation.Bean
import org.springframework.context.annotation.Configuration

@EnableConfigurationProperties(MyRetroProperties::class)
@Configuration
class MyRetroConfiguration {
    @Bean
    fun ready(retroBoardService: RetroBoardService):
            ApplicationListener<ApplicationReadyEvent> {
```

```
return ApplicationListener<ApplicationReadyEvent> { _:
ApplicationReadyEvent ->
    val id = retroBoardService.save(
        RetroBoard(name = "Spring Boot Conference")
    ).id!!
    with(retroBoardService) {
        addCardToRetroBoard(
            id, Card(comment = "Spring Boot Rocks!",
            cardType = CardType.HAPPY, retroBoardId = id)
        )
        addCardToRetroBoard(
            id, Card(comment = "Meet everyone in person",
            cardType = CardType.HAPPY, retroBoardId = id)
        )
        addCardToRetroBoard(
            id, Card(comment = "When is the next one?",
            cardType = CardType.MEH, retroBoardId = id)
        )
        addCardToRetroBoard(
            id, Card(comment = "Not enough time to talk to
            everyone",
            cardType = CardType.SAD, retroBoardId = id)
        )
    }
}
}
```

The MyRetroConfiguration class changes the way we save some initial data. It uses the RetroBoardService to do the job, and, as you can imagine, the RetroBoardService uses the RetroBoardRepository interface (as a field is injected in the constructor).

Next, open/create the application.properties file. See Listing 5-17.

Listing 5-17. src/main/resources/application.properties

```
# DataSource
spring.datasource.generate-unique-name=false
```

```
spring.datasource.name=test-db
# SQL init
spring.sql.init.mode=always
logging.level.org.springframework.jdbc.core.JdbcTemplate=DEBUG
```

The only new addition to application.properties from the previous chapter is the logging, and this includes a DEBUG over the JdbcTemplate class. Why? Because at the end, the JdbcTemplate is the one executing all the SQL statements. When you start the app, you should see some of the SQL queries being executed (which is a way to see if you need to improve how you are modeling the classes or do a better job in normalizing some of the relationships).

The schema.sql file and the advice.*, exception.*, service.*, and web.* packages and classes are the same as in Chapter 4, so there's no need to add them here.

Running the My Retro App

You can run the My Retro App in your IDE or you can execute the following command:

```
./gradlew clean bootRun
```

In the output, you should see that Docker Compose will start the PostgreSQL service and you should see part of the SQL queries being executed, thanks to the logging property.

```
...
Executing SQL update and returning generated keys
DEBUG [main] o.s.jdbc.core.JdbcTemplate          : Executing prepared SQL
                                                    statement [INSERT INTO
                                                    "retro_board" ("name")
                                                    VALUES (?)]
 INFO [main] c.a.myretro.advice.RetroBoardAdvice: [ADVICE] findById
DEBUG [main] o.s.jdbc.core.JdbcTemplate          : Executing prepared
                                                    SQL query
DEBUG [main] o.s.jdbc.core.JdbcTemplate          : Executing prepared SQL
                                                    statement [SELECT "retro_
                                                    board"."id" AS "id",
                                                    "retro_board"."name"
                                                    AS "name" FROM "retro_
```

```
                                              board" WHERE "retro_
                                              board"."id" = ?]
DEBUG [main] o.s.jdbc.core.JdbcTemplate     : Executing prepared
                                              SQL query
DEBUG [main] o.s.jdbc.core.JdbcTemplate     : Executing prepared
                                              SQL statement [SELECT
                                              "card"."id" AS "id",
                                              "card"."comment" AS
                                              "comment", "card"."card_
                                              type" AS "card_type",
                                              "card"."retro_board_id"
                                              AS "retro_board_id",
                                              "card"."id" AS "id"
                                              FROM "card" WHERE
                                              "card"."retro_board_
                                              id" = ?]
DEBUG [main] o.s.jdbc.core.JdbcTemplate     : Executing prepared
                                              SQL update
...
```

Now you can open your browser and go to http://localhost:8080/retros or execute the following command:

```
curl -s  http://localhost:8080/retros | jq .
[
  {
    "id": "8e2d85d3-2521-45d0-975c-2753bac964c5",
    "name": "Spring Boot Conference",
    "cards": {
      "9aa89e63-d85d-41bc-af5e-ad6fd41d9447": {
        "id": "9aa89e63-d85d-41bc-af5e-ad6fd41d9447",
```

```
            "comment": "Spring Boot Rocks!",
            "cardType": "HAPPY"
          },
          "57e89fec-5720-4207-8de6-d2c11470b422": {
            "id": "57e89fec-5720-4207-8de6-d2c11470b422",
            "comment": "Not enough time to talk to everyone",
            "cardType": "SAD"
          },
          "f0ba172b-396e-471b-bff3-84eb5fd15934": {
            "id": "f0ba172b-396e-471b-bff3-84eb5fd15934",
            "comment": "When is the next one?",
            "cardType": "MEH"
          },
          "c29d3809-688b-4102-a65a-7fdfc2062875": {
            "id": "c29d3809-688b-4102-a65a-7fdfc2062875",
            "comment": "Meet everyone in person",
            "cardType": "HAPPY"
          }
        }
      }
    }
]
```

Note that in the `Card` element the `retroBoardId` is not printed out, and this is because of the `@JsonIgnore` annotation in the `Card` class.

You now know how Spring Boot uses the Spring Data technology: it auto-configures all the `DataSource`, `JdbcTemplate`, and everything underneath, initializes the database by finding a `schema.sql` or `data.sql` (it's important to use `spring.sql.init. mode=always` to allow the database initialization to kick in), and enables the repositories (`@EnableJdbcRepositories`) without revealing where to find them.

Next, let's review how Spring Boot relies on Spring Data JPA to create awesome apps using this technology.

Spring Data JPA

The *Jakarta Persistence API (JPA)* (formerly known as *Java Persistence API*) is not a tool or framework, but a set of specifications that define concepts for any implementer. Like Spring Data JDBC, Spring Data JPA can be used as an ORM tool. And now, with the JPA 3 specification, JPA can be extended to be used for NoSQL databases. The difference between JDBC and JPA is that in JPA you need to think not in terms of relationships but in terms of the rules of persistence of the Java or Kotlin code. In JDBC, you need to manually translate your code back and forth to relational tables, columns, and keys.

If you use plain JPA in a non-Spring application, you still need to do a lot of coding and a lot of configuration in your app, such as handling connection and session management, handling transaction setup and management, defining mapping and persistence units with XML files, defining the JPA implementation to be used, and much more.

Spring Data JPA eliminates most of this effort by auto-configuring the implementation of the data access layers. The main feature of Spring Data JPA is that developers only need to write repository interfaces and, if needed, any custom finder methods. Spring Data JPA takes care of the implementation. Here are some of its other features:

- Spring programming model

- The choice of using the `CrudRepository` interface or the `JpaRepository` interfaces

- Spring Data Extension with the support for `Querydsl` extension predicates and thus type-safe JPA queries

- Repository query-based methods, based on several keywords (`findBy<field-name>`, `deleteBy<field-name>`, `findBy<field-name>And<other-field-name>`, etc.) together with the field names of the domain classes

- Transparent auditing of domain classes

- Pagination support, dynamic query execution, and the ability to integrate custom data access code through several interfaces with the `PagingAndSortingRepository`

- Callbacks and events

- Customization of individual repositories

- Validation of @Query annotated queries at bootstrap time, providing control of customization to what you really need

- JavaConfig-based repository configuration using the @EnableJpaRepositories annotation

- Powerful extensions to extend Spring Data JPA, such as the use of Hibernate Envers for auditing/revisions

Spring Data JPA with Spring Boot

Using Spring Data JPA in a Spring app (no Spring Boot) requires adding some configuration (JavaConfig or XML), declaring DataSource, PlatformTransactionManager, and LocalContainerEntityManagerFactoryBean, and using the @EnableJpaRepositories and @EnableTransactionManagement annotations in the class where you are using the @Configuration annotation.

Thanks to Spring Boot auto-configuration, you don't need to do anything. It works just by adding the spring-boot-starter-data-jpa starter dependency. Spring Boot allows you to overwrite the defaults by providing spring.jpa.* properties. Another cool feature that Spring Boot provides is the default registration of OpenEntityManagerInViewInterceptor, which applies the *Open EntityManager in View* pattern to allow for lazy loading in web views.

By default, Spring Boot uses Hibernate JPA implementation, which also brings an enterprise-grade level for data applications.

The following sections show how you can use Spring Data JPA with Spring Boot in your applications.

Users App with Spring Boot and Spring Data JPA

Remember that you have access to the code, so if you want to start from scratch, you can go to the Spring Initializr (https://start.spring.io) and accept the default settings apart from choosing Kotlin. Set the Group field to com.apress and the Artifact and Name fields to users. For dependencies, add Web, Validation, JPA, H2, and PostgreSQL. Download the project, unzip it, and import it into your favorite IDE. This section covers only the classes that have changed from previous sections. By the end of this section, you should have the structure shown in Figure 5-3.

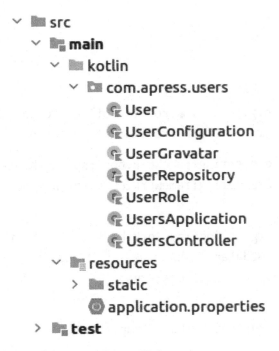

∨ ▪ src
    ∨ ▪ **main**
        ∨ ▪ kotlin
            ∨ ▪ com.apress.users
                ⍟ User
                ⍟ UserConfiguration
                ⍟ UserGravatar
                ⍟ UserRepository
                ⍟ UserRole
                ⍟ UsersApplication
                ⍟ UsersController
        ∨ ▪ resources
            > ▪ static
                ⚙ application.properties
    > ▪ **test**

Figure 5-3. *Users App with Spring Data JPA*

Importantly, you no longer need the schema.sql file. Spring Boot with Spring Data JPA takes care of creating the database tables, as described in the following sections.

Start by opening the build.gradle file and replacing its contents with the contents shown in Listing 5-18.

Listing 5-18. The build.gradle File

```
import org.jetbrains.kotlin.gradle.tasks.KotlinCompile
plugins {
    id 'org.springframework.boot' version '3.2.3'
    id 'io.spring.dependency-management' version '1.1.4'
    id 'org.jetbrains.kotlin.jvm' version '2.0.20-RC'
    id "org.jetbrains.kotlin.plugin.spring" version "2.0.20-RC"
    // <- simplifies spring proxying
}

group = 'com.apress'
version = '0.0.1-SNAPSHOT'
sourceCompatibility = '17'
```

```
repositories {
    mavenCentral()
}

dependencies {
    implementation "org.jetbrains.kotlin:kotlin-stdlib-jdk8"
    implementation "org.jetbrains.kotlin:kotlin-reflect"

    implementation 'org.springframework.boot:spring-boot-starter-web'
    implementation 'org.springframework.boot:spring-boot-starter-
    validation'

    implementation 'org.springframework.boot:spring-boot-starter-data-jpa'
    runtimeOnly 'com.h2database:h2'
    runtimeOnly 'org.postgresql:postgresql'

    // Web
    implementation 'org.webjars:bootstrap:5.2.3'

    testImplementation 'org.springframework.boot:spring-boot-starter-test'
}
tasks.named('test') {
    useJUnitPlatform()
}

test {
    testLogging {
        events "passed", "skipped", "failed"
        showExceptions true
        exceptionFormat "full"
        showCauses true
        showStackTraces true
        showStandardStreams = false
    }
}

//    kotlin {
//        jvmToolchain(17)
//    }
```

```
tasks.withType(KotlinCompile).configureEach {
    kotlinOptions {
        freeCompilerArgs = ['-Xjsr305=strict']
        jvmTarget = '17'
    }
}
```

As you can see, this code uses the spring-boot-starter-data-jpa starter dependency and two drivers.

Next, let's look at the domain class. Open/Create the User class. See Listing 5-19.

Listing 5-19. src/main/kotlin/apress/com/users/User.kt

```
package com.apress.users

import jakarta.persistence.*
import jakarta.validation.constraints.NotBlank
import jakarta.validation.constraints.Pattern

@Entity(name = "USERS")
class User(
    @GeneratedValue(strategy = GenerationType.IDENTITY)
    @Id
    var id: Long? = null,

    @get:NotBlank(message = "Email cannot be empty")
    var email:  String? = null,

    @get:NotBlank(message = "Name cannot be empty")
    var name:  String? = null,

    var gravatarUrl: String? = null,

    @get:Pattern(
        message = "Password must be at least 8 characters long and contain
        at least one number, one uppercase, one lowercase and one special
        character",
        regexp = "^(?=.*[0-9])(?=.*[a-z])(?=.*[A-Z])(?=.*[@#$%^&+=!])(?=\\
        S+$).{8,}$"
    )
```

```
    var password:  String? = null,

    var userRole: MutableList<UserRole>? = null,

    var active:Boolean = false
) {
    @PrePersist
    private fun prePersist() {
        gravatarUrl = gravatarUrl ?: UserGravatar.getGravatarUrlFromEmai
        l(email!!)
        userRole = userRole ?: mutableListOf(UserRole.INFO)
    }
}
```

Listing 5-19 shows that the User class includes the following annotations (all of which are from the jakarta.persistence.* package):

- @Entity: This annotation marks the class as an entity and accepts a parameter that will be used to set the name of the table—in this case, the USERS table.

- @Id: This annotation is required to set the class identity, which is the primary key in the database.

- @GeneratedValue: This annotation is used to set the Id generation strategy. It accepts as a parameter which strategy to use. This choice will depend on your database engine. If your database doesn't support an identity column, you can use the GenerationType. SEQUENCE strategy. If your database does support an identity column, you can use any of these: GenerationType.TABLE (indicates that the persistence provider must assign primary keys for the entity using an underlying database table to ensure uniqueness), GenerationType. UUID (indicates that the persistence provider must assign primary keys for the entity by generating an RFC 4122 Universally Unique Identifier), or GenerationType.AUTO (indicates that the persistence provider should pick an appropriate strategy for the database).

- @PrePersist: This annotation marks the method as a callback for the corresponding lifecycle event. There are many more of these callback annotation markers, including @PreUpdate, @PreRemove, @PostUpddate, @PostRemove, @PostPersist, and @PostLoad.

Next, open/create the UserRepository interface. See Listing 5-20.

Listing 5-20. src/main/kotlin/apress/com/users/UserRepository.kt

```
package com.apress.users

import org.springframework.data.repository.CrudRepository
import org.springframework.transaction.annotation.Transactional

interface UserRepository : CrudRepository<User, Long> {
    fun findByEmail(email: String): User?

    @Transactional
    fun deleteByEmail(email: String?)
}
```

The UserRepository interface extends from the CrudRepository...wait...what? We used the same interface in Listing 5-4. We could use the JPA-related interface, but we will use it in the My Retro App project. Remember that the CrudRepository interface has several methods declared and that Spring Data will take care of the implementation. Also note that the @Transactional annotation has been added, which allows you to have a thread-safe call.

Next, open the application.properties file and replace its contents with the contents shown in Listing 5-21.

Listing 5-21. src/main/resources/application.properties

```
# H2
spring.h2.console.enabled=true
# DataSource
spring.datasource.generate-unique-name=false
spring.datasource.name=test-db
# JPA
spring.jpa.show-sql=true
```

```
spring.jpa.generate-ddl=true
spring.jpa.hibernate.ddl-auto=update
spring.jpa.properties.hibernate.format_sql=true
```

The new additions to the application.properties file are two spring.jpa.* properties, the first of which will show every SQL statement executed and the second of which will help auto-generate the DDL for your database. This is awesome, because you no longer have to worry about creating a schema.sql file!

The spring.jpa.hibernate.ddl-auto property provides the following values:

- update: Updates the schema if necessary.

- create: Creates the schema and destroys the previous data.

- create-drop: Creates the schema and then destroys the schema at the end of the session.

- none: Disables the DDL handling.

- validate: Validates the schema and makes no changes to the database.

As you can see, the DDL generation support covers different scenarios. The other classes—UserConfiguration, UserGravatar, UserRole, and UsersController—and the UsersHttpRequestTests test remain the same.

Testing and Running the Users App

You can run the tests in your IDE or by using the following command:

```
./gradlew clean test
UsersHttpRequestTests > userEndPointFindUserShouldReturnUser() PASSED
UsersHttpRequestTests > userEndPointDeleteUserShouldReturnVoid() PASSED
UsersHttpRequestTests > indexPageShouldReturnHeaderOneContent() PASSED
UsersHttpRequestTests > userEndPointPostNewUserShouldReturnUser() PASSED
UsersHttpRequestTests >
usersEndPointShouldReturnCollectionWithTwoUsers() PASSED
```

You can run the Users App in your IDE or use the following command:

```
./gradlew bootRun
...
Hibernate:
    create table users (
        id bigint generated by default as identity,
        active boolean not null,
        email varchar(255),
        gravatar_url varchar(255),
        name varchar(255),
        password varchar(255),
        user_role tinyint array,
        primary key (id)
    )
...
```

This output shows that the JPA/Hibernate SQL statements are being executed when saving the data (in the UserConfiguration class).

My Retro App Using Spring Boot and Spring Data JPA

Next, let's look at what you need to do to use Spring Data JPA in the My Retro App. We add all the classes that are important to review; remember that you have access to the source code. If you want to start from scratch, go to the Spring Initializr (https://start.spring.io) and start an empty project. Set the Group field to com.apress and the Artifact and Name fields to myretro. For dependencies, add Web, Validation, JPA, Docker Compose, Processor, and PostgreSQL. Download the project, unzip it, and import it into your favorite IDE. By the end of this section, you should have the structure shown in Figure 5-4.

Figure 5-4. *My Retro App with Spring Data JPA*

As you can see, you no longer need `schema.sql`. Spring Boot with Spring Data JPA takes care of creating the database's tables.

Open the `build.gradle` file and replace its contents with the contents shown in Listing 5-22.

Listing 5-22. build.gradle

```
import org.jetbrains.kotlin.gradle.tasks.KotlinCompile
plugins {
    id 'org.springframework.boot' version '3.2.3'
    id 'io.spring.dependency-management' version '1.1.4'
    id 'org.jetbrains.kotlin.jvm' version '2.0.20-RC'
```

```
    id "org.jetbrains.kotlin.plugin.spring" version "2.0.20-RC"
    // <- simplifies spring proxying
}

group = 'com.apress'
version = '0.0.1-SNAPSHOT'
sourceCompatibility = '17'

repositories {
    mavenCentral()
}

dependencies {
    implementation "org.jetbrains.kotlin:kotlin-stdlib-jdk8"
    implementation "org.jetbrains.kotlin:kotlin-reflect"

    implementation 'org.springframework.boot:spring-boot-starter-web'
    implementation 'org.springframework.boot:spring-boot-starter-
    validation'
    implementation 'org.springframework.boot:spring-boot-starter-aop'

    implementation 'org.springframework.boot:spring-boot-starter-data-jpa'
    developmentOnly 'org.springframework.boot:spring-boot-docker-compose'

    annotationProcessor 'org.springframework.boot:spring-boot-
    configuration-processor'

    runtimeOnly 'org.postgresql:postgresql'

    // Web
    implementation 'org.webjars:bootstrap:5.2.3'

    testImplementation 'org.springframework.boot:spring-boot-starter-test'
}

tasks.named('test') {
    useJUnitPlatform()
}

//      kotlin {
//          jvmToolchain(17)
```

```
//    }
tasks.withType(KotlinCompile).configureEach {
    kotlinOptions {
        freeCompilerArgs = ['-Xjsr305=strict']
        jvmTarget = '17'
    }
}
```

As you can see, this code includes the `spring-boot-starter-data-jpa` and `spring-boot-docker-compose` starter dependencies.

Next, open/create the `board` package and the `Card` and `RetroBoard` classes. Listing 5-23 shows the `Card` class.

Listing 5-23. src/main/kotlin/apress/com/myretro/board/Card.kt

```
package com.apress.myretro.board

import com.fasterxml.jackson.annotation.JsonIgnore
import jakarta.persistence.*
import jakarta.validation.constraints.NotBlank
import jakarta.validation.constraints.NotNull
import java.util.*

@Entity
data class Card(
    @GeneratedValue(strategy = GenerationType.UUID)
    @Id val id: UUID? = null,

    @get:NotBlank
    var comment: String? = null,

    @Enumerated(EnumType.STRING)
    @get:NotNull
    var cardType: CardType? = null,

    @ManyToOne
    @JoinColumn(name = "retro_board_id")
    @JsonIgnore
    var retroBoard: RetroBoard? = null
)
```

Let's analyze the `Card` class annotations and see what changed from the previous versions:

- **@Entity**: This annotation marks the class as an entity. This annotation comes from the `jakarta.persistence.*` package. By default, the name of the table is CARD.

- **@GeneratedValue**: This annotation is used to set the `Id` generation strategy. It accepts as a parameter which strategy to use; this will depend on your database engine. This example uses the UUID.

- **@Id**: This annotation is required to set the class identity, which is the primary key in the database. This annotation also comes from the `jakarta.persistence.*` package.

- **@Enumerated**: This annotation specifies that a property or field should be persisted as an enumerated type. It accepts a value of `EnumType`, `ORDINAL`, or `STRING`. With this setting, it will generate the following SQL statement (this is just a snippet):

```
create table card (
        id uuid not null,
        retro_board_id uuid,
        card_type varchar(255) not null check (card_type in
        ('HAPPY','MEH','SAD')),
        comment varchar(255),
        primary key (id)
    )
```

- **@ManyToOne**: This annotation specifies a single-valued association to another entity class that has many-to-one multiplicity. There is also the @ManyToMany, @OneToOne, and @OneToMany.

- **@JoinColumn**: This annotation specifies a column for joining an entity association or element collection. In this case, we are identifying which column to join, `retro_board_id`. Remember that the `NamingStrategy` takes place, using snake case to create the fields. You can see that in the previous snippet.

As previously mentioned, with JPA, you need to take care of the objects and the dependencies. In this case, we have a dependency of the RetroBoard class, shown in Listing 5-24.

Listing 5-24. src/main/kotlin/apress/com/myretro/board/RetroBoard.kt

```kotlin
package com.apress.myretro.board

import jakarta.persistence.*
import jakarta.validation.constraints.NotBlank
import java.util.*

@Entity
data class RetroBoard(
    @GeneratedValue(strategy = GenerationType.UUID)
    @Id
    var id: UUID? = null,

    @get:NotBlank(message = "A name must be provided")
    var name: String? = null,

    @OneToMany(mappedBy = "retroBoard")
    val cards: MutableList<Card> = mutableListOf()
)
```

Note in Listing 5-24 that we are still using the required annotations—@Entity and @Id. We also are using the new @OneToMany annotation, which knows how to get all the Cards based on the RetroBoard id. The @OneToMany annotation specifies a many-valued association with one-to-many multiplicity.

Next, open/create the persistence package and the CardRepository and RetroBoardRepository classes, as shown in Listings 5-25 and 5-26, respectively.

Listing 5-25. src/main/kotlin/apress/com/myretro/persistence/CardRepository.kt

```kotlin
package com.apress.myretro.persistence

import com.apress.myretro.board.Card
import org.springframework.data.jpa.repository.JpaRepository
import java.util.*

interface CardRepository : JpaRepository<Card, UUID>
```

Listing 5-26. src/main/kotlin/apress/com/myretro/persistence/
RetroBoardRepository.kt

```
package com.apress.myretro.persistence

import com.apress.myretro.board.RetroBoard
import org.springframework.data.jpa.repository.JpaRepository
import java.util.*

interface RetroBoardRepository : JpaRepository<RetroBoard, UUID>
```

Listings 5-25 and 5-26 show that the `CardRepository` and `RetroBoardRepository` interfaces are both extending from the `JpaRepository` interface, which is all about JPA. Take a look at the following snippet:

```
public interface JpaRepository<T, ID> extends ListCrudRepository<T, ID>, ListPagingAndSortingRepository<T, ID>, QueryByExampleExecutor<T> {
    void flush();
    <S extends T> S saveAndFlush(S entity);
    <S extends T> List<S> saveAllAndFlush(Iterable<S> entities);
    void deleteAllInBatch(Iterable<T> entities);
    void deleteAllByIdInBatch(Iterable<ID> ids);
    void deleteAllInBatch();
    T getReferenceById(ID id);
    @Override
    <S extends T> List<S> findAll(Example<S> example);
    @Override
    <S extends T> List<S> findAll(Example<S> example, Sort sort);
}
```

As you can see, `JpaRepository` extends from other interfaces that allow paging and sorting, and from `CrudRepository`, which brings in the methods you already know.

Next, open/create the `service` package and the `RetroBoardService` class. See Listing 5-27.

Listing 5-27. src/main/kotlin/apress/com/myretro/service/
RetroBoardService.kt

```kotlin
package com.apress.myretro.service

import com.apress.myretro.board.Card
import com.apress.myretro.board.RetroBoard
import com.apress.myretro.exception.CardNotFoundException
import com.apress.myretro.exception.RetroBoardNotFoundException
import com.apress.myretro.persistence.CardRepository
import com.apress.myretro.persistence.RetroBoardRepository
import org.springframework.beans.factory.annotation.Autowired
import org.springframework.stereotype.Service
import java.util.*
import java.util.function.Consumer
import java.util.function.Function
import java.util.function.Supplier
import kotlin.jvm.optionals.getOrNull

@Service
class RetroBoardService {
    @Autowired
    lateinit var retroBoardRepository: RetroBoardRepository

    @Autowired
    lateinit var cardRepository: CardRepository

    fun save(domain: RetroBoard): RetroBoard {
        return retroBoardRepository.save<RetroBoard>(domain)
    }

    fun findById(uuid: UUID): RetroBoard =
        retroBoardRepository.findById(uuid).get()

    fun findAll(): Iterable<RetroBoard> =
        retroBoardRepository.findAll()

    fun delete(uuid: UUID) {
        retroBoardRepository.deleteById(uuid)
    }
```

```kotlin
fun findAllCardsFromRetroBoard(uuid: UUID): Iterable<Card> =
    findById(uuid).cards

fun addCardToRetroBoard(uuid: UUID, card: Card): Card {
    return card.apply {
        retroBoardRepository.findById(uuid).getOrNull()?.also {
            this.retroBoard = it
        }?:throw RetroBoardNotFoundException()
        cardRepository.save<Card>(this)
    }
}

fun addMultipleCardsToRetroBoard(uuid: UUID, cards: Collection<Card>) {
    val retroBoard: RetroBoard = findById(uuid)
    cards.forEach{ card: Card -> card.retroBoard = retroBoard }
    cardRepository.saveAll(cards)
}

fun findCardByUUID(uuidCard: UUID): Card =
    cardRepository.findById(uuidCard).getOrNull()?:throw CardNotFound
    Exception()

fun saveCard(card: Card): Card {
    return cardRepository.save<Card>(card)
}

fun removeCardByUUID(cardUUID: UUID) {
    cardRepository.deleteById(cardUUID)
}
}
```

As you can see, the RetroBoardService class is very straightforward. In this case, we are using two repositories, the CardRepository and RetroBoardRepository interfaces, as part of the dependencies that will be injected by Spring.

Next, open the application.properties file and replace its contents with the contents shown in Listing 5-28.

Listing 5-28. src/main/resources/application.properties

```
# DataSource
spring.datasource.generate-unique-name=false
spring.datasource.name=test-db
# JPA
spring.jpa.show-sql=true
spring.jpa.generate-ddl=true
spring.jpa.hibernate.ddl-auto=create-drop
spring.jpa.properties.hibernate.format_sql=true
```
spring.jpa.properties.hibernate.dialect=org.hibernate.dialect.
PostgreSQLDialect

The only new property is `hibernate.dialect`, which is included to show that you can specify a dialect. However, this is not necessary, because when the auto-configuration kicks in, it already knows that you are using PostgreSQL.

The `advice`, `config`, `exception`, and `web` packages and their classes are the same ones from the previous sections and chapters. As previously noted, you can access the source code from the Apress website (`https://www.apress.com/gp/services/source-code`).

Running the My Retro App

You can run My Retro App in your IDE or you can execute the following command:

```
./gradlew clean bootRun
```

In the output you should see that Docker Compose will start up the PostgreSQL service and you should see part of the SQL queries being executed. Note that the JPA generates three tables—`card`, `retro_board`, and `retro_board_card`—which is the result of how we create the classes and relationships.

Now you can either open your browser and go to `http://localhost:8080/retros` or execute the following command:

```
curl -s  http://localhost:8080/retros | jq .
[
  {
    "id": "57964a9a-9b56-453d-925a-64f63b502a48",
```

```
  "name": "Spring Boot Conference",
  "cards": [
    {
      "id": "080d4feb-8f84-4fc7-b6c3-9da741291846",
      "comment": "Spring Boot Rocks!",
      "cardType": "HAPPY"
    },
    {
      "id": "6a642199-ca5f-4d25-9242-1fe3301cf49d",
      "comment": "Meet everyone in person",
      "cardType": "HAPPY"
    },
    {
      "id": "5b4fd29f-89a8-4842-9381-6a0ed4cddb4f",
      "comment": "When is the next one?",
      "cardType": "MEH"
    },
    {
      "id": "91a49f48-a99b-4163-a0c7-230aa0142dc2",
      "comment": "Not enough time to talk to everyone",
      "cardType": "SAD"
    }
  ]
}
]
```

As you can see, `Card` is not printing out the `retroBoard` instance due to the `@JsonIgnore` annotation.

That's it, you're now aware of the power of JPA. But is there something simpler?

Spring Data REST

Spring Data REST, another project under the umbrella of Spring Data, provides an easy way to build hypermedia-driven REST web services using the interface repositories. When you include Spring Data REST, it will analyze all your domain models and create all the necessary HTTP resources for aggregates contained in your models. In other words, it will generate the REST controllers (with the Hypertext Application Language as the media type) having access to HTTP methods (such as POST, GET, PUT, PATCH, and so on) for your application.

The following are some of the most common features of Spring Data REST:

- Exposes a discoverable REST API based on your domain model

- Uses HAL+JSON by default (Hypertext Application Language)

- Exposes collection, item, and any association resources that represent your model

- Supports pagination via navigational links

- Creates search resources for query methods defined in your repositories

- Exposes metadata about the model discovered as Application-Level Profile Semantics (ALPS) and JSON Schema

- Brings a HAL Explorer to exposed metadata

- Currently supports JPA, MongoDB, Neo4j, Solr, Cassandra, and Gemfire

- Allows customizations of the default resources exposed

Spring Data REST with Spring Boot

If you want to use Spring Data REST with Spring Boot, you need to add the spring-boot-starter-data-rest starter along with the supported technologies. All the auto-configuration will set up everything for you to use the REST API from your models. There's no need to do anything else—it's that simple.

Users App Using Spring Boot and Spring Data REST

You have access to the code, so if you want to start from scratch, you can go to the Spring Initializr (https://start.spring.io) and accept the defaults. Set the Group field to com.apress and the Artifact and Name fields to users. For dependencies, add Web, Validation, JPA, Data REST, and H2. Download the project, unzip it, and import it into your favorite IDE. We present only the classes that changed from the previous sections. By the end of this section, you should have the structure shown in Figure 5-5.

Figure 5-5. *Users App with JPA and Data REST*

Notice in particular that this no longer includes the UsersController class or static content!

Start by opening the build.gradle file and replacing its contents with the contents shown in Listing 5-29.

Listing 5-29. The build.gradle File

```
import org.jetbrains.kotlin.gradle.tasks.KotlinCompile
plugins {
    id 'org.springframework.boot' version '3.2.3'
    id 'io.spring.dependency-management' version '1.1.4'
    id 'org.jetbrains.kotlin.jvm' version '2.0.20-RC'
    id "org.jetbrains.kotlin.plugin.spring" version "2.0.20-RC"
    // <- simplifies spring proxying
}

group = 'com.apress'
version = '0.0.1-SNAPSHOT'
sourceCompatibility = '17'
```

```
repositories {
    mavenCentral()
}

dependencies {
    implementation "org.jetbrains.kotlin:kotlin-stdlib-jdk8"
    implementation "org.jetbrains.kotlin:kotlin-reflect"

    implementation 'org.springframework.boot:spring-boot-starter-web'
    implementation 'org.springframework.boot:spring-boot-starter-
    validation'

    implementation 'org.springframework.boot:spring-boot-starter-data-jpa'

    implementation 'org.springframework.boot:spring-boot-starter-data-rest'
    implementation 'org.springframework.data:spring-data-rest-hal-explorer'

    runtimeOnly 'com.h2database:h2'

    // Web
    implementation 'org.webjars:bootstrap:5.2.3'

    testImplementation 'org.springframework.boot:spring-boot-starter-test'
}

tasks.named('test') {
    useJUnitPlatform()
}

test {
    testLogging {
        events "passed", "skipped", "failed"
        showExceptions true
        exceptionFormat "full"
        showCauses true
        showStackTraces true
        showStandardStreams = false
    }
}
```

```
//    kotlin {
//        jvmToolchain(17)
//    }
tasks.withType(KotlinCompile).configureEach {
    kotlinOptions {
        freeCompilerArgs = ['-Xjsr305=strict']
        jvmTarget = '17'
    }
}
```

We've added the spring-boot-starter-data-rest, spring-data-rest-hal-explorer, and, of course, spring-boot-starter-data-jpa starter dependencies.

Next, open/create the UserRepository interface. See Listing 5-30.

Listing 5-30. src/main/kotlin/apress/com/users/UserRepository.kt

```
package com.apress.users

import org.springframework.data.repository.CrudRepository
import org.springframework.data.repository.PagingAndSortingRepository

interface UserRepository : CrudRepository<User, Long>,
                           PagingAndSortingRepository<User, Long> {
    fun findByEmail(email: String): User?
}
```

We've only removed the delete method and extended the PaginAndSortingRespository interface. This interface is also part of Spring Data (the core) and can be used along with JPA.

The User, UserConfiguration, UserGravatar, and UserRole classes haven't changed from the Spring Data JPA project, nor has the application.properties file (and, yes, we removed the UsersController class). Modifying the UserRepository wasn't necessary, but we wanted to show you the effects of having pagination and sorting. And that's it, just a minimal change!

Note   When you run the Users App, Spring Data REST inspects your application and gets your repositories. Based on the domain classes, it will create several endpoints that accept any HTTP requests. The access will be using the domain model (in this case, the User class), and it will generate the /users endpoint (which is lowercase and plural, thanks to the Evo Inflector library). The response will be always based on HAL+JSON media type/content-type, so you need to know how to handle those responses.

Running the Users App

Normally you would test the app before running it, but we want to run it first to show you the result of including the spring-data-rest-hal-explorer starter dependency and discuss the benefits that it brings to the app.

Either run the application in your IDE or run it using the following command:

./gradlew clean bootRun

Open your browser and go to http://localhost:8080. You should see the HAL Explorer, as shown in Figure 5-6.

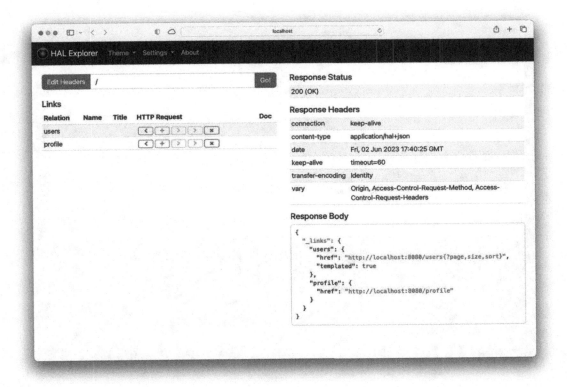

Figure 5-6. *Users App http://localhost:8080 with HAL Explorer*

By default, you have access to the HAL Explorer in the root endpoint /. If you click the < symbol in the users row (in the left pane below the HTTP Request), you will see a dialog box asking for parameters, as shown in Figure 5-7.

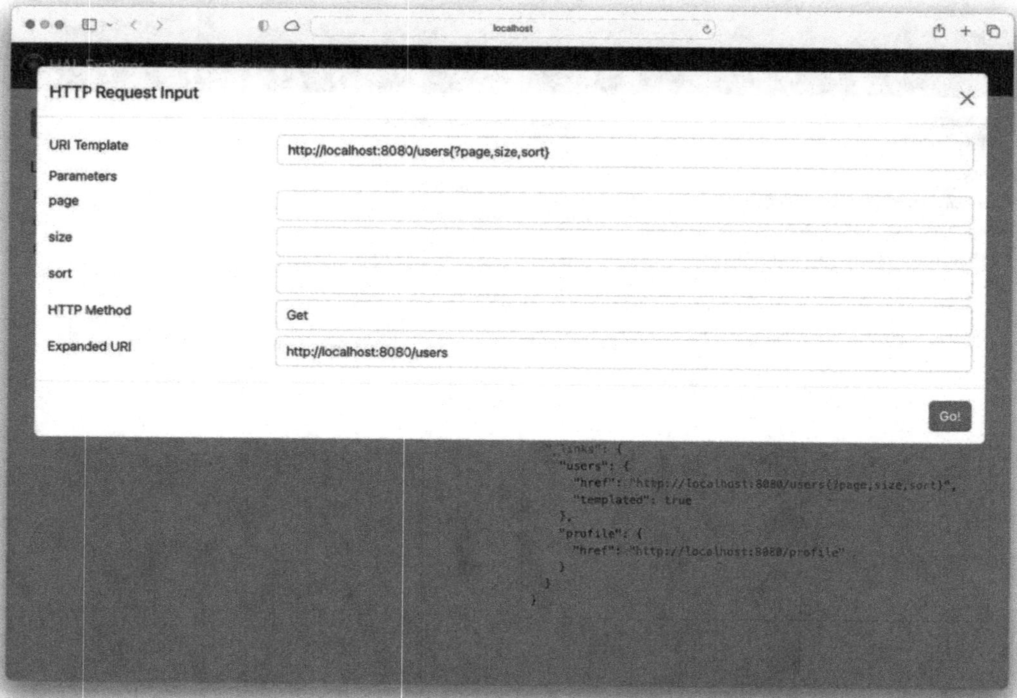

Figure 5-7.   *Users App with HAL Explorer: The Users dialog*

If you click the Go! button, you will see the updated HAL Explorer window, as shown in Figure 5-8.

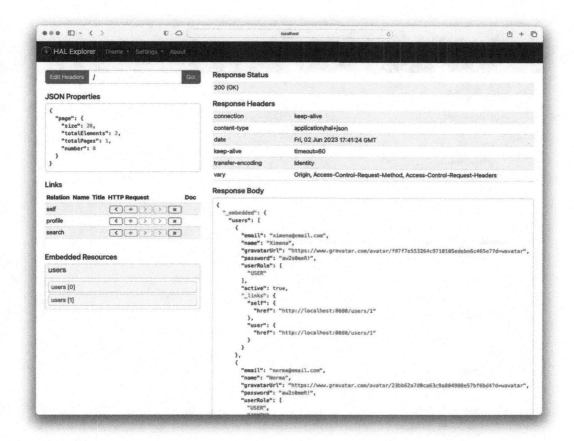

Figure 5-8. *Users App HAL Explorer: The user's HAL hyperlinks*

Notice that the response has more metadata, with new keywords; that's the HAL. response. If you click users[0] in the left pane under Embedded Resources, you should see the window in Figure 5-9.

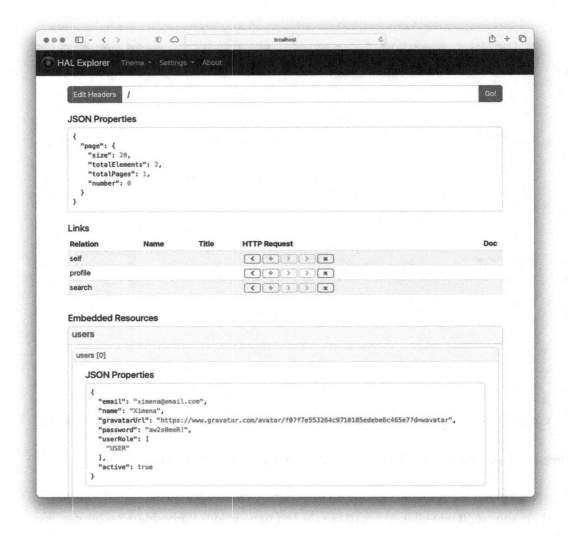

Figure 5-9. *Users App HAL Explorer: Embedded Resources - users[0]*

This is awesome, because now you have an API that is discoverable by other clients. Take a moment to click around and look at the HAL format. If you want to take a look at the command line, open a terminal and execute the following:

```
curl -s  http://localhost:8080/users | jq .
{
  "_embedded": {
    "users": [
      {
```

```
    "email": "ximena@email.com",
    "name": "Ximena",
    "gravatarUrl": "https://www.gravatar.com/avatar/f07f7e553264c971010
5edebe6c465e7?d=wavatar",
    "password": "aw2sOmeR!",
    "userRole": [
      "USER"
    ],
    "active": true,
    "_links": {
      "self": {
        "href": "http://localhost:8080/users/1"
      },
      "user": {
        "href": "http://localhost:8080/users/1"
      }
    }
  },
  {
    "email": "norma@email.com",
    "name": "Norma",
    "gravatarUrl": "https://www.gravatar.com/avatar/23bb62a7d0ca63c
9a804908e57bf6bd4?d=wavatar",
    "password": "aw2sOmeR!",
    "userRole": [
      "USER",
      "ADMIN"
    ],
    "active": true,
    "_links": {
      "self": {
        "href": "http://localhost:8080/users/2"
      },
      "user": {
        "href": "http://localhost:8080/users/2"
```

```
        }
      }
    }
  ]
},
"_links": {
  "self": {
    "href": "http://localhost:8080/users?page=0&size=20"
  },
  "profile": {
    "href": "http://localhost:8080/profile/users"
  },
  "search": {
    "href": "http://localhost:8080/users/search"
  }
},
"page": {
  "size": 20,
  "totalElements": 2,
  "totalPages": 1,
  "number": 0
}
}
```

Before you continue, analyze the response and all the elements. In particular, notice that there is a "_links" element and that it declares the "search" endpoint. This endpoint was created thanks to the findByEmail method declaration in the UserRepository, so you can search for an email using the following command:

curl -s "http://localhost:8080/users/search/findByEmail?email=ximena@email. com" | jq .

```
{
  "email": "ximena@email.com",
  "name": "Ximena",
  "gravatarUrl": "https://www.gravatar.com/avatar/f07f7e553264c9710105edebe
  6c465e7?d=wavatar",
```

```json
  "password": "aw2s0meR!",
  "userRole": [
    "USER"
  ],
  "active": true,
  "_links": {
    "self": {
      "href": "http://localhost:8080/users/1"
    },
    "user": {
      "href": "http://localhost:8080/users/1"
    }
  }
}
```

It will return the user and the self-links (that help navigate to an individual record). If you are in a browser, you can access http://localhost:8080/users and get all the user records. If you install the JSON Viewer plugin, you can click any of the links displayed on the page. See Figure 5-10.

Figure 5-10. *Users App http://localhost:8080/users : JSON viewer plugin*

Testing the Users App

Now it's time to test the app using integration testing. In this case, it's a little different from what you have seen in previous sections and chapters. This test uses new classes that support the HAL/HATEOAS media type.

Open/create the `UsersHttpRequestTests` class and replace/add the content in Listing 5-31.

Listing 5-31. src/test/kotlin/apress/com/users/UsersHttpRequestTests.kt

```kotlin
package com.apress.users

import com.fasterxml.jackson.core.JsonProcessingException
import com.fasterxml.jackson.databind.ObjectMapper
import org.assertj.core.api.Assertions
import org.junit.jupiter.api.BeforeEach
import org.junit.jupiter.api.Test
import org.springframework.beans.factory.annotation.Autowired
import org.springframework.boot.test.context.SpringBootTest
import org.springframework.boot.test.web.client.TestRestTemplate
import org.springframework.core.ParameterizedTypeReference
import org.springframework.hateoas.CollectionModel
import org.springframework.hateoas.EntityModel
import org.springframework.hateoas.MediaTypes
import org.springframework.http.*

@SpringBootTest(webEnvironment = SpringBootTest.WebEnvironment.RANDOM_PORT)
class UsersHttpRequestTests {
    private var baseUrl: String? = null

    @Autowired
    private lateinit var restTemplate: TestRestTemplate

    @BeforeEach
    @Throws(Exception::class)
    fun setUp() {
        baseUrl = "/users"
    }

    @Test
    @Throws(Exception::class)
    fun usersEndPointShouldReturnCollectionWithTwoUsers() {
        val response: ResponseEntity<CollectionModel<EntityModel<User>>> =
            restTemplate.exchange(
                baseUrl,
                HttpMethod.GET,
```

```
                    null,
                    object : ParameterizedTypeReference<CollectionModel
                    <EntityModel<User>>>() {})
        Assertions.assertThat(response).isNotNull()
        Assertions.assertThat(response.statusCode).isEqualTo(HttpStatus.OK)
        Assertions.assertThat(response.body).isNotNull()
        Assertions.assertThat(response.headers.getContentType()).
            isEqualTo(MediaTypes.HAL_JSON)
        Assertions.assertThat(response.body!!.content.size).isGreaterThanOr
        EqualTo(2)
    }

    @Test
    @Throws(Exception::class)
    fun userEndPointPostNewUserShouldReturnUser() {
        val createHeaders = HttpHeaders()
        createHeaders.contentType = MediaTypes.HAL_JSON
        val user: User = User(
            email="dummy@email.com",
            name="Dummy",
            gravatarUrl="https://www.gravatar.com/avatar/23bb62a7d0ca63c
            9a804908e57bf6bd4?d=wavatar",
            password = "aw2s0meR!",
            userRole = mutableListOf(UserRole.USER),
            active=true)
        val createRequest = HttpEntity(convertToJson(user), createHeaders)
        val response: ResponseEntity<EntityModel<User>> = restTemplate.
        exchange(
            baseUrl,
            HttpMethod.POST,
            createRequest,
            object : ParameterizedTypeReference<EntityModel<User>>() {})
        Assertions.assertThat(response).isNotNull()
        Assertions.assertThat(response.statusCode).isEqualTo(HttpStatus.
        CREATED)
```

```kotlin
        val userResponse = response.body!!
        Assertions.assertThat(userResponse).isNotNull()
        Assertions.assertThat(userResponse.content).isNotNull()
        Assertions.assertThat(userResponse.getLink("self")).isNotNull()
        Assertions.assertThat(userResponse.content!!.email).
        isEqualTo(user.email)
    }

    @Test
    @Throws(Exception::class)
    fun userEndPointDeleteUserShouldReturnVoid() {
        restTemplate.delete("$baseUrl/1")
        val response: ResponseEntity<CollectionModel<EntityModel<User>>> =
            restTemplate.exchange(
                baseUrl,
                HttpMethod.GET,
                null,
                object :
ParameterizedTypeReference<CollectionModel<EntityModel<User>>>() {})
        Assertions.assertThat(response).isNotNull()
        Assertions.assertThat(response.statusCode).isEqualTo(HttpStatus.OK)
        Assertions.assertThat(response.body).isNotNull()
        Assertions.assertThat(response.headers.getContentType()).
            isEqualTo(MediaTypes.HAL_JSON)
        Assertions.assertThat(response.body!!.content.size).isGreaterThanOr
        EqualTo(1)
    }

    @Test
    @Throws(Exception::class)
    fun userEndPointFindUserShouldReturnUser() {
        val email = "ximena@email.com"
        val response: ResponseEntity<EntityModel<User>> = restTemplate.
        exchange(
            "$baseUrl/search/findByEmail?email={email}",
            HttpMethod.GET,
```

```
                null,
                object : ParameterizedTypeReference<EntityModel<User>>() {},
                email
        )
        Assertions.assertThat(response.statusCode).isEqualTo(HttpStatus.OK)
        val users = response.body!!
        Assertions.assertThat(users).isNotNull()
        Assertions.assertThat(users.content!!.email).isEqualTo(email)
    }

    @Throws(JsonProcessingException::class)
    private fun convertToJson(user: User): String {
        val objectMapper = ObjectMapper()
        return objectMapper.writeValueAsString(user)
    }
}
```

The UsersHttpRequestTests test class is now using classes from the org.
springframework.hateoas.* package. The spring-boot-starter-data-rest starter
dependency that we added includes the spring-hateoas library, which contains the
necessary classes to handle the HAL+JSON type: CollectionModel and EntityModel.
Note that you can get the references, the links, and all the declaration that the
response has.

You can run the test using your IDE or using the following command:

```
./gradlew clean test
UsersHttpRequestTests > userEndPointFindUserShouldReturnUser() PASSED
UsersHttpRequestTests > userEndPointDeleteUserShouldReturnVoid() PASSED
UsersHttpRequestTests > userEndPointPostNewUserShouldReturnUser() PASSED
UsersHttpRequestTests >
usersEndPointShouldReturnCollectionWithTwoUsers() PASSED
```

My Retro App Using Spring Boot and Spring Data REST

Now it's My Retro App's turn to benefit from Spring Data REST. Again, you can use the
code or you can start from scratch by going to the Spring Initializr (https://start.
spring.io). You can use an empty project, but again, make sure to set the Group field to

com.apress and the Artifact and Name fields to myretro. For dependencies, add Web, Validation, JPA, Docker Compose, Data REST, and PostgreSQL. Download the project, unzip it, and import it into your favorite IDE. By the end of this section, you should have the structure shown in Figure 5-11.

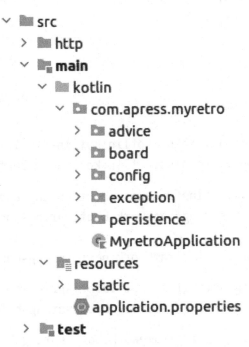

Figure 5-11. *My Retro App with Spring Data JPA and REST*

You already know what's missing, right? Yes, the web and service packages and classes are gone! You don't need them anymore. So, what changed?

Open the build.gradle file and replace its contents with the contents shown in Listing 5-32.

Listing 5-32. build.gradle

```
import org.jetbrains.kotlin.gradle.tasks.KotlinCompile
plugins {
    id 'org.springframework.boot' version '3.2.3'
    id 'io.spring.dependency-management' version '1.1.4'
    id 'org.jetbrains.kotlin.jvm' version '2.0.20-RC'
    id "org.jetbrains.kotlin.plugin.spring" version "2.0.20-RC"
```

```
    // <- simplifies spring proxying
}

group = 'com.apress'
version = '0.0.1-SNAPSHOT'
sourceCompatibility = '17'

repositories {
    mavenCentral()
}

dependencies {
    implementation "org.jetbrains.kotlin:kotlin-stdlib-jdk8"
    implementation "org.jetbrains.kotlin:kotlin-reflect"

    implementation 'org.springframework.boot:spring-boot-starter-web'
    implementation 'org.springframework.boot:spring-boot-starter-
    validation'
    implementation 'org.springframework.boot:spring-boot-starter-aop'

    implementation 'org.springframework.boot:spring-boot-starter-data-jpa'
    implementation 'org.springframework.boot:spring-boot-starter-data-rest'

    developmentOnly 'org.springframework.boot:spring-boot-docker-compose'

    annotationProcessor 'org.springframework.boot:spring-boot-
    configuration-processor'

    runtimeOnly 'org.postgresql:postgresql'

    // Web
    implementation 'org.webjars:bootstrap:5.2.3'

    testImplementation 'org.springframework.boot:spring-boot-starter-test'
}

tasks.named('test') {
    useJUnitPlatform()
}

//    kotlin {
```

```
//          jvmToolchain(17)
//      }
tasks.withType(KotlinCompile).configureEach {
    kotlinOptions {
        freeCompilerArgs = ['-Xjsr305=strict']
        jvmTarget = '17'
    }
}
```

The only addition is the `spring-boot-starter-data-rest` starter dependency. The `advice`, `board`, `config`, `exception`, and `persistence` packages and their classes remain the same. Of course, we removed the `service` and `web` packages and their classes.

Run the My Retro App

To run the My Retro App, use your IDE or the following command:

```
./gradlew clean bootRun
```

What happens if you point your browser to `http://localhost:8080/retros`? You will get a `404 - Not Found` error, but why? We have been using the `/retros` as an endpoint, so what happened? Recall that Spring Data REST reviews your repositories and changes the names of the domain classes to lowercase and plural to create the endpoints, so in this case, you have the `/retroBoards` and `/cards` endpoints.

If you go to `http://localhost:8080/retroBoards`, you will get all the `RetroBoard` records. You can also use the following command:

```
curl -s http://localhost:8080/retroBoards | jq .
{
  "_embedded": {
    "retroBoards": [
      {
        "name": "Spring Boot Conference",
        "_links": {
          "self": {
            "href": "http://localhost:8080/retroBoards/fc873a23-15ee-42f6-
            b9f4-bfbab4537ff4"
          },
```

```json
    "retroBoard": {
        "href": "http://localhost:8080/retroBoards/fc873a23-15ee-42f6-
        b9f4-bfbab4537ff4"
      },
      "cards": {
        "href": "http://localhost:8080/retroBoards/fc873a23-15ee-42f6-
        b9f4-bfbab4537ff4/cards"
      }
     }
    }
   }
  ]
 },
 "_links": {
   "self": {
     "href": "http://localhost:8080/retroBoards?page=0&size=20"
   },
   "profile": {
     "href": "http://localhost:8080/profile/retroBoards"
   }
 },
 "page": {
   "size": 20,
   "totalElements": 1,
   "totalPages": 1,
   "number": 0
 }
}
```

Look at the _embedded and _links data, which refer, respectively, to retroBoards (plural) and retroBoard (singular). However, when using HAL by default, the HAL auto-configuration will pluralize the class and create an endpoint in the form of /retroBoards (camel case), but your clients connect to /retros. How could you switch this back? There is a solution to this. Open the RetroBoardRepository interface and add the code shown in Listing 5-33.

Listing 5-33. src/main/kotlin/apress/com/myretro/persistence/
RetroBoardRepository.kt

```kotlin
package com.apress.myretro.persistence

import com.apress.myretro.board.RetroBoard
import org.springframework.data.jpa.repository.JpaRepository
import org.springframework.data.rest.core.annotation.RepositoryRestResource
import java.util.*

@RepositoryRestResource(path = "retros",
    itemResourceRel = "retros", collectionResourceRel = "retros")
interface RetroBoardRepository : JpaRepository<RetroBoard, UUID>
```

The modified RetroBoardRepository interface now includes the
@RepositoryRestResource annotation. It takes three parameters:

- path: This parameter creates the endpoint you want, called /retros.

- itemResourceRel: This parameter changes the name in the "_links"
  to "retros" (instead of "retroBoard").

- collectionResourceRel: This parameter changes the name in "_
  embedded" from "retroBoards" to "retros".

Rerun the app by going to http://localhost:8080/retros or by using the following
command:

```
curl -s http://localhost:8080/retros | jq .
{
  "_embedded": {
    "retros": [
      {
        "name": "Spring Boot Conference",
        "_links": {
          "self": {
            "href": "http://localhost:8080/retros/e800d409-9295-4565-bf4b-
            f3b95ff32eff"
          },
          "retros": {
```

```
            "href": "http://localhost:8080/retros/e800d409-9295-4565-bf4b-
            f3b95ff32eff"
          },
          "cards": {
            "href": "http://localhost:8080/retros/e800d409-9295-4565-bf4b-
            f3b95ff32eff/cards"
          }
        }
      }
    ]
  },
  "_links": {
    "self": {
      "href": "http://localhost:8080/retros?page=0&size=20"
    },
    "profile": {
      "href": "http://localhost:8080/profile/retros"
    }
  },
  "page": {
    "size": 20,
    "totalElements": 1,
    "totalPages": 1,
    "number": 0
  }
}
```

Before you continue, and if you are in the browser, you can look at the /profile/
retros endpoint in your browser or command line. That will give you the ALPS
(Application-Level Profile Semantics) and JSON Schema:

```
curl -s -H 'Accept:application/schema+json' http://localhost:8080/profile/
retros | jq .
{
  "title": "Retro board",
  "properties": {
```

```
    "cards": {
      "title": "Cards",
      "readOnly": false,
      "type": "string",
      "format": "uri"
    },
    "name": {
      "title": "Name",
      "readOnly": false,
      "type": "string"
    }
  },
  "definitions": {},
  "type": "object",
  "$schema": "http://json-schema.org/draft-04/schema#"
}
```

With these options, you can expose your API to the public.

Summary

This chapter covered Spring Data JDBC, Spring Data JPA, and Spring Data REST and explained how Spring Boot helps you remove all the extra configuration by using the auto-configuration based on the dependencies. You learned the following:

- Spring Data (the core) uses repository interfaces, such as `CrudRepository` and `PagingAndSortingRepository` (others include `ListCrudRepository`, `ListPagingAndSortingRepository`, `Repository`, `NoRepositoryBean`, and `RepositoryDefinition`).

- In Spring Data JDBC, you need to focus on relationships, but in Spring Data JPA, you need to focus on object composition.

- JDBC is limited to many-to-many relationships, but you can still perform the job using SQL statements.

- You learned that JDBC can initialize the database. Spring Boot can look at the classpath and if it finds `schema.sql` or `data.sql`, it can create the table and add data.

- JPA can generate tables based on the `spring.jpa.*` properties, and thanks to the Spring Boot auto-configuration, all the interface repositories are enabled.

- You also learned about a REST implementation based on Spring Data REST, and how Spring Data REST with Spring Boot helps you configure everything so that it works like plug and play.

- With Spring Data REST, you can have out-of-the-box web controllers that expose many endpoints.

Chapter 6 covers the NoSQL databases.

CHAPTER 6

Spring Data NoSQL with Spring Boot

Felipe Gutierrez[a*]

[a] 4109 Rillcrest Grove Way Fuquay Varina, NC 27526-3562, Albuquerque, NM, USA

Spring Data MongoDB

Spring Data MongoDB implements the Spring programming model for the MongoDB document type database. One of the most important features of Spring Data MongoDB is that it offers the POJO (plain old Java object) model for interacting with collections by using well-known repository interfaces.

The following are some of the many features of Spring Data MongoDB:

- Full configuration through JavaConfig classes or XML configuration files

- The well-known data exception management translation from Spring Data Access

- Life-cycle callbacks and events

- Implementation of the `Repository`, `CrudRepository`, and `MongoRepository` interfaces

- Custom query methods and `Querydsl` integration

- MapReduce integration

- Annotation-based mapping metadata (using the `@Document` annotation to specify your domain class and the `@Id` annotation to specify the identifier or key)

© Peter Späth, Felipe Gutierrez 2025

P. Späth and F. Gutierrez, *Pro Spring Boot 3 with Kotlin*, https://doi.org/10.1007/979-8-8688-1131-9_6

- `MongoTemplate` and `MongoOperations` classes to help with all the boilerplate to connect and execute actions on MongoDB

- Low-level mapping using the `MongoReader` and `MongoWriter` abstractions

Spring Data MongoDB with Spring Boot

If you want to use MongoDB with Spring Boot, you need to include the `spring-boot-starter-data-mongodb` starter dependency. The Spring Boot auto-configuration will set up all the necessary defaults to connect to a MongoDB database and will identify all the repositories and domain classes that are required for your application.

This auto-configuration will set up the `MongoDatabaseFactory` with the default URI: `mongodb://localhost/test`. You can use an injected `MongoTemplate` and `MongoOperations` classes, and if you want to change these defaults, you can modify this behavior by using the `spring.data.mongodb.*` properties.

Users App with Spring Data MongoDB and Spring Boot

If you are following along, you can reuse some of the code from the previous versions. Or you can start from scratch by going to the Spring Initializr (`https://start.spring.io`) and generating a base project (no dependencies), but make sure to set the Group field to `com.apress` and the Artifact and Name Fields to `users`. Download the project, unzip it, and import it into your favorite IDE. By the end of this section, you should have the structure shown in Figure 6-1.

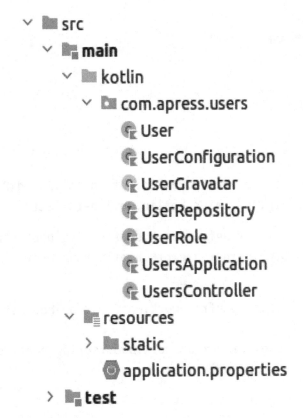

Figure 6-1. *Users App with Spring Data MongoDB with Spring Boot*

Open the build.gradle file and replace its contents with the contents shown in
Listing 6-1.

Listing 6-1. The build.gradle File

```
import org.jetbrains.kotlin.gradle.tasks.KotlinCompile

plugins {
    id 'org.springframework.boot' version '3.2.3'
    id 'io.spring.dependency-management' version '1.1.4'
    id 'org.jetbrains.kotlin.jvm' version '2.0.20-RC'
    id "org.jetbrains.kotlin.plugin.spring" version "2.0.20-RC"
    // <- simplifies spring proxying
}
```

```
group = 'com.apress'
version = '0.0.1-SNAPSHOT'
sourceCompatibility = '17'

repositories {
    mavenCentral()
}

dependencies {
    implementation "org.jetbrains.kotlin:kotlin-stdlib-jdk8"
    implementation "org.jetbrains.kotlin:kotlin-reflect"

    implementation 'org.springframework.boot:spring-boot-starter-web'
    implementation 'org.springframework.boot:spring-boot-starter-
    validation'

    implementation 'org.springframework.boot:spring-boot-starter-
    data-mongodb'
    developmentOnly 'org.springframework.boot:spring-boot-docker-compose'

    // Web
    implementation 'org.webjars:bootstrap:5.2.3'

    testImplementation 'org.springframework.boot:spring-boot-starter-test'
}

tasks.named('test') {
    useJUnitPlatform()
}

test {
    testLogging {
        events "passed", "skipped", "failed"
        showExceptions true
        exceptionFormat "full"
        showCauses true
        showStackTraces true
        showStandardStreams = false
    }
```

```
}
//    kotlin {
//        jvmToolchain(17)
//    }
tasks.withType(KotlinCompile).configureEach {
    kotlinOptions {
        freeCompilerArgs = ['-Xjsr305=strict']
        jvmTarget = '17'
    }
}
```

Note that the spring-boot-starter-data-mongodb and spring-boot-docker-compose starter dependencies are included. The Spring Boot auto-configuration feature will use the defaults to configure everything to connect to the MongoDB engine and perform the necessary operations and interaction.

Next, create/open the User class; it should look like Listing 6-2.

Listing 6-2. src/main/kotlin/apress/com/users/User.kt

```
package com.apress.users

import jakarta.validation.constraints.NotBlank
import jakarta.validation.constraints.Pattern
import org.springframework.data.annotation.Id
import org.springframework.data.mongodb.core.mapping.Document

@Document
data class User(
    @Id
    @get:NotBlank(message = "Email can not be empty")
    var email: String? = null,

    @get:NotBlank(message = "Name can not be empty")
    var name: String? = null,

    var gravatarUrl: String? = null,

    @get:Pattern(
```

```kotlin
    message = "Password must be at least 8 characters long and contain
    at least one number, one uppercase, one lowercase and one special
    character",
    regexp = "^(?=.*[0-9])(?=.*[a-z])(?=.*[A-Z])(?=.*[@#$%^&+=!])(?=\\
    S+$).{8,}$"
)
var password: String? = null,

var userRole: Collection<UserRole>? = null,
var active:Boolean = false
)
)
```

Do you know what changed compared to the previous version of the User class (in JPA, shown in Listing 5-19)? You now use the @Document annotation (instead of @Entity) that belongs to the `org.springframework.data.mongo.*` package. The @Document annotation identifies the class as a domain object so that it can be persisted into the MongoDB database. And practically that's it.

Next, create/open the UserRepository interface. See Listing 6-3.

Listing 6-3. src/main/kotlin/apress/com/users/UserRepository.kt

```kotlin
package com.apress.users

import org.springframework.data.repository.CrudRepository

interface UserRepository : CrudRepository<User, String>
```

As you can see, this class hasn't changed at all, we still extend from the CrudRepository interface. There is the MongoRepository, but we are going to use that in the My Retro App project. The objective here is to show that you can still use your base without too much effort when migrating from one technology to another.

Next, create/open the UsersController class. See Listing 6-4.

Listing 6-4. src/main/kotlin/apress/com/users/UsersController.kt

```kotlin
package com.apress.users

import org.springframework.beans.factory.annotation.Autowired
import org.springframework.http.HttpStatus
import org.springframework.http.ResponseEntity
```

```kotlin
import org.springframework.validation.FieldError
import org.springframework.validation.ObjectError
import org.springframework.web.bind.MethodArgumentNotValidException
import org.springframework.web.bind.annotation.*
import org.springframework.web.servlet.support.ServletUriComponentsBuilder
import java.net.URI
import java.time.LocalDateTime
import java.time.format.DateTimeFormatter
import java.util.function.Consumer

@RestController
@RequestMapping("/users")
class UsersController {
    @Autowired
    private lateinit var userRepository: UserRepository

    @get:GetMapping
    val all: ResponseEntity<Iterable<User>>
        get() = ResponseEntity.ok(userRepository.findAll())

    @GetMapping("/{email}")
    @Throws(Throwable::class)
    fun findUserById(@PathVariable email: String): ResponseEntity<User> =
        ResponseEntity.of<User>(userRepository.findById(email))

    @RequestMapping(method = [RequestMethod.POST, RequestMethod.PUT])
    fun save(@RequestBody user: User): ResponseEntity<User> {
        userRepository!!.save(user)
        val location: URI = ServletUriComponentsBuilder
            .fromCurrentRequest()
            .path("/{email}")
            .buildAndExpand(user.email)
            .toUri()
        return ResponseEntity.created(location).body<User>(user)
    }

    @DeleteMapping("/{email}")
    @ResponseStatus(HttpStatus.NO_CONTENT)
```

```
    fun save(@PathVariable email: String) =
        userRepository.deleteById(email)

    @ExceptionHandler(MethodArgumentNotValidException::class)
    @ResponseStatus(HttpStatus.BAD_REQUEST)
    fun handleValidationExceptions(ex: MethodArgumentNotValidException):
            Map<String, String> =
        ex.bindingResult.allErrors.associate { error: ObjectError ->
            (error as FieldError).field to (error.getDefaultMessage() ?:
            "undef")
        }.toMutableMap()
}
```

The UsersController class hasn't changed either. It's the same as the previous versions. But, note that you can directly use the UserRepository that will be injected by Spring.

Next, create/open the UserConfiguration class. See Listing 6-5.

Listing 6-5. src/main/kotlin/apress/com/users/UserConfiguration.kt

```
package com.apress.users

import org.springframework.boot.context.event.ApplicationReadyEvent
import org.springframework.context.ApplicationListener
import org.springframework.context.annotation.Bean
import org.springframework.context.annotation.Configuration
import org.springframework.data.mongodb.core.mapping.event.
BeforeConvertCallback
import java.util.*

@Configuration
class UserConfiguration : BeforeConvertCallback<User> {
    @Bean
    fun init(userRepository: UserRepository):
            ApplicationListener<ApplicationReadyEvent> {
        return ApplicationListener<ApplicationReadyEvent> { _:
        ApplicationReadyEvent ->
            userRepository.save(
```

```kotlin
            User(
                email="ximena@email.com",
                name="Ximena",
                password="aw2sOmeR!",
                userRole = mutableListOf(UserRole.USER),
                active = true)
        )
        userRepository.save(
            User(
                email="norma@email.com",
                name="Norma",
                password="aw2sOmeR!",
                userRole = mutableListOf(UserRole.USER,UserRole.ADMIN),
                active=true)
        )
    }
}

override fun onBeforeConvert(entity: User, collection: String): User {
    entity.gravatarUrl = entity.gravatarUrl ?:
        UserGravatar.getGravatarUrlFromEmail(entity.email!!)
    entity.userRole = entity.userRole ?: listOf(UserRole.INFO)
    return entity
}
}
```

The UserConfiguration class is implementing the BeforeConvertCallback interface, where you can add your logic before the entity is saved into the MongoDB database. You need to implement the onBeforeConvert method. Note that instead of creating another class for the callback event, you can use your configuration class to add the necessary implementation. Also note that this class is initializing some documents (as in previous versions) using ApplicationReadyEvent and using the UserRepository interface.

Next, create/open the docker-compose.yaml file. See Listing 6-6.

Listing 6-6. The docker-compose.yaml File

```
version: "3.1"
services:
  mongo:
    image: mongo
    restart: always
    environment:
      MONGO_INITDB_DATABASE: retrodb
    ports:
      - "27017:27017"
```

The docker-compose.yaml file ensures that your MongoDB database is up and running when executing the application. Remember that this file is used only in development (not testing).

We are finished here. The UserGravatar and UserRole classes have no changes. The application.properties file must be empty; you don't need to specify anything there.

Testing the Users App

To test the Users App, create/open the UsersHttpRequestTests class. See Listing 6-7.

Listing 6-7. src/test/kotlin/apress/com/users/UsersHttpRequestTests.kt

```
package com.apress.users

import org.assertj.core.api.Assertions
import org.junit.jupiter.api.Test
import org.springframework.beans.factory.annotation.Autowired
import org.springframework.beans.factory.annotation.Value
import org.springframework.boot.test.context.SpringBootTest
import org.springframework.boot.test.web.client.TestRestTemplate

@SpringBootTest(
    webEnvironment = SpringBootTest.WebEnvironment.RANDOM_PORT,
    properties = ["spring.data.mongodb.database=retrodb"]
)
class UsersHttpRequestTests {
```

```kotlin
@Value("\${local.server.port}")
private var port = 0

private val BASE_URL = "http://localhost:"
private val USERS_PATH = "/users"

@Autowired
private lateinit var restTemplate: TestRestTemplate

@Test
fun indexPageShouldReturnHeaderOneContent() {
    Assertions.assertThat(
        restTemplate.getForObject(
            BASE_URL + port,
            String::class.java
        )
    ).contains("Simple Users Rest Application")
}

@Test
fun usersEndPointShouldReturnCollectionWithTwoUsers() {
    val response: Collection<*> =
        restTemplate.getForObject(BASE_URL + port + USERS_PATH,
                Collection::class.java)
    Assertions.assertThat(response.size).isEqualTo(2)
}

@Test
fun userEndPointPostNewUserShouldReturnUser() {
    val user: User = User(
        email="dummy@email.com",
        name="Dummy",
        gravatarUrl="https://www.gravatar.com/avatar/23bb62a7d0ca63
        c9a804908e57bf6bd4?d=wavatar",
        password="aw2sOmeR!",
        userRole = mutableListOf(UserRole.USER),
        active=true)
```

```
        val response = restTemplate.postForObject(BASE_URL + port +
        USERS_PATH,
                user, User::class.java)
        Assertions.assertThat(response).isNotNull()
        Assertions.assertThat(response.email).isEqualTo(user.email)
        val users: Collection<*> =
            restTemplate.getForObject(BASE_URL + port + USERS_PATH,
                    Collection::class.java)
        Assertions.assertThat(users.size).isGreaterThanOrEqualTo(2)
    }

    @Test
    fun userEndPointDeleteUserShouldReturnVoid() {
        restTemplate.delete("$BASE_URL$port$USERS_PATH/norma@email.com")
        val users: Collection<*> =
            restTemplate.getForObject<Collection<*>>(BASE_URL + port +
            USERS_PATH,
                Collection::class.java)
        Assertions.assertThat(users.size).isLessThanOrEqualTo(2)
    }

    @Test
    fun userEndPointFindUserShouldReturnUser() {
        val user = restTemplate.getForObject(
                "$BASE_URL$port$USERS_PATH/ximena@email.com",
                User::class.java)
        Assertions.assertThat(user).isNotNull()
        Assertions.assertThat(user.email).isEqualTo("ximena@email.com")
    }
}
```

The UsersHttpRequestTests class is the same as in the previous versions, but there is an interesting point to note here. The previous section left the application. properties file empty. The spring-boot-docker-compose dependency we added works for development only, so to use most of these defaults from Spring Boot, you have to add the name of the database (retrodb) you are going to use; otherwise, the name will be test.

To run the tests, you first need to start MongoDB. You can do so using your IDE (VS Code and IntelliJ both have plugins for running `docker-compose` files) or through the command line:

```
docker compose up -d
```

This command will use the `docker-compose` dependency and start the `mongodb` service in the background. Next, you can run the test with the following:

```
./gradlew clean test
```

You should get the following output:

```
UsersHttpRequestTests > userEndPointFindUserShouldReturnUser() PASSED
UsersHttpRequestTests > userEndPointDeleteUserShouldReturnVoid() PASSED
UsersHttpRequestTests > indexPageShouldReturnHeaderOneContent() PASSED
UsersHttpRequestTests > userEndPointPostNewUserShouldReturnUser() PASSED
UsersHttpRequestTests >
usersEndPointShouldReturnCollectionWithTwoUsers() PASSED
```

You can now stop `docker compose` with this command:

```
docker compose down
```

It would be nice to have this `docker compose` feature working as test support, right? You'll see how to do that in the testing chapter (Chapter 8) with *Test Containers.*

Running the Users App

To run the Users App, first make sure you don't have `docker compose` running—the Users App will run this for you. Then run the following command:

```
./gradlew clean bootRun
...
INFO -[              main] ..eLifecycleManager : Using Docker Compose file ..
INFO -[utReader-stderr] ...core.DockerCli   : Container users-
mongo-1  Created
INFO -[utReader-stderr] ...core.DockerCli   : Container users-
mongo-1  Starting
```

```
INFO -[utReader-stderr] ...core.DockerCli   : Container users-
mongo-1  Started
...
```

The output shows that the container just started up. Now open another terminal and use the following command:

```
curl -s http://localhost:8080/users | jq .
  {
    "email": "ximena@email.com",
    "name": "Ximena",
    "gravatarUrl": "https://www.gravatar.com/avatar/f07f7e553264c9710105ede
    be6c465e7?d=wavatar",
    "password": "aw2sOmeR!",
    "userRole": [
      "USER"
    ],
    "active": true
  },
  {
    "email": "dummy@email.com",
    "name": "Dummy",
    "gravatarUrl": "https://www.gravatar.com/avatar/23bb62a7d0ca63c9a80490
    8e57bf6bd4?d=wavatar",
    "password": "aw2sOmeR!",
    "userRole": [
      "USER"
    ],
    "active": true
  },
  {
    "email": "norma@email.com",
    "name": "Norma",
    "gravatarUrl": "https://www.gravatar.com/avatar/23bb62a7d0ca63c9a80490
    8e57bf6bd4?d=wavatar",
    "password": "aw2sOmeR!",
```

```
    "userRole": [
      "USER",
      "ADMIN"
    ],
    "active": true
  }
]
```

Based on the previous versions and how the Users App works, switching from JPA to MongoDB was very straightforward, with minimal changes necessary. And in this version, you used the docker-compose dependency to use MongoDB.

If you want to run this app using a remote MongoDB database, you need to add the spring.data.mongo.* properties to the application.properties file, similar to the following:

```
# MongoDB
spring.data.mongodb.uri=mongodb://retroadmin:aw2s0me@other-server:27017/ret
rodb?directConnection=true&serverSelectionTimeoutMS=2000&authSource=admin&a
ppName=mongosh+1.7.1
spring.data.mongodb.database=retrodb
```

where the mongodb URI looks like this:

```
mongodb://<username>:<password>@<remote-server>:<port>/<database>[?...]
```

In the connection URL, you must specify the username and the password as one of the parameters in the authorization source, that is admin as default value. Just check your URI details with your administrator.

My Retro App with Spring Data MongoDB Using Spring Boot

Let's switch to the My Retro App project and see what you need to do to use the MongoDB persistence. If you are following along, you can reuse some of the code from the previous versions. Or you can start from scratch by going to the Spring Initializr (https://start.spring.io), generating a base project (no dependencies), and setting

the Group field to com.apress and the Artifact and Name fields to myretro. Download
the project, unzip it, and import it into your favorite IDE. By the end of this section, you
should have the structure shown in Figure 6-2.

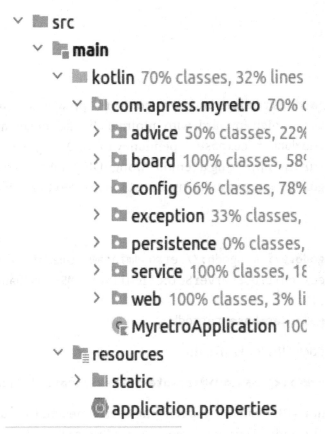

Figure 6-2. *My Retro App with Spring Data MongoDB with Spring Boot*

As you can see, some of the packages and their classes remain the same as the
previous versions. We want to show you the persistence package, which contains
the RetroBoardPersistenceCallback (as a separate) class and implements
BeforeConvertCallback to perform an operation before the document is persisted in
MongoDB.

Open the build.gradle file and replace the contents with the contents shown in
Listing 6-8.

Listing 6-8. The build.gradle File

```
import org.jetbrains.kotlin.gradle.tasks.KotlinCompile
plugins {
    id 'org.springframework.boot' version '3.2.3'
    id 'io.spring.dependency-management' version '1.1.4'
    id 'org.jetbrains.kotlin.jvm' version '2.0.20-RC'
    id "org.jetbrains.kotlin.plugin.spring" version "2.0.20-RC"
    // <- simplifies spring proxying
}

group = 'com.apress'
version = '0.0.1-SNAPSHOT'
sourceCompatibility = '17'

repositories {
    mavenCentral()
}

dependencies {
    implementation "org.jetbrains.kotlin:kotlin-stdlib-jdk8"
    implementation "org.jetbrains.kotlin:kotlin-reflect"

    implementation 'org.springframework.boot:spring-boot-starter-web'
    implementation 'org.springframework.boot:spring-boot-starter-
    validation'
    implementation 'org.springframework.boot:spring-boot-starter-aop'
    implementation 'com.fasterxml.uuid:java-uuid-generator:4.0.1'

    implementation 'org.springframework.boot:spring-boot-starter-
    data-mongodb'
    developmentOnly 'org.springframework.boot:spring-boot-docker-compose'

    annotationProcessor 'org.springframework.boot:spring-boot-
    configuration-processor'

    // Web
    implementation 'org.webjars:bootstrap:5.2.3'
```

```
    testImplementation 'org.springframework.boot:spring-boot-starter-test'
}

tasks.named('test') {
    useJUnitPlatform()
}

//    kotlin {
//        jvmToolchain(17)
//    }
tasks.withType(KotlinCompile).configureEach {
    kotlinOptions {
        freeCompilerArgs = ['-Xjsr305=strict']
        jvmTarget = '17'
    }
}
```

As you can see, the `build.gradle` file uses the `spring-boot-starter-data-mongodb` starter dependency.

Next, create/open the `board` package and the `Card` class and `CardType` enum, as shown in Listings 6-9 and 6-10, respectively.

Listing 6-9. src/main/kotlin/apress/com/myretro/board/Card.kt

```kotlin
package com.apress.myretro.board

import jakarta.validation.constraints.NotBlank
import jakarta.validation.constraints.NotNull

data class Card(
    @get:NotNull
    var id: java.util.UUID? = null,

    @get:NotBlank
    var comment: String? = null,

    @get:NotNull
    var cardType: CardType? = null
)
```

Listing 6-10. src/main/kotlin/apress/com/myretro/board/CardType.kt

```
package com.apress.myretro.board
enum class CardType {
    HAPPY,MEH,SAD
}
```

As you can see, the Card and CardType classes haven't changed from the base version. This does not use any persistence mechanism or annotation.

Next, create/open the RetroBoard class. See Listing 6-11.

Listing 6-11. src/main/kotlin/apress/com/myretro/board/RetroBoard.kt

```
package com.apress.myretro.board

import jakarta.validation.constraints.NotBlank
import jakarta.validation.constraints.NotNull
import org.springframework.data.annotation.Id
import org.springframework.data.mongodb.core.mapping.Document
import java.util.*

@Document
data class RetroBoard(
    @Id
    @get:NotNull
    var id:  UUID? = null,

    @get:NotBlank(message = "A name must be provided")
    var name: String? = null,

    var cards: MutableList<Card>? = null
){
    fun addCard(card: Card) {
        cards = cards ?: mutableListOf()
        cards!!.add(card)
    }

    fun addCards(cards: List<Card>) {
        this.cards = this.cards ?: mutableListOf()
        this.cards!!.addAll(cards)
```

```
    }

    fun removeCard(cardId: UUID) {
        if (cards == null) return
        cards!!.removeIf { card: Card -> card.id == cardId }
    }
}
```

The `@Document` annotation makes the `RetroBoard` class ready for MongoDB, and the `@Id` annotation creates an identifier, which in this case is the UUID type. Listing 6-11 also adds some helper methods for adding cards—the `addCard` and `addCards` methods.

Next, create/open the `persistence` package, the `RetroBoardPersistenceCallback` class, and the `RetroBoardRepository` interface. Listing 6-12 shows the `RetroBoardPersistenceCallback` class.

Listing 6-12. src/main/kotlin/apress/com/myretro/persistence/
RetroBoardPersistenceCallback.kt

```
package com.apress.myretro.persistence

import com.apress.myretro.board.RetroBoard
import org.springframework.data.mongodb.core.mapping.event.
BeforeConvertCallback
import org.springframework.stereotype.Component
import java.util.*

@Component
class RetroBoardPersistenceCallback : BeforeConvertCallback<RetroBoard> {
    override fun onBeforeConvert(retroBoard: RetroBoard, s: String):
    RetroBoard =
        retroBoard.also { it.id = it.id ?: UUID.randomUUID() }
}
```

Listing 6-12 shows the `RetroBoardPersistenceCallback` class. Note that this implements the `BeforeConvertCallback` interface. Did you remember this in the Users App? We declared in the same Java config (`UserConfiguration` class; see Listing 6-5). The difference is that here, we are creating a separate class. Which is better? Whichever makes sense for your application, really. And, of course, for this class to work, you need to mark it as a Spring Bean by using the `@Component` annotation.

Listing 6-13 shows the RetroBoardRepository interface.

Listing 6-13. src/main/kotlin/apress/com/myretro/persistence/
RetroBoardRepository.kt

```
package com.apress.myretro.persistence

import com.apress.myretro.board.RetroBoard
import org.springframework.data.mongodb.repository.MongoRepository
import org.springframework.data.mongodb.repository.Query
import java.util.*

interface RetroBoardRepository : MongoRepository<RetroBoard, UUID> {
    @Query("{'id': ?0}")
    abstract override fun findById(id: UUID): Optional<RetroBoard>

    @Query("{}, { cards: { \$elemMatch: { _id: ?0 } } }")
    abstract fun findRetroBoardByCardId(cardId: UUID): Optional<RetroBoard>
}
```

Listing 6-13 follows the *Spring Data application model*, the use of repositories, so that you don't need to worry about the implementation. In this case, we are using a specific repository, MongoRepository, which changed the signatures from the traditional Repository or CrudRepository. It's defined like this:

```
public interface MongoRepository<T, ID>
        extends ListCrudRepository<T, ID>, ListPagingAndSortingRepository
        <T, ID>, QueryByExampleExecutor<T> {
    <S extends T> S insert(S entity);
    <S extends T> List<S> insert(Iterable<S> entities);
    <S extends T> List<S> findAll(Example<S> example);
    <S extends T> List<S> findAll(Example<S> example, Sort sort);
}
```

And guess what? Because the RetroBoardRepository interface extends the ListCrudRepository interface, which in turn extends from CrudRepository, you have access to the methods that you are accustomed to using. The RetroBoardRepository interface is defining the findById method but is using the @Query annotation that accepts a String value in which you can add the JavaScript code to query MongoDB. The

RetroBoardRepository interface is also declaring the findRetroBoardByCardId method with its @Query annotation and the query to be executed. As you can see, you need this type of method because you use the Card as an aggregate to the RetroBoard. Again, this is just an example of what you can do to get the relationship from the RetroBoard and Card classes applying the MongoDB context.

Next, create/open the service package and the RetroBoardService class, as shown in Listing 6-14.

Listing 6-14. src/main/kotlin/apress/com/myretro/service/ RetroBoardService.kt

```kotlin
package com.apress.myretro.service

import com.apress.myretro.board.Card
import com.apress.myretro.board.RetroBoard
import com.apress.myretro.exception.CardNotFoundException
import com.apress.myretro.persistence.RetroBoardRepository
import org.springframework.beans.factory.annotation.Autowired
import org.springframework.stereotype.Service
import java.util.*
import kotlin.jvm.optionals.getOrNull

@Service
class RetroBoardService {
    @Autowired
    lateinit var retroBoardRepository: RetroBoardRepository

    fun save(domain: RetroBoard): RetroBoard =
        domain.also { it.cards = it.cards ?: mutableListOf() }.run {
            retroBoardRepository.save<RetroBoard>(this)
        }

    fun findById(uuid: UUID): RetroBoard =
        retroBoardRepository.findById(uuid).get()

    fun findAll(): Iterable<RetroBoard> =
        retroBoardRepository.findAll()

    fun delete(uuid: UUID) =
        retroBoardRepository.deleteById(uuid)
```

```kotlin
fun findAllCardsFromRetroBoard(uuid: UUID): Iterable<Card> =
    findById(uuid).cards!!

fun addCardToRetroBoard(uuid: UUID, card: Card): Card {
    if (card.id == null) card.id = UUID.randomUUID()
    val retroBoard: RetroBoard = findById(uuid)
    retroBoard.addCard(card)
    retroBoardRepository.save<RetroBoard>(retroBoard)
    return card
}

fun addMultipleCardsToRetroBoard(uuid: UUID, cards: List<Card>) {
    val retroBoard: RetroBoard = findById(uuid)
    retroBoard.addCards(cards)
    retroBoardRepository.save<RetroBoard>(retroBoard)
}

fun findCardByUUID(uuidCard: UUID): Card {
        val result: Optional<RetroBoard> =
         retroBoardRepository.findRetroBoardByCardId(uuidCard)
    return result.getOrNull()?.cards?.firstOrNull{ it.id ==
    uuidCard } ?:
        throw CardNotFoundException()
}

fun removeCardByUUID(uuid: UUID, cardUUID: UUID) {
    val retroBoard: RetroBoard = findById(uuid)
    retroBoard.removeCard(cardUUID)
    retroBoardRepository.save<RetroBoard>(retroBoard)
}
}
```

As you can see, the RetroBoardService class uses RetroBoardRepository and the declared methods in the interface. Also note that this time we are taking care of the UUID in the save and addCardToRetroBoard methods. Again, this is another example demonstrating that the UUID can be managed in the callbacks or events, and it's up to you to decide where it makes the most sense.

Next, create/open the config package and the MyRetroConfiguration class. See Listing 6-15.

Listing 6-15. src/main/kotlin/apress/com/myretro/config/
MyRetroConfiguration.kt

```kotlin
package com.apress.myretro.config

import com.apress.myretro.board.Card
import com.apress.myretro.board.CardType
import com.apress.myretro.board.RetroBoard
import com.apress.myretro.service.RetroBoardService
import org.springframework.boot.context.event.ApplicationReadyEvent
import org.springframework.boot.context.properties.
EnableConfigurationProperties
import org.springframework.context.ApplicationListener
import org.springframework.context.annotation.Bean
import org.springframework.context.annotation.Configuration
import java.util.*

@EnableConfigurationProperties(MyRetroProperties::class)
@Configuration
class MyRetroConfiguration {
    @Bean
    fun ready(retroBoardService: RetroBoardService):
            ApplicationListener<ApplicationReadyEvent> {
        return ApplicationListener<ApplicationReadyEvent> { _:
        ApplicationReadyEvent ->
            val retroBoardId = UUID.fromString("9dc9b71b-a07e-418b-
            b972-40225449aff2")
            retroBoardService.save(
                RetroBoard(
                    id=retroBoardId,
                    name="Spring Boot Conference",
                    cards = mutableListOf(
                        Card(id=UUID.fromString(
                            "bb2a80a5-a0f5-4180-a6dc-80c84bc014c9"),
                            comment="Spring Boot Rocks!",
                            cardType=CardType.HAPPY),
                        Card(id=UUID.randomUUID(),
```

```
                        comment="Meet everyone in person",
                        cardType=CardType.HAPPY),
                    Card(id=UUID.randomUUID(),
                        comment="When is the next one?",
                        cardType=CardType.MEH),
                    Card(id=UUID.randomUUID(),
                        comment="Not enough time to talk to everyone",
                        cardType=CardType.SAD)
                )
            )
        )
    }
  }
}
```

Note in Listing 6-15 that we are using the ready event and adding some data using the RetroBoardService.

The advice, exception, and web packages and classes remain the same as in previous versions. The rest of the config package classes also remain the same (MyRetroProperties and UsersConfiguration classes).

Next, create/open the docker-compose.yaml file that uses the mongo service, as shown in Listing 6-16.

Listing 6-16. The docker-compose.yaml File

```
version: "3.1"
services:
  mongo:
    image: mongo
    restart: always
    environment:
      MONGO_INITDB_DATABASE: retrodb
    ports:
      - "27017:27017"
```

As you can see, this file is the same as in the Users App project.

At this point, the `application.properties` file just contains a single entry—`spring.docker.compose.file = ./myretro/docker-compose.yaml`—which points to the Docker file. Other than that, it remains empty, but you need to add properties after you run the app, as described in the following section.

Running My Retro App

To run the application, use your IDE or run it from the terminal with the following command:

```
./gradlew clean bootRun
```

If you direct your browser to `http://localhost:8080/retros` or execute the following `curl` command line, you'll get an error:

```
curl -s http://localhost:8080/retros | jq .
{
  "timestamp": "2023-06-06T21:10:08.737+00:00",
  "status": 500,
  "error": "Internal Server Error",
  "path": "/retros"
}
```

If you look at the console (where the My Retro App project is running), you'll see this error:

```
org.springframework.core.convert.ConverterNotFoundException: No converter found capable of converting from type [org.bson.types.Binary] to type [java.util.UUID]
```

Before we solve this issue, let's connect to the running container with another Mongo container and use the Mongo client (`mongosh`). You can execute the following command:

```
docker run -it --rm --network myretro_default mongo mongosh --host mongo retrodb
```

First, you need to identify the network where the MongoDB container is running. If you are using docker compose, you can get the network information with the following command:

```
docker network ls
NETWORK ID      NAME                DRIVER    SCOPE
cee592df7cc9    bridge              bridge    local
2ac86d937732    educates            bridge    local
087927a8ef8c    host                host      local
83b09c37d02e    kind                bridge    local
3e5ded7b4095    minikube            bridge    local
757602f101d2    myretro_default     bridge    local
38898bbc5491    none                null      local
3c0967bf62b8    test-scdf_default   bridge    local
71d99f2d6934    users_default       bridge    local
```

You can see that the name of the network is myretro_default. Then, we are using the command mongosh pointing to the mongo host (this comes from the docker-compose.yaml) and the name of the database, retrodb. Within the mongosh client, if you run this:

```
retrodb> db.retroBoard.find({});
[{
    _id: Binary(Buffer.from("8b417ea01bb7c99df2af4954224072b9", "hex"), 3),
    name: 'Spring Boot Conference',
    cards: [
      {
        _id: Binary(Buffer.from("8041f5a0a5802abbc914c04bc880dca6",
        "hex"), 3),
        comment: 'Spring Boot Rocks!',
        cardType: 'HAPPY'
      },
      {
        _id: Binary(Buffer.from("dd448b729c5fa1a0c6ab3919ffc48b84",
        "hex"), 3),
        comment: 'Meet everyone in person',
        cardType: 'HAPPY'
      },
```

```
    {
      _id: Binary(Buffer.from("094924fee8d3ef9d60bef876439eeeb4",
      "hex"), 3),
      comment: 'When is the next one?',
      cardType: 'MEH'
    },
    {
      _id: Binary(Buffer.from("a6401bca1b9f6cda0a1ff95bd2dc61b9",
      "hex"), 3),
      comment: 'Not enough time to talk to everyone',
      cardType: 'SAD'
    }
  ],
  _class: 'com.apress.myretro.board.RetroBoard'
  }
]
```

The output indicates that the MongoDB representation of the UUID is the
Binary(Buffer.from) object and that Spring doesn't know about it or know how to
handle it. But there is an easy fix. You can add the property shown in Listing 6-17 to the
application.properties file.

Listing 6-17. src/main/resource/application.properties

```
# MongoDB
spring.data.mongodb.uuid-representation=standard
```

One of the main formats that MongoDB uses is Binary JSON (BSON), which extends
the capabilities of JSON with additional data types and binary encodings. And in
this case, it tries to use its own "hex" binary representation for the UUID, but with this
property, you can use the standard UUID format.

Before you rerun My Retro App, you need to drop the values from the collection
with this:

```
retrofb> db.retroBoard.drop({});
true
```

This is necessary because you are using docker compose and it creates a volume that is reused every time you run the app and the container is started up. If you rerun to the My Retro App project after adding this property to the application.properties file, you can execute the curl command:

```
curl -s http://localhost:8080/retros | jq .
[
  {
    "id": "9dc9b71b-a07e-418b-b972-40225449aff2",
    "name": "Spring Boot Conference",
    "cards": [
      {
        "id": "bb2a80a5-a0f5-4180-a6dc-80c84bc014c9",
        "comment": "Spring Boot Rocks!",
        "cardType": "HAPPY"
      },
      {
        "id": "bf2e263e-b698-43a9-adc7-bec07e94c8fd",
        "comment": "Meet everyone in person",
        "cardType": "HAPPY"
      },
      {
        "id": "130441b7-6b77-465e-b879-006163de5279",
        "comment": "When is the next one?",
        "cardType": "MEH"
      },
      {
        "id": "92c7d841-9e2a-40b1-847c-362fb5fe53cc",
        "comment": "Not enough time to talk to everyone",
        "cardType": "SAD"
      }
    ]
  }
]
```

If you are curious about how it looks in Mongo, execute the following command (in the Mongo client, it is connected to the Mongo database):

```
retrodb> db.retroBoard.find({});
[
  {
    _id: new UUID("9dc9b71b-a07e-418b-b972-40225449aff2"),
    name: 'Spring Boot Conference',
    cards: [
      {
        _id: new UUID("bb2a80a5-a0f5-4180-a6dc-80c84bc014c9"),
        comment: 'Spring Boot Rocks!',
        cardType: 'HAPPY'
      },
      {
        _id: new UUID("bf2e263e-b698-43a9-adc7-bec07e94c8fd"),
        comment: 'Meet everyone in person',
        cardType: 'HAPPY'
      },
      {
        _id: new UUID("130441b7-6b77-465e-b879-006163de5279"),
        comment: 'When is the next one?',
        cardType: 'MEH'
      },
      {
        _id: new UUID("92c7d841-9e2a-40b1-847c-362fb5fe53cc"),
        comment: 'Not enough time to talk to everyone',
        cardType: 'SAD'
      }
    ],
    _class: 'com.apress.myretro.board.RetroBoard'
  }
]
```

Now you can see the data using the UUID. Did you notice the _class element? This is provided by Spring as metadata, so mapping between Mongo documents and classes is easy.

Note   You can find the complete source code for this book at the Apress website: `https://www.apress.com/gp/services/source-code`.

Spring Data Redis

Spring Data Redis is another NoSQL in-memory data structure data store, with support for key/value maps, lists, sets, sorted sets, bitmaps, hyperloglogs, and much more. Redis can also be used for pub/sub messaging, because it is fast. It has various additional features, such as scalability and high availability. Some of its uses include session management, real-time analytics, task queues, caching, chat applications, leaderboard, and more.

Spring Data Redis provides a lot of low-level and high-level abstractions to interact with Redis from Spring applications. These are some of its many features:

- Spring programming model.

- RedisTemplate, a class based on template implementation that provides high-level abstraction for performing various Redis operations, exception translation, and serialization. It also provides the StringRedisTemplate, which allows string-focused operations.

- Easy connection across multiple Redis drivers (Lettuce and Jedis).

- Exception translation to Spring's portable Data Access exception hierarchy.

- Pub/sub support (such as a MessageListenerContainer for message-driven POJOs).

- Support for Redis Cluster and Redis Sentinel.

- Reactive API support for the Lettuce driver.

- JDK, String, JSON, and Spring Object/XML mapping serializers.

- JDK Collection implementations on top of Redis.

- Redis implementation for Spring 3.1 cache abstraction.

- Repository interfaces including support for custom query methods using @EnableRedisRepositories.

- Stream support.

Spring Data Redis with Spring Boot

By using Spring Data Redis with Spring Boot, you get the auto-configuration for Lettuce and Jedis clients and all the abstraction provided by Spring Data Redis. If you want to use Spring Data Redis in your Spring Boot app, you need to add the `spring-boot-starter-data-redis` starter dependency. If you intend to use Spring Data Redis only, without Spring Boot, and you are using the repository programming model, you need to use the `@EnableRedisRepositories` annotation in your `JavaConfig` class. Of course, if you are using Spring Boot, there's no need for this annotation because Spring Boot takes care of the configuration.

The next sections explain what you need to do in your projects to use Redis as data persistence, starting with the Users App.

Users App with Spring Data Redis Using Spring Boot

Again, you can reuse some of the code from previous versions or you can start from scratch by going to the Spring Initializr (`https://start.spring.io`) and generating a base project (no dependencies); as always, make sure to set the Group field to `com.apress` and the Artifact and Name fields to `users`. Download the project, unzip it, and import it into your favorite IDE. By the end of this section, you should have the structure shown in Figure 6-3.

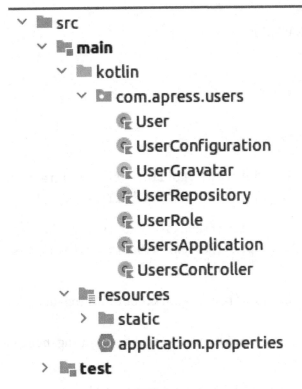

Figure 6-3. *Users App with Spring Data Redis with Spring Boot*

As you can see, we are going to use docker compose with Redis so that it's easy to test and run the application.

Start by opening the build.gradle file and replacing the contents with the contents shown in Listing 6-18.

Listing 6-18. The build.gradle File

```
import org.jetbrains.kotlin.gradle.tasks.KotlinCompile
plugins {
    id 'org.springframework.boot' version '3.2.3'
    id 'io.spring.dependency-management' version '1.1.4'
    id 'org.jetbrains.kotlin.jvm' version '2.0.20-RC'
    id "org.jetbrains.kotlin.plugin.spring" version "2.0.20-RC"
    // <- simplifies spring proxying
}
```

```
group = 'com.apress'
version = '0.0.1-SNAPSHOT'
sourceCompatibility = '17'

repositories {
    mavenCentral()
}

dependencies {
    implementation "org.jetbrains.kotlin:kotlin-stdlib-jdk8"
    implementation "org.jetbrains.kotlin:kotlin-reflect"

    implementation 'org.springframework.boot:spring-boot-starter-web'
    implementation 'org.springframework.boot:spring-boot-starter-
    validation'

    implementation 'org.springframework.boot:spring-boot-starter-
    data-redis'
    developmentOnly 'org.springframework.boot:spring-boot-docker-compose'

    // Web
    implementation 'org.webjars:bootstrap:5.2.3'

    testImplementation 'org.springframework.boot:spring-boot-starter-test'
}

tasks.named('test') {
    useJUnitPlatform()
}

test {
    testLogging {
        events "passed", "skipped", "failed"
        showExceptions true
        exceptionFormat "full"
        showCauses true
        showStackTraces true
        showStandardStreams = false
    }
}
```

```
//    kotlin {
//        jvmToolchain(17)
//    }
tasks.withType(KotlinCompile).configureEach {
    kotlinOptions {
        freeCompilerArgs = ['-Xjsr305=strict']
        jvmTarget = '17'
    }
}
```

We are adding the `spring-boot-starter-data-redis` and `spring-boot-docker-compose` starter dependencies, which will allow Spring Boot to use the auto-configuration feature to set up everything about Redis—from connections to all the necessary classes to do any interaction.

Next, create/open the User class. See Listing 6-19.

Listing 6-19. src/main/kotlin/apress/com/users/User.kt

```
package com.apress.users

import jakarta.validation.constraints.NotBlank
import org.springframework.data.annotation.Id
import org.springframework.data.redis.core.RedisHash

@RedisHash("USERS")
data class User(
    @Id
    @get:NotBlank(message = "Email can not be empty")
    var email:  String? = null,

    @get:NotBlank(message = "Name can not be empty")
    var name:  String? = null,

    var gravatarUrl: String? = null,

    @get:NotBlank(message = "Password can not be empty")
    var password:  String? = null,

    var userRole: Collection<UserRole>? = null,
    var active:Boolean = false
)
```

The User class is now marked with the @RedisHashMark annotation, which accepts a String value that will be the prefix that distinguishes it from other domain classes. This annotation marks objects as aggregate roots to be stored in the Redis hash.

Next, create/open the UserRepository interface, as shown in Listing 6-20.

Listing 6-20. src/main/kotlin/apress/com/users/UserRepository.kt

```
package com.apress.users
import org.springframework.data.repository.CrudRepository
interface UserRepository : CrudRepository<User,String>
```

As you can see, the UserRepository interface is the same as in previous versions, extending from the CrudRepository interface, which (as you already know) comes with several methods that will be implemented by Spring Data core and the Redis abstractions.

Next, create/open the UsersController class. See Listing 6-21.

Listing 6-21. src/main/kotlin/apress/com/users/UsersController.kt

```
package com.apress.users

import org.springframework.beans.factory.annotation.Autowired
import org.springframework.http.HttpStatus
import org.springframework.http.ResponseEntity
import org.springframework.validation.FieldError
import org.springframework.validation.ObjectError
import org.springframework.web.bind.MethodArgumentNotValidException
import org.springframework.web.bind.annotation.*
import org.springframework.web.servlet.support.ServletUriComponentsBuilder
import java.net.URI

@RestController
@RequestMapping("/users")
class UsersController {
    @Autowired
    private lateinit var userRepository: UserRepository

    @get:GetMapping
    val all: ResponseEntity<Iterable<User>>
```

```kotlin
    get() = ResponseEntity.ok(userRepository.findAll())

@GetMapping("/{email}")
@Throws(Throwable::class)
fun findUserById(@PathVariable email: String): ResponseEntity<User> =
    ResponseEntity.of(userRepository.findById(email))

@RequestMapping(method = [RequestMethod.POST, RequestMethod.PUT])
fun save(@RequestBody user: User): ResponseEntity<User> {
    with(user){
        gravatarUrl = gravatarUrl ?: UserGravatar.getGravatarUrlFromEma
        il(email!!)
        userRole = userRole ?: setOf(UserRole.INFO)
    }
    userRepository.save(user)
    val location: URI = ServletUriComponentsBuilder
        .fromCurrentRequest()
        .path("/{email}")
        .buildAndExpand(user.email)
        .toUri()
    return ResponseEntity.created(location).body(user)
}

@DeleteMapping("/{email}")
@ResponseStatus(HttpStatus.NO_CONTENT)
fun delete(@PathVariable email: String) =
    userRepository.deleteById(email)

@ExceptionHandler(MethodArgumentNotValidException::class)
@ResponseStatus(HttpStatus.BAD_REQUEST)
fun handleValidationExceptions(ex: MethodArgumentNotValidException):
        Map<String, String> =
    ex.bindingResult.allErrors.associate { error: ObjectError ->
        (error as FieldError).field to (error.getDefaultMessage() ?:
        "undef")
    }.toMutableMap()
}
```

The UsersController class is the same as the previous versions. Note that the UserRepository is used, and it will be injected when the application starts.

Next, create/open the UserConfiguration class. See Listing 6-22.

Listing 6-22. src/main/kotlin/apress/com/users/UserConfiguration.kt

```kotlin
package com.apress.users

import org.springframework.boot.context.event.ApplicationReadyEvent
import org.springframework.context.ApplicationListener
import org.springframework.context.annotation.Bean
import org.springframework.context.annotation.Configuration

@Configuration
class UserConfiguration {
    @Bean
    fun init(userRepository: UserRepository):
            ApplicationListener<ApplicationReadyEvent> {
        return ApplicationListener<ApplicationReadyEvent> { _:
        ApplicationReadyEvent ->
            userRepository.save(
                User(
                    email="ximena@email.com",
                    name="Ximena",
                    gravatarUrl="https://www.gravatar.com/avatar/23bb62a7d0
                    ca63c9a804908e57bf6bd4?d=wavatar",
                    password="aw2sOmeR!",
                    userRole = mutableListOf(UserRole.USER),
                    active = true)
            )
            userRepository.save(
                User(
                    email="norma@email.com",
                    name="Norma",
                    gravatarUrl="https://www.gravatar.com/avatar/f07f
                    7e553264c9710105edebe6c465e7?d=wavatar",
                    password="aw2sOmeR!",
```

```
            userRole = mutableListOf(UserRole.USER,UserRole.ADMIN),
            active=true)
        )
    }
  }
}
```

In the `UserConfiguration` class, we are adding some users, and in this case we are also adding the `gravatarUrl` field value. In Spring Data Redis, there are no callbacks or events before persisting any object, so you can add the `gravatarUrl` field value either manually in the controller when receiving the object by using the data class' constructor and named parameters or by creating a service that takes care of it before saving. So, as you can see, you have options, and for now you can add it in the configuration.

The `UserGravatar` and `UserRole` classes are the same as in previous versions. The `application.properties` file is empty except for `spring.docker.compose.file = ./users/docker-compose.yaml`. Remember that the auto-configuration will use the default connection parameters. If you want to override them, you can set the `spring.data.redis.*` properties as environment variables, either from the command line or in the `application.properties` file.

Testing the Users App

To test the Users App, create/open the `UsersHttpRequestTests` class. See Listing 6-23.

Listing 6-23. src/test/kotlin/apress/com/users/UsersHttpRequestTests.kt

```
package com.apress.users

import org.assertj.core.api.Assertions
import org.junit.jupiter.api.Test
import org.springframework.beans.factory.annotation.Autowired
import org.springframework.beans.factory.annotation.Value
import org.springframework.boot.test.context.SpringBootTest
import org.springframework.boot.test.web.client.TestRestTemplate

@SpringBootTest(webEnvironment = SpringBootTest.WebEnvironment.RANDOM_PORT)
class UsersHttpRequestTests {
```

```kotlin
@Value("\${local.server.port}")
private val port = 0

private val BASE_URL = "http://localhost:"
private val USERS_PATH = "/users"

@Autowired
private lateinit var restTemplate: TestRestTemplate

@Test
@Throws(Exception::class)
fun indexPageShouldReturnHeaderOneContent() {
    Assertions.assertThat(
        restTemplate.getForObject(
            BASE_URL + port,
            String::class.java
        )
    ).contains("Simple Users Rest Application")
}

@Test
@Throws(Exception::class)
fun usersEndPointShouldReturnCollectionWithTwoUsers() {
    val response: Collection<User> =
        restTemplate.getForObject(BASE_URL + port + USERS_PATH,
            Collection::class.java) as Collection<User>
    Assertions.assertThat(response.size).isEqualTo(2)
}

@Test
@Throws(Exception::class)
fun userEndPointPostNewUserShouldReturnUser() {
    val user: User = User(
        email="dummy@email.com",
        name="Dummy",
        gravatarUrl="https://www.gravatar.com/avatar/23bb62a7d0ca63c
9a804908e57bf6bd4?d=wavatar",
        password="aw2s0meR!",
```

```kotlin
        userRole = mutableListOf(UserRole.USER),
        active=true)
    val response = restTemplate.postForObject(BASE_URL + port +
    USERS_PATH,
        user, User::class.java)
    Assertions.assertThat(response).isNotNull()
    Assertions.assertThat(response.email).isEqualTo(user.email)
    val users: Collection<User> =
        restTemplate.getForObject(BASE_URL + port + USERS_PATH,
            Collection::class.java) as Collection<User>
    Assertions.assertThat(users.size).isGreaterThanOrEqualTo(2)
}

@Test
@Throws(Exception::class)
fun userEndPointDeleteUserShouldReturnVoid() {
    restTemplate.delete("$BASE_URL$port$USERS_PATH/norma@email.com")
    val users: Collection<User> =
        restTemplate.getForObject(BASE_URL + port + USERS_PATH,
            Collection::class.java) as Collection<User>
    Assertions.assertThat(users.size).isLessThanOrEqualTo(2)
}

@Test
@Throws(Exception::class)
fun userEndPointFindUserShouldReturnUser() {
    val user = restTemplate.getForObject(
        "$BASE_URL$port$USERS_PATH/ximena@email.com", User::class.java)
    Assertions.assertThat(user).isNotNull()
    Assertions.assertThat(user.email).isEqualTo("ximena@email.com")
}
}
```

As you can see, the UsersHttpRequestTests class has not changed. To begin the test, you need to have Redis up and running. You can use your IDE to run the docker-compose.yaml service or execute the following in the command line:

```
docker compose up -d
```

Once Redis is up and running, you can run the tests by using the IDE or the following command:

```
./gradlew clean test
UsersHttpRequestTests > userEndPointFindUserShouldReturnUser() PASSED
UsersHttpRequestTests > userEndPointDeleteUserShouldReturnVoid() PASSED
UsersHttpRequestTests > indexPageShouldReturnHeaderOneContent() PASSED
UsersHttpRequestTests > userEndPointPostNewUserShouldReturnUser() PASSED
UsersHttpRequestTests > usersEndPointShouldReturnCollectionWithTwoUsers()
                        PASSED
```

Running the Users App

Before you run the application, make sure Redis (from docker compose) is stopped. Then you can run the app by using your IDE or the following command:

```
./gradlew clean bootRun
```

First docker compose starts, then the application. Next, you can direct your browser to http://localhost:8080/users or use the following command:

```
curl -s http://localhost:8080/users | jq .
[
  {
    "email": "ximena@email.com",
    "name": "Ximena",
    "gravatarUrl": "https://www.gravatar.com/avatar/23bb62a7d0ca63c9a80490
8e57bf6bd4?d=wavatar",
    "password": "aw2s0meR!",
    "userRole": [
      "USER"
    ],
    "active": true
  },
  {
    "email": "norma@email.com",
    "name": "Norma",
```

```
      "gravatarUrl": "https://www.gravatar.com/avatar/f07f7e553264c9710105ede
      be6c465e7?d=wavatar",
      "password": "aw2s0meR!",
      "userRole": [
        "USER",
        "ADMIN"
      ],
      "active": true
   }
]
```

If you are curious, you can use the Redis CLI and take a peek at how Spring Data Redis saves the data. You can execute the following command:

```
docker run -it --rm --network users_default redis:alpine redis-cli -h redis
```

This command uses the users_default network and the redis:alpine image by passing the execution to redis-cli with the -h (host) flag and redis (the name of the service, declared in docker-compose.yaml). After the command is executed, you should get the redis:6379> prompt. Then you can look at the keys by executing the KEYS command:

```
redis:6379> KEYS *
1) "USERS"
2) "USERS:norma@email.com"
3) "USERS:ximena@email.com"
```

You can get the type, for example:

```
redis:6379> TYPE "USERS:norma@email.com"
hash
```

You can get the keys of the hash using the following command:

```
redis:6379> HKEYS "USERS:norma@email.com"
1) "email"
2) "active"
3) "_class"
4) "userRole.[1]"
```

```
5) "password"
6) "userRole.[0]"
7) "gravatarUrl"
8) "name"
```

You can get the values of that hash with the following:

```
redis:6379> HVALS "USERS:norma@email.com"
1) "norma@email.com"
2) "1"
3) "com.apress.users.User"
4) "ADMIN"
5) "aw2sOmeR!"
6) "USER"
7) "https://www.gravatar.com/avatar/f07f7e553264c9710105edebe6c465e7?
   d=wavatar"
8) "Norma"
```

You can also get a specific field with this:

```
redis:6379> HGET "USERS:norma@email.com" name
"Norma"
```

Play around with the commands in the Redis client (you can view the documentation at https://redis.io/commands/).

The next section looks at using Spring Data Redis in the My Retro App project.

My Retro App with Spring Data Redis Using Spring Boot

If you are following along, you can reuse some of the code from the previous versions. Or you can start from scratch by going to the Spring Initializr (https://start.spring.io) and generating a base project (no dependencies); just make sure you have set the Group field to com.apress and the Artifact and Name fields to myretro. Download the project, unzip it, and import it into your favorite IDE. By the end of this section, you should have the structure shown in Figure 6-4.

Figure 6-4. My Retro App with Spring Data Redis with Spring Boot

Open the build.gradle file and replace the contents with the contents shown in Listing 6-24.

Listing 6-24. The build.gradle File

```
import org.jetbrains.kotlin.gradle.tasks.KotlinCompile
plugins {
    id 'org.springframework.boot' version '3.2.3'
    id 'io.spring.dependency-management' version '1.1.4'
    id 'org.jetbrains.kotlin.jvm' version '2.0.20-RC'
    id "org.jetbrains.kotlin.plugin.spring" version "2.0.20-RC"
    // <- simplifies spring proxying
}
```

```
group = 'com.apress'
version = '0.0.1-SNAPSHOT'
sourceCompatibility = '17'

repositories {
    mavenCentral()
}

dependencies {
    implementation "org.jetbrains.kotlin:kotlin-stdlib-jdk8"
    implementation "org.jetbrains.kotlin:kotlin-reflect"

    implementation 'org.springframework.boot:spring-boot-starter-web'
    implementation 'org.springframework.boot:spring-boot-starter-
    validation'
    implementation 'org.springframework.boot:spring-boot-starter-aop'

    implementation 'org.springframework.boot:spring-boot-starter-
    data-redis'
    developmentOnly 'org.springframework.boot:spring-boot-docker-compose'

    annotationProcessor 'org.springframework.boot:spring-boot-
    configuration-processor'

    // Web
    implementation 'org.webjars:bootstrap:5.2.3'

    testImplementation 'org.springframework.boot:spring-boot-starter-test'
}
tasks.named('test') {
    useJUnitPlatform()
}

//    kotlin {
//        jvmToolchain(17)
//    }
tasks.withType(KotlinCompile).configureEach {
    kotlinOptions {
```

```
        freeCompilerArgs = ['-Xjsr305=strict']
        jvmTarget = '17'
    }
}
```

Listing 6-24 shows that we included the spring-boot-starter-data-redis starter dependency and docker compose.

Next, create/open the board package and the RetroBoard class. See Listing 6-25.

Listing 6-25. src/main/kotlin/apress/com/myretro/board/RetroBoard.kt

```
package com.apress.myretro.board

import jakarta.validation.constraints.NotBlank
import jakarta.validation.constraints.NotNull
import org.springframework.data.annotation.Id
import org.springframework.data.redis.core.RedisHash
import java.util.*

@RedisHash("RETRO_BOARD")
data class RetroBoard(
    @Id
    @get:NotNull
    var id: UUID? = null,

    @get:NotBlank(message = "A name must be provided")
    var name: String? = null,

    var cards: MutableList<Card>? = null
)
```

Listing 6-25 shows the RetroBoard class. Note that it is marked using the @RedisHash annotation using the RETRO_BOARD parameter. This will identify the hash for Redis. Also, we are using the @Id annotation to mark an identifier, which is used to establish the key for that hash value (as in the Users App).

Next, create/open the persistence package and the RetroBoardRepository interface. See Listing 6-26.

Listing 6-26. src/main/kotlin/apress/com/myretro/persistence/
RetroBoardRepository.kt

```
package com.apress.myretro.persistence

import com.apress.myretro.board.RetroBoard
import org.springframework.data.repository.CrudRepository
import java.util.*

interface RetroBoardRepository : CrudRepository<RetroBoard, UUID>
```

We are using `CrudRepository`, which is the same as in the other versions, and we are using the Spring Data core to implement this interface on our behalf using all the Redis operations.

The `advice`, `config`, `exception`, `service`, and `web` packages and all their classes remain the same as the previous versions, and in the `board` package, the `Card` and `CardType` also remain the same. Also, the `application.properties` file is empty except for `spring.docker.compose.file = ./myretro/docker-compose.yaml`. So, to sum it up, the only significant change was the addition of the `@RedisHash` annotation to the `RetroBoard` class.

Running My Retro App

To run the application, you can use the IDE or the following command:

```
./gradlew clean bootRun
```

Then, point your browser to `http://localhost:8080/retros` or execute the following command:

```
curl -s http://localhost:8080/retros | jq .
[
  {
    "id": "9dc9b71b-a07e-418b-b972-40225449aff2",
    "name": "Spring Boot Conference",
    "cards": [
      {
        "id": "bb2a80a5-a0f5-4180-a6dc-80c84bc014c9",
```

```
      "comment": "Spring Boot Rocks!",
      "cardType": "HAPPY"
    },
    {
      "id": "e39cd241-4c75-41c8-9750-8b01e8225774",
      "comment": "Meet everyone in person",
      "cardType": "HAPPY"
    },
    {
      "id": "e8947c01-fd30-4f78-81cf-31acf5cfd46b",
      "comment": "When is the next one?",
      "cardType": "MEH"
    },
    {
      "id": "ce228247-d414-4cf9-8356-dbccb89f9370",
      "comment": "Not enough time to talk to everyone",
      "cardType": "SAD"
    }
  ]
 }
]
```

If you want to know how it is represented in Redis, you can run the following Docker container client to run the redis-cli:

```
docker run -it --rm --network myretro_default redis:alpine redis-cli
-h redis
```

Notice that we are using the myretro_default network that was generated when the application ran.

You can review the Redis commands next. You can review the keys with the following Redis commands:

```
redis:6379> keys *
1) "RETRO_BOARD"
2) "RETRO_BOARD:9dc9b71b-a07e-418b-b972-40225449aff2"
```

You can review the values with these commands:

```
redis:6379> hvals "RETRO_BOARD:9dc9b71b-a07e-418b-b972-40225449aff2"
 1) "com.apress.myretro.board.RetroBoard"
 2) "HAPPY"
 3) "Spring Boot Rocks!"
 4) "bb2a80a5-a0f5-4180-a6dc-80c84bc014c9"
 5) "HAPPY"
 6) "Meet everyone in person"
 7) "08821ce0-79ed-4dd4-ad8d-c6d0e841738f"
 8) "MEH"
 9) "When is the next one?"
10) "edf4dcc7-c800-48e2-bf2d-0af41b5c3a23"
11) "SAD"
12) "Not enough time to talk to everyone"
13) "7545e981-4042-4f9f-8986-78ff92242c3c"
14) "9dc9b71b-a07e-418b-b972-40225449aff2"
15) "Spring Boot Conference"
```

You can view the keys with these commands:

```
redis:6379> Hkeys "RETRO_BOARD:9dc9b71b-a07e-418b-b972-40225449aff2"
 1) "_class"
 2) "cards.[0].cardType"
 3) "cards.[0].comment"
 4) "cards.[0].id"
 5) "cards.[1].cardType"
 6) "cards.[1].comment"
 7) "cards.[1].id"
 8) "cards.[2].cardType"
 9) "cards.[2].comment"
10) "cards.[2].id"
11) "cards.[3].cardType"
12) "cards.[3].comment"
13) "cards.[3].id"
14) "id"
15) "name"
```

And you can view the field values with these commands:

```
redis:6379> hget "RETRO_BOARD:9dc9b71b-a07e-418b-b972-40225449aff2" "cards.
[3].cardType"
"SAD"
```

Note that the `Card` domain class is set as keys using a composition, the name of the instance pluralized to `cards`, the array notation, and the `Card` field name.

So, that's how you run your applications using Spring Data Redis and Spring Boot. Of course, here we are using the repository programming model, but you can use the `RedisTemplate` or `StringRedisTemplate` directly, or any other operation classes directly, such as `HashOperation`, `ListOperations`, `ZSetOperations`, and so on.

Summary

This chapter covered MongoDB and Redis as NoSQL databases, and you learned how they are based in the Spring Data core project and how they expose the same repository programming model, making this easier with minimal changes just in the domain classes.

You learned that Spring Boot uses the auto-configuration feature to set the default connection parameters and enable extra features for NoSQL databases, and the only thing you are required to do is add these dependencies.

You also learned with both projects (Users App and My Retro App) what to do to mark the classes with the right annotation (@Document, @RedisHash) and use the core such as @Id annotation and the `CrudRepository` interface. Again, only minimal changes are needed if you let Spring Data do the work for you.

Chapter 7 explores Spring Reactor and explains how to create Reactive applications.

CHAPTER 7

Spring Boot Reactive

Felipe Gutierrez[a*]

　[a] 4109 Rillcrest Grove Way Fuquay Varina, NC 27526-3562, Albuquerque, NM, USA

Reactive Systems

In the past decade, the software industry has responded to the demands of mobile and cloud computing by improving software development processes to produce software that is more stable, more robust, more resilient, and more flexible to accept more modern demands, not only by users (using the desktop or the web) but by a variety of devices (mobile phones, sensors, etc.). Accommodating these new workloads has many challenges, which is why a group of organizations worked together to produce a manifesto to cover many aspects of today's data demands.

The Reactive Manifesto

The Reactive Manifesto (`https://www.reactivemanifesto.org/`) was published on September 16, 2014. It defines the characteristics of reactive systems. Reactive systems are flexible, loosely coupled, and scalable. They are more tolerant to failure, and when a failure occurs, they deal with it by applying patterns to avoid disaster.

To paraphrase the Reactive Manifesto, Reactive systems have the following characteristics:

- *Responsive*: Reactive systems respond in a timely manner, if possible. They focus on providing fast and consistent response times and establishing reliable upper bounds for delivering a consistent quality of service.

© Peter Späth, Felipe Gutierrez 2025

P. Späth and F. Gutierrez, *Pro Spring Boot 3 with Kotlin*, https://doi.org/10.1007/979-8-8688-1131-9_7

- *Resilient*: Reactive systems apply replication, containment, isolation, and delegation patterns to achieve resilience. They contain failures through isolation so that failures do not affect other parts of the system or other systems. Recovery must be from another system, so that high availability (HA) is ensured.

- *Elastic*: Reactive systems are responsive under any kind of workload. They can react to changes in the input rate by increasing or decreasing the resources allocated to service these inputs. They should not have any bottlenecks, meaning they have the capability to shard or replicate components and distribute inputs to them. Reactive systems must support predictive algorithms, which ensures cost-effective elasticity on commodity hardware.

- *Message driven*: Reactive systems rely on asynchronous messaging to establish a boundary between components, making sure that the systems are loosely coupled, isolated, and location transparent. Reactive systems must support load management, elasticity, and flow control by providing a back-pressure pattern when needed. The communication must be nonblocking to allow recipients to consume resources while active, which leads to lower system overhead.

After the publication of the Reactive Manifesto, different initiatives started to emerge and implement frameworks and libraries that help many developers around the world. Reactive Streams (`https://www.reactive-streams.org/`) is a specification that defines four simple interfaces: `Publisher<T>`, a provider of an unbounded number of sequenced elements, publishing them according to the demand of the subscriber; `Subscriber<T>`, which subscribes to the publisher; `Subscription`, which represents the one-to-one lifecycle of a subscriber subscribing to a publisher; and `Processor`, which is the processing stage for both *Subscriber* and *Publisher*. Reactive Streams also has different implementations, such as *ReactiveX RXJava* (`https://github.com/ReactiveX/RxJava`), *Akka Streams* (`https://akka.io`), *Ratpack* (`https://ratpack.io`), *Vert.x* (`https://vertx.io`), *Slick* (`https://scala-slick.org/`), *Project Reactor* (`https://projectreactor.io`), *Reactive Relational Database Connectivity (R2DBC)* (`https://r2dbc.io/`), and many more.

The Reactive Streams API has its own implementation in the Java 9 SDK release; in other words, as of December 2017, Reactive Streams version 1.0.2 is part of JDK9.

Project Reactor

Project Reactor 3.5.x is a library that is built around the Reactive Streams specification, bringing the Reactive programming paradigm to JVM. Reactive programming is a paradigm that is an event-based model, where data is pushed to the consumer as it becomes available; it deals with asynchronous sequences of events. Offering fully asynchronous and nonblocking patterns, reactive programming is an alternative to the limited ways of doing async code in the JDK (callbacks, APIs, and the Future<V> interface).

Reactor is a full, nonblocking reactive programming framework that manages back pressure and integrates interaction with the Java 8+ functional APIs (CompletableFuture, Stream, and Duration). Reactor provides two reactive composable asynchronous APIs: Flux [N] (for N elements) and Mono [0|1] (for 0 or 1 elements). Reactor can be used to develop microservices architectures because it offers interprocess communication (IPC) with reactor-ipc components and backpressure-ready network engines for HTTP (including WebSockets, TCP, and UDP). Reactive encoding and decoding are also fully supported.

Mono<T>, an Asynchronous [0|1] Result

Mono<T> is a specialized Publisher<T> interface that emits one item, and it can optionally terminate with onComplete or onError signals. You can apply operators to manipulate the item (see Figure 7-1).

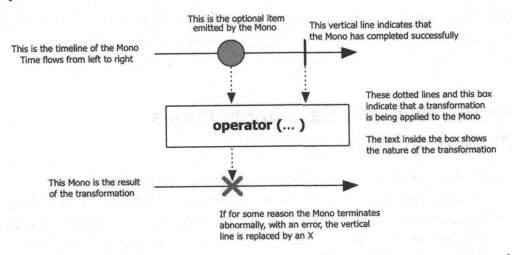

Figure 7-1. Mono [0/1] (Source: https://projectreactor.io documentation)

Flux<T>: An Asynchronous Sequence of [0|N] Items

Flux<T> is a Publisher<T> that represents an asynchronous sequence of 0 to N emitted items that can optionally terminate by using onComplete or an onError signal (see Figure 7-2).

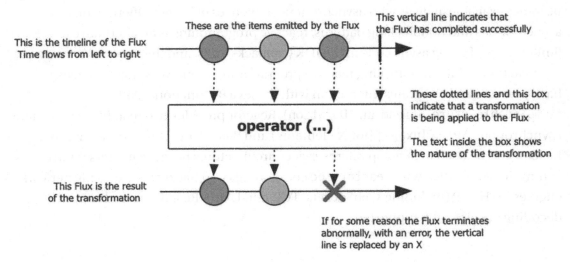

Figure 7-2. *Flux [0/N] (Source: https://projectreactor.io documentation)*

Project Reactor provides processors, operators, and timers that can sustain a high throughput rate on tens of millions of messages per second with a low memory footprint.

Note   If you want to know more about Project Reactor, peruse its documentation at https://projectreactor.io/docs/core/release/reference/.

Reactive Web and Data Applications with Spring Boot

By using Spring Boot, creating your Reactive apps is simple. Spring Boot provides auto-configuration of all your web and data reactive apps using Web Flux, by adding the spring-boot-starter-webflux starter and any reactive data dependencies. When you create a project in the Spring Initializr (https://start.spring.io), click Add Dependencies and type **reactive**. You will get a list of dependencies similar to Figure 7-3.

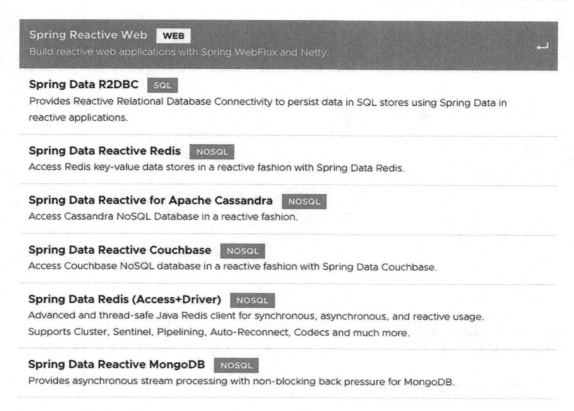

Figure 7-3. *Spring Initializr Reactive dependencies*

You can use any programming style model, from using annotations to functional programming, and use the Reactive types of `Mono<T>` or `Flux<T>` classes for your responses. When you are using Spring Boot with Spring Reactive Web (a.k.a. WebFlux), the application container used is Netty by default (no more Tomcat). You can switch to Undertow instead.

Figure 7-4 depicts the respective programming models when you are using Spring MVC or Spring WebFlux.

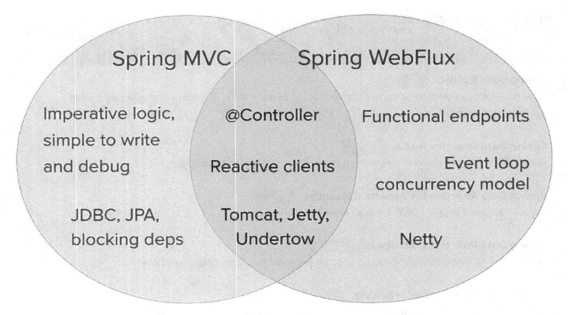

Figure 7-4. *Applicability of Spring MVC WebFlux (Source: https://docs. spring.io/spring-framework/reference/web/webflux/new-framework.html)*

As you can see, you have options, from using functional to annotated endpoints.

Users App with Spring Boot Reactive

For the Users App, we are going to use WebFlux and R2DBC with H2 and functional programming for the endpoints, which will be a little different from the previous versions. You can start from scratch by going to the Spring Initializr (https://start. spring.io) and generating a base project (no dependencies). Make sure to set the group field to com.apress and the Artifact and Name fields to users. Download the project, unzip it, and import it into your favorite IDE. By the end of this section, you should have the structure shown in Figure 7-5.

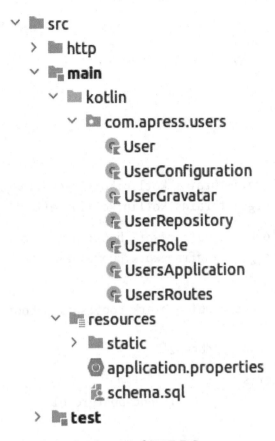

Figure 7-5. *Users App with Web Flux and R2DBC*

Next, open the build.gradle file and replace its contents with the contents shown in Listing 7-1.

Listing 7-1. The build.gradle File

```
import org.jetbrains.kotlin.gradle.tasks.KotlinCompile
plugins {
    id 'org.springframework.boot' version '3.2.3'
    id 'io.spring.dependency-management' version '1.1.4'
    id 'org.jetbrains.kotlin.jvm' version '2.0.20-RC'
    id "org.jetbrains.kotlin.plugin.spring" version "2.0.20-RC"
    // <- simplifies spring proxying
}
```

```
group = 'com.apress'
version = '0.0.1-SNAPSHOT'
sourceCompatibility = '17'

repositories {
    mavenCentral()
}

dependencies {
    implementation "org.jetbrains.kotlin:kotlin-stdlib-jdk8"
    implementation "org.jetbrains.kotlin:kotlin-reflect"

    implementation 'org.springframework.boot:spring-boot-starter-webflux'
    implementation 'org.springframework.boot:spring-boot-starter-
    validation'

    implementation 'org.springframework.boot:spring-boot-starter-
    data-r2dbc'
    runtimeOnly 'io.r2dbc:r2dbc-h2'

    // Reactive Postgres
    //runtimeOnly 'org.postgresql:r2dbc-postgresql'

    // Web
    implementation 'org.webjars:bootstrap:5.2.3'

    testImplementation 'org.springframework.boot:spring-boot-starter-test'
    testImplementation 'io.projectreactor:reactor-test'

}

tasks.named('test') {
    useJUnitPlatform()
}

test {
    testLogging {
        events "passed", "skipped", "failed"
        showExceptions true
        exceptionFormat "full"
```

```
        showCauses true
        showStackTraces true
        showStandardStreams = false
    }
}

//    kotlin {
//        jvmToolchain(17)
//    }
tasks.withType(KotlinCompile).configureEach {
    kotlinOptions {
        freeCompilerArgs = ['-Xjsr305=strict']
        jvmTarget = '17'
    }
}
```

Listing 7-1 shows the necessary dependencies to use WebFlux and R2DBC. Note that you need to include the DB driver (in this example, it will use the H2 database) and add the Reactive driver (in this case, the r2dbc-h2 driver). If H2 is not a good option for you, you can switch to the Reactive PostgreSQL r2dbc-postgresql dependency. Also notice that we are using the reactor-test dependency, which allows us to test new types such as Flux and Mono.

Next, create/open the User class. See Listing 7-2.

Listing 7-2. src/main/kotlin/apress/com/users/User.kt

```
package com.apress.users

import jakarta.validation.constraints.NotBlank
import org.springframework.data.annotation.Id
import org.springframework.data.relational.core.mapping.Table
import java.util.*

@Table("PEOPLE")
@JvmRecord
data class User(
    @Id
    val id: UUID?,
```

```
    @get:NotBlank(message = "Email cannot be empty")
    val email:  String?,

    @get:NotBlank(message = "Name cannot be empty")
    val name:  String?,

    val gravatarUrl: String?,

    @get:NotBlank(message = "Password cannot be empty")
    val password:  String?,

    val userRole: Collection<UserRole>,
    val active: Boolean
) {
    fun withGravatarUrl(email: String): User {
        val url = UserGravatar.getGravatarUrlFromEmail(email)
        return User(UUID.randomUUID(), email, name, url, password,
        userRole, active)
    }
}
```

We are using the @Table annotation with the PEOPLE value, which will be the name of the table. We are also using the @Id annotation. Note that we are using the Spring Data core, a common use case for these domain classes.

Next, create/open the UserRepository interface. See Listing 7-3.

Listing 7-3. src/main/kotlin/apress/com/users/UserRepository.kt

```
package com.apress.users

import org.springframework.data.repository.reactive.ReactiveCrudRepository
import reactor.core.publisher.Mono
import java.util.*

interface UserRepository : ReactiveCrudRepository<User, UUID> {
    fun findByEmail(email: String): Mono<User>
    fun deleteByEmail(email: String): Mono<Void>
}
```

In Listing 7-3, we are using a new extended interface, ReactiveCrudRepository, which takes the domain class (in this case, the User) and the identifier (in this case, a UUID).

Next, create/open the UserRoutes class. See Listing 7-4.

Listing 7-4. src/main/kotlin/apress/com/users/UserRoutes.kt

```kotlin
package com.apress.users

import org.springframework.beans.factory.annotation.Autowired
import org.springframework.context.annotation.Bean
import org.springframework.context.annotation.Configuration
import org.springframework.web.reactive.function.BodyExtractors
import org.springframework.web.reactive.function.server.*
import reactor.core.publisher.*

@Configuration
class UsersRoutes {
    @Autowired
    private lateinit var userRepository: UserRepository

    @get:Bean
    val usersRoute: RouterFunction<ServerResponse>
        get() = RouterFunctions.route(
            RequestPredicates.GET("/users")
        ) { _: ServerRequest ->
            ServerResponse.ok()
                .body<User, Flux<User>>(userRepository.findAll(),
                User::class.java)
        }

    @Bean
    fun postUserRoute(): RouterFunction<ServerResponse> {
        return RouterFunctions.route(
            RequestPredicates.POST("/users")
        ) { request: ServerRequest ->
            request
                .body<Mono<User>>(BodyExtractors.toMono(User::class.java))
```

317

```
                    .flatMap { entity: User -> userRepository.save(entity) }
                    .then(ServerResponse.ok().build())
        }
    }

    @Bean
    fun findUserByEmail(): RouterFunction<ServerResponse> {
        return RouterFunctions.route(
            RequestPredicates.GET("/users/{email}")
        ) { request: ServerRequest ->
            ServerResponse.ok()
                .body<User, Mono<User>>(
                    userRepository.findByEmail(request.pathVariable
                    ("email")),
                    User::class.java
                )
        }
    }

    @Bean
    fun deleteUserByEmail(): RouterFunction<ServerResponse> {
        return RouterFunctions.route(
            RequestPredicates.DELETE("/users/{email}")
        ) { request: ServerRequest ->
            userRepository.deleteByEmail(request.pathVariable("email"))
            ServerResponse.noContent().build()
        }
    }
}
```

In Listing 7-4, we are defining the routes for the endpoints and configuring the
server responses, all in the UserRoutes class (this is different from the previous
versions, in which we have two separated files for defining routes and another for the
responses). Note that this is a JavaConfig class and that we are marking it with the
@Configuration annotation, meaning that we need to declare beans with the @Bean
annotation. We are using the RouterFunction with the ServerResponse type and using
the route configuration to accept a request and return a ServerResponse. This all is

very straightforward because we are based on the Spring Data core with the repositories programming model (meaning that Spring Data is doing the implementation of the ReactiveCrudRepository interface on our behalf).

Because we are using ServerResponse, this wraps all the responses—either Flux<T> or Mono<T> classes, depending on the response from the Reactive database.

If we were just using Project Reactor to access the database (without Spring R2DBC), we would need to write something like the following code snippet:

```
val connectionFactory = ConnectionFactories
            .get("r2dbc:h2:mem:///testdb")
Mono.from(connectionFactory.create())
    .flatMapMany { connection: Connection ->
        connection
            .createStatement("SELECT name FROM PEOPLE WHERE email = $1")
            .bind("$1", "norma@email.com")
            .execute()
    }
    .flatMap { result: Result ->
        result
            .map{ row: Row, rowMetadata: RowMetadata? ->
                row.get(
                    "name",
                    String::class.java
                )
            }
    }
    .doOnNext { x: String? -> println(x) }
    .subscribe()
```

Next, create/open the UserConfiguration class. See Listing 7-5.

Listing 7-5. src/main/kotlin/apress/com/users/UserConfiguration.kt

```
package com.apress.users

import org.springframework.boot.CommandLineRunner
import org.springframework.context.annotation.Bean
import org.springframework.context.annotation.Configuration
```

```kotlin
import org.springframework.data.r2dbc.mapping.event.BeforeConvertCallback
import org.springframework.data.relational.core.sql.SqlIdentifier
import org.springframework.stereotype.Component
import reactor.core.publisher.Mono
import java.time.Duration
import java.util.*

@Configuration
class UserConfiguration {
    @Component
    inner class GravatarUrlGeneratingCallback :
    BeforeConvertCallback<User> {
        override fun onBeforeConvert(user: User, sqlIdentifier:
        SqlIdentifier):
                Mono<User> {
            return Mono.just(
                if (user.id == null && user.gravatarUrl.isNullOrEmpty())
                    user.withGravatarUrl(user.email!!)
                else user
            )
        }
    }

    @Bean
    fun init(userRepository: UserRepository): CommandLineRunner {
        return CommandLineRunner { _: Array<String> ->
            userRepository.saveAll(
                listOf(
                    User(null,
                        "ximena@email.com",
                        "Ximena",
                        null,
                        "aw2s0me",
                        listOf(UserRole.USER),
                        true),
                    User(
```

```
                    null,
                    "norma@email.com",
                    "Norma",
                    null,
                    "aw2s0me",
                    listOf(UserRole.USER, UserRole.ADMIN),
                    true
                )
            )
        ).blockLast(Duration.ofSeconds(10))
    }
  }
}
```

Let's analyze the `UserConfiguration` class:

- **BeforeConvertCallback**: We are declaring this inner class, which implements the `BeforeConvertCallback` interface. We have been implementing it in previous versions (for the data persistence apps), and in this case we are declaring it as an inner class instead of having a separate class (which option you use is up to you and where you want to have certain logic). In this method, we are checking for the `gravatarUrl` field and setting it if it's null.

- **CommandLineRunner**: Instead of using the `ApplicationListener` (which will listen for the `ApplicationReadyEvent`), we are using the `CommandLineRunner` interface as a reminder that we have options for how we execute code when the application is ready.

Next, create/open the `schema.sql` file, shown in Listing 7-6.

Listing 7-6. src/main/resources/schema.sql

```
drop table if exists people cascade;
create table people (
    id uuid default random_uuid() not null,
    email varchar(255) not null,
    active boolean not null,
```

```
gravatar_url varchar(255),
name varchar(255),
password varchar(255),
user_role VARCHAR(100) array,
primary key (id));
```

If you want to use PostgreSQL, you need to change to the uuid_generate_v4() and enable the plugin that handles those functions:

```
CREATE EXTENSION IF NOT EXISTS "uuid-ossp";
```

The UserGravatar and UserRole classes remain the same as in the previous versions. The application.properties file is empty. Remember that Spring Boot will do all the auto-configuration, which means that it will initialize the database with the SQL statements found in the schema.sql file and it will set all the default values needed for the connection.

Testing the Users App

To test the Users App, you need to use a different client that accepts the Flux<T> or Mono<T> types. Specifically, you need the reactor-test dependency in the build. gradle file (Listing 7-1). So, create/open the UsersHttpRequestTests class. See Listing 7-7.

Listing 7-7. src/test/kotlin/apress/com/users/UsersHttpRequestTests.kt

```
package com.apress.users

import org.assertj.core.api.Assertions
import org.junit.jupiter.api.Test
import org.springframework.beans.factory.annotation.Autowired
import org.springframework.boot.test.context.SpringBootTest
import org.springframework.test.web.reactive.server.WebTestClient
import reactor.core.publisher.Mono
import java.util.*
import java.util.function.Consumer
```

```kotlin
@SpringBootTest(webEnvironment = SpringBootTest.WebEnvironment.RANDOM_PORT)
class UsersHttpRequestTests {
    @Autowired
    private val webTestClient: WebTestClient? = null

    @Test
    @Throws(Exception::class)
    fun indexPageShouldReturnHeaderOneContent() {
        webTestClient!!.get().uri("/")
            .exchange()
            .expectStatus().isOk()
            .expectBody(String::class.java)
            .value { value: String ->
                Assertions.assertThat(value)
                    .contains("Simple Users Rest Application") }
    }

    @Test
    @Throws(Exception::class)
    fun usersEndPointShouldReturnCollectionWithTwoUsers() {
        webTestClient!!.get().uri("/users")
            .exchange().expectStatus().isOk()
            .expectBody(Collection::class.java).value(Consumer {
                collection: Collection<*> ->
                Assertions.assertThat(collection.size).isGreater
                ThanOrEqualTo(3)
            })
    }

    @Test
    @Throws(Exception::class)
    fun userEndPointPostNewUserShouldReturnUser() {
        webTestClient!!.post().uri("/users")
            .body(
                Mono.just(
                    User(
                        null,
```

```
                            "dummy@email.com",
                            "Dummy",
                            null,
                            "aw2s0me",
                            Arrays.asList(UserRole.USER),
                            true
                        )
                ), User::class.java
            )
            .exchange().expectStatus().isOk()
    }

    @Test
    @Throws(Exception::class)
    fun userEndPointDeleteUserShouldReturnVoid() {
        webTestClient!!.delete().uri("/users/norma@email.com")
            .exchange().expectStatus().isNoContent()
    }

    @Test
    @Throws(Exception::class)
    fun userEndPointFindUserShouldReturnUser() {
        webTestClient!!.get().uri("/users/ximena@email.com")
            .exchange().expectStatus().isOk()
            .expectBody(User::class.java).value { user: User ->
                Assertions.assertThat(user).isNotNull()
                Assertions.assertThat(user.email).isEqualTo("ximena
                @email.com")
            }
    }
}
```

Listing 7-7 is using the WebTestClient class instead of the TestRestTemplate class. The WebTestClient class is a client for testing web servers; it uses the WebClient class internally to perform requests. The WebTestClient class provides a fluent API, using get(), post(), and delete() methods that allow you to easily configure your tests. This client can connect not only to any server over HTTP, but also to any WebFlux app.

To run your test, you can use your IDE or the following command:

```
./gradlew clean test
UsersHttpRequestTests > userEndPointFindUserShouldReturnUser() PASSED
UsersHttpRequestTests > userEndPointDeleteUserShouldReturnVoid() PASSED
UsersHttpRequestTests > indexPageShouldReturnHeaderOneContent() PASSED
UsersHttpRequestTests > userEndPointPostNewUserShouldReturnUser() PASSED
UsersHttpRequestTests > usersEndPointShouldReturnCollectionWithTwoUsers()
                        PASSED
```

Running the Users App

Run the Users App by using your IDE or by executing the following command:

```
./gradlew clean bootRun
```

Next, point your browser to http://localhost:8080/users or open another terminal and use the following curl command:

```
curl -s http://localhost:8080/users | jq .
{
    "id": "9ca8bbbe-4814-4223-9dc9-1c6aec783e43",
    "email": "ximena@email.com",
    "name": "Ximena",
    "gravatarUrl": "https://www.gravatar.com/avatar/f07f7e553264c9710105ede
be6c465e7?d=wavatar",
    "password": "aw2s0me",
    "userRole": [
      "USER"
    ],
    "active": true
  },
  {
    "id": "f1e5570d-15f4-41e6-bb87-de333871232c",
    "email": "norma@email.com",
    "name": "Norma",
```

```
    "gravatarUrl": "https://www.gravatar.com/avatar/23bb62a7d0ca63c9a80490
    8e57bf6bd4?d=wavatar",
    "password": "aw2s0me",
    "userRole": [
      "USER",
      "ADMIN"
    ],
    "active": true
  }
]
```

Note   If you want more information about Spring R2DBC, visit the reference documentation at `https://docs.spring.io/spring-data/r2dbc/docs/current/reference/html/#reference`.

My Retro App with Spring Boot Reactive

Switching to the My Retro App project, we are going to use Reactive MongoDB persistence and the annotation-based controller endpoints. If you are following along, you can reuse some of the code from the previous versions. Or you can start from scratch by going to the Spring Initializr (`https://start.spring.io`) and generating a base project (no dependencies). Make sure to set the Group field to `com.apress` and the Artifact and Name fields to `myretro`. Download the project, unzip it, and import it into your favorite IDE. By the end of this section, you should have the structure shown in Figure 7-6.

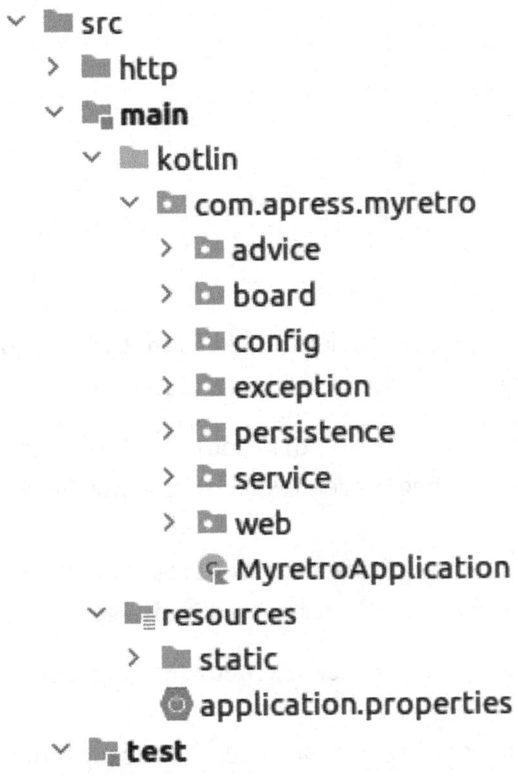

```
∨ ■ src
    > ■ http
    ∨ ■ main
        ∨ ■ kotlin
            ∨ ■ com.apress.myretro
                > ■ advice
                > ■ board
                > ■ config
                > ■ exception
                > ■ persistence
                > ■ service
                > ■ web
                    ■ MyretroApplication
        ∨ ■ resources
            > ■ static
                ■ application.properties
    ∨ ■ test
```

Figure 7-6. *My Retro App with WebFlux/MongoDB*

The My Retro App project's final structure is very similar to the MongoDB version. Open the build.gradle file. See Listing 7-8.

Listing 7-8. The build.gradle File

```
import org.jetbrains.kotlin.gradle.tasks.KotlinCompile
plugins {
    id 'org.springframework.boot' version '3.2.3'
    id 'io.spring.dependency-management' version '1.1.4'
    id 'org.jetbrains.kotlin.jvm' version '2.0.20-RC'
    id "org.jetbrains.kotlin.plugin.spring" version "2.0.20-RC"
    // <- simplifies spring proxying
}
```

```
group = 'com.apress'
version = '0.0.1-SNAPSHOT'
sourceCompatibility = '17'

repositories {
    mavenCentral()
}

dependencies {
    implementation "org.jetbrains.kotlin:kotlin-stdlib-jdk8"
    implementation "org.jetbrains.kotlin:kotlin-reflect"

    implementation 'org.springframework.boot:spring-boot-starter-webflux'
    implementation 'org.springframework.boot:spring-boot-starter-
    validation'
    implementation 'org.springframework.boot:spring-boot-starter-aop'
    implementation 'com.fasterxml.uuid:java-uuid-generator:4.0.1'

    implementation 'org.springframework.boot:spring-boot-starter-data-
    mongodb-reactive'
    developmentOnly 'org.springframework.boot:spring-boot-docker-compose'

    annotationProcessor 'org.springframework.boot:spring-boot-
    configuration-processor'

    // Web
    implementation 'org.webjars:bootstrap:5.2.3'

    testImplementation 'org.springframework.boot:spring-boot-starter-test'
    testImplementation 'io.projectreactor:reactor-test'
}

tasks.named('test') {
    useJUnitPlatform()
}

//    kotlin {
//        jvmToolchain(17)
//    }
```

```
tasks.withType(KotlinCompile).configureEach {
    kotlinOptions {
        freeCompilerArgs = ['-Xjsr305=strict']
        jvmTarget = '17'
    }
}
```

Listing 7-8 shows the build.gradle dependencies, including the new spring-boot-starter-data-mongodb-reactive starter dependency added to this file.

Create/open the board package and the Card, CardType, and RetroBoard classes. See Listings 7-9, 7-10, and 7-11, respectively.

Listing 7-9. src/main/kotlin/apress/com/myretro/board/Card.kt

```
package com.apress.myretro.board

import java.util.*

data class Card(
    var id: UUID? = null,
    var comment: String? = null,
    var cardType: CardType? = null
)
```

Listing 7-10. src/main/kotlin/apress/com/myretro/board/CardType.kt

```
package com.apress.myretro.board
enum class CardType {
    HAPPY,MEH,SAD
}
```

Listing 7-11. src/main/kotlin/apress/com/myretro/board/RetroBoard.kt

```
package com.apress.myretro.board

import org.springframework.data.annotation.Id
import org.springframework.data.mongodb.core.mapping.Document
import java.util.*
```

```kotlin
@Document
data class RetroBoard(
    @Id
    var id: UUID? = null,

    var name: String? = null,

    var cards: MutableList<Card>? = null
){
    fun addCard(card: Card) = ensureCardsExist().add(card)

    fun addCards(cards: Collection<Card>) = ensureCardsExist().
    addAll(cards)

    private fun ensureCardsExist() = this.run {
        cards = cards ?: mutableListOf(); cards!! }
}
```

The Card class and CardType enum remain the same, but the RetroBoard class now includes the @Document and @Id annotations. The @Document annotation marks the class as a persistence domain for the MongoDB, and the @Id annotation adds an identifier to the document, in this case the UUID.

Next, create/open the persistence package, the RetroBoardRepository interface, and the RetroBoardPersistenceCallback class. Listing 7-12 shows the RetroBoardRepository interface.

Listing 7-12. src/main/kotlin/apress/com/myretro/persistence/
RetroBoardRepository.kt

```kotlin
package com.apress.myretro.persistence

import com.apress.myretro.board.RetroBoard
import org.springframework.data.mongodb.repository.Query
import org.springframework.data.mongodb.repository.ReactiveMongoRepository
import reactor.core.publisher.Mono
import java.util.*

interface RetroBoardRepository : ReactiveMongoRepository<RetroBoa
rd, UUID> {
```

```
@Query("{'id': ?0}")
override fun findById(id: UUID): Mono<RetroBoard>

@Query("{}, { cards: { \$elemMatch: { _id: ?0 } } }")
fun findRetroBoardByIdAndCardId(cardId: UUID): Mono<RetroBoard>
}
```

Listing 7-12 shows that the RetroBoardRepository interface includes the following:

- ReactiveMongoRepository: This is a Mongo-specific interface with reactive support. It extends from the ReactiveCrudRepository, ReactiveSortingRepository, and ReactiveQueryByExampleExecutor interfaces. It brings all the usual methods (insert, save, find*, etc.) but in this case using the Flux and Mono types. Spring Data and Project Reactor will implement these interfaces using all the reactive support.

- Mono<RetroBoard>: As in previous versions, you can define your own find* methods and even use your own queries, in this case using the MongoDB query language. We are using the @Query annotation to define a particular query that will find a Card by its UUID among all the retroBoard objects. Of course, this approach is not the best because you can narrow your search if you facilitate the retroBoard UUID or do a different map reduce option. The idea here is that you can extend, use, and create your own custom queries.

Listing 7-13 shows the RetroBoardPersistenceCallback class.

Listing 7-13. src/main/kotlin/apress/com/myretro/persistence/
RetroBoardPersistenceCallback.kt

```
package com.apress.myretro.persistence

import com.apress.myretro.board.RetroBoard
import org.reactivestreams.Publisher
import org.slf4j.LoggerFactory
import org.springframework.data.mongodb.core.mapping.event.
    ReactiveBeforeConvertCallback
import org.springframework.stereotype.Component
```

```kotlin
import reactor.core.publisher.Mono
import java.util.*

@Component
class RetroBoardPersistenceCallback : ReactiveBeforeConvertCallback<Ret
roBoard> {
    override fun onBeforeConvert(entity: RetroBoard, collection: String):
            Publisher<RetroBoard> {
        with(entity) {
            id = id ?: UUID.randomUUID()
            cards = cards ?: mutableListOf()
            LOG.info("[CALLBACK] onBeforeConvert {}", this)
        }
        return Mono.just(entity)
    }
    companion object {
        val LOG = LoggerFactory.getLogger(RetroBoardPersistenceCallback::
        class.java)
    }
}
```

Notice in the `RetroBoardPersistenceCallback` class that we are now using the `ReactiveBeforeConvertCallback` interface. This interface has a method, called `onBeforeConvert`, that expects to return a `Publisher`. This method will be used to add a UUID when a `RetroBoard` entity doesn't have one. Also note that we are returning a `Mono`, in this case with the `Mono.just()` method. Again, this is one way to implement this business rule, but you can add logic to the service if you prefer. With the code in Listing 7-13, we are making our service as clean as possible.

Next, open/create the `advice` package and the `RetroBoardAdvice` class. See Listing 7-14.

Listing 7-14. src/main/kotlin/apress/com/myretro/advice/RetroBoardAdvice.kt

```kotlin
package com.apress.myretro.advice

import com.apress.myretro.board.RetroBoard
import com.apress.myretro.exception.RetroBoardNotFoundException
import org.aspectj.lang.ProceedingJoinPoint
```

```
import org.aspectj.lang.annotation.Around
import org.aspectj.lang.annotation.Aspect
import org.slf4j.LoggerFactory
import org.springframework.stereotype.Component
import reactor.core.publisher.Mono
import java.util.*

@Component
@Aspect
class RetroBoardAdvice {
    @Around(
        "execution(* com.apress.myretro.persistence.RetroBoardRepository.
        findById(..))"
    )
    @Throws(Throwable::class)
    fun checkFindRetroBoard(proceedingJoinPoint: Proceeding
    JoinPoint): Any {
        LOG.info("[ADVICE] {}", proceedingJoinPoint.signature.name)
        try {
            return proceedingJoinPoint.proceed(
                arrayOf<Any>(
                    UUID.fromString(proceedingJoinPoint.args[0].toString())
                )
            ) as Mono<RetroBoard>
        }catch (e:NullPointerException) {
            throw RetroBoardNotFoundException()
        }
    }

    companion object {
        val LOG = LoggerFactory.getLogger(RetroBoardAdvice::class.java)
    }
}
```

The RetroBoardAdvice class will help intercept the calls to avoid any other errors (we are removing some concerns from the main code, to avoid code tangling and scattering). Because we are using Reactive programming, we need to use either the Flux type or Mono type, and in this case we are using the Mono type.

Next, create/open the service package with the RetroBoardService class. See
Listing 7-15.

Listing 7-15. src/main/kotlin/apress/com/myretro/service/
RetroBoardService.kt

```kotlin
package com.apress.myretro.service

import com.apress.myretro.board.Card
import com.apress.myretro.board.RetroBoard
import com.apress.myretro.persistence.RetroBoardRepository
import org.springframework.beans.factory.annotation.Autowired
import org.springframework.stereotype.Service
import reactor.core.publisher.Flux
import reactor.core.publisher.Mono
import java.util.*

@Service
class RetroBoardService {
    @Autowired
    lateinit var retroBoardRepository: RetroBoardRepository

    fun save(domain: RetroBoard): Mono<RetroBoard> =
        retroBoardRepository.save(domain)

    fun findById(uuid: UUID): Mono<RetroBoard> =
        retroBoardRepository.findById(uuid)

    fun findAll(): Flux<RetroBoard> =
        retroBoardRepository.findAll()

    fun delete(uuid: UUID): Mono<Void> =
        retroBoardRepository.deleteById(uuid)

    fun findAllCardsFromRetroBoard(uuid: UUID): Flux<Card> =
        findById(uuid).flatMapIterable(RetroBoard::cards)

    fun addCardToRetroBoard(uuid: UUID, card: Card): Mono<Card> =
        findById(uuid).flatMap<Card>{ retroBoard: RetroBoard ->
            card.id = card.id ?: UUID.randomUUID()
```

```kotlin
        retroBoard.cards!!.add(card)
        save(retroBoard).thenReturn<Card>(card)
    }

    fun findCardByUUID(uuidCard: UUID): Mono<Card> =
        retroBoardRepository.findRetroBoardByIdAndCardId(uuidCard)
            .flatMapIterable(RetroBoard::cards)
            .filter{ card -> card.id == uuidCard }
            .next()

    fun removeCardByUUID(uuid: UUID, cardUUID: UUID): Mono<Void> {
        findById(uuid)
            .doOnNext { retroBoard: RetroBoard ->
                retroBoard.cards!!.removeIf { card -> card.id == cardUUID }
            }
            .flatMap { entity: RetroBoard ->
                save(entity)
            }
            .subscribe()
        return Mono.empty()
    }
}
}
```

In Listing 7-15 we are using the RetroBoardRepository interface that will be injected by Spring. We are using either the Flux or Mono type depending on the service method. Every method will emit an entity type (either Flux or Mono), and somehow we need to subscribe to them. But how or where? Some of the methods interact with (i.e., are transformed by) the entities using flatMap or flatMapIterable, and even so, we are emitting these types.

We are creating a method called removeCardFromRetroBoard; take a moment and analyze it. First, we are using the findById method (in this case, the retroBoard), which will emit a Mono<RetroBoard> entity if found. Then, we can remove it using the doOnNext method, which will emit a modified Mono<RetroBoard> entity (because we are removing the Card by UUID if found). Finally, we can apply a transformation using the flatMap method (this transformation will emit a Mono<RetroBoard>). The transformation will be just to save it. Remember that you are dealing with Reactive entities, so it's necessary to subscribe() to the flow. Finally, we return just an empty Mono entity.

Next, create/open the web package and the RetroBoardController class, shown in Listing 7-16.

Listing 7-16. src/main/kotlin/apress/com/myretro/web/ RetroBoardController.kt

```kotlin
package com.apress.myretro.web

import com.apress.myretro.board.Card
import com.apress.myretro.board.RetroBoard
import com.apress.myretro.service.RetroBoardService
import org.springframework.beans.factory.annotation.Autowired
import org.springframework.http.HttpStatus
import org.springframework.web.bind.annotation.*
import reactor.core.publisher.Flux
import reactor.core.publisher.Mono
import java.util.*

@RestController
@RequestMapping("/retros")
class RetroBoardController {
    @Autowired
    private lateinit var retroBoardService: RetroBoardService

    @get:GetMapping
    val allRetroBoards: Flux<RetroBoard>
        get() = retroBoardService.findAll()

    @PostMapping
    fun saveRetroBoard(@RequestBody retroBoard: RetroBoard):
    Mono<RetroBoard> =
        retroBoardService.save(retroBoard)

    @GetMapping("/{uuid}")
    fun findRetroBoardById(@PathVariable uuid: UUID): Mono<RetroBoard> =
        retroBoardService.findById(uuid)

    @GetMapping("/{uuid}/cards")
    fun getAllCardsFromBoard(@PathVariable uuid: UUID): Flux<Card> =
        retroBoardService.findAllCardsFromRetroBoard(uuid)
```

```
@PutMapping("/{uuid}/cards")
fun addCardToRetroBoard(@PathVariable uuid: UUID, @RequestBody
card: Card):
        Mono<Card> =
    retroBoardService.addCardToRetroBoard(uuid, card)

@GetMapping("/cards/{uuidCard}")
fun getCardByUUID(@PathVariable uuidCard: UUID): Mono<Card> =
    retroBoardService.findCardByUUID(uuidCard)

@ResponseStatus(HttpStatus.NO_CONTENT)
@DeleteMapping("/{uuid}/cards/{uuidCard}")
fun deleteCardFromRetroBoard(@PathVariable uuid: UUID,
        @PathVariable uuidCard: UUID): Mono<Void> =
    retroBoardService.removeCardByUUID(uuid, uuidCard)
}
```

In the RetroBoardController class, we are using *annotation-based programming* to create the web endpoints, and in this case every endpoint will expose either Flux or Mono types. This class uses RetroBoardService and we are still emitting these types without subscription. This is because Spring WebFlux takes care of the subscription for the Reactive controllers.

Next, create/open the config package and the MyRetroConfiguration class, shown in Listing 7-17.

Listing 7-17. src/main/kotlin/apress/com/myretro/config/ MyRetroConfiguration.kt

```
package com.apress.myretro.config

import com.apress.myretro.advice.RetroBoardAdvice
import com.apress.myretro.board.Card
import com.apress.myretro.board.CardType
import com.apress.myretro.board.RetroBoard
import com.apress.myretro.service.RetroBoardService
import org.slf4j.LoggerFactory
import org.springframework.boot.context.event.ApplicationReadyEvent
```

```kotlin
import org.springframework.boot.context.properties.
EnableConfigurationProperties
import org.springframework.context.ApplicationListener
import org.springframework.context.annotation.Bean
import org.springframework.context.annotation.Configuration
import java.util.*

@EnableConfigurationProperties(MyRetroProperties::class)
@Configuration
class MyRetroConfiguration {
    @Bean
    fun ready(retroBoardService: RetroBoardService):
            ApplicationListener<ApplicationReadyEvent> {
        return ApplicationListener<ApplicationReadyEvent> { _:
        ApplicationReadyEvent ->
            LOG.info("Application Ready Event")
            val retroBoardId = UUID.fromString("9dc9b71b-a07e-418b-
            b972-40225449aff2")
            retroBoardService.save(
                RetroBoard(
                    id=retroBoardId,
                    name="Spring Boot Conference",
                    cards = mutableListOf(
                        Card(id=UUID.fromString(
                                "bb2a80a5-a0f5-4180-a6dc-80c84bc014c9"),
                            comment="Spring Boot Rocks!",
                            cardType= CardType.HAPPY),
                        Card(id=UUID.randomUUID(),
                            comment="Meet everyone in person",
                            cardType= CardType.HAPPY),
                        Card(id=UUID.randomUUID(),
                            comment="When is the next one?",
                            cardType= CardType.MEH),
                        Card(id=UUID.randomUUID(),
                            comment="Not enough time to talk to everyone",
                            cardType= CardType.SAD)
```

```
            )
          )
        ).subscribe()
      }
    }
    companion object {
        val LOG = LoggerFactory.getLogger(MyRetroConfiguration::class.java)
    }
}
```

The MyRetroConfiguration class is using the RetroBoardService, and we are saving a retroBoard. Note that the save method emits an entity. To save that entity, you need to subscribe, and that's why you use the subscribe() method. Again, in the Reactive controllers, you don't need to subscribe because Spring WebFlux will take care of that.

The exception package is like the other versions; the MyRetroProperties and UsersConfiguration haven't changed. You can reuse these classes.

Next, create/open the application.properties file. See Listing 7-18.

Listing 7-18. src/main/resources/application.properties

```
# MongoDB
spring.data.mongodb.uuid-representation=standard
spring.data.mongodb.database=retrodb
spring.data.mongodb.repositories.type=reactive

spring.docker.compose.file = ./myretro/docker-compose.yaml
```

The only property in application.properties that is important here is spring. data.mongodb.uuid-representation. Recall that it is important because MongoDB uses its own implementation to deal with UUID objects, and if you want to use the UUID, you need to use this property. Also notice that we specified the name of the database. If you don't set the name, Spring Boot auto-configuration will use test by default, but you need to change it in your database setup (docker-compose.yaml). Also, we are using a property to set the repositories to reactive, even though this is set by Spring Boot auto-configuration.

Next, create/open the docker-compose.yaml file. See Listing 7-19.

Listing 7-19. The docker-compose.yaml File

```
version: "3.1"
services:
  mongo:
    image: mongo
    restart: always
    environment:
      MONGO_INITDB_DATABASE: retrodb
    ports:
      - "27017:27017"
```

The docker-compose.yaml file is the same as the previous version—nothing different is needed to use Reactive programming.

Running My Retro App

You can run My Retro App by using the IDE or the following command:

./gradlew clean bootRun

You should see the Docker containers starting up and the Netty server ready to accept requests. You can do some testing using VS Code (and the REST Client plugin called humao. rest-client). Or, if you are using the IntelliJ Enterprise Edition, you have it by default.

Create/open the myretro.http file. See Listing 7-20.

Listing 7-20. src/http/myretro.http

```
### Get All Retro Boards
GET http://localhost:8080/retros
Content-Type: application/json
### Get Retro Board
GET http://localhost:8080/retros/9dc9b71b-a07e-418b-b972-40225449aff2
Content-Type: application/json
### Get All Cards from Retro Board
GET http://localhost:8080/retros/9dc9b71b-a07e-418b-b972-40225449aff2/cards
Content-Type: application/json
### Get Single Card No Retro Board
```

```
GET http://localhost:8080/retros/cards/bb2a80a5-a0f5-4180-a6dc-80c84bc014c9
Content-Type: application/json
### Create a Retro Board
POST http://localhost:8080/retros
Content-Type: application/json
{
  "name": "Spring Boot Videos 2024"
}
### Add Card to Retro
PUT http://localhost:8080/retros/9dc9b71b-a07e-418b-b972-40225449aff2/cards
Content-Type: application/json
{
  "comment": "We are back in business",
  "cardType": "HAPPY"
}
### Delete Card from Retro
DELETE http://localhost:8080/retros/9dc9b71b-a07e-418b-b972-40225449aff2/
cards/bb2a80a5-a0f5-4180-a6dc-80c84bc014c9
Content-Type: application/json
```

The `myretro.http` file allows you to execute REST calls to different endpoints. The "Testing the Users App" section already covered the `WebClient` and `WebTestClient` classes; you can create your own integration test.

Summary

Now you know what to do when you need to create a Reactive application with Spring Boot and Project Reactor. This chapter explained Reactive programming and the many implementations from different frameworks.

You learned about Project Reactor and how it exposes the new `Flux` and `Mono` types to make it easier for your application to emit new flows of streaming data.

You saw the different ways to create a web API using functional or annotation-based reactive applications, where you emit the results using `Flux` or `Mono`. Although we didn't mention it, you can still use something like `Mono<ResponseEntity<RetroBoard>>` to return a response that can have custom HTTP headers, for example.

Chapter 8 explains how to test with Spring Boot.

CHAPTER 8

Spring Boot Testing

Felipe Gutierrez[a*]

[a] 4109 Rillcrest Grove Way Fuquay Varina, NC 27526-3562, Albuquerque, NM, USA

Spring Testing Framework

One of the main ideas of the Spring Framework is to encourage developers to create simple and loosely coupled classes and to program to interfaces, making the software more robust and extensible. The Spring Framework provides the tools for making unit and integration testing easy (actually, you don't need Spring to test the functionality of your system if you program to interfaces). In other words, your application should be testable using either the JUnit or TestNG test engine with objects (by simple instantiation using the new operator)—without Spring or any other container.

The Spring Framework has several testing packages that help create unit and integration testing for applications. It offers unit testing by providing several mock objects (`Environment`, `PropertySource`, JNDI, Servlet; Reactive: `ServerHttpRequest` and `ServerHttpResponse` test utilities) that help you test your code in isolation.

One of the most commonly used testing features of the Spring Framework is integration testing. Its primary's goals are

- Managing the Spring IoC container caching between test execution

- Transaction management

- Dependency injection of test fixture instances

- Spring-specific base classes

The Spring Framework provides an easy way to do testing by integrating the `ApplicationContext` in the tests. The Spring testing module offers several ways to use the `ApplicationContext`, programmatically and through annotations:

© Peter Späth, Felipe Gutierrez 2025

P. Späth and F. Gutierrez, *Pro Spring Boot 3 with Kotlin*, https://doi.org/10.1007/979-8-8688-1131-9_8

- BootstrapWith: A class-level annotation that configures how the Spring TestContext Framework is bootstrapped.

- @ContextConfiguration: Defines class-level metadata to determine how to load and configure an ApplicationContext for integration tests. This is a must-have annotation for your classes because that's where the ApplicationContext loads all your bean definitions.

- @WebAppConfiguration: A class-level annotation to declare that the ApplicationContext that loads for an integration test should be a WebApplicationContext.

- @ActiveProfile: A class-level annotation to declare which bean definition profile(s) should be active when loading an ApplicationContext for an integration test.

- @TestPropertySource: A class-level annotation that configures the locations of property files and inline properties that are added to the PropertySources in the Environment for an ApplicationContext loaded for an integration test.

- @DirtiesContext: Indicates that the underlying Spring ApplicationContext has been modified or corrupted during the execution of a test (for example, the state of a singleton bean has changed) and should be closed.

The Spring Framework offers many more annotations, including @TestExecutionListeners, @Commit, @Rollback, @BeforeTransaction, @AfterTransaction, @Sql, @SqlGroup, @SqlConfig, @Timed, @Repeat, @IfProfileValue, and so forth.

As you can see, you have a lot of choices when you test with the Spring Framework. Normally, you always use the @RunWith annotation, which wires up all the test framework goodies. For example, the following code shows how you can do unit/ integration testing using just Spring:

```
@RunWith(SpringRunner.class)
@ContextConfiguration({"/app-config.xml", "/test-data-access-config.xml"})
@ActiveProfiles("dev")
@Transactional
class UsersTests {
```

```
        @Test
        fun userPersistenceTest(){
//...
}
}
```

Let's now explore the Spring Boot set of features that enable you to create better unit, integration, and isolation tests (per layer) with ease.

Spring Boot Testing Framework

Spring Boot uses the power of the Spring Testing Framework by enhancing and adding new annotations and features that make testing easier for developers.

If you want to start using all the testing features provided by Spring Boot, you only need to add the `spring-boot-starter-test` dependency with a scope test to your application. This dependency is already in place if you used the Spring Initializr (https://start.spring.io) to create your projects.

The `spring-boot-starter-test` dependency provides several test frameworks that play very well with all the Spring Boot testing features: Junit 5, AssertJ, Hamcrest, Mockito, JSONassert, JsonPath, and the Spring Test and Spring Boot Test utilities and integration support for Spring Boot applications. If you are using a different test framework, it likely will also play very nicely with the Spring Boot Test module; you only need to include those dependencies manually.

Spring Boot provides the `@SpringBootTest` annotation, which simplifies the way you can test Spring apps. Normally, with Spring testing, you must add several annotations to test a particular feature or functionality of your app, but not in Spring Boot. The `@SpringBootTest` annotation's `webEnvironment` parameter accepts values such as `RANDOM_PORT` or `DEFINED_PORT`, `MOCK`, and `NONE`. The `@SpringBootTest` annotation also defines `properties` (properties that you want to test for different values), `args` (for arguments you normally passed in the command line, such `@SpringBootTest(args = "--app.name=Users"))`, `classes` (a list of classes in which you declared your beans using the `@Configuration` annotation), and `useMainMethod`, with values such as `ALWAYS` and `WHEN_AVAILABLE` (meaning that it will use the `main` method of the application to set the `ApplicationContext` to run the tests).

The following sections show you some of the main test classes from the two different projects that you have been developing in this book.

Note   This chapter uses the code in the 08-testing folder. You have access to the code at this Apress website: https://www.apress.com/gp/services/source-code.

Testing Web Apps with a Mock Environment

The @SpringBootTest annotation by default uses a mock environment, meaning that it doesn't start the server. Nevertheless, it's ready for testing web endpoints. To use this feature, you need to use the MockMvc class along with the @AutoConfigurationMockMvc annotation as a marker for the test class. This annotation will configure the MockMvc class and all its dependencies, such as filters, security (if any), and so forth. If you were using just Spring (no Spring Boot), you could use the MockMvc class, but you would need to do some extra steps because it relies on WebApplicationContext. Fortunately, with Spring Boot, you only need to inject it with the @Autowired annotation.

Let's look at the Users App project in the test folder. The name of the class is UserMockMvcTests. See Listing 8-1.

Listing 8-1.   src/test/kotlin/apress/com/users/UserMockMvcTests.kt

```
package com.apress.users
```

```
import org.hamcrest.Matchers
import org.junit.jupiter.api.Test
import org.springframework.beans.factory.annotation.Autowired
import org.springframework.boot.test.autoconfigure.web.servlet.
AutoConfigureMockMvc
import org.springframework.boot.test.context.SpringBootTest
import org.springframework.test.context.ActiveProfiles
import org.springframework.test.web.servlet.MockMvc
import org.springframework.test.web.servlet.request.MockMvcRequestBuilders
import org.springframework.test.web.servlet.result.MockMvcResultMatchers
```

```kotlin
@SpringBootTest
@AutoConfigureMockMvc
@ActiveProfiles("mockMvc")
class UserMockMvcTests {
    @Autowired
    private lateinit var mockMvc: MockMvc

    @Test
    @Throws(Exception::class)
    fun createUserTests() {
        val location = mockMvc.perform(
            MockMvcRequestBuilders.post("/users")
                .contentType("application/json")
                .content(
                    """
                    {
                        "email": "dummy@email.com",
                        "name": "Dummy",
                        "password": "aw2sOmeR!",
                        "gravatarUrl": "https://www.gravatar.com/avatar/
                        fb651279f4712e209991e05610dfb03a?d=wavatar",
                        "userRole": ["USER"],
                        "active": true
                    }
                    """.trimIndent()
                )
        )
            .andExpect(MockMvcResultMatchers.status().isCreated())
            .andExpect(MockMvcResultMatchers.header().exists("Location"))
            .andReturn().response.getHeader("Location")
        mockMvc.perform(MockMvcRequestBuilders.get(location!!))
            .andExpect(MockMvcResultMatchers.status().isOk())
            .andExpect(MockMvcResultMatchers.jsonPath("$.email").exists())
```

```kotlin
            .andExpect(MockMvcResultMatchers.jsonPath("$.active").
            value(true))
    }

    @Throws(Exception::class)
    @Test
    fun allUsersTests() {
        mockMvc.perform(MockMvcRequestBuilders.get("/users"))
            .andExpect(MockMvcResultMatchers.status().isOk())
            .andExpect(MockMvcResultMatchers.jsonPath("$[0].name").
            value("Dummy"))
            .andExpect(
                MockMvcResultMatchers.jsonPath("$..active")
                    .value<Iterable<Boolean>>(Matchers.hasItem(true))
            )
            .andExpect(MockMvcResultMatchers
                .jsonPath("$[*]").value(Matchers.hasSize<Any>(1)))
    }
}
```

Let's analyze the UserMockMvcTests class:

- @SpringBootTest: This annotation is essential for testing with Spring
  Boot. It provides the SpringBootContextLoader as the default
  ContextLoader. It searches for all the @Configuration classes,
  allows custom Environment properties, and can register either
  a TestRestTemplate (which we used in previous chapters when
  running the tests) or a WebTestClient (for Reactive apps, such as
  MongoDB). As mentioned, it also accepts parameters where you can
  add the type of web environment—by default, MOCK–arguments, and
  properties.

- @AutoConfigureMockMvc: This annotation creates the MockMvc bean
  that can be injected to perform all the server-side testing, among
  other features, such as filters, security, and so on.

- @ActiveProfiles: This annotation helps run only the defined beans under the name set (in this case mockMvc). This is helpful when you have a lot of testing and you need a certain behavior. This annotation will activate the mockMvc profile. Normally, in every configuration class, you can add the @Profile({"<profile-name>"}) annotation to specify which beans are needed for such profile(s).

- MockMvc: This bean class is the entry point for all the server-side testing, and it supports request builders and result matchers that can be combined with different test libraries such as Mockito, Hamcrest, and AssertJ, among others.

- MockMvcRequestBuilders: The MockMvc class has a perform method that accepts a request builder, and the MockMvcRequestBuilders class provides a fluent API where you can perform the get, post, put, and so on. These request builders accept the URI in the form of a path (it's not necessary to add the complete URL), and you can build on whatever request you need, such as adding headers, content type, content, and so on. This is because it returns a MockHttpServletRequestBuilder class, which includes a lot of customization for the request.

- Hamcrest and MockMvcResultMatchers: After calling the perform method (from MockMvc), you have access to a ResultsActions interface, where you can add all the expectations on the results of the executed request. This includes the andExpect(ResultMatcher), andExpectAll(ResultMatcher...), andDo(ResultHandler), and andReturn() methods. The andReturn() method returns a MvcResult interface, which is also a fluent API where you can get anything that brings the request (content, headers, etc.). Because some of these methods require a ResultMatcher interface, you can find implementation using the Hamcrest library (such as contains, hasSize, etc.). In our tests, we use the jsonPath result matchers that allow us to interact with the JSON response.

It's important to mention that these tests need something extra that allows them to use the repositories, which is covered in the following sections.

Using Mocking and Spying Beans

Spring Boot testing includes two annotations that allow you to mock Spring Beans, which is helpful when some of these beans depend on external services, such a third-party REST endpoints, database connections, and so forth. If one of these services is unavailable, these annotations can help. First look at the UserMockBeanTests class. See Listing 8-2.

Listing 8-2. src/test/kotlin/apress/com/users/UserMockBeanTests.kt

```
package com.apress.users

import org.junit.jupiter.api.Test
import org.mockito.ArgumentMatchers
import org.mockito.Mockito
import org.springframework.beans.factory.annotation.Autowired
import org.springframework.boot.test.autoconfigure.web.servlet.
AutoConfigureMockMvc
import org.springframework.boot.test.context.SpringBootTest
import org.springframework.boot.test.mock.mockito.MockBean
import org.springframework.http.MediaType
import org.springframework.test.context.ActiveProfiles
import org.springframework.test.web.servlet.MockMvc
import org.springframework.test.web.servlet.request.MockMvcRequestBuilders
import org.springframework.test.web.servlet.result.MockMvcResultMatchers

@SpringBootTest
@AutoConfigureMockMvc
@ActiveProfiles("mockBean")
class UserMockBeanTests {
    @Autowired
    private lateinit var mockMvc: MockMvc

    @MockBean
    private lateinit var userRepository: UserRepository

    @Test
    @Throws(Exception::class)
```

```kotlin
fun saveUsers() {
    val user = UserBuilder.createUser()
        .withName("Dummy")
        .withEmail("dummy@email.com")
        .active()
        .withRoles(UserRole.USER)
        .withPassword("aw3sOm3R!")
        .build()
    Mockito.'when'<Any>(userRepository.save(ArgumentMatchers.any()))
        .thenReturn(user)
    mockMvc.perform(
        MockMvcRequestBuilders.post("/users")
            .contentType(MediaType.APPLICATION_JSON)
            .content(
                """
    {
                    "email": "dummy@email.com",
                    "name": "Dummy",
                    "password": "aw2sOmeR!",
                    "gravatarUrl": "https://www.gravatar.com/avatar/
                    fb651279f4712e209991e05610dfb03a?d=wavatar",
                    "userRole": ["USER"],
                    "active": true
                }
                """.trimIndent()
            )
    )
        .andExpect(MockMvcResultMatchers.status().isCreated())
        .andExpect(MockMvcResultMatchers.jsonPath("$.name").
        value(user.name))
        .andExpect(MockMvcResultMatchers.jsonPath("$.email").
        value(user.email))
        .andExpect(MockMvcResultMatchers.jsonPath("$.userRole").
        isArray())
```

```
        .andExpect(MockMvcResultMatchers.jsonPath("$.userRole[0]").
        value("USER"))
    Mockito.verify(userRepository, Mockito.times(1)).save(
        Mockito.any(
            User::class.java
        )
    )
  }
}
```

The `UserMockBeanTests` class includes the following:

- `@MockBean`: This annotation mocks the object that's marked, enabling you to add the necessary behavior and outcome for that object. It replaces the object implementation, so it can be easily customized. To use this bean, you need to use a framework such as Mockito. In the test in Listing 8-2, we are mocking the `when()` `UserRepository` object, meaning that we don't need any connection or anything related to the database; basically, we are mocking its behavior.

- `Mockito.*`: The Mockito library helps you add the behavior to the mock bean (in this case, the `UserRepository`) with the `thenReturn()` methods. Then we can verify the behavior after we perform the call with the `verify()` method. Note that the Mockito library has a lot of useful fluent APIs. In this test, we are specifying that when the `UserRepository` uses the `save` method (with any value), it will return the user we specified, then at the end we verify that our mock bean was called once when saving the `User` object.

Remember, the `@MockBean` will replace the actual bean with a mock implementation that is easy to modify to get the desired behavior.

Next, take a look at the `UserSpyBeanTests` class, shown in Listing 8-3.

Listing 8-3. src/test/kotlin/apress/com/users/UserSpyBeanTests.kt

```
package com.apress.users

import org.junit.jupiter.api.Test
import org.mockito.Mockito
import org.springframework.beans.factory.annotation.Autowired
```

```kotlin
import org.springframework.boot.test.autoconfigure.web.servlet.
AutoConfigureMockMvc
import org.springframework.boot.test.context.SpringBootTest
import org.springframework.boot.test.mock.mockito.SpyBean
import org.springframework.test.context.ActiveProfiles
import org.springframework.test.web.servlet.MockMvc
import org.springframework.test.web.servlet.request.MockMvcRequestBuilders
import org.springframework.test.web.servlet.result.MockMvcResultMatchers
import java.util.*

@SpringBootTest
@AutoConfigureMockMvc
@ActiveProfiles("spyBean")
class UserSpyBeanTests {
    @Autowired
    private lateinit var mockMvc: MockMvc

    @SpyBean
    private lateinit var userRepository: UserRepository

    @Test
    @Throws(Exception::class)
    fun testGetAllUsers() {
        val mockUsers: List<User> = listOf(
            UserBuilder.createUser()
                .withName("Ximena")
                .withEmail("ximena@email.com")
                .build(),
            UserBuilder.createUser()
                .withName("Norma")
                .withEmail("norma@email.com")
                .build()
        )
        Mockito.doReturn(mockUsers).'when'(userRepository)!!.findAll()
        mockMvc.perform(MockMvcRequestBuilders.get("/users"))
            .andExpect(MockMvcResultMatchers.status().isOk())
            .andExpect(MockMvcResultMatchers.jsonPath("$[0].name").
            value("Ximena"))
```

```
        .andExpect(MockMvcResultMatchers.jsonPath("$[1].name").
        value("Norma"))
    Mockito.verify(userRepository).findAll()
  }
}
```

Let's analyze the `UserSpyBeanTests` class:

- `@SpyBean`: This annotation creates a spy bean. A *spy bean* is similar to a mock object, but it retains the original behavior of the real bean. It allows you to intercept and verify method invocations and specify specific behavior for selected methods while keeping the rest of the methods intact. In the example in Listing 8-3, we use the `doReturn()` method when the `UserRepository` instance is used, and when we call the `findAll()` method. At the end, we are verifying that the actual `findAll()` method was called.

Testcontainers

Testcontainers (`https://testcontainers.com/`) is an open source framework that allows you to run some services in a Docker container through unit testing frameworks. Spring Boot now has the capability to use Testcontainers with ease, without any configuration. You simply include two dependencies in your Maven or Gradle build files: `org.springframework.boot:spring-boot-testcontainers` and `org.testcontainers:junit-jupiter` (with `scope test` for Maven and `testImplementation` for Gradle).

Previous chapters demonstrated the use of the `spring-boot-docker-compose` feature, which reads a `docker-compose.yaml` file provided the developer and allows you to run your app by creating the necessary environment. Recall that this feature works only when running the app, not when executing the tests. So, the solution is Testcontainers!

With Testcontainers, Spring Boot introduces the following annotations:

- `@Testcontainers`: Starts and stops the containers; this annotation looks for every `@Container` annotation.

- `@Container`: Sets up all the necessary configuration that is required for the Testcontainers framework to initialize.

- **@ServiceConnection**: Takes care of creating the default connection
  details to be used with your application. In this case, it depends
  on which technology you use. For example, in this chapter, we are
  using Postgres for the Users App project and MongoDB for the My
  Retro App project, so we must include the necessary Testcontainers
  dependency—`org.testcontainers:postgresql` or `org.
  testcontainers:mongodb`, respectively.

You will find out that, with Testcontainers in Spring Boot, it will normally take some
time to pull down the image (if it's not there) and start the testing. For this behavior, the
Spring Boot team also created the `@RestartScope` annotation. It allows you to re-create
the container (keep it running) when your app is restarted if you are using Spring Boot
Dev Tools. One of the main features of Dev Tools is that you can use it in your favorite
IDE and it will restart your app in any new file modification when it's saved. The normal
steps without Dev Tools include modifying your app, saving it, and then either stopping
or restarting it. With Spring Boot Dev Tools, you don't need to do this, because it
automatically restarts the app when the file is saved.

So, let's look at how to use Testcontainers with Spring Boot. The following snippet
shows you how to use the `@Testcontainers`, `@Container`, and `@ServiceConnection`
annotations and how to enable the PostgreSQL container:

```
@SpringBootTest
@Testcontainers
class UserTests {
    companion object {
        @Container
        @ServiceConnection
        val PostgreSQLContainer<*> postgreSQLContainer =
            PostgreSQLContainer("postgres:latest")
    }
    // Your test here ...
}
```

In the following sections, you'll see this as part of the test.

Spring Boot Testing Slices

So far, the book hasn't used integration testing because you normally need the whole server to do such tests. In some other chapters we used this a lot, and we use the TestRestTemplate to perform some calls to the web application using the SpringBootTest.WebEnvironment.RANDOM_PORT to get the port and such.

Spring Boot offers a way to test only the layers you need instead of testing the whole environment. Suppose you only need to parse the JSON response and verify that the serialization was done correctly, the values of the field match, and so forth. With Spring Boot, you don't need the whole environment for that. The Spring Boot slice testing feature allows you to test every layer separately, including the controller layer, the data layer, and the domain layer.

- @WebMvcTest

  Purpose: Tests Spring MVC controllers in isolation.

  Includes: Web layer components (controllers, filters, view resolvers, etc.).

  Excludes: Service layer, repository layer, and other non-web components.

  Suitable For: Testing the behavior of controllers, request mappings, validation, and rendering views (if applicable).

- @DataJpaTest

  Purpose: Tests Spring Data JPA repositories in isolation.

  Includes: JPA repositories, entity classes, and related configuration.

  Excludes: Service layer, web layer, and other non-JPA components.

  Suitable For: Testing repository CRUD operations, queries, and custom repository methods.

- @JdbcTest

  Purpose: Tests data access code that uses plain JDBC (without Spring Data JPA).

  Includes: DataSource configuration, JDBC templates, and SQL scripts.

Excludes: JPA repositories, web layer, and other non-JDBC components.

Suitable For: Testing low-level JDBC operations, SQL scripts, and data access logic not using JPA.

- `@JsonTest`

  Purpose: Tests JSON serialization and deserialization.

  Includes: Jackson or Gson configurations and custom serializers/ deserializers.

  Excludes: Web layer, data access layers, and other non-JSON components.

  Suitable For: Verifying correct serialization and deserialization of your objects to and from JSON.

- `@RestClientTest`

  Purpose: Tests Spring's RestTemplate- or WebClient-based REST clients.

  Includes: REST client beans, error handling configurations, and related components.

  Excludes: Web layer (server-side), data access layers, and other non-REST client components.

  Suitable For: Verifying REST client configurations, request building, response handling, and error scenarios.

- `@DataMongoTest`

  Purpose: Tests Spring Data MongoDB repositories in isolation.

  Includes: MongoDB repositories, entity classes, and related configuration.

  Excludes: Web layer, JPA components, and other non-MongoDB components.

  Suitable For: Testing repository operations with MongoDB, queries, and custom repository methods.

- @SpringBootTest (Special Case)

  Purpose: Not strictly a "slice," but provides a way to test the full application context.

  Includes: All Spring Beans and configurations.

  Suitable For: End-to-end tests or integration tests that need the complete application context.

Let's start by looking at the @JsonTest annotation.

@JsonTest

@JsonTest is an annotation that allows you to test your JSON serialization and deserialization. This annotation also auto-configures the right mapper support if it finds any of these libraries in your classpath: Jackson, Gson, or JSONB.

Listing 8-4 shows the UserJsonTest class.

Listing 8-4. src/test/kotlin/apress/com/users/UserJsonTest.kt

```
package com.apress.users

import com.apress.users.UserGravatar.getGravatarUrlFromEmail
import jakarta.validation.ConstraintViolationException
import jakarta.validation.Validation
import org.assertj.core.api.Assertions.*
import org.junit.jupiter.api.Test
import org.springframework.beans.factory.annotation.Autowired
import org.springframework.boot.test.autoconfigure.json.JsonTest
import org.springframework.boot.test.json.JacksonTester
import java.io.IOException

@JsonTest
class UserJsonTests {
    @Autowired
    private lateinit var jacksonTester: JacksonTester<User>
```

```kotlin
@Test
@Throws(IOException::class)
fun serializeUserJsonTest() {
    val user =
    UserBuilder.createUser(Validation.buildDefaultValidatorFactory().
    validator)
        .withEmail("dummy@email.com")
        .withPassword("aw2s0me")
        .withName("Dummy")
        .withRoles(UserRole.USER)
        .active().build()
    val json = jacksonTester.write(user)
    assertThat(json).extractingJsonPathValue("$.email")
        .isEqualTo("dummy@email.com")
    assertThat(json).extractingJsonPathArrayValue<Any>("$.
    userRole").size()
        .isEqualTo(1)
    assertThat(json).extractingJsonPathBooleanValue("$.active").
    isTrue()
    assertThat(json).extractingJsonPathValue("$.gravatarUrl").
    isNotNull()
    assertThat(json).extractingJsonPathValue("$.gravatarUrl").
    isEqualTo(
        getGravatarUrlFromEmail(user.email!!)
    )
}

@Test
@Throws(IOException::class)
fun serializeUserJsonFileTest() {
    val user =
    UserBuilder.createUser(Validation.buildDefaultValidatorFactory().
    validator)
        .withEmail("dummy@email.com")
        .withPassword("aw2s0me")
        .withName("Dummy")
```

```kotlin
            .withRoles(UserRole.USER)
            .active().build()
        println(user)
        val json = jacksonTester.write(user)

        // You need to add the user.json file in the
        // src/test/resources/com/apress/users folder
        assertThat(json).isEqualToJson("user.json")
    }

    @Test
    @Throws(Exception::class)
    fun deserializeUserJsonTest() {
        val userJson = """
                {
                    "email": "dummy@email.com",
                    "name": "Dummy",
                    "password": "aw2sOme",
                    "userRole": ["USER"],
                    "active": true
                }
            """.trimIndent()
        val user = jacksonTester.parseObject(userJson)
        assertThat(user.email).isEqualTo("dummy@email.com")
        assertThat(user.password).isEqualTo("aw2sOme")
        assertThat(user.active).isTrue()
    }

    @Test
    fun userValidationTest() {
        assertThatExceptionOfType(
            ConstraintViolationException::class.java
        ).isThrownBy {
            UserBuilder.createUser(Validation.buildDefault
            ValidatorFactory().validator)
                .withEmail("dummy@email.com")
```

```
            .withName("Dummy")
            .withRoles(UserRole.USER)
            .active().build()
    }

    // Junit 5
    val exception: Exception = org.junit.jupiter.api.Assertions.
    assertThrows(
        ConstraintViolationException::class.java
    ) {
        UserBuilder.createUser(Validation.buildDefault
        ValidatorFactory().validator)
            .withName("Dummy")
            .withRoles(UserRole.USER)
            .active().build()
    }
    val expectedMessage = "email: Email cannot be empty"
    assertThat(exception.message).contains(expectedMessage)
    }
}
```

The UserJsonTest class includes the following:

- @JsonTest: This annotation marks this class as only JSON serialization. It auto-configures the test based on what's in the classpath and on what dependency library you are using—Jackson (comes with spring-boot-starter-web as default), Jsonb, or Gson.

- JacksonTester: This class takes care of the *serialization* and *deserialization* of the domain class. It uses the Jackson library (the default) and the ObjectMapper class to do the serialization.

- JsonContent: This class includes the content from a JSON tester, which is useful to get the values from the serialization.

- UserBuilder: This class receives a Validation class, which helps inspect and validate the values of fields marked with @NotBlank or @NotNull annotations.

- Validation: This class belongs to the Jakarta validation package. It helps review and validate the fields marked with annotations, such as @NotBlank, @NoNull, and so on.

- assertThat: We are using the AssertJ package to use the assertations for serialization and deserialization in this class.

- assertThatExceptionOfType: This class helps identify the type of error or exception thrown during testing. In Listing 8-4, we are creating a User class that doesn't comply with the @NotBlank annotation, and because of that, this class identifies it as a ConstraintViolationException exception.

- assertThrows: We can do the same with this assertThrows call. This is a different way to accomplish the same asserts.

As you can see, doing tests on your domain is simpler than ever—no more waiting for a response or a particular service—and you can test your own domain schemas by doing serialization and deserialization of your classes. Also note that you can test against JSON files, in this case the user.json file. This file must be placed in the src/test/resources/com/apress/users folder in order to be picked up by the test framework.

@WebMvcTest

If you can do standalone domain/schemas tests, you might wonder if you can do them over your web controllers? Yes, you can! You can use the @WebMvcTest annotation to test only the web endpoint—the controllers. The @WebMvcTest annotation auto-configures all the Spring MVC infrastructure, but it will be limited just to the @RestController, the annotated classes, the Filter interface implementations, and all other web-related classes. By default, the annotation sets the webEnvironment to MOCK, which means that this annotation inherits from the @AutoConfigureMockMvc, which in turn means that you can use the MockMvc class.

Listing 8-5 shows the UserControllerTests class.

Listing 8-5. src/main/kotlin/apress/com/users/UserControllerTests.kt

```kotlin
package com.apress.users

import com.fasterxml.jackson.databind.ObjectMapper
import org.junit.jupiter.api.Test
import org.mockito.Mockito
import org.springframework.beans.factory.annotation.Autowired
import org.springframework.boot.test.autoconfigure.web.servlet.WebMvcTest
import org.springframework.boot.test.mock.mockito.MockBean
import org.springframework.http.MediaType
import org.springframework.test.web.servlet.MockMvc
import org.springframework.test.web.servlet.request.
MockMvcRequestBuilders as MMRB
import org.springframework.test.web.servlet.result.MockMvcResultHandlers
import org.springframework.test.web.servlet.result.MockMvcResultMatchers
import java.util.*

@WebMvcTest(controllers = [UsersController::class])
class UserControllerTests {
    @Autowired
    private lateinit var mockMvc: MockMvc

    @MockBean
    private lateinit var userRepository: UserRepository

    @Throws(Exception::class)
    @Test
    fun allUsersTest() {
            Mockito.'when'(userRepository.findAll()).thenReturn(
                listOf(
                    UserBuilder.createUser()
                        .withName("Ximena")
                        .withEmail("ximena@email.com")
                        .active()
                        .withRoles(UserRole.USER, UserRole.ADMIN)
                        .withPassword("aw3sOm3R!")
                        .build(),
```

```kotlin
                            UserBuilder.createUser()
                                .withName("Norma")
                                .withEmail("norma@email.com")
                                .active()
                                .withRoles(UserRole.USER)
                                .withPassword("aw3sOm3R!")
                                .build()
                    )
                )
            mockMvc.perform(MMRB.get("/users"))
                .andDo(MockMvcResultHandlers.print())
                .andExpect(MockMvcResultMatchers.status().isOk())
                .andExpect(MockMvcResultMatchers.content()
                    .contentType(MediaType.APPLICATION_JSON))
                .andExpect(MockMvcResultMatchers.jsonPath("$[0].active").
                value(true))
        }

    @Test
    @Throws(Exception::class)
    fun newUserTest() {
        val user = UserBuilder.createUser()
            .withName("Dummy")
            .withEmail("dummy@email.com")
            .active()
            .withRoles(UserRole.USER, UserRole.ADMIN)
            .withPassword("aw3sOm3R!")
            .build()
        Mockito.'when'(userRepository.save<User>(user)).thenReturn(user)
        mockMvc.perform(
            MMRB.post("/users")
                .content(toJson(user))
                .contentType(MediaType.APPLICATION_JSON)
        )
            .andDo(MockMvcResultHandlers.print())
            .andExpect(MockMvcResultMatchers.status().isCreated())
```

```kotlin
        .andExpect(MockMvcResultMatchers.content()
            .contentType(MediaType.APPLICATION_JSON))
        .andExpect(MockMvcResultMatchers.jsonPath("$.email")
            .value("dummy@email.com"))
}

@Test
@Throws(Exception::class)
fun findUserByEmailTest() {
    val user = UserBuilder.createUser()
        .withName("Dummy")
        .withEmail("dummy@email.com")
        .active()
        .withRoles(UserRole.USER, UserRole.ADMIN)
        .withPassword("aw3sOm3R!")
        .build()
    Mockito.'when'<Optional<User>>(userRepository.findById
    (user.email!!))
            .thenReturn(
        Optional.of<User>(user)
    )
    mockMvc.perform(
        MMRB.get("/users/{email}", user.email)
            .contentType(MediaType.APPLICATION_JSON)
    )
        .andDo(MockMvcResultHandlers.print())
        .andExpect(MockMvcResultMatchers.status().isOk())
        .andExpect(MockMvcResultMatchers.content()
            .contentType(MediaType.APPLICATION_JSON))
        .andExpect(MockMvcResultMatchers.jsonPath("$.email")
            .value("dummy@email.com"))
}

@Test
@Throws(Exception::class)
fun deleteUserByEmailTest() {
```

```
        val user = UserBuilder.createUser()
            .withEmail("dummy@email.com")
            .build()
        Mockito.doNothing().'when'<UserRepository?>(userRepository)
            .deleteById(user.email!!)
        mockMvc.perform(MMRB.delete("/users/{email}", user.email))
            .andExpect(MockMvcResultMatchers.status().isNoContent())
    }

    companion object {
        private fun toJson(obj: Any?): String = ObjectMapper().
        writeValueAsString(obj)
    }
}
```

The UserControllerTests class includes the following:

- @WebMvcvTest: This annotation inherits the @AutoConfiguraMockMvc annotation, so it's ready to use the MockMvc class, which also means that the webEnvironment is a MOCK. Thanks to this, we can test our web controllers without starting up the complete server to do some testing. You can declare more controllers in this annotation.

- MockMvc: As you know, this class is the entry point for the server side of the Spring MVC test support. In this case, it allows us to perform HTTP method requests on our controllers.

- @MockBean: This annotation will mock the bean behavior. This is helpful when you don't want to wait for an external service to be ready, because you can mock the behavior. In this case, we are mocking the UserRepository.

- Mockito.*: We are using the when().thenReturn to prepare our call and then perform the calls and expect the results. Also, we are using the doNothing().when() calls. As you can see, the Mockito library offers a nice fluent API that you can use in these scenarios.

Before you continue to the next section, take time to review the @WebMvcTest annotation and the UserControllerTests class in depth.

@DataJpaTest

With this annotation, you can test everything about the JPA technology. It auto-configures all the repositories and the needed entities for you to test without starting a web server or any other dependency. In other words, @DataJpaTest is dedicated to testing the data layer. It also sets the spring.jpa.show-sql property to true so that you can see the queries when the tests are been executed. Listing 8-6 shows the UserJpaRepositoryTests class.

Listing 8-6. src/test/kotlin/apress/com/users/UserJpaRepositoryTests.kt

```kotlin
package com.apress.users

import org.assertj.core.api.Assertions.*
import org.junit.jupiter.api.Test
import org.springframework.beans.factory.annotation.Autowired
import org.springframework.boot.test.autoconfigure.jdbc.
AutoConfigureTestDatabase
import org.springframework.boot.test.autoconfigure.orm.jpa.DataJpaTest
import org.springframework.boot.testcontainers.service.connection.
ServiceConnection
import org.springframework.context.annotation.Import
import org.testcontainers.containers.PostgreSQLContainer
import org.testcontainers.junit.jupiter.Container
import org.testcontainers.junit.jupiter.Testcontainers

@Import(UserConfiguration::class)
@Testcontainers
@AutoConfigureTestDatabase(replace = AutoConfigureTestDatabase.
Replace.NONE)
@DataJpaTest
class UserJpaRepositoryTests {
    @Autowired
    var userRepository: UserRepository? = null
    @Test
    fun findAllTest() {
        val expectedUsers = userRepository!!.findAll()
```

```
        assertThat(expectedUsers).isNotEmpty()
        assertThat(expectedUsers).isInstanceOf(Iterable::class.java)
        assertThat(expectedUsers).element(0).isInstanceOf(User::class.java)
        assertThat(expectedUsers).element(0).matches(User::active)
    }

    @Test
    fun saveTest() {
        val dummyUser = UserBuilder.createUser()
            .withName("Dummy")
            .withEmail("dummy@email.com")
            .active()
            .withRoles(UserRole.INFO)
            .withPassword("aw3sOm3R!")
            .build()
        val expectedUser = userRepository!!.save<User>(dummyUser)
        assertThat(expectedUser).isNotNull()
        assertThat(expectedUser).isInstanceOf(User::class.java)
        assertThat(expectedUser).hasNoNullFieldsOrProperties()
        assertThat(expectedUser.active).isTrue()
    }

    @Test
    fun findByIdTest() {
        val expectedUser = userRepository!!.findById("norma@email.com")
        assertThat(expectedUser).isNotNull()
        assertThat(expectedUser.get()).isInstanceOf(User::class.java)
        assertThat(expectedUser.get().active).isTrue()
        assertThat(expectedUser.get().name).isEqualTo("Norma")
    }

    @Test
    fun deleteByIdTest() {
        var expectedUser = userRepository!!.findById("ximena@email.com")
        assertThat(expectedUser).isNotNull()
        assertThat(expectedUser.get()).isInstanceOf(User::class.java)
        assertThat(expectedUser.get().active).isTrue()
```

```
        assertThat(expectedUser.get().name).isEqualTo("Ximena")
        userRepository!!.deleteById("ximena@email.com")
        expectedUser = userRepository!!.findById("ximena@email.com")
        assertThat(expectedUser).isNotNull()
        assertThat(expectedUser).isEmpty()
    }

    companion object {
        @Container
        @ServiceConnection
        var postgreSQLContainer: PostgreSQLContainer<*> =
            PostgreSQLContainer("postgres:latest")
    }
}
```

The `UserJpaRepositoryTests` class includes the following:

- **@DataJpaTest**: This annotation auto-configures everything related to the JPA, from the repositories to the `EntityManager` (required as part of the JPA implementation), and even inherits from the `@Transactional` annotation, meaning that you are making sure your tests are completely transactional. With this annotation, you don't need a web layer to perform any of this against your data persistence.

- **@Import**: One of the cool features of Spring is that you can import specific configurations with this annotation. In this case, we are importing the `UserConfiguration` where we are adding users.

- **@Testcontainers**: As described, this annotation starts and stops the containers; this annotation looks for every `@Container` defined annotation. In this case, we are marking this class as `Testcontainers`, and this will look for any `@Container` annotation and set up the environment for running the specified container image.

- **@AutoConfigureTestDatabase**: When testing the data layer, it is normally better to use an in-memory database, because it's fast and efficient. But sometimes you need to do testing over a real database, and in this case, the `@AutoConfigureTestDatabase` annotation will not use the embedded auto-configuration, but instead will follow what you specified in `@Container` and `@ServerConnection`.

- `@Container`, `@ServerConnection`, `PostgreSQLContainer`: You already know these annotations. All these annotations will auto-configure the start and stop of the PostgreSQL container, the `DataSource` interface that needed connection parameters, such as `username`, `password`, `url`, `dialect`, `driverClass`, and so on.

- `Assertions.*`: In this class, we are using AssertJ, which comes with a fluent API for doing assertions.

Spring Boot not only has support for the JPA, but it also has the following annotations (and many more) that follow the same pattern. Isolate your tests based on the technology you need to test for:

- `@JdbcTest`: For tests related to `JdbcTemplate` programming; covered in Chapters 4 and 5

- `@DataJdbcTest`: For tests on the Spring Data repositories

- `@JooqTest`: For all jOOQ-related tests

- `@DataNeo4jTest`: For Spring Data Neo4J–related tests

- `@DataRedisTest`: For all Spring Data Redis–related tests

- `@DataLdapTest`: For LDAP tests

@WebFluxTest

If you have a Reactive web app with Spring Boot WebFlux, you can test it using the `@WebFluxTest` annotation, which will auto-configure all the web-related beans and annotations for a WebFlux application. It auto-configures the `WebTestClient` interface to perform any exchange/request to the WebFlux endpoints, and it plays well with the `@MockBean` annotation for any services or repositories.

Listing 8-7 shows the `RetroBoardWebFluxTests` class.

Listing 8-7. src/test/kotlin/apress/com/myretro/ RetroBoardWebFluxTests.kt

```
package com.apress.myretro

import com.apress.myretro.board.Card
import com.apress.myretro.board.CardType
import com.apress.myretro.board.RetroBoard
```

```
import com.apress.myretro.service.RetroBoardService
import com.apress.myretro.web.RetroBoardController
import org.junit.jupiter.api.Test
import org.mockito.Mockito
import org.springframework.beans.factory.annotation.Autowired
import org.springframework.boot.test.autoconfigure.web.reactive.WebFluxTest
import org.springframework.boot.test.mock.mockito.MockBean
import org.springframework.http.HttpHeaders
import org.springframework.http.MediaType
import org.springframework.test.web.reactive.server.WebTestClient
import org.springframework.web.reactive.function.BodyInserters
import reactor.core.publisher.Flux
import reactor.core.publisher.Mono
import java.util.*

@WebFluxTest(controllers = [RetroBoardController::class])
class RetroBoardWebFluxTests {
    @MockBean
    lateinit var retroBoardService: RetroBoardService

    @Autowired
    private lateinit var webClient: WebTestClient

    @Test
    fun allRetroBoardTest() {
        Mockito.'when'(retroBoardService.findAll()).thenReturn(
            Flux.just(
                RetroBoard(
                    UUID.randomUUID(), "Simple Retro", mutableListOf(
                        Card(UUID.randomUUID(), "Happy to be here",
                            CardType.HAPPY),
                        Card(UUID.randomUUID(), "Meetings everywhere",
                            CardType.SAD),
                        Card(UUID.randomUUID(), "Vacations?",
                            CardType.MEH),
                        Card(UUID.randomUUID(), "Awesome Discounts",
                            CardType.HAPPY),
                        Card(UUID.randomUUID(), "Missed my train",
```

371

```
                                    CardType.SAD)
                        )
                    )
                )
            )
        webClient.get()
            .uri("/retros")
            .accept(MediaType.APPLICATION_JSON)
            .exchange()
            .expectStatus().isOk()
            .expectBody().jsonPath("$[0].name").isEqualTo
            ("Simple Retro")
        Mockito.verify(retroBoardService, Mockito.times(1)).findAll()
    }

    @Test
    fun findRetroBoardByIdTest() {
        val uuid = UUID.randomUUID()
        Mockito.'when'(retroBoardService.findById(uuid)).thenReturn(
            Mono.just(
                RetroBoard(
                    uuid, "Simple Retro", mutableListOf(
                        Card(UUID.randomUUID(), "Happy to be here",
                        CardType.HAPPY),
                        Card(UUID.randomUUID(), "Meetings everywhere",
                        CardType.SAD),
                        Card(UUID.randomUUID(), "Vacations?",
                        CardType.MEH),
                        Card(UUID.randomUUID(), "Awesome Discounts",
                        CardType.HAPPY),
                        Card(UUID.randomUUID(), "Missed my train",
                        CardType.SAD)
                    )
                )
            )
        )
```

```kotlin
    webClient.get()
        .uri("/retros/{uuid}", uuid.toString())
        .header(HttpHeaders.ACCEPT, MediaType.APPLICATION_JSON_VALUE)
        .exchange()
        .expectStatus().isOk()
        .expectBody(RetroBoard::class.java)
    Mockito.verify(retroBoardService, Mockito.times(1)).findById(uuid)
}

@Test
fun saveRetroBoardTest() {
    val retroBoard = RetroBoard()
    retroBoard.name = "Simple Retro"
    Mockito.'when'(retroBoardService.save(retroBoard))
        .thenReturn(Mono.just(retroBoard))
    webClient.post()
        .uri("/retros")
        .contentType(MediaType.APPLICATION_JSON)
        .body(BodyInserters.fromValue(retroBoard))
        .exchange()
        .expectStatus().isOk()
    Mockito.verify(retroBoardService, Mockito.times(1)).save
    (retroBoard)
}

@Test
fun deleteRetroBoardTest() {
    val uuid = UUID.randomUUID()
    Mockito.'when'(retroBoardService.delete(uuid)).thenReturn
    (Mono.empty())
    webClient.delete()
        .uri("/retros/{uuid}", uuid.toString())
        .exchange()
        .expectStatus().isOk()
    Mockito.verify(retroBoardService, Mockito.times(1)).delete(uuid)
}
}
```

The `RetroBoardWebFluxTests` class includes the following:

- `@WebFluxTests`: This annotation configures everything related to a WebFlux application, looking for `@Controller`, `Filter`, and so on. You can add the controller you want to test. In this case, it is the `RetroBoardController` class. This test isolates from the data layer, testing only the web layer.

- `WebTestClient`: Recall from Chapter 7 that this class is used for testing HTTP and WebFlux endpoints; it returns mocks of the response, making it easier to do the assertions and test your classes.

- `Mockito.*`: Again, we are using the Mockito library not only to prepare our call but also to verify that the call was executed appropriately.

@DataMongoTest

Similar to its support for SQL testing, Spring Boot provides testing support for NoSQL databases, such as the `@DataMongoTest` annotation to test only the MongoDB data layer.

Listing 8-8 shows the `RetroBoardMongoTests` class.

Listing 8-8. src/main/kotlin/apress/com/myretro/RetroBoardMongoTests.kt

```
package com.apress.myretro

import com.apress.myretro.board.RetroBoard
import com.apress.myretro.persistence.RetroBoardRepository
import org.assertj.core.api.Assertions.*
import org.junit.jupiter.api.Test
import org.springframework.beans.factory.annotation.Autowired
import org.springframework.boot.test.autoconfigure.data.mongo.DataMongoTest
import org.springframework.test.context.ActiveProfiles
import org.springframework.test.context.DynamicPropertyRegistry
import org.springframework.test.context.DynamicPropertySource
import org.testcontainers.containers.MongoDBContainer
import org.testcontainers.junit.jupiter.Container
import reactor.test.StepVerifier
import java.util.*
```

```kotlin
@ActiveProfiles("mongoTest")
@DataMongoTest
class RetroBoardMongoTests {
    @Autowired
    lateinit var retroBoardRepository: RetroBoardRepository

    @Test
    fun saveRetroTest() {
        val namex = "Spring Boot 3 Retro"
        val retroBoard = RetroBoard().apply {
            id = UUID.randomUUID()
            name = namex
        }
        val retroBoardResult = retroBoardRepository.insert
        (retroBoard).block()
        assertThat(retroBoardResult).isNotNull()
        assertThat(retroBoardResult!!.id).isInstanceOf(UUID::class.java)
        assertThat(retroBoardResult.name).isEqualTo(namex)
    }

    @Test
    fun findRetroBoardById() {
        val retroBoard = RetroBoard().apply {
            id = UUID.randomUUID()
            name = "Migration Retro"
        }
        val retroBoardResult = retroBoardRepository.insert
        (retroBoard).block()
        assertThat(retroBoardResult).isNotNull()
        assertThat(retroBoardResult!!.id).isInstanceOf(UUID::class.java)
        val retroBoardMono = retroBoardRepository.findById
        (retroBoardResult.id!!)
        StepVerifier
            .create(retroBoardMono)
            .assertNext { retro: RetroBoard ->
                assertThat(retro).isNotNull()
```

375

```
                assertThat(retro).isInstanceOf(RetroBoard::class.java)
                assertThat(retro.name).isEqualTo("Migration Retro")
            }
            .expectComplete()
            .verify()
    }

    companion object {
        @Container
        var mongoDBContainer = MongoDBContainer("mongo:latest")

        init {
            mongoDBContainer.start()
        }

        @DynamicPropertySource
        @JvmStatic
        fun setProperties(registry: DynamicPropertyRegistry) {
            registry.add("spring.data.mongodb.uri") { mongoDBContainer.
            replicaSetUrl }
        }
    }
}
```

The RetroBoardMongoTests class includes the following:

- @DataMongoTest: This annotation auto-configures the Mongo layer,
  where it finds all classes related to Mongo data layer, from domain
  classes to repositories.

- @ActiveProfiles: This annotation sets the profile for a mongoTest.
  It's useful for isolating tests.

- @Container: You also know this annotation, which starts and stops
  the container. In this case, we statically declared the MongoDB
  container and omitted the @Testcontainers annotation, simply to
  demonstrate another way to achieve the same result.

- @DynamcPropertiesSource: With the @ServiceConnection
  annotation (introduced earlier in the chapter), the test sets the
  right Mongo connection properties (the defaults). In this case, we
  are using another approach—a dynamic way to set the connection
  properties using the @DynamicPropertiesSource annotation. With
  this annotation, you can override all the defaults. Note that for Kotlin
  it is important to add the @JvmStatic annotation, otherwise Spring
  won't see it.

Using Testcontainers to Run Your Spring Boot Applications

So far, we have been using the spring-boot-docker-compose dependency to run
the apps and the spring-boot-testcontainers dependency for testing. With
Testcontainers, Spring Boot provides a way to run your app without needing to
use docker-compose, directly from a container. How? It's very easy. Open the
RetroBoardTestConfiguration class shown in Listing 8-9.

Listing 8-9. src/main/kotlin/apress/com/myretro/
RetroBoardTestConfiguration.kt

```
package com.apress.myretro

import org.springframework.boot.SpringApplication
import org.springframework.boot.devtools.restart.RestartScope
import org.springframework.boot.testcontainers.service.connection.
ServiceConnection
import org.springframework.context.annotation.Bean
import org.springframework.context.annotation.Configuration
import org.springframework.context.annotation.Profile
import org.testcontainers.containers.MongoDBContainer

@Profile("!mongoTest")
@Configuration
class RetroBoardTestConfiguration {
    @Bean
```

```kotlin
@RestartScope
@ServiceConnection
fun mongoDBContainer(): MongoDBContainer {
    return MongoDBContainer("mongo:latest")
}

companion object {
    @JvmStatic
    fun main(args: Array<String>) {
        SpringApplication.from { obj: Array<String> ->
                MyretroApplication.main(obj) }.run(*args)
    }
}
}
```

Let's analyze the `RetroBoardTestConfiguration` class:

- `@RestartScope`: Every time you run your application, the container restarts, and one way to avoid this situation is to use the `spring-boot-devtools` dependency. `@RestartScope` will then prevent the container from restarting for every test method you have in your tests. The time required to run the tests will be shorter because you don't need to wait for the container to restart.

- `@ServiceConnection`: As you know, this annotation sets up all the connection parameters from the container you are trying to run, so you don't need to worry about these parameters.

- `SpringApplication.from`: This is very important! Notice that we are using a main method (yes, another entry point for our application), and in this case, instead of using the `SpringApplication.run()` method, we are using the `SpringApplication.from()` method. It points to our main class (in this case, `MyretroApplication::main`).

Summary

This chapter explained the unit and integration testing support in Spring Boot. You discovered that Spring Boot testing is based on the Spring Framework Testing Framework, and that Spring Boot auto-configuration helps configure a lot of that testing.

You also learned that Spring Boot testing includes slice testing, which enables you to test all layers in isolation and by technology—from your domain classes with the `@JsonTest` annotation, to the web controllers with `@WebMvcTest`, all the way to the data layer with `@DataJpaTest` annotations.

This chapter also introduced you to the Testcontainers Framework and how it can help not only for testing but also for running your application. You saw many ways to perform testing, thanks to the Spring Boot Testing Framework, which offers the choice of using AssertJ, Mockito, Hamcrest, and many more libraries.

PART II

Spring Cloud Data Flow: Internals

CHAPTER 9

Spring Boot Security

Felipe Gutierrez[a*]

[a] 4109 Rillcrest Grove Way Fuquay Varina, NC 27526-3562, Albuquerque, NM, USA

Spring Security

The Spring Security Framework provides *authentication* and *authorization*, as well as ways to prevent common attacks such cross-site request forgery (CSRF) and cross-origin resource sharing (CORS), among others. It also supports integration with different technologies, such as Spring Data, cryptography, concurrency, Spring MVC, Spring Web Flux, WebSockets, observability, and much more. The Spring Security team has been working very hard to create ways to secure applications with ease, such as by simplifying how you expose security to your code and, recently, by launching the Spring Authorization Server, a framework that supports implementation of OAuth2 and similar specifications.

One of the most important features of the Spring Security Framework is that it implements and uses the *chain-of-responsibility design pattern*, which allows you to easily add your own custom logic to secure your apps.

Before we get into the details, let's review the main Spring Security architecture, depicted in Figure 9-1, to see how it works and how you can use it to secure your apps.

© Peter Späth, Felipe Gutierrez 2025

P. Späth and F. Gutierrez, *Pro Spring Boot 3 with Kotlin*, https://doi.org/10.1007/979-8-8688-1131-9_9

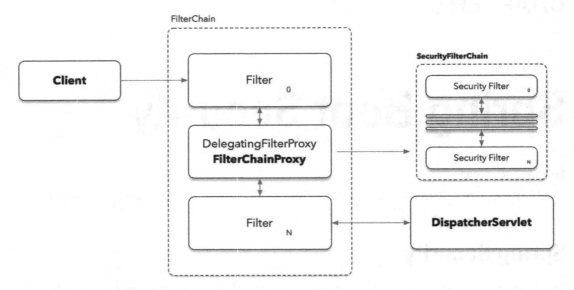

Figure 9-1. *The Spring Security architecture*

Let's review each part of the Spring Security architecture:

- *Client*: This is any client, from a web-based browser to any device that can use HTTP, WebSockets, and so on.

- `FilterChain`: The Spring Security servlet is based on servlet filters, so when a client makes a request, the Spring container will create a `FilterChain` that contains `Filter` instances and the servlet instance (`DispatcherServlet`) to accept any incoming requests (`HttpServletRequest`) and return a response (`HttpServletResponse`). You will have multiple filters for different purposes, not only for security but for your own business logic.

- `DelegatingFilterProxy` > `FilterChainProxy`: Spring provides a `Filter` named `DelegatingFilterProxy` that delegates an instance of `FilterChainProxy`, which is the main class that Spring Security provides to apply default security features to the application. You can also add your own `SecurityFilterChain` with your own custom rules for authentication and authorization.

- SecurityFilterChain: The SecurityFilterChain interface is used
  by the FilterChainProxy class. This is where you specify your own
  custom rules for authentication and authorization. This is where
  the Spring Security Filter will create the necessary instances that
  allow your custom security to be placed. The SecurityFilterChain
  is where you provide what to secure by HTTP method (GET, POST,
  DELETE, PATCH, etc.), by URL pattern (e.g., /users/**, /retros/
  admin/**, etc.), and much more. You can add as many filters as you
  need. In fact, there are also defaults, such as CsrfFilter (provided
  with the HttpSecurity.csrf call), BasicAuthenticationFilter
  (provided with HttpSecurity.httpBasic), and
  AuthorizationFilter (provided when the HttpSecurity.
  authorizationHttpRequests is called). This chapter revisit these
  filters and shows how to configure them. Another important filter
  in the SecurityFilterChain is ExceptionTranslationFilter;
  it allows the translation of the AccessDeniedException and
  AuthenticationException responses.

- DispatcherServlet: This is the core component that handles all
  incoming web requests. It acts as the "front controller," receiving
  requests, determining the appropriate handler (controller), and
  delegating request processing to that handler. Think of it as the
  central traffic controller directing incoming web requests to their
  correct destinations within your Spring application. When a web
  request arrives, Spring Security's filters intercept it before it reaches
  the DispatcherServlet. These filters handle authentication
  (verifying user identity) and authorization (checking permissions),
  ensuring that only authorized requests are forwarded to the
  DispatcherServlet for further processing. Once security checks
  pass, the DispatcherServlet takes over, finding the correct controller
  method to handle the request and generating the response.

Now that you know a little more about how Spring Security helps secure your
applications, let's start with the Users App and My Retro App projects with Spring Boot.

Spring Security with Spring Boot

This chapter covers the MVC (Servlet) and Reactive integrations with the book's two projects and explains how they will interact. This section provides a brief overview of how Spring Security works in Spring Boot and how to add security to an existing application.

Start by opening your `build.gradle` file and adding the security dependencies shown in the following snippet:

build.gradle - snippet

```
// ...
implementation 'org.springframework.boot:spring-boot-starter-security'
testImplementation 'org.springframework.security:spring-security-test'
//...
```

When Spring Boot runs, it will find these dependencies and auto-configure everything necessary to secure your apps. If there is no custom configuration (no `SecurityFilterChain` declared), auto-configuration provides several default beans that will make every access to your application secure, by requiring a username and password. By default, Spring Security auto-configuration creates the `UserDetailsService` bean, which provides the user details for authentication. It generates the `user` username and randomly generates a password that will be printed out in the console logs. Something similar to the following snippet:

```
...
Using generated security password: 2a569843-122a-4559-a245-60f5ab2b6c51
...
```

Auto-configuration also creates the `HttpSecurity` bean that, by default, requires all requests to be authenticated, and it sets the `PasswordEncoder` to use the BCrypt (algorithm) password encoder as the default. If you try to access your application either by using an external client or through a web browser, you will be prompted for a username (`user`) and password (from the console output).

This only covers authentication, but what about authorization? Don't worry, as this is covered in the "Adding Security to My Retro App" section later in this chapter.

In the following section, we start using a UI application that is written using jQuery and (of course) HTML.

Adding Security to Users App

This section shows you not only how to secure Users App but also how to connect it to a UI app. This UI app is written using HTML and jQuery, something simple and quick. Of course, you are welcome to add any other UI framework, such as Angular, VueJS, React, and so on.

First, let's talk about the backend, the Users App project. If you are following along, you can open the Users App project in your favorite IDE, open the `build.gradle` file, and add the needed security dependencies. See Listing 9-1.

Listing 9-1. The build.gradle File

```
import org.jetbrains.kotlin.gradle.tasks.KotlinCompile
plugins {
    id 'org.springframework.boot' version '3.2.3'
    id 'io.spring.dependency-management' version '1.1.4'
    id 'org.jetbrains.kotlin.jvm' version '2.0.20-RC'
    id "org.jetbrains.kotlin.plugin.spring" version "2.0.20-RC"
    // <- simplifies spring proxying
}

group = 'com.apress'
version = '0.0.1-SNAPSHOT'
sourceCompatibility = '17'

repositories {
    mavenCentral()
}

dependencies {
    implementation "org.jetbrains.kotlin:kotlin-stdlib-jdk8"
    implementation "org.jetbrains.kotlin:kotlin-reflect"

    implementation 'org.springframework.boot:spring-boot-starter-web'
    implementation 'org.springframework.boot:spring-boot-starter-
    validation'
    implementation 'org.springframework.boot:spring-boot-starter-security'
    implementation 'org.springframework.boot:spring-boot-starter-data-jpa'
```

```
    runtimeOnly 'com.h2database:h2'
    runtimeOnly 'org.postgresql:postgresql'

    // Web
    implementation 'org.webjars:bootstrap:5.2.3'

    testImplementation 'org.springframework.boot:spring-boot-starter-test'
    testImplementation 'org.springframework.security:spring-security-test'
}

tasks.named('test') {
    useJUnitPlatform()
}

test {
    testLogging {
        events "passed", "skipped", "failed" //, "standardOut",
        "standardError"

        showExceptions true
        exceptionFormat "full"
        showCauses true
        showStackTraces true

        // Change to 'true' for more verbose test output
        showStandardStreams = false
    }
}

//    kotlin {
//        jvmToolchain(17)
//    }
tasks.withType(KotlinCompile).configureEach {
    kotlinOptions {
        freeCompilerArgs = ['-Xjsr305=strict']
        jvmTarget = '17'
    }
}
```

Note in Listing 9-1 that `postgresql` and `h2` are both included. By default, we are going to use the H2 database. In this project, we are going to skip the default behavior for the Spring Security auto-configuration with Spring Boot. We are going to create a custom authentication for all the requests with a few users that will be persistent in-memory only. Of course, this is just one way to do it, but the reality is that you will find that authentication normally involves a persistence mechanism, and we are going to cover that too, so don't worry about it too much at this point.

Next, open/create the `UserSecurityConfig` class, shown in Listing 9-2.

Listing 9-2. src/main/kotlin/com/apress/users/security/UserSecurityConfig.kt

```kotlin
package com.apress.users.security

import org.springframework.context.annotation.Bean
import org.springframework.context.annotation.Configuration
import org.springframework.security.config.Customizer
import org.springframework.security.config.annotation.web.builders.
HttpSecurity
import org.springframework.security.config.annotation.web.configurers.
CsrfConfigurer
import org.springframework.security.core.userdetails.User
import org.springframework.security.crypto.bcrypt.BCryptPasswordEncoder
import org.springframework.security.crypto.password.PasswordEncoder
import org.springframework.security.provisioning.InMemoryUserDetailsManager
import org.springframework.security.provisioning.UserDetailsManager
import org.springframework.security.web.SecurityFilterChain


@Configuration
class UserSecurityConfig {
    @Bean
    @Throws(Exception::class)
    fun filterChain(http: HttpSecurity): SecurityFilterChain {
        http
            .csrf { csrf: CsrfConfigurer<HttpSecurity> -> csrf.disable() }
            .authorizeHttpRequests(Customizer { auth ->
                auth.anyRequest().authenticated()
            })
```

```kotlin
            .httpBasic(Customizer.withDefaults())
        return http.build()
    }

    @Bean
    fun userDetailsManager(passwordEncoder: PasswordEncoder):
    UserDetailsManager {
        val admin = User
            .builder()
            .username("admin")
            .password(passwordEncoder.encode("admin"))
            .roles("ADMIN", "USER")
            .build()
        val manager = User
            .builder()
            .username("manager@email.com")
            .password(passwordEncoder.encode("aw2sOmeR!"))
            .roles("ADMIN", "USER")
            .build()
        val user = User
            .builder()
            .username("user@email.com")
            .password(passwordEncoder.encode("aw2sOmeR!"))
            .roles("USER")
            .build()
        return InMemoryUserDetailsManager(manager, user, admin)
    }

    @Bean
    fun passwordEncoder(): PasswordEncoder {
        return BCryptPasswordEncoder()
    }
}
```

The `UserSecurityConfig` class includes the following:

- `SecurityFilterChain`: We are declaring a `SecurityFilterChain` bean, which will provide all the configuration for this application. This is where you can declare the security filters to use and even create your own custom filter.

- `HttpSecurity`: This class allows the configuration of all the web-based security for specific HTTP requests. If nothing is provided (default), the security will be applied to all requests. It can be configured to specific requests using `RequestMatcher` patterns, custom filters implementations, and much more.

- `csrf`: In this code, we are declaring that the `CsrfFilter` (with `csrf()` method call) needs to be disabled. (This is just for now; but for production purposes, it should always be enabled to avoid any surprises!) In Spring Security, CSRF (cross-site request forgery) protection is enabled by default. However, there are valid reasons why you might want to disable it in certain scenarios:

  - If your API is stateless (doesn't rely on server-side sessions) and uses token-based authentication (like JWT), then CSRF attacks are not a concern. Since each request carries its own authentication token, there's no session cookie for an attacker to exploit.

  - If your API is primarily consumed by non-browser clients (e.g., mobile apps, other backend services), then CSRF attacks are not relevant. CSRF exploits browser behavior, and non-browser clients typically don't send cookies with requests.

  - You might have specific endpoints in your application that don't change state (e.g., GET requests that only retrieve data). These endpoints are less susceptible to CSRF attacks, and disabling CSRF protection for them can simplify development and testing. Disabling CSRF protection should be done with caution. If your application has stateful endpoints that are accessible via browsers, disabling CSRF opens it up to potential CSRF attacks.

- authorizeHttpRequests: This method provides a way to configure AuthorizationManagerRequestMatcherRegister, a Customizer that allows you to declare endpoint match patterns, specific HTTP methods requests (GET, POST, PUT, DELETE, PATCH, OPTIONS, etc.), and a combination of both to secure your application. If nothing is provided, (as you saw earlier) it will secure all incoming requests by default. With the usage of authorizedHttpRequests, we are configuring the AuthorizationFilter.

- httpBasic: We are calling this method to configure BasicAuthenticationFilter, where either the username/password or authentication token is required for authentication.

So, that's how you configure the SecurityFilterChain, by providing some default or custom behavior to secure the app. It's important to remember that we are only using authentication, not authorization yet. Next, we have two more beans declarations:

- UserDetailsManager/InMemoryUserDetailsManager: This interface allows you to create new users and update existing ones. This interface extends from the UserDetailsService, which (in our opinion) is the heart of authentication and authorization because you can add any implementation here, from in-memory (with InMemoryUserDetailsManager) to JDBC, LDAP, and much more. In this code, we use UserDetails to create a user with the User.builder() method call and provide the username, password, and roles (you can add more properties, such as accountExpired, credentialsExpired, disabled, accountLocked and PasswordEncoder).

- PasswordEncoder/BCryptPasswordEncoder: This bean declares how the password should be persisted, by declaring an encoder algorithm. In this case, it uses the BCryptPasswordEncoder class, where the *log round* (which controls the amount of work required to hash a password) is set to 10 by default. It can be configured to anywhere between 4 and 31. The higher the log round, the more work required, and the more secure the hash will be.

That's it! That's how you add authentication to Users App.

Users App Web Controller

If you are interested in reviewing the source code, you can find it in the chapter 09-security folder; there is a new method at the end that will respond to the /{email}/ gravatar endpoint, by returning the URL based on the user's username/email. We can calculate the hash needed to provide the ID for the gravatar, but we want to make an external call when integrating the My Retro App project with the Users App project later in this chapter.

Note   You have access to all the source code at the Apress website or here: https://github.com/felipeg48/pro-spring-boot-3rd.

Let's test the Users App security!

Testing Security in Users App

Spring Security provides different ways to test your code. This section starts with an integration test, using the well-known TestRestTemplate class from the previous chapters.

Open/create the UsersHttpRequestTests class. See Listing 9-3.

Listing 9-3. src/test/kotlin/com/apress/users/UsersHttpRequestTests.kt

```
package com.apress.users

import com.apress.users.model.User
import com.apress.users.model.UserRole
import org.assertj.core.api.Assertions.*
import org.junit.jupiter.api.Test
import org.springframework.beans.factory.annotation.Autowired
import org.springframework.boot.test.context.SpringBootTest
import org.springframework.boot.test.web.client.TestRestTemplate
import java.util.*

@SpringBootTest(webEnvironment = SpringBootTest.WebEnvironment.RANDOM_PORT)
class UsersHttpRequestTests {
    private val USERS_PATH = "/users"
```

```kotlin
@Autowired
private lateinit var restTemplate: TestRestTemplate

@Test
@Throws(Exception::class)
fun indexPageShouldReturnHeaderOneContent() {
    val html = restTemplate.withBasicAuth(
        "manager@email.com", "aw2sOmeR!").getForObject("/",
        String::class.java)
    assertThat(html).contains("Simple Users Rest Application")
}

@Test
@Throws(Exception::class)
fun usersEndPointShouldReturnCollectionWithTwoUsers() {
    val response: Collection<User> = restTemplate.withBasicAuth(
            "manager@email.com", "aw2sOmeR!")
        .getForObject(USERS_PATH, Collection::class.java) as
        Collection<User>
    assertThat(response.size).isGreaterThan(1)
}

@Test
@Throws(Exception::class)
fun userEndPointPostNewUserShouldReturnUser() {
    val user = User(
        "dummy@email.com", "Dummy",
        "https://www.gravatar.com/avatar/23bb62a7d0ca63c9a804908e57bf6
        bd4?d=wavatar",
        "SomeOtherAw2sOmeR!", mutableListOf(UserRole.USER), true
    )
    val response = restTemplate.withBasicAuth("manager@email.com",
    "aw2sOmeR!")
        .postForObject(USERS_PATH, user, User::class.java)
    assertThat(response).isNotNull()
    assertThat(response.email).isEqualTo(user.email)
    val users: Collection<User> = restTemplate.withBasicAuth(
```

```kotlin
                "manager@email.com", "aw2sOmeR!")
            .getForObject(USERS_PATH, Collection::class.java) as
            Collection<User>
        assertThat(users.size).isGreaterThanOrEqualTo(2)
    }

    @Test
    @Throws(Exception::class)
    fun userEndPointDeleteUserShouldReturnVoid() {
        restTemplate.withBasicAuth(
            "manager@email.com", "aw2sOmeR!").delete("$USERS_PATH/norma@
            email.com")
        val users: Collection<User> = restTemplate.withBasicAuth(
                "manager@email.com", "aw2sOmeR!")
            .getForObject(USERS_PATH, Collection::class.java) as
            Collection<User>
        assertThat(users.size).isLessThanOrEqualTo(2)
    }

    @Test
    @Throws(Exception::class)
    fun userEndPointFindUserShouldReturnUser() {
        val user = restTemplate.withBasicAuth(
                "manager@email.com", "aw2sOmeR!").getForObject(
            "$USERS_PATH/ximena@email.com", User::class.java
        )
        assertThat(user).isNotNull()
        assertThat(user.email).isEqualTo("ximena@email.com")
    }
}
```

Listing 9-3 shows the integration test when adding security to your app. The only difference from previous chapters is that we are now using the TestRestTemplate with the withBasicAuth method, which receives the username and password as parameters. And because Users App is configured with basic authentication, this method is exactly what you need here. If you run the tests, they will pass.

Mocking Security Tests

Mocking is another way to test security when you need to isolate the behavior of a particular object. This way, you can simulate the behavior of the real object, in this case security, and simply focus on part of the business logic.

Open/create the UserMockMvcTests class. See Listing 9-4.

Listing 9-4. src/test/kotlin/com/apress/users/UserMockMvcTests.kt

```kotlin
package com.apress.users

import org.hamcrest.Matchers
import org.junit.jupiter.api.Test
import org.springframework.beans.factory.annotation.Autowired
import org.springframework.boot.test.autoconfigure.web.servlet.
AutoConfigureMockMvc
import org.springframework.boot.test.context.SpringBootTest
import org.springframework.security.test.context.support.WithMockUser
import org.springframework.test.web.servlet.MockMvc
import org.springframework.test.web.servlet.request.MockMvcRequestBuilders
import org.springframework.test.web.servlet.result.MockMvcResultMatchers

@SpringBootTest
@WithMockUser
@AutoConfigureMockMvc
class UserMockMvcTests {
    @Autowired
    private lateinit var mockMvc: MockMvc

    @Test
    @Throws(Exception::class)
    fun createUserTests() {
        val location = mockMvc.perform(
            MockMvcRequestBuilders.post("/users")
                .contentType("application/json")
                .content(
                    """
                    {
```

```
                                 "email": "dummy@email.com",
                                 "name": "Dummy",
                                 "password": "aw2s0meR!",
                                 "gravatarUrl":
"https://www.gravatar.com/avatar/fb651279f4712e209991e05610dfb03a?d
=wavatar",
                                 "userRole": ["USER"],
                                 "active": true
                             }
                         """.trimIndent()
                )
        )
            .andExpect(MockMvcResultMatchers.status().isCreated())
            .andExpect(MockMvcResultMatchers.header().exists("Location"))
            .andReturn().response.getHeader("Location")
        mockMvc.perform(MockMvcRequestBuilders.get(location!!))
            .andExpect(MockMvcResultMatchers.status().isOk())
            .andExpect(MockMvcResultMatchers.jsonPath("$.email").exists())
            .andExpect(MockMvcResultMatchers.jsonPath("$.active").
            value(true))
    }

    @Throws(Exception::class)
    @Test
    fun allUsersTests() {
        mockMvc.perform(MockMvcRequestBuilders.get("/users"))
            .andExpect(MockMvcResultMatchers.status().isOk())
            .andExpect(MockMvcResultMatchers.jsonPath("$[0].name").
            value("Ximena"))
            .andExpect(
                MockMvcResultMatchers.jsonPath("$..active")
                    .value<Iterable<Boolean>>(Matchers.hasItem(true))
            )
    }
}
```

The `UserMockMvcTests` class includes the following:

- `@AutoConfigureMockMvc`: As you know, this annotation configures the `MockMvc` object for testing web apps.

- `MockMvc`: As you know, this object simulates any HTTP requests and responses without using the real web server. In this case, we use the `POST` and `GET` HTTP requests.

- `@WithMockUser`: This annotation comes with the `spring-security-test` dependency and it allows us to mock the user in the security context. In this case, you can test functionality without worrying about getting authenticated. Of course, if you remove this annotation, the tests will fail. The `@WithMockUser` annotation accepts parameters. For example, you can use it like this: `@WithMockUser(username = "user", password = "password", roles = "USER")`, where you can make sure that the user is authenticated or has the needed permission. And it can live as a class annotation, affecting every test method, or by method if you require more control in your mocking.

Now you know that you have options for testing security, either unit or integration testing.

Using Persistence for Security Authentication in Users App

You just saw that you can do security authentication with users in-memory, but in a real-world scenario, the users are in a database. Fortunately, Spring Security provides an easy way to use a standard JDBC implementation for `UserDetailsService`. It requires you to provide the username, password, account status (enable or disable), and roles. The SQL schema shown in Listing 9-5 follows this standard implementation.

Listing 9-5. SQL Schema for Spring Security

```
create table users(
    username varchar_ignorecase(50) not null primary key,
    password varchar_ignorecase(50) not null,
    enabled boolean not null
```

```
);
create table authorities (
    username varchar_ignorecase(50) not null,
    authority varchar_ignorecase(50) not null,
    constraint fk_authorities_users foreign key(username) references users
    (username)
);
create unique index ix_auth_username on authorities (username,authority);
```

Spring Security provides a dedicated schema depending on the engine used (PostgreSQL, Oracle, MySQL, etc.). You can find more details here: `https://docs.spring.io/spring-security/reference/servlet/appendix/database-schema.html`.

If you want to use the default schema, you simply need to change the return type of `UserDetailsManager` to `JdbcUserDetailsManager` in the `UserSecurityConfig` class.

Open the `UserSecurityConfig` class and replace all the code with the contents in Listing 9-6.

Listing 9-6. src/main/kotlin/com/apress/users/security/UserSecurityConfig.kt

```kotlin
package com.apress.users.security
import org.springframework.context.annotation.Bean
import org.springframework.context.annotation.Configuration
import org.springframework.jdbc.datasource.embedded.EmbeddedDatabaseBuilder
import org.springframework.jdbc.datasource.embedded.EmbeddedDatabaseType
import org.springframework.security.config.Customizer
import org.springframework.security.config.annotation.web.builders.
HttpSecurity
import org.springframework.security.config.annotation.web.configurers.
CsrfConfigurer
import org.springframework.security.core.userdetails.User
import org.springframework.security.core.userdetails.jdbc.JdbcDaoImpl
import org.springframework.security.crypto.bcrypt.BCryptPasswordEncoder
import org.springframework.security.crypto.password.PasswordEncoder
import org.springframework.security.provisioning.JdbcUserDetailsManager
import org.springframework.security.provisioning.UserDetailsManager
import org.springframework.security.web.SecurityFilterChain
import javax.sql.DataSource
```

```kotlin
@Configuration
class UserSecurityConfig {
    @Bean
    @Throws(Exception::class)
    fun filterChain(http: HttpSecurity): SecurityFilterChain {
        http
            .csrf { csrf: CsrfConfigurer<HttpSecurity> -> csrf.disable() }
            .authorizeHttpRequests(Customizer { auth ->
                auth.anyRequest().authenticated()
            })
            .httpBasic(Customizer.withDefaults())
        return http.build()
    }

    @Bean
    fun dataSource(): DataSource {
        return EmbeddedDatabaseBuilder()
            .setType(EmbeddedDatabaseType.H2)
            .addScript(JdbcDaoImpl.DEFAULT_USER_SCHEMA_DDL_LOCATION)
            .build()
    }

    @Bean
    fun userDetailsManager(passwordEncoder: PasswordEncoder,
            dataSource: DataSource?): UserDetailsManager {
        val admin = User
            .builder()
            .username("admin")
            .password(passwordEncoder.encode("admin"))
            .roles("ADMIN", "USER")
            .build()
        val manager = User
            .builder()
            .username("manager@email.com")
            .password(passwordEncoder.encode("aw2sOmeR!"))
            .roles("ADMIN", "USER")
```

```
            .build()
    val user = User
        .builder()
        .username("user@email.com")
        .password(passwordEncoder.encode("aw2sOmeR!"))
        .roles("USER")
        .build()
    val users = JdbcUserDetailsManager(dataSource)
    users.createUser(admin)
    users.createUser(manager)
    users.createUser(user)
    return users
}

@Bean
fun passwordEncoder(): PasswordEncoder {
    return BCryptPasswordEncoder()
}
}
```

Listing 9-6 shows the new UserSecurityConfig class. Note that SecurityFilter
Chain didn't change; only DataSource and JdbcUserDetailsManager did.

That's it. If you run the same unit and integration tests, they should pass without
any issues.

Using Custom Persistence for Your Authentication Security

This section shows you how you can use your own custom models to supply part of the
authentication and authorization for your apps. In this case, Users App already comes
with the required info that Spring Security needs. Of course, this model brings extra
information that is valuable just for this domain, but it can also be used for security
(authentication and authorization) purposes.

To use this model, you need to replace all code in the UserSecurityConfig class with
the code shown in Listing 9-7.

Listing 9-7. src/main/kotlin/com/apress/users/security/UserSecurityConfig.kt

```kotlin
package com.apress.users.security
import com.apress.users.repository.UserRepository
import org.springframework.context.annotation.Bean
import org.springframework.context.annotation.Configuration
import org.springframework.security.authentication.AuthenticationProvider
import org.springframework.security.authentication.dao.
DaoAuthenticationProvider
import org.springframework.security.config.Customizer
import org.springframework.security.config.annotation.web.builders.
HttpSecurity
import org.springframework.security.config.annotation.web.configurers.
CsrfConfigurer
import org.springframework.security.web.SecurityFilterChain

@Configuration
class UserSecurityConfig {
    @Bean
    @Throws(Exception::class)
    fun filterChain(http: HttpSecurity,
            authenticationProvider: AuthenticationProvider?):
            SecurityFilterChain {
        http
            .csrf { csrf: CsrfConfigurer<HttpSecurity> -> csrf.disable() }
            .authorizeHttpRequests(Customizer { auth ->
                auth.anyRequest().authenticated()
            })
            .authenticationProvider(authenticationProvider)
            .httpBasic(Customizer.withDefaults())
        return http.build()
    }

    @Bean
    fun authenticationProvider(userRepository: UserRepository?):
            AuthenticationProvider {
        val provider = DaoAuthenticationProvider()
```

```
    provider.setUserDetailsService(UserSecurityDetailsService
    (userRepository!!))
    return provider
  }
}
```

Let's review the modified `UserSecurityConfig` class:

- `AuthenticationProvider`: In this example, we use our own database, which will serve data for authentication and authorization. We need to specify a provider that will do this type of authentication. You can provide multiple `AuthenticationProvider` instances that are managed by `ProviderManager`. In fact, Spring Security already has `DaoAuthenticationProvider`, `JwtAuthenticationProvider` (if you want to handle JWT tokens), `LdapAuthenticationProvider`, `CasAuthenticationProvider`, and more. You can also create your own custom authentication provider.

- `DaoAuthenticationProvider`: One of the main benefits of using an `AuthenticationProvider` is that it implements what you require, and you only need to provide the logic to get the data—in this case the username/password and authorities/roles. In this example, we are setting up `UserSecurityDetailsService`, which uses `UserRepository` where the data lives.

- `UserSecurityDetailsService`/`UserRepository`: In this example we are declaring a new instance of the `UserSecurityDetailsService` class. It requires `UserRepository`. This class implements `UserDetailsService`, which will hold the data for the authentication process—in this case the username, the password, the `authorities` or `roles`, and other properties that can be useful when the authentication is happening.

Next, open/create the `UserSecurityDetailsService` class. See Listing 9-8.

Listing 9-8. src/main/kotlin/com/apress/users/security/
UserSecurityDetailsService.kt

```kotlin
package com.apress.users.security

import com.apress.users.exception.UserNotFoundException
import com.apress.users.model.User
import com.apress.users.model.UserRole
import com.apress.users.repository.UserRepository
import org.springframework.beans.factory.annotation.Autowired
import org.springframework.security.core.userdetails.UserDetails
import org.springframework.security.core.userdetails.UserDetailsService
import org.springframework.security.core.userdetails.
UsernameNotFoundException
import org.springframework.security.crypto.factory.PasswordEncoderFactories
import org.springframework.security.crypto.password.PasswordEncoder
import java.util.function.Supplier

class UserSecurityDetailsService(var userRepository: UserRepository) :
        UserDetailsService {
    @Throws(UsernameNotFoundException::class)
    override fun loadUserByUsername(username: String): UserDetails {
        val user: User = userRepository.findById(username)
            .orElseThrow{ UserNotFoundException() }
        val passwordEncoder: PasswordEncoder =
            PasswordEncoderFactories.createDelegatingPasswordEncoder()
        return org.springframework.security.core.userdetails.User
            .withUsername(username)
            .roles(
                *user.userRole!!.map { obj: UserRole -> obj.toString()
                }.toTypedArray()
            )
            .password(passwordEncoder.encode(user.password))
            .accountExpired(!user.active)
            .build()
    }
}
```

In the `UserSecurityDetailsService` class, we are implementing the
`UserDetailsService` that we'll use to retrieve the username, the password, and other
useful properties for authentication. In this case, we use the `User.active` property to set
the `accountExpired` property as an example, and we use the `UserRole` instance to collect
a list of roles.

Now you know that there are different ways to configure authentication with Spring
Security, from the default approach with the `user` username and the randomly generated
password in the console, to using in-memory and persistence (using the default schema
or a custom schema), and even to using LDAP. If you implement `UserDetails`, you can
plug in anything you want in order to provide authentication and authorization.

Connecting a UI to Users App

Now it's time to connect a UI to Users App. In the source code under `resources/`, you
will find a folder named `users-ui` that includes all the HTML, JavaScript (jQuery), and
necessary assets to have a UI for Users App. Before continuing with the UI and backend
code, take some time to review it and analyze what is happening.

Let's first look at the `login.js` file and review part of its code, shown in Listing 9-9.

Listing 9-9. Snippet from users-ui/assets/js/login.js

```
...
$('#btn__login').click(function(e) {
    e.preventDefault();
    let user_email = $('input[name="user_email"]').val();
    let user_password = $('input[name="user_password"]').val();
    $.ajax({
        url: 'http://localhost:8080/users/'+user_email,
        method: 'GET',
        headers: {
            'Authorization': 'Basic ' + btoa(user_email + ':' + user_password),
            'Content-Type': 'application/json'
        }
    })
    .done(function( response, textStatus, xhr ) {
    // ....
}
```

Note that in the $.ajax call, we use the /users/{email} endpoint for the url value. Perhaps you are thinking that this is unusual, because it could be /authenticate or something similar, and yes, you could do that, but to illustrate how this UI works, we use that endpoint as part of the authentication.

Another important part of the code is the headers value, where we use the HTTP Authorization header and the btoa() method, which allows us to encode to base64 the string we are sending, in this case the username and password. When we receive the response from the backend, we get it in the done function.

Now switch to Users App (the backend) and modify/create the UserSecurityConfig class. See Listing 9-10.

Listing 9-10. src/main/kotlin/com/apress/users/security/UserSecurityConfig.kt

```kotlin
package com.apress.users.security
import com.apress.users.repository.UserRepository
import org.springframework.context.annotation.Bean
import org.springframework.context.annotation.Configuration
import org.springframework.security.authentication.AuthenticationProvider
import org.springframework.security.authentication.dao.
DaoAuthenticationProvider
import org.springframework.security.config.Customizer
import org.springframework.security.config.annotation.web.builders.
HttpSecurity
import org.springframework.security.config.annotation.web.configurers.
CorsConfigurer
import org.springframework.security.config.annotation.web.configurers.
CsrfConfigurer
import org.springframework.security.web.SecurityFilterChain
import org.springframework.web.cors.CorsConfiguration
import org.springframework.web.cors.CorsConfigurationSource
import org.springframework.web.cors.UrlBasedCorsConfigurationSource

@Configuration
class UserSecurityConfig {
    @Bean
    @Throws(Exception::class)
    fun filterChain(
```

```kotlin
    http: HttpSecurity, authenticationProvider: AuthenticationProvider?,
    corsConfigurationSource: CorsConfigurationSource?
): SecurityFilterChain {
    http
        .csrf { csrf: CsrfConfigurer<HttpSecurity> -> csrf.disable() }
        .cors { cors: CorsConfigurer<HttpSecurity?> ->
            cors.configurationSource(corsConfigurationSource) }
        .authorizeHttpRequests{ auth ->
            auth.anyRequest().authenticated()
        }
        .authenticationProvider(authenticationProvider)
        .formLogin(Customizer.withDefaults())
        .httpBasic(Customizer.withDefaults())
    return http.build()
}

@Bean
fun corsConfigurationSource(): CorsConfigurationSource {
    val configuration = CorsConfiguration().apply {
        allowedOrigins = mutableListOf("*")
        allowedMethods = mutableListOf("*")
        allowedHeaders = mutableListOf("*")
    }
    return UrlBasedCorsConfigurationSource().apply {
        registerCorsConfiguration(" / * *", configuration)
    }
}

@Bean
fun authenticationProvider(userRepository: UserRepository):
        AuthenticationProvider {
    val provider = DaoAuthenticationProvider()
    provider.setUserDetailsService(UserSecurityDetailsService
    (userRepository))
    return provider
}
}
```

Listing 9-10 shows the modified `UserSecurityConfig` class that works with the UI. Let's review it:

- `cors`: As mentioned, Spring Security provides support for cross-origin resource sharing, which blocks any script from connecting or making calls using AJAX to a different origin. In this case, the requests won't be happening in the same origin, because they will be made using the UI (which lives in a different server), so we need to provide access to it and we need to declare some rules by using `CorsConfigurationSource`.

- `formLogin`: We are also adding a new way to authenticate as part of the `SecurityFilterChain`—in this case as `formLogin` with its defaults. So, if we try to get directly into the `/users` endpoint, Spring Security will respond with a login page requesting a username and password.

- `CorsConfigurationSource/CorsConfiguration/UrlBasedCors ConfigurationSource`: We are creating the `CorsConfigurationSource` bean to declare the origins, headers, and methods of the requests to identify where they are coming from. In this case, we are enabling everything just for demonstration purposes, but when there are clients embedded in your apps, you must restrain and configure security in such a way as to prevent hacking.

Users Frontend/Backend: Let's Give It a Try!

Run the two apps in the UI. First, make sure that Users App (backend) is up and running. Then, in your `users-ui`, you can use Python or any other app that can serve those HTML files. If you are using an IDE for the UI, it should have a way to run your apps. If you are using the JetBrains WebStorm IDE, for example, simply right-click the `index.html` file and select Run. If you are using VS Code, you can use the Live Server plugin and click (in the status bar) the Go Live button, which will launch a browser window in port 5500.

Using Python, go to the root of the `users-ui` folder and execute the following command:

```
python3 -m http.server
```

This opens the 8000 port. If you open your browser and go to `http://localhost:8000`, you will see the UI in Figure 9-2.

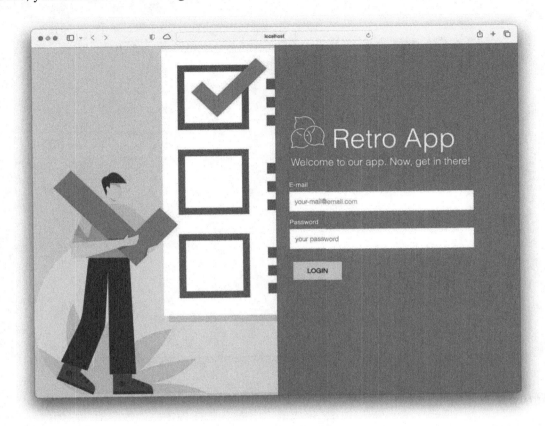

Figure 9-2. *http://localhost:8000: The Users/Retro App*

Figure 9-2 shows the Users/Retro App. Right now we are using the Retro App view to see the users, so it's not an error. You can log in with the following credentials:

`manager@email.com/aw2sOmeR!`

After successfully logging in, you should see the Users screen in Figure 9-3.

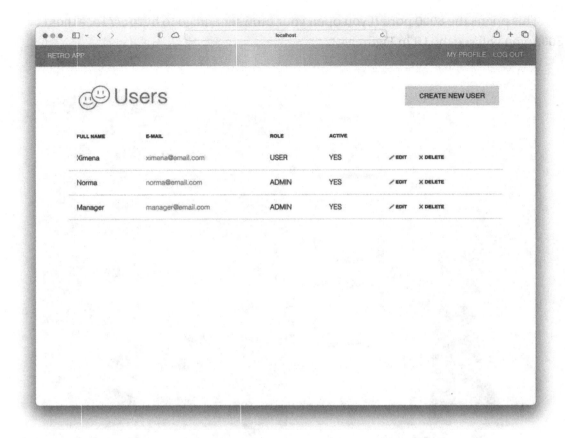

Figure 9-3. *Users page*

If you want to test its functionality, go ahead and experiment. The listed users are the ones that we set in the backend in the UserConfig class.

Note   If you find a bug/issue in the UI or have a suggestion for an improvement, let us know. You can write a pull request here: https://github.com/felipeg48/pro-spring-boot-3rd.

If you now try to access the backend directly, at http://localhost:8080, you will see the login page in Figure 9-4.

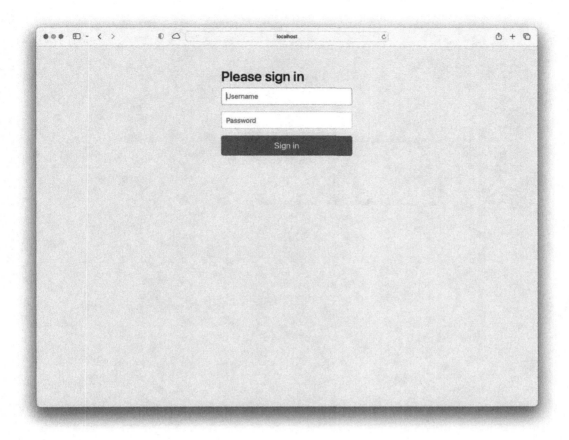

Figure 9-4. *Users App backend (http://localhost:8080)*

Figure 9-4 shows the default implementation of the formLogin declaration set in the SecurityFilterChain. If you provide the credentials, you will see a list of users in JSON format, as shown in Figure 9-5.

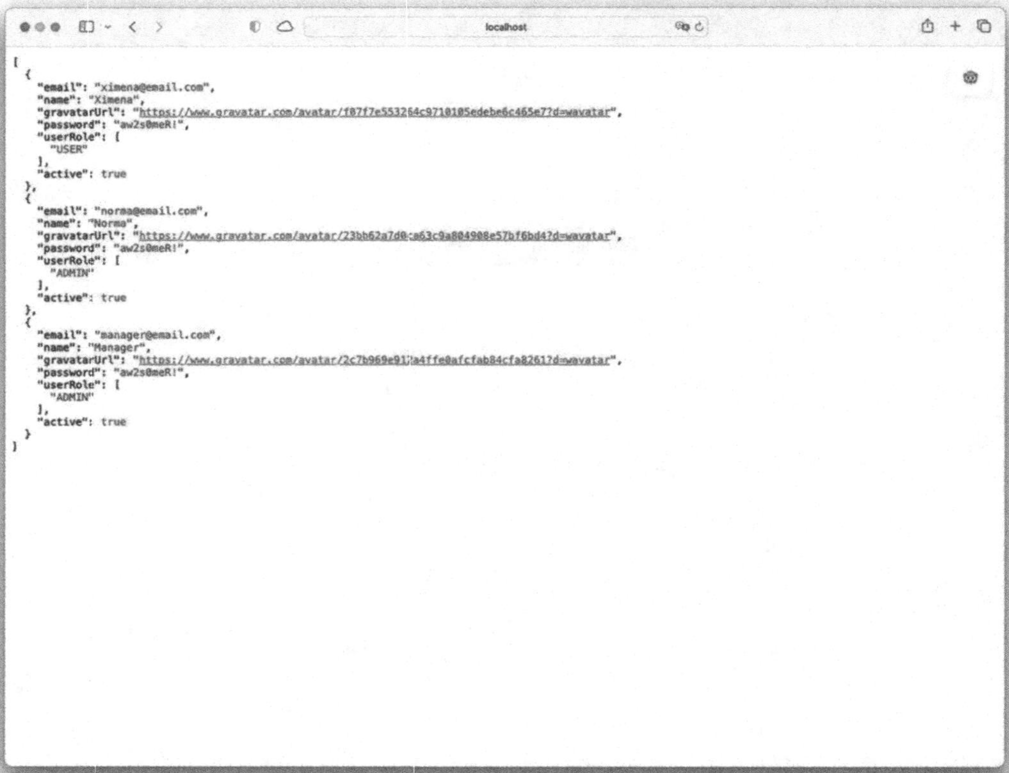

Figure 9-5. *List of users in JSON format, displayed after authenticating*

Now you know how to integrate an external UI into your Users App using Spring Security with Spring Boot! Before moving on to the next section, keep in mind that we discussed only *authentication* in this section. The following sections cover *authorization*.

Adding Security to My Retro App

My Retro App is an integration of a Reactive technology, and Spring Security with Spring Boot provides the similar auto-configuration when the dependencies are based on WebFlux. The main idea is that you are going to connect both apps—Users App will provide user information lookup, and My Retro App will secure that information (User info) based on the security configuration that will be defining in this section. In My Retro App, we'll define authentication and authorization, as depicted in Figure 9-6.

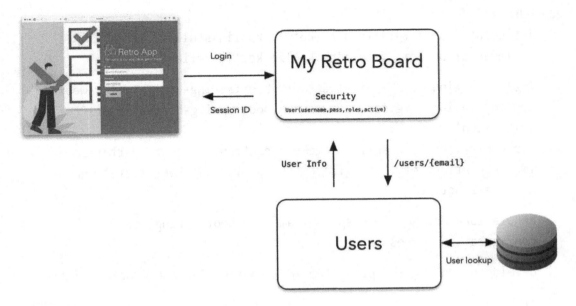

Figure 9-6. *My Retro App security flow*

Next, we review the source code, which you can find in the 09-security/myretro folder. If you open the build.gradle file, you will see the code shown in Listing 9-11.

Listing 9-11. build.gradle

```
import org.jetbrains.kotlin.gradle.tasks.KotlinCompile
plugins {
    id 'org.springframework.boot' version '3.2.3'
    id 'io.spring.dependency-management' version '1.1.4'
    id 'org.jetbrains.kotlin.jvm' version '2.0.20-RC'
    id "org.jetbrains.kotlin.plugin.spring" version "2.0.20-RC"
    // <- simplifies spring proxying
}

group = 'com.apress'
version = '0.0.1-SNAPSHOT'
sourceCompatibility = '17'

repositories {
    mavenCentral()
}
```

```
dependencies {
    implementation "org.jetbrains.kotlin:kotlin-stdlib-jdk8"
    implementation "org.jetbrains.kotlin:kotlin-reflect"

    implementation 'org.springframework.boot:spring-boot-starter-webflux'
    implementation 'org.springframework.boot:spring-boot-starter-
    validation'
    implementation 'org.springframework.boot:spring-boot-starter-security'
    implementation 'org.springframework.boot:spring-boot-starter-data-
    mongodb-reactive'

    annotationProcessor 'org.springframework.boot:spring-boot-
    configuration-processor'

    developmentOnly 'org.springframework.boot:spring-boot-docker-compose'

    // Web
    implementation 'org.webjars:bootstrap:5.2.3'
    implementation 'org.webjars:webjars-locator-core'

    // DevTools
    implementation        'org.springframework.boot:spring-boot-devtools'
    testImplementation 'org.springframework.boot:spring-boot-
    testcontainers'
    testImplementation 'org.testcontainers:junit-jupiter'
    testImplementation 'org.testcontainers:mongodb'

    testImplementation 'org.springframework.boot:spring-boot-starter-test'
    testImplementation 'org.springframework.security:spring-security-test'
    testImplementation 'io.projectreactor:reactor-test'
}

tasks.named('test') {
    useJUnitPlatform()
}

test {
    testLogging {
        events "passed", "skipped", "failed" //, "standardOut",
        "standardError"
```

```
        showExceptions true
        exceptionFormat "full"
        showCauses true
        showStackTraces true

        // Change to 'true' for more verbose test output
        showStandardStreams = false
    }
}

//    kotlin {
//        jvmToolchain(17)
//    }
tasks.withType(KotlinCompile).configureEach {
    kotlinOptions {
        freeCompilerArgs = ['-Xjsr305=strict']
        jvmTarget = '17'
    }
}
```

Listing 9-11 shows the spring-boot-starter-security dependencies added to the build.gradle file.

Next, open/create the UserClient class. See Listing 9-12.

Listing 9-12. src/main/kotlin/apress/com/myretro/client/UserClient.kt

```
package com.apress.myretro.client

import com.apress.myretro.config.MyRetroProperties
import org.springframework.http.HttpHeaders
import org.springframework.stereotype.Component
import org.springframework.web.reactive.function.client.WebClient
import reactor.core.publisher.Mono

@Component
class UserClient(webClientBuilder: WebClient.Builder, props:
MyRetroProperties) {
    private val webClient: WebClient = webClientBuilder
        .baseUrl(props.users!!.server!!)
```

```
        .defaultHeaders { headers: HttpHeaders ->
            headers.setBasicAuth(
                props.users!!.username!!,
                props.users!!.password!!
            )
        }
        .build()

    fun getUserInfo(email: String): Mono<User> {
        return webClient.get()
            .uri("/users/{email}", email)
            .retrieve()
            .bodyToMono(User::class.java)
    }

    fun getUserGravatar(email: String?): Mono<String> {
        return webClient.get()
            .uri("/users/{email}/gravatar", email)
            .retrieve()
            .bodyToMono(String::class.java)
    }
}
```

The UserClient class is marked as a Spring Bean with the @Component annotation, which will make it available when needed. This class is like the RestTemplate class but for Reactive applications. It has its own way to deal with the WebFlux components, such as Flux and Mono types, and it can be used in non-Reactive apps as well. The UserClient class has two methods that use the WebClient class:

- The getUserInfo method will use the /users/{email} endpoint to retrieve user information by sending an email (as a parameter of the method). In the header configuration, you can use the *basic authentication* required by Users App (or Users Service in this case) to access its API. We are using the MyRetroProperties class, which is constructed by Spring and is expecting the server, port, username, and password properties. (You can look at the MyRetroProperties class to review these properties and the `application.properties` file.) In other words, to secure My Retro App, you need to have some users, and Users App holds such information, so we use Users App as an authentication and authorization mechanism for My Retro App. To authenticate, we use the `WebClient` class, which will access the Users Service.

- The `getUserGravatar` method will be used to retrieve the image (based on the email) and uses the `WebClient` to communicate to the Users Service.

Notice that both methods are calling a non-Reactive app, and they are transforming the response into a `Mono` type.

Next, open/create the `RetroBoardSecurityConfig` class. See Listing 9-13.

Listing 9-13. src/main/kotlin/apress/com/myretro/security/ RetroBoardSecurityConfig.kt

```
package com.apress.myretro.security

import com.apress.myretro.client.User
import com.apress.myretro.client.UserClient
import com.apress.myretro.client.UserRole
import org.springframework.context.annotation.Bean
import org.springframework.context.annotation.Configuration
import org.springframework.core.io.buffer.DataBuffer
import org.springframework.http.HttpMethod
import org.springframework.http.HttpStatusCode
import org.springframework.http.ReactiveHttpOutputMessage
import org.springframework.security.authentication.BadCredentialsException
import org.springframework.security.authentication.
ReactiveAuthenticationManager
import org.springframework.security.authentication.
UsernamePasswordAuthenticationToken
import org.springframework.security.config.Customizer
import org.springframework.security.config.web.server.ServerHttpSecurity
import org.springframework.security.core.Authentication
import org.springframework.security.core.GrantedAuthority
```

```
import org.springframework.security.core.authority.SimpleGrantedAuthority
import org.springframework.security.web.server.SecurityWebFilterChain
import org.springframework.security.web.server.WebFilterExchange
import org.springframework.security.web.server.authentication.
    ServerAuthenticationSuccessHandler
import org.springframework.web.cors.CorsConfiguration
import org.springframework.web.cors.reactive.CorsConfigurationSource
import org.springframework.web.cors.reactive.
UrlBasedCorsConfigurationSource
import org.springframework.web.server.WebSession
import reactor.core.publisher.Flux
import reactor.core.publisher.Mono
import java.util.stream.Collectors

@Configuration
class RetroBoardSecurityConfig {
    @Bean
    @Throws(Exception::class)
    fun securityWebFilterChain(
        http: ServerHttpSecurity,
        reactiveAuthenticationManager: ReactiveAuthenticationManager?,
        corsConfigurationSource: CorsConfigurationSource?
    ): SecurityWebFilterChain {
        http
            .csrf{ csrf: ServerHttpSecurity.CsrfSpec -> csrf.disable() }
            .cors{ cors: ServerHttpSecurity.CorsSpec ->
                    cors.configurationSource(corsConfigurationSource) }
            .authorizeExchange { auth: ServerHttpSecurity.
            AuthorizeExchangeSpec ->
                auth
                    .pathMatchers(HttpMethod.POST, "/retros/**").
                    hasRole("ADMIN")
                    .pathMatchers(HttpMethod.DELETE, "/retros/**").
                    hasRole("ADMIN")
                    .pathMatchers("/retros/**").hasAnyRole("USER", "ADMIN")
                    .pathMatchers("/", "/webjars/**").permitAll()
```

```kotlin
            }
            .authenticationManager(reactiveAuthenticationManager)
            .formLogin{ formLoginSpec: ServerHttpSecurity.FormLoginSpec ->
                formLoginSpec.authenticationSuccessHandler(
                    serverAuthenticationSuccessHandler()
                )
            }
            .httpBasic(Customizer.withDefaults())
        return http.build()
}

@Bean
fun serverAuthenticationSuccessHandler():
ServerAuthenticationSuccessHandler {
    return ServerAuthenticationSuccessHandler {
            webFilterExchange: WebFilterExchange, authentication:
            Authentication ->
        webFilterExchange.exchange.session
            .flatMap{ session: WebSession ->
                val (email, name, password, gravatarUrl) =
                    authentication.details as User
                val body = """
            {
                "email": "%s",
                "name": "%s",
                "password": "%s",
                "userRole": "%s",
                "gravatarUrl": "%s",
                "active": %s
            }
            """.trimIndent().format(
                    email,
                    name,
                    password,
                    authentication.authorities.stream()
```

```kotlin
                        .map { obj: GrantedAuthority -> obj.authority }
                        .map { role: String -> role.
                        replace("ROLE_", "") }
                        .collect(Collectors.joining(",")),
                    gravatarUrl, true)
                webFilterExchange.exchange.response.setStatusCode(
                    HttpStatusCode.valueOf(200))
                val response: ReactiveHttpOutputMessage =
                    webFilterExchange.exchange.response
                response.headers.add("Content-Type",
                "application/json")
                response.headers.add("X-MYRETRO",
                    "SESSION=" + session.id + "; Path=/; HttpOnly;
                    SameSite=Lax")
                val dataBufferPublisher: DataBuffer =
                    response.bufferFactory().wrap(body.toByteArray())
                response.writeAndFlushWith(
                    Flux.just<DataBuffer>(dataBufferPublisher)
                    .windowUntilChanged())
            }
        }
    }

    @Bean
    fun corsConfigurationSource(): CorsConfigurationSource {
        val configuration = CorsConfiguration().apply {
            allowedMethods = mutableListOf("GET", "POST", "PUT", "DELETE",
            "OPTIONS")
            allowedHeaders = mutableListOf(
                "x-ijt",
                "Set-Cookie",
                "Cookie",
                "Content-Type",
                "X-MYRETRO",
                "Allow",
                "Authorization",
```

```
        "Access-Control-Allow-Origin",
        "Access-Control-Allow-Credentials",
        "Access-Control-Allow-Headers",
        "Access-Control-Allow-Methods",
        "Access-Control-Expose-Headers",
        "Access-Control-Max-Age",
        "Access-Control-Request-Headers",
        "Access-Control-Request-Method",
        "Origin",
        "X-Requested-With",
        "Accept",
        "Accept-Encoding",
        "Accept-Language",
        "Host",
        "Referer",
        "Connection",
        "User-Agent"
    )
    exposedHeaders = mutableListOf(
        "x-ijt",
        "Set-Cookie",
        "Cookie",
        "Content-Type",
        "X-MYRETRO",
        "Allow",
        "Authorization",
        "Access-Control-Allow-Origin",
        "Access-Control-Allow-Credentials",
        "Access-Control-Allow-Headers",
        "Access-Control-Allow-Methods",
        "Access-Control-Expose-Headers",
        "Access-Control-Max-Age",
        "Access-Control-Request-Headers",
        "Access-Control-Request-Method",
        "Origin",
```

```
            "X-Requested-With",
            "Accept",
            "Accept-Encoding",
            "Accept-Language",
            "Host",
            "Referer",
            "Connection",
            "User-Agent"
        )
        allowedOriginPatterns = mutableListOf("http://localhost:*")
        allowCredentials = true
    }
    val source = UrlBasedCorsConfigurationSource()
    source.registerCorsConfiguration("/**", configuration)
    return source
}

@Bean
fun reactiveAuthenticationManager(userClient: UserClient):
        ReactiveAuthenticationManager {
    return ReactiveAuthenticationManager { authentication:
    Authentication ->
        val username = authentication.name
        val password = authentication.credentials.toString()
        val userResult: Mono<User> = userClient.getUserInfo(username)
        userResult.flatMap{ user: User ->
            if (user.password == password) {
                val grantedAuthorities: List<GrantedAuthority> =
                user.userRole.stream()
                    .map { obj: UserRole -> obj.name }
                    .map { str: String -> "ROLE_$str" }
                    .map { role: String? ->
                        SimpleGrantedAuthority(
                            role
                        )
                    }
```

```
                    .collect(Collectors.toList<GrantedAuthority>())
                val authenticationToken =
                    UsernamePasswordAuthenticationToken(
                        username, password, grantedAuthorities)
                authenticationToken.details = user
                return@flatMap Mono.just<Username
                PasswordAuthenticationToken>
                    (authenticationToken)
            } else {
                return@flatMap Mono.error<Authentication>
                    (BadCredentialsException("Invalid username or
                    password"))
            }
        }
    }
}
}
```

The RetroBoardSecurityConfig class includes the following:

- SecurityWebFilterChain: This interface is familiar, right? In Users
  App, we use the SecurityFilterChain interface for *Servlet web
  apps*, and in this case, we use *WebFlux* (*Reactive web apps*), so we
  need to use its counterpart, the SecurityWebFilterChain interface,
  which deals with Mono and Flux types. It has the same behavior as
  SecurityFilterChain. It will help declare any custom filters we
  need. In our example, we also require the ServerHttpSecurity,
  ReactiveAuthenticationManager, and CorsConfigurationSource
  beans as parameters of the method.

- ServerHttpSecurity: Very similar to its counterpart (the
  HttpSecurity class), the ServerHttpSecurity class configures all
  the security for specific requests. By default (if not used), the security
  will be applied to all requests (it will get the username the user
  defines and the password printed out in the logs). In this case, we are
  defining certain rules:

- We are disabling the CSRF filter.

- We are configuring the CORS filter.

- We are defining security access for the `/retros/*` endpoint requests. We are adding the `POST` and `DELETE` methods with the `ADMIN` role, and any of these `USER` or `ADMIN` roles for the other HTTP request, such as `GET`. We are also permitting any `/` and `/webjars/**` endpoints that correspond to the `index. html` page and resources such as images and CSS or JS scripts. Also, we are using a `ReactiveAuthenticationManager,` and defining *form* and *basic* authentication.

- `ReactiveAuthenticationManager`: This bean helps contact Users App. An important detail here is that we are using `Mono` and `Flux` types, so we need to use some of these reactive methods and do the appropriate handling to get the needed value. `ReactiveAuthenticationManager` is a functional interface that defines the `Mono<Authentication> authenticate(Authentication)` method. When we get the request, we can get the information, in this case the username and password, then we can use the `UserClient` to get the `User` info and return the `Mono<Authentication>`. This is done by creating the `UsernamePasswordAuthenticationToken` or by throwing an exception with `BadCredentialsException`. This is part of the authentication process. It's also important to know that the `UsernamePasswordAuthenticationToken` class extends the `AbstractAuthenticationToken` abstract class, which has the `Object` details, where we add the `User` info (retrieved by the `UserClient` class) and use it in the `authenticationSuccessHandler` as part of its configuration.

- `CorsConfigurationSource`: This interface defines the `CorsConfiguration getCorsConfiguration(ServerWebExchange)` method, which we can configure by adding the headers and origins and allowing credentials for specific endpoints. In this case, we are using everything with the `/**` syntax.

- ServerAuthenticationSuccessHandler: We are going to
  use an external login page (see Figure 9-6), which requires
  us to add some configuration for it to work. We need to
  define authenticationSuccessHandler. We are declaring a
  ServerAuthenticationSuccessHandler bean. This interface declares
  the Mono<Void> onAuthenticationSuccess(WebFilterExchange,
  Authentication) method, and it gets invoked when the application
  authenticates successfully. All of this is necessary because the UI will
  point to the /login endpoint, and this configuration will generate the
  necessary SESSION ID that is required for subsequent calls. In other
  words, this call will have the response that the UI needs—in this case
  the JSON object that is expecting to contain all the User info—so it
  can apply the necessary logic to the frontend to differentiate between
  the ADMIN and USER roles.

As you can see, you need to add more configuration for Reactive web apps, but
the primary purpose of using Spring Security is the same, and Spring Boot helps a lot
by removing the boilerplate that would be needed if you were using only Spring apps.
Before you proceed to the next section, review the code and analyze it at your own pace.
Remember that it includes authentication and authorization by integrating both apps—
Users App to retrieve user information, and My Retro App to apply the security based on
the rules set in the ServerHttpSecurity configuration.

Next, let's test the My Retro App.

Unit Testing My Retro App Security for Authorization

To test My Retro App, we are going to perform a unit test rather than an integration
test. However, we use the @MockBean used in Chapter 8 for integration testing to test the
authorization that we set for some of the endpoints because we are going to do a mock
authentication.

Open/create the RetroBoardWebFluxTests class. See Listing 9-14.

Listing 9-14. src/test/kotlin/apress/com/myretro/RetroBoardWebFluxTests.kt

```kotlin
package com.apress.myretro

import com.apress.myretro.board.Card
import com.apress.myretro.board.CardType
import com.apress.myretro.board.RetroBoard
import com.apress.myretro.client.UserClient
import com.apress.myretro.security.RetroBoardSecurityConfig
import com.apress.myretro.service.RetroBoardService
import com.apress.myretro.web.RetroBoardController
import org.junit.jupiter.api.Test
import org.mockito.Mockito
import org.springframework.beans.factory.annotation.Autowired
import org.springframework.boot.test.autoconfigure.web.reactive.WebFluxTest
import org.springframework.boot.test.mock.mockito.MockBean
import org.springframework.context.annotation.Import
import org.springframework.http.HttpHeaders
import org.springframework.http.MediaType
import org.springframework.security.test.context.support.WithMockUser
import org.springframework.test.web.reactive.server.WebTestClient
import org.springframework.web.reactive.function.BodyInserters
import reactor.core.publisher.Flux
import reactor.core.publisher.Mono
import java.util.*

@Import(RetroBoardSecurityConfig::class)
@WithMockUser
@WebFluxTest(controllers = [RetroBoardController::class])
class RetroBoardWebFluxTests {
    @MockBean
    private lateinit var retroBoardService: RetroBoardService

    @MockBean
    private lateinit var userClient: UserClient

    @Autowired
    private lateinit var webClient: WebTestClient
```

```kotlin
@Test
fun allRetroBoardTest() {
        Mockito.'when'(retroBoardService.findAll()).thenReturn(
            Flux.just(
                RetroBoard(
                    UUID.randomUUID(), "Simple Retro", mutableListOf(
                        Card(UUID.randomUUID(),
                            "Happy to be here", CardType.HAPPY),
                        Card(UUID.randomUUID(),
                            "Meetings everywhere", CardType.SAD),
                        Card(UUID.randomUUID(),
                            "Vacations?", CardType.MEH),
                        Card(UUID.randomUUID(),
                            "Awesome Discounts", CardType.HAPPY),
                        Card(UUID.randomUUID(),
                            "Missed my train", CardType.SAD)
                    )
                )
            )
        )
        webClient.get()
            .uri("/retros")
            .accept(MediaType.APPLICATION_JSON)
            .exchange()
            .expectStatus().isOk()
            .expectBody().jsonPath("$[0].name").
            isEqualTo("Simple Retro")
        Mockito.verify(retroBoardService, Mockito.times(1)).findAll()
    }

@Test
fun findRetroBoardByIdTest() {
    val uuid = UUID.randomUUID()
    Mockito.'when'(retroBoardService.findById(uuid)).thenReturn(
        Mono.just(
            RetroBoard(
```

```
                    uuid, "Simple Retro", mutableListOf(
                        Card(UUID.randomUUID(), "Happy to be here",
                        CardType.HAPPY),
                        Card(UUID.randomUUID(), "Meetings everywhere",
                        CardType.SAD),
                        Card(UUID.randomUUID(), "Vacations?",
                        CardType.MEH),
                        Card(UUID.randomUUID(), "Awesome Discounts",
                        CardType.HAPPY),
                        Card(UUID.randomUUID(), "Missed my train",
                        CardType.SAD)
                    )
                )
            )
        )
    webClient.get()
        .uri("/retros/{uuid}", uuid.toString())
        .header(HttpHeaders.ACCEPT, MediaType.APPLICATION_JSON_VALUE)
        .exchange()
        .expectStatus().isOk()
        .expectBody(RetroBoard::class.java)
    Mockito.verify(retroBoardService, Mockito.times(1)).findById(uuid)
}

@Test
@WithMockUser(roles = ["ADMIN"])
fun saveRetroBoardTest() {
    val retroBoard = RetroBoard().apply {
        name = "Simple Retro"
    }
    Mockito.'when'(retroBoardService.save(retroBoard))
        .thenReturn(Mono.just(retroBoard))
    webClient.post()
        .uri("/retros")
        .contentType(MediaType.APPLICATION_JSON)
        .body(BodyInserters.fromValue(retroBoard))
```

```
        .exchange()
        .expectStatus().isOk()
    Mockito.verify(retroBoardService, Mockito.times(1)).
    save(retroBoard)
}

@Test
@WithMockUser(roles = ["ADMIN"])
fun deleteRetroBoardTest() {
    val uuid = UUID.randomUUID()
    Mockito.'when'(retroBoardService.delete(uuid)).thenReturn(Mono.
    empty())
    webClient.delete()
        .uri("/retros/{uuid}", uuid.toString())
        .exchange()
        .expectStatus().isOk()
    Mockito.verify(retroBoardService, Mockito.times(1)).delete(uuid)
}
}
```

The `RetroBoardWebFluxTests` class includes the following annotations:

- `@MockBean`: We use this annotation in two main classes, `RetroBoardService` and `UserClient`, because we want to apply the authorization and see if the roles work.

- `@WithMockUser`: We use this annotation at the class level, but in the `saveRetroBoardTest` and `deleteRetroBoardTest` methods, we overwrite it by adding the `roles` parameter and defining the `ADMIN` role. If you remove this annotation from these methods, the tests will fail.

If you run these tests, they should pass without any issues. Again, as shown at the end of Listing 9-14, the unit testing is completed by mocking some services, but testing the authorization is one of the important key elements added to this project.

Putting Everything Together: UI, Users App, and Retro App

To put everything together, we use the My Retro App UI (frontend app), which you can find in the resources/myretro-ui folder. Review and analyze it before running it.

Let's first review an important file that includes the security configuration. Open/ create the login.js file in the myretro-ui folder. See Listing 9-15.

Listing 9-15. myretro-ui/assets/js/login.js

```javascript
$(function() {
  $('#btn_login').click(function(e) {
    e.preventDefault();
    let user_email = $('input[name="user_email"]').val();
    let user_password = $('input[name="user_password"]').val();
    $.ajax({
      url: 'http://localhost:8081/login',
      method: 'POST',
        data: {
                username: user_email,
                password: user_password
        },
      xhrFields: {
          withCredentials: true
      },
    headers:{
      'Access-Control-Allow-Origin': '*'
    }
  })
      .done(function( response, textStatus, xhr ) {
        console.log(response)
        if(xhr.status === 200 &&
            response.active === true &&
            response.email === user_email &&
            response.password === user_password ) {
          let isAdmin = response.userRole.includes("ADMIN");
```

```
        localStorage.setItem('ls_name', response.name);
        localStorage.setItem('ls_email', response.email);
        localStorage.setItem('ls_gravatar', response.gravatarUrl);
        localStorage.setItem('ls_role', response.userRole);
        document.cookie = xhr.getResponseHeader('x-myretro');
        console.log(xhr.getAllResponseHeaders());
        if (isAdmin){
          window.location.href = "admin-dashboard.html";
        }else {
          window.location.href = "admin-users.html";
        }
        return;
      }
    });
  });
});
```

In the $.ajax call in login.js, we use the POST HTTP method and point to the /login endpoint. We didn't specify this endpoint in the My Retro App project, but Spring Security defines it by default. The same happens for the /logout endpoint. Also note that we use xhrFields.withCredentials, which allows us to send credentials (cookies, headers, and TLS client certificates) for cross-site access control requests (remember that this is an external app, the UI, so we must do this). After a successful login, it will save the session ID for subsequent calls.

Now it's time to run the app and see if it works. These are the three main steps to make it work:

1. Run Users App, which will run on port 8080.

2. Run My Retro App, which will run on port 8081.

3. Run myretro-ui using the index.html file. You can use your IDE (such as VS Code or WebStorm) or Python.

If you use Python, you need to be in the root of the myretro-ui folder; then execute the following command:

```
python3 -m http.server
```

This will open port 8000. Now you can go to your browser and open it. You should see the Login page shown in Figure 9-7.

Figure 9-7. *Login page for My Retro App (the same as for Users App)*

Enter manager@email.com in the Email field and aw2s0meR! in the Password field and then click the Login button.

You should see the dashboard of My Retro App, shown in Figure 9-8, where you can manage Retros or Users.

Figure 9-8. My Retro App after a successful login

> **Note**   This is just to test security, and does not include much functionality. Play
> around with the apps. If you find any UI bugs, let us know, or you can help by
> submitting your own PR in GitHub with more UI details: `https://github.com/`
> `felipeg48/pro-spring-boot-3rd`.

Adding a Social Login with OAuth2

Many applications require users to authenticate and be authorized by third-party
entities, and the entities are often social media platforms such as Facebook, Google, X
(formally Twitter), GitHub, and so forth. This section shows you how to configure Users
App to authenticate through GitHub. It takes you step by step through the configuration,
and you will discover that the process is very simple when you use Spring Boot, because
it wires everything up so that you can use any social media entities.

By using a social media platform, you are providing a single sign-on (SSO) capability. This allows you to simplify registration and logins for your end users. By using a social media login mechanism, you get some useful features:

- Email verification
- User profiles
- One-click experience

Social media is the most popular way to communicate to the world, so this capability potentially brings more registrations and more traffic to your applications. Let's get started with Users App.

Social Login to Users App

You have access to the code, so go ahead and import the Users App project in 09-security-social/users to your favorite IDE. Then, open the build.gradle file. See Listing 9-16.

Listing 9-16. The build.gradle File

```
import org.jetbrains.kotlin.gradle.tasks.KotlinCompile
plugins {
    id 'org.springframework.boot' version '3.2.3'
    id 'io.spring.dependency-management' version '1.1.4'
    id 'org.jetbrains.kotlin.jvm' version '2.0.20-RC'
    id "org.jetbrains.kotlin.plugin.spring" version "2.0.20-RC"
    // <- simplifies spring proxying
}

group = 'com.apress'
version = '0.0.1-SNAPSHOT'
sourceCompatibility = '17'

repositories {
    mavenCentral()
}
```

```
dependencies {
    implementation "org.jetbrains.kotlin:kotlin-stdlib-jdk8"
    implementation "org.jetbrains.kotlin:kotlin-reflect"

    implementation 'org.springframework.boot:spring-boot-starter-web'
    implementation 'org.springframework.boot:spring-boot-starter-
    validation'
    implementation 'org.springframework.boot:spring-boot-starter-security'
    implementation 'org.springframework.boot:spring-boot-starter-data-jpa'
    implementation 'org.springframework.boot:spring-boot-starter-
    oauth2-client'

    runtimeOnly 'com.h2database:h2'
    runtimeOnly 'org.postgresql:postgresql'

    // Web
    implementation 'org.webjars:bootstrap:5.2.3'

    testImplementation 'org.springframework.boot:spring-boot-starter-test'
    testImplementation 'org.springframework.security:spring-security-test'
}

tasks.named('test') {
    useJUnitPlatform()
}

test {
    testLogging {
        events "passed", "skipped", "failed" //, "standardOut",
        "standardError"

        showExceptions true
        exceptionFormat "full"
        showCauses true
        showStackTraces true

        // Change to 'true' for more verbose test output
        showStandardStreams = false
    }
}
```

```
//    kotlin {
//        jvmToolchain(17)
//    }
tasks.withType(KotlinCompile).configureEach {
    kotlinOptions {
        freeCompilerArgs = ['-Xjsr305=strict']
        jvmTarget = '17'
    }
}
```

Listing 9-16 shows that we are adding the familiar `spring-boot-starter-security`
and the new `spring-boot-starter-oauth2-client` dependency to the dependencies.
Once Spring Boot identifies this new dependency (through auto-configuration), it
will wire up everything that your app needs to use this social login mechanism via the
OAuth2 protocol and client.

Next, open/create the `UserSecurityConfig` class. See Listing 9-17.

Listing 9-17. src/main/kotlin/apress/com/users/security/UserSecurityConfig.kt

```
package com.apress.users.security

import org.springframework.context.annotation.Bean
import org.springframework.context.annotation.Configuration
import org.springframework.security.config.Customizer
import org.springframework.security.config.annotation.web.builders.
HttpSecurity
import org.springframework.security.config.annotation.web.configurers.
AuthorizeHttpRequestsConfigurer.AuthorizationManagerRequestMatcherRegistry
import org.springframework.security.config.annotation.web.configurers.
CsrfConfigurer
import org.springframework.security.config.annotation.web.configurers.
LogoutConfigurer
import org.springframework.security.web.SecurityFilterChain
import org.springframework.security.web.csrf.CookieCsrfTokenRepository
import org.springframework.security.web.util.matcher.AntPathRequestMatcher

@Configuration
class UserSecurityConfig {
```

```
@Bean
@Throws(Exception::class)
fun filterChain(http: HttpSecurity): SecurityFilterChain {
    http
        .csrf { c: CsrfConfigurer<HttpSecurity?> ->
            c.csrfTokenRepository(CookieCsrfTokenRepository.
            withHttpOnlyFalse()) }
        .authorizeHttpRequests{ auth ->
                auth.requestMatchers(
                        AntPathRequestMatcher("/index.html"),
                        AntPathRequestMatcher("/webjars/**"),
                        AntPathRequestMatcher("/error")
                    ).permitAll()
                    .anyRequest().authenticated()
        }
        .logout { l: LogoutConfigurer<HttpSecurity?> ->
            l.logoutSuccessUrl("/index.html").permitAll() }
        .oauth2Login(Customizer.withDefaults())
    return http.build()
    }
}
```

Let's review the `UserSecurityConfig` class. First, we define the security filter by providing the `SecurityFilterChain` bean and configuring the `HttpSecurity` class. We configure the CSRF filter and set the token repository `withHttpOnlyFalse`, which is necessary in the Spring Security OAuth2 client because it allows the CSRF token to be read by JavaScript. (GitHub needs this feature.) Also, we are permitting access to the `index.html` page, the `/error` endpoint, and the assets that live in the `/webjars/**` path; everything else should be authenticated. We had declared the `/logout` and redirected to the home (`/index.html`) with no security. Finally, the `aouth2Login(Customizer. withDefaults())` configuration uses the social login mechanism to go to the GitHub page and tell you that you are about to access Users App and you need to provide the right permissions. After gaining access, you are allowed to use the Users App endpoints. Behind the scenes, Spring Boot configures everything that is necessary to start the OAuth2 protocol with GitHub. See Figure 9-9.

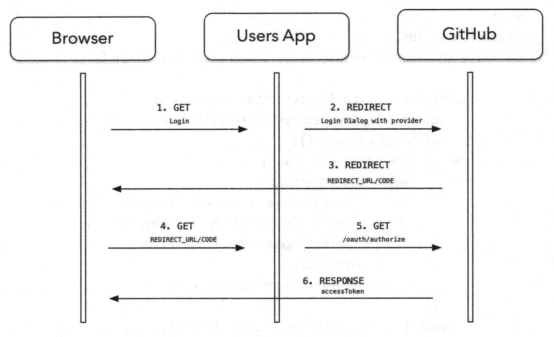

Figure 9-9. *Sequence diagram for Social Login*

Next, open/create the `application.yaml` file. See Listing 9-18.

Listing 9-18. src/main/resources/application.yaml

```
spring:
  h2:
    console:
      enabled: true
  datasource:
    generate-unique-name: false
    name: test-db
  jpa:
    show-sql: true
  security:
    oauth2:
      client:
        registration:
          github:
```

```
        client-id: ${GITHUB_CLIENT_ID}
        client-secret: ${GITHUB_CLIENT_SECRET}
        scope:
          - user:email
          - https://github.com/login/oauth/authorize
logging:
  level:
    org:
      springframework:
        security: DEBUG
```

Listing 9-18 shows the application.yaml properties. The important part are the security.oauth2.client.* properties. We use the registration.github.* so we need to provide the client-id and the client-secret keys. In this case, Spring Boot reads this file and looks for such keys using the GITHUB_CLIENT_ID and GITHUB_CLIENT_SECRET environment variables. Keeping your secret and password keys as environment variables or secrets is a best practice if you are using the Kubernetes infrastructure for deployment.

Use this process to get these keys:

1. Go to https://github.com/settings/developers and sign in. If you don't have an account, click the link to create an account (it's free), create your account, and then sign in. Make sure you are authenticated.

2. Click the New OAuth App button on the right and fill out the required information on the registration form (see Figure 9-10).

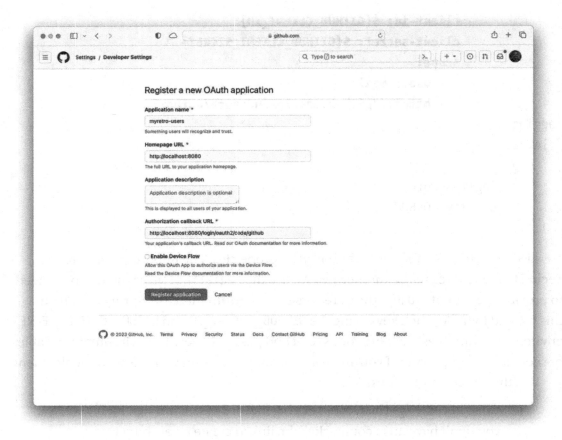

Figure 9-10. *Registering a new OAuth app on GitHub*

- Application name: `myretro-users`

- Home page URL: `http://localhost:8080`

- Authorization callback URL: `http://localhost:8080/login/oauth2/code/github`

3. Click the Register Application button. You will see the page shown in Figure 9-11.

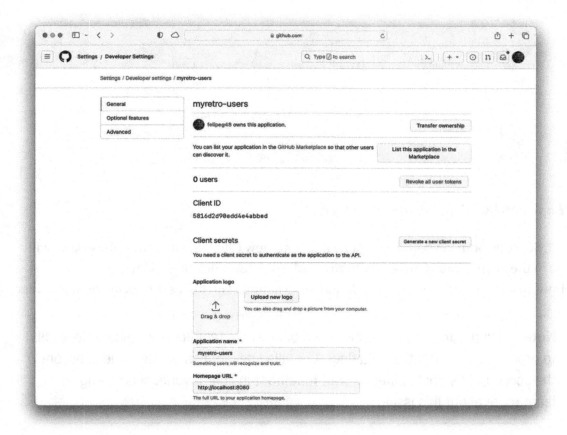

Figure 9-11. *New OAuth app*

4. In the Client Secrets section, click the Generate a New Client
    Secret button. Copy the key that is displayed there. See
    Figure 9-12.

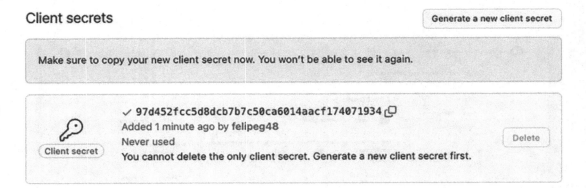

Figure 9-12. *Copying the client secret*

So, copy both keys—the Client ID and your new Client Secrets keys (these keys will be in the environment variable you saw earlier). Then, click the Update Application button, and that's it. Users App will update to include GitHub as the social login provider.

Note   Using `localhost` for the home page and a redirect URL frequently leads to problems in an OAuth2 data flow. A detailed description of this issue is beyond the scope of this book. Enter **oauth2 localhost** in your favorite search engine to learn more about this issue.

Running Users App with Social Login

Now it's time to run Users App and see the results of the new login functionality. Before you run Users App, make sure you set the `GITHUB_CLIENT_ID` and `GITHUB_CLIENT_SECRET` environment variables with the Client ID and Client secret key from the GitHub pages. You can use your IDE to set those variables (consult your IDE's documentation for help).

If you are working from the command line, you can use something like this:

```
GITHUB_CLIENT_ID=xxxx GITHUB_CLIENT_SECRET=xxxx ./gradlew clean bootRUN
```

For example, we are using IntelliJ, so we can configure the environment variables in the Run/Debug Configurations dialog box, as shown in Figure 9-13.

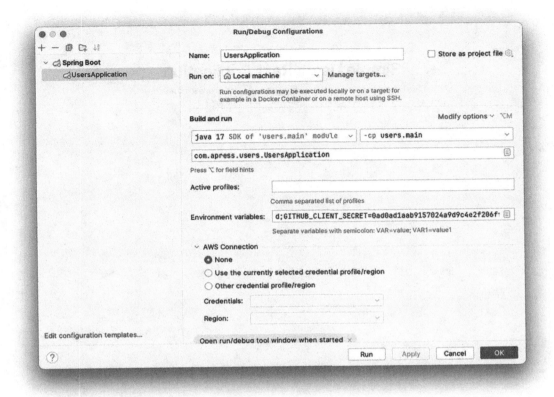

Figure 9-13. *IntelliJ Run/Debug Configurations dialog box*

Once you have Users App up and running, open your browser and go to http://localhost:8080. You will see the home page in Figure 9-14.

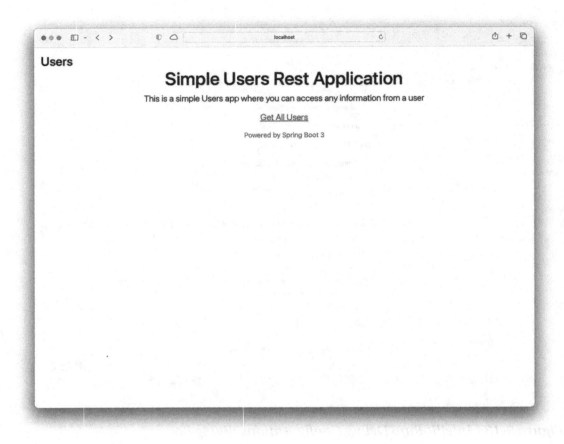

Figure 9-14. *Home page at http://localhost:8080*

Click the Get All Users link. You will be redirected to a GitHub page similar to the one shown in Figure 9-15.

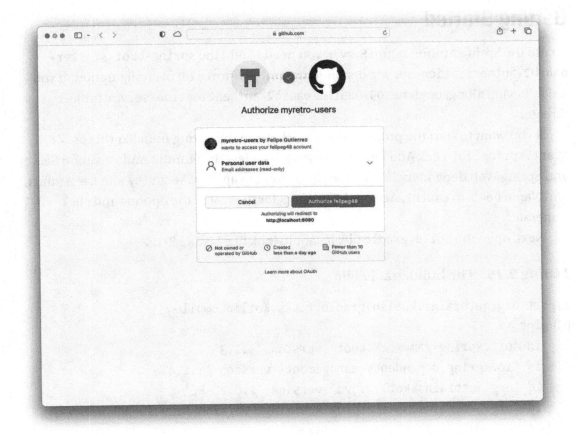

Figure 9-15. *GitHub prompt for authorization*

You need to log in and then authorize `myretro-users` to use the email for read only. After you accept the authorization, you will see the JSON response with all the users.

That's it! Now you have a social login for the Users App project. If you review it, it's very simple. Remember that behind the scenes, Spring Boot is doing most of the heavy lifting with the Spring Security Framework.

The Spring Authorization Server

The Spring Security team recently released the new *Spring Authorization Server*, which provides the implementation of the OAuth2.1 and OpenID Connect 1.0 specifications. Of course, it is built on top of the Spring Security Framework. You can get more insight here: `https://spring.io/projects/spring-authorization-server`.

Getting Started

To use the Spring Authorization Server, you need to add the `spring-boot-starter-oauth2-authorization-server` dependency and perform a bit of configuration. If you are following along, open the `09-oauth2/oauth2-authentication-server` project directory.

If you want to start the project from scratch, go to the Spring Initializr (`https://start.spring.io`), click Add Dependencies, and select the OAuth2 Authorization Server and Spring Web dependencies. Set the Group field to `apress.security` and the Artifact and Name fields to `oauth2`. Accept the defaults for the rest of the options and click Generate.

Next, open the `build.gradle` file; it should look like Listing 9-19.

Listing 9-19. The build.gradle File

```
import org.jetbrains.kotlin.gradle.tasks.KotlinCompile
plugins {
    id 'org.springframework.boot' version '3.2.3'
    id 'io.spring.dependency-management' version '1.1.4'
    id 'org.jetbrains.kotlin.jvm' version '2.0.20-RC'
    id "org.jetbrains.kotlin.plugin.spring" version "2.0.20-RC"
    // <- simplifies spring proxying
}

group = 'com.apress.security'
version = '0.0.1-SNAPSHOT'

java {
    sourceCompatibility = '17'
}

repositories {
    mavenCentral()
}

dependencies {
    implementation "org.jetbrains.kotlin:kotlin-stdlib-jdk8"
    implementation "org.jetbrains.kotlin:kotlin-reflect"
```

```
    implementation 'org.springframework.boot:spring-boot-starter-web'
    implementation 'org.springframework.boot:spring-boot-starter-security'
    implementation 'org.springframework.boot:'+
        'spring-boot-starter-oauth2-authorization-server'
    testImplementation 'org.springframework.boot:spring-boot-starter-test'
}

tasks.named('test') {
    useJUnitPlatform()
}

//    kotlin {
//        jvmToolchain(17)
//    }
tasks.withType(KotlinCompile).configureEach {
    kotlinOptions {
        freeCompilerArgs = ['-Xjsr305=strict']
        jvmTarget = '17'
    }
}
```

Next, we are going to add users that will be authenticated in the Spring Authorization Server. Open/create the Oauth2Config class. See Listing 9-20.

Listing 9-20. src/main/kotlin/apress/security/oauth2/Oauth2Config.kt

```
package com.apress.security.oauth2

import org.springframework.context.annotation.Bean
import org.springframework.context.annotation.Configuration
import org.springframework.security.core.userdetails.User
import org.springframework.security.crypto.bcrypt.BCryptPasswordEncoder
import org.springframework.security.crypto.password.PasswordEncoder
import org.springframework.security.provisioning.InMemoryUserDetailsManager

@Configuration
class Oauth2Config {
    @Bean
    fun inMemoryUserDetailsManager(passwordEncoder: PasswordEncoder):
```

447

```
        InMemoryUserDetailsManager {
    val admin = User
        .builder()
        .username("admin")
        .password(passwordEncoder.encode("admin"))
        .authorities("users.read", "users.write")
        .build()
    val manager = User
        .builder()
        .username("manager@email.com")
        .password(passwordEncoder.encode("aw2s0meR!"))
        .authorities("users.read", "users.write")
        .build()
    val user = User
        .builder()
        .username("user@email.com")
        .password(passwordEncoder.encode("aw2s0meR!"))
        .authorities("users.read")
        .build()
    return InMemoryUserDetailsManager(manager, user, admin)
}

@Bean
fun passwordEncoder(): PasswordEncoder {
    return BCryptPasswordEncoder()
}
}
```

Note that we use the InMemoryUserDetailsManager for simplicity, but you already know how to use JDBC.

Finally, we need to add the configuration. Open/create the application.yaml file and use the contents shown in Listing 9-21.

Listing 9-21. src/main/resources/application.yaml

```
## Server
server:
  port: ${PORT:9000}
## Logging
logging:
  level:
    org.springframework.security: trace
## Bcrypt - Cost Factor 10
## https://bcrypt.online/
## Spring Security
spring:
  security:
    oauth2:
      authorizationserver:
        client:
          users-client:
            registration:
              client-name: "Users' Client"
              client-id: "users-client"
              client-secret: "$2y$10$4Da3ibamZ5Jo34gs7HUhLuNmbPdEhxqWrR9
              v/Z.qosEmWbYYVHCZe"
              client-authentication-methods:
                - "client_secret_basic"
              authorization-grant-types:
                - "authorization_code"
                - "refresh_token"
                - "client_credentials"
              redirect-uris:
                - "http://127.0.0.1:8181/login/oauth2/code/users-client-
                authorization-code"
                - "http://127.0.0.1:8181/users"
              post-logout-redirect-uris:
                - "http://127.0.0.1:8181/"
              scopes:
```

```yaml
              - "openid"
              - "profile"
              - "users.read"
              - "users.write"
          require-authorization-consent: true
    myretro-client:
      registration:
        client-name: "MyRetro Client"
        client-id: "myretro-client"
        client-secret: "$2y$10$KzJqWNyybMyX8.oEJNAGI.YRI4M/
        FuOZcizXQboZ4YDfQfzG9ZmrK"
        client-authentication-methods:
          - "client_secret_basic"
        authorization-grant-types:
          - "authorization_code"
          - "refresh_token"
          - "client_credentials"
        redirect-uris:
          - "http://127.0.0.1:8080/login/oauth2/code/myretro-client-
            authorization-code"
        post-logout-redirect-uris:
          - "http://127.0.0.1:8080/"
        scopes:
          - "openid"
          - "profile"
          - "retros:read"
          - "retros:write"
      require-authorization-consent: true
```

In the application.yaml file, we define the oauth2 configuration needed for the two projects. The idea is that both projects can use the Spring Authorization Server as the authentication and authorization mechanism instead of having that logic locally. Review the configuration.

It's important to note that, after the spring.security.oauth2.authorizationserver. client.* properties, you specify your custom registration. In this case, it's users-client.* (for Users App) and myretro-client.* (for My Retro App).

Look at the `client-secret` property. It's hashed using BCrypt as the algorithm, with a cost factor of 10. The actual word is `secret`, and its BCrypt hash is `$2y$10$7jJ/Gil7n5tlQJOuSbMiMOcrxH7m9SmSwtBwdFS4XEzBHUCJkYeQG`. You can use the Bcrypt Hash Generator at `https://bcrypt.online/` to hash any other secret.

Also, look at the `redirect-uris` (some of them must be used in the apps that will be authenticated against the server) and the `scopes` that are required to consent to the access to the page. These will be displayed once you log in.

That's it! The process is similar to the process described in the previous section for creating access in the GitHub Developer page, where the `client-id` and `client-secret` were generated by GitHub.

Now you can run your Spring Authorization Server app. It will start listening on the port 9000.

Using the Spring Authentication Server with Users App

To use the Spring Authorization Server with Users App, you need to add two dependencies: `spring-boot-starter-oauth2-authorization-server` and `spring-boot-starter-oauth2-client`. You can open the `09-oauth2/users` project and import it into your favorite IDE.

Open the `build.gradle` file. It should look like Listing 9-22.

Listing 9-22. The build.gradle File

```
import org.jetbrains.kotlin.gradle.tasks.KotlinCompile
plugins {
    id 'org.springframework.boot' version '3.2.3'
    id 'io.spring.dependency-management' version '1.1.4'
    id 'org.jetbrains.kotlin.jvm' version '2.0.20-RC'
    id "org.jetbrains.kotlin.plugin.spring" version "2.0.20-RC"
    // <- simplifies spring proxying
}

group = 'com.apress'
version = '0.0.1-SNAPSHOT'
sourceCompatibility = '17'

repositories {
```

```
    mavenCentral()
}

dependencies {
    implementation "org.jetbrains.kotlin:kotlin-stdlib-jdk8"
    implementation "org.jetbrains.kotlin:kotlin-reflect"

    implementation 'org.springframework.boot:spring-boot-starter-web'
    implementation 'org.springframework.boot:spring-boot-starter-webflux'
    implementation 'org.springframework.boot:spring-boot-starter-
    validation'
    implementation 'org.springframework.boot:spring-boot-starter-security'
    implementation 'org.springframework.boot:'+
        'spring-boot-starter-oauth2-authorization-server'
    implementation "org.springframework.boot:spring-boot-starter-
    oauth2-client"
    implementation 'org.springframework.boot:spring-boot-starter-data-jpa'

    runtimeOnly 'com.h2database:h2'
    runtimeOnly 'org.postgresql:postgresql'

    // Web
    implementation 'org.webjars:bootstrap:5.2.3'
    implementation 'org.webjars:webjars-locator-core'

    testImplementation 'org.springframework.boot:spring-boot-starter-test'
    testImplementation 'org.springframework.security:spring-security-test'
}

tasks.named('test') {
    useJUnitPlatform()
}

test {
    testLogging {
        events "passed", "skipped", "failed" //, "standardOut",
        "standardError"

        showExceptions true
```

```
        exceptionFormat "full"
        showCauses true
        showStackTraces true

        // Change to 'true' for more verbose test output
        showStandardStreams = false
    }
}

//    kotlin {
//        jvmToolchain(17)
//    }
tasks.withType(KotlinCompile).configureEach {
    kotlinOptions {
        freeCompilerArgs = ['-Xjsr305=strict']
        jvmTarget = '17'
    }
}
```

Next, open the UserSecurityConfig class. See Listing 9-23.

Listing 9-23. src/main/kotlin/apress/com/users/security/UserSecurityConfig.kt

```
package com.apress.users.security

import org.springframework.context.annotation.Bean
import org.springframework.context.annotation.Configuration
import org.springframework.security.config.Customizer
import org.springframework.security.config.annotation.web.builders.
HttpSecurity
import org.springframework.security.config.annotation.web.builders.
WebSecurity
import org.springframework.security.config.annotation.web.configuration.
WebSecurityCustomizer
import org.springframework.security.config.annotation.web.configurers.
CorsConfigurer
import org.springframework.security.config.annotation.web.configurers.
CsrfConfigurer
```

```kotlin
import org.springframework.security.config.annotation.web.configurers.
oauth2.client.OAuth2LoginConfigurer
import org.springframework.security.config.annotation.web.configurers.
oauth2.server.resource.OAuth2ResourceServerConfigurer
import org.springframework.security.web.SecurityFilterChain
import org.springframework.web.cors.CorsConfiguration
import org.springframework.web.cors.CorsConfigurationSource
import org.springframework.web.cors.UrlBasedCorsConfigurationSource

@Configuration
class UserSecurityConfig {
    @Bean
    fun webSecurityCustomizer(): WebSecurityCustomizer {
        return WebSecurityCustomizer { web: WebSecurity ->
            web.ignoring().requestMatchers("/webjars/**") }
    }

    @Bean
    @Throws(Exception::class)
    fun filterChain(http: HttpSecurity,
            corsConfigurationSource: CorsConfigurationSource?):
            SecurityFilterChain {
        http
            .csrf { csrf: CsrfConfigurer<HttpSecurity> -> csrf.disable() }
            .cors { cors: CorsConfigurer<HttpSecurity?> ->
                cors.configurationSource(corsConfigurationSource) }
            .authorizeHttpRequests{ auth ->
                auth
                    .requestMatchers("/users/**").hasAnyAuthority(
                        "SCOPE_users.read", "SCOPE_users.write")
                    .requestMatchers("/logout").permitAll()
            }
            .oauth2Login { login: OAuth2LoginConfigurer<HttpSecurity?> ->
                login
                    .loginPage("/oauth2/authorization/users-client-
                    authorization-code")
```

```kotlin
                .defaultSuccessUrl("/users")
                .permitAll()
        }
        .oauth2ResourceServer {
            config: OAuth2ResourceServerConfigurer<HttpSecurity?> ->
                config.jwt(Customizer.withDefaults()) }
    return http.build()
}

@Bean
fun corsConfigurationSource(): CorsConfigurationSource {
    val configuration = CorsConfiguration()
    configuration.allowedOrigins = mutableListOf("*")
    configuration.setAllowedMethods(mutableListOf("*"))
    configuration.allowedHeaders = mutableListOf("*")
    val source = UrlBasedCorsConfigurationSource()
    source.registerCorsConfiguration("/**", configuration)
    return source
}
}
```

Note that the requestMatchers() method now includes SCOPE_users.read and
SCOPE_users.write. By convention, SCOPE_ is used when you are using OAuth2 (and
ROLE_ is used when you are using a database or other authentication and authorization
mechanisms). When the Spring Authorization Server provides the scopes (based on the
configuration shown in Listing 9-21), notice that they are not with the SCOPE_. Spring
Security will add them and they must match the ones you provide.

Also notice in Listing 9-23 that we now have the oauth2Login that we are configuring
with .loginPage("/oauth2/authorization/users-client-authorization-code").
These values must match the ones declared in Listing 9-21. There is no special
configuration for the resource server (with oauth2ResourceServer), so the default will
be sufficient.

Next, to see the required configuration, open the application.properties file. See
Listing 9-24.

Listing 9-24. src/main/resources/application.properties

```
# Server
server.port=${PORT:8181}
oauth2.server.port=${OAUTH2_PORT:9000}
# H2 Console
spring.h2.console.enabled=false
# Datasource
spring.datasource.generate-unique-name=false
spring.datasource.name=test-db
# JPA
spring.jpa.show-sql=true
## Authorization Server
spring.security.oauth2.resourceserver.jwt.issuer-uri=http://localhost:9000
## Client Registration
spring.security.oauth2.client.registration.users-client-authorization-code.
provider=spring
spring.security.oauth2.client.registration.users-client-authorization-code.
client-id=users-client
spring.security.oauth2.client.registration.users-client-authorization-code.
client-secret=secret
spring.security.oauth2.client.registration.users-client-authorization-code.
authorization-grant-type=authorization_code
spring.security.oauth2.client.registration.users-client-authorization-code.
redirect-uri=http://127.0.0.1:8181/login/oauth2/code/{registrationId}
spring.security.oauth2.client.registration.users-client-authorization-code.
scope=openid,profile,users.read,users.write
spring.security.oauth2.client.registration.users-client-authorization-code.
client-name=users-client-authorization-code
# Provider
spring.security.oauth2.client.provider.spring.issuer-uri=http://
localhost:9000
# Logging
logging.level.org.springframework.security=TRACE
```

One of the most important pieces in Listing 9-24 are the `*.client.registration.*` properties. The names of these properties must exactly match the names of the `*.users-client-authorization-code.*` properties when we declared the `redirect-uris` in Listing 9-21.

In the Spring Authorization Server, we declared `http://127.0.0.1:8181/login/oauth2/code/users-client-authorization-code`, the last segment of which (`users-client-authorization-code`) must be part of the registration properties.

We are also declaring that the provider is the Spring Authorization Server, `http://localhost:9000`. Again, this configuration is the same as the one in the "Social Login to Users App" section with GitHub.

Running Users App

Before running Users App, make sure the Spring Authorization Server is up and running. Then run Users App, and you should see some activity in the log console for the Spring Authorization Server.

Once Users App is running, open your browser and go to `http://localhost:8181/users`. It will automatically redirect you to a login page (`http://localhost:9000/login`). See Figure 9-16.

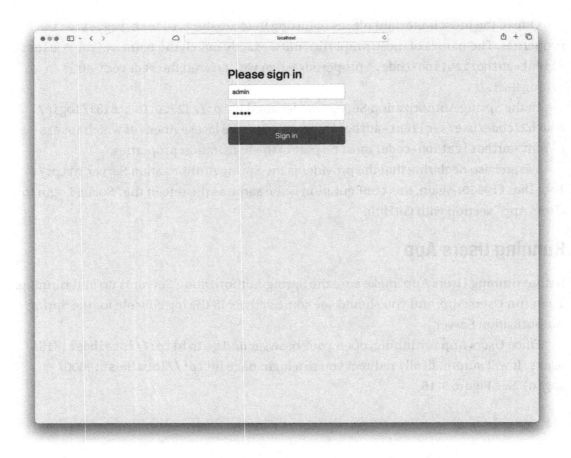

Figure 9-16. *http://localhost:8181/users is automatically redirected to http://localhost:9000/login*

In the fields, enter the `admin` and `admin` credentials. These are set in the Spring Authorization Server (see the configuration in Listing 9-20).

Click the Sign In button. You will be redirected to the Consent Required page shown in Figure 9-17.

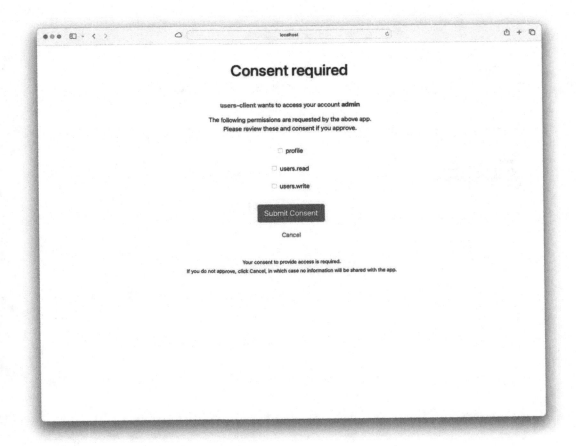

Figure 9-17. *Consent Required page*

On the Consent Required page, you need to select what you want to share as part of the authorization process. Of course, the /users endpoint requires users.read or users.write, which will be transformed to SCOPE_users.read and SCOPE_users.write, respectively.

Once you click Submit Consent, you will be presented with the original request, as shown in http://localhost:8181/users. See Figure 9-18.

Figure 9-18. *The /users endpoint access after acceptance*

And that's it! You now have another option if your company wants to use the Spring Authorization Server as a mechanism for authentication and authorization.

Wait... What About My Retro App?

My Retro App follows the same pattern described for Users App in the previous section. You are encouraged to open and review it (located in the `09-oauth2/myretro` directory). You will find a small change in the scopes: whereas they are declared as `retros:read` and `retros:write` in Users App, in My Retro App they are declared as `users.read` and `users.write` (i.e., with periods instead of colons). This difference is to show you that there is no rule of thumb on how you label your security scopes—that particular requirement depends on the business rules of the company.

Summary

This chapter covered a lot of Spring Security and explained how Spring Boot helps auto-configure most of the beans required for its functionality. You learned different ways to secure your web apps.

You learned how to configure Spring Security for servlets and Reactive web applications. You learned that you can provide any kind of security simply by using `UserDetails`, from in-memory, to JDBC, and even custom security.

You learned that Spring Security works with the chain of responsibility pattern and gives you the ability to provide your own filter, simply by providing the `SecurityFilterChain` (for Servlet web apps) or `SecurityWebFilterChain` (for Reactive web apps) beans and their configurations to secure your requests using roles or scopes.

You learned how to include a social login mechanism in your apps and how to connect them. And finally, you learned about the new Spring Authorization Server—how it works and how to configure it.

Chapter 10 explores the details of messaging with Spring Boot.

CHAPTER 10

Messaging with Spring Boot

Felipe Gutierrez[a*]

[a] 4109 Rillcrest Grove Way Fuquay Varina, NC 27526-3562, Albuquerque, NM, USA

Messaging As a Concept

Messaging is a way for different parts of a computer system, or even different systems, to communicate with each other. Messaging is used in many ways, from instant messaging or email, to enterprise applications.

Messaging can be *synchronous*, meaning that the sender and receiver must both be available at the same time, or *asynchronous*, meaning that the sender and receiver can communicate at different times. Messaging can also be *publish-and-subscribe (pub/sub)*, meaning that messages are published to a topic and any interested subscribers can receive them, or *peer-to-peer*, meaning that messages are sent directly from one sender to one receiver.

Messaging is a very powerful way to build distributed systems because it allows different parts of a system to communicate with each other without having to be tightly coupled. This means that changes to one part of the system do not necessarily affect the other parts.

Using Spring Boot to create messaging systems is easy due to the abstractions that simplify how these systems are built. Spring Boot provides several features that make it easy to develop and manage messaging applications, including support for popular messaging brokers such as RabbitMQ, Apache Kafka, Apache Pulsar, and Apache ActiveMQ.

The examples in this chapter show you how to use Spring Boot to build messaging applications using different technologies and messaging brokers.

© Peter Späth, Felipe Gutierrez 2025
P. Späth and F. Gutierrez, *Pro Spring Boot 3 with Kotlin*, https://doi.org/10.1007/979-8-8688-1131-9_10

Messaging with Spring Boot

The Spring Framework contains a dedicated technology for messaging, which you can find as a dependency (`spring-messaging`). Around 2013/2014, all the core messaging was part of the Spring Integration technology, but the Spring Integration team decided to move it to the core-level package, so it would be easy for future messaging technologies to use such components. Thanks to the Spring Integration team, we now have an amazing technology that can help developers integrate different systems—not only internally or locally but also remotely.

The Spring Messaging technology provides a simple model for implementing complex enterprise integration solutions with ease. It also facilitates asynchronous and message-driven behavior by promoting components that are loosely coupled for modularity and testability and more easily separating the concerns between business logic and integration logic. All this promotes reusability and portability.

These are some of the main components of the `spring-messaging` technology:

- Message: This interface belongs to the `org.springframework.messaging` package and defines a generic wrapper for any Java/Kotlin object. It has a payload and headers. Consider the following code snippet:

```
package org.springframework.messaging
interface Message<T> {
    fun getPayload():T
    fun getHeaders():MessageHeaders
}
```

  The `getHeaders()` method returns a `MessageHeaders` class that implements the `Map<String, Object>` and `Serializable` interfaces. This class includes several useful properties, such as ID, `timestamp`, `correlation ID`, and `return address`, among others. Thanks to these properties, serialization and deserialization can happen. More about this later in the chapter.

- `MessageChannel`: This is a functional interface that defines an overload method called `send` (and it uses the `Message` interface as a parameter) and uses it as a pipe (in a pipe-filter architecture). This interface can be used in point-to-point and publish-and-subscribe scenarios. The following snippet defines it:

```
package org.springframework.messaging;
@FunctionalInterface
public interface MessageChannel {
    long INDEFINITE_TIMEOUT = -1;
    default boolean send(Message<?> message) {
        return send(message, INDEFINITE_TIMEOUT);
    }
    boolean send(Message<?> message, long timeout);
}
```

- *Message endpoint*: As the name suggests, a *message endpoint* is not an interface or class but rather an endpoint through which *inbound* and *outbound* messages pass and can be enhanced, filtered, and more. You can see a message endpoint as a filter. Spring Messaging and the other messaging technologies covered in this chapter use this concept. To mention some of them: *message transformer, message filter, message router, splitter, aggregator, service activator, channel adapter,* and *endpoint bean names.*

Note   If you want more insight, check out *Spring Boot Messaging* (Apress, 2017; https://link.springer.com/book/10.1007/978-1-4842-1224-0), which will help you understand not only this concept about messaging but also other messaging technologies.

Using spring-messaging with Spring Boot is even easier, because all the manual configuration that you normally do in a regular Spring app is performed by Spring Boot auto-configuration.

This intro to spring-messaging explains how the different technologies—such as JMS, AMQP, Kafka, and Pulsar by Spring—are very similar in context and explains what is happening behind the scenes.

Events with Spring Boot

In our opinion, *events* are an essential way to implement messaging across modules or components within your applications, and normally they are used internally, in your business logic. That said, before we delve into the specific message broker technologies, let's start with events and see how easy it is to use them with Spring Boot.

One of the main features of the Spring Framework is its event handling. The event handling in the Spring ApplicationContext is provided through the ApplicationEvent class and the ApplicationListener interface.

In fact, every time your Spring Boot app starts, there are many events happening in the Spring ApplicationContext, and you can listen to such events. For example, the Spring Framework provides some built-in events, such as ContextRefreshedEvent, ContextStartedEvent, ContextStoppedEvent, and ContextClosedEvent, among others. And, of course, Spring Boot provides its own built-in events, such as ApplicationReadyEvent, which happens when your app is ready. The CommandLineRunner or ApplicationRunner interface implementations run if they are found in your code, and these provide such an event. (Does this sound familiar? Tip: Check your configuration classes.) Other built-in events include ApplicationStartingEvent, ApplicationFailedEvent, and many more (some of these events are listeners of the Spring events, that send anything that your application needs).

The steps for using events in Spring are as follows:

1. Create your event by extending the ApplicationEvent class.

2. Implement the ApplicationEventPublishAware interface and use the ApplicationEventPublisher class to publish your ApplicationEvent (from the previous step).

3. Implement the ApplicationListener based on your event.

4. Implement the onApplicationEvent method.

However, there is a simpler way. Spring also provides annotation-based event listeners with the @EventListener annotation and asynchronous listeners with the combination of the @Async annotation—these help you create your own custom events with ease.

Adding Events to Users App

Let's add two events to the Users App project:

- **UserActivatedEvent**: Sent when a **User** changes its status to active or inactive.

- **UserRemovedEvent**: Sent when a **User** is removed from the database.

You have access to the code at the Apress website or here: `https://github.com/ felipeg48/pro-spring-boot-3rd`. You can use the code from the `ch10-messaging-events/users` folder. Or you can use any other Users App project.

We are going to create a new package named `events`. Open/create the `UserActivatedEvent` and `UserRemovedEvent` classes with the code shown in Listings 10-1 and 10-2, respectively.

Listing 10-1. src/main/kotlin/com/apress/users/events/UserActivatedEvent.kt

```kotlin
package com.apress.users.events

data class UserActivatedEvent(
    var email: String? = null,
    var active:Boolean? = false
)
```

As you can see in Listing 10-1, the `UserActivatedEvent` class is a very simple POJO (plain old Java object). `UserRemovedEvent` in Listing 10-2 is also very simple.

Listing 10-2. src/main/kotlin/com/apress/users/events/UserRemovedEvent.kt

```kotlin
package com.apress.users.events

import java.time.LocalDateTime

data class UserRemovedEvent(
    var email: String? = null,
    var removed: LocalDateTime? = null
)
```

Next, create the `UserLogs` class; it will be the listener of such events. See Listing 10-3.

Listing 10-3. src/main/kotlin/com/apress/users/events/UserLogs.kt

```kotlin
package com.apress.users.events

import org.slf4j.LoggerFactory
import org.springframework.context.event.EventListener
import org.springframework.scheduling.annotation.Async
import org.springframework.stereotype.Component

@Component
class UserLogs {
    @Async
    @EventListener
    fun userActiveStatusEventHandler(event: UserActivatedEvent) {
        LOG.info("User {} active status: {}", event.email, event.active)
    }

    @Async
    @EventListener
    fun userDeletedEventHandler(event: UserRemovedEvent) {
        LOG.info("User {} DELETED at {}", event.email, event.removed)
    }

    companion object {
        private val LOG = LoggerFactory.getLogger(UserLogs::class.java)
    }
}
```

The `UserLogs` class is marked with the `@Component` annotation, so the other two annotations—`@Async` and `@EventListener`—are registered in the app context. This will enable the methods to listen to such events. Right now, these events are logged into the console, but in reality these events could be saved or could send a message to an external broker.

Next, open/create the `UserService` class. See Listing 10-4.

Listing 10-4. src/main/kotlin/com/apress/users/service/UserService.kt

```kotlin
package com.apress.users.service

import com.apress.users.events.UserActivatedEvent
import com.apress.users.events.UserRemovedEvent
import com.apress.users.model.User
import com.apress.users.repository.UserRepository
import org.springframework.beans.factory.annotation.Autowired
import org.springframework.context.ApplicationEventPublisher
import org.springframework.stereotype.Service
import java.time.LocalDateTime
import java.util.*

@Service
class UserService {
    @Autowired
    private lateinit var userRepository: UserRepository

    @Autowired
    private lateinit var publisher: ApplicationEventPublisher

    val allUsers: Iterable<User>
      get() = userRepository.findAll()

    fun findUserByEmail(email: String): Optional<User> =
        userRepository.findById(email)

    fun saveUpdateUser(user: User): User =
        userRepository.save<User>(user).also {
            publisher.publishEvent(UserActivatedEvent(it.email, it.active))
        }

    fun removeUserByEmail(email: String) =
        userRepository.deleteById(email).also {
            publisher.publishEvent(UserRemovedEvent(email, LocalDateTime.
            now()))
        }
}
```

Listing 10-4 shows that the UserService class is marked with the @Service annotation. We are also using the ApplicationEventPublisher class. This class will help publish the events with the publishEvent method.

That's it. Very easy, right? If you run the UsersHttpRequestTests tests, you will see something like this in the console logs:

```
...
2023-10-11T14:29:31.535-04:00  INFO 47670 --- [   Test worker] com.apress.
users.events.UserLogs          : User dummy@email.com active status: false
2023-10-11T14:29:31.542-04:00  INFO 47670 --- [   Test worker] com.
apress.users.events.UserLogs          : User dummy@email.com DELETED at
2023-10-11T14:29:31.541750
```

The configuration for My Retro App is similar. Look at the 10-messaging-events/myretro folder and the events and service packages. Very simple.

JMS with Spring Boot

This section shows how you can integrate Java Message Service with Spring Boot apps, using the book's two main projects. JMS has been around since the late 1980s and is still used by quite a few big companies, primarily financial institutions. JMS was developed by Sun Microsystems, and then it went to the Java Community Process (JCP) with Oracle for development of version 2.0. JMS continues to evolve and is currently part of the *Jakarta EE ecosystem* and named *Jakarta Messaging*. JMS 3.0 is still under development.

It's important to know that JMS supports both the *point-to-point* and *publish-and-subscribe* messaging models. In a point-to-point model, the *queue* is the hub of communication, and in the publish-and-subscribe model, the *topic* is the hub. See Figure 10-1.

point-to-point

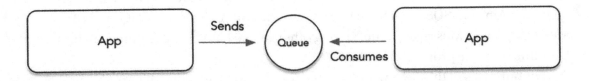

publish-and-subscribe

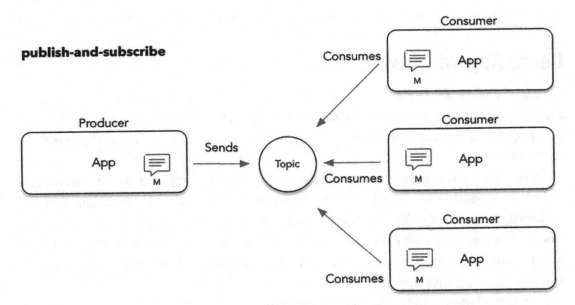

Figure 10-1. *Point-to-point and publish-and-subscribe messaging models*

The Spring Framework supports JMS with several useful classes that can provide the message publishing and consuming. The JmsTemplate class wraps up all the boilerplate code for connecting, sessioning, multithreading, reconnecting, and much more. The JdbcTemplate class will be practically the same as in Chapters 4 and 5, but for messaging of course. Spring also provides several annotations that can build consumers with ease, such as the @JmsListener annotation. If you want to do manual message handling, the SimpleMessageListenerContainer annotation gives you more control over your messaging solution.

Which Broker Are We Using?

Currently, in the IT market there are many JMS broker implementations available, including Amazon SQS, Apache ActiveMQ Classic and Artemis, IBM MQ, and JBoss Messaging Open Message Queue, among others. Each has special features, such as handling multiple protocols besides JMS.

For purposes of this demonstration, we use the Apache ActiveMQ Artemis broker. This broker includes the latest JMS implementation, plus it comes with new protocol implementations such as AMQP, STOMP, MQTT, OpenWire, and additional features. If you want to know more about ActiveMQ Artemis, go to `https://activemq.apache.org/components/artemis/`. The code used here is the same for any other broker you choose. The important broker-specific information is the broker URL and credentials.

Users App with JMS

Let's start with Users App and see how easy it's to add JMS to this project. You can get the code from the Apress website or from the GitHub repo: `https://github.com/felipeg48/pro-spring-boot-3rd`. You can find the code in the `10-messaging-jms/users` folder.

If you are starting from scratch with the Spring Initializr (`https://start.spring.io`), click Add Dependencies, type **JMS** in the search field, and choose the Spring for Apache ActiveMQ Artemis dependency. Add the Web, Validation, JPA, H2, PostgreSQL, and Docker Compose Support dependencies. Set the Group ID field to `com.apress` and the Artifact and Name fields to `users`. Then, click Generate, download the project, unzip it, and import it into your favorite IDE.

Open the `build.gradle` file. See Listing 10-5.

Listing 10-5. The build.gradle File

```
import org.jetbrains.kotlin.gradle.tasks.KotlinCompile
plugins {
    id 'org.springframework.boot' version '3.2.3'
    id 'io.spring.dependency-management' version '1.1.4'
    id 'org.jetbrains.kotlin.jvm' version '2.0.20-RC'
    id "org.jetbrains.kotlin.plugin.spring" version "2.0.20-RC"
    // <- simplifies spring proxying
}
```

```
group = 'com.apress'
version = '0.0.1-SNAPSHOT'
sourceCompatibility = '17'

repositories {
    mavenCentral()
}

dependencies {
    implementation "org.jetbrains.kotlin:kotlin-stdlib-jdk8"
    implementation "org.jetbrains.kotlin:kotlin-reflect"

    implementation 'org.springframework.boot:spring-boot-starter-web'
    implementation 'org.springframework.boot:spring-boot-starter-
    validation'

    implementation 'org.springframework.boot:spring-boot-starter-artemis'
    implementation 'com.fasterxml.jackson.datatype:jackson-datatype-jsr310'

    developmentOnly 'org.springframework.boot:spring-boot-docker-compose'

    implementation 'org.springframework.boot:spring-boot-starter-data-jpa'
    runtimeOnly 'com.h2database:h2'
    runtimeOnly 'org.postgresql:postgresql'

    // Web
    implementation 'org.webjars:bootstrap:5.2.3'

    testImplementation 'org.springframework.boot:spring-boot-starter-test'
}
tasks.named('test') {
    useJUnitPlatform()
}

//    kotlin {
//        jvmToolchain(17)
//    }
tasks.withType(KotlinCompile).configureEach {
    kotlinOptions {
```

```
        freeCompilerArgs = ['-Xjsr305=strict']
        jvmTarget = '17'
    }
}
```

Because the spring-boot-starter-artemis dependency is in the build.gradle file, Spring Boot will auto-configure ConnectionFactory (with the default broker-url, mode, and other properties), JmsTemplate, MessageConverter (default for classes that implement Serializable, are Map or String type based), and other important classes. The jackson-datatype-jsr310 dependency will help with the event serialization that has the LocalDateTime as a property/field. We are also using the spring-boot-docker-compose dependency, so we can run the app and it will look for the docker-compose. yaml file and start the services we need.

We are going to use the events from the previous section, and we need to add some features that will help us add the JSON serialization. Next, open/create the UserRemovedEvent class. See Listing 10-6.

Listing 10-6. src/main/kotlin/com/apress/users/events/UserRemovedEvent.kt

```
package com.apress.users.events

import com.fasterxml.jackson.annotation.JsonFormat
import com.fasterxml.jackson.databind.annotation.JsonSerialize
import com.fasterxml.jackson.datatype.jsr310.ser.LocalDateTimeSerializer
import java.time.LocalDateTime

data class UserRemovedEvent(
    var email: String? = null,

    @get:JsonFormat(pattern = "yyyy-MM-dd HH:mm:ss")
    @get:JsonSerialize(using = LocalDateTimeSerializer::class)
    var removed: LocalDateTime? = null
)
```

We added the @JsonFormat and @JsonSerialize annotations to the UserRemovedEvent class. These annotations help serialize LocalDateTime with the format yyy-MM-dd HH:mm:ss. If you were to remove it, you would have come a long way (unnecessary information, in our opinion) to express something as simple as that.

Next, the UserActivatedEvent class is the same as shown in Listing 10-1, so there's no need to present it again.

Next, open/create the UserLogs class. See Listing 10-7.

Listing 10-7. src/main/kotlin/com/apress/users/events/UserLogs.kt

```kotlin
package com.apress.users.events

import com.apress.users.jms.UserJmsConfig
import org.slf4j.LoggerFactory
import org.springframework.beans.factory.annotation.Autowired
import org.springframework.context.event.EventListener
import org.springframework.jms.core.JmsTemplate
import org.springframework.scheduling.annotation.Async
import org.springframework.stereotype.Component

@Component
class UserLogs {
    @Autowired
    private lateinit var jmsTemplate: JmsTemplate

    @Async
    @EventListener
    fun userActiveStatusEventHandler(event: UserActivatedEvent) {
        jmsTemplate.convertAndSend(UserJmsConfig.DESTINATION_
        ACTIVATED, event)
        LOG.info("User {} active status: {}", event.email, event.active)
    }

    @Async
    @EventListener
    fun userDeletedEventHandler(event: UserRemovedEvent) {
        jmsTemplate.convertAndSend(UserJmsConfig.DESTINATION_
        REMOVED, event)
        LOG.info("User {} DELETED at {}", event.email, event.removed)
    }
```

```kotlin
    companion object {
        private val LOG = LoggerFactory.getLogger(UserLogs::class.java)
    }
}
```

Listing 10-7 shows that now we not only are listening for the events but also sending the events as messages by using the JmsTemplate and calling the convertAndSend method. This method is overloaded to accept different values, and here we are using the destination. (The destination is the name of the *queue*, because this is a point-to-point model; in the publish-and-subscribe model, it would be the name of the *topic*.) The queue is DESTINATION_ACTIVATED=activated-users and DESTINATION_REMOVED=removed-users and it that will receive the message and the actual message (either UserActivatedEvent or UserRemovedEvent) as a second value. The JmsTemplate uses the fire-and-forget pattern unless you indicate that you need an immediate response (sendAndReceive). It will convert the message using a message converter, by default it will try to execute the implementation of the MessageConverter interface. It will also attempt to discover if the message is a String, Map<?,?>, Serializable, or byte[] type. If it can't discover the type, it will throw a MessageConversionException.

We need to send these events as JSON. To do that, we can tell the JmsTemplate to use a JSON message converter. Next, open/create the UserJmsConfig class. See Listing 10-8.

Listing 10-8. src/main/kotlin/com/apress/users/jms/UserJmsConfig.kt

```kotlin
package com.apress.users.jms

import org.springframework.context.annotation.Bean
import org.springframework.context.annotation.Configuration
import org.springframework.jms.support.converter.
MappingJackson2MessageConverter
import org.springframework.jms.support.converter.MessageConverter
import org.springframework.jms.support.converter.MessageType

@Configuration
class UserJmsConfig {
    @Bean
    fun messageConverter(): MessageConverter =
        MappingJackson2MessageConverter().apply {
            setTypeIdPropertyName("_type")
```

```
        setTargetType(MessageType.TEXT)
    }

    companion object {
        const val DESTINATION_ACTIVATED = "activated-users"
        const val DESTINATION_REMOVED = "removed-users"
    }
}
```

The UserJmsConfig class is marked using the @Configuration annotation, which will be picked up when the application starts and helps Spring look for any @Bean definition and configures it accordingly. In this class, we are defining two constants, DESTINATION_ACTIVATED=activated-users and DESTINATION_REMOVED=removed-users, which are the names of the queues (or the *topics*, depending on the model used). By default, Spring Boot creates these queues when the JmsTemplate executes the convertAndSend method, so there is no need to create the queues manually or programmatically. Of course, you can override the default if you want.

We are defining the MessageConverter; we are overriding it because, by default, Spring Boot will configure this bean. We are creating a MappingJackson2MessageConverter. We are setting the target type as TEXT, meaning that our event object will be sent as text in JSON format, and we are defining a TypeId that will help the converter identify which class type it needs to do the serialization and deserialization. The TypeId can be any text you like; this is just a hint for the converter (it could be _class_, _id_, or custom, for example). In this case, we are using _type.

Next, open/create the docker-compose.yaml file. See Listing 10-9.

Listing 10-9. docker-compose.yaml

```
version: "3"
services:
  artemis:
    container_name: artemis
    hostname: artemis
    image: apache/activemq-artemis:latest-alpine
    platform: linux/amd64
    restart: always
    environment:
```

477

```
    EXTRA_ARGS: "--nio --relax-jolokia --http-host 0.0.0.0"
  ports:
    - "61616:61616"
    - "8161:8161"
```

As you can see, the docker-compose.yaml file is very straightforward. When the app starts and sees the spring-boot-docker-compose dependency, it will look for this file and start the services.

By default, the Apache ActiveMQ Artemis credentials are artemis/artemis, so it's necessary to provide the spring.artermis.* properties in the application.properties file. See Listing 10-10.

Listing 10-10. src/main/resources/application.properties

```
spring.h2.console.enabled=true
spring.datasource.generate-unique-name=false
spring.datasource.name=test-db
# JMS Remote
spring.artemis.user=artemis
spring.artemis.password=artemis
#spring.artemis.broker-url=tcp://localhost:61616
#spring.artemis.mode=native

spring.docker.compose.file: ./users/docker-compose.yaml
```

Now we are ready to publish the events as JSON messages to the JMS broker.

Running Users App

Go ahead and run the Users App project. It will start by starting the services from the docker-compose.yaml file. You should see the logs from the events:

```
...
User ximena@email.com active status: true
User norma@email.com active status: false
User dummy@email.com active status: false
User dummy@email.com DELETED at 2023-10-12T15:43:10.798841
...
```

Remember that this is happening because, in the `UserConfiguration` class, we have the `CommandLineRunner init(UserService)` bean declaration that will be executed once the app is ready. The `UserService` has the event publisher, and the `UserLogs` class will log the appropriate events.

Let's now look at the ActiveMQ Artemis broker. Open your browser and go to `http://localhost:8161` to access the ActiveMQ Artemis Management console. See Figure 10-2.

Figure 10-2. *The ActiveMQ Artemis Management console (`http://` `localhost:8161`)*

As previously indicated, the username and password are both `artemis`. After you enter them and click Log In, expand the navigation pane, select addresses, and click the Queues tab, as shown in Figure 10-3. You will see the `activated-users` and `removed-users` queues with some messages (indicated in the Message Count column).

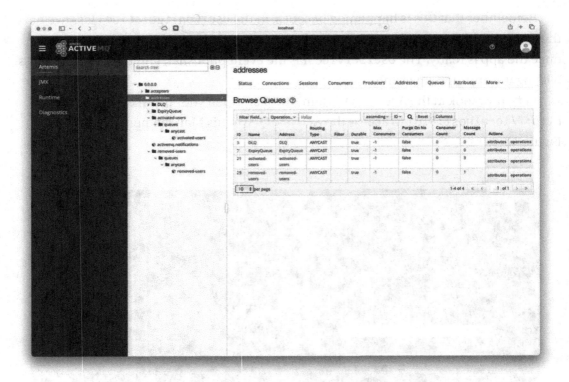

Figure 10-3. *The Queues tab of the ActiveMQ Artemis Management console*

Select the `activated-users` queue in the navigation pane to see the messages that are in the queue at that moment. See Figure 10-4.

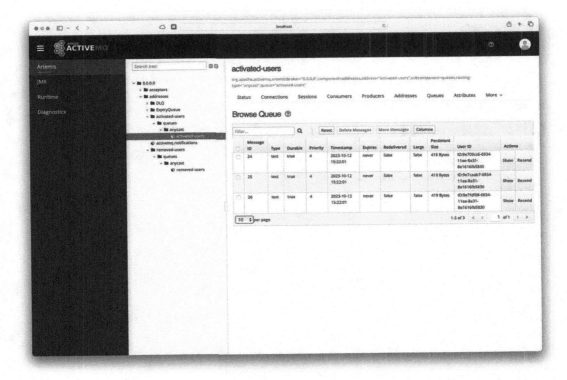

Figure 10-4. *Message list for the activated-users queue*

Now you can select one of the messages and view its contents. Figure 10-5 shows an example of an open message.

Note   If you use the finished sources, you have to temporarily disable (comment them out) the @JmsListener in the UserEventListeners class to see those messages in the queue browser.

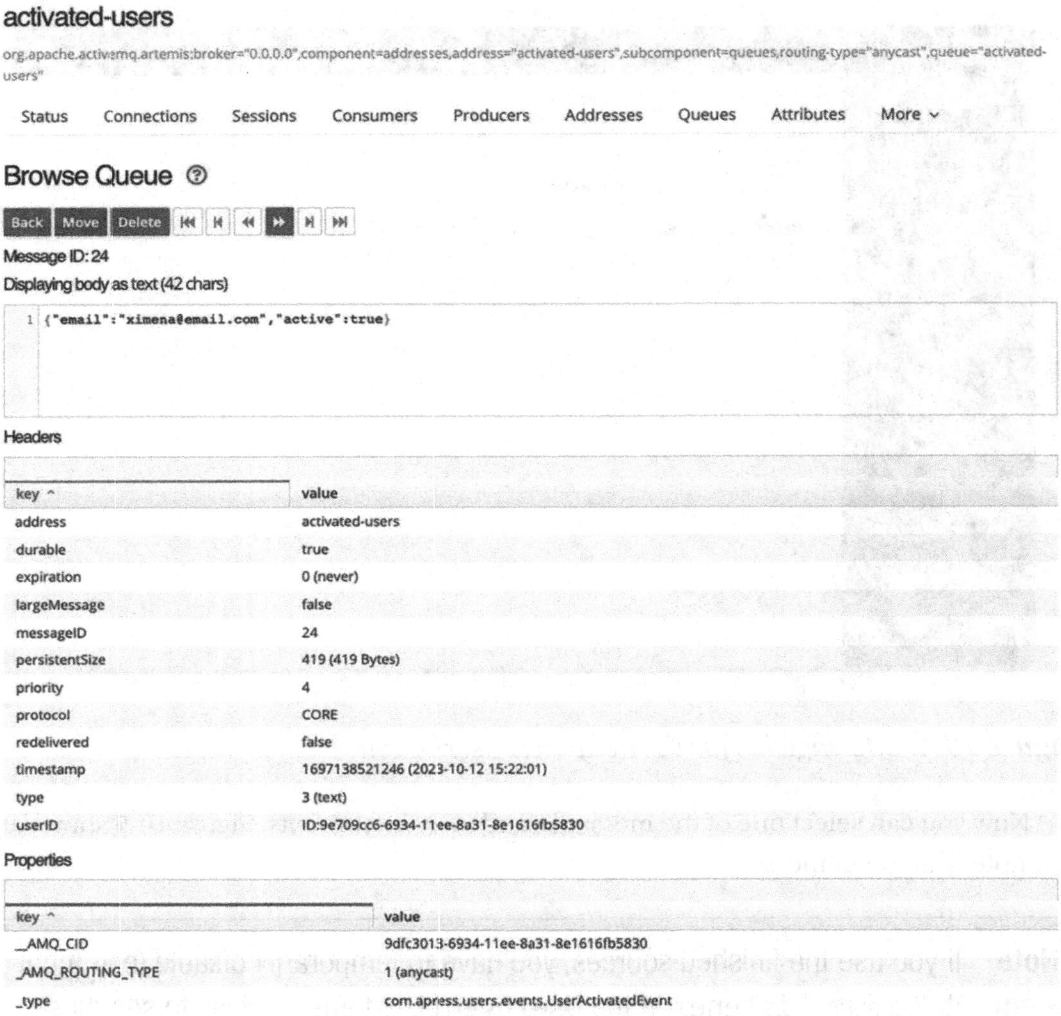

activated-users

org.apache.activemq.artemis:broker="0.0.0.0",component=addresses,address="activated-users",subcomponent=queues,routing-type="anycast",queue="activated-users"

Status	Connections	Sessions	Consumers	Producers	Addresses	Queues	Attributes	More ∨

Browse Queue ⑦

Back	Move	Delete	⏮	ᴵ◀	◀◀	▶▶	▶ᴵ	⏭

Message ID: 24

Displaying body as text (42 chars)

```
1  {"email":"ximena@email.com","active":true}
```

Headers

key ^	value
address	activated-users
durable	true
expiration	0 (never)
largeMessage	false
messageID	24
persistentSize	419 (419 Bytes)
priority	4
protocol	CORE
redelivered	false
timestamp	1697138521246 (2023-10-12 15:22:01)
type	3 (text)
userID	ID:9e709cc6-6934-11ee-8a31-8e1616fb5830

Properties

key ^	value
__AMQ_CID	9dfc3013-6934-11ee-8a31-8e1616fb5830
_AMQ_ROUTING_TYPE	1 (anycast)
_type	com.apress.users.events.UserActivatedEvent

Figure 10-5. *An activated-users message example*

The message is in JSON format. Look at the Headers and Properties sections. The Properties section shows the _type key and the com.apress.users.events. UserActivatedEvent value. Remember that this property is useful for providing a hint to MessageConverter for deserialization (and serialization) when using a listener.

Next, select the removed-users queue in the navigation pane and open a message. You'll see something like the example in Figure 10-6.

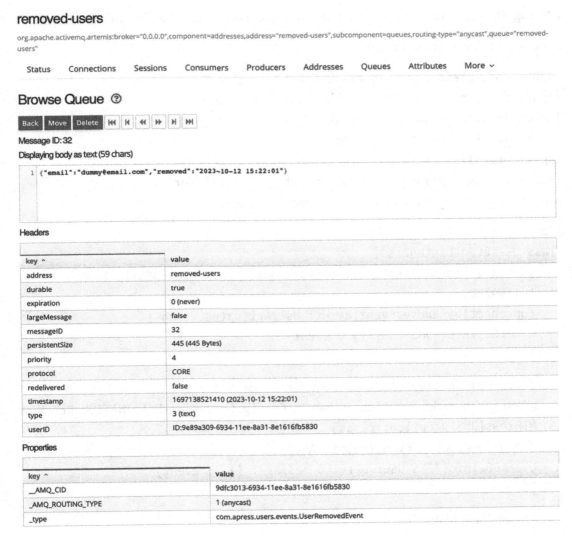

Figure 10-6. *A removed-users message example*

Note in Figure 10-6 that the event message uses the JSON format for `LocalDateTime`:
`yyyy-MM-dd HH:mm:ss`. This is in `UserRemovedEvent` and the `@JsonFormat(pattern =`
`"yyyy-MM-dd HH:mm:ss")` annotation.

Listen for Incoming User Events with JMS

Next, create/open the `UserEventListeners` class. See Listing 10-11.

Listing 10-11. src/main/kotlin/com/apress/users/jms/UserEventListeners.kt

```kotlin
package com.apress.users.jms

import com.apress.users.events.UserActivatedEvent
import jakarta.jms.JMSConnectionFactoryDefinition
import jakarta.jms.JMSException
import jakarta.jms.JMSSessionMode
import org.slf4j.LoggerFactory
import org.springframework.jms.annotation.JmsListener
import org.springframework.stereotype.Component

@Component
class UserEventListeners {
    @JmsListener(destination = UserJmsConfig.Companion.DESTINATION_
    ACTIVATED)
    fun onActivatedUserEvent(event: UserActivatedEvent) {
        LOG.info("JMS User {}", event)
    }

    // Generic ActiveMQMessage > jakarta.jms.Message
    @JmsListener(destination = UserJmsConfig.Companion.DESTINATION_REMOVED)
    @Throws(JMSException::class)
    fun onRemovedUserEvent(event: Any?) {
        LOG.info("JMS User DELETED message: {} ", event)
    }

    companion object {
        private val LOG = LoggerFactory.getLogger(UserEventListeners::c
        lass.java)
    }
}
```

Let's review the UserEventListeners class:

- @Component: This annotation is necessary for Spring to wire up every
  listener.

- @JmsListener: This annotation needs the destination name (queue
  or topic); it has more parameters, but this one will be enough.

- onActivatedUserEvent: This method accepts UserActivatedEvent as a parameter value, which will be passed once the message is received and converted (deserialization) from JSON to object.

- onRemovedUserEvent: This method accepts an Object (this is on purpose) because we want to show you what type of object is being received.

Rerunning Users App

If you run Users App again with the new changes thus far, you will get the following output:

```
...
JMS User UserActivatedEvent(email=ximena@email.com, active=true)
JMS User UserActivatedEvent(email=norma@email.com, active=false)
JMS User UserActivatedEvent(email=dummy@email.com, active=false)
JMS User DELETED message: ActiveMQMessage[ID:93288cbb-6937-11ee-8a2a-8
e1616fb5830]:PERSISTENT/ClientMessageImpl[messageID=98, durable=true,
address=removed-users,userID=93288cbb-6937-11ee-8a2a-8e1616fb5830,propertie
s=TypedProperties[__AMQ_CID=92b75453-6937-11ee-8a2a-8e1616fb5830,_type=com.
apress.users.events.UserRemovedEvent,_AMQ_ROUTING_TYPE=1]]
...
```

The onRemovedUserEvent(Object) object gets ActiveMQMessage (this class implements the jakarta.jms.Message interface). Review this message and notice that it comes with a lot of information that can be useful for other business logic. You probably are wondering how to use the actual UserRemovedEvent object instead of the generic, right? The answer, next.

If you change the signature, as in the following snippet:

```
@JmsListener(destination = UserJmsConfig.DESTINATION_REMOVED)
fun onRemovedUserEvent(event:UserRemovedEvent) {
    LOG.info("JMS User DELETED message: {} ", event)
}
```

You will get a `MessageConversionException` message saying that it cannot deserialize the `LocalDateTime` object. Although we configured `MessageConverter`, we need to tell it (by creating a custom `MessageConverter`) how to deserialize it. By default, `com.fasterxml.jackson.databind.ObjectMapper` is configured with its default (for serialization, this is easy, but not for deserialization), but we need to add a way to handle the `LocalDateTime` type.

In the `UserJmsConfig` class, replace the `MessageConverter` declaration, as shown in the following snippet:

```
@Bean
fun messageConverter(): MessageConverter {
    val mapper = ObjectMapper()
    mapper.registerModule(JavaTimeModule())
    val converter = MappingJackson2MessageConverter()
    converter.setTypeIdPropertyName("_type")
    converter.setTargetType(MessageType.TEXT)
    converter.setObjectMapper(mapper)
    return converter
}
```

And that's it! Now you can use the `onRemovedUserEvent(UserRemovedEvent event)` signature and everything will work.

Remember that a JMS listener is normally another app that consumes messages asynchronously and does some processing with the messages. Here, we have the producer and consumer in the same base code. One use case for this project would be to notify My Retro App when a user has been created or deleted and, for example, do a server push to refresh the web page.

You now know how to use the JMS point-to-point model with ActiveMQ Artemis. The next section explores how to use the JMS publish-and-subscribe model (refer to Figure 10-1).

Using JMS Topics with My Retro App

Using JMS with My Retro App to listen for events that occur in Users App is a good example of the publish-and-subscribe model. A user is either activated or not, and if a user is removed from the system, the app must send the events and act accordingly. JMS implements the pub/sub model by using *topics*. In other words, we need to subscribe to any of those events.

You can find the source code in the 10-messaging-jms/myretro folder. Or, if you are starting from scratch using the Spring Initializr (https://start.spring.io), add the same dependencies mentioned in the "Users App with JMS" section.

Open/create the build.gradle file, as shown in Listing 10-12.

Listing 10-12. The build.gradle File

```
import org.jetbrains.kotlin.gradle.tasks.KotlinCompile
plugins {
    id 'org.springframework.boot' version '3.2.3'
    id 'io.spring.dependency-management' version '1.1.4'
    id 'org.jetbrains.kotlin.jvm' version '2.0.20-RC'
    id "org.jetbrains.kotlin.plugin.spring" version "2.0.20-RC"
    // <- simplifies spring proxying
}

group = 'com.apress'
version = '0.0.1-SNAPSHOT'
sourceCompatibility = '17'

repositories {
    mavenCentral()
}

dependencies {
    implementation "org.jetbrains.kotlin:kotlin-stdlib-jdk8"
    implementation "org.jetbrains.kotlin:kotlin-reflect"

    implementation 'org.springframework.boot:spring-boot-starter-web'
    implementation 'org.springframework.boot:spring-boot-starter-
    validation'

    implementation 'org.springframework.boot:spring-boot-starter-artemis'
    implementation 'com.fasterxml.jackson.datatype:jackson-datatype-jsr310'

    implementation 'org.springframework.boot:spring-boot-starter-data-jpa'

    annotationProcessor 'org.springframework.boot:spring-boot-
    configuration-processor'
```

```
    runtimeOnly 'com.h2database:h2'
    runtimeOnly 'org.postgresql:postgresql'

    testImplementation 'org.springframework.boot:spring-boot-starter-test'
}

tasks.named('test') {
    useJUnitPlatform()
}

//    kotlin {
//        jvmToolchain(17)
//    }
tasks.withType(KotlinCompile).configureEach {
    kotlinOptions {
        freeCompilerArgs = ['-Xjsr305=strict']
        jvmTarget = '17'
    }
}
```

Listing 10-12 shows that we are using the spring-boot-starter-artemis and jackson-datatype-jsr310 dependencies. We don't need spring-boot-docker-compose here because we are going to connect to the one that Users App is using.

Note   The code base used here (My Retro App project) is using the spring-boot-starter-data-jpa (not Reactive in this case).

Next, open/create the UserEvent class. See Listing 10-13.

Listing 10-13.   src/main/kotlin/com/apress/myretro/jms/UserEvent.kt

```
package com.apress.myretro.jms

import com.fasterxml.jackson.annotation.JsonFormat
import com.fasterxml.jackson.annotation.JsonIgnoreProperties
import com.fasterxml.jackson.databind.annotation.JsonSerialize
import com.fasterxml.jackson.datatype.jsr310.ser.LocalDateTimeSerializer
import java.time.LocalDateTime
```

```kotlin
@JsonIgnoreProperties(ignoreUnknown = true)
data class UserEvent(
    var email: String? = null,
    var action: String? = null,
    var active:Boolean = false,

    @JsonFormat(pattern = "yyyy-MM-dd HH:mm:ss")
    @JsonSerialize(using = LocalDateTimeSerializer::class)
    private var removed: LocalDateTime? = null
)
```

You can think of the UserEvent class as a merger of the information from the UserActivatedEvent and UserRemovedEvent classes from Users App. Note also that we have a new field—action: String—which will hold the event action description (Activated or Removed). This can be useful for new features. We are also using the @Js onIgnoreProperties(ignoreUnknown = true) annotation, which can be useful when listening for JSON data that might not have the same fields.

Next, open/create the UserEventListeners class. See Listing 10-14.

Listing 10-14. src/main/kotlin/com/apress/myretro/jms/UserEventListeners.kt

```kotlin
package com.apress.myretro.jms

import org.slf4j.LoggerFactory
import org.springframework.jms.annotation.JmsListener
import org.springframework.jms.annotation.JmsListeners
import org.springframework.stereotype.Component

@Component
class UserEventListeners {
    @JmsListeners(
        JmsListener(destination = "\${jms.user-events.queue.1}"),
        JmsListener(destination = "\${jms.user-events.queue.2}")
    )
    fun onUserEvent(userEvent: UserEvent?) {
        LOG.info("UserEventListeners.onUserEvent: {}", userEvent)
    }
```

```
    companion object {
        private val LOG = LoggerFactory.getLogger(UserEventListeners::
        class.java)
    }
}
```

The UserEventListeners class includes the following annotations (a few of which should be familiar to you) and method:

- @Component: This annotation marks the class as a Spring Bean, and it is necessary for the other annotations to get registered as well.

- @JmsListeners: This annotation accepts multiple @JmsListener annotations. This is useful in this case because we have only one message to receive, the UserEvent object.

- @JmsListener: This annotation is useful to connect to the topics (or queues, in a point-to-point model), and in this case we are using some properties that are external and will be found in the application.properties file.

- onUserEvent: This method is marked as a listener and it will receive the UserEvent messages.

Next, create/open the UserEventConfig class. See Listing 10-15.

Listing 10-15. src/main/kotlin/com/apress/myretro/jms/UserEventConfig.kt

```
package com.apress.myretro.jms

import com.fasterxml.jackson.core.JsonProcessingException
import com.fasterxml.jackson.databind.ObjectMapper
import com.fasterxml.jackson.datatype.jsr310.JavaTimeModule
import jakarta.jms.JMSException
import jakarta.jms.Message
import jakarta.jms.Session
import org.springframework.context.annotation.Bean
import org.springframework.context.annotation.Configuration
import org.springframework.jms.support.converter.MessageConversionException
import org.springframework.jms.support.converter.MessageConverter
```

```kotlin
@Configuration
class UserEventConfig {
    @Bean
    fun messageConverter(): MessageConverter {
        return object : MessageConverter {
            @Throws(JMSException::class, MessageConversionException::class)
            override fun toMessage('object': Any, session: Session):
            Message {
                throw UnsupportedOperationException("Not supported yet.")
            }

            @Throws(JMSException::class, MessageConversionException::class)
            override fun fromMessage(message: Message): Any {
                val mapper = ObjectMapper()
                mapper.registerModule(JavaTimeModule())
                val type = message.getStringProperty("_type")
                return mapper
                    .readValue(message.getBody(String::class.java),
                        UserEvent::class.java)
                    .apply {
                        action =
                            if (type.contains("Removed")) "Removed" else
                            "Activated"
                    }
            }
        }
    }
}
```

The UserEventConfig class includes the following:

- @Configuration: As you know, this annotation helps Spring look for @Bean definitions and configure them accordingly.

- MessageConverter: This bean is necessary; we don't need the default because we are dealing with JSON objects, and for some of them we need to do the deserialization. We are returning a new implementation of the MessageConverter. This interface provides two methods to implement—toMessage (which we don't need because we are not sending any messages; we are just receiving) and fromMessage. We are using the jackson library to use the ObjectMapper, both because we need to use the JavaTimeModule (due the LocalDateTime type we are using) and because we need to fill out the action field with Activated or Removed based on the event.

Take a moment to carefully review the code in Listing 10-15.

Next, open the application.properties file. See Listing 10-16.

Listing 10-16. src/main/resources/application.properties

```
server.port=${PORT:8181}
## Data
spring.h2.console.enabled=true
spring.datasource.generate-unique-name=false
spring.datasource.name=test-db
# spring.jpa.show-sql=true
## JMS Remote
#spring.artemis.broker-url=tcp://localhost:61616
#spring.artemis.mode=native
spring.artemis.user=artemis
spring.artemis.password=artemis
## JMS Topic
spring.jms.pub-sub-domain=true
## User Event Queues
jms.user-events.queue.1=activated-users
jms.user-events.queue.2=removed-users
```

At the end of the file, note that two queues are listed. The values are injected in the @JmsListener annotations; these are the topic's names. We have changed from *queues* (point-to-point) to *topics* (pub/sub). It's as easy as setting the spring.jms.pub-sub-domain=true property, and that's it. Of course, it's important that the sender/publisher of the message also sets this value. This means that Users App needs to use this property as well.

Running My Retro App

To run My Retro App, you need to do the following:

1. Go to Users App and add the `spring.jms.pub-sub-domain=true` property to the `application.properties` file and start the application. This runs the `docker-compose.yaml` file and launches the ActiveMQ Artemis service. If you are curious, look at the queues in the ActiveMQ Artemis console (`http://localhost:8161`, credentials `artemis/artemis`); they will be the same, but you will find some duplicates with a Router type of *MULTICAST* (this feature is related to ActiveMQ Artemis). This will allow Users App to subscribe multiple consumers so they can receive the messages published to these queues (or topics in this case).

2. Run My Retro App.

3. Add a user to the Users API. You can use the `user.http` file with the HTTP client from VS Code or IntelliJ to test the API. Or in a terminal, you can execute this:

```
curl -i -s -d '{"name":"Dummy","email":"dummy@email.com",
"password":"aw2s0meR!","userRole":["INFO"],"active":true}' \
-H "Content-Type: application/json" \
http://localhost:8080/users
HTTP/1.1 201
Location: http://localhost:8080/users/dummy@email.com
Content-Type: application/json
Transfer-Encoding: chunked
Date: Fri, 13 Oct 2023 19:31:30 GMT
{"email":"dummy@email.com","name":"Dummy","gravatarUrl":null,
"password":"aw2s0meR!","userRole":["INFO"],"active":true}
```

If you check the logs on both apps, you will see the following in My Retro App:

```
UserEventListeners.onUserEvent: UserEvent(email=dummy@email.com,
action=Activated, active=true, removed=null)
```

You can now delete the users you just created, using this command:

```
curl -i -s -XDELETE http://localhost:8080/users/dummy@email.com
HTTP/1.1 204
Date: Fri, 13 Oct 2023 19:35:05 GMT
```

Then, in the logs, you will see the following:

```
UserEventListeners.onUserEvent: UserEvent(email=dummy@email.com,
action=Removed, active=false, removed=2023-10-13T15:35:05)
```

Each log sets the action, either `Activated` or `Removed`.

You now know how to enable topics (pub/sub) using JMS. The next section looks at another messaging implementation—AMQP with Spring Boot.

AMQP with Spring Boot

Early messaging protocols, such as those developed by Sun Microsystems, Oracle, IBM, and Microsoft, were proprietary, making it difficult to mix technologies or programming languages.

In response to this challenge, a team at JPMorgan Chase created the Advanced Message Queuing Protocol (AMQP). AMQP is an open standard application layer protocol for message-oriented middleware (MOM). AMQP is a wire-level protocol, which means that applications can use any technology or programming language to communicate with AMQP-compliant messaging brokers.

There are many different AMQP messaging brokers available, but RabbitMQ is one of the most popular. RabbitMQ is easy to use and scale and is very fast, so we use it in this section.

Installing RabbitMQ

Before we discuss RabbitMQ, you can install it (this is optional), even though we are going to use Docker Compose to play with it. If you are using macOS or Linux, use the brew command to install it:

```
$ brew upgrade
$ brew install rabbitmq
```

If you are using another UNIX system or a Windows system, go to the RabbitMQ website and use the installers (`https://www.rabbitmq.com/docs/download`). RabbitMQ is written in Erlang, so its major dependency is to install the Erlang runtime in your system. Nowadays, all the RabbitMQ installers come with all the Erlang dependencies. Make sure the executables are in your `PATH` variable (for Windows and Linux, depending on the OS you are using). If you are using `brew`, you don't need to worry about setting the `PATH` variable.

RabbitMQ/AMQP: Exchanges, Bindings, and Queues

AMQP defines three concepts that are a little different from the JMS world, but very easy to understand. AMQP defines *exchanges*, which are entities to which the messages are sent. Every exchange takes a message and routes it to zero or more *queues*. This routing involves an algorithm that is based on the exchange type and rules, called *bindings*.

AMPQ defines five exchange types (in addition to the default type): *Direct, Fanout, Topic, Consistent Hash*, and *Headers*. Figure 10-7 shows these different exchange types.

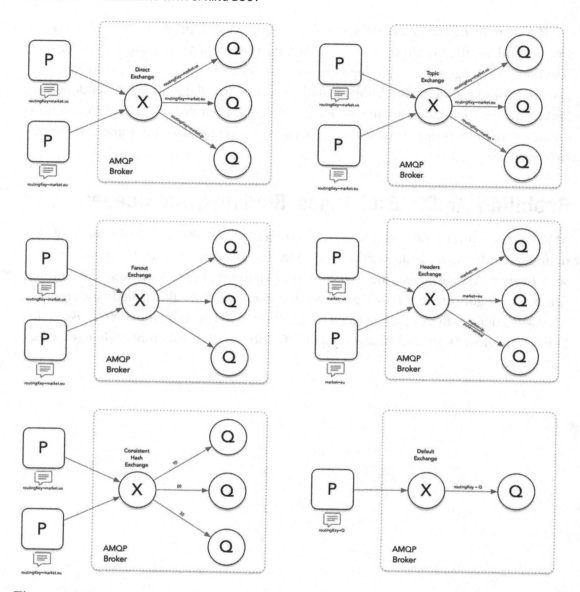

Figure 10-7. *AMQP exchanges, bindings, and queues*

The main idea of AMPQ is to send a message to an exchange, including a routing key, and then the exchange, based on its type, will deliver the message to the queue (or it won't if the routing key doesn't match).

The *default exchange* is bound automatically to every queue. The *direct exchange* is bound to a queue by a *routing key*; you can see this exchange type as one-to-one binding. The *topic exchange* is similar to the *direct exchange*; the only difference is that in its *binding* you can add a wildcard into its *routing key.* You can use the * (asterisk symbol), which matches exactly one word in a routing key, or you can use the # (hash symbol), which matches zero or more words in a routing key, or any other combination.

The *headers exchange* is like the topic exchange; the only difference is that the binding is based on the message headers (this is a very powerful exchange, and you can do all and any expressions for its headers). The *fanout exchange* copies the message to all the bound queues; you can see this exchange as a message broadcast. The Consistent Hash Exchange is a specialized exchange type that distributes messages across multiple queues using a consistent hashing algorithm. This ensures that messages with the same routing key are consistently sent to the same queue, even when queues are added or removed. This makes it ideal for scaling out consumers while maintaining message ordering within specific groups (defined by the routing key).

You can get more information about these concepts and exchange types at `https://rabbitmq.com/tutorials/amqp-concepts.html`.

Using AMQP with RabbitMQ in Users App

Now it's time to use the power of RabbitMQ in Users App. You can download the source (from the `10-messaging-rmq/users` folder), or if you are using the Spring Initializr (`https://start.spring.io`), make sure to select Spring for RabbitMQ, Web, JPA, Validation, Docker Compose, H2, and PostgreSQL as dependencies. Set the Group field to `com.apress` and the Artifact and Name fields to `users`. Then generate the project, download it, unzip it, and import it into your favorite IDE.

Open the `build.gradle` file, which should look like Listing 10-17.

Listing 10-17. The build.gradle File

```
import org.jetbrains.kotlin.gradle.tasks.KotlinCompile
plugins {
    id 'org.springframework.boot' version '3.2.3'
    id 'io.spring.dependency-management' version '1.1.4'
    id 'org.jetbrains.kotlin.jvm' version '2.0.20-RC'
    id "org.jetbrains.kotlin.plugin.spring" version "2.0.20-RC"
    // <- simplifies spring proxying
}
```

```
group = 'com.apress'
version = '0.0.1-SNAPSHOT'
sourceCompatibility = '17'

repositories {
    mavenCentral()
}

dependencies {
    implementation "org.jetbrains.kotlin:kotlin-stdlib-jdk8"
    implementation "org.jetbrains.kotlin:kotlin-reflect"

    implementation 'org.springframework.boot:spring-boot-starter-web'
    implementation 'org.springframework.boot:spring-boot-starter-
    validation'

    implementation 'org.springframework.boot:spring-boot-starter-amqp'
    implementation 'com.fasterxml.jackson.datatype:jackson-datatype-jsr310'

    developmentOnly 'org.springframework.boot:spring-boot-docker-compose'

    implementation 'org.springframework.boot:spring-boot-starter-data-jpa'
    runtimeOnly 'com.h2database:h2'
    runtimeOnly 'org.postgresql:postgresql'

    // Web
    implementation 'org.webjars:bootstrap:5.2.3'

    testImplementation 'org.springframework.boot:spring-boot-starter-test'
}

tasks.named('test') {
    useJUnitPlatform()
}

//     kotlin {
//         jvmToolchain(17)
//     }
tasks.withType(KotlinCompile).configureEach {
    kotlinOptions {
```

```
        freeCompilerArgs = ['-Xjsr305=strict']
        jvmTarget = '17'
    }
}
```

The important dependencies here are `spring-boot-amqp` and `jackson-datatype-jsr310`, which will help us deal with the `LocalDateTime` serialization and deserialization.

When Spring Boot starts, it will identify the AMQP dependency and auto-configure all the necessary default Spring Beans that will help connect to the RabbitMQ broker.

Next, open/create the events package and the `UserActivatedEvent` and `UserRemovedEvent` classes that we are going to send to RabbitMQ. They are similar to the same classes in the previous sections, but we want to show you more alternatives. The choice of how to configure these classes will depend on your business logic. See Listings 10-18 and 10-19.

Listing 10-18. src/main/kotlin/com/apress/users/events/UserActivatedEvent.kt

```kotlin
package com.apress.users.events

data class UserActivatedEvent(
    var email: String? = null,
    var active:Boolean? = false,
    var action:String? = "ACTIVATION_STATUS"
)
```

Listing 10-19. src/main/kotlin/com/apress/users/events/UserRemovedEvent.kt

```kotlin
package com.apress.users.events

import com.fasterxml.jackson.annotation.JsonFormat
import java.time.LocalDateTime

data class UserRemovedEvent(
    var email: String? = null,
    @JsonFormat(shape = JsonFormat.Shape.STRING, pattern = "yyyy-MM-dd
    HH:mm:ss")
    var removed: LocalDateTime? = null,
    var action:String? = "REMOVED"
)
```

As you can see, we are now adding the actions as properties in both classes. This is an easy way to cheat instead of discovering the action based on the name, as we did previously.

Publishing Messages to RabbitMQ

This section shows how to publish messages to RabbitMQ. Remember that a publisher requires the following steps: open a connection (to the RabbitMQ broker), create a channel, and send the message to an exchange. Fortunately, these steps are simplified with spring-amqp and Spring Boot.

Next, open/create the UserLogs class. See Listing 10-20.

Listing 10-20. src/main/kotlin/com/apress/users/events/UserLogs.kt

```kotlin
package com.apress.users.events

import com.apress.users.amqp.UserRabbitConfiguration
import org.slf4j.LoggerFactory
import org.springframework.amqp.rabbit.core.RabbitTemplate
import org.springframework.beans.factory.annotation.Autowired
import org.springframework.context.event.EventListener
import org.springframework.scheduling.annotation.Async
import org.springframework.stereotype.Component

@Component
class UserLogs {
    @Autowired
    private lateinit var rabbitTemplate: RabbitTemplate

    @Async
    @EventListener
    fun userActiveStatusEventHandler(event: UserActivatedEvent) {
        rabbitTemplate.convertAndSend(UserRabbitConfiguration.
        USERS_ACTIVATED, event)
        LOG.info("User {} active status: {}", event.email, event.active)
    }

    @Async
    @EventListener
```

```kotlin
fun userDeletedEventHandler(event: UserRemovedEvent) {
    rabbitTemplate.convertAndSend(UserRabbitConfiguration.
    USERS_REMOVED, event)
    LOG.info("User {} DELETED at {}", event.email, event.removed)
}

companion object {
    private val LOG = LoggerFactory.getLogger(UserLogs::class.java)
}
}
```

Listing 10-20 shows that the UserLogs class is similar to its configuration in the previous section (see Listing 10-7), but in this case we are using the RabbitTemplate class. This class implements the Template design pattern, removing the boilerplate of connecting to the broker, session management, message conversion (based on the Spring Boot auto-configuration use of the SimpleMessageConverter), reconnecting when there is an error, retries, connection pool, channels, and much more.

In this example, RabbitTemplate is using the convertAndSend method. It accepts the *routing key* as the first parameter (in this case, either users.activated or users. removed) and the event as the second parameter. This method has many overloads, so you can choose the one that best fits your business logic.

Note   We previously noted that a publisher always connects to an Exchange, and in this class an Exchange is specified, but it will be declared in the RestTemplate configuration. Therefore, using the convertAndSend method is easier.

Next, open/create the UserRabbitConfiguration class. See Listing 10-21.

Listing 10-21. src/main/kotlin/com/apress/users/amqp/ UserRabbitConfiguration.kt

```kotlin
package com.apress.users.amqp;

import com.fasterxml.jackson.databind.ObjectMapper;
import com.fasterxml.jackson.datatype.jsr310.JavaTimeModule;
import org.springframework.amqp.core.Binding;
```

```
import org.springframework.amqp.core.Queue;
import org.springframework.amqp.core.TopicExchange;
import org.springframework.amqp.rabbit.connection.ConnectionFactory;
import org.springframework.amqp.rabbit.core.RabbitTemplate;
import org.springframework.amqp.support.converter.
Jackson2JsonMessageConverter;
import org.springframework.context.annotation.Bean;
import org.springframework.context.annotation.Configuration;

@Configuration
class UserRabbitConfiguration {
    @Bean
    fun rabbitTemplate(connectionFactory: ConnectionFactory):
    RabbitTemplate =
        RabbitTemplate(connectionFactory).apply {
            setExchange("USERS")
            messageConverter = Jackson2JsonMessageConverter(
                ObjectMapper().registerModule(JavaTimeModule()))
        }

    @Bean
    fun exchange(): TopicExchange =
        TopicExchange(USERS_EXCHANGE)

    @Bean
    fun userStatusQueue(): Queue =
        Queue(USERS_STATUS_QUEUE, true, false, false)

    @Bean
    fun userRemovedQueue(): Queue =
        Queue(USERS_REMOVED_QUEUE, true, false, false)

    @Bean
    fun userStatusBinding(): Binding =
        Binding(USERS_STATUS_QUEUE,
            Binding.DestinationType.QUEUE, USERS_EXCHANGE,
            USERS_ACTIVATED, null)
```

```kotlin
@Bean
fun userRemovedBinding(): Binding =
    Binding(USERS_REMOVED_QUEUE,
        Binding.DestinationType.QUEUE, USERS_EXCHANGE,
        USERS_REMOVED, null)

companion object {
    const val USERS_EXCHANGE = "USERS"
    const val USERS_STATUS_QUEUE = "USER_STATUS"
    const val USERS_REMOVED_QUEUE = "USER_REMOVED"
    const val USERS_ACTIVATED = "users.activated"
    const val USERS_REMOVED = "users.removed"
}
}
```

Let's review the UserRabbitConfiguration class:

- @Configuration: Again, this annotation is a marker for the class that prompts Spring Boot to configure any @Bean declared in this class.

- ConnectionFactory: This interface gathers all the necessary values from the auto-configuration, such as host (where the RabbitMQ broker is running), username, password, virtualhost, and any listeners. This interface implementation is required for the RabbitTemplate class.

- RabbitTemplate: This class implements all the necessary logic to open a connection (a pool of connections), channels (a pool of channels), and retries (in case of connection lost to the broker), and it can be used to override and set new values. In this case, we set the exchange (a topic exchange named USERS). We also override the message converter using the Jackson2JsonMessageConverter class.

- Jackson2JsonMessageConverter: This class has a hierarchy that extends some abstract classes and implements the MessageConverter interface. Here we use it to convert our event into JSON format and we register the JavaTimeModule class module, which will deal with the LocalDateTime format.

- TopicExchange: This class creates a durable *topic exchange*, which will allow us to create some keys that may contain some regular expressions and use the routing capabilities that RabbitMQ offers by default with this type of *exchange*.

- Queue: We declare two queues, USERS_STATUS and USERS_ REMOVED. These queues have the properties of durable set to true (which means that in case of a crash or restart, the queue is still there), exclusive set to false (which means that we can use multiple consumers for this queue), and autodelete set to false (which means that even if a consumer gets disconnected from the queue, the queue will be there).

- Binding: As depicted in Figure 10-7, every *exchange* is connected to a *queue* through a *binding* that might have (depending on the *exchange*) a *routing key*. In this case, we are creating a *binding* per *queue* and assigning a *routing key* (users.activated and users. removed).

It's important to note that we are creating the exchange, queues, and bindings programmatically, but you can create them manually in the RabbitMQ web console.

Next, add/open the docker-compose.yaml file. See Listing 10-22.

Listing 10-22. docker-compose.yaml

```
version: "3"
services:
  rabbitmq:
    container_name: rabbitmq
    hostname: rabbitmq
    image: rabbitmq:management-alpine
    restart: always
    ports:
      - "15672:15672"
      - "5672:5672"
```

Running Users App with RabbitMQ

To run Users App with RabbitMQ, you can use the command line or your IDE. When you run it, you will see the following in the console:

```
...
Created new connection: rabbitConnectionFactory#7fff419d:0/
SimpleConnection@6f5f892c [delegate=amqp://guest@127.0.0.1:5672/,
localPort=63724]
UserLogs: User ximena@email.com active status: true
UserLogs: User norma@email.com active status: false
UserLogs: User dummy@email.com active status: false
UserLogs: User dummy@email.com DELETED at 2023-10-19T15:57:46.049020
...
```

Let's review what just happened. Open your browser and point it to `http://localhost:15672`, which is the RabbitMQ web console. See Figure 10-8.

Figure 10-8. *The RabbitMQ web console (`http://localhost:15672`) login page*

The credentials are guest/guest. Log in to see the RabbitMQ web console screen shown in Figure 10-9.

Figure 10-9. *The main page of the RabbitMQ web console*

From this console, you can see statistics in real time, view all the messages that are passing through, and get consumption information or any other important properties, such as memory, disk space, and much more. Next, click the Exchanges tab. See Figure 10-10.

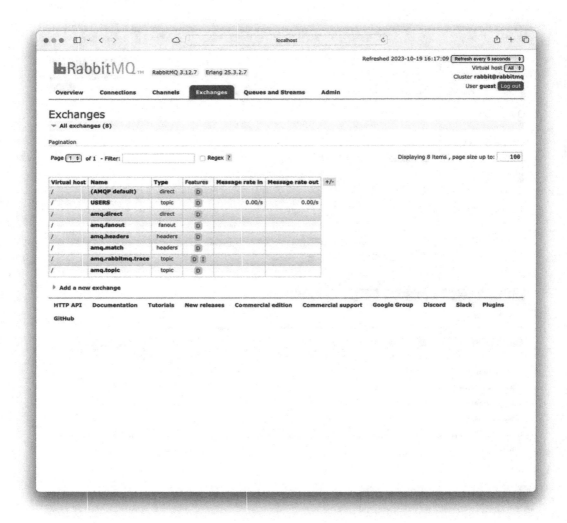

Figure 10-10. *RabbitMQ web console Exchanges tab*

By default, several exchanges are predefined. Note that the USERS exchange (type topic) is declared.

Next, click the Queues and Streams tab. See Figure 10-11.

Figure 10-11. *The Queues and Streams tab of the RabbitMQ web console*

The USER_STATUS and USER_REMOVED queues are defined as *classic queue*, which is just fine. There is also a *quorum queue*, which can be used when you need more high availability and are doing clustering.

Next, click the USER_STATUS queue to see the details shown in Figure 10-12.

Figure 10-12. *The USER_STATUS queue of the RabbitMQ web console*

You should have some messages there. Scroll down the page and expand the Get Message section. Click the Get Message(s) button, and you should see something like Figure 10-13.

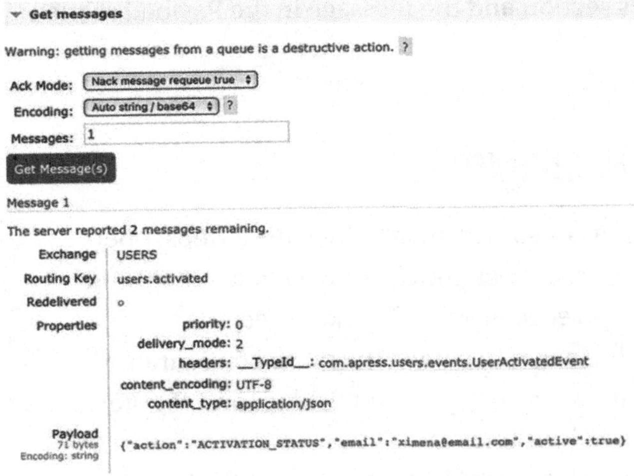

Figure 10-13. *The USER_STATUS queue with the Get Messages section expanded*

The Payload section at the bottom shows the event message converted into JSON format. In the Properties section, note that in the headers field there is a key of __ TypeId__ and its value is com.apress.users.event.UserActivatedEvent. This is like TypeId in JMS, but it is not necessary to explicitly declare it here—Spring AMQP will generate it by default.

If you review the message from the USER_REMOVED queue, you should see something like Figure 10-14.

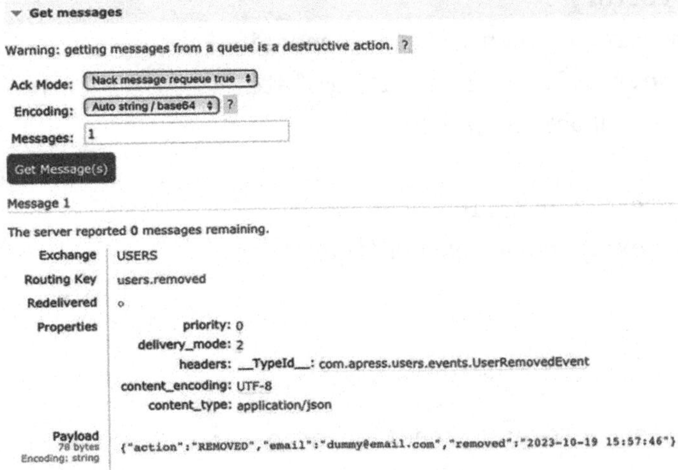

Figure 10-14. *The USER_REMOVED queue with the Get Messages area expanded*

The headers field in the Properties section and the message in the Payload section indicate we have what we need.

Now you can stop your Users App.

Consuming Messages from RabbitMQ

To consume messages from RabbitMQ, a consumer must follow these steps: open a connection (to the RabbitMQ broker), create a channel, connect to a queue, and consume the message (with auto-acknowledge or manual acknowledge).

We are consuming events in JSON format, so we need the same configuration as in the JMS configuration—we need to override the default listener and register JavaTimeModule to be used for the deserialization.

It's time to create the final version of the UserRabbitConfiguration class. See Listing 10-23.

Listing 10-23. src/main/kotlin/com/apress/users/amqp/ UserRabbitConfiguration.kt

```
package com.apress.users.amqp

import com.fasterxml.jackson.databind.ObjectMapper
import com.fasterxml.jackson.datatype.jsr310.JavaTimeModule
import org.springframework.amqp.rabbit.config.
SimpleRabbitListenerContainerFactory
import org.springframework.amqp.rabbit.connection.ConnectionFactory
import org.springframework.amqp.rabbit.core.RabbitTemplate
import org.springframework.amqp.support.converter.
Jackson2JsonMessageConverter
import org.springframework.context.annotation.Bean
import org.springframework.context.annotation.Configuration

@Configuration
class UserRabbitConfiguration {
    @Bean
    fun rabbitTemplate(connectionFactory: ConnectionFactory):
    RabbitTemplate =
        RabbitTemplate(connectionFactory).apply {
            setExchange("USERS")
```

```kotlin
        messageConverter = Jackson2JsonMessageConverter(
            ObjectMapper().registerModule(JavaTimeModule()))
    }

    @Bean
    fun rabbitListenerContainerFactory(connectionFactory:
    ConnectionFactory?):
            SimpleRabbitListenerContainerFactory =
        SimpleRabbitListenerContainerFactory().apply {
            setConnectionFactory(connectionFactory)
            setMessageConverter(Jackson2JsonMessageConverter(ObjectMapper()
                .registerModule(JavaTimeModule())))
    }

    companion object {
        const val USERS_EXCHANGE = "USERS"
        const val USERS_STATUS_QUEUE = "USER_STATUS"
        const val USERS_REMOVED_QUEUE = "USER_REMOVED"
        const val USERS_ACTIVATED = "users.activated"
        const val USERS_REMOVED = "users.removed"

    }
}
```

Listing 10-23 shows that we removed the exchange, queue, and binding
beans; we will show you another way to create them. Next, we are declaring
SimpleRabbitListernerContainerFactory (very similar to the JMS version), using the
well-known ConnectionFactory, and registering JavaTimeModule.

Next, open/create the UserListeners class. See Listing 10-24.

Listing 10-24. src/main/kotlin/com/apress/users/amqp/UserListeners.kt

```kotlin
package com.apress.users.amqp

import com.apress.users.events.UserActivatedEvent
import com.apress.users.events.UserRemovedEvent
import org.slf4j.LoggerFactory
import org.springframework.amqp.rabbit.annotation.Exchange
import org.springframework.amqp.rabbit.annotation.Queue
```

```kotlin
import org.springframework.amqp.rabbit.annotation.QueueBinding
import org.springframework.amqp.rabbit.annotation.RabbitListener
import org.springframework.stereotype.Component

@Component
class UserListeners {
    @RabbitListener(
        bindings = [QueueBinding(
            value = Queue(
                name = UserRabbitConfiguration.USERS_STATUS_QUEUE,
                durable = "true",
                autoDelete = "false"
            ),
            exchange = Exchange(name = UserRabbitConfiguration.USERS_
            EXCHANGE, type = "topic"),
            key = arrayOf(UserRabbitConfiguration.USERS_ACTIVATED)
        )]
    )
    fun userStatusEventProcessing(activatedEvent: UserActivatedEvent) {
        LOG.info("[AMQP - Event] Activated Event Received: {}",
        activatedEvent)
    }

    @RabbitListener(
        bindings = [QueueBinding(
            value = Queue(
                name = UserRabbitConfiguration.USERS_REMOVED_QUEUE,
                durable = "true",
                autoDelete = "false"
            ),
            exchange = Exchange(name = UserRabbitConfiguration.USERS_
            EXCHANGE, type = "topic"),
            key = arrayOf(UserRabbitConfiguration.USERS_REMOVED)
        )]
    )
```

```kotlin
fun userRemovedEventProcessing(removedEvent: UserRemovedEvent) {
    LOG.info("[AMQP - Event] Activated Event Received: {}",
    removedEvent)
}

companion object {
    private val LOG = LoggerFactory.getLogger(UserListeners::
    class.java)
}
}
```

The UserListeners class includes the following annotations:

- @RabbitMQListener: This annotation creates a RabbitListener that will take the default implementation unless overridden. In this case we are creating SimpleRabbitListenerContainerFactory, which will bring our own MessageConverter configuration (in this case, the Jackson2JsonMessageConverter). With this annotation you can define queues, exchanges, and bindings (through other annotations), making this simpler and more readable code because you know where the listener is consuming from.

- @QueueBinding: This annotation allows you to create a binding from the exchange to the queue. One of the benefits here is that if the queue, exchange, and bindings are not present, this annotation will attempt to create them.

- @Queue: This annotation allows you to declare a queue in the broker with some properties, such as durable and autodelete, among others. If the queue is not in the broker, this annotation will attempt to create it.

- @Exchange: This annotation declares an exchange in the broker with some properties. If the exchange is not present in the broker, this annotation will attempt to create it.

Note   If for some reason you change a property (any property) of a queue (for example, set `durable` to `true` the first time and then to `false` the next time), the queue will fail. Be sure to carefully design the types of exchanges, routing keys, and queue types and properties you will use to avoid any errors.

Running Users App with RabbitMQ to Consume Messages

If you run Users App with RabbitMQ, you will have a publisher and consumers, and you will get the following output:

```
...
User ximena@email.com active status: true
User norma@email.com active status: false
User dummy@email.com active status: false
[AMQP - Event] Activated Event Received: UserActivatedEvent(action=ACTIVATI
ON_STATUS, email=ximena@email.com, active=true)
[AMQP - Event] Activated Event Received: UserActivatedEvent(action=ACTIVATI
ON_STATUS, email=norma@email.com, active=false)
[AMQP - Event] Activated Event Received: UserActivatedEvent(action=ACTIVATI
ON_STATUS, email=dummy@email.com, active=false)
User dummy@email.com DELETED at 2023-10-19T17:27:26.442656
[AMQP - Event] Activated Event Received: UserRemovedEvent(action=REMOVED,
email=dummy@email.com, removed=2023-10-19T17:27:26)
...
```

Awesome! You now know how to use RabbitMQ for messaging. Of course, this is just a tiny bit of what you can do with it. Continue reading to discover other features.

Using RabbitMQ in My Retro App to Consume User Events

Now that we've established how to consume messages from RabbitMQ (based on Users App and its User Events), we can replicate the same pattern in My Retro App. We need to declare `SimpleRabbitListenerContainerFactory`, add the `@RabbitListener` annotation to a method that will receive the two events, and create the event classes—basically just copy and paste from Users App, right? But we haven't explored one of the best features of RabbitMQ, its routing capabilities. If your intention is to capture every event from your users, you don't need to create a class per event or a listener per event. Instead, you can use the *topic exchange* capability to route messages based on the routing key, and because this is a *topic* type, you can use wildcards for the keys. See Figure 10-15.

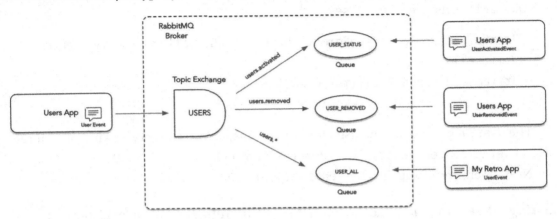

***Figure 10-15.** Users App interaction with My Retro App via topic exchange*

Figure 10-15 shows the interaction that we'll have with Users App. Recall that we've just created consumers that are listening for the UserActivadedEvent (based on the routing key users.activated that is bound to the USERS_STATUS queue) and the UserRemovedEvent (based on the users.removed routing key that is bound to the USER_REMOVED queue). We are going to create another queue (named USER_ALL) that will receive the copy of the two events (UserActivatedEvent or UserRemovedEvent), and this is based on the users.* routing key. This is a wildcard that works only with *topic exchanges,* thereby allowing us to have more flexibility for any type of routing.

You can open or create the My Retro App project based on the JPA. You can find the code in the 10-messageing-amqp/myretro folder.

Open/create the UserEvent class. See Listing 10-25.

Listing 10-25. src/main/kotlin/com/apress/myretro/amqp/UserEvent.kt

```
package com.apress.myretro.amqp

import com.fasterxml.jackson.annotation.JsonFormat
import com.fasterxml.jackson.annotation.JsonIgnoreProperties
import java.time.LocalDateTime
```

```kotlin
@JsonIgnoreProperties(ignoreUnknown = true)
data class UserEvent(
    var action: String? = null,
    var email: String? = null,
    var active:Boolean = false,

    @JsonFormat(shape = JsonFormat.Shape.STRING, pattern = "yyyy-MM-dd
    HH:mm:ss")
    var removed: LocalDateTime? = null
)
```

The UserEvent class will be used for both events; as you can see, it's kind of a merge of the UserActivatedEvent and UserRemovedEvent fields.

Next, open/create the UserListener class. See Listing 10-26.

Listing 10-26. src/main/kotlin/com/apress/myretro/amqp/UserListener.kt

```kotlin
package com.apress.myretro.amqp

import org.slf4j.LoggerFactory
import org.springframework.amqp.rabbit.annotation.Exchange
import org.springframework.amqp.rabbit.annotation.Queue
import org.springframework.amqp.rabbit.annotation.QueueBinding
import org.springframework.amqp.rabbit.annotation.RabbitListener
import org.springframework.stereotype.Component

@Component
class UserListener {
    @RabbitListener(
        bindings = [QueueBinding(
            value = Queue(
                name = USERS_ALL_QUEUE,
                durable = "true",
                autoDelete = "false"
            ),
            exchange = Exchange(name = USERS_EXCHANGE, type = "topic"),
            key = [USERS_ALL]
        )]
```

```kotlin
)
fun userStatusEventProcessing(userEvent: UserEvent?) {
    LOG.info("[AMQP - Event] Received: {}", userEvent)
}

companion object {
    private const val USERS_ALL = "users.*"
    private const val USERS_ALL_QUEUE = "USER_ALL"
    private const val USERS_EXCHANGE = "USERS"
    private val LOG = LoggerFactory.getLogger(UserListener::class.java)
}
}
```

Listing 10-26 shows that the UserListener class is almost the same as in Users App, but here we are declaring the new USER_ALL queue, the binding between the queue and the USERS exchange using the users.* routing key, which allows us to receive a copy of every event message, and the users.activated and users.removed messages. To use the topic exchange and its routing capabilities effectively, it is important to have a good naming convention for your routing keys, which is why we named them with the prefix users.. This enables us to use users.status.activated, users.status.removed, users.status.deactivated, users.admin.activated, and users.admin.deactivated, in the future, and even have some wildcards such as users.*.activated (this will include the users.status.activated and users.admin.activated). The topic exchange also accepts the # symbol, which will match zero or more words, and the * symbol, which will match one word.

Next, open/create the UserRabbitConfiguration class. See Listing 10-27.

Listing 10-27. src/main/kotlin/com/apress/myretro/amqp/
UserRabbitConfiguration.kt

```kotlin
package com.apress.myretro.amqp

import com.fasterxml.jackson.databind.ObjectMapper
import com.fasterxml.jackson.datatype.jsr310.JavaTimeModule
import org.springframework.amqp.rabbit.config.
SimpleRabbitListenerContainerFactory
import org.springframework.amqp.rabbit.connection.ConnectionFactory
```

```
import org.springframework.amqp.support.converter.
Jackson2JsonMessageConverter
import org.springframework.context.annotation.Bean
import org.springframework.context.annotation.Configuration

@Configuration
class UserRabbitConfiguration {
    @Bean
    fun rabbitListenerContainerFactory(connectionFactory:
    ConnectionFactory?):
            SimpleRabbitListenerContainerFactory {
        val factory = SimpleRabbitListenerContainerFactory()
        factory.setConnectionFactory(connectionFactory)
        factory.setMessageConverter(
            Jackson2JsonMessageConverter(
                ObjectMapper()
                    .registerModule(JavaTimeModule())
            )
        )
        return factory
    }
}
```

As we did earlier for the `UserRabbitConfiguration` class, we are declaring the `SimpleRabbitListenerContainerFactory` bean and configuring `MessageConverter` with `Jackson2JsonMessageConverter` to register `JavaTimeModule`, which will help with the deserialization of the `LocalDateTime` type.

Running My Retro App to Listen for User Events from RabbitMQ

Make sure you have Users App up and running; Users App has the `docker-compose.yaml` file that will be used by Spring Boot to start the RabbitMQ broker.

Next, run My Retro App. You can check out the RabbitMQ web console and see that there are three queues, as shown in Figure 10-16.

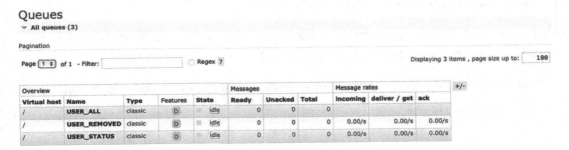

Queues
- All queues (3)

Pagination

Page [1 ◆] of 1 - Filter: [   ]   □ Regex ?   Displaying 3 items , page size up to: [100]

Overview					Messages			Message rates			+/-
Virtual host	Name	Type	Features	State	Ready	Unacked	Total	incoming	deliver / get	ack	
/	USER_ALL	classic	D	idle	0	0	0				
/	USER_REMOVED	classic	D	idle	0	0	0	0.00/s	0.00/s	0.00/s	
/	USER_STATUS	classic	D	idle	0	0	0	0.00/s	0.00/s	0.00/s	

Figure 10-16. *RabbitMQ web console with three queues*

Next, send a new user to the terminal with the following command:

```
curl -i -s -d '{"name":"Dummy","email":"dummy@email.com","password":
"aw2sOmeR!","userRole":["INFO"],"active":true}' \
-H "Content-Type: application/json" \
http://localhost:8080/users
HTTP/1.1 201
Location: http://localhost:8080/users/dummy@email.com
Content-Type: application/json
Transfer-Encoding: chunked
Date: Sat, 21 Oct 2023 17:32:34 GMT
{"email":"dummy@email.com","name":"Dummy","gravatarUrl":null,"password":
"aw2sOmeR!","userRole":["INFO"],"active":true}
```

If you check out the My Retro console, you should have this event:

```
[AMQP - Event] Received: UserEvent(action=ACTIVATION_STATUS, email=dummy@
email.com, active=true, removed=null)
```

You can also experiment with deleting a user using the following command:

```
curl -i -s -XDELETE http://localhost:8080/users/dummy@email.com
HTTP/1.1 204
Date: Sat, 21 Oct 2023 17:34:12 GMT
```

The My Retro App console will show the following:

```
[AMQP - Event] Received: UserEvent(action=REMOVED, email=dummy@email.com,
active=false, removed=2023-10-21T13:34:12)
```

Nice; you've now integrated both apps/services that use events sent to RabbitMQ as your message broker.

WebSockets with Spring Boot

WebSockets is one of our favorite technologies because it allows near real-time event processing. WebSockets is a communication protocol that provides full-duplex channels over TCP. The WebSockets protocol defines two types of messages—text and binary—and it is normally used with the definition of a subprotocol that sends and receives messages.

One of the most interesting parts about this protocol is that there is a handshake between the client and the server. It starts with the client sending an HTTP request with special headers that allow a direct connection through TCP using a unique hash key between the client and server. The communication can then start by sending and receiving WebSockets data frames. This is how it looks behind the scenes:

```
Client request:
GET /chat HTTP/1.1
Upgrade: websocket
Connection: Upgrade
Sec-WebSocket-Key: dGhlIHNhbXBsZSBub25jZSB3aGljaCBrZXk=
Server response:
HTTP/1.1 101 Switching Protocols
Upgrade: websocket
Connection: Upgrade
Sec-WebSocket-Accept: s3pPLMBiTxaQ9kYGzzh5fWusIqFw=
```

In this section, we use Spring's STOMP (Simple Text-Oriented Messaging Protocol) support (as the subprotocol) and see how Spring WebSockets acts as the STOMP broker to clients using Spring Boot.

Adding WebSockets to Users App

To add WebSockets to Users App, simply add the `spring-boot-starter-websocket` dependency, which will be enough for Spring Boot to auto-configure all the necessary defaults. This will provide a WebSockets communication framework that enables you to create event-driven and real-time applications with ease.

You can use the code in the `10-messaging-websockets/users` folder or you can start from scratch with the Spring Initializr (`https://start.spring.io`). For the latter, add the WebSockets, Validation, JPA, H2, and Postgresql dependencies, set the Group field to `com.apress`, and set the Artifact and Name fields to `users`. Then generate and download the project, unzip it, and import it into your favorite IDE. The main codebase will be from the Users Web/JPA.

You also need to add some extra dependencies, so open the `build.gradle` file. See Listing 10-28.

Listing 10-28. The build.gradle File

```
import org.jetbrains.kotlin.gradle.tasks.KotlinCompile
plugins {
    id 'org.springframework.boot' version '3.2.3'
    id 'io.spring.dependency-management' version '1.1.4'
    id 'org.jetbrains.kotlin.jvm' version '2.0.20-RC'
    id "org.jetbrains.kotlin.plugin.spring" version "2.0.20-RC"
    // <- simplifies spring proxying
}

group = 'com.apress'
version = '0.0.1-SNAPSHOT'
sourceCompatibility = '17'

repositories {
    mavenCentral()
}

dependencies {
    implementation "org.jetbrains.kotlin:kotlin-stdlib-jdk8"
    implementation "org.jetbrains.kotlin:kotlin-reflect"
```

```
    implementation 'org.springframework.boot:spring-boot-starter-websocket'
    implementation 'org.springframework.boot:spring-boot-starter-
    validation'

    implementation 'org.webjars:webjars-locator-core'
    implementation 'org.webjars:sockjs-client:1.5.1'
    implementation 'org.webjars:stomp-websocket:2.3.4'

    implementation 'com.fasterxml.jackson.datatype:jackson-datatype-jsr310'

    implementation 'org.springframework.boot:spring-boot-starter-data-jpa'
    runtimeOnly 'com.h2database:h2'
    runtimeOnly 'org.postgresql:postgresql'

    // Web
    implementation 'org.webjars:bootstrap:5.2.3'
    implementation 'org.webjars:jquery:3.7.1'

    testImplementation 'org.springframework.boot:spring-boot-starter-test'
}

tasks.named('test') {
    useJUnitPlatform()
}

//      kotlin {
//          jvmToolchain(17)
//      }
tasks.withType(KotlinCompile).configureEach {
    kotlinOptions {
        freeCompilerArgs = ['-Xjsr305=strict']
        jvmTarget = '17'
    }
}
```

Listing 10-28 shows that we are only using spring-boot-starter-websocket; all the web dependencies come with the websocket dependency, so there is no need to declare them. We are also using sockjs-client and stomp-websocket, which will help on the UI (client) side. We are going to send JSON messages, so we need the jackson-datatype-jsr310 dependency as well.

Next, open/create the UserSocket class. See Listing 10-29.

Listing 10-29. src/main/kotlin/com/apress/users/web/socket/UserSocket.kt

```kotlin
package com.apress.users.web.socket

import org.springframework.beans.factory.annotation.Autowired
import org.springframework.messaging.core.MessageSendingOperations
import org.springframework.stereotype.Component
import java.time.LocalDateTime
import java.time.format.DateTimeFormatter

@Component
class UserSocket {
    @Autowired
    private lateinit var messageSendingOperations: MessageSendingOperatio
    ns<String>

    fun userLogSocket(event: Map<String, Any>) {
        val map: Map<String, Any> = mapOf(
                "event" to event,
                "version" to "1.0",
                "time" to LocalDateTime.now().
                    format(DateTimeFormatter.ofPattern("yyyy-MM-dd
                    HH:mm:ss"))
        )
        messageSendingOperations.convertAndSend("/topic/user-logs", map)
    }
}
```

The important element in the UserSocket class is the MessageSendingOperations interface, which belongs to the org.springframework.messaging.core package from the spring-message dependency. This interface is a common way to send messages regardless of the technology used; you can think of it as a high-level communication. You can use any protocol you need—in fact, Spring JMS and Spring AMQP use this interface for specialization of the JmsMessageOperations and RabbitMessageOperations interfaces, respectively, for sending messages.

You can see that we are sending a Map<String, Object> as a message or event; you can send anything really, but we wanted to show you that you can send basic classes, such as a Map.

Next, open/create the UserSocketConfiguration class. As you can imagine, you need to do some configuration. See Listing 10-30.

Listing 10-30. src/main/kotlin/com/apress/users/web/socket/ UserSocketConfiguration.kt

```
package com.apress.users.web.socket

import org.springframework.context.annotation.Configuration
import org.springframework.messaging.simp.config.MessageBrokerRegistry
import org.springframework.web.socket.config.annotation.
EnableWebSocketMessageBroker
import org.springframework.web.socket.config.annotation.
StompEndpointRegistry
import org.springframework.web.socket.config.annotation.
    WebSocketMessageBrokerConfigurer

@Configuration
@EnableWebSocketMessageBroker
class UserSocketConfiguration : WebSocketMessageBrokerConfigurer {
    override fun configureMessageBroker(config: MessageBrokerRegistry) {
        config.enableSimpleBroker("/topic")
        config.setApplicationDestinationPrefixes("/app")
    }

    override fun registerStompEndpoints(registry: StompEndpointRegistry) {
        registry.addEndpoint("/logs").withSockJS()
    }
}
```

The `UserSocketConfiguration` class includes the following:

- `@Configuration`: We need this class to be part of the configuration when the app starts, so we need to mark it with this annotation.

- `@EnableWebSocketMessageBroker`: We need this annotation because we are going to do some *broker-backed* messaging over WebSockets using a higher-level messaging subprotocol. In other words, we are going to be the broker that handles the STOMP protocol over WebSockets.

- `WebSocketMessageBrokerConfigurer`: This interface is useful because it defines methods for configuring message handling through simple protocols, such as STOMP. With this implementation, we define our message converters, custom return value handlers, STOMP endpoints, the usage of the `MessageChannel` from the core of `spring-messaging`, and much more.

- `MessageBrokerRegistry`: This is one of the parameters of the `ConfigureMessageBroker` method implementation, and it helps configure the message broker options. In this case we are configuring the broker destination prefix with `/topic` and the application destination prefix with `/app`.

- `StompEndpointRegistry`: This is a contract for registering STOMP over WebSockets endpoints and in this case the `/logs` endpoint.

This completes the backend. Yes, that's it! Next, let's look at things from the UI side.

Using the WebSockets Client in Users App to Consume Events

Next, open/create the `app.js` file; it will contain the client side. See Listing 10-31.

Listing 10-31. src/main/resources/static/js/app.js

```
let stompClient = null;
function connect() {
    let socket = new SockJS('/logs');
    stompClient = Stomp.over(socket);
    stompClient.connect({}, function (frame) {
```

```
                    console.log('Connected: ' + frame);
                    stompClient.subscribe('/topic/user-logs', function
                    (response) {
                            console.log(response);
                            showLogs(response.body);
                    });
        });
}
function showLogs(message) {
    $("#logs").append("<tr><td>" + message + "</td></tr>");
}
$(function () {
    connect();
});
```

The app.js file is a plain JavaScript file in which we are using the jQuery library.
We are using the SockJS class, which comes from the socks-client JavaScript
dependency. The SockJS class is using the /logs endpoint we defined in the
UserSocketConfiguration class (Listing 10-30). We are also creating the Stomp client,
which will allow us to connect and subscribe to any incoming message into the /topic/
user-logs destination. This was configured in the UserSocketConfiguration and
UserSocket classes (Listing 10-29) when we used the convertAndSend method call. Once
we get the user event, we use the showLogs method and append it to the #logs HTML
element (this is a <div/> element).

Next, open/create the index.html file. See Listing 10-32.

Listing 10-32. src/main/resources/static/index.html

```
<!DOCTYPE html>
<html lang="en">
<head>
    <meta charset="UTF-8">
    <link rel="stylesheet" type="text/css"
          href="webjars/bootstrap/5.2.3/css/bootstrap.min.css">
    <script src="/webjars/jquery/3.7.1/jquery.min.js"></script>
    <script src="/webjars/sockjs-client/1.5.1/sockjs.min.js"></script>
    <script src="/webjars/stomp-websocket/2.3.4/stomp.min.js"></script>
```

```html
<script src="/js/app.js"></script>
    <title>Welcome - Users App</title>
</head>
<body class="d-flex h-100 text-center">
<div class="cover-container d-flex w-100 h-100 p-3 mx-auto flex-column">
    <header class="mb-auto">
        <div>
            <h3 class="float-md-start mb-0">Users</h3>
        </div>
    </header>
    <main class="px-3">
        <h1>Simple Users Rest Application</h1>
        <p class="lead">This is a simple Users app where you can access any
        information from a user</p>
        <p class="lead">
            <a href="/users">Get All Users</a>
        </p>
    </main>
    <footer class="mt-auto text-black-50">
        <p>Powered by Spring Boot 3</p>
        <table>
            <div id="logs">
            </div>
        </table>
    </footer>
</div>
</body>
</html>
```

Listing 10-32 shows that we are using the jQuery, sockjs, and the stomp libraries
that are embedded in the org.webjars dependencies. We are also using a <div/> with
id=logs, which will be the element we are appending to the user event message that we
receive from the server.

Running Users App with WebSockets

You are now ready to see Users App with WebSockets in action. Run Users App, either from the command line or using your IDE, and then open your browser and point it to http://localhost:8080. Next, open the web developer console. All browsers have them.

The web developer console should show something similar to Figure 10-17.

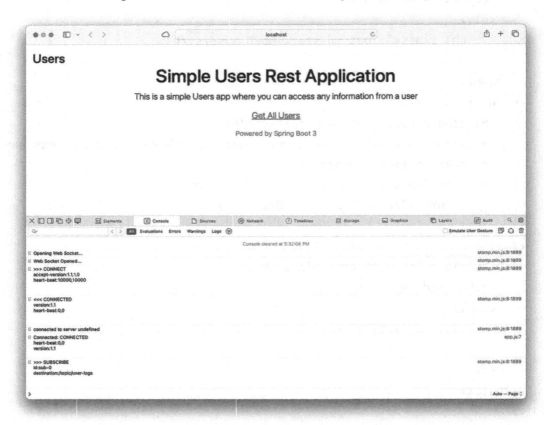

Figure 10-17. *Web developer console (http://localhost:8080)*

You should see that you are connected to the server and the destination /topic/user-logs. If you add and remove a user using this command line:

```
curl -i -s -d '{"name":"Dummy","email":"dummy@email.com","password":
"aw2sOmeR!","userRole":["INFO"],"active":true}' \
-H "Content-Type: application/json" \
http://localhost:8080/users
curl -i -s -XDELETE http://localhost:8080/users/dummy@email.com
```

you should see something similar to Figure 10-18 in the web developer console.

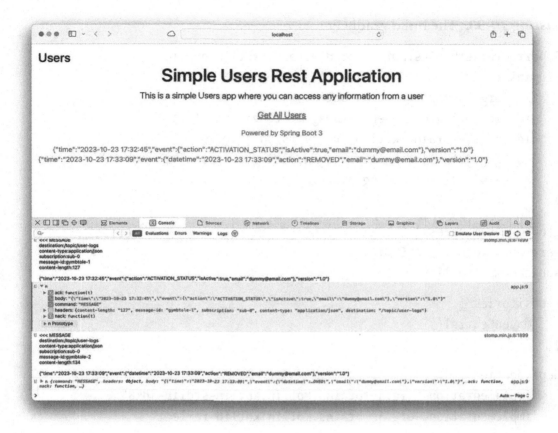

Figure 10-18. *User events in the web developer console*

Figure 10-18 shows the result of adding and deleting a user. Notice that the message comes in JSON format.

Using WebSockets in My Retro App to Consume Events

One of the more common questions students ask is whether they can use WebSockets from My Retro App and receive User events. Of course they can, so let's do it.

If you are starting from scratch, you can follow the same process as in the previous sections. Be sure to add the spring-boot-starter-websocket dependency and, of course, the others we are using in this project. You can use the code in the 10-messaging-websocket/myretro folder.

Open the build.gradle file. See Listing 10-33.

Listing 10-33. The build.gradle File

```
import org.jetbrains.kotlin.gradle.tasks.KotlinCompile
plugins {
    id 'org.springframework.boot' version '3.2.3'
    id 'io.spring.dependency-management' version '1.1.4'
    id 'org.jetbrains.kotlin.jvm' version '2.0.20-RC'
    id "org.jetbrains.kotlin.plugin.spring" version "2.0.20-RC"
    // <- simplifies spring proxying
}

group = 'com.apress'
version = '0.0.1-SNAPSHOT'
sourceCompatibility = '17'

repositories {
    mavenCentral()
}

dependencies {
    implementation "org.jetbrains.kotlin:kotlin-stdlib-jdk8"
    implementation "org.jetbrains.kotlin:kotlin-reflect"

    implementation 'org.springframework.boot:spring-boot-starter-websocket'
    implementation 'org.springframework.boot:spring-boot-starter-
    validation'

    implementation 'com.fasterxml.jackson.datatype:jackson-datatype-jsr310'

    implementation 'org.springframework.boot:spring-boot-starter-data-jpa'

    annotationProcessor 'org.springframework.boot:spring-boot-
    configuration-processor'

    runtimeOnly 'com.h2database:h2'
    runtimeOnly 'org.postgresql:postgresql'

    testImplementation 'org.springframework.boot:spring-boot-starter-test'
}
```

```
tasks.named('test') {
    useJUnitPlatform()
}

//    kotlin {
//        jvmToolchain(17)
//    }
tasks.withType(KotlinCompile).configureEach {
    kotlinOptions {
        freeCompilerArgs = ['-Xjsr305=strict']
        jvmTarget = '17'
    }
}
```

Next, open/create the Event and UserEvent classes. See Listings 10-34 and 10-35, respectively.

Listing 10-34. src/main/kotlin/com/apress/myretro/web/socket/Event.kt

```
package com.apress.myretro.web.socket

import com.fasterxml.jackson.annotation.JsonFormat
import java.time.LocalDateTime

data class Event(
    var version: String? = null,

    @get:JsonFormat(shape = JsonFormat.Shape.STRING, pattern = "yyyy-MM-dd
    HH:mm:ss")
    var time: LocalDateTime? = null,

    var event: UserEvent? = null
)
```

Listing 10-35. src/main/kotlin/com/apress/myretro/web/socket/UserEvent.kt

```
package com.apress.myretro.web.socket

import com.fasterxml.jackson.annotation.JsonFormat
import com.fasterxml.jackson.annotation.JsonIgnoreProperties
import java.time.LocalDateTime
```

```kotlin
@JsonIgnoreProperties(ignoreUnknown = true)
data class UserEvent(
    var email: String? = null,
    var active:Boolean = false,
    var action: String? = null,

    @get:JsonFormat(shape = JsonFormat.Shape.STRING, pattern = "yyyy-MM-dd
    HH:mm:ss")
    var datetime: LocalDateTime? = null
)
```

We need to create the Event and UserEvent classes because we are sending a
composite event message. We also need to use the @JsonFormat annotation to create a
standard data-time pattern that comes from the user service.

Next, open/create the consumer, which is the UserSocketClient class. See
Listing 10-36.

Listing 10-36. src/main/kotlin/com/apress/myretro/web/socket/
UserSocketClient.kt

```kotlin
package com.apress.myretro.web.socket

import org.slf4j.LoggerFactory
import org.springframework.messaging.simp.stomp.StompCommand
import org.springframework.messaging.simp.stomp.StompHeaders
import org.springframework.messaging.simp.stomp.StompSession
import org.springframework.messaging.simp.stomp.StompSessionHandlerAdapter
import org.springframework.stereotype.Component

@Component
class UserSocketClient : StompSessionHandlerAdapter() {
    override fun afterConnected(session: StompSession,
            connectedHeaders: StompHeaders) {
        LOG.info("Client connected: headers {}", connectedHeaders)
        session.subscribe(TOPIC, this)
    }
```

```kotlin
override fun handleFrame(headers: StompHeaders, payload: Any?) {
    LOG.info("Client received: payload {}, headers {}", payload, headers)
}

override fun handleException(
    session: StompSession, command: StompCommand?,
    headers: StompHeaders, payload: ByteArray, exception: Throwable
) {
    LOG.error(
        "Client error: exception {}, command {}, payload {}, headers {}",
        exception.message, command, payload, headers
    )
}

override fun handleTransportError(session: StompSession, exception:
Throwable) {
    LOG.error("Client transport error: error {}", exception.message)
}

companion object {
    private const val TOPIC = "/topic/user-logs"
    private val LOG = LoggerFactory.getLogger(UserSocketClient::
    class.java)
}
}
```

The UserSocketClient class is important because you need to handle the session, manage any exceptions, and receive the message (*payload*). You can see this class as a low-level way to get the insight of the WebSockets frames. Let's review it:

- @Component: We need this class as a Spring Bean, so we need to mark it using the @Component annotation.

- StompSessionHandlerAdapter: This is an abstract adapter that doesn't have a default implementation because, normally, you must deal with the session and the socket frame yourself. This abstract class implements the StompSessionHandler interface, so you need to implement how you want to manage the exceptions and errors that come from the frame or the session, and what else needs to be done when the connection is successful (afterConnected method).

- `StompSession`: This interface will be implemented behind the scenes. This interface sends and receives messages and creates subscriptions. In this case, the `afterConnected` method uses `StompSession` to subscribe to the `/topic/users-logs` destination.

- `StompHeaders`: This is the same as the `Headers` message you saw in previous sections. This class will implement a `MultiValueMap` interface. This contains useful information, such as content-type, content-length, receipt, host, and more. These properties are necessary for the protocol.

Next, open/create the `UserSocketMessageConverter` class. See Listing 10-37.

Listing 10-37. src/main/kotlin/com/apress/myretro/web/socket/
UserSocketMessageConverter.kt

```kotlin
package com.apress.myretro.web.socket

import com.fasterxml.jackson.databind.ObjectMapper
import com.fasterxml.jackson.datatype.jsr310.JavaTimeModule
import org.slf4j.LoggerFactory
import org.springframework.messaging.Message
import org.springframework.messaging.MessageHeaders
import org.springframework.messaging.converter.MessageConverter
import org.springframework.stereotype.Component

@Component
class UserSocketMessageConverter : MessageConverter {
    override fun fromMessage(message: Message<*>, targetClass:
    Class<*>): Any? {
        val mapper: ObjectMapper = ObjectMapper().registerModule(Java
        TimeModule())
        var userEvent: Event? = null
        try {
            val m = String((message.payload as ByteArray))
            userEvent = mapper.readValue(m, Event::class.java)
        } catch (ex: Exception) {
            LOG.error("Cannot Deserialize - {}", ex.message)
```

```kotlin
        }
        return userEvent
    }

    override fun toMessage(payload: Any, headers: MessageHeaders?):
    Message<*> {
        throw UnsupportedOperationException()
    }

    companion object {
        private val LOG =
            LoggerFactory.getLogger(UserSocketMessageConverter::class.java)
    }
}
```

The UserSocketMessageConverter class includes the following:

- @Component: We need this custom MessageConverter as a Spring
  Bean, so we need to mark it using the @Component annotation.

- MessageConverter: As you know, this is how we create our custom
  MessageConverter. We only need to implement the fromMessage
  method, which is where we register the JavaTimeModule that will deal
  with the LocalDateTime type when deserializing.

Next, open/create the UserSocketConfiguration class. See Listing 10-38.

Listing 10-38. src/main/kotlin/com/apress/myretro/web/socket/
UserSocketConfiguration.kt

```kotlin
package com.apress.myretro.web.socket

import com.apress.myretro.config.RetroBoardProperties
import org.springframework.beans.factory.annotation.Autowired
import org.springframework.context.annotation.Bean
import org.springframework.context.annotation.Configuration
import org.springframework.messaging.simp.stomp.StompSessionHandler
import org.springframework.web.socket.client.WebSocketClient
import org.springframework.web.socket.client.standard.
StandardWebSocketClient
```

```kotlin
import org.springframework.web.socket.messaging.WebSocketStompClient
import org.springframework.web.socket.sockjs.client.
RestTemplateXhrTransport
import org.springframework.web.socket.sockjs.client.SockJsClient
import org.springframework.web.socket.sockjs.client.Transport
import org.springframework.web.socket.sockjs.client.WebSocketTransport

@Configuration
class UserSocketConfiguration {
    @Autowired
    private lateinit var retroBoardProperties: RetroBoardProperties

    @Bean
    fun webSocketStompClient(
        webSocketClient: WebSocketClient,
        userSocketMessageConverter: UserSocketMessageConverter,
        userSocketClient: StompSessionHandler
    ): WebSocketStompClient {
        val webSocketStompClient = WebSocketStompClient(webSocketClient)
        webSocketStompClient.messageConverter = userSocketMessageConverter
//        webSocketStompClient.connect(
//            retroBoardProperties.usersService!!.hostname +
//                retroBoardProperties.usersService!!.basePath,
//            userSocketClient
//        )
        webSocketStompClient.connectAsync(
            retroBoardProperties.usersService!!.hostname +
            retroBoardProperties.usersService!!.basePath,
            userSocketClient
        )
        return webSocketStompClient
    }

    @Bean
    fun webSocketClient(): WebSocketClient {
        val transports: MutableList<Transport> = mutableListOf(
            WebSocketTransport(StandardWebSocketClient()),
```

538

```
            RestTemplateXhrTransport()
        )
        return SockJsClient(transports)
    }
}
```

The UserSocketConfiguration class will help us establish a connection to Users App. We need a client, in this case a WebSockets/STOMP client, so let's review the class:

- RetroBoardProperties: This class binds the external properties in which we can hold information about the remote server (hostname) and its path (basePath). In this case, we need to declare the properties, either in the application.properties file or as environment variables (your choice).

- StompSessionHandler: This class defines the custom StompSessionHandler, in this case the UserSocketClient class (see Listing 10-36). This class is needed as a parameter to connect to the WebSocketStompClient.

- WebSocketClient: This interface is essential because it initiates the WebSockets request. It requires a list of transports that will be responsible for managing the protocol—in this case, the SockJS based on the RestTemplate.

- WebSocketStompClient: This class uses the STOMP over WebSockets protocol and gets connected via WebSocketClient. This is the main core of the protocol handler, where the lifecycle starts. It requires the session handler (see Listing 10-36) as part of its constructor. This class connects to the WebSocket server by calling the connect method and passing the URI (the remote server based on the RetroBoardProperties values). It also defines how it will be connected (WebSocketClient).

In the UserSocketConfiguration, we used the RetroBoardProperties class, which binds the properties declared in the application.properties file. Open/create the application.properties file. See Listing 10-39.

Listing 10-39. src/main/resources/application.properties

```
# Port
server.port=${PORT:8081}
# Data
spring.h2.console.enabled=true
spring.datasource.generate-unique-name=false
spring.datasource.name=test-db
#spring.jpa.show-sql=true
# My Retro Properties
myretro.users-service.hostname=http://localhost:8080
myretro.users-service.base-path=/logs
```

Listing 10-39 shows the users-service.* properties that are necessary to connect to the WebSockets/STOMP server that lives in Users App.

Running My Retro App Using WebSockets/STOMP

Now it's time to run both apps and see how they interact. Make sure Users App is up and running; it should run in port 8080. Run the My Retro App project. Once it is up and running, take a look at the Users App console. The last output should be something similar to this:

```
WebSocketSession[1 current WS(1)-HttpStream(0)-HttpPoll(0), 1 total, 0
closed abnormally (0 connect failure, 0 send limit, 0 transport error)],
stompSubProtocol[processed CONNECT(1)-CONNECTED(1)-DISCONNECT(0)],
stompBrokerRelay[null], inboundChannel[pool size = 0, active threads
= 0, queued tasks = 0, completed tasks = 6], outboundChannel[pool
size = 0, active threads = 0, queued tasks = 0, completed tasks = 1],
sockJsScheduler[pool size = 8, active threads = 1, queued tasks = 2,
completed tasks = 428]
WebSocketSession[1 current WS(1)-HttpStream(0)-HttpPoll(0), 1 total, 0
closed abnormally (0 connect failure, 0 send limit, 0 transport error)],
stompSubProtocol[processed CONNECT(1)-CONNECTED(1)-DISCONNECT(0)],
stompBrokerRelay[null], inboundChannel[pool size = 0, active threads = 0,
queued tasks = 0, completed tasks = 6], outboundChannel[pool size = 0, active
threads = 0, queued tasks = 0, completed tasks = 1], sockJsScheduler[pool
size = 8, active threads = 1, queued tasks = 2, completed tasks = 861]
```

540

This means that there is a connection established between the Users App and the My Retro App projects. Now use the previous command to send a new `User`:

```
curl -i -s -d '{"name":"Dummy","email":"dummy@email.com","password":
"aw2sOmeR!","userRole":["INFO"],"active":true}' \
-H "Content-Type: application/json" \
http://localhost:8080/users
```

With this command, you will see the following output in the My Retro App console:

```
2023-10-27T17:01:01.811-04:00  INFO 53760 --- [lient-AsyncIO-2]
c.a.myretro.web.socket.UserSocketClient  : Client received: payload
Event(version=1.0, time=2023-10-27T17:00:53, event=UserEvent(email=dummy@
email.com, active=false, action=ACTIVATION_STATUS, datetime=null)),
headers {destination=[/topic/user-logs], content-type=[application/json],
subscription=[0], message-id=[c0396b652a9f42c3884d9f4666b8115d-4], content-
length=[127]}
```

You are getting the payload (in this case, the `Event` type). If you remove the user:

```
curl -I -s -XDELETE http://localhost:8080/users/dummy@email.com
```

you will get something like this:

```
2023-10-27T17:01:55.261-04:00  INFO 53760 --- [lient-AsyncIO-5]
c.a.myretro.web.socket.UserSocketClient  : Client received: payload
Event(version=1.0, time=2023-10-27T17:01:55, event=UserEvent(email=dummy@
email.com, active=false, action=REMOVED, datetime=2023-10-27T17:01:55)),
headers {destination=[/topic/user-logs], content-type=[application/json],
subscription=[0], message-id=[c0396b652a9f42c3884d9f4666b8115d-5], content-
length=[134]}
```

Nice! You now know how to use WebSockets between apps.

RSocket with Spring Boot

RSocket is one of the newest technologies being used for messaging. This technology is an application protocol for multiplexed, duplex communication over TCP, WebSockets, and stream transports. RSocket has different interaction models:

- *Request/response*: You send a message, and you get a message back.

- *Request/stream*: You send a message, and you get back a stream of messages.

- *Fire-and-forget*: You send a message, and you get no response.

- *Channel*: A stream of messages is sent in both directions.

Some of the key features of the RSocket protocol are Reactive Streams semantics, request throttling, session resumption, fragmentation and reassembly of large messages, and keepalive frames (heartbeats). When using RSocket with Spring, the `spring-messaging` module supplies `RSocketRequester` and the annotated responders such as the `@MessageMapping` annotation.

This section uses the request/response interaction model to demonstrate another way to establish interaction with the book's two apps. Let's get started and see how easy it is to add RSocket technologies to Users App and My Retro App.

Using RSocket with Users App with Spring Boot

You can find all the source code in the `10-messaging-rsocket/users` folder. We are going to use WebFlux code from previous chapters. If you are starting from scratch with the Spring Initializr (`https://start.spring.io`), set the Group field to `com.apress` and the Artifact and Name fields to `users`. Add the RSocket, WebFlux, Validation, R2DBC, and H2 dependencies. Generate and download the project, unzip it, and import it into your favorite IDE.

Let's start with the `build.gradle` file. It should look like Listing 10-40.

Listing 10-40. The build.gradle File

```
import org.jetbrains.kotlin.gradle.tasks.KotlinCompile
plugins {
    id 'org.springframework.boot' version '3.2.3'
    id 'io.spring.dependency-management' version '1.1.4'
    id 'org.jetbrains.kotlin.jvm' version '2.0.20-RC'
    id "org.jetbrains.kotlin.plugin.spring" version "2.0.20-RC"
    // <- simplifies spring proxying
}
```

```
group = 'com.apress'
version = '0.0.1-SNAPSHOT'
sourceCompatibility = '17'

repositories {
    mavenCentral()
}

dependencies {
    implementation "org.jetbrains.kotlin:kotlin-stdlib-jdk8"
    implementation "org.jetbrains.kotlin:kotlin-reflect"

    implementation 'org.springframework.boot:spring-boot-starter-webflux'
    implementation 'org.springframework.boot:spring-boot-starter-rsocket'
    implementation 'org.springframework.boot:spring-boot-starter-
    validation'

    implementation 'com.fasterxml.jackson.datatype:jackson-datatype-jsr310'

    implementation 'org.springframework.boot:spring-boot-starter-
    data-r2dbc'
    runtimeOnly 'io.r2dbc:r2dbc-h2'
    runtimeOnly 'org.postgresql:r2dbc-postgresql'

    // Web
    implementation 'org.webjars:bootstrap:5.2.3'

    testImplementation 'org.springframework.boot:spring-boot-starter-test'
    testImplementation 'io.projectreactor:reactor-test'
}

tasks.named('test') {
    useJUnitPlatform()
}

//      kotlin {
//          jvmToolchain(17)
//      }
tasks.withType(KotlinCompile).configureEach {
    kotlinOptions {
```

```
        freeCompilerArgs = ['-Xjsr305=strict']
        jvmTarget = '17'
    }
}
```

We are adding the `spring-boot-starter-webflux`, `spring-boot-starter-rsocket`, and `r2dbc-h2` (database) dependencies to the `build.gradle` file.

Next, open/create the `UserRSocket` class. See Listing 10-41.

Listing 10-41. src/main/kotlin/com/apress/users/rsocket/UserRSocket.kt

```kotlin
package com.apress.users.rsocket

import com.apress.users.model.User
import com.apress.users.service.UserService
import org.springframework.beans.factory.annotation.Autowired
import org.springframework.messaging.handler.annotation.MessageMapping
import org.springframework.stereotype.Controller
import reactor.core.publisher.Flux
import reactor.core.publisher.Mono

@Controller
class UserRSocket {
    @Autowired
    private lateinit var userService: UserService

    @MessageMapping("new-user")
    fun newUser(user: User): Mono<User> =
        userService.saveUpdateUser(user)

    @get:MessageMapping("all-users")
    val allUsers: Flux<User>
        get() = userService.allUsers

    @MessageMapping("user-by-email")
    fun findUserByEmail(email: String): Mono<User> =
        userService.findUserByEmail(email)
```

```
@MessageMapping("remove-user-by-email")
fun removeUserByEmail(email: String): Mono<Void> =
    userService.removeUserByEmail(email).let {
        Mono.empty()
    }
}
```

The important feature in the UserRSocket class is the @MessageMapping annotation, which is a responder in an RSocket app. It's like the annotations you are used to, such as @GetMapping, @PostMapping, and so on. With this annotation, you need to define a *destination*, and it can accept other parameters, such as java.security.Principal, @Header, @Payload, and so on. The annotated method can return a STOMP over WebSockets value or a custom definition with the @SendTo or @SendToUser annotations. In this case, we are using Mono and Flux types.

Next, open the application.properties file, the contents of which should be similar to Listing 10-42.

Listing 10-42. src/main/resources/application.properties

```
# RSocket
spring.rsocket.server.port=9898
# R2DBC
spring.r2dbc.properties.initialization-mode=always
spring.r2dbc.generate-unique-name=false
spring.r2dbc.name=retro-db
# Logging
logging.level.org.springframework.r2dbc=DEBUG
```

In the application.properties file, the important property is spring.rsocket. server.port, which maps to port 9898.

And that's it! You don't need anything else. Basically, when Spring Boot finds the spring-boot-starter-rsocket dependency, it will auto-configure the RSocketServer, the handler, the message converter, and so forth with the default values. In this case, it will also register all the destinations based on the @MessageMapping annotation responders.

Running Users App with RSocket and Spring Boot

You can now run Users App. You don't need to do anything special here. The most important information is in the logs. Once you run the app (either from the command line with ./gradlew bootRun or from your IDE), take a look at the logs. You should see something similar to the following:

```
...
--- [           main] o.s.b.web.embedded.netty.NettyWebServer  : Netty
started on port 8080
--- [           main] o.s.b.rsocket.netty.NettyRSocketServer   : Netty
RSocket started on port(s): 9898
--- [           main] com.apress.users.UsersApplication        : Started
UsersApplication in 2.576 seconds
```

Remember that this is a WebFlux app, so the Netty server is used and configured by default by Spring Boot. A NettyRSockerServer is also being started, and it's listening on port 9898.

Add some users from the command line:

```
curl -i -s -d '{"name":"Dummy","email":"dummy@email.com","password":
"aw2sOmeR!","userRole":["INFO"],"active":true}' \
-H "Content-Type: application/json" \
http://localhost:8080/users
curl -i -s -d '{"name":"Ximena","email":"ximena@email.com","password":
"aw2sOmeR!","userRole":["INFO","ADMIN"],"active":true}' \
-H "Content-Type: application/json" \
http://localhost:8080/users
```

Now you are ready to request RSocket messages.

Requesting RSocket Messages in My Retro App

This section explains what you need to do to incorporate the RSocket technology into My Retro App. If you downloaded the code, take a look at the 10-messagin-rsocket/ myretro folder. If you are starting from scratch with the Spring Initializr (https:// start.spring.io), set the Group field to com.apress and the Artifact and Name fields to myretro. Add the RSocket, WebFlux, Validation, Mongo Reactive, and Docker Compose dependencies. Generate and download the project, unzip it, and import it into your favorite IDE.

Let's start with the build.gradle file. See Listing 10-43.

Listing 10-43. The build.gradle File

```
import org.jetbrains.kotlin.gradle.tasks.KotlinCompile
plugins {
    id 'org.springframework.boot' version '3.2.3'
    id 'io.spring.dependency-management' version '1.1.4'
    id 'org.jetbrains.kotlin.jvm' version '2.0.20-RC'
    id "org.jetbrains.kotlin.plugin.spring" version "2.0.20-RC"
    // <- simplifies spring proxying
}

group = 'com.apress'
version = '0.0.1-SNAPSHOT'
sourceCompatibility = '17'

repositories {
    mavenCentral()
}

dependencies {
    implementation "org.jetbrains.kotlin:kotlin-stdlib-jdk8"
    implementation "org.jetbrains.kotlin:kotlin-reflect"

    implementation 'org.springframework.boot:spring-boot-starter-webflux'
    implementation 'org.springframework.boot:spring-boot-starter-rsocket'
    implementation 'org.springframework.boot:spring-boot-starter-
    validation'

    implementation 'com.fasterxml.jackson.datatype:jackson-datatype-jsr310'

    implementation 'org.springframework.boot:spring-boot-starter-data-
    mongodb-reactive'

    annotationProcessor 'org.springframework.boot:spring-boot-
    configuration-processor'
```

```
    developmentOnly 'org.springframework.boot:spring-boot-docker-compose'

    testImplementation 'org.springframework.boot:spring-boot-starter-test'
}

tasks.named('test') {
    useJUnitPlatform()
}

//    kotlin {
//        jvmToolchain(17)
//    }
tasks.withType(KotlinCompile).configureEach {
    kotlinOptions {
        freeCompilerArgs = ['-Xjsr305=strict']
        jvmTarget = '17'
    }
}
```

Listing 10-43 shows that we are using the spring-boot-starter-rsocket dependency.

Next, open/create the User and UserRole classes, shown in Listings 10-44 and 10-45, respectively.

Listing 10-44. src/main/kotlin/com/apress/myretro/rsocket/User.kt

```
package com.apress.myretro.rsocket

import com.fasterxml.jackson.annotation.JsonIgnoreProperties
import java.util.*

@JsonIgnoreProperties(ignoreUnknown = true)
data class User(
    var id: UUID? = null,
    var email: String? = null,
    var name: String? = null,
    var gravatarUrl: String? = null,
    var userRole: MutableCollection<UserRole> = mutableListOf(),
    var active:Boolean = false
)
```

Listing 10-45. src/main/kotlin/com/apress/myretro/rsocket/UserRole.kt

```
package com.apress.myretro.rsocket
enum class UserRole {
    USER, ADMIN, INFO
}
```

As you can see, the User and UserRole classes are the same as in the Users App project.

Next, open/create the UserClient interface. See Listing 10-46.

Listing 10-46. src/main/kotlin/com/apress/myretro/rsocket/UserClient.kt

```
package com.apress.myretro.rsocket

import org.springframework.messaging.rsocket.service.RSocketExchange
import org.springframework.stereotype.Component
import reactor.core.publisher.Flux

@Component
interface UserClient {
    @get:RSocketExchange("all-users")
    val allUsers: Flux<User>
}
```

The UserClient interface is marking a method with the @RSocketExchange annotation, which defines the RSocket endpoint called all-users. Behind the scenes and thanks to Spring Boot, this endppoint will be able to reach out to the RSocket server and look for that destination (responder)—in this case, Users App. For now, we are going to reach out to only one destination. You can do the same for any other destination (@MessageMapping).

Next, open/create the Config class. See Listing 10-47.

Listing 10-47.   src/main/kotlin/com/apress/myretro/rsocket/Config.kt

```kotlin
package com.apress.myretro.rsocket

import org.slf4j.LoggerFactory
import org.springframework.beans.factory.annotation.Value
import org.springframework.boot.CommandLineRunner
import org.springframework.context.annotation.Bean
import org.springframework.context.annotation.Configuration
import org.springframework.messaging.rsocket.RSocketRequester
import org.springframework.messaging.rsocket.service.
RSocketServiceProxyFactory

@Configuration
class Config {
    @Bean
    fun getRSocketServiceProxyFactory(
        requestBuilder: RSocketRequester.Builder,
        @Value("\${myretro.users-service.host:localhost}") host: String,
        @Value("\${myretro.users-service.port:9898}") port: Int
    ): RSocketServiceProxyFactory =
        requestBuilder.tcp(host, port).let {
            RSocketServiceProxyFactory.builder(it).build()
        }

    @Bean
    fun getClient(factory: RSocketServiceProxyFactory): UserClient =
        factory.createClient(UserClient::class.java)

    @Bean
    fun commandLineRunner(userClient: UserClient): CommandLineRunner =
        CommandLineRunner { _: Array<String> ->
            userClient.allUsers.doOnNext { user: User -> LOG.info
            ("User: {}", user) }
                .subscribe()
        }
```

```
companion object {
    private val LOG = LoggerFactory.getLogger(Config::class.java)
}
```
}

Let's review the `Config` class:

- `RSocketRequester.Builder`: This interface is configured by Spring Boot auto-configuration. This is an RSocket wrapper that can send and return objects. It can route and prepare other useful metadata. In this case, we are using the values of the `myretro.user-service.*` properties (to get the host and port where the RSocket server is running) to create an `RSocketRequester` object. This object can create the factory we need.

- `RSocketServiceProxyFactory`: This is a factory for creating a client proxy based on the RSocket service interface that is used with the `@RSocketExchange` methods (`UserClient` interface).

- `UserClient`: This interface is an RSocket service. Behind the scenes, an implementation does all the work of connecting, sending, receiving, and so on, to the RSocket server.

Note that we are using `CommandLineRunner`, which means that when the app is ready, it will execute the code. In this case, it will use the `UserClient#getAllUsers` method to make a request to the `all-users` destination that lives in Users App.

Next, open the `application.properties` file, shown in Listing 10-48.

Listing 10-48. src/main/resources/application.properties

```
# MongoDB
#spring.data.mongodb.uri=mongodb://retroadmin:aw2s0me@127.0.0.1:27017/retro
db?directConnection=true&serverSelectionTimeoutMS=2000&authSource=admin&app
Name=mongosh+1.7.1
#spring.data.mongodb.database=retrodb
# App
server.port=8081
# Users Service
myretro.users-service.host=localhost
```

myretro.users-service.port=9898

spring.docker.compose.file: ./myretro/docker-compose.yaml

In the application.properties file, we define the users-service properties to indicate where the RSocket server is running. In this case, it's in the same machine (localhost) and port 9898.

Finally, we need to add the docker-compose.yaml file. Remember that we use the spring-boot-docker-compose dependency, so it can start up the MongoDB service. See Listing 10-49.

Listing 10-49. docker-compose.yaml

```
version: "3.1"
services:
  mongo:
    image: mongo
    restart: always
    environment:
      MONGO_INITDB_DATABASE: retrodb
    ports:
      - "27017:27017"
```

Running the RSocket Requester in My Retro App with Spring Boot

It's time to run the RSocket requester in My Retro App. You can do this from the command line or in your IDE. After you run it, you should see the following output:

```
...
--- User: User(id=7d8f43c1-4911-4945-8a5d-301b365e82ce, email=dummy@email.
com, name=Dummy, gravatarUrl=https://www.gravatar.com/avatar/fb651279f471
2e209991e05610dfb03a?d=wavatar, userRole=[INFO], active=true)
--- User: User(id=2074203e-add0-40ca-95c2-82b2a23e1f13, email=ximena@email.
com, name=Ximena, gravatarUrl=https://www.gravatar.com/avatar/f07f7e55326
4c9710105edebe6c465e7?d=wavatar, userRole=[INFO, ADMIN], active=true)
...
```

As you can see, we are requesting to the all-users destination, using RSocket!

Other Messaging Frameworks

In the Apress GitHub repository for this book (`https://www.apress.com/gp/services/source-code`) or in this personal GitHub repository (`https://github.com/felipeg48/pro-spring-boot-3rd`), you can find additional examples of messaging frameworks, including Kafka, Redis, and more. Covering them all would require a second entire book. Stay tuned for more code and features in the repo. The most important element of developing this kind of application is that it should reflect the Spring way to create apps, because it allows you to use Spring/Spring Boot and simple messaging solutions using this programming style.

Summary

In this chapter you learned about different messaging technologies that can help you create synchronous and asynchronous messaging systems. You discovered that the main core of Spring Messaging is in the `spring-messaging` module, and when you use it with Spring Boot, the auto-configuration will set all the defaults, including connecting, sessioning, reconnecting, message converting, and much more.

You also learned that the `spring-messaging` module includes interfaces and implementations, such as the `Template` design pattern, that are implemented in every technology. These interfaces bring concrete class implementations such as `JmsTemplate`, `RabbitTemplate`, `RedisTemplate`, and `PulsarTemplate` (and many more) that help you take care of the business logic. That way, you don't have to spend time on the underlying technology, making development much easier.

CHAPTER 11

Spring Boot Actuator

Felipe Gutierrez[a*]
ᵃ 4109 Rillcrest Grove Way Fuquay Varina, NC 27526-3562, Albuquerque, NM, USA

What Is Spring Boot Actuator?

Spring Boot Actuator is a powerful tool that can help developers in various ways, including:

- *Monitoring application health*: Actuator provides a set of endpoints that expose key metrics about the health of a Spring Boot application, such as CPU usage, memory consumption, and thread pool utilization. This information can help developers identify potential performance issues and take corrective actions before they impact users.

- *Debugging and troubleshooting*: Actuator provides endpoints that allow developers to dump thread stacks, inspect environment variables, and view logs. This information can be invaluable when debugging and troubleshooting issues in a running application.

- *Enabling remote management*: Actuator can be configured to expose endpoints over HTTPS, allowing developers to manage and monitor their applications remotely. This can be particularly useful for applications deployed in production environments.

- *Integrating with external monitoring tools*: Actuator can be configured to export metrics to external monitoring tools, such as Prometheus or Grafana. This allows developers to centralize their monitoring data and gain deeper insights into application performance. All this is thanks to the Micrometer technology (`https://micrometer.io/`).

555

© Peter Späth, Felipe Gutierrez 2025
P. Späth and F. Gutierrez, *Pro Spring Boot 3 with Kotlin*, https://doi.org/10.1007/979-8-8688-1131-9_11

- *Customizing actuator endpoints*: Actuator provides a flexible API that allows developers to create custom endpoints to expose additional information or functionality from their applications.

As developers, Spring Boot Actuator can help with these tasks:

- *Identify performance bottlenecks*: By monitoring CPU, memory, and thread pool usage, developers can identify performance bottlenecks in their applications.

- *Detect memory leaks*: Actuator's dump endpoints allow developers to inspect the heap and identify memory leaks.

- *Troubleshoot database connectivity issues*: Actuator's connection pool metrics can help developers identify database connectivity issues.

- *Track application startup and shutdown*: Actuator's lifecycle events endpoint provides insights into application startup and shutdown behavior.

- *Monitor application security*: Actuator's security endpoints provide information about the security configuration of the application.

Overall, Spring Boot Actuator is a valuable tool for developers that can help them monitor, debug, troubleshoot, and manage their Spring Boot applications. Let's start adding Spring Boot Actuator to the main apps.

Users App with Spring Boot Actuator

This section starts with Users App. You have access to the source code in the 11-actuator/users folder. If you want to start from scratch, we are going to use Users App with JPA. In the Spring Initializr (https://start.spring.io), set the Group field to com.apress and the Artifact and Name fields to users. Add the Web, Validation, Data JPA, Actuator, H2, and PostgreSQL dependencies. Generate and download the project, unzip it, and import it into your favorite IDE.

Let's check the build.gradle file. See Listing 11-1.

Listing 11-1. The build.gradle File

```
import org.jetbrains.kotlin.gradle.tasks.KotlinCompile
plugins {
    id 'org.springframework.boot' version '3.2.3'
    id 'io.spring.dependency-management' version '1.1.4'
    id "com.gorylenko.gradle-git-properties" version "2.4.1"
    id 'org.jetbrains.kotlin.jvm' version '2.0.20-RC'
    id "org.jetbrains.kotlin.plugin.spring" version "2.0.20-RC"
    // <- simplifies spring proxying
}

group = 'com.apress'
version = '0.0.1-SNAPSHOT'
sourceCompatibility = '17'

configurations {
    compileOnly {
        extendsFrom annotationProcessor
    }
}

repositories {
    mavenCentral()
}

springBoot {
    buildInfo()
}

dependencies {
    implementation "org.jetbrains.kotlin:kotlin-stdlib-jdk8"
    implementation "org.jetbrains.kotlin:kotlin-reflect"

    implementation 'org.springframework.boot:spring-boot-starter-web'
    implementation 'org.springframework.boot:spring-boot-starter-
    validation'

    implementation 'org.springframework.boot:spring-boot-starter-data-jpa'
```

```
    implementation 'org.springframework.boot:spring-boot-starter-actuator'

    implementation 'org.springframework.boot:spring-boot-starter-security'

    //implementation 'org.springframework.boot:spring-boot-starter-amqp'

    runtimeOnly 'com.h2database:h2'
    runtimeOnly 'org.postgresql:postgresql'

    annotationProcessor 'org.springframework.boot:spring-boot-
    configuration-processor'

    // Web
    implementation 'org.webjars:bootstrap:5.2.3'

    testImplementation 'org.springframework.boot:spring-boot-starter-test'
}
//    kotlin {
//        jvmToolchain(17)
//    }
tasks.withType(KotlinCompile).configureEach {
    kotlinOptions {
        freeCompilerArgs = ['-Xjsr305=strict']
        jvmTarget = '17'
    }
}

tasks.named('test') {
    useJUnitPlatform()
}
```

The only new dependency is the spring-boot-starter-actuator. Just by adding this, the Spring Boot auto-configuration will set up all the Actuator defaults. This means that you instantly have *production-ready features*! Spring Boot Actuator defines several endpoints that allow you to have out-of-the-box, production-ready features, such as metrics, environment variables, events, sessions, thread dumps, scheduled tasks, loggers, health indicators, and much more.

/actuator

By default, Spring Boot Actuator defines the /actuator endpoint as a prefix for other actuator endpoints. The only Actuator endpoint enabled is mapped to the /actuator/health endpoint, which is responsible for showing the application health information.

Note   If you started from scratch, you can copy the version of Users App that incorporates the JPA technology.

Let's run the application. No modification is required. Adding the spring-boot-starter-actuator dependency is sufficient. You can run Users App either by using your IDE or by running the following command from the command line:

```
./gradlew bootRun
...
...
INFO 11418 --- [main] o.s.b.a.e.web.EndpointLinksResolver        : Exposing 1
endpoint(s) beneath base path '/actuator'
...
...
```

Notice the log about exposing the /actuator endpoint.

Now open your browser and go to http://localhost:8080/actuator. You should see the /actuator endpoint (prefix) response, as shown in Figure 11-1. If you are using the downloaded sources, you first have to enter these security credentials: "admin"/"admin". We cover security later.

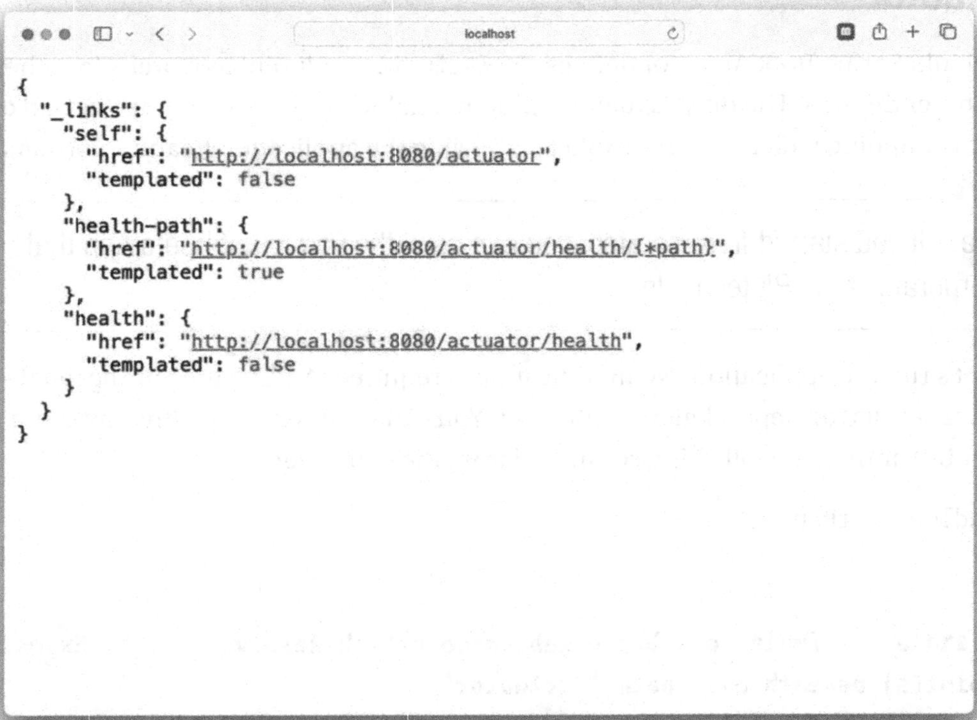

Figure 11-1. *Default prefix /actuator (http://localhost:8080/actuator)*

The /actuator endpoint (prefix) response is a HATEOAS (Hypermedia As The Engine Of Application State) response. One of its main features is that it includes resource links that can be accessed directly in the browser and can be used for more specialized jobs, such as web scraping, to find out how the app defines its API, and much more. Click the last reference, http://localhost:8080/actuator/health, to see the following response:

```
{
  "status": "UP"
}
```

The /actuator/health endpoint can provide detailed information about the health of the application. We show you more details about this endpoint in later sections. For now, this endpoint is the only one that is enabled by default.

Configuring /Actuator Endpoints

You can configure, override, enable, and do much more to the actuator endpoints. As you saw, the prefix of the actuator is /actuator and you can easily override it with the following property:

management.endpoints.web.base-path

You can add this property to the application.properties file and assign it the /users-system-management value. See Listing 11-2.

Listing 11-2. src/main/resources/application.properties

```
# Spring Properties
spring.h2.console.enabled=true
spring.datasource.generate-unique-name=false
spring.datasource.name=test-db
# Actuator Config
management.endpoints.web.base-path=/users-system-management
# Spring Info
spring.application.name=Users App
```

Listing 11-2 shows that we also added a new property, called spring.application.name, with the Users App value, which is for testing some of the features of Spring Boot Actuator later in the chapter.

After the preceding property change, rerun Users App and point your browser to http://localhost:8080/users-system-management. See Figure 11-2.

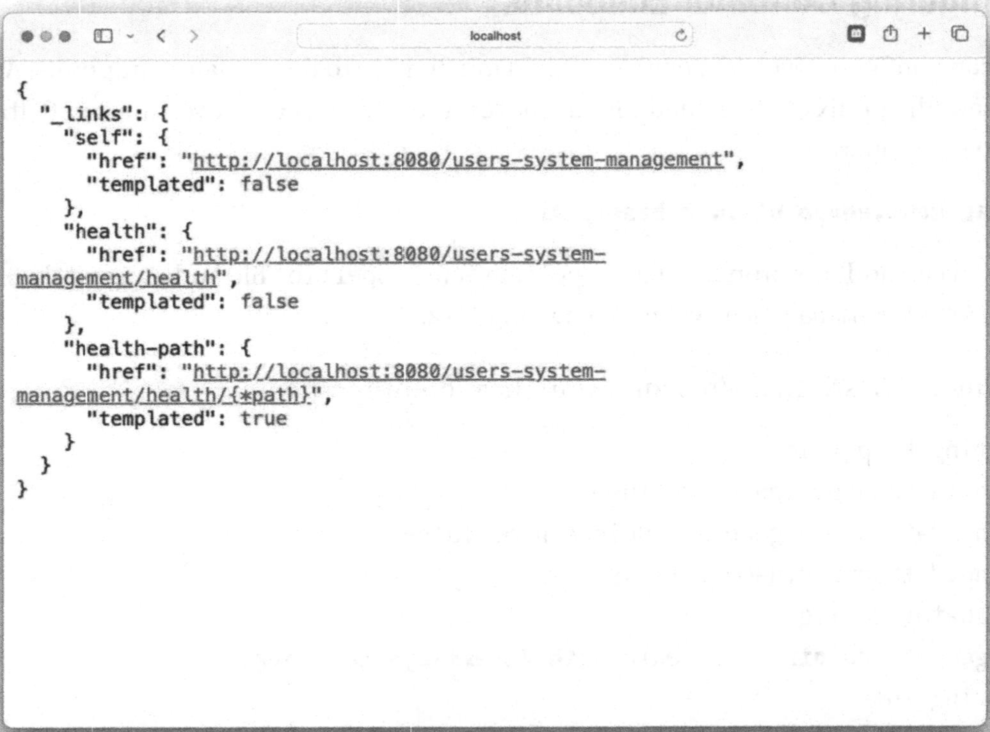

Figure 11-2. *http://localhost:8080/users-system-management*

The `management.endpoints.web.*` properties have more ways to override the defaults, and we are going to review them soon.

Next, comment out the property you just added by putting a # before the property declaration, so that you can work just with the `/actuator` (a short prefix).

Using Spring Profiles for Actuator Endpoints

Before continuing with Spring Boot Actuator, let's use the Spring profiles to test the Actuator features. Create a blank file named `application-actuator.properties` in the `src/main/resources` folder, in the same location as the `application.properties` file.

Enabling Actuator Endpoints

So far, we have just worked with the `/actuator/health` endpoint, which is the default. Now it's time to review the other endpoints. Spring Boot Actuator has a convention for its endpoints with the pattern `/actuator/{id}`, where the `{id}` is the endpoint you want to access. In other words, each feature has its own ID, and to use the endpoints, you need to enable them with the following property:

`management.endpoints.web.exposure.[include|exclude]``=<id>[,<id>]|*`

You can choose to enable them all by using this syntax:

`management.endpoints.web.exposure.include=*`

Or you can enable each actuator feature individually, separated by commas if you want to enable more than one. For example:

`management.endpoints.web.exposure.include=health,info,env,shutdown,bea`
`ns,metrics`

By default, these endpoints are also exposed through Java Management Extensions (JMX). You can also include or exclude actuator endpoints for JMX with this syntax:

`management.endpoints.jmx.exposure.[include|exclude]=[*|<id>[,<id>]`

For example, to include all actuator endpoints you would use this:

`management.endpoints.jmx.exposure.include=*`

/actuator/info

This actuator endpoint provides general information about your application, and accessing it only requires a GET request to `/actuator/info`. One of the cool things you can do with this endpoint is get the information about the Git (branch, commit, etc.) and the build (artifact, version, group), and you can even have your own information about your app. In other words, you can add anything you want that makes sense for your app after the `info.*` property.

Add the properties shown in Listing 11-3 to the `application-actuator.properties` file.

Listing 11-3. src/main/resources/application-actuator.properties

```
management.endpoints.web.exposure.include=health, info
# Actuator Info
management.info.env.enabled=true
info.application.name=${spring.application.name}
info.developer.name=Felipe
info.developer.email=felipe@email.com
info.api.version=1.0
```

Listing 11-3 shows the properties added to the application-actuator.properties file. First, note that we are exposing just the health and info endpoints. We are also enabling the info environment (with management.info.env.enabled=true) and adding useful information for Users App with the info.* properties. We are calling the base (application.properties) with the info.application.name property.

Next, let's run this application. First make sure to add the profile either as an environment variable (SPRING_PROFILES_ACTIVE=actuator) or as a parameter. If you are using an IDE, check in your IDE documentation how to set a profile. In IntelliJ, in the top menu, choose Run ➤ Edit Configurations and then find the Active Profiles field. Or you can set the environment variable in your OS. If you are running your app from the command line, you can execute the following:

```
./gradlew bootRun --args='--spring.profiles.active=actuator'
```

If you direct your browser to http://localhost:8080/actuator/info, you will see something similar to the code shown in Figure 11-3.

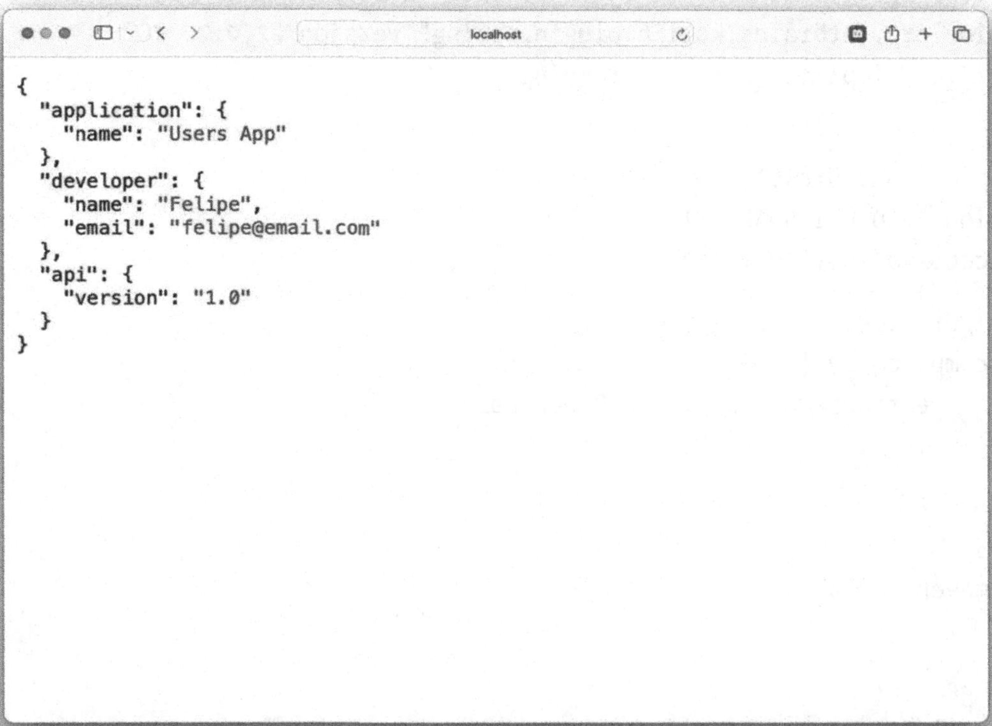

Figure 11-3. */actuator/info endpoint*

To enable Git and build info, you need to add a plugin for the Git information (`com.gorylenko.gradle-git-properties`) and add a call for the build info (`buildInfo()`) to the `build.gradle` file. See Listing 11-4.

Listing 11-4. The build.gradle File

```
import org.jetbrains.kotlin.gradle.tasks.KotlinCompile
plugins {
    id 'org.springframework.boot' version '3.2.3'
    id 'io.spring.dependency-management' version '1.1.4'
    // GIT property exposure to Actuator works only, if this is a GIT
    repo. If not,
    // comment this line out, otherwise you'll get a build error:
    id "com.gorylenko.gradle-git-properties" version "2.4.1"
```

```
    id 'org.jetbrains.kotlin.jvm' version '2.0.20-RC'
    id "org.jetbrains.kotlin.plugin.spring" version "2.0.20-RC"
    // <- simplifies spring proxying
}

group = 'com.apress'
version = '0.0.1-SNAPSHOT'
sourceCompatibility = '17'

configurations {
    compileOnly {
        extendsFrom annotationProcessor
    }
}

repositories {
    mavenCentral()
}

springBoot {
    buildInfo()
}

dependencies {
    implementation "org.jetbrains.kotlin:kotlin-stdlib-jdk8"
    implementation "org.jetbrains.kotlin:kotlin-reflect"

    implementation 'org.springframework.boot:spring-boot-starter-web'
    implementation 'org.springframework.boot:spring-boot-starter-
    validation'

    implementation 'org.springframework.boot:spring-boot-starter-data-jpa'

    implementation 'org.springframework.boot:spring-boot-starter-actuator'

    implementation 'org.springframework.boot:spring-boot-starter-security'

    //implementation 'org.springframework.boot:spring-boot-starter-amqp'

    runtimeOnly 'com.h2database:h2'
    runtimeOnly 'org.postgresql:postgresql'
```

```
    annotationProcessor 'org.springframework.boot:spring-boot-
configuration-processor'

    // Web
    implementation 'org.webjars:bootstrap:5.2.3'

    testImplementation 'org.springframework.boot:spring-boot-starter-test'
}
//    kotlin {
//        jvmToolchain(17)
//    }
tasks.withType(KotlinCompile).configureEach {
    kotlinOptions {
        freeCompilerArgs = ['-Xjsr305=strict']
        jvmTarget = '17'
    }
}

tasks.named('test') {
    useJUnitPlatform()
}
```

Listing 11-4 shows the build.gradle file where we added the plugin necessary for the Git information and the call for the build information.

You can now rerun Users App. Don't forget the actuator profile. From now on, we are going to use this profile, so be ready. Once you rerun your app, go to http:// localhost:8080/actuator/info. You will see something like Figure 11-4.

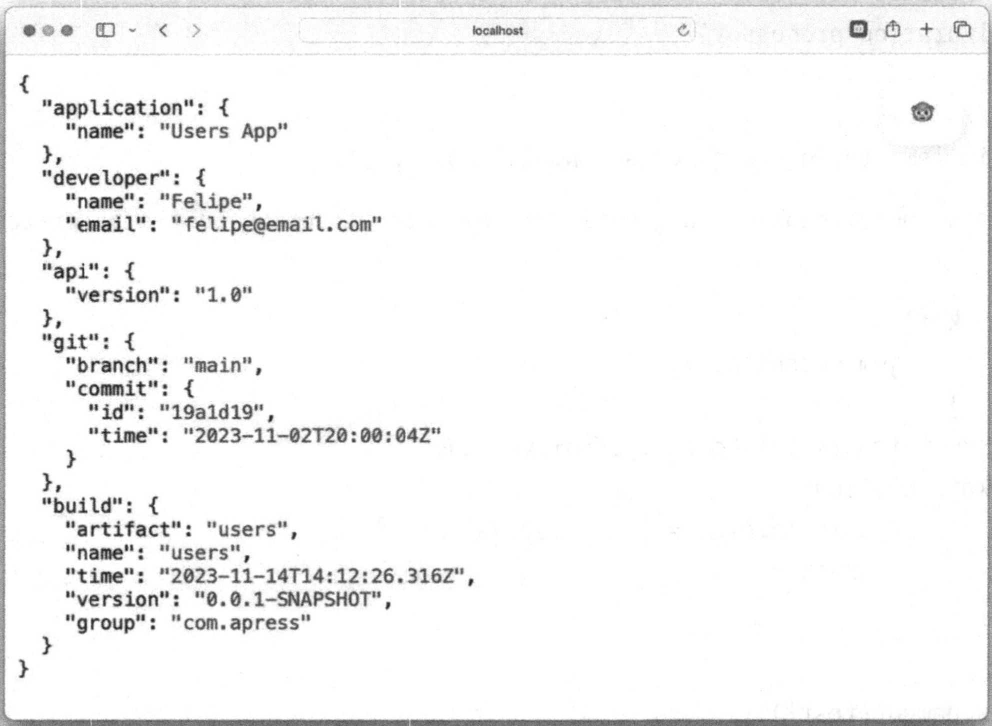

```
{
  "application": {
    "name": "Users App"
  },
  "developer": {
    "name": "Felipe",
    "email": "felipe@email.com"
  },
  "api": {
    "version": "1.0"
  },
  "git": {
    "branch": "main",
    "commit": {
      "id": "19a1d19",
      "time": "2023-11-02T20:00:04Z"
    }
  },
  "build": {
    "artifact": "users",
    "name": "users",
    "time": "2023-11-14T14:12:26.316Z",
    "version": "0.0.1-SNAPSHOT",
    "group": "com.apress"
  }
}
```

Figure 11-4. */actuator/info with Git and build information*

Figure 11-4 shows you the /actuator/info endpoint with the Git and build info. You can get more details from the Git info. You can view the user, messages, remote, tags, and so on. To enable the full details, add the following property:

```
management.info.git.mode=full
```

/actuator/env

This actuator endpoint provides information about the application's environment. This is useful when you want to see what environment variables your app can access. To test it, you can add it to the list of endpoints:

```
management.endpoints.web.exposure.include=health,info,env
```

You can access this endpoint with the following GET request to /actuator/env, and you should see output similar to what's shown here:

```
curl -s http://localhost:8080/actuator/env | jq .
{
  "activeProfiles": [
    "actuator"
  ],
  "propertySources": [
    {
      "name": "server.ports",
      "properties": {
        "local.server.port": {
          "value": "******"
        }
      }
    },
    {
      "name": "servletContextInitParams",
      "properties": {}
    },
    {
      "name": "systemProperties",
      "properties": {
        "java.specification.version": {
          "value": "******"
        },
        "sun.jnu.encoding": {
          "value": "******"
        },
...
...
}
```

/actuator/beans

This endpoint provides information about the application's Spring Beans. You can get access to this endpoint with the following GET request to /actuator/beans. This is useful when you want to see if your configuration picks up the declared beans or if you have any conditional beans that need to be present depending on your business conditions.

```
curl -s http://localhost:8080/actuator/beans | jq .
{
  "contexts": {
    "Users App": {
      "beans": {
        "userLogs": {
          "aliases": [],
          "scope": "singleton",
          "type": "com.apress.users.events.UserLogs",
          "resource": "file [/Users/felipeg/Progs/Books/pro-spring-
          boot-3rd/java/11-actuator/users/build/classes/java/main/com/
          apress/users/events/UserLogs.class]",
          "dependencies": [
            "logEventEndpoint"
          ]
        ...
        ...
        "jdbcTemplate": {
          "aliases": [],
          "scope": "singleton",
          "type": "org.springframework.jdbc.core.JdbcTemplate",
          "resource": "class path resource [org/springframework/boot/
          autoconfigure/jdbc/JdbcTemplateConfiguration.class]",
          "dependencies": [
            "dataSourceScriptDatabaseInitializer",
            "org.springframework.boot.autoconfigure.jdbc.
            JdbcTemplateConfiguration",
            "dataSource",
```

```
        "spring.jdbc-org.springframework.boot.autoconfigure.jdbc.
        JdbcProperties"
      ]
    }
  }
}
}
}
```

/actuator/conditions

This endpoint provides information about the evaluation of conditions in the configuration and auto-configuration classes. In other words, any classes marked with the @Configuration annotation and other conditional annotations will be evaluated and the information provided will be shown here. To access this endpoint, you can use the following GET request to /actuator/conditions:

```
curl -s http://localhost:8080/actuator/conditions | jq .
{
  "contexts": {
    "Users App": {
      "positiveMatches": {
    ...
    ...
        "BeansEndpointAutoConfiguration": [
          {
            "condition": "OnAvailableEndpointCondition",
            "message": "@ConditionalOnAvailableEndpoint marked as exposed
            by a 'management.endpoints.jmx.exposure' property"
          }
        ],
    ...
    ...
        "JacksonAutoConfiguration.JacksonObjectMapperConfiguration": [
          {
            "condition": "OnClassCondition",
```

```
            "message": "@ConditionalOnClass found required
            class 'org.springframework.http.converter.json.
            Jackson2ObjectMapperBuilder'"
        }
    ],
    ...
    ...
  }
}
```

/actuator/configprops

This endpoint provides all the information about the classes that provide configuration properties—in other words, classes marked with the @ConfigurationProperties annotation. You can run a GET request to the /actuator/configprops:

```
curl -s http://localhost:8080/actuator/configprops | jq .
{
  "contexts": {
    "Users App": {
      "beans": {
        "spring.jpa-org.springframework.boot.autoconfigure.orm.jpa.
        JpaProperties": {
          "prefix": "spring.jpa",
          "properties": {
            "mappingResources": ,
            "showSql": "******",
            "generateDdl": "******",
            "properties": {}
          },
          "inputs": {
            "mappingResources": [],
            "showSql": {},
            "generateDdl": {},
            "properties": {}
          }
```

```
      },
      ...

    ...
      "dataSource": {
        "prefix": "spring.datasource.hikari",
        "properties": {
          "error": "******"
        },
        "inputs": {
          "error": {}
        }
      },
      ...
        ....
      }
    }
  }
}
```

/actuator/heapdump

This endpoint provides the heap dump from the running app's JVM. To access this information, you can run the following GET request to the /actuator/heapdump. It's important to know that this endpoint has a lot of information and the response is in binary format. You might prefer to use the -O option in the curl command to generate a file named heapdump:

```
curl -s http://localhost:8080/actuator/heapdump -O
```

There are several software tools available for analyzing Java heap dump files. Eclipse Memory Analyzer (MAT), VisualVM, and Jhat are a few of the most popular options.

/actuator/threaddump

This endpoint provides the thread dump as JSON format from the running app's JVM. To access this information, you can run a GET request to the /actuator/threaddump:

```
curl -s http://localhost:8080/actuator/threaddump | jq .
```

```
{
  "threads": [
    {
      "threadName": "Reference Handler",
      "threadId": 2,
      "blockedTime": -1,
      "blockedCount": 7,
      "waitedTime": -1,
      "waitedCount": 0,
      "lockOwnerId": -1,
      "daemon": true,
      "inNative": false,
      "suspended": false,
      "threadState": "RUNNABLE",
      "priority": 10,
      "stackTrace": [
        {
          "moduleName": "java.base",
          "moduleVersion": "17.0.5",
          "methodName": "waitForReferencePendingList",
          "fileName": "Reference.java",
          "lineNumber": -2,
          "nativeMethod": true,
          "className": "java.lang.ref.Reference"
        },
        {
          "moduleName": "java.base",
          "moduleVersion": "17.0.5",
          "methodName": "processPendingReferences",
          "fileName": "Reference.java",
          "lineNumber": 253,
          "nativeMethod": false,
          "className": "java.lang.ref.Reference"
        },
        {
```

```
            "moduleName": "java.base",
            "moduleVersion": "17.0.5",
            "methodName": "run",
            "fileName": "Reference.java",
            "lineNumber": 215,
            "nativeMethod": false,
            "className": "java.lang.ref.Reference$ReferenceHandler"
          }
        ],
        "lockedMonitors": [],
        "lockedSynchronizers": []
      },
      ...
      ...
      ...
    ]
}
```

/actuator/mappings

This endpoint provides all the information about the request mappings, which is everything that is marked with @RestController or @Controller or is manually defined. To access this information, you can run a GET request to the /actuator/mappings:

```
curl -s http://localhost:8080/actuator/mappings | jq .
{
  "contexts": {
    "Users App": {
      "mappings": {
        "dispatcherServlets": {
          "dispatcherServlet": [
            {
              "handler": "Actuator web endpoint 'configprops'",
              "predicate": "{GET [/actuator/configprops], produces
              [application/vnd.spring-boot.actuator.v3+json || application/
              vnd.spring-boot.actuator.v2+json || application/json]}",
              "details": {
```

```
          ...
        }
    },
      ...
      ...
    {
        "handler": "Actuator web endpoint 'health'",
        "predicate": "{GET [/actuator/health], produces [application/
        vnd.spring-boot.actuator.v3+json ‖ application/vnd.spring-
        boot.actuator.v2+json ‖ application/json]}",
        "details": {
          ....
        }
    },
      ...
      ....
    {
        "handler": "com.apress.users.web.
        UsersController#save(String)",
        "predicate": "{DELETE [/users/{email}]}",
        "details": {
          ...
        }
    },
    {
        "handler": "com.apress.users.web.UsersController#getAll()",
        "predicate": "{GET [/users]}",
        "details": {
            ...
        }
    },
    {
        "handler": "ResourceHttpRequestHandler [classpath
        [META-INF/resources/webjars/]]",
        "predicate": "/webjars/**"
```

```
    },
    {
      "handler": "ResourceHttpRequestHandler [classpath [META-
      INF/resources/], classpath [resources/], classpath [static/],
      classpath [public/], ServletContext ",
      "predicate": "/**"
    }
  ]
},
"servletFilters": [
    ...
    ...
]
  }
  }
  }
}
```

/actuator/loggers

This endpoint provides the information about the logging level that was set for the application. To access this information, you can run a GET request to the /actuator/loggers:

```
curl -s http://localhost:8080/actuator/loggers | jq .
{
  "levels": [
    "OFF",
    "ERROR",
    "WARN",
    "INFO",
    "DEBUG",
    "TRACE"
  ],
  "loggers": {
    "ROOT": {
```

```
      "configuredLevel": "INFO",
      "effectiveLevel": "INFO"
    },
    ...
    ...
  },
  "groups": {
    "web": {
      "members": [
        "org.springframework.core.codec",
        "org.springframework.http",
        "org.springframework.web",
        "org.springframework.boot.actuate.endpoint.web",
        "org.springframework.boot.web.servlet.ServletContext
        InitializerBeans"
      ]
    },
    "sql": {
      "members": [
        "org.springframework.jdbc.core",
        "org.hibernate.SQL",
        "org.jooq.tools.LoggerListener"
      ]
    }
  }
}
```

/actuator/metrics

This endpoint provides a list of the metrics that you can access by adding the respective name to the end of the endpoint. These metrics have useful information about your application, the system, and the JVM. If you add the Micrometer dependency with Prometheus and Grafana, you can export these metrics as well. Interesting, right? You are going to see this in action in the next sections. For now, check out the following examples. To access this information, you can run a GET request to the /actuator/metrics:

```
curl -s http://localhost:8080/actuator/metrics | jq .
{
  "names": [
    "application.ready.time",
    "application.started.time",
    "disk.free",
    "disk.total",
    "executor.active",
    "executor.completed",
    "executor.pool.core",
    "executor.pool.max",
    "executor.pool.size",
    "executor.queue.remaining",
    "executor.queued",
    "hikaricp.connections",
    "hikaricp.connections.acquire",
    "hikaricp.connections.active",
    "hikaricp.connections.creation",
    "hikaricp.connections.idle",
    "hikaricp.connections.max",
    "hikaricp.connections.min",
    "hikaricp.connections.pending",
    "hikaricp.connections.timeout",
    "hikaricp.connections.usage",
    "http.server.requests",
    "http.server.requests.active",
    "jdbc.connections.active",
    "jdbc.connections.idle",
    "jdbc.connections.max",
    "jdbc.connections.min",
    "jvm.buffer.count",
    "jvm.buffer.memory.used",
    "jvm.buffer.total.capacity",
    "jvm.classes.loaded",
    "jvm.classes.unloaded",
```

```
        "jvm.compilation.time",
        "jvm.gc.live.data.size",
        "jvm.gc.max.data.size",
        "jvm.gc.memory.allocated",
        "jvm.gc.memory.promoted",
        "jvm.gc.overhead",
        "jvm.gc.pause",
        "jvm.info",
        "jvm.memory.committed",
        "jvm.memory.max",
        "jvm.memory.usage.after.gc",
        "jvm.memory.used",
        "jvm.threads.daemon",
        "jvm.threads.live",
        "jvm.threads.peak",
        "jvm.threads.started",
        "jvm.threads.states",
        "logback.events",
        "process.cpu.usage",
        "process.files.max",
        "process.files.open",
        "process.start.time",
        "process.uptime",
        "spring.data.repository.invocations",
        "system.cpu.count",
        "system.cpu.usage",
        "system.load.average.1m",
        "tomcat.sessions.active.current",
        "tomcat.sessions.active.max",
        "tomcat.sessions.alive.max",
        "tomcat.sessions.created",
        "tomcat.sessions.expired",
        "tomcat.sessions.rejected"
    ]
}
```

For example, you can get metrics info about the JVM with /jvm.info:

```
curl -s http://localhost:8080/actuator/metrics/jvm.info | jq .
{
  "name": "jvm.info",
  "description": "JVM version info",
  "measurements": [
    {
      "statistic": "VALUE",
      "value": 1.0
    }
  ],
  "availableTags": [
    {
      "tag": "vendor",
      "values": [
        "GraalVM Community"
      ]
    },
    {
      "tag": "runtime",
      "values": [
        "OpenJDK Runtime Environment"
      ]
    },
    {
      "tag": "version",
      "values": [
        "17.0.5+8-jvmci-22.3-b08"
      ]
    }
  ]
}
```

More about this endpoint very soon!

/actuator/shutdown

This endpoint gracefully shuts down the application. To make /shutdown work, you need to include it in the management.endpoints.web.exposure.include property and enable it. For example:

```
management.endpoints.web.exposure.include=health,info,event-
config,env,shutdown
management.endpoint.shutdown.enabled=true
```

After these settings, you can run an HTTP POST request to the /actuator/shutdown:

```
curl -s -XPOST http://localhost:8080/actuator/shutdown
{"message":"Shutting down, bye..."}
```

You need to be very careful with the shutdown setting. The best way will be to secure it. Only admins should be able to do this. And, yes, you can add security to this. We show you how in the next section.

Note   This section introduced the most commonly used actuator endpoints. There are many more endpoints, but they are enabled when the right dependency is in place and auto-configuration is executed. We talk about several of these endpoints in the following sections.

Adding Security

Any actuator endpoint can have sensitive information that you don't want to share, in which case the best option is to secure your site and the actuator endpoints. Let's add security to Users App.

To the build.gradle file, add the following dependency:

```
implementation 'org.springframework.boot:spring-boot-starter-security'
```

If you run the application and try to access the actuator endpoint, you will be prompted for a username and password, the user will be user and the password is the one that was printed out in the console.

...

```
WARN 25992 --- [            main] .s.s.UserDetailsServiceAutoConfiguration :
Using generated security password: a84b06a6-1c99-4fb8-969d-6b969f73580a
This generated password is for development use only. Your security
configuration must be updated before running your application in
production.
INFO 25992 --- [            main] o.s.b.a.e.web.EndpointLinksResolver        :
Exposing 16 endpoint(s) beneath base path '/actuator'

...

...
```

Of course, you already knew this from Chapter 8. However, you can add some security configuration so that you don't have to rely on the password each time you restart the app. Open/create the UserSecurityAuditConfiguration class. See Listing 11-5.

Listing 11-5. src/main/kotlin/com/apress/users/config/
UserSecurityAuditConfiguration.kt

```kotlin
package com.apress.users.config

import org.springframework.boot.actuate.audit.AuditEventRepository
import org.springframework.boot.actuate.audit.InMemoryAuditEventRepository
import org.springframework.context.annotation.Bean
import org.springframework.context.annotation.Configuration
import org.springframework.security.config.Customizer
import org.springframework.security.config.annotation.web.builders.
HttpSecurity
import org.springframework.security.config.annotation.web.configurers.
CsrfConfigurer
import org.springframework.security.core.userdetails.User
import org.springframework.security.crypto.bcrypt.BCryptPasswordEncoder
import org.springframework.security.crypto.password.PasswordEncoder
import org.springframework.security.provisioning.InMemoryUserDetailsManager
import org.springframework.security.provisioning.UserDetailsManager
import org.springframework.security.web.SecurityFilterChain
import org.springframework.security.web.servlet.util.matcher.
MvcRequestMatcher
import org.springframework.web.servlet.handler.HandlerMappingIntrospector
```

```kotlin
@Configuration
class UserSecurityAuditConfiguration {
    @Bean
    fun auditEventRepository(): AuditEventRepository {
        return InMemoryAuditEventRepository()
    }

    // Enable this if you want the Home page to be publicly accessible
    /*
    @Bean
    fun webSecurityCustomizer(introspector: HandlerMappingIntrospector?):
            WebSecurityCustomizer? {
        val mvcMatcherBuilder = MvcRequestMatcher.Builder(introspector)
        return WebSecurityCustomizer { web: WebSecurity ->
            web.ignoring().requestMatchers(
                mvcMatcherBuilder.pattern("/webjars/ **"),
                mvcMatcherBuilder.pattern("/index.html"),
                mvcMatcherBuilder.pattern("/")
            )
        }
    }
     */

    @Bean
    @Throws(Exception::class)
    fun securityFilterChain(http: HttpSecurity,
            introspector: HandlerMappingIntrospector?): SecurityFilterChain {
        val mvcMatcherBuilder = MvcRequestMatcher.Builder(introspector)
        http
            .csrf { csrf: CsrfConfigurer<HttpSecurity> -> csrf.disable() }
            .authorizeHttpRequests{ auth ->
                auth
                    .requestMatchers(mvcMatcherBuilder.pattern
                    ("/actuator/**"))
                    .hasRole("ACTUATOR")
//.requestMatchers(mvcMatcherBuilder.pattern("/management/**")).
hasRole("ACTUATOR")
```

584

```kotlin
                .anyRequest().authenticated()
        }
        .formLogin(Customizer.withDefaults())
        .httpBasic(Customizer.withDefaults())
    return http.build()
}

@Bean
fun userDetailsManager(passwordEncoder: PasswordEncoder):
UserDetailsManager {
    val admin = User
        .builder()
        .username("admin")
        .password(passwordEncoder.encode("admin"))
        .roles("ADMIN", "USER", "ACTUATOR")
        .build()
    val manager = User
        .builder()
        .username("manager")
        .password(passwordEncoder.encode("manager"))
        .roles("ADMIN", "USER")
        .build()
    val user = User
        .builder()
        .username("user")
        .password(passwordEncoder.encode("user"))
        .roles("USER")
        .build()
    return InMemoryUserDetailsManager(manager, user, admin)
}

@Bean
fun passwordEncoder(): PasswordEncoder {
    return BCryptPasswordEncoder()
}
}
```

In the UserSecurityAuditConfiguration class, we are setting the ACTUATOR role, which can access only the /actuator/** endpoints, and the user admin is the only one with that role. If you rerun Users App, the /actuator/** endpoints will be secure.

/actuator/auditevents

Spring Boot Actuator provides the /actuator/auditevents endpoint when Spring Security is enabled; this allows you to audit every time there is an authentication *success, failure,* or *access denied* event. To use this endpoint, it's necessary to define an AuditEventRepository bean that includes a convenient way to store these events in memory with the InMemoryAuditEventRepository class (an implementation of the AuditEventRepository interface).

In the UserSecurityAuditConfiguration class (see Listing 11-5), add the following bean declaration:

```
@Bean
fun auditEventRepository() =
    InMemoryAuditEventRepository()
```

That's the only thing you need. When the app starts the auto-configuration and determines that you have security and the AuditEventRepository bean declared, it will enable the /actuator/auditevents endpoint and it will save every event in memory.

Next, rerun Users App and try to access it with different users and an incorrect password. Take a look at the events with the following command:

```
curl -s -u admin:admin http://localhost:8080/actuator/auditevents | jq .
{
  "events": [
    {
      "timestamp": "2023-11-20T19:04:28.683151Z",
      "principal": "manager",
      "type": "AUTHENTICATION_SUCCESS",
      "data": {
        "details": {
          "remoteAddress": "0:0:0:0:0:0:0:1"
        }
      }
    },
```

```json
{
    "timestamp": "2023-11-20T19:04:34.975087Z",
    "principal": "manager",
    "type": "AUTHORIZATION_FAILURE",
    "data": {
      "details": {
        "remoteAddress": "0:0:0:0:0:0:0:1"
      }
    }
  },
  {
    "timestamp": "2023-11-20T19:04:54.906022Z",
    "principal": "admin",
    "type": "AUTHENTICATION_SUCCESS",
    "data": {
      "details": {
        "remoteAddress": "0:0:0:0:0:0:0:1"
      }
    }
  }
 ]
}
```

Remember that admin/admin is the only one that has the ACTUATOR role. If you want to use your app in a production environment, you need to add your own implementation of the AuditEventRepository class and perhaps save this into a database.

If you want to have more control, you can always listen for these events. An AuditApplicationEvent class is being used for these events, and you can listen to it as well. If you want, you can add the following code to the UserLogs class (we are going to use it later as well):

```
@EventListener
fun on(event:AuditApplicationEvent) {
    log.info("Audit: {}", event);
}
```

In the source code, you can find the complete class in the `11-actuator/users` folder
(`src/main/kotlin/com/apress/users/events/UserLogs.kt`).

If you rerun your application after this change and try to log in, you will get
something similar to the following output:

```
INFO 26910 --- [nio-8080-exec-1] com.apress.users.events.UserLogs
: Audit Event: org.springframework.boot.actuate.audit.listener.AuditApp
licationEvent[source=AuditEvent [timestamp=2023-11-20T20:00:02.559298Z,
principal=admin, type=AUTHENTICATION_SUCCESS, data={details=WebAuthenticati
onDetails [RemoteIpAddress=127.0.0.1, SessionId=null]}]]
```

You now know how to add security to the Actuator endpoints and take advantage of
the audit events.

Implementing Custom Actuator Endpoints

Implementing a custom actuator endpoint is easy! To show you how easy it is, let's add
a simple feature to Users App. We are going to add prefix and postfix characters when
there is a log event so that we can identify the event immediately.

First, open/create the `LogEventConfig` class, which will hold the feature data, in this
case the prefix and postfix characters that we are going to use. See Listing 11-6.

Listing 11-6. src/main/kotlin/com/apress/users/actuator/LogEventConfig.kt

```
package com.apress.users.actuator

data class LogEventConfig (
    var enabled:Boolean = true,
    var prefix:String = ">> ",
    var postfix:String = " <<"
)
```

Listing 11-6 shows the `LogEventConfig` class. The simple `LogEventConfig` class
shows that the respective default prefix and postfix values are `>>` and `<<`. As you can see,
it's very simple.

Next, open/create the `LogEventEndpoint` class. See Listing 11-7.

Listing 11-7. src/main/kotlin/com/apress/users/actuator/LogEventEndpoint.kt

```kotlin
package com.apress.users.actuator

import org.springframework.boot.actuate.endpoint.annotation.Endpoint
import org.springframework.boot.actuate.endpoint.annotation.ReadOperation
import org.springframework.boot.actuate.endpoint.annotation.WriteOperation
import org.springframework.lang.Nullable
import org.springframework.stereotype.Component

@Component
@Endpoint(id = "event-config")
class LogEventEndpoint {
    private val config = LogEventConfig()

    @ReadOperation
    fun config(): LogEventConfig = config

    @WriteOperation
    fun eventConfig(@Nullable enabled: Boolean?, @Nullable prefix: String?,
            @Nullable postfix: String?) {
        if (enabled != null) config.enabled = enabled
        if (prefix != null) config.prefix = prefix
        if (postfix != null) config.postfix = postfix
    }

    val isEnable: Boolean
        get() = config.enabled
}
```

The LogEventEndpoint class includes the following annotations:

- @Endpoint: This annotation allows you to create a custom actuator endpoint. It's necessary to provide an id that doesn't collide with the others, in this case event-config. This annotation creates the /actuator/event-config endpoint, and it will be available via the web (through HTTP) and JMX. If you need it only for the web, you can use the @WebEndpoint annotation; if you need it only for JMX, use @JmxEndpoint. In this case, we want it for both, so we are using @Endpoint.

- `@ReadOperation`: This annotation marks a method that will return a value with a response status of 200 (OK); if this method doesn't return a value, the response status will be 404 (Not Found). This annotation can be accessed through a GET HTTP method. In this case, we are returning the values of the `LogEventConfig` object.

- `@WriteOperation`: This annotation marks a method that accepts simple type parameters; they cannot accept custom objects, and this is because the endpoints should be agnostic and they go through a conversion process. This operation accepts only an HTTP POST method. If this operation returns a value, the response status will be 200 (OK); if it doesn't return a value, it will return a response status of 204 (No Content). The parameters are marked with the `@Nullable` annotation (it can be `@javax.annotation.Nullable` or `@org.springframework.lang.Nullable`) because in the JMX context, the parameters are required by default, but they can be optional by adding `@Nullable`.

This class is marked as `@Component`, meaning that it will be picked up by Spring Boot auto-configuration and set as a Spring Bean.

Even though we didn't use it, there is a `@DeleteOperation` annotation that accepts a DELETE HTTP method. If this returns a value, it will produce a status of 200 (OK), and if does not return a value, it will respond with status 204 (No Content).

In our example, in the `@ReadOperation` annotation we are just returning an object, so it will produce an `application/json` content-type, but we can return an `org.springframework.core.io.Resource`, which will produce an `application/octect-stream` content-type.

Next, open the `UserLogs` class. See Listing 11-8.

Listing 11-8. src/main/kotlin/com/apress/users/events/UserLogs.kt

```
package com.apress.users.events

import com.apress.users.actuator.LogEventEndpoint
import org.slf4j.LoggerFactory
import org.springframework.beans.factory.annotation.Autowired
import org.springframework.boot.actuate.audit.listener.
AuditApplicationEvent
```

```kotlin
import org.springframework.context.event.EventListener
import org.springframework.scheduling.annotation.Async
import org.springframework.stereotype.Component

@Component
class UserLogs {
    @Autowired
    private lateinit var logEventEndpoint: LogEventEndpoint

    @Async
    @EventListener
    fun userActiveStatusEventHandler(event: UserActivatedEvent) {
        if (logEventEndpoint.isEnable) LOG.info(
            "{} User {} active status: {} {}", logEventEndpoint.config().
            prefix,
            event.email, event.active, logEventEndpoint.config().postfix
        ) else LOG.info("User {} active status: {}", event.email,
        event.active)
    }

    @Async
    @EventListener
    fun userDeletedEventHandler(event: UserRemovedEvent) {
        if (logEventEndpoint.isEnable) LOG.info(
            "{} User {} DELETED at {} {}", logEventEndpoint.config().prefix,
            event.email, event.removed, logEventEndpoint.config().postfix
        ) else LOG.info("{} User {} DELETED at {} {}", event.email, event.
        removed)
    }

    @EventListener
    fun on(event: AuditApplicationEvent?) {
        LOG.info("Audit Event: {}", event)
    }

    companion object {
        private val LOG = LoggerFactory.getLogger(UserLogs::class.java)
    }
}
```

In the `UserLogs` class, we are using the `LogEventEndpoint` class and its values for the prefix (>> default value) and postfix (<< default value). We are verifying that the endpoint is enabled to add these prefix and postfix characters. We have the audit security listener at the end.

Next, enable /actuator/event-config in the `application-actuator.properties` file with this syntax:

`management.endpoints.web.exposure.include=health,info,`**`event-`**
`config``,env,shutdown`

This property is enabling the endpoints by ID, but keep in mind that you can use * to add all endpoints. We are enabling the `event-config` endpoint.

Next, run it. Once it is up and running, you can check out the new custom endpoint with this:

```
curl -s -u admin:admin http://localhost:8080/actuator/event-config | jq .
{
  "enabled": true,
  "prefix": ">> ",
  "postfix": " <<"
}
```

Nice! If you add a new user, like so:

```
curl -XPOST -H "Content-Type: application/json" -d '{"email":"felipe@email.
com","name":"Felipe","gravatarUrl":"https://www.gravatar.com/avatar/23bb62a
7d0ca63c9a804908e57bf6bd5?d=wavatar","password":"awesome","userRole":["USER
","ADMIN"],"active":true}' http://localhost:8080/users
```

you should see something like this in the console output:

```
>>  User felipe@email.com active status: true  <<
```

Next, let's change the prefix and postfix characters. You can either use an HTTP POST request or use JMX. An HTTP POST request is as simple as executing the following command:

```
curl -i -u admin:admin -H"Content-Type: application/json" -XPOST
-d'{"prefix":"[ ","postfix":"]"}' http://localhost:8080/actuator/
event-config
```

We are changing the characters of the prefix to [and the postfix to]. You can verify the change with this:

```
curl -s -u admin:admin http://localhost:8080/actuator/event-config | jq .
{
  "enabled": true,
  "prefix": "[ ",
  "postfix": "]"
}
```

If you delete the previous user:

```
curl -s -u admin:admin -XDELETE http://localhost:8080/users/felipe@
email.com
```

you should see this in the console output:

```
[  User felipe@email.com DELETED at 2023-11-21T11:14:54.639662 ]
```

Easy! right? Next, you see how to use JMX in this case.

Accessing Custom Endpoints with JMX

Java Management Extensions (JMX) is a technology that lets you manage and monitor Java/Kotlin applications and resources. It provides a standard way to expose information about your running application (like performance metrics or configuration settings) and allows you to change those settings dynamically. Think of it as a control panel for your application, accessible remotely, that gives you insights into its health and lets you tweak it while it's running. Spring Boot Actuator leverages JMX to expose operational information about your running application. If you add `spring.jmx.enabled=true` to the `application-actuator.properties` file, Actuator automatically registers its endpoints as JMX MBeans (Managed Beans), making them accessible through JMX clients like JConsole. This allows you to monitor and manage your application remotely, including health checks, metrics, configuration details, thread dumps, and more. Essentially, JMX serves as a communication channel for Actuator to provide valuable insights and control over your application's runtime behavior. You can now use the JMX console in your app. In your terminal, execute the following command to open the window shown in Figure 11-5:

```
jconsole
```

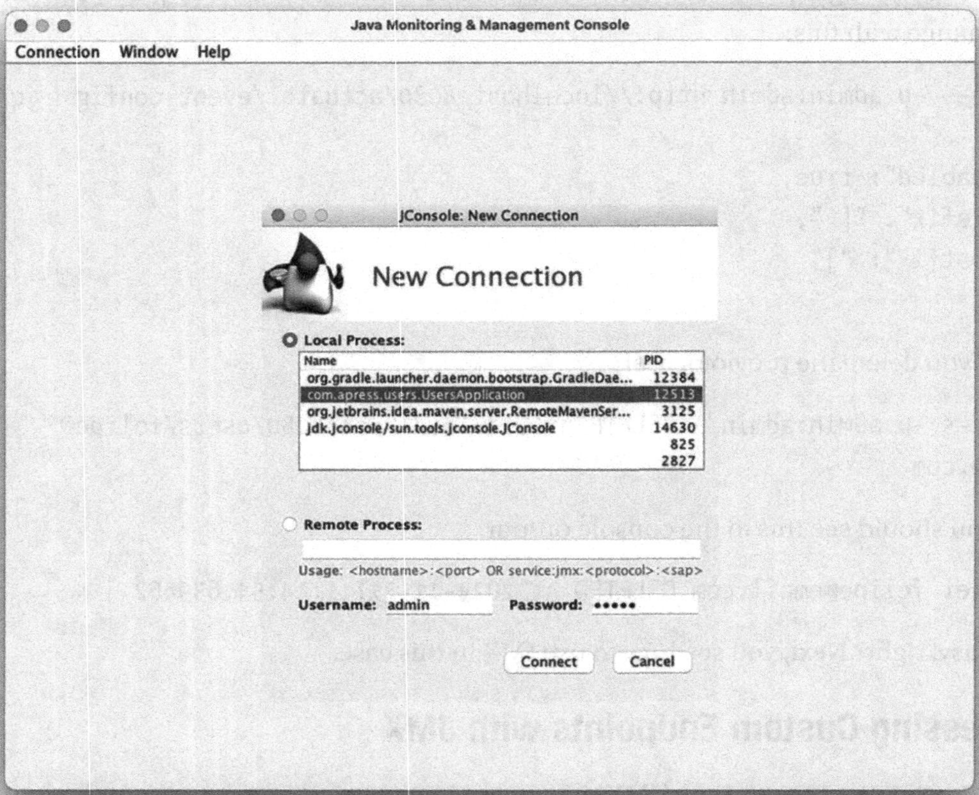

Figure 11-5. *The JConsole*

JConsole is a graphical interface that is compliant with the JMX specification, and it's used for JVM instrumentation to observe the performance and resource consumption of the applications running on the JVM.

As shown in Figure 11-5, in the Local Process field, select `com.apress.users.`
`UsersApplication`, enter `admin` in the Username and Password fields, and click Connect. Then you should see something like Figure 11-6, with the Overview tab displayed by default.

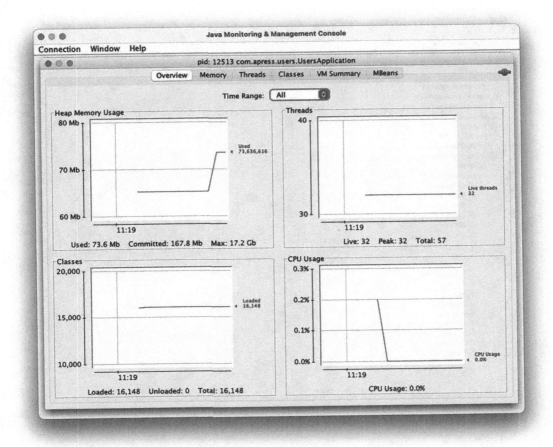

Figure 11-6. *The JConsole Overview tab*

Select the last tab, MBeans (Managed Beans). As shown in Figure 11-7, in the navigation pane on the left, expand the `org.springframework.boot` ➤ Endpoint ➤ `Event-config` ➤ Operations node and you'll see that we have enabled the /event-config endpoint and the read (`config`) and write (`eventConfig`) operations.

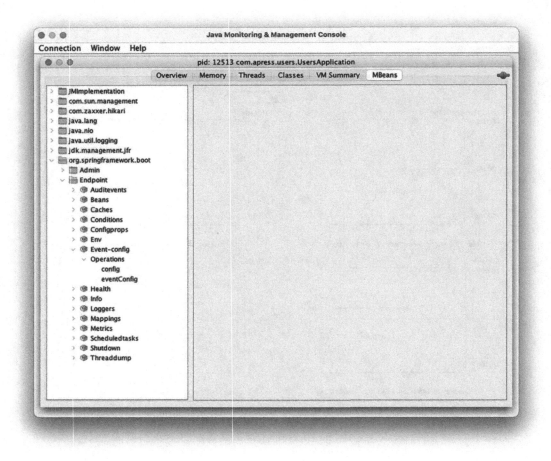

Figure 11-7. *The JConsole MBeans tab*

Click the `config` operation to see the information about the read operation, the return type (`Map`), and so forth, as shown in Figure 11-8.

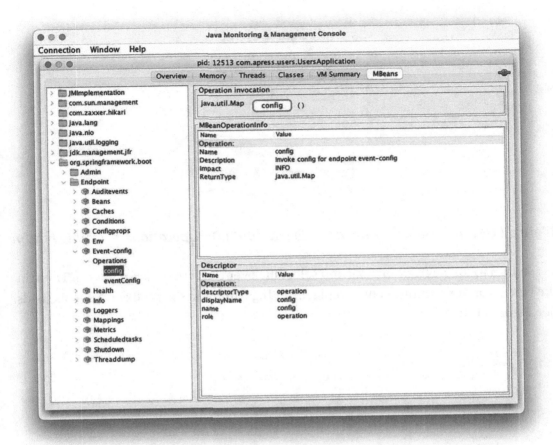

Figure 11-8. *The JConsole MBeans tab expanded to Event-config ➤ Operations ➤ config*

If you click the Config button in the Operation Invocation section, you will see the pop-up window shown in Figure 11-9.

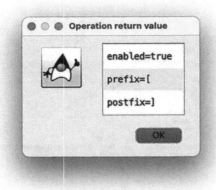

Figure 11-9. *JConsole* ➤ *MBeans* ➤ *Event Config* ➤ *Operations* ➤ *Config button*

Return to the navigation pane and select the eventConfig write operation. Then, in the Operation Invocation section, replace String with ** in the prefix and postfix fields. See Figure 11-10.

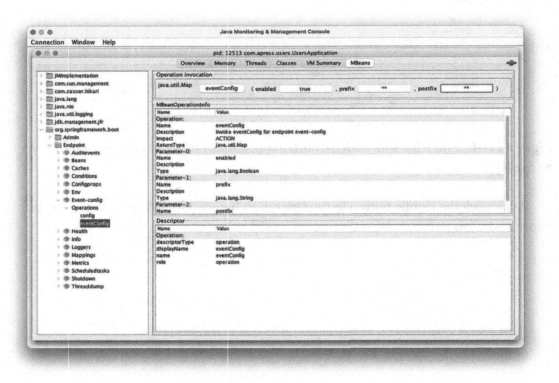

Figure 11-10. *JMX Console* ➤ *Event Config* ➤ *Operations*

Next, click the Eventconfig button to the left and that will set the new values for prefix and postfix. You can check them out by selecting Config in the navigation pane, or you can add a new user. Use the same command as before:

```
curl -XPOST -H "Content-Type: application/json" -d '{"email":"felipe@email.
com","name":"Felipe","gravatarUrl":"https://www.gravatar.com/avatar/23bb62a
7d0ca63c9a804908e57bf6bd5?d=wavatar","password":"awesome","userRole":
["USER","ADMIN"],"active":true}' http://localhost:8080/users
```

After executing this command, you should see the following in your console output:

```
** User felipe@email.com active status: true **
```

This is how you interact with JMX and the actuator endpoints. Before you close the JConsole, browse around and view the other endpoints.

More Spring Boot Actuator Configuration

This section introduces several additional configuration options that Spring Boot Actuator offers.

CORS Support

To enable protection against cross-origin resource sharing (CORS), use the following properties syntax:

```
management.endpoints.web.cors.allowed-origins=<*|<site1[,site2]>>
management.endpoints.web.cors.allowed-methods=<*|[http-methods[,]]>
```

For example:

```
management.endpoints.web.cors.allowed-origins=*
management.endpoints.web.cors.allowed-methods=GET,POST,PUT,DELETE,OPTIONS
```

Changing the Server Address, Port, and Base Path

Changing the server port, address, and base path of Spring Boot Actuator can be a good practice for security reasons. Consider the following example:

```
management.server.port=8282
management.server.address=127.0.0.1
management.server.base-path=/management
```

First, we are changing the port to 8282, meaning that Spring Boot Actuator will start serving at that port. We are also defining the address as 127.0.01 (localhost), which can be useful if you have multiple network interfaces, because you can use a special address only for the Spring Boot Actuator endpoints that won't be publicly available just for internal use. Finally, we are changing the base path to /management, meaning that access to Spring Boot Actuator will be http://localhost:8282/management/actuator.

If you want to run Users App with this new configuration, it's important to add the new base path to the security with the following line of code:

```
.requestMatchers(mvcMatcherBuilder.pattern("/management/**")).
hasRole("ACTUATOR")
```

Using SSL with Spring Boot Actuator

You can add an SSL to Spring Boot Actuator with the following properties:

```
management.server.ssl.enabled=true
management.server.ssl.key-store=classpath:keystore.p12
management.server.ssl.key-store-password=changeit
management.server.ssl.key-password=changeit
management.server.ssl.key-store-type=PKCS12
management.server.ssl.key-alias=tomcat
```

Configuring Endpoints

Several actuator endpoints have read operations, such as /actuator/metrics, /actuator/beans, /actuator/env, and so on, and these endpoints can cache their values for a period of time. You can control this time period with the following actuator property syntax:

```
management.endpoint.<id>.cache.time-to-live=<period-of-time>
```

The following is an example:

```
management.endpoint.beans.cache.time-to-live=10s
management.endpoint.metrics.cache.time-to-live=10s
management.endpoint.env.cache.time-to-live=10s
```

Overview of /actuator/health

This endpoint is one of the most important features of Spring Boot Actuator because it can help you determine if your app is up or down based on the health of some subsystems or business rules. As previously mentioned, this endpoint is activated by default, so when you access it, you will see something like this:

```
curl -u admin:admin -s http://localhost:8080/actuator/health | jq .
{
  "status": "UP"
}
```

This is just enough for external systems or clients that make sure their systems are up and running and respond correctly. When you deploy your app into the cloud (described in Chapter 13) to a Kubernetes environment, for example, Spring Boot will auto-configure extra details for the /actuator/health endpoint and it will create /actuator/health/liveness and /actuator/health/readiness, so it's easy for you to expose this in your YAML deployment files.

One nice feature of the /actuator/health endpoint is that it not only can expose more information about the app, but it also enables you to create a custom health indicator and build the necessary status and report it back. If you need more information, you can adjust the details with the following syntax:

management.endpoint.health.show-details=<never,when_authorized|always>

If you don't set this property, by default it is never. In this case and because we are using Spring Security, we can use the when_authorized value. We can have even more granular access to the roles by using the following property syntax:

```
management.endpoint.health.roles=<role-name[,]>
```

You can add this to the application-actuator.properties file:

management.endpoint.health.show-details=when_authorized
management.endpoint.health.roles=ACTUATOR

If you rerun Users App and execute the following command, you will see output similar to what's shown here:

```
curl -u admin:admin -s http://localhost:8080/actuator/health | jq .
{
  "status": "UP",
  "components": {
    "db": {
      "status": "UP",
      "details": {
        "database": "H2",
        "validationQuery": "isValid()"
      }
    },
    "diskSpace": {
      "status": "UP",
      "details": {
        "total": 1000240963584,
        "free": 97917366272,
        "threshold": 10485760,
        "path": "/Users/felipeg/Progs/Books/pro-spring-boot-3rd/java/11-
        actuator/users/.",
        "exists": true
      }
    },
    "ping": {
      "status": "UP"
    }
  }
}
```

Note that this output also shows components such as db, diskSpace, and ping. Those are health indictors, which are discussed next.

Health Indicators

One of the benefits of using Spring Boot Actuator and the /actuator/health endpoint is that there are several health indicators that you can add out-of-the-box to give you details of your application's health. In this case, the db (where you can see the engine used, in this case H2, and the validation query that is executed to see if the database is alive) and the diskspace (where you can see the details of where this is executed, free space, etc.) are some of them.

These components get all the health information that is collected from HealthContributorRegistry, by default all the HealthContributor implementations defined in the app context, and in our case in the Users App ApplicationContext.

Other built-in health indicators that you can use are cassandra, couchbase, elasticsearch, hazelcast, influxdb, jms, ldap, mail, mongo, neo4j, ping, rabbit, and redis.

Let's run an experiment and see our app in action. In the build.gradle file, in the dependencies section, add the following dependency:

```
implementation 'org.springframework.boot:spring-boot-starter-amqp'
```

We are adding AMQP to our project, even though we don't have any code. Rerun the app and go to the /actuator/health endpoint (you will get some errors about connecting, but disregard them for now):

```
curl -u admin:admin -s http://localhost:8080/actuator/health | jq .
{
  "status": "DOWN",
  "components": {
    "db": {
      "status": "UP",
      "details": {
        "database": "H2",
        "validationQuery": "isValid()"
      }
    },
    "diskSpace": {
      "status": "UP",
      "details": {
```

```
          "total": 1000240963584,
          "free": 97769340928,
          "threshold": 10485760,
          "path": "/Users/felipeg/Progs/Books/pro-spring-boot-3rd/java/11-
          actuator/users/.",
          "exists": true
        }
      },
      "ping": {
        "status": "UP"
      },
      "rabbit": {
        "status": "DOWN",
        "details": {
          "error": "org.springframework.amqp.AmqpConnectException: java.net.
          ConnectException: Connection refused"
        }
      }
    }
  }
}
```

You now have the rabbit component (based on the amqp dependency) with the details, and because a RabbitMQ broker is not running, it reports DOWN, and the main health status of the app is also DOWN. In other words, this status bubbles up to the main health details of your app. However, you can change the order in which the status is presented so that the status of the app indicates UP even though the status of the rabbit component is DOWN. Of course, there is a way to indicate the status is UP even though the rabbit component is DOWN (maybe it is not essential that rabbit is up due to some of your business rules). To define the order, set the following property:

management.endpoint.health.status.order=fatal,down,out-of-service,unknown,up

The management.endpoint.health.status.order property defines the preceding status order by default, so if you omit the down value like this:

management.endpoint.health.status.order=fatal,out-of-service,unknown,up

and then rerun the app, the main status should be UP, even though the `rabbit` component is reporting DOWN. If you want to see the status of the `rabbit` component as UP, you can start a RabbitMQ through a Docker command and rerun the app:

```
docker run -d --rm --name rabbit -p 15672:15672 -p 5672:5672
rabbitmq:management-alpine
curl -u admin:admin -s http://localhost:8080/actuator/health | jq .
{
  "status": "UP",
  "components": {
    "db": {
      "status": "UP",
      "details": {
        "database": "H2",
        "validationQuery": "isValid()"
      }
    },
    "diskSpace": {
      "status": "UP",
      "details": {
        "total": 1000240963584,
        "free": 97315823616,
        "threshold": 10485760,
        "path": "/Users/felipeg/Progs/Books/pro-spring-boot-3rd/java/11-
        actuator/users/.",
        "exists": true
      }
    },
    "ping": {
      "status": "UP"
    },
    "rabbit": {
      "status": "UP",
      "details": {
```

```
      "version": "3.12.9"
    }
  }
 }
}
```

The `rabbit` component is now reporting the status as UP and the version. If you want, you can stop the RabbitMQ with this command:

```
docker stop rabbit
```

You can also comment out the `amqp` dependency we added to the `build.gradle` file, because you no longer need it.

If you want to add your own custom health indicator, you have a few options, as discussed in the next section.

A Custom Health Indicator for Users App

As previously explained, all the health information is collected from `HealthContributorRegistry`, which contains implementations of the `HealthContributor` interface. `HealthContributor` is an empty interface, basically a marker that is agnostic of what you will be reporting as health status. Spring Boot Actuator provides a `HealthIndicator` interface that you can implement to build up a health status.

Open/create the `EventsHealthIndicator` class. This class will use `LogEventEndpoint` and check out if it's enabled or not. See. Listing 11-9.

Listing 11-9. src/main/kotlin/com/apress/users/actuator/ EventsHealthIndicator.kt

```
package com.apress.users.actuator

import org.springframework.beans.factory.annotation.Autowired
import org.springframework.boot.actuate.health.Health
import org.springframework.boot.actuate.health.HealthIndicator
import org.springframework.boot.actuate.health.Status
import org.springframework.stereotype.Component
```

```
@Component
class EventsHealthIndicator : HealthIndicator {
    @Autowired
    private lateinit var logEventEndpoint: LogEventEndpoint

    override fun health(): Health {
        return if (check()) Health.up().build() else  // Custom Status
            Health.status(Status("EVENTS-DOWN", "Events are turned
            off!")).build()

        // Status
        //return Health.status(Status.DOWN).build();
    }

    private fun check(): Boolean {
        return logEventEndpoint.isEnable
    }
}
```

Listing 11-9 shows that the EventsHealthIndicator class implements the
HealthIndicator interface, which is a functional interface that has a default method of
getHealth(boolean) and the health() method that we are overriding. We are checking
whether our endpoint (/actuator/event-config) is enabled or not, and based on
the results, we can build up our status. If it's not enabled, we create a new Status with
EVENTS-DOWN and a description stating Events are turned off!.

Also notice that the EventsHealthIndicator class is marked as @Component, so it
will be picked up by the Spring Boot and Actuator auto-configuration, and this class
will be part of the HealthContributorRegistry as an events component, which is
a naming convention. In other words, your custom health indicator must end with
HealthIndicator. The syntax is <Name>HealthIndicator, and because the name is
EventsHealthIndicator, it will be registered as events.

Next, in the application-actuator.properties file, enable the endpoint and add a
new status order:

management.endpoints.web.exposure.include=health,info,**event-
config**,env,shutdown
management.endpoint.health.status.order=**events-down**,fatal,down,out-of-
service,unknown,up

The order in which we added the events-down correlates to the new status that we created in Listing 11-9 (EVENTS-DOWN).

Next, run Users App and go to the /actuator/health endpoint:

```
curl -u admin:admin -s http://localhost:8080/actuator/health | jq .
{
  "status": "UP",
  "components": {
    "db": {
      "status": "UP",
      "details": {
        "database": "H2",
        "validationQuery": "isValid()"
      }
    },
    "diskSpace": {
      "status": "UP",
      "details": {
        "total": 1000240963584,
        "free": 98204057600,
        "threshold": 10485760,
        "path": "/Users/felipeg/Progs/Books/pro-spring-boot-3rd/java/11-
        actuator/users/.",
        "exists": true
      }
    },
    "events": {
        "status": "UP"
      },
    "ping": {
      "status": "UP"
    }
  }
}
```

Now our custom health indicator appears in the /actuator/health endpoint. What happens if we disable this endpoint? You can do this by using JMX with JConsole, or run a POST request to change the value, or set the default field value to false (in the LogEventConfig class).

You will get the following output:

```
curl -u admin:admin -s http://localhost:8080/actuator/health | jq .
{
  "description": "Events are turned off!",
    "status": "EVENTS-DOWN",
  "components": {
    "db": {
      "status": "UP",
      "details": {
        "database": "H2",
        "validationQuery": "isValid()"
      }
    },
    "diskSpace": {
      "status": "UP",
      "details": {
        "total": 1000240963584,
        "free": 98187304960,
        "threshold": 10485760,
        "path": "/Users/felipeg/Progs/Books/pro-spring-boot-3rd/java/11-
        actuator/users/.",
        "exists": true
      }
    },
    "events": {
        "description": "Events are turned off!",
        "status": "EVENTS-DOWN"
      },
    "ping": {
```

```
      "status": "UP"
    }
  }
}
```

As you can see, the status order took precedence and we can say that, because the events are down, our app status is down as well. Remember that here we are using a custom Status with the EVENTS-DOWN value.

My Retro App with Spring Boot Actuator Observability: Metrics, Logs, and Tracing

This section discusses observability and explains how to add this new concept to My Retro App. Observability is a way to observe internally what is going on in your running system from the outside—normally through logs, metrics, and traces. Spring Boot, with the power of Spring Boot Actuator and Micrometer, helps you add observability out-of-the-box.

As indicated, you need to use the Spring Boot Actuator and Micrometer framework dependencies. Micrometer provides a vendor-neutral API for collecting and exposing metrics. It supports a variety of monitoring systems, including Prometheus, Datadog, Graphite, InfluxDB, and many more. You can get more info at the main site of Micrometer (https://micrometer.io) and in its documentation (https://micrometer.io/docs).

Let's dig into some of the most common use cases for using observability with Spring Boot and add them to My Retro App.

Adding Observability to My Retro App

You have access to the source code in the 11-actuator/myretro folder. If you want to start from scratch, we are going to use the Users with JPA. In the Spring Initializr (https://start.spring.io), set the Group field to com.apress and the Artifact and Name fields to users. Add the Web, WebFlux, Validation, Data JPA, Actuator, H2, PostgreSQL, Prometheus, Distributed Tracing, Zipkin, and Docker Compose Support dependencies. Generate and download the project, unzip it, and import it into your favorite IDE.

Let's check the build.gradle file. See Listing 11-10.

Listing 11-10. The build.gradle File

```
import org.jetbrains.kotlin.gradle.tasks.KotlinCompile
plugins {
    id 'org.springframework.boot' version '3.2.3'
    id 'io.spring.dependency-management' version '1.1.4'
    id 'org.jetbrains.kotlin.jvm' version '2.0.20-RC'
    id "org.jetbrains.kotlin.plugin.spring" version "2.0.20-RC"
    // <- simplifies spring proxying
}

group = 'com.apress'
version = '0.0.1-SNAPSHOT'
sourceCompatibility = '17'

configurations {
    compileOnly {
        extendsFrom annotationProcessor
    }
}

repositories {
    mavenCentral()
}

dependencies {
    implementation "org.jetbrains.kotlin:kotlin-stdlib-jdk8"
    implementation "org.jetbrains.kotlin:kotlin-reflect"

    implementation 'org.springframework.boot:spring-boot-starter-web'
    implementation 'org.springframework.boot:spring-boot-starter-webflux'
    implementation 'org.springframework.boot:spring-boot-starter-
    validation'
    implementation 'org.springframework.boot:spring-boot-starter-data-jpa'
    implementation 'org.springframework.boot:spring-boot-starter-actuator'
    implementation 'org.springframework.boot:spring-boot-starter-aop'
```

```
    runtimeOnly      'com.github.loki4j:loki-logback-appender:1.4.1'
    implementation 'io.micrometer:micrometer-tracing-bridge-brave'
    implementation 'io.zipkin.reporter2:zipkin-reporter-brave'
    implementation    'net.ttddyy.observation:datasource-micrometer-spring-
    boot:1.0.2'

    runtimeOnly 'com.h2database:h2'
    runtimeOnly 'org.postgresql:postgresql'
    runtimeOnly 'io.micrometer:micrometer-registry-jmx'
    runtimeOnly 'io.micrometer:micrometer-registry-prometheus'

    developmentOnly 'org.springframework.boot:spring-boot-docker-compose'

    annotationProcessor 'org.springframework.boot:spring-boot-
    configuration-processor'

    testImplementation 'org.springframework.boot:spring-boot-starter-test'
}

tasks.named('test') {
    useJUnitPlatform()
}

//     kotlin {
//         jvmToolchain(17)
//     }
tasks.withType(KotlinCompile).configureEach {
    kotlinOptions {
        freeCompilerArgs = ['-Xjsr305=strict']
        jvmTarget = '17'
    }
}
```

Listing 11-10 shows that we are using additional dependencies that will help us bring observability to our application. Important to note here is that we are adding the Web and WebFlux dependencies, so what happens if we try to run the app? What does Spring Boot do? We will explain why we need this and how to configure Spring Boot to use only one particular type of web application. Note that we also need the spring-boot-starter-aop, loki-logback-appender, and datasource-micrometer-spring-boot dependencies. The aop dependency will be essential for the observability code we are adding; the loki-logback-appender dependency will be for the logs; and the datasource-micrometer-spring-boot dependency will be for the database observability.

Adding Custom Metrics and Observations

As you know, Spring Boot Actuator comes with some default metrics that allow you to know more about the memory consumption, CPU, threads, JVM statistics, and much more. However, sometimes these metrics are not sufficient to measure and observe some logic within our application.

The combination of Spring Boot Actuator and Micrometer allows you to add custom metrics and observations to your apps with ease. For example, in My Retro App, we can add counters that allow us to know how many times a particular endpoint was hit, as well as observe what is happening behind the scenes.

Let's start by opening/creating the RetroBoardMetricsInterceptor class. See Listing 11-11.

Listing 11-11. src/main/kotlin/com/apress/myretro/metrics/ RetroBoardMetricsInterceptor.kt

```kotlin
package com.apress.myretro.metrics

import io.micrometer.core.instrument.MeterRegistry
import jakarta.servlet.http.HttpServletRequest
import jakarta.servlet.http.HttpServletResponse
import org.slf4j.LoggerFactory
import org.springframework.web.servlet.HandlerInterceptor

class RetroBoardMetricsInterceptor(val registry: MeterRegistry) :
HandlerInterceptor {
    @Throws(Exception::class)
    override fun afterCompletion(
        request: HttpServletRequest,
        response: HttpServletResponse,
        handler: Any,
        ex: Exception?
    ) {
```

```
        val URI: String = request.requestURI
        val METHOD: String = request.method
        if (!URI.contains("prometheus")) {
            LOG.info("URI: $URI METHOD: $METHOD")
            registry.counter("retro_board_api", "URI", URI,
                "METHOD", METHOD).increment()
        }
    }

    companion object {
        private val LOG =
            LoggerFactory.getLogger(RetroBoardMetricsInterceptor::
            class.java)
    }
}
```

In the RetroBoardMetricsInterceptor class, we are implementing a
HandlerInterceptor interface. This interface is part of the org.springframework.
web.servlet package, and we can use it to intercept every request. It has some default
implementation, and we are overriding the afterCompletion method. One of the key
elements in this class is the MeterRegistry instance (an abstract class that creates and
manages your application's set of meters, such as counters, gauges, task timers, and
much more), which allows us to use a counter.incremet method that aggregates the
value to the defined name (in this case, retro_board_api) and accepts some event tags
(key/value pairs) for tracking (in this case, URI=METHOD). In other words, there will be
a metric named retro_board_api that will increment its counter every time there is a
request to the app endpoint and its value is different from the prometheus string.

Next, open/create the RetroBoardMetrics class. See Listing 11-12.

Listing 11-12. src/main/kotlin/com/apress/myretro/metrics/
RetroBoardMetrics.kt

```
package com.apress.myretro.metrics

import io.micrometer.core.instrument.Counter
import io.micrometer.core.instrument.MeterRegistry
import io.micrometer.observation.ObservationRegistry
import io.micrometer.observation.aop.ObservedAspect
```

```kotlin
import org.springframework.context.annotation.Bean
import org.springframework.context.annotation.Configuration
import org.springframework.web.servlet.handler.MappedInterceptor

@Configuration
class RetroBoardMetrics {
    @Bean
    fun observedAspect(registry: ObservationRegistry): ObservedAspect =
        ObservedAspect(registry)

    @Bean
    fun retroBoardCounter(registry: MeterRegistry): Counter =
        Counter.builder("retro_boards").description("Number of Retro Boards")
            .register(registry)

    @Bean
    fun metricsInterceptor(registry: MeterRegistry): MappedInterceptor =
        MappedInterceptor(arrayOf("/**"), RetroBoardMetricsInterceptor
        (registry))
}
```

Let's review the RetroBoardMetrics class:

- @Configuration: First, it's important to know that we need to enable these metrics, and a way to do that is to create a configuration class. You can add these beans in a main configuration class, but in this case, we wanted to demonstrate that you can use the @Configuration annotation to create your own project-specific class (RetroBoardMetrics in this example) in which to add these beans. (More on this when we extend this project by creating our own spring-boot-starter.)

- ObservedAspect/ObservationRegistry: The ObservedAspect class is an aspect for intercepting methods that have the @Observerd annotation, or all the methods in a class marked with this annotation. With this annotation, you will observe the execution of the method code, giving you a trace ID and a span (the time interval between events). And because we needed to be part of the metrics exposure, it is necessary to add the ObservationRegistry, which will include all the context to create the observation we need.

615

- Counter/MeterRegistry: The Counter bean increases values monotonically. This Counter interface extends from the Meter interface to provide a fluent API to create a custom metric meter. In this case, we need to give it a name (retro_boards) and a description, and then we need to register it using the MeterRegistry abstract class that creates and manages our app's set of meters. In this case, we are going to use this counter every time there is a new RetroBoard added to the system.

- MappedInterceptor: This bean uses the RetroBoardMetricsInterceptor class (see Listing 11-11), which wraps a HandlerInterceptor and uses URL patterns to determine whether it applies to a given request, and in this case all the /** except for the ones that contain the string prometheus.

As you can see, the declaration to add observability and metrics is very straightforward.

Adding an External Request with the New @HttpExchange

In this section, we configure My Retro App to call Users App by using the @HttpExchange annotation. This annotation is part of the Spring Framework 6 web core package and it allows you to define declarative HTTP services using Java/Kotlin interfaces. We cover the @HttpExchange annotation more in later chapters, but for now, let's create a simple interface that will call the Users App endpoint.

Open/create the UserClient interface. See Listing 11-13.

Listing 11-13. src/main/kotlin/com/apress/myretro/client/UserClient.kt

```
package com.apress.myretro.client

import com.apress.myretro.client.model.User
import org.springframework.web.bind.annotation.PathVariable
import org.springframework.web.service.annotation.GetExchange
import org.springframework.web.service.annotation.HttpExchange
import reactor.core.publisher.Flux
import reactor.core.publisher.Mono
```

```
@HttpExchange(url = "/users", accept = ["application/json"],
    contentType = "application/json")
interface UserClient {
    @get:GetExchange
    val allUsers: Flux<User>

    @GetExchange("/{email}")
    fun getById(@PathVariable email: String): Mono<User>
}
```

As you can see, the UserClient interface is very straightforward. You annotate your interface with @HttpExchange; it accepts parameters such as the url, contentType, accept, and method. Then you define method-specific annotations such as @GetExchange, @PostExchange, @PutExchange, @PatchExchange, @DeleteExchange, and more.

In Listing 11-13 we are using the Reactive WebFlux types such as Mono and Flux. Very straightforward.

Next, open/create the User class and the UserRole enum. See Listings 11-14 and 11-15, respectively.

Listing 11-14. src/main/kotlin/com/apress/myretro/client/model/User.kt

```
package com.apress.myretro.client.model

@JvmRecord
data class User(
    val email: String,
    val name: String,
    val gravatarUrl: String,
    val password: String,
    val userRole: Collection<UserRole>,
    val active: Boolean
)
```

Listing 11-15. src/main/kotlin/com/apress/myretro/client/model/UserRole.kt

```
package com.apress.myretro.client.model
enum class UserRole {
    USER, ADMIN, INFO
}
```

Next, open/create the UserClientConfig class. See Listing 11-16.

Listing 11-16. src/main/kotlin/com/apress/myretro/client/UserClientConfig.kt

```
package com.apress.myretro.client

import org.springframework.beans.factory.annotation.Value
import org.springframework.context.annotation.Bean
import org.springframework.context.annotation.Configuration
import org.springframework.http.HttpHeaders
import org.springframework.web.reactive.function.client.WebClient
import org.springframework.web.reactive.function.client.support.
WebClientAdapter
import org.springframework.web.service.invoker.HttpServiceProxyFactory

@Configuration
class UserClientConfig {
    @Bean
    fun webClient(
        @Value("\${users.app.url}") baseUrl: String,
        @Value("\${users.app.username}") username: String,
        @Value("\${users.app.password}") password: String
    ): WebClient {
        return WebClient.builder()
            .defaultHeaders { header: HttpHeaders ->
                header.setBasicAuth(
                    username, password
                )
            }
            .baseUrl(baseUrl)
            .build()
    }
```

```kotlin
@Bean
fun userClient(webClient: WebClient): UserClient {
    val httpServiceProxyFactory = HttpServiceProxyFactory.builderFor(
        WebClientAdapter.create(
            webClient
        )
    ).build()
    return httpServiceProxyFactory.createClient(UserClient::class.java)
}
}
```

The `UserClientConfig` class includes the following:

- `@Configuration`: Here we declared another configuration class that deals only with the client. This is a good practice when you have different dependencies.

- `WebClient`: You already know about this class and how you can use it to do the request calls to external services. Note that we are also adding the basic authorization header necessary for our Users service (remember that Users App already has security dependencies).

- `HttpServiceProxyFactory`: We are declaring our `UserClient` interface (see Listing 11-13) that uses the `@HttpExchange` annotation and declares the `@GetExchange` annotations for the endpoints. The `HttpServiceProxyFactory` will create a client proxy from an HTTP service based on the mentioned annotations.

Next, open/create the `RetroBoardAndCardService` class. See Listing 11-17.

Listing 11-17. src/main/kotlin/com/apress/myretro/service/
RetroBoardAndCardService.kt

```kotlin
package com.apress.myretro.service

import com.apress.myretro.board.RetroBoard
import com.apress.myretro.client.UserClient
import com.apress.myretro.client.model.User
import com.apress.myretro.events.RetroBoardEvent
```

```
import com.apress.myretro.events.RetroBoardEventAction
import com.apress.myretro.exceptions.RetroBoardNotFoundException
import com.apress.myretro.persistence.RetroBoardRepository
import io.micrometer.core.instrument.Counter
import io.micrometer.observation.annotation.Observed
import org.slf4j.LoggerFactory
import org.springframework.beans.factory.annotation.Autowired
import org.springframework.context.ApplicationEventPublisher
import org.springframework.stereotype.Service
import java.time.LocalDateTime
import java.util.*

@Service
@Observed(name = "retro-board-service", contextualName = "retroBoardAnd
CardService")
class RetroBoardAndCardService {
    @Autowired
    private lateinit var retroBoardRepository: RetroBoardRepository
    @Autowired
    private lateinit var eventPublisher: ApplicationEventPublisher
    @Autowired
    private lateinit var retroBoardCounter: Counter
    @Autowired
    private lateinit var userClient: UserClient

    // Uncomment this to see the effect of the @Observed annotation
    // (Custom Observation))
    //@Observed(name = "retro-boards",contextualName = "allRetroBoards")
    fun allRetroBoards():List<RetroBoard> {
        LOG.info("Getting all retro boards")
        return retroBoardRepository.findAll()
    }

    // Uncomment this to see the effect of the @Observed annotation
    // (Custom Observation))
    //@Observed(name = "retro-board-id",contextualName =
    "findRetroBoardById")
```

```kotlin
fun findRetroBoardById(uuid: UUID): RetroBoard {
    LOG.info("Getting retro board by id: {}", uuid)
    return retroBoardRepository.findById(uuid)
        .orElseThrow{ RetroBoardNotFoundException() }
}

fun saveOrUpdateRetroBoard(retroBoard: RetroBoard): RetroBoard {
    val retroBoardResult: RetroBoard =
        retroBoardRepository.save<RetroBoard>(retroBoard)
    eventPublisher.publishEvent(
        RetroBoardEvent(
            retroBoardResult.retroBoardId,
            RetroBoardEventAction.CHANGED,
            LocalDateTime.now()
        )
    )
    retroBoardCounter.increment()
    return retroBoardResult
}

fun deleteRetroBoardById(uuid: UUID) {
    retroBoardRepository.deleteById(uuid)
    eventPublisher.publishEvent(
        RetroBoardEvent(uuid, RetroBoardEventAction.DELETED,
        LocalDateTime.now()))
}

//@Observed(name = "users",contextualName = "allUsers")
fun allUsers() {
    LOG.info("Getting all users")
    userClient.allUsers.subscribe(
        { user: User? -> LOG.info("User: {}", user) },
        { error: Throwable? -> LOG.error("Error: {}", error.
        toString()) },
        { LOG.info("Completed") }
    )
}
```

```kotlin
    companion object {
        private val LOG = LoggerFactory.getLogger(RetroBoardAndCardService:
        :class.java)
    }
}
```

Listing 11-17 shows that we are marking the `RetroBoardAndCardService` class using the `@Observed` annotation, meaning that every method call will have its own observation. We are also using the `allUsers()` method to call the `UserClient`.

Next, open/create the `RetroBoardController` class. It is basically the same as in the previous chapters, but here we need to add the call to get all the users from Users App. See Listing 11-18.

Listing 11-18. src/main/kotlin/com/apress/myretro/web/
RetroBoardController.kt

```kotlin
package com.apress.myretro.web

import com.apress.myretro.board.RetroBoard
import com.apress.myretro.service.RetroBoardAndCardService
import org.springframework.beans.factory.annotation.Autowired
import org.springframework.http.HttpStatus
import org.springframework.http.ResponseEntity
import org.springframework.web.bind.annotation.*
import org.springframework.web.util.UriComponentsBuilder
import java.net.URI
import java.util.*

@RestController
@RequestMapping("/retros")
class RetroBoardController {
    @Autowired
    private lateinit var retroBoardAndCardService: RetroBoardAndCardService

    @get:GetMapping
    val allRetroBoards: ResponseEntity<Iterable<RetroBoard>>
        get() = ResponseEntity.ok(retroBoardAndCardService.
        allRetroBoards())
```

```kotlin
@GetMapping("/{uuid}")
fun findRetroBoardById(@PathVariable uuid: UUID):
ResponseEntity<RetroBoard> =
    ResponseEntity.ok(retroBoardAndCardService.findRetroBoard
    ById(uuid))

@RequestMapping(method = [RequestMethod.POST, RequestMethod.PUT])
fun saveRetroBoard(
    @RequestBody retroBoard: RetroBoard,
    componentsBuilder: UriComponentsBuilder
): ResponseEntity<RetroBoard> {
    val saveOrUpdateRetroBoard: RetroBoard =
        retroBoardAndCardService.saveOrUpdateRetroBoard(retroBoard)
    val uri: URI =
        componentsBuilder.path("/{uuid}").buildAndExpand(saveOrUpdate
        RetroBoard
        .retroBoardId).toUri()
    return ResponseEntity.created(uri).body(saveOrUpdateRetroBoard)
}

@DeleteMapping("/{uuid}")
@ResponseStatus(HttpStatus.NO_CONTENT)
fun deleteRetroBoardById(@PathVariable uuid: UUID): ResponseEntity<*> {
    retroBoardAndCardService.deleteRetroBoardById(uuid)
    return ResponseEntity.noContent().build<Any>()
}

@get:GetMapping("/users")
val allUsers: ResponseEntity<Void>
    // External Call
    get() {
        retroBoardAndCardService.allUsers()
        return ResponseEntity.ok().build()
    }
}
```

Listing 11-18 shows that the only method we'll be calling with the endpoint /retros/ users will be the getAllUsers method, which calls the services that use the UserClient to call the Users App service.

Adding Logging Using Grafana Loki

The logs are sent to the standard output, but you also can stream them to an external entity for further analysis, and because we added the loki-logback-appender as a dependency, we can use Grafana Loki (https://grafana.com/oss/loki/) to aggregate the logs to store or query them to get insights into the system in a centralized console. To do this, we need to add an XML configuration to the project.

Open/create the logback-spring.xml file in the resources folder. See Listing 11-19.

Listing 11-19. src/main/resources/logback-spring.xml

```xml
<?xml version="1.0" encoding="UTF-8"?>
<configuration>
    <include resource="org/springframework/boot/logging/logback/base.xml"/>
    <springProperty scope="context" name="appName" source="spring.
    application.name"/>
    <appender name="LOKI" class="com.github.loki4j.logback.Loki4jAppender">
        <http>
            <url>http://localhost:3100/loki/api/v1/push</url>
        </http>
        <format>
            <label>
                <pattern>application=${appName},host=${HOSTNAME},level=%lev
                el</pattern>
            </label>
            <message>
                <pattern>${FILE_LOG_PATTERN}</pattern>
            </message>
            <sortByTime>true</sortByTime>
        </format>
    </appender>
    <root level="INFO">
```

```
    <appender-ref ref="LOKI"/>
  </root>
</configuration>
```

In the `logback-spring.xml` file, we first need to declare a property that will be an identifier for our logs. We are following the recommended practice and sticking with the name of the application using the `spring.application.name` property from Spring Boot. Next, we are declaring the actual configuration of the log appender with the name LOKI. The first and most important part is where to stream the logs in this case we are using the Grafana Loki service (discussed in more detail a bit later) at the `http://localhost:3100/loki/api/v1/push` endpoint. We are declaring the pattern that the log will have (it's important to establish a good pattern for your apps). For our purposes, just using the application's name, the host, and the level will be sufficient. The level will be the `logging.pattern.correlation` property that we are going to set next.

Next, let's add some properties. Open the `application.properties` file. See Listing 11-20.

Listing 11-20. src/main/resources/application.properties

```
## DataSource
spring.h2.console.enabled=true
spring.datasource.generate-unique-name=false
spring.datasource.name=test-db
spring.jpa.show-sql=true
## Server
server.port=9081
## Docker Compose
spring.docker.compose.readiness.wait=never
## Application
spring.main.web-application-type=servlet
spring.application.name=my-retro-app
logging.pattern.correlation=[${spring.application.name:},%X{traceId:-},%X{spanId:-}]
## Actuator Info
info.developer.name=Felipe
info.developer.email=felipe@email.com
info.api.version=1.0
```

```
management.endpoint.env.enabled=true
## Actuator
management.endpoints.web.exposure.include=health,info,metrics,prometheus
## Actuator Observations
management.observations.key-values.application=${spring.application.name}
## Actuator Metrics
management.metrics.distribution.percentiles-histogram.http.server.
requests=true
## Actuator Tracing
management.tracing.sampling.probability=1.0
## Actuator Prometheus
management.prometheus.metrics.export.enabled=true
management.metrics.use-global-registry=true
## Users App Service
users.app.url=http://localhost:8080
users.app.username=admin
users.app.password=admin

spring.docker.compose.file: ./myretro/docker-compose.yaml
```

Let's review some of these properties in the application.properties file.

Remember that we added the Web and WebFlux dependencies? Well, our app actually needs to be run as a Servlet app (not Reactive), so we added the spring.main. web-application-type=servlet property.

Another important property is spring.docker.compose.readiness.wait=never. Because we are going to use multiple services and some of them don't have the readiness, this value must set to never. Another key will be the logging.pattern. correlation, which will be injected in the log level, the one we declared in the logback-spring.xml file (see Listing 11-19).

Review the Actuator properties, which are very straightforward to follow. Both prometheus properties are by default, but we wanted to show you that they can be overridden when needed. We are also using percentiles, which is data that we need to expose to create the necessary graphs. The observation will be based on the key application that has the name of the app (my-retro-app). And the sampling that we need is always 1.0 (100%) of the times.

Last, we are declaring the users.app.* properties that are used to retrieve the user information.

Declaring Services in Docker Compose

Next, open/create the docker-compose.yaml file. See Listing 11-21.

Listing 11-21. The docker-compose.yaml File

```
version: '3'
services:
  tempo:
    image: grafana/tempo
    extra_hosts: [ 'host.docker.internal:host-gateway' ]
    ports:
      - "14268"
      - "9411:9411"
    volumes:
      - ./services/tempo/tempo.yaml:/etc/tempo.yaml:ro
      - ./services/tempo/tempo-data:/tmp/tempo
    command: [ "-config.file=/etc/tempo.yaml" ]
  loki:
    image: grafana/loki
    extra_hosts: [ 'host.docker.internal:host-gateway' ]
    ports:
      - "3100:3100"
    command: [ "-config.file=/etc/loki/local-config.yaml" ]
    environment:
      - JAEGER_AGENT_HOST=tempo
      - JAEGER_ENDPOINT=http://tempo:14268/api/traces
      - JAEGER_SAMPLER_TYPE=const
      - JAEGER_SAMPLER_PARAM=1
  prometheus:
    image: prom/prometheus
    extra_hosts: ['host.docker.internal:host-gateway']
    volumes:
      - ./services/prometheus/prometheus.yml:/etc/prometheus/
      prometheus.yml:ro
    command:
```

```
      - '--config.file=/etc/prometheus/prometheus.yml'
      - '--enable-feature=exemplar-storage'
    ports:
      - "9090:9090"
  grafana:
    image: grafana/grafana
    extra_hosts: ['host.docker.internal:host-gateway']
    environment:
      - GF_AUTH_ANONYMOUS_ENABLED=true
      - GF_AUTH_ANONYMOUS_ORG_ROLE=Admin
      - GF_AUTH_DISABLE_LOGIN_FORM=true
    volumes:
      - ./services/grafana/datasources:/etc/grafana/provisioning/
      datasources:ro
      - ./services/grafana/dashboards:/etc/grafana/provisioning/
      dashboards:ro
    ports:
      - "3000:3000"
```

Take a moment to review the docker-compose.yaml file, which is very straightforward. In this case, we need four services—Prometheus (for metrics), Grafana (for graphics), Grafana Loki (for logs), and Grafana Tempo (for tracing).

In Listing 11-21, some of the services have a volumes parameter declared and pointing to a directory structure services/ folder. Let's review them:

- services/prometheus/prometheus.yml:

```
global:
  scrape_interval: 2s
  evaluation_interval: 2s
scrape_configs:
  - job_name: 'prometheus'
    static_configs:
      - targets: [ 'host.docker.internal:9090' ]
  - job_name: 'retroBoard'
    metrics_path: '/actuator/prometheus'
    static_configs:
      - targets: ['host.docker.internal:9081']
```

This file has the configuration where Prometheus will get its information. We are using `host.docker.internal:9090`, which points to the host machine and the endpoint; in this case, `/actuator/prometheus`.

- `services/grafana/datasources/datasources.yaml`:

```yaml
apiVersion: 1
datasources:
  - name: Prometheus
    type: prometheus
    access: proxy
    url: http://prometheus:9090
    editable: false
    jsonData:
      httpMethod: POST
      exemplarTraceIdDestinations:
        - name: trace_id
          datasourceUid: tempo
  - name: Tempo
    type: tempo
    access: proxy
    orgId: 1
    url: http://tempo:3200
    basicAuth: false
    isDefault: true
    version: 1
    editable: false
    apiVersion: 1
    uid: tempo
    jsonData:
      httpMethod: GET
      tracesToLogs:
        datasourceUid: 'loki'
  - name: Loki
    type: loki
    uid: loki
```

```
access: proxy
orgId: 1
url: http://loki:3100
basicAuth: false
isDefault: false
version: 1
editable: false
apiVersion: 1
jsonData:
  derivedFields:
    -   datasourceUid: tempo
        matcherRegex: \[.+,(.+?),
        name: TraceID
        url: $${__value.raw}
```

For Grafana to show graphics, it's necessary to declare some data sources from which it will pick up all the information. We are declaring the three data sources that are going to be useful for our metrics (Prometheus), our logs (Loki), and our tracing (Tempo).

- services/grafana/dashboards/dashboard.yml, log_traces_ metrics.json, spring_boot_statistics.json: These files declare the dashboards that we are going to use for our observability. This can be manually created using the Grafana web interface, but we are adding these files here so you don't have to. In the next section, we show you how to import some existing dashboards from the community.

- services/tempo/tempo.yaml:

```
server:
  http_listen_port: 3200
distributor:
  receivers:
    zipkin:
storage:
  trace:
```

```
    backend: local
    local:
      path: /tmp/tempo/blocks
```

This file will set the Grafana Tempo listening port and the storage for the logs, in this case using the local directory.

Ready to Run!

It's time to run both apps. Start Users App and make sure it is up and running. Next, run My Retro App, which will start the docker compose by running each service. Wait until you can see that the app is ready to be used.

If you take a look at the console, you will see something similar to this:

```
[my-retro-app] [                  main] [my-retro-app,656a4219c89834979593
2a1ae70f316b,95932a1ae70f316b]
```

This is the log we declared in the logback-spring.xml file (see Listing 11-19): first, the application name, then the host, then the level (which in this case is the correlation pattern), the name of the app, the trace ID, and the time span for the tracing.

Next, execute the curl commands. They allow you to generate some logs, metrics, and tracing. For example:

```
curl -s http://localhost:9081/retros | jq .
[
  {
    "retroBoardId": "163c859d-9238-463c-a14b-f245e380ec92",
    "name": "Spring Boot 3 Retro",
    "cards": [
      {
        "cardId": "33f23935-1cbd-46b7-a276-195fa2ebdd3e",
        "comment": "Nice to meet everybody",
        "cardType": "HAPPY",
        "created": "2023-12-01 15:29:13",
        "modified": "2023-12-01 15:29:13"
      },
      {
        "cardId": "e9afa712-6f32-4f85-a4c5-7aa6af62e754",
```

```
      "comment": "When are we going to travel?",
      "cardType": "MEH",
      "created": "2023-12-01 15:29:13",
      "modified": "2023-12-01 15:29:13"
    },
    {
      "cardId": "ba87ca9e-164a-45d3-87c5-30f4fdad25a2",
      "comment": "When are we going to travel?",
      "cardType": "SAD",
      "created": "2023-12-01 15:29:13",
      "modified": "2023-12-01 15:29:13"
    }
  ],
  "created": "2023-12-01 15:29:13",
  "modified": "2023-12-01 15:29:13"
  }
]
```

curl -s http://localhost:9081/retros/163c859d-9238-463c-a14b-f245e380ec92 | jq .

```
{
  "retroBoardId": "163c859d-9238-463c-a14b-f245e380ec92",
  "name": "Spring Boot 3 Retro",
  "cards": [
    {
      "cardId": "33f23935-1cbd-46b7-a276-195fa2ebdd3e",
      "comment": "Nice to meet everybody",
      "cardType": "HAPPY",
      "created": "2023-12-01 15:29:13",
      "modified": "2023-12-01 15:29:13"
    },
    {
      "cardId": "e9afa712-6f32-4f85-a4c5-7aa6af62e754",
      "comment": "When are we going to travel?",
      "cardType": "MEH",
      "created": "2023-12-01 15:29:13",
```

```
      "modified": "2023-12-01 15:29:13"
    },
    {
      "cardId": "ba87ca9e-164a-45d3-87c5-30f4fdad25a2",
      "comment": "When are we going to travel?",
      "cardType": "SAD",
      "created": "2023-12-01 15:29:13",
      "modified": "2023-12-01 15:29:13"
    }
  ],
  "created": "2023-12-01 15:29:13",
  "modified": "2023-12-01 15:29:13"
}
```

curl -i http://localhost:9081/retros/users
```
HTTP/1.1 200
Content-Length: 0
Date: Fri, 01 Dec 2023 21:13:46 GMT
```

Execute these commands multiple times. Then you'll be ready to continue and see what happen with these requests.

Observing with Grafana and Prometheus—Metrics, Logs, and Tracing

Now that My Retro App is up and running, open a browser and go to the Prometheus service: http://localhost:9090/targets. See Figure 11-11.

Figure 11-11. *Prometheus (http://localhost:9090/targets)*

Figure 11-11 shows the Prometheus service with the two endpoints declared. In this case, the /actuator/prometheus endpoint is where all the metrics of My Retro App live.

Next, open Grafana: http://localhost:3000. See Figure 11-12.

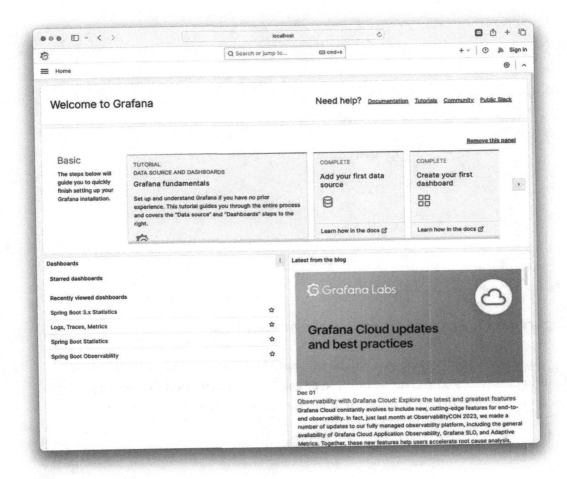

Figure 11-12. *The Grafana home page*

Figure 11-12 shows that you are automatically logged in with Admin credentials (based on the environment variables set in the docker-compose.yaml file).

Next, click the "hamburger" icon in the top-left corner and select Explore, as shown in Figure 11-13.

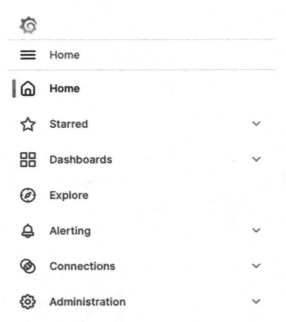

Figure 11-13. *Opening the main menu to select Explore*

After you click Explore, you will be presented with a page that contains all of Grafana's services. They can be queried to get useful information. In the drop-down menu to the right of Outline, shown in Figure 11-14, select Loki.

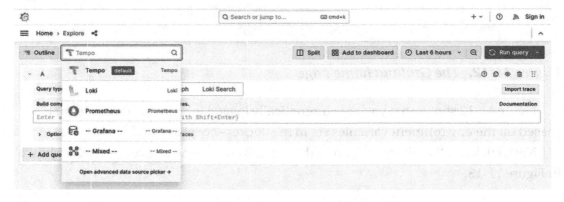

Figure 11-14. *Prometheus Tempo and Loki Dashboard*

Next, go to the A query. Select `application` and `my-retro-app` in the Label Filters drop-down list boxes, as shown in Figure 11-15. Then, click the Run Query button in the upper right.

Figure 11-15. *Loki application/my-retro query*

Figure 11-15 shows the logs of the application, which are sorted by time (newest first). Review them.

In the same query pane under Label Filters, in the Line Contains section, add `Getting all users`, as shown in Figure 11-16, and then click the Run Query button again. You will see something like the results in Figure 11-16.

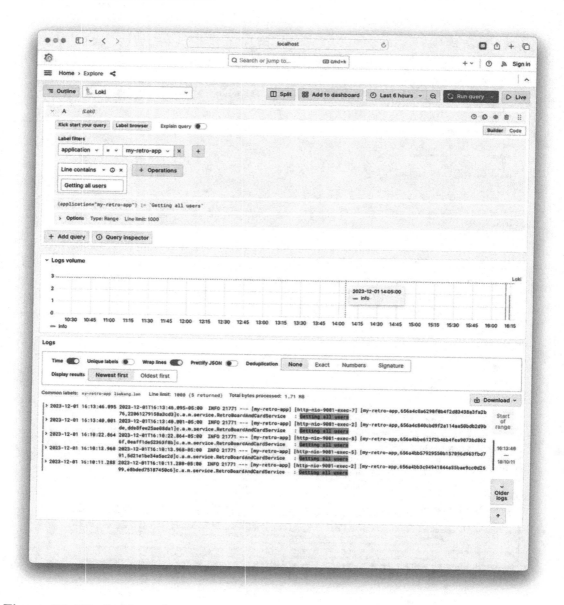

Figure 11-16. *Loki application/my-retro-app/Getting all users query*

This new query shows all the requests that we did to the /retros/users endpoint.

If you click one of the Getting all users logs, you will see something similar to Figure 11-17.

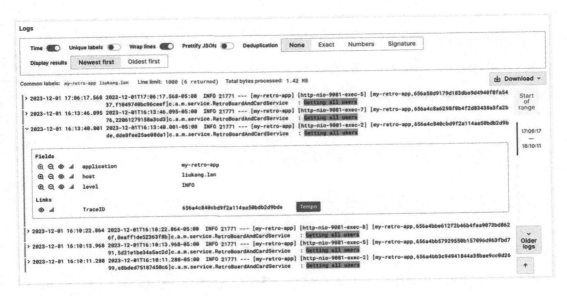

Figure 11-17. *Log details*

Next, click the Tempo button to reveal the trace, which shows what happened when this endpoint was requested. See Figure 11-18.

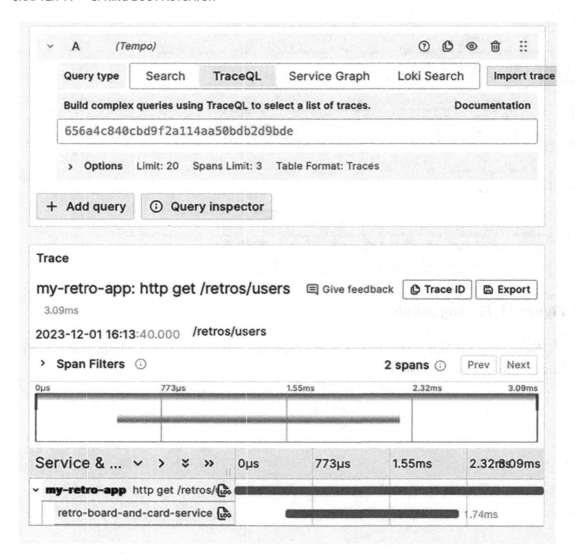

Figure 11-18. Tempo ➤ Trace ID / Spans ➤ /retros/users

You can play around and click the requests made and see how much time it takes to reach the other service. Go back to the Loki pane and change the Line Contains field to Getting all retro boards. Click one of the logs to see the trace that was made to the database. See Figure 11-19.

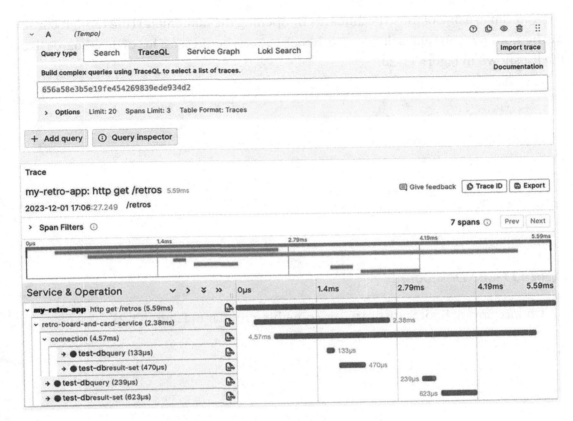

Figure 11-19. *Tempo* ➤ *Trace ID / Spans* ➤ */retros*

As you can see, we are getting more insight into our application. We can react to any bottleneck or any other process that we deem to be taking more time than expected. Take a moment to investigate what else you can do with these views.

What About External Resources: Memory, CPU, and Storage?

Glad you asked! How can you see the metrics of an app, like the memory, CPU, storage, threads, and more? There are different ways to do this, and normally you need to use Prometheus as the data source and start adding views to a dashboard. Even though this is a fun thing to do, we provided you with two dashboards that we took from the guy behind Micrometer and Spring Boot Actuator, Jonatan Ivanov! Thanks to Jonatan. We also found a useful dashboard from Sai Subramanyam, which includes awesome articles from programming techies!

You can use one of those dashboards by opening the main menu (the top-left corner, the hamburger icon) and selecting Dashboards. You should see a list of dashboards like the list shown in Figure 11-20.

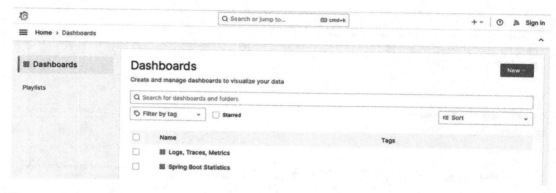

Figure 11-20. *Dashboards*

Choose Spring Boot Statistics to see something similar to Figure 11-21.

Figure 11-21. *Spring Boot Statistics displaying Prometheus metrics*

You can also import other dashboards from `https://grafana.com/grafana/dashboards/`. You can search for Spring Boot (in the search field displaying Search Dashboards) and you will find many! Return to the Dashboards page (see Figure 11-20), click the New button in the top-right corner, and select Import. You will see a page like Figure 11-22.

Import dashboard

Import dashboard from file or Grafana.com

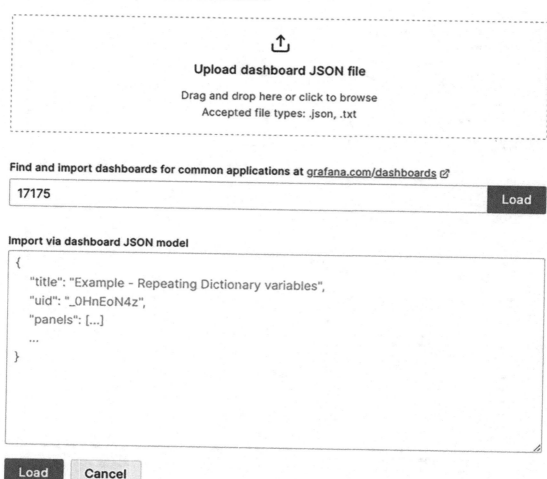

Figure 11-22. *Importing dashboards*

In the Find and Import Dashboards field, add the **17175** ID (Spring Boot Observability, `https://grafana.com/grafana/dashboards/17175-spring-boot-observability/`) and then click the Load button. This will take you to the page shown in Figure 11-23, where you select the data sources that are already defined, such as Prometheus and Loki. Select them and then click Import.

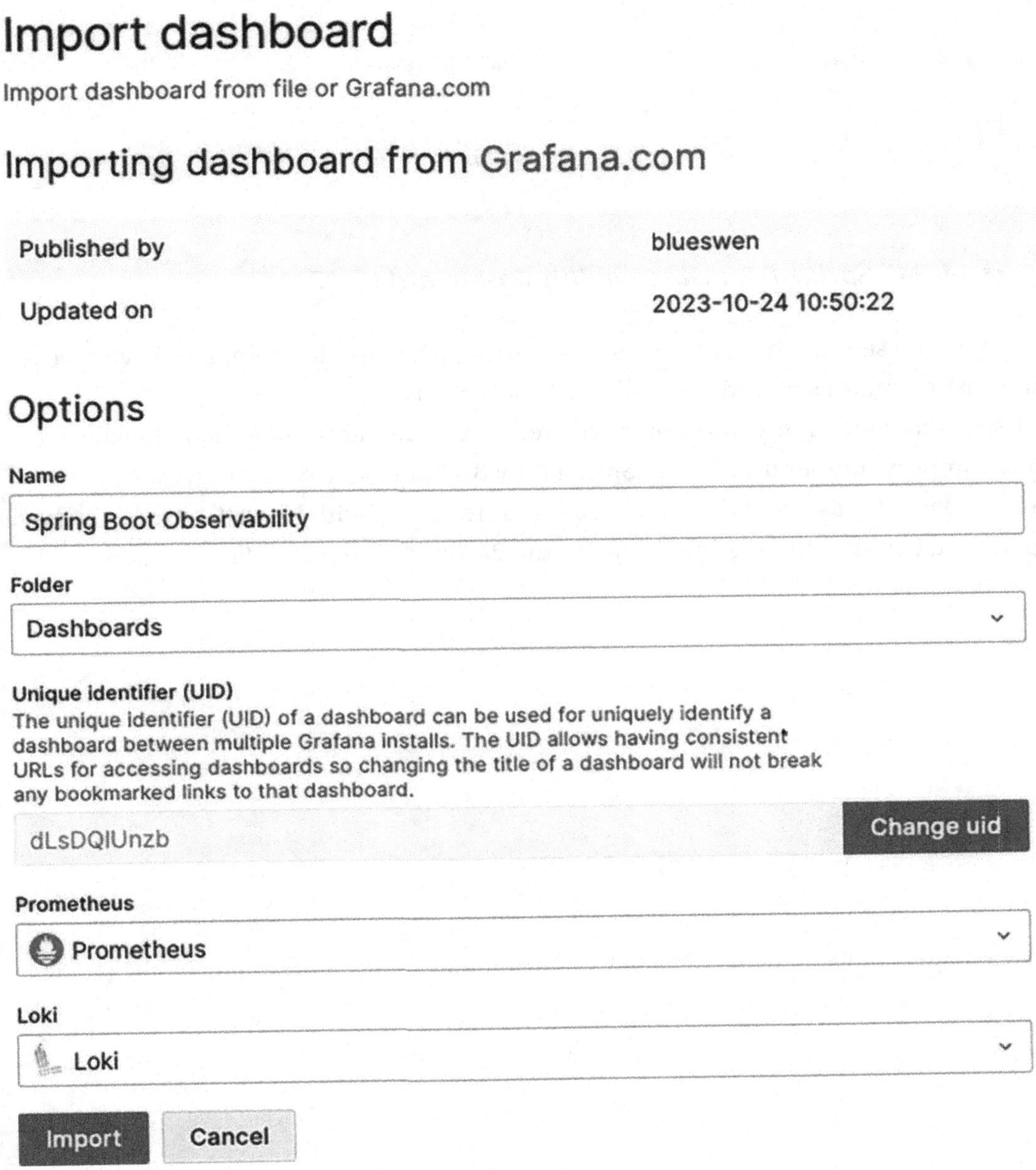

Import dashboard

Import dashboard from file or Grafana.com

Importing dashboard from Grafana.com

Published by	blueswen
Updated on	2023-10-24 10:50:22

Options

Name

Spring Boot Observability

Folder

Dashboards ⌄

Unique identifier (UID)
The unique identifier (UID) of a dashboard can be used for uniquely identify a
dashboard between multiple Grafana installs. The UID allows having consistent
URLs for accessing dashboards so changing the title of a dashboard will not break
any bookmarked links to that dashboard.

dLsDQIUnzb   Change uid

Prometheus

🔘 Prometheus ⌄

Loki

🗼 Loki ⌄

Import   Cancel

Figure 11-23. *Spring Boot Observability dashboard ID 17175*

You should see something like the dashboard shown in Figure 11-24.

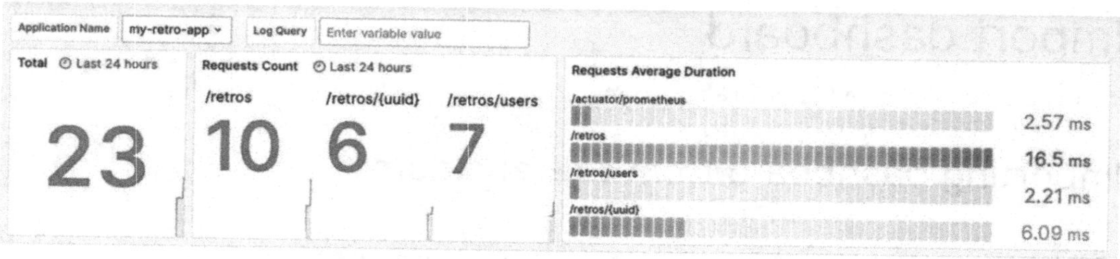

Figure 11-24. Spring Boot Observability dashboard ID 17175

As you can see, you have more options in this dashboard. It's helpful to have access to the custom metrics that we did with the Counter class.

Experiment with more dashboards or create new ones and share them. Finally, you can import another dashboard, Spring Boot 3.x Statistics (https://grafana.com/grafana/dashboards/19004-spring-boot-statistics/), with ID 19004. Once you have imported it, you should see something like the dashboard shown in Figure 11-25.

Figure 11-25. *Spring Boot 3.x Statistics dashboard ID 19004*

As demonstrated in this section, you have many ways to add observability to your projects (logs, metrics, and tracing), all in one console such as Grafana, thanks to the power of Spring Boot Actuator and Micrometer.

Summary

In this chapter you explored the most commonly used Actuator endpoints and discovered how easy it is to add production-ready features to your application. You learned how to implement your own metrics with the `Counter` and `Request` interceptors, and how to create your own custom health indicators.

You also learned how to add observability to your apps so they will react when something is wrong (high memory consumption, slow process, etc) by understanding what is happening to your application. You learned how to check out the logs, do tracing, and observe the metrics not only of the app, but of the whole computer.

Finally, you learned how to integrate multiple services, including Prometheus, Grafana, Loki, and Tempo.

CHAPTER 12

Spring Boot Native and AOT

Felipe Gutierrez[a*]

[a] 4109 Rillcrest Grove Way Fuquay Varina, NC 27526-3562, Albuquerque, NM, USA

What Is Spring AOT?

Spring AOT (Ahead-of-Time) is a new feature introduced in Spring Framework 6 designed to optimize application startup time and reduce runtime overhead, particularly for large and complex applications.

Spring AOT does the following:

- *Early analysis*: AOT processes the application context at build time, performing many of the tasks that traditionally happen during runtime. This includes analyzing bean definitions, resolving dependencies, and verifying configurations.

- *Code generation*: AOT generates optimized code based on the build-time analysis, which is executed during runtime. This reduces the amount of work done at startup, leading to faster startup times.

- *Reduces reflection*: AOT reduces the reliance on reflection, which can be a bottleneck for startup performance, especially for native images generated by GraalVM.

Here's how Spring AOT is used:

- *Build-time processing*: AOT processing is typically done as part of the project's build process using the Spring Boot build plugins (Maven or Gradle).

© Peter Späth, Felipe Gutierrez 2025
P. Späth and F. Gutierrez, *Pro Spring Boot 3 with Kotlin*, https://doi.org/10.1007/979-8-8688-1131-9_12

- *Runtime execution*: The generated AOT code is then included in the application and used during runtime startup.

- *GraalVM Native Images*: AOT is essential for creating GraalVM Native Images of Spring applications, as native images require ahead-of-time compilation and have restrictions on reflection usage.

Spring AOT is necessary for the following reasons:

- *Performance optimization*: AOT can significantly improve the startup time of Spring applications, especially for large projects with complex configurations.

- *Resource efficiency*: AOT reduces the memory footprint and CPU usage of Spring applications at runtime.

- *GraalVM native image compatibility*: AOT is a prerequisite for creating GraalVM Native Images, which offer even faster startup times and smaller memory footprints.

Use Spring AOT for the following:

- *Large applications*: AOT is most beneficial for large and complex Spring applications where startup time and resource usage are significant concerns.

- *Microservices*: AOT can be useful for microservices architectures where fast startup times are crucial for scaling and responsiveness.

- *GraalVM Native Images*: If you want to build GraalVM Native Images of your Spring application, AOT is mandatory.

Be aware of the following caveats:

- *Reduced flexibility*: AOT imposes some restrictions on dynamic behaviors, such as conditional bean definitions based on runtime conditions.

- *Compatibility*: Not all Spring features are fully compatible with AOT yet, so it's important to check the documentation for limitations.

What Is GraalVM?

GraalVM is a high-performance platform for running applications written in various languages, including Java, Kotlin, JavaScript, Python, Ruby, and more. It offers several key features:

- *High performance*: GraalVM can significantly improve the execution speed of Java and Kotlin applications compared to traditional JVMs. This is achieved through a combination of optimizations, such as ahead-of-time (AOT) compilation and dynamic language support, which we review in the following sections with Spring Boot.

- *Multilanguage support*: GraalVM can run applications written in various languages, eliminating the need for separate runtimes for each language. This makes it a versatile platform for developing polyglot applications.

- *Native Images*: GraalVM can compile Java/Kotlin applications into standalone executables, which can be launched without a JVM. This can further improve performance and reduce memory consumption.

- *Java on Truffle*: GraalVM uses the Truffle framework for dynamic language support. This allows you to run languages like JavaScript and Python alongside Java in the same runtime environment. (Also, as we discovered, you can create your own language more easily than ever. If you decide to do so, share it with the world!)

- *Open source*: GraalVM is available as an open source project under the GNU General Public License.

Benefits of Using GraalVM

The following are some of the benefits that GraalVM offers:

- *Faster application startup and execution*: GraalVM can significantly improve the performance of your Java/Kotlin applications, leading to faster startup times and improved responsiveness.

- *Reduced memory footprint*: GraalVM's Native Image technology can reduce the memory footprint of your applications by up to 50 percent.

- *Simplified deployment*: GraalVM's single runtime environment eliminates the need to manage multiple runtimes for different languages.

- *Polyglot application development*: GraalVM allows you to develop applications using various languages, making it easier to build complex and flexible solutions.

- *Improved portability*: GraalVM's Native Image technology allows you to build portable applications that can run on any platform without a JVM.

GraalVM is available for various platforms, including Linux, macOS, Windows, and ARM. You can download the latest version from the GraalVM website: `https://www.graalvm.org/downloads/`. You learn how to install GraalVM in the section entitled "Creating GraalVM Native Apps" later in the chapter.

Did you know that you can run your Java/Kotlin applications using just GraalVM? Yes, you can run your existing applications on GraalVM with no code changes. Simply use the `graalvm` command instead of the standard `java` command. Explore the GraalVM documentation, which provides comprehensive information about the platform, including tutorials, guides, and API references: `https://www.graalvm.org/latest/docs/introduction/`.

Examples of Using GraalVM

Here are some examples of how GraalVM can be used in different scenarios:

- Microservices:

  - GraalVM's fast startup times and low memory footprint make it ideal for building microservices.

  - Its support for multiple languages allows you to use the best language for each service.

  - Native Image allows you to create self-contained microservices that are easy to deploy and manage.

- Serverless computing:

  - GraalVM's small footprint and fast startup times make it well suited for serverless environments.

  - Its support for multiple languages allows you to build serverless functions in the language of your choice.

- Polyglot applications:

  - GraalVM allows you to mix and match different languages within the same application.

  - This can be useful for applications that need to interact with different platforms or technologies.

- High-performance computing:

  - GraalVM's advanced compilers and optimizations can significantly improve the performance of computationally intensive applications.

  - This can be valuable for scientific computing, machine learning, and other high-performance workloads.

- Desktop applications:

  - GraalVM can be used to build native desktop applications with faster startup times and lower memory footprint.

  - This is useful for applications that require high performance and responsiveness.

Here are some specific examples of projects that use GraalVM:

- **Spring Boot:** Spring Boot offers a GraalVM Native Image extension that allows you to build self-contained Spring Boot applications.

- **Apache Kafka:** The open source streaming platform Apache Kafka can be built with GraalVM for improved performance and scalability.

- **GraalVM Enterprise:** Oracle offers a commercial version of GraalVM with additional features and support, including subscription-based access to Oracle JDK and Oracle Cloud Infrastructure integration.

These are just a few examples of how GraalVM can be used. With its unique features and capabilities, GraalVM is a powerful tool that can help developers build faster, more efficient, and more flexible applications.

Spring, Spring Boot, and GraalVM

Now that you know more about GraalVM, it's important to review some key differences between JVM and GraalVM, learn how Spring and Spring Boot support GraalVM, and explore what Spring does with the code to make it easy for GraalVM to generate the native application.

As you know, GraalVM analyzes the code at compile time to generate the native application based on your OS. If you are on Windows, GraalVM generates an .exe file, and if you're using a UNIX environment, it generates the binary for that UNIX OS. For this to work, you must let GraalVM know in advance how your application is built. If you have dynamic logic in your app (which we do in the book's project apps, because Spring and Spring Boot have dynamic capabilities at runtime, such as auto-configuration and proxy creation for the Spring Beans), you must provide hints in JSON format to let GraalVM know what to do with all these classes.

The following are some of the key differences between JVM and GraalVM:

- *Static analysis*: GraalVM performs static analysis of the application at build time from the main entry point. This means that if there is code that cannot be reached, then that code won't be part of the native executable.

- *Classpath fixed*: The classpath must be fixed and cannot be changed at build time.

- *No lazy class loading*: GraalVM doesn't know about dynamic components or any other way to instantiate a class, so you need to tell GraalVM what to do with these resources, serialization, and dynamic proxies. In the executable, all the classes will be loaded into memory at startup.

- *Limitations*: GraalVM still has limitations with some of the Java or Kotlin features. The Spring Boot GitHub site has a Spring Boot with GraalVM page (under the Wiki tab) that provides more details about what is supported and what is not: `https://github.com/spring-projects/spring-boot/wiki/Spring-Boot-with-GraalVM`.

AOT Processing in Spring

As mentioned, GraalVM needs help identifying any dynamic component of your application to ensure that the component is part of the final native compiled version. One of the benefits of using Spring with GraalVM is that it has a mechanism that will generate the files that identify an app's dynamic components.

There is a small limitation to this mechanism. Due to the dynamic part of Spring, it is important to note that any configuration/bean declaration marked with the @Profile annotation has its limitations. (@Profile is used in Spring to activate beans conditionally based on active profiles, which are often determined at runtime and the GraalVM's closed-world assumption conflicts with this dynamic behavior. When building a native image, GraalVM needs to know upfront which profiles will be active and which beans should be included in the image.) To address this limitation, you need to add extra configuration so that the AOT processing can process any profile you need for your native applications.

If you are using Maven, this is what you need to do if you are using profiles (for example):

```
<profile>
    <id>native</id>
    <build>
        <pluginManagement>
            <plugins>
                <plugin>
                    <groupId>org.springframework.boot</groupId>
                    <artifactId>spring-boot-maven-plugin</artifactId>
                    <executions>
                        <execution>
                            <id>process-aot</id>
                            <configuration>
                                <profiles>profile-cloud,profile-
                                security,profile-staging</profiles>
                            </configuration>
                        </execution>
                    </executions>
                </plugin>
```

```
            </plugins>
        </pluginManagement>
    </build>
</profile>
```

If you are using Gradle, you need to use the following syntax for the profiles:

```
tasks.withType(org.springframework.boot.gradle.tasks.aot.ProcessAot).
configureEach {
    args('--spring.profiles.active=profile-cloud,profile-security,profile-
    staging')
}
```

Also important to note is that if you have properties that change when a bean is created, GraalVM can't identify those changes. This means that if you have any @ Configuration with @ConditionalOnProperty annotations (we haven't covered this annotation yet, but we will when we extend Spring Boot) and any .enable property, it won't be supported out of the box. The good news is that Spring can help with that by using its AOT processing!

When the Spring AOT engine is processing your application, it will generate

- The necessary Java source code that GraalVM will understand

- Bytecode for the dynamic proxies

- GraalVM JSON files (called HINT files):

    - Resources (resource-config.json)

    - Reflection (reflect-config.json)

    - Serialization (serialization-config.json)

    - JNI (jni-config.json)

    - Java Proxy (proxy-config.json)

These files will be generated in the target/spring-aot/main/resources folder (if you are using Maven) or in the build/generated/aotResources folder (if you are using Gradle) and they will be placed in the META-INF/native-image file, where GraalVM will pick them up to generate the native image.

Creating GraalVM Native Apps

To create a native app, you need to prepare your environment/computer by installing the GraalVM tools. Our recommendation is to install the *Liberica Native Image Kit (NIK)* from `https://bell-sw.com/pages/downloads/native-image-kit`. There are three NIK versions, corresponding to the JDK 11, 17, and 21 versions, and because we are using the latest version of Spring Boot 3.x, we require, at minimum, the JDK 17 version. You can choose NIK 23-JDK 17 or NIK 23-JDK 21.

If you are using macOS or Linux, you can install it using SDKMAN! (`https://sdkman.io/`) by executing the following command (for example):

```
sdk install java 22.3.4.r17-nik
```

Note   You can check out the available *graalvm/Liberica* versions using `sdk list java`. You will see the versions in the last column.

Make sure your terminal/environment is using that version by executing the following command:

```
java -version
openjdk version "17.0.9" 2023-10-17 LTS
OpenJDK Runtime Environment GraalVM 22.3.4 (build 17.0.9+11-LTS)
OpenJDK 64-Bit Server VM GraalVM 22.3.4 (build 17.0.9+11-LTS, mixed mode,
sharing)
```

If you are using Windows, follow the instructions in this blog post that was created by the GraalVM team for Windows users: `https://medium.com/graalvm/using-graalvm-and-native-image-on-windows-10-9954dc071311`. Or, you can follow the instructions from the Windows installer in the Liberica site: `https://bell-sw.com/pages/downloads/native-image-kit`.

You are now set with the GraalVM tools.

Creating a Native Users App

This section explains how to create a Native Users App. If you are following along and want to use the provided source code, go to the `12-native-aot/users` folder. If you want to start from scratch with the Spring Initializr (`https://start.spring.io`), add the GraalVM Native Support, Web, JPA, Validation, Actuator, H2, and PostgreSQL dependencies. Set the Group field to com.apress and the Artifact and Name fields to users. Click the Generate button, download the project, unzip it, and import it into your favorite IDE.

Open the build.gradle file. See Listing 12-1.

Listing 12-1. The build.gradle File

```
import org.jetbrains.kotlin.gradle.tasks.KotlinCompile
plugins {
    id 'java'
    id 'org.springframework.boot' version '3.2.3'
    id 'io.spring.dependency-management' version '1.1.4'
    id 'org.hibernate.orm' version '6.4.1.Final'
    id 'org.graalvm.buildtools.native' version '0.9.28'
    id 'org.jetbrains.kotlin.jvm' version '2.0.20-RC'
    id "org.jetbrains.kotlin.plugin.spring" version "2.0.20-RC"
    // <- simplifies spring proxying
}

group = 'com.apress'
version = '0.0.1-SNAPSHOT'
sourceCompatibility = '17'

configurations {
    compileOnly {
        extendsFrom annotationProcessor
    }
}

repositories {
    mavenCentral()
}

dependencies {
    implementation "org.jetbrains.kotlin:kotlin-stdlib-jdk8"
    implementation "org.jetbrains.kotlin:kotlin-reflect"

    implementation 'org.springframework.boot:spring-boot-starter-web'
```

```
    implementation 'org.springframework.boot:spring-boot-starter-validation'

    implementation 'org.springframework.boot:spring-boot-starter-data-jpa'

    implementation 'org.springframework.boot:spring-boot-starter-actuator'

    runtimeOnly 'com.h2database:h2'
    runtimeOnly 'org.postgresql:postgresql'

    annotationProcessor 'org.springframework.boot:spring-boot-
    configuration-processor'

    // Web
    implementation 'org.webjars:bootstrap:5.2.3'

    testImplementation 'org.springframework.boot:spring-boot-starter-test'
}
tasks.named('test') {
    useJUnitPlatform()
}

hibernate {
    enhancement {
        enableAssociationManagement = true
    }
}

//    kotlin {
//        jvmToolchain(17)
//    }
tasks.withType(KotlinCompile).configureEach {
    kotlinOptions {
        freeCompilerArgs = ['-Xjsr305=strict']
        jvmTarget = '17'
    }
}

tasks.named('test') {
    useJUnitPlatform()
}
```

Listing 12-1 shows that the plugins section of the build.gradle file now includes the org.graalvm.buildtools.native plugin, which will help you generate the native application. We are going to use the solution from Chapter 11. If you are starting from scratch, you can copy and paste the same code. If you are using the 12-native-aot/ users folder code, no modifications are necessary. You should have the folder structure shown in Figure 12-1.

Figure 12-1. *Users App structure*

Before continuing, make sure the code works. You can run it from the command line or from your IDE.

Note   The AOT compiler cannot handle Kotlin's data class' very well, so it's better to avoid them. Also take a closer look at the startup class. It looks different from our other projects. See https://github.com/spring-projects/ spring-boot/wiki/Spring-Boot-with-GraalVM for more limitations.

Next, we create the Native Users App. Open a terminal and execute the following command at the root of the users project:

```
export JAVA_HOME=/path/to/graalsvm
./gradlew nativeCompile

...

...
BUILD SUCCESSFUL in 1m 45s
9 actionable tasks: 4 executed, 5 up-to-date
```

The first line makes sure that Gradle uses the correct compiler. Shown is the LINUX variant. For Windows, you'd use something like set ... This can take up to 15 minutes depending on your computer's processor and memory (be patient if you have an old computer). We used a Mac with an M3 chip, so it was fast.

If you are using Maven, you can execute the following command:

```
./mvnw -Pnative native:compile
```

The preceding build command (either Gradle or Maven) will generate the executable in the build/native/nativeCompile/users folder for Gradle or in the users/target/ users folder for Maven.

Let's review what happens before we run the application. There are several stages that happen when you execute the previous command. First, the AOT processing starts and generates all the necessary JSON config files (proxy-config.json, reflect-config. json, resource-config.json, and so on), and then the GraalVM native compilation occurs (remember that the config files are required for GraalVM to know what your app is using to create the native app). At this stage, there are six internal steps: initializing, building, parsing methods, inlining methods, compiling methods, and creating more classes. You should have a structure similar to Figure 12-2 for Gradle or similar to Figure 12-3 for Maven.

Figure 12-2. *Files and folder structure after using Gradle with GraalVM as the native build*

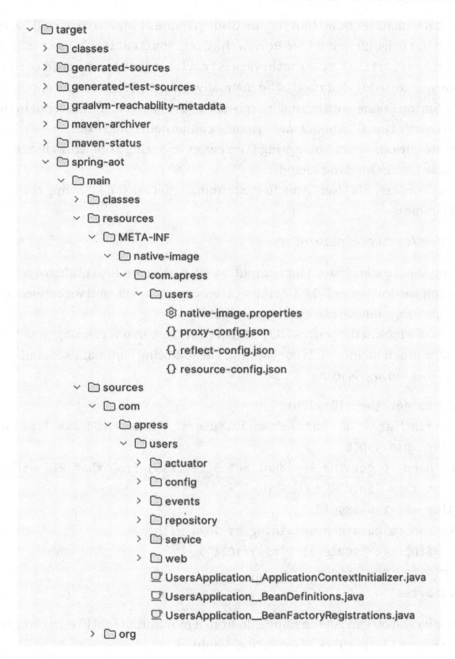

Figure 12-3. *Files and folder structure after using Maven with GraalVM as the native build*

Note that whichever build tool you are using (Gradle or Maven), you will have the same result but in a different folder. Review the UsersApplication_*.java source code. In the UsersApplication__BeanFactoryRegistrations.java file, you will see all the beans that you are using that need to be manually registered to make the application work. The Spring Framework normally registers all the beans at runtime, but in this case, we need to notify GraalVM about any dynamic components or proxies.

If you are curious about how Spring Framework or Spring Boot works behind the scenes, these classes hold the secret!

You can now execute Users App. In the terminal, execute the following command (if you used Gradle):

```
build/native/nativeCompile/users
```

The app should start faster. Our computer took 0.08 seconds to initialize versus 4.5 seconds if we do regular JVM. Of course, Users App is small, and we cannot see the benefits right away, but we can check its memory.

If you take a look at the process ID (PID) of Users App that is running, you can discover how much memory it is consuming. The following commands identify the total megabytes that the app is using:

```
# We need to get the PID with:
pid=$(ps -fea | grep -E 'nativeCompile.*users' | head -n1 | awk '{print $2}')
# In my case pid=99008
# Then we need to get the Resident Set Size (RSS) from that PID with:
rss=$(ps -o rss= "$pid" | tail -n1)
# The value was rss=189948
# Then we can calculate by dividing by 1024 with:
mem_usage=$(bc <<< "scale=1; ${rss}/1024")
echo $mem_usage megabytes
186.3 megabytes
```

Alternatively, you can get the same info from a monitoring tool like top/htop for UNIX (see Figure 12-4) or Task Manager for Windows.

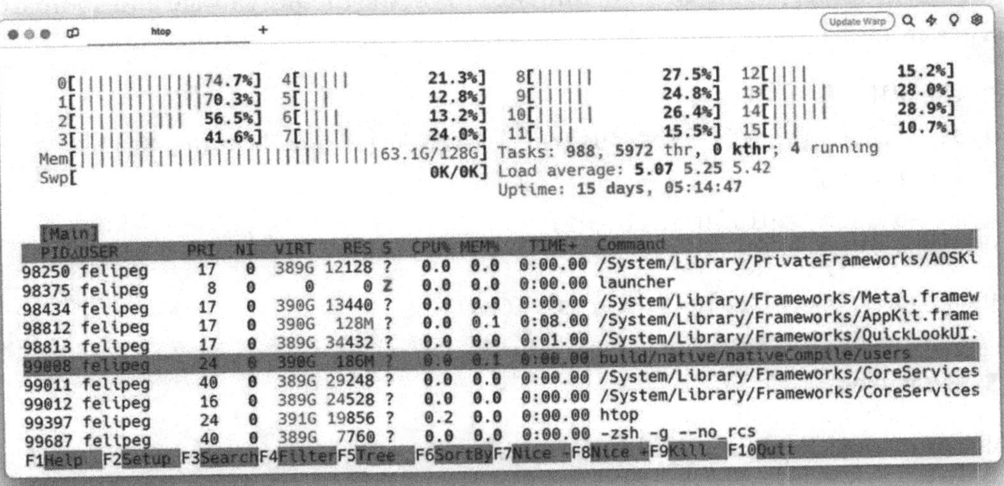

Figure 12-4. *UNIX htop showing PID 99008 with 186M*

Because Users App has the Actuator dependency and it's enabled in the application.properties file, you can safely execute the REST call to gracefully turn off Users App:

```
curl -si -XPOST http://localhost:8080/actuator/shutdown
HTTP/1.1 200
Content-Type: application/vnd.spring-boot.actuator.v3+json
Transfer-Encoding: chunked
Date: Fri, 12 Jan 2024 01:22:44 GMT
{"message":"Shutting down, bye..."}
```

Next, let's compare this with the actual JVM. To do this, just build the project to create the JAR file. You can use the following command:

```
./gradlew build
```

You can then run the app with this command:

```
java -jar build/libs/users-0.0.1-SNAPSHOT.jar
```

It should take between four to eight seconds to start. Again, this is low compared perhaps to a bigger app (more code, more services, etc).

Next, you can repeat the UNIX commands to get the memory usage and compare it. It will get around 420MB:

```
# Get the PID
pid=$(ps -fea | grep -E 'libs.*users' | tail -n1 | awk '{print $2}')
# Getting the RSS
rss=$(ps -o rss= "$pid" | tail -n1)
# Get the Memory usage
mem_usage=$(bc <<< "scale=1; ${rss}/1024")
echo $mem_usage megabytes
416.5 megabytes
```

As you can see, JVM uses double the memory. You can use your monitor tool of choice. Figure 12-5 shows the results in htop.

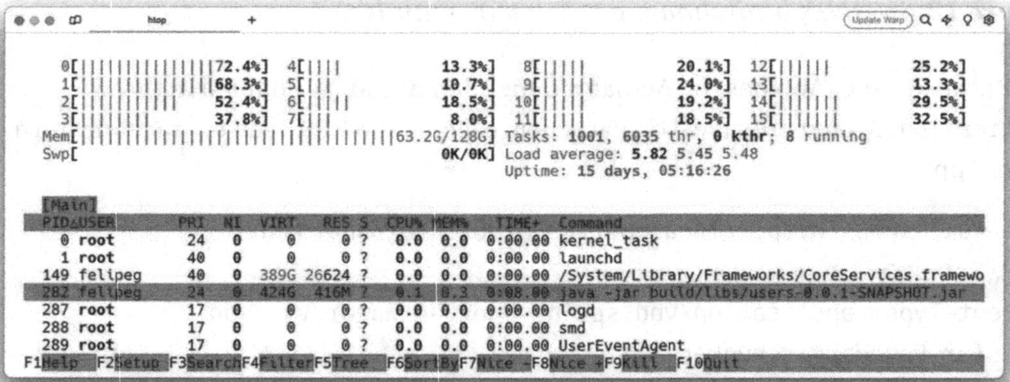

Figure 12-5. *UNIX htop showing PID 282 with 416M*

You can also use JConsole to see the values, as shown in Figures 12-6 and 12-7.

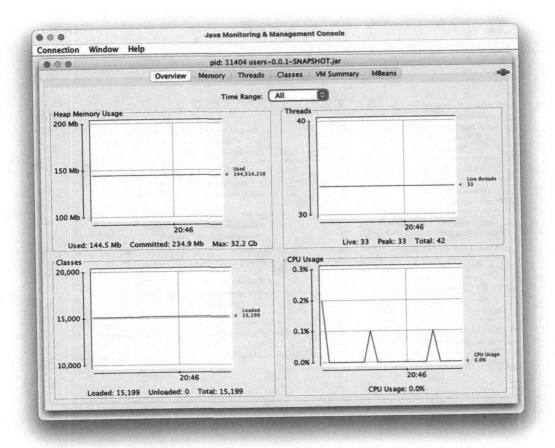

Figure 12-6. *JConsole showing memory usage*

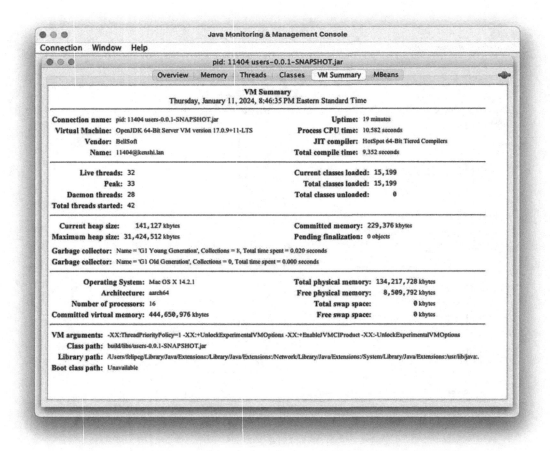

Figure 12-7. *JConsole showing commited virtual memory of 444MB*

As you can see, there is a big difference between the JVM and a native app. Plus, if you start playing around with the API, you will also see some benefits in performance when using a native app over a JVM.

You can now shut down Users App by making a POST request to the /actuator/ shutdown endpoint.

Creating a Native My Retro App

In this section, we create a native version of My Retro App. If you downloaded the source code, you can find it in the 12-native-aot/myretro folder. If are starting from scratch with the Spring Initializr (https://start.spring.io), add the GraalVM Native Support,

Web, WebFlux, JPA, Validation, Docker Compose Support, Actuator, H2, and PostgreSQL dependencies. Set the Group field to com.apress and the Artifact and Name fields to myretro. Click the Generate button, download the project, unzip it, and import it into your favorite IDE.

We are going to use the same code from the previous chapter, so if you are starting from scratch, you can copy and paste the structure. Of course, we need to make a couple of modifications, which we will show and explain to you.

Start by opening the build.gradle file. See Listing 12-2.

Listing 12-2. The build.gradle File

```
import org.jetbrains.kotlin.gradle.tasks.KotlinCompile
plugins {
    id 'java'
    id 'org.springframework.boot' version '3.2.3'
    id 'io.spring.dependency-management' version '1.1.4'
    id 'org.hibernate.orm' version '6.4.1.Final'
    id 'org.graalvm.buildtools.native' version '0.9.28'
    id 'org.jetbrains.kotlin.jvm' version '2.0.20-RC'
    id "org.jetbrains.kotlin.plugin.spring" version "2.0.20-RC"
    // <- simplifies spring proxying
}

group = 'com.apress'
version = '0.0.1-SNAPSHOT'
sourceCompatibility = '17'

configurations {
    compileOnly {
        extendsFrom annotationProcessor
    }
}

repositories {
    mavenCentral()
}

dependencies {
```

```
    implementation "org.jetbrains.kotlin:kotlin-stdlib-jdk8"
    implementation "org.jetbrains.kotlin:kotlin-reflect"

    implementation 'org.springframework.boot:spring-boot-starter-web'
    implementation 'org.springframework.boot:spring-boot-starter-webflux'
    implementation 'org.springframework.boot:spring-boot-starter-
    validation'
    implementation 'org.springframework.boot:spring-boot-starter-data-jpa'
    implementation 'org.springframework.boot:spring-boot-starter-actuator'
    implementation 'org.springframework.boot:spring-boot-starter-aop'

    runtimeOnly     'com.github.loki4j:loki-logback-appender:1.4.1'
    implementation 'io.micrometer:micrometer-tracing-bridge-brave'
    implementation 'io.zipkin.reporter2:zipkin-reporter-brave'
    implementation  'net.ttddyy.observation:datasource-micrometer-spring-
    boot:1.0.2'

    runtimeOnly 'com.h2database:h2'
    runtimeOnly 'org.postgresql:postgresql'
    runtimeOnly 'io.micrometer:micrometer-registry-jmx'
    runtimeOnly 'io.micrometer:micrometer-registry-prometheus'

    developmentOnly 'org.springframework.boot:spring-boot-docker-compose'

    annotationProcessor 'org.springframework.boot:spring-boot-
    configuration-processor'

    testImplementation 'org.springframework.boot:spring-boot-starter-test'
}
tasks.named('test') {
    useJUnitPlatform()
}

hibernate {
    enhancement {
        enableAssociationManagement = true
    }
}
```

```
//    kotlin {
//        jvmToolchain(17)
//    }
tasks.withType(KotlinCompile).configureEach {
    kotlinOptions {
        freeCompilerArgs = ['-Xjsr305=strict']
        jvmTarget = '17'
    }
}
```

Listing 12-2 shows that we are using some of the actuator and micrometer dependencies. We are also using the org.graalvm.buildtools.native plugin, which will help us create the native app.

As mentioned, this project requires some modifications. Remember that My Retro App communicates with Users App through the UserClient interface. See Listing 12-3.

Listing 12-3. src/main/kotlin/com/apress/myretro/client/UserClient.kt

```
package com.apress.myretro.client

import com.apress.myretro.client.model.User
import org.springframework.web.bind.annotation.PathVariable
import org.springframework.web.service.annotation.GetExchange
import org.springframework.web.service.annotation.HttpExchange
import reactor.core.publisher.Flux
import reactor.core.publisher.Mono

@HttpExchange(url = "/users", accept = ["application/json"],
    contentType = "application/json")
interface UserClient {
    @get:GetExchange
    val allUsers: Flux<User>

    @GetExchange("/{email}")
    fun getById(@PathVariable email: String): Mono<User>
}
```

In the UserClient interface, we are using the @HttpExchange annotation to declare how we are going to consume the /users endpoint. And, of course, we need to configure the UserClientConfig class to use this client in the code. See Listing 12-4.

Listing 12-4. src/main/kotlin/com/apress/myretro/client/UserClientConfig.kt

```kotlin
package com.apress.myretro.client

import com.apress.myretro.config.RetroBoardProperties
import org.springframework.context.annotation.Bean
import org.springframework.context.annotation.Configuration
import org.springframework.http.HttpHeaders
import org.springframework.web.reactive.function.client.WebClient
import org.springframework.web.reactive.function.client.support.
WebClientAdapter
import org.springframework.web.service.invoker.HttpServiceProxyFactory

@Configuration
class UserClientConfig {
    @Bean
    fun webClient(retroBoardProperties: RetroBoardProperties): WebClient {
        return WebClient.builder()
            .defaultHeaders { header: HttpHeaders ->
                header.setBasicAuth(
                    retroBoardProperties.usersService!!.username!!,
                    retroBoardProperties.usersService!!.password!!
                )
            }
            .baseUrl(retroBoardProperties.usersService!!.baseUrl!!)
            .build()
    }

    @Bean
    fun userClient(webClient: WebClient?): UserClient {
        val httpServiceProxyFactory = HttpServiceProxyFactory.builderFor(
            WebClientAdapter.create(
                webClient!!
            )
```

```
    )
        .build()
        return httpServiceProxyFactory.createClient(UserClient::class.java)
    }
}
```

Listing 12-4 shows the configuration needed to access a WebClient instance. You have seen this in Chapter 11, but this time we are using the RetroBoardProperties to use the username, password, and baseUrl properties to identify where Users App is running (and although Users App currently doesn't have security, this is how we would add it to the WebClient).

Next, look at the RetroBoardProperties and UsersService classes, shown in Listings 12-5 and 12-6, respectively. These classes define the configuration properties that we will use for the connection to Users App.

Listing 12-5. src/main/kotlin/com/apress/myretro/config/
RetroBoardProperties.kt

```kotlin
package com.apress.myretro.config

import org.springframework.boot.context.properties.ConfigurationProperties
import org.springframework.boot.context.properties.
NestedConfigurationProperty

@ConfigurationProperties(prefix = "myretro")
class RetroBoardProperties {
    @NestedConfigurationProperty
    var usersService: UsersService? = null
}
```

Listing 12-6. src/main/kotlin/com/apress/myretro/config/UsersService.kt

```kotlin
package com.apress.myretro.config

open class UsersService(
    open var baseUrl: String? = null,
    open var basePath: String? = null,
    open var username: String? = null,
    open var password: String? = null
)
```

The `RetroBoardProperties` and `UsersService` classes should be familiar, but `RetroBoardProperties` includes a new annotation, `@NestedConfigurationProperty`. This annotation is a *must* if you have nested properties and want to create a native app. Although Spring helps us with the AOT processing, nested properties in this form (`RetroBoardProperties` and `UsersService`) won't be detectable and won't be bindable, which is why this annotation is essential in this case.

You can test this app later for a native app; you can comment out the `@NestedConfigurationProperty` and compile it (it will compile but it won't run). The `RetroBoardProperties` class is a dependency for the `WebClient` to be created, so it must be initialized, and if you don't have this marker (`@NestedConfigurationProperty` annotation), GraalVM will compile and create the native app. But then it will fail when it runs because no values are bindable to the properties.

The `application.properties` file is shown in Listing 12-7.

Listing 12-7. src/main/resources/application.properties

```
## DataSource
spring.h2.console.enabled=true
spring.datasource.generate-unique-name=false
spring.datasource.name=test-db
spring.jpa.show-sql=true
## Server
server.port=9081
## Docker Compose
spring.docker.compose.readiness.wait=never
## Application
spring.main.web-application-type=servlet
spring.application.name=my-retro-app
logging.pattern.correlation=[${spring.application.name:},%X{traceId:-
},%X{spanId:-}]
## Actuator Info
info.developer.name=Felipe
info.developer.email=felipe@email.com
info.api.version=1.0
management.endpoint.env.enabled=true
## Actuator
```

```
management.endpoints.web.exposure.include=health,info,metrics,prometheus,
shutdown,configprops,env,trace
## Enable shutdown endpoint
management.endpoint.shutdown.enabled=true
## Actuator Observations
management.observations.key-values.application=${spring.application.name}
## Actuator Metrics
management.metrics.distribution.percentiles-histogram.http.server.
requests=true
## Actuator Tracing
management.tracing.sampling.probability=1.0
## Actuator Prometheus
management.prometheus.metrics.export.enabled=true
management.metrics.use-global-registry=true
## Docker
spring.docker.compose.file: ./myretro/docker-compose.yaml
## Users App Service
myretro.users-service.base-url=http://localhost:8080
myretro.users-service.base-path=/users
myretro.users-service.username=admin
myretro.users-service.password=admin
```

The new additions to the application.properties file are the final four lines, which define the nested properties to connect to Users App.

It's now time to convert My Retro App into a native app. To do this, we first must start up all the service dependencies we have; remember that this app connects to Grafana/Loki. You should have in the root directory (12-native-aot/myretro) the docker-compose.yaml file with all the necessary service declarations.

In a terminal window, you can start the services with this command:

```
docker compose up -d
```

Once the services start, execute the following:

```
export JAVA_HOME=/path/to/graalsvm
./gradlew nativeCompile
...
```

...

```
BUILD SUCCESSFUL in 1m 11s
10 actionable tasks: 10 executed
```

When we compiled the app, we used GraalVM 21 (instead of 17), which includes an extra step (performing analysis), but that didn't take too much time, and it likely did some good stuff by internally optimizing everything. As you can see in the preceding output, it took around 30 seconds less, even though My Retro App is bigger than Users App.

Make sure Users App is up and running. Then you can execute the following:

```
build/native/nativeCompile/myretro
...
...
Completed initialization in 1 ms
```

Next, try it by accessing some of the resources. Also check that access to Users App works by going to the /retros/users endpoint. You should see all the users that are being consumed from Users App in the console.

Let's check out how much memory was consumed:

```
# Get the PID
pid=$(ps -fea | grep -E 'Compile.*myretro' | tail -n1 | awk '{print $2}')
# Getting the RSS
rss=$(ps -o rss= "$pid" | tail -n1)
# Get the Memory usage
mem_usage=$(bc <<< "scale=1; ${rss}/1024")
echo $mem_usage megabytes
238.4 megabytes
```

Only 238.4MB for My Retro App. Let's compare it to a JVM as well. But first, shut down the app with this command:

```
curl -s -XPOST http://localhost:9081/actuator/shutdown
{"message":"Shutting down, bye..."}
```

Next, build it with this command:

```
./gradlew clean build
```

And run it with this command:

```
java -jar build/libs/myretro-0.0.1-SNAPSHOT.jar
```

Once it's started, check the memory usage with this command:

```
# Get the PID
pid=$(ps -fea | grep -E 'libs.*myretro | tail -n1 | awk '{print $2}')
# Getting the RSS
rss=$(ps -o rss= "$pid" | tail -n1)
# Get the Memory usage
mem_usage=$(bc <<< "scale=1; ${rss}/1024")
echo $mem_usage megabytes
```

511.2 megabytes

Yes, it's double again (memory usage). You can gracefully shut down My Retro App with this command:

```
curl -s -XPOST http://localhost:9081/actuator/shutdown
{"message":"Shutting down, bye..."}
```

Note   Getting the PID (process ID) can be tricky. It depends on the OS and how it shows you the info. The command (for example $ `ps -aux`) sometimes goes to the head and sometimes to the tail of the output, so just be careful in choosing the right PID of your app.

Remember that you also can use Grafana (`http://localhost:3000`) and the Spring Boot Statistics Dashboard to compare the performance of the native application and the JVM.

GraalVM Native Images, wait... What?

You have just seen the power of GraalVM to create a native application that will increase performance, provide faster starts, and improve memory usage. All of this can be very useful when you deploy an app in the cloud.

GraalVM also can help with these deployments, faster restarts, and much more by combining the power of Cloud Native Buildpacks (CNBs; see `https://buildpacks.io/`) that Spring Boot provides to create Docker images with ease.

Docker image creation has been part of the Spring Boot plugin (Gradle or Maven build tools) since version 2.3.0. By default, it creates an Open Container Initiative (OCI; see `https://opencontainers.org/`) image using CNBs. In fact, simply using the Spring Boot Plugin is sufficient to create a Docker image. If you don't have the GraalVM dependency, the Spring Boot plugin by default will create a JAR and use that artifact to create the Docker image, meaning that the process behind the scenes will install the JRE so your JAR can work.

If you include the GraalVM dependency plugin called `org.graalvm.buildtools.native`, it will start the AOT process and will create the Docker image with your native application, making this a native image. The next section explains what you need to do to create a native image for your projects.

Creating Native Image for Users App

Creating a native image is as simple as executing the following command:

```
./gradlew bootBuildImage
```

That's it. It will start by executing the AOT process and creating the native application. Then it will use the Cloud Native Buildpacks to create the Docker image. By default, it will generate the `docker.io/library/users:0.0.1-SNAPSHOT` tag, which means that you can run your app with the following command:

```
docker run --rm -p 8080:8080 --platform linux/amd64 docker.io/library/
users:0.0.1-SNAPSHOT
```

In this command, `--rm` removes the image when we stop it and `-p` exports the 8080 port to the local 8080 (syntax: `HOST-POST:CONTAINER-PORT`). We are including the `--platform` parameter because we are using a Mac Silicon (M3-chip) and the Buildpacks are using Linux AMD 64, and we need to emulate it, which is the function of this parameter. Finally, the long name is the default image name.

If you prefer to add your own tag or name convention, you can add the `imageName` parameter in the command line. For example, Felipe's Docker ID is `felipeg48`, so he could generate the image like this:

```
./gradlew bootBuildImage --imageName=felipeg48/users:v0.0.1
```

This will create the image so that it can be run like this (a bit shorter than the original command):

```
docker run --rm -p 8080:8080 --platform linux/amd64 felipeg48/users:v0.0.1
```

You can also publish your image by adding the publishImage parameter. You need to be authenticated to publish the image:

```
./gradlew bootBuildImage --imageName=felipeg48/users:v0.0.1 --publishImage
```

Alternatively, you can add configuration directly to the build.gradle file:

```
tasks.named("bootBuildImage") {
    imageName.set("felipeg48/users:v0.0.1")
    publish = true
    docker {
        publishRegistry {
            username = "felipe48"
            password = "myAwesome$ecret"
        }
    }
}
```

Note   If you are using Maven, you can create your native image with ./mvnw -Pnative spring-boot:build-image.

Inspecting the User's Native Image

Let's take peek inside the Docker image we have just created. To do so, download a tool named dive from https://github.com/wagoodman/dive. You can execute it like this:

```
dive felipeg48/users:v0.0.1
```

You will see something similar to Figure 12-8.

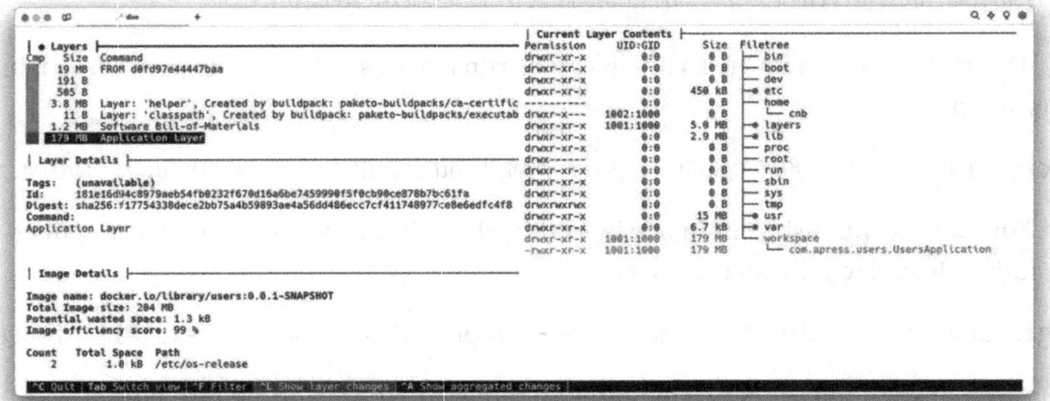

Figure 12-8. *Using the dive tool*

The dive tool provides a visualization of the layers inside the Docker image. You can navigate with the Tab key to the different sections. For example, as shown in Figure 12-8, in the Layers section you can select the Application Layer (with the up/down arrow keyboard keys). From the Current Layer Contents pane, you can see the path of the application, which in this case is the /workspace/com.apress.users.UsersApplication executable.

Feel free to inspect every layer. In the Current Layer Contents pane, you can collapse the folders using the spacebar.

Creating a My Retro App Native Image

You can create this native image using the same process as previously described, but remember that you need to start docker compose up from your terminal.

You can go to the My Retro source code and execute the following command in a terminal:

```
./gradlew bootBuildImage
```

As before, this will generate the docker.io/library/myretro:0.0.1-SNAPSHOT image. However, running the image in this context will be different, because you need access to the same network where all the services are.

When you executed the docker compose up, by default it created a bridged network, which is easy to see if you execute the following command:

```
docker network list
NETWORK ID      NAME            DRIVER    SCOPE
f97e915ba54a    bridge          bridge    local
cf3efd768256    host            host      local
2c3b202a4106    myretro_default bridge    local
7540438ac56c    none            null      local
```

It uses the name of the folder in which you executed docker compose up and appends _default to its name. To connect to that network, we are going to use the --network=<name> parameter in the docker run command. To run the My Retro native image, execute the following:

```
docker run --rm -p 9081:9081 --network myretro_default --platform linux/
amd64 docker.io/library/myretro:0.0.1-SNAPSHOT
```

That's it! If you try to execute the /retros/users endpoint now, it will produce an error telling you that it's not reachable. Do you know why? Well, this is because the Users container image needs to run in the same network bridge as My Retro App. You can stop the Users container and run it like this:

```
docker run --rm -p 8080:8080 --network myretro_default --platform linux/
amd64 felipeg48/users:v0.0.1
```

And that's it.

Inspecting the My Retro Native Image

Again, you can take a peek at the My Retro native image by using the dive command:

```
dive docker.io/library/myretro:0.0.1-SNAPSHOT
```

Figure 12-9 shows the result.

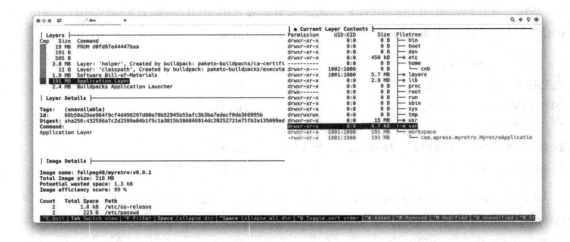

Figure 12-9. *The dive tool with My Retro native image*

You can stop the images by making a POST request to the /actuator/ shutdown endpoint and executing the docker compose down command.

Testing Native Apps and Images

If you want to test your apps when creating the native app/image, you can do so with the following commands.

If you are using Maven:

```
./mvnw -PnativeTest test
```

If you are using Gradle:

```
./gradle nativeTest
```

AOT Processing with Custom Hints

When you have your own custom AOP (Aspect Oriented Programming) or any other dynamic code (e.g. using reflection), other resources (configuration files, etc.), proxies, or serialization process in your app, it all might be skipped by the AOT processing if you don't let the AOT know how your app works. The Spring AOT engine gives you a few different ways to provide *custom hints*. You can implement custom hints from

the RuntimeHintsRegistrar functional interface via the registerHints method.
Or, if your app relies on binding, you can use the @RegisterReflectionForBinding
annotation over your JSON serialization bean, for example, or WebClient, RestClient, or
RestTemplate directly.

```
class MyCustomRuntimeHintsRegistrar : RuntimeHintsRegistrar {
    override fun registerHints(hints: RuntimeHints,
    classLoader:ClassLoader?) {
        hints.resources().registerPattern("my-data.csv")
        hints.serialization().registerType(MySerializableConverter::
        class.java)
    }
}
@Configuration
class RetroBoardCustomHintsConfiguration {
    @Bean
    @RegisterReflectionForBinding(RetroBoard::class)
    @ImportRuntimeHints(MyCustomRuntimeHintsRegistrar::class)
    fun peopleListener(objectMapper: ObjectMapper, @Value("classpath:/my-
    data.csv") csv: Resource)
            : ApplicationListener<ApplicationReadyEvent> {
        return ApplicationListener<ApplicationReadyEvent>
        {
            InputStreamReader(csv.inputStream).use {
                val csvData = FileCopyUtils.copyToString(it)
                csvData.split(System.lineSeparator())
                    .map { line -> line.split(",") }
                    .map { row -> RetroBoard().apply {
                        retroBoardId= UUID.fromString(row[0]);
                        name=row[1] }
                    }
                    .map { retroBoard ->
                        objectMapper.writeValueAsString(retroBoard)
                    }
```

```
                    .forEach(System.out::println)
            }
        }
    }
}
```

As you can see, this is very straightforward, but before moving forward, let's analyze it:

- RuntimeHintsRegistrar: You need to implement this functional interface by adding code to the registerHints method. Normally, you would add any reflections, serializations, resources (in this example, the my-data.csv resource), and proxies.

- @RegisterReflectionForBinding: If you have a class that will be binding values with some serialization, it's important to use the @RegisterReflectionForBinding annotation so it can be picked up by the AOT processing.

- @ImportRuntimeHints: This annotation tells the AOT processing which classes are ready for custom hints with the RuntimeHintsRegistrar.

Remember, if you don't add this annotation or register these custom hints, they won't be picked up by the AOT processing.

Summary

This chapter covered how to create GraalVM native applications and native images to use with containers such as Docker. You learned that, with native apps, you can improve performance, reduce memory consumption, and provide faster starts.

Remember that you need to have GraalVM installed on your system, and only by using the org.graalvm.buildtools.native plugin can you create a native app or a native image.

Chapter 13 launches into the cloud with a discussion of Spring Cloud.

CHAPTER 13

Spring Cloud with Spring Boot

Felipe Gutierrez[a*]

[a] 4109 Rillcrest Grove Way Fuquay Varina, NC 27526-3562, Albuquerque, NM, USA

Challenges Addressed by Spring Cloud

Spring Cloud addresses various challenges in the development of microservices and distributed systems, including but not limited to the following:

- *Service discovery and registration*: Simplifies the registration and discovery of microservices within a distributed system.

- *Load balancing*: Provides tools for load balancing requests across multiple instances of microservices to ensure efficient resource utilization.

- *Configuration management*: Offers solutions for managing configuration settings across microservices in a centralized and dynamic manner.

- *Circuit breakers*: Implements patterns such as the Circuit Breaker pattern (discussed later in the chapter) to handle faults and failures gracefully, therefore preventing cascading failures in distributed systems.

- *Routing and API gateway*: Facilitates the implementation of routing and API gateway patterns for efficient communication between microservices.

685

© Peter Späth, Felipe Gutierrez 2025
P. Späth and F. Gutierrez, *Pro Spring Boot 3 with Kotlin*, https://doi.org/10.1007/979-8-8688-1131-9_13

- *Distributed tracing*: Supports distributed tracing to monitor and analyze requests as they traverse through various microservices.

- *Fault tolerance*: Introduces mechanisms for handling faults and failures in a resilient manner, enhancing the overall robustness of distributed systems.

- *Security*: Provides tools for securing communication between microservices and managing authentication and authorization.

Spring Cloud leverages various technologies and components to address the challenges mentioned. The following are some of the key technologies:

- *Netflix OSS components*: Integrates with several Netflix Open Source Software (OSS) components, such as Eureka for service discovery, Ribbon for client-side load balancing, and Hystrix for circuit breakers.

- *Spring Cloud Config*: Enables centralized configuration management for microservices, allowing dynamic updates without requiring application restarts.

- *Spring Cloud Sleuth*: Integrates with distributed tracing systems, providing insights into the flow of requests across microservices. Although this project is still available as a standalone project at `https://spring.io/projects/spring-cloud`, the core has been moved to the Micrometer project. If you want to learn more about Spring Cloud Sleuth and use the latest versions of Spring Boot, the recommendation is to use *micrometer tracing* instead (`https://docs.micrometer.io/tracing/reference/index.html`).

- *Spring Cloud Stream*: Simplifies the development of event-driven microservices by providing abstractions for message-driven communication.

- *Spring Cloud Security*: Offers tools for securing microservices through authentication, authorization, and other security mechanisms.

- *Spring Cloud Bus*: Facilitates the propagation of configuration changes across microservices in a distributed system.

- *Spring Cloud Contract*: Supports consumer-driven contract testing to ensure compatibility between microservices.

- *Spring Cloud Kubernetes*: An extension of the Spring Cloud framework that streamlines the development of microservices for Kubernetes environments. It provides abstractions and integrations that simplify common tasks such as service discovery, configuration management, load balancing, and more, ensuring seamless compatibility with Kubernetes-native features.

- *Spring Cloud Function*: Provides a convenient and flexible framework for building serverless applications and functions. It leverages the strengths of the Spring ecosystem, promotes a consistent development model, and supports multiple programming languages and function as a service (FaaS) providers, allowing developers to focus on writing business logic without being tightly coupled to the underlying infrastructure.

- *Spring Cloud Gateway*: Offers a versatile and extensible gateway solution that facilitates the development of microservices architectures. It addresses the challenges of routing, filtering, load balancing, and other cross-cutting concerns, providing a central point for managing and controlling external access to microservices.

Covering all the projects under the Spring Cloud umbrella is beyond the scope of this book. If you want to know about other projects, look at the Spring Cloud documentation:

`https://spring.io/projects/spring-cloud/`.

This chapter digs deeper into some of the most commonly used Spring Cloud technologies and explains how to use them in the book's two main projects—the Users App and My Retro App projects.

Microservices

Microservices refers to an architectural style for developing software applications as a collection of small, independent, and loosely coupled services. Each microservice represents a specific business capability and runs as a separate process, communicating with other microservices through well-defined APIs. Microservices architecture aims to enhance scalability, maintainability, and agility by breaking down complex applications into smaller, independently deployable and scalable services. However, it also introduces challenges like service discovery, load balancing, and distributed tracing. Spring Cloud provides a comprehensive set of tools and libraries that address these challenges, making it easier to build and manage microservices-based applications on the Java platform.

Twelve-Factor App Practices and Spring Boot/ Spring Cloud Relationship

The Twelve-Factor App (`https://12factor.net/`) is a set of best practices and principles for building modern, scalable, and maintainable web applications. Developers at Heroku, a cloud platform as a service (PaaS) provider, formulated these practices and they have become widely adopted in the software development industry. While initially designed for monolithic applications, many of the practices and principles align well with the microservices architecture.

Here's a quick summary of how microservices relate to the Twelve-Factor App practices and how Spring Boot and Spring Cloud implement them:

1. *Codebase*: Each microservice has its own codebase, managed independently.

   - *Spring Boot:* Supports the development of standalone, executable JARs and WARs, making it easy to manage a single codebase.

   - *Spring Cloud:* Enhances the development of microservices architectures, allowing developers to manage multiple codebases for independent microservices.

2. *Dependencies*: Each microservice manages its dependencies, minimizing shared dependencies.

   - *Spring Boot:* Leverages a dependency management system, making it explicit about project dependencies. Developers can easily manage and isolate dependencies.

   - *Spring Cloud:* Integrates with Spring Boot, providing additional features for building distributed systems and managing dependencies between microservices.

3. *Config*: Externalize configuration, allowing dynamic changes without code modifications.

   - *Spring Boot:* Encourages externalized configuration, allowing developers to use `application.properties` or `application.yaml` files for configuration. The configuration can be easily overridden using environment variables.

   - *Spring Cloud:* Extends Spring Boot's configuration capabilities by providing tools for centralized and dynamic configuration management across microservices.

4. *Backing services*: Microservices interact with databases, queues, and other services as separate entities.

   - *Spring Boot:* Easily integrates with various backing services such as databases, message brokers, and caches. It supports configuration properties for connecting to external services.

   - *Spring Cloud:* Facilitates the interaction with and discovery of backing services using components like service discovery and client-side load balancing.

5. *Build, release, run*: Microservices are independently built, released, and run.

   - *Spring Boot:* Provides an embedded web server, making it easy to package applications as standalone JAR files. The build and run processes are streamlined, simplifying deployment.

   - *Spring Cloud:* Builds on Spring Boot's capabilities to enhance the deployment and scaling of microservices, supporting dynamic routing and load balancing.

6. *Processes*: Microservices are designed to be stateless, allowing for easy scalability and resilience.

   - *Spring Boot:* Supports the creation of stateless applications. State is typically managed by external services, and the framework facilitates the development of RESTful stateless APIs.

   - *Spring Cloud:* Complements Spring Boot in developing stateless microservices, adhering to the distributed nature of cloud-native applications.

7. *Port binding*: Microservices expose APIs and communicate over well-defined ports.

   - *Spring Boot:* Applications can be configured to listen on specific ports, and the framework provides an embedded web server for easy port binding.

   - *Spring Cloud:* Integrates with Spring Boot to manage ports and facilitate communication between microservices using well-defined APIs.

8. *Concurrency*: Microservices scale independently, enabling efficient resource utilization.

   - *Spring Boot:* Supports the creation of concurrent, stateless components. The application can be easily scaled horizontally by deploying multiple instances.

   - *Spring Cloud*: Works seamlessly with Spring Boot to scale microservices independently, providing tools for service discovery and load balancing.

9. *Disposability*: Microservices are designed to be disposable, allowing for quick deployment and scaling.

   - *Spring Boot:* Enables fast startup and graceful shutdown, aligning with the disposability principle. It's designed to be suitable for cloud-native environments.

   - *Spring Cloud:* Aligns with Spring Boot's disposability features, enabling the rapid scaling and deployment of microservices.

10. *Dev/prod parity*: Aim for consistency among development, testing, and production environments.

    - *Spring Boot:* Provides a consistent development model across different environments, minimizing the disparity among development, testing, and production environments.

    - *Spring Cloud:* Ensures consistency in development, testing, and production environments, promoting a unified development and deployment model.

11. *Logs*: Microservices generate logs that are often aggregated into centralized systems for monitoring.

    - *Spring Boot:* Integrates with logging frameworks and provides flexible logging configurations, allowing logs to be treated as event streams. Centralized logging can be easily implemented.

    - *Spring Cloud:* Integrates with Spring Boot to support centralized logging, ensuring that logs can be treated as event streams in a distributed system.

12. *Admin processes*: Administrative tasks can be executed independently for each microservice.

    - *Spring Boot*: Supports the implementation of admin or management tasks as one-off processes, separate from the main application logic.

    - *Spring Cloud:* Provides additional tools for managing and monitoring distributed systems, supporting administrative processes and tasks.

Spring Boot and Spring Cloud complement each other to implement the Twelve-Factor App principles effectively, particularly in the context of building cloud-native applications and microservices architectures. They provide a cohesive and comprehensive framework for developing, deploying, and managing modern, scalable applications.

Cloud Development

So far with the two projects—Users App and My Retro App—we have been developing microservices that complement each other to create a complete solution, and the projects work independently of each other, meaning that we can access Users App directly or through My Retro App. If you review the Twelve-Factor App practices again with these projects in mind, you'll discover that we cover all of them, providing a perfect scenario for cloud development—but what does "cloud development" actually mean?

Cloud development refers to the entire process of building, testing, deploying, and running software applications in the cloud instead of on physical, onsite servers. It leverages the resources and services provided by cloud computing platforms like Amazon Web Services (AWS), Microsoft Azure, and Google Cloud Platform (GCP).

Some key characteristics of cloud development include:

- *Location independence*: Development and deployment happen within the cloud platform, accessible from anywhere with an Internet connection.

- *Scalability*: Resources like storage, computing power, and memory can be easily scaled up or down based on demand.

- *Flexibility*: Cloud platforms offer a wide range of services and tools that can be integrated into the development process.

- *Collaboration*: Teams can work together on projects in real time regardless of their physical location.

- *Cost-effectiveness*: Cloud platforms eliminate the need for upfront hardware investments and provide pay-as-you-go pricing.

There are two main approaches to cloud development:

- *Cloud-based development*: This involves using traditional development tools and methodologies but deploying the application to the cloud.

- *Cloud-native development*: This involves designing and building applications specifically for the cloud, taking advantage of its unique characteristics. And, yes, we've seen some of this in the previous chapter with GraalVM.

Cloud development offers several advantages over traditional on-premises development, including the following:

- *Reduced costs*: Eliminates hardware and maintenance costs

- *Increased agility*: Faster development and deployment cycles

- *Improved scalability*: Easier to handle fluctuating demand

- *Enhanced collaboration*: Enables teams to work together more effectively

- *Greater innovation*: Provides access to a wider range of tools and services

However, it's important to also consider the potential challenges of cloud development, such as:

- *Vendor lock-in*: Dependence on a specific cloud provider

- *Security concerns*: Reliant on implementation of robust security measures

- *Network reliability*: Reliant on Internet connectivity

Overall, cloud development is a growing trend that offers many benefits for organizations of all sizes. If you're considering moving to the cloud, carefully evaluate your needs and choose a platform that meets your requirements.

Using Spring Cloud Technologies

This section explores the following Spring Cloud technologies that can be used on any local system (for development purposes) or in any cloud platform:

- *Spring Cloud Consul* for service discovery and external configuration management. HashiCorp Consul, a widely-adopted service networking solution, excels at service discovery, health checking, and configuration management in distributed systems. Recognizing its power, Spring Cloud Consul seamlessly integrates Consul into the Spring ecosystem. This enables Spring Boot applications to leverage Consul for service discovery and external configuration management, providing a robust foundation for building resilient and scalable microservices architectures.

- *Spring Cloud Vault* for database connections and secrets. HashiCorp Vault is a powerful secrets management tool that provides secure storage and access control for sensitive data like passwords, API keys, and certificates. Spring Cloud Vault, a module within the Spring Cloud project, simplifies the integration of Vault into Spring Boot applications. This integration enables applications to securely retrieve and manage secrets stored in Vault, bolstering security practices and eliminating the need to hardcode sensitive information in application configurations.

- *Spring Cloud OpenFeign* for request/response communication between microservices

- *Spring Cloud Gateway* with some of its features such as filters with *load balancing* and *circuit breakers*

We chose these Spring Cloud technologies because they are the most commonly used in the IT industry for cloud development.

For purposes of this discussion, assume that we are using Amazon Web Services, Google Cloud, or the Microsoft Azure cloud infrastructure and using only compute instances (virtual machines) to deploy the apps (Users App and My Retro Apps). The apps need to be distributed and have multiple instances, because we need high availability, access to external configuration, and security for sensitive information (for example, by requiring credentials to connect to a database). Figure 13-1 depicts the overall cloud architecture that we'll implement in this chapter.

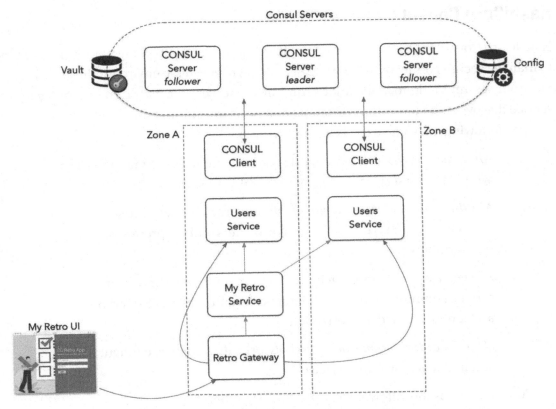

Figure 13-1. *The Users App and My Retro App cloud architecture*

Figure 13-1 shows that we need two instances of the Users App Service, and a gateway that can help us reach out to these services. That way, the UI or client will only know one address to do some requests, and not every single service address and port.

HashiCorp Consul and Spring Cloud Consul

The Spring Cloud Consul technology is integrated into the HashiCorp Consul technology, so let's start by understanding what Consul is and exploring some of its use cases, features, and benefits.

Note   In this discussion, "Consul" without "HashiCorp" or "Spring Cloud" preceding it always refers to HashiCorp Consul.

HashiCorp Consul

HashiCorp Consul (`https://www.consul.io/`) is a service networking platform designed to manage secure connectivity between services across diverse environments, including on-premises, multi-cloud, and various runtimes. It serves as a central control plane for service discovery, secure communication, and network automation.

The following are some use cases for Consul:

- *Microservices architectures*: Easily connect and manage microservices with dynamic service discovery and health checks.

- *Multi-cloud and hybrid deployments*: Ensure consistent service connectivity across different cloud providers and on-premises infrastructure.

- *API gateways and service meshes*: Implement secure service-to-service communication with features like automatic TLS encryption and identity-based authorization.

- *Network automation*: Automate network infrastructure configuration and updates based on service changes.

Consul includes the following features (among others):

- *Service discovery*: Register and locate services using DNS, HTTP, or gRPC interfaces.

- *Health checks*: Monitor service health and automatically deregister unhealthy instances.

- *Secure communication*: Enable service-to-service encryption with mutual TLS (mTLS) and identity-based authorization.

- *Key-value store*: Store configuration and secrets securely within Consul.

- *Multi-data center support*: Scale Consul across multiple data centers or regions seamlessly.

- *Service mesh integration*: Integrate with existing service meshes like Linkerd or Istio.

- *API gateway*: Manage traffic and access control for services within Consul Service Mesh.

- *Network automation*: Automate network infrastructure configuration based on service changes.

Benefits of Consul include:

- *Simplified service management*: Centrally manage service discovery, health checks, and security.

- *Increased agility*: Accelerate service deployment and scaling with multi-platform support.

- *Improved operational efficiency*: Automate tasks and gain centralized visibility into services.

- *Enhanced security*: Enforce least privilege access and enable secure communication.

Using HashiCorp Consul

This section uses Docker to start the Consul server and a Consul client. Consul requires a server-client architecture that enables it to provide features like distributed consensus, high availability, security, and efficient management, which wouldn't be possible with just clients alone. This architecture ensures reliability, scalability, and security for service discovery and networking in various scenarios.

To start the Consul server, execute the following command:

```
docker run \
    -d \
    -p 8500:8500 \
    -p 8600:8600/udp \
    --rm \
    --name=consul-server \
    consul:1.15.4 agent -server -ui -node=server-1 -bootstrap-expect=1
    -client=0.0.0.0
```

Note   At the time of this writing, the Consul version is 1.15.4. You can check the Docker Hub for the latest version: `https://hub.docker.com/_/consul`.

Next, we determine the address the client needs to connect to the server. Execute the following command:

```
docker exec consul-server consul members
```

The output of this command is the default Docker IP address (normally `172.17.0.2`). We can now start the client and use the IP address:

```
docker run \
    --name=consul-client --rm -d \
    consul:1.15.4 agent -node=client-1 -retry-join=172.17.0.2
```

Because we are going to use Consul as an external configuration mechanism, we need to add some keys. For this aim, you can either use Consul's REST API or install the Consul CLI tool to interact with it (`https://developer.hashicorp.com/consul/docs/install`).

The following command adds the necessary key/value pairs:

`curl -X PUT -d 'admin' http://localhost:8500/v1/kv/`**config/users-service/db/username**
`curl -X PUT -d 'mysecretpassword' http://localhost:8500/v1/kv/`**config/users-service/db/password**

It's important to note that we are using a very specific way to add these key/value pairs. We are following the Spring Cloud Consul convention, which requires this syntax:

```
config/<application-name>/<your-properties>
config/<application-name>,<profiles>/<your-properties>
```

In this case, we are using `users-service` as the application name (`spring.application.name`) and `db.username` and `db.password` as properties. These properties are for the database.

Also add the following properties (we are using the Consul CLI in this case):

```
consul kv put config/users-service/user/reportFormat PDF
consul kv put config/users-service/user/emailSubject 'Welcome to the Users
Service!'
consul kv put config/users-service/user/emailFrom 'users@email.com'
consul kv put config/users-service/user/emailTemplate '
Thanks for choosing Users Service
We have a REST API that you can use to integrate with your Apps.
Thanks from the Users App team.'
```

You can also use the Web UI, shown in Figure 13-2, by pointing your browser to
`http://localhost:8500`.

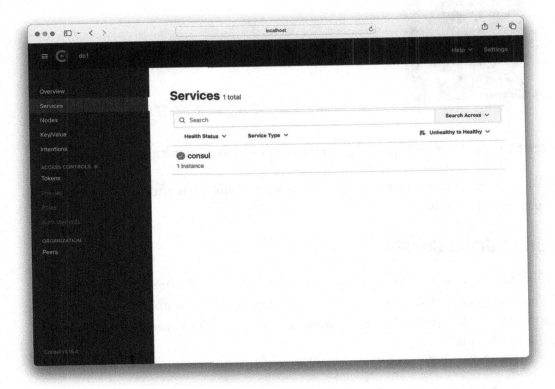

Figure 13-2. *HashiCorp Consul Web UI (`http://localhost:8500`)*

If you look at the Key/Value section, you should see the `db.*` and `user.*` properties
defined, as shown in Figure 13-3.

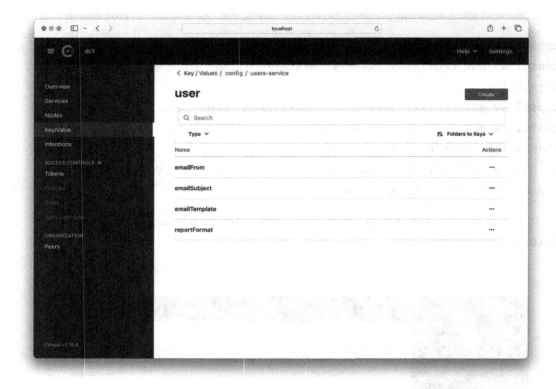

Figure 13-3. *Consul Key/Value section (config/users-service/user properties)*

Let's now review what Spring Cloud Consul technology is and how it can help you use HashiCorp Consul.

Spring Cloud Consul

Spring Cloud Consul is a library that seamlessly integrates Spring Boot applications with HashiCorp Consul. It leverages Consul's capabilities to simplify service discovery, communication, and configuration management within microservices architectures built with Spring.

Some of the key features of Spring Cloud Consul are

- *Simplified service discovery:*

    - Automatically registers and discovers Spring Boot applications.

    - Utilizes annotations to integrate service discovery features without manual configuration.

- Supports Spring Cloud Load Balancer for intelligent routing and Ribbon for client-side load balancing.

- Integrates with Spring Cloud Gateway for dynamic API gateway routing.

- *Robust configuration management:*

  - Leverages Consul's key-value store for centralized configuration management.

  - Uses Spring Environment to access configuration values stored in Consul.

  - Dynamically updates configurations across all services without individual redeploys.

- *Secure service communication:*

  - Enables strong mutual TLS (mTLS) encryption by leveraging Consul's built-in security features.

  - Enforces identity-based authorization for secure access control.

- *Distributed control bus:*

  - Utilizes Consul's events to trigger actions across the microservice environment.

  - Sends and receives events for coordination and notification purposes.

- *Integration with other Spring Cloud projects:*

  - Works seamlessly with other Spring Cloud projects, such as Spring Cloud Netflix for advanced features like Hystrix resilience.

The benefits of using Spring Cloud Consul include the following:

- *Reduced development time*: Simplifies service discovery and configuration management through annotations and auto-configuration.

- *Improved developer experience*: Provides a familiar Spring approach to working with Consul, minimizing the learning curve.

- *Enhanced reliability and scalability*: Leverages Consul's high availability and multi-data center support for robust microservices.

- *Increased security*: Enforces secure communication and authorization within your microservices architecture.

In essence, Spring Cloud Consul bridges the gap between Spring Boot applications and Consul, empowering developers to build resilient, scalable, and secure microservices with ease.

Using Spring Cloud Consul in Users App

This section explains how to add Spring Cloud Consul to Users App and reviews the service discovery feature and the external configuration. External configuration using tools such as Consul and Spring Cloud Consul provides significant advantages for microservices architectures. It fosters increased agility, enhanced security, improved maintainability, and simplified scaling, contributing to the overall success of your microservice ecosystem.

Let's start with Users App. The source code for this chapter is in the 13-cloud/ users folder. If you want to start from scratch with the Spring Initializr (https://start. spring.io), set the Group field to com.apress and the Artifact and Name fields to users. Then add JPA, PostgreSQL, Web, Validation, Actuator, Consul Configuration, and Consul Discovery as dependencies. Leave all other settings as their defaults. Then, generate and download the project, unzip it, and import it into your favorite IDE.

Let's start by opening the build.gradle file See Listing 13-1.

Listing 13-1. The build.gradle File

```
import org.jetbrains.kotlin.gradle.tasks.KotlinCompile
plugins {
    id 'java'
    id 'org.springframework.boot' version '3.2.3'
    id 'io.spring.dependency-management' version '1.1.4'
    id 'org.hibernate.orm' version '6.4.1.Final'
    id 'org.graalvm.buildtools.native' version '0.9.28'
    id 'org.jetbrains.kotlin.jvm' version '2.0.20-RC'
    id "org.jetbrains.kotlin.plugin.spring" version "2.0.20-RC"
    // <- simplifies spring proxying
```

```
}
group = 'com.apress'
version = '0.0.1-SNAPSHOT'

java {
    sourceCompatibility = '17'
}

configurations {
    compileOnly {
        extendsFrom annotationProcessor
    }
}

ext {
    set('springCloudVersion', "2023.0.0")
}

repositories {
    mavenCentral()
}

dependencyManagement {
    imports {
        mavenBom "org.springframework.cloud:spring-cloud-dependencies:$
        {springCloudVersion}"
    }
}

dependencies {
    implementation "org.jetbrains.kotlin:kotlin-stdlib-jdk8"
    implementation "org.jetbrains.kotlin:kotlin-reflect"

    implementation 'org.springframework.boot:spring-boot-starter-web'
    implementation 'org.springframework.boot:spring-boot-starter-
    validation'
    implementation 'org.springframework.boot:spring-boot-starter-data-jpa'
    implementation 'org.springframework.boot:spring-boot-starter-actuator'
```

```
    // Consul
    implementation 'org.springframework.cloud:spring-cloud-starter-consul-
    config'
    implementation 'org.springframework.cloud:spring-cloud-starter-consul-
    discovery'

    // Vault
    //implementation 'org.springframework.cloud:spring-cloud-vault-config-
    databases'
    //implementation 'org.springframework.cloud:spring-cloud-starter-vault-
    config'

    // Streaming
    //implementation 'org.springframework.boot:spring-boot-starter-amqp'
    //implementation 'org.springframework.cloud:spring-cloud-stream'
    //implementation 'org.springframework.cloud:spring-cloud-stream-
    binder-rabbit'
    //implementation 'org.springframework.integration:spring-integration-file'

    runtimeOnly 'org.postgresql:postgresql'

    annotationProcessor 'org.springframework.boot:spring-boot-configuration-
    processor'

    // Web
    implementation 'org.webjars:bootstrap:5.2.3'

    // Test
    testImplementation 'org.springframework.boot:spring-boot-starter-test'
    //testImplementation 'org.springframework.amqp:spring-rabbit-test'
    //testImplementation 'org.springframework.cloud:spring-cloud-stream-
    test-binder'
}

tasks.named('test') {
    useJUnitPlatform()
}

hibernate {
  enhancement {
```

```
        enableAssociationManagement = true
    }
}

tasks.named("bootBuildImage") {
    builder = "dashaun/builder:tiny"
    environment = ["BP_NATIVE_IMAGE" : "true"]
}

//     kotlin {
//         jvmToolchain(17)
//     }
tasks.withType(KotlinCompile).configureEach {
    kotlinOptions {
        freeCompilerArgs = ['-Xjsr305=strict']
        jvmTarget = '17'
    }
}
```

Listing 13-1 shows that we are using the Maven BOM (bill of materials), which allows us to get the spring-cloud-dependencies that we need. In this case, that's spring-cloud-starter-consul-config (for external configuration) and spring-cloud-starter-consul-discovery (for service discovery).

Next, create/open the UserProperties class. See Listing 13-2.

Listing 13-2. src/main/kotlin/com/apress/users/config/UserProperties.kt

```
package com.apress.users.config

import org.springframework.boot.context.properties.ConfigurationProperties

//@RefreshScope
@ConfigurationProperties(prefix = "user")
open class UserProperties {
    open var reportFormat: String? = null
    open var emailSubject: String? = null
    open var emailFrom: String? = null
    open var emailTemplate: String? = null
}
```

Listing 13-2 shows that we are marking the UserProperties class as @ ConfigurationProperties, meaning that the value will be bound at startup. These values are kept in an external storage, in this case, the Consul server. That's why we needed to create, for example, the config/users-service/user/reportFormat key and its value PDF.

Next, open/create the application.yaml file. See Listing 13-3.

Listing 13-3. src/main/resources/application.yaml

```
spring:
  application:
    name: users-service
  config:
    import: consul://
  datasource:
    url: jdbc:postgresql://localhost:5432/users_db?sslmode=disable
    username: ${db.username}
    password: ${db.password}
  jpa:
    generate-ddl: true
    show-sql: true
    hibernate:
      ddl-auto: update
info:
  developer:
    name: Felipe
    email: felipe@email.com
  api:
    version: 1.0
management:
  endpoints:
    web:
      exposure:
        include: health,info,event-config,shutdown,configprops,beans
  endpoint:
    configprops:
```

```
      show-values: always
    health:
      show-details: always
      status:
        order: events-down, fatal, down, out-of-service, unknown, up
    shutdown:
      enabled: true
  info:
    env:
      enabled: true
server:
  port: ${PORT:8080}
```

The `application.yaml` file includes the following:

- `spring.application.name`: This property is a *must* because the configuration is based on a naming convention, so the name must be set here. In this case, we set the name to `users-service`.

- `spring.config.import`: This property informs Spring Boot that part of the configuration is located in the Consul server, so the value is set to `consul://`.

- `spring.datasource.username` and `spring.datasource.password`: These properties refer to `${db.username}` and `${db.password}`, respectively. The values will be taken from the `config/users-service/db/username` key/value and `config/users-service/db/password` respectively.

- `management.endpoint.configprops.show-values`: By default, the `/configpros` actuator endpoint masks all the properties' values, but we are setting this key to `always` to show the properties because we are going to see a very cool feature for the configuration properties.

We've previously covered the other properties in Listing 13-3, so we don't revisit them here.

Running Users App with Spring Consul

To run Users App, we need to run the PostgreSQL database first. Execute the following command to start the PostgreSQL database:

```
docker run --name postgres --rm \
 -p 5432:5432 \
 --platform linux/amd64 \
 -e POSTGRES_PASSWORD=mysecretpassword \
 -e POSTGRES_USER=admin \
 -e POSTGRES_DB=users_db \
 -d postgres
```

After the DB is up and running, you can run your application. Set the PORT to 8091, either by using your IDE (every IDE has a way to set the environment variables) or by executing the following command:

```
PORT=8091 ./gradlew bootRun
```

Everything should work! If you look at the Services section of the Consul UI (http://localhost:8500/ui/dc1/services), you should see users-service listed (with "1 instance" below it). See Figure 13-4.

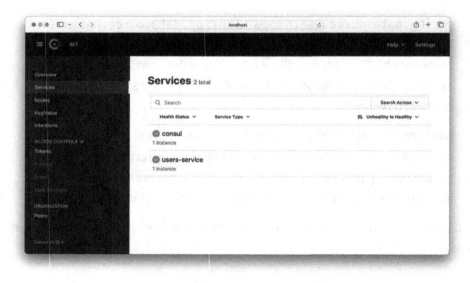

Figure 13-4. *Consul UI Services section (http://localhost:8500/ui/dc1/services)*

What happened? Because we added the `spring-cloud-starter-consul-discovery` dependency, Spring Boot and the Spring Cloud Consul auto-configuration automatically registered this service in the HashiCorp Consul, making this available to be discovered by other services. And because we added the `spring-cloud-starter-consul-config` dependency and set the `spring.config.import` key to `consul://`, it will get all the properties from the Consul Config storage based on the naming convention `config/users-service/*` for properties. When it sees the `db.username`, the value will be picked up from `consul://config/users-service/db/username` or when it sees the `user.reportFormat` (from the `UserProperties` class), it will get its value from `consul://config/users-service/user/reportFormat`. Very nice, right?

Going back to the browser, if you click `users-service`, you will see something like Figure 13-5.

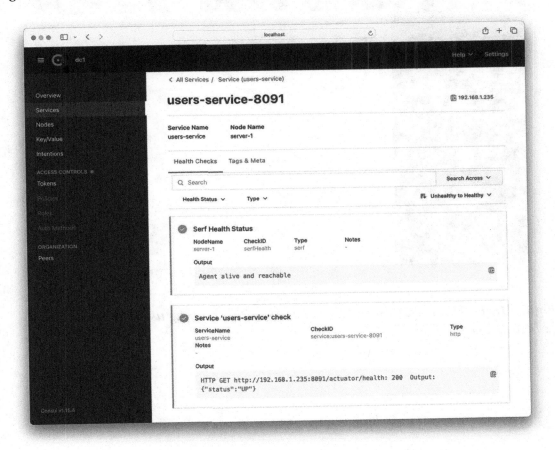

Figure 13-5. *Consul UI displaying users-service-8091*

Consul uses the `spring-boot-actuator` endpoint (`/actuator/health`) to determine if the service is alive.

What happens if you have multiple instances of Users App? Well, you can open another terminal and run another instance using the following command:

```
PORT=8092 ./gradlew bootRun
```

If you look at the Services section of the Consul UI again, you will see that it's been updated to appear as shown in Figure 13-6, with "2 instances" under `users-service`. Click `users-service` and you will see the two services listed, as shown in Figure 13-7.

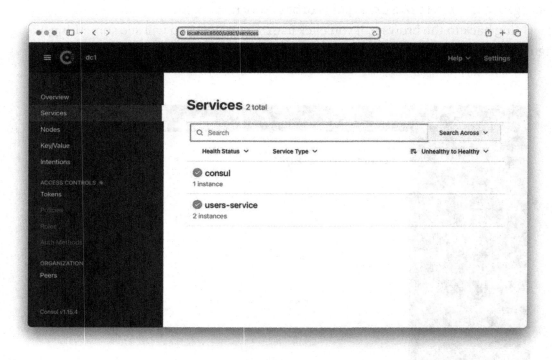

Figure 13-6. *Updated Consul UI Services section showing users-service (2 instances)*

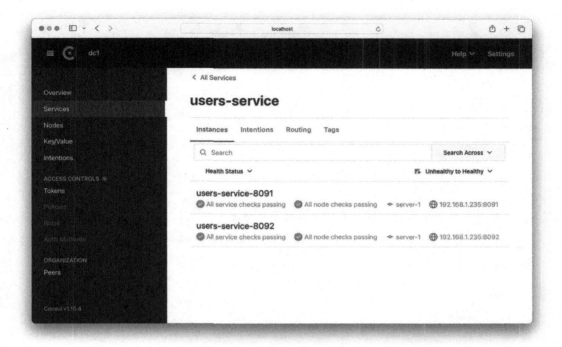

Figure 13-7. *Consul UI displaying users-service-8091 and users-service-8092*

Reviewing the UserProperties

Next, let's review the `UserProperties` class using the actuator. Point your browser to the `http://localhost:8091/actuator/configprops` endpoint. As shown in Figure 13-8, you should see the values we entered before (in Consul).

711

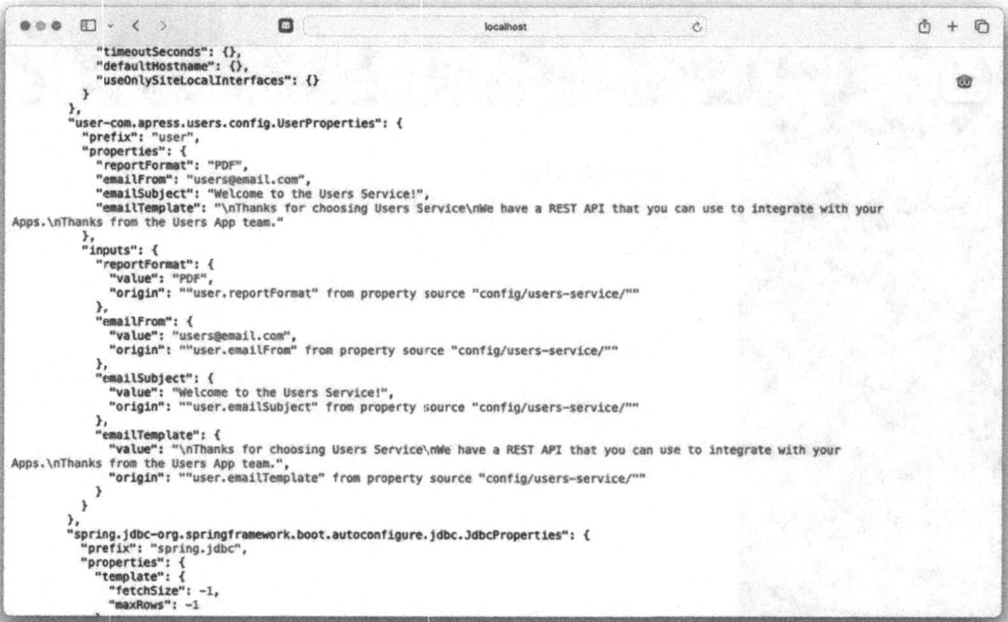

Figure 13-8. *http://localhost:8091/actuator/configprops*

If you need to change a property when the app is running, you will need to restart the app. But one of the nice features of using the combination of Spring Boot and Spring Cloud Consul is that Spring Boot provides the @RefreshScope annotation, which allows you to change the value of a property and Spring Boot will take care of re-creating the bean that has this marker and reflect the new value. For example, suppose you have something like the following:

```
@Configuration
class UserConfigurationExample {
    @Value("${message}")
    var message:String
    ...
}
```

This configuration will look for config/users-service/message, and it won't change even though you changed it in Consul. This is because it was set and used at the beginning of the app. If you need to change this behavior and use a new value set, then you need to use the @RefreshScope annotation:

```
@RefreshScope
@Configuration
class UserConfigurationExample {
   @Value("${message}")
   var message:String
   ...
}
```

Using a YAML Format Instead of a Key/Value Pair as a Configuration

If you review the application.yaml file again (see Listing 13-3), you might wonder whether you can format everything as YAML in Consul. The answer is *yes*, you can add a whole YAML blob instead of key/value pairs. To activate this feature, you need to set the property format to YAML in the application.yaml file:

```
spring:
  cloud:
    consul:
      config:
        format: YAML
```

Then you need to add a data key and set all the YAML. You need to add the config/users-service/data key and add the following as a value:

```
spring:
  datasource:
    url: jdbc:postgresql://localhost:5432/users_db?sslmode=disable
    username: admin
    password: mysecretpassword
  jpa:
    generate-ddl: true
    show-sql: true
    hibernate:
      ddl-auto: update
  info:
    developer:
```

713

```yaml
    name: Felipe
    email: felipe@email.com
  api:
    version: 1.0
management:
  endpoints:
    web:
     exposure:
        include: health,info,event-config,shutdown,configprops,beans
    endpoint:
    configprops:
      show-values: always
    health:
      show-details: always
      status:
        order: events-down, fatal, down, out-of-service, unknown, up
    shutdown:
      enabled: true
  info:
    env:
      enabled: true
user:
  reportFormat: PDF
  emailSubject: 'Welcome to the User Services'
  emailFrom: 'user@email.com'
  emailTemplate: 'Thanks for choosing Users Service'
```

Now you add the username and password database credentials to the YAML (config/users-service/data value) and the user.* properties. See Figure 13-9.

Figure 13-9. *Consul UI Key/Value section displaying config/users-service/ data key*

The `application.yaml` file will have the content in Listing 13-4.

Listing 13-4. src/main/resources/application.yaml

```
spring:
  application:
    name: users-service
  config:
    import: consul://
  cloud:
    config:
      format: YAML
server:
  port: ${PORT:8080}
```

As you can see, everything is externalized now. Of, you can also play with the Spring Profiles (e.g., test, dev, prod, etc.) and make this more configurable.

Using Spring Cloud Consul in My Retro App

This section explains how to add Spring Cloud Consul capabilities to My Retro App. The source code is in the 13-cloud/myretro folder. We are going to reuse the code from the Spring Boot Actuator chapter (Chapter 11) and make a few modifications. If you want to start from scratch with the Spring Initializr (https://start.spring.io), set the Group field to com.apress and the Artifact and Name fields to myretro. Then add JPA, H2, Web, Validation, Actuator, Consul Configuration, Consul Discovery, and OpenFeign as dependencies. Leave all other settings as their defaults. Finally, generate and download the project, unzip it, and import it into your favorite IDE.

Start by opening the build.gradle file. See Listing 13-5.

Listing 13-5. The build.gradle File

```
import org.jetbrains.kotlin.gradle.tasks.KotlinCompile
plugins {
    id 'java'
    id 'org.springframework.boot' version '3.2.3'
    id 'io.spring.dependency-management' version '1.1.4'
    id 'org.hibernate.orm' version '6.4.1.Final'
    id 'org.graalvm.buildtools.native' version '0.9.28'
```

```
    id 'org.jetbrains.kotlin.jvm' version '2.0.20-RC'
    id "org.jetbrains.kotlin.plugin.spring" version "2.0.20-RC"
    // <- simplifies spring proxying
}

group = 'com.apress'
version = '0.0.1-SNAPSHOT'
sourceCompatibility = '17'

configurations {
    compileOnly {
        extendsFrom annotationProcessor
    }
}

repositories {
    mavenCentral()
}

ext {
    set('springCloudVersion', "2023.0.0")
}

dependencies {
    implementation "org.jetbrains.kotlin:kotlin-stdlib-jdk8"
    implementation "org.jetbrains.kotlin:kotlin-reflect"

    implementation 'org.springframework.boot:spring-boot-starter-web'
    implementation 'org.springframework.boot:spring-boot-starter-
    validation'
    implementation 'org.springframework.boot:spring-boot-starter-data-jpa'
    implementation 'org.springframework.boot:spring-boot-starter-actuator'

    // Consul
    implementation 'org.springframework.cloud:spring-cloud-starter-
    consul-config'
    implementation 'org.springframework.cloud:spring-cloud-starter-consul-
    discovery'
```

```
    // OpenFeign
    implementation 'org.springframework.cloud:spring-cloud-starter-
    openfeign'

    // Kubernetes
    implementation 'org.springframework.cloud:spring-cloud-starter-
    kubernetes-client-all'

    runtimeOnly 'com.h2database:h2'
    runtimeOnly 'io.micrometer:micrometer-registry-prometheus'

    annotationProcessor 'org.springframework.boot:spring-boot-
    configuration-processor'

    testImplementation 'org.springframework.boot:spring-boot-starter-test'
}

dependencyManagement {
    imports {
        mavenBom "org.springframework.cloud:spring-cloud-dependencies:
        ${springCloudVersion}"
    }
}

tasks.named('test') {
    useJUnitPlatform()
}

hibernate {
  enhancement {
    enableAssociationManagement = true
  }
}

tasks.named("bootBuildImage") {
    builder = "dashaun/builder:tiny"
    environment = ["BP_NATIVE_IMAGE" : "true"]
}
```

```
//    kotlin {
//        jvmToolchain(17)
//    }
tasks.withType(KotlinCompile).configureEach {
    kotlinOptions {
        freeCompilerArgs = ['-Xjsr305=strict']
        jvmTarget = '17'
    }
}
```

Listing 13-5 shows that we are adding the `spring-cloud-start-consul` dependencies as well as the `spring-cloud-starter-openfeign` and `spring-cloud-starter-kubernetes-client-all` dependencies to `build.gradle`. We discuss the Kubernetes client in the last section of this chapter, which will clarify why you need to include it here.

If you remember, My Retro App has a way to communicate with Users App, and in Chapter 12, we used the `@HttpExchange` and `@GetExchange` annotations, which simplify the way to connect to other services' APIs. This time we are going to use a different approach.

Using OpenFeign in My Retro App

Spring Cloud OpenFeign is a library that simplifies consuming RESTful web services by declaratively defining client interfaces annotated with Spring MVC annotations. It automatically generates clients based on these interfaces, handling tasks like these:

- HTTP request mapping based on annotations like `@GetMapping` and `@PostMapping`

- Parameter decoding and encoding using Spring's `HttpMessageConverters`

- Feign interceptor integration for custom request/response processing

- Hystrix fault tolerance for resilient service calls

The following are some of the key features of Spring Cloud OpenFeign:

- *Declarative interface-based clients*: Write interfaces, not low-level HTTP code, for a cleaner and more concise approach.

- *Spring MVC annotations*: Leverage familiar Spring MVC annotations for intuitive syntax and integration.

- *Default encoder and decoder support*: Use Spring's default message converters for seamless data handling.

- *Support for Feign interceptors*: Integrate custom interceptors for additional processing and logging.

- *Hystrix integration*: Automatically enable Hystrix fault tolerance for resilient service calls.

- *Load balancing support*: Integrate with Spring Cloud Load Balancer for intelligent service discovery and routing.

- *Service discovery integration*: Work with various service discovery tools like Eureka and Consul.

- *OAuth2 Support*: Simplify secure communication with OAuth2-protected services.

- *Micrometer support*: Monitor and collect metrics from Feign clients using Micrometer.

- *Spring Data support*: Use Spring Data repositories directly with Feign clients for convenient data access.

- *Spring* `@RefreshScope` *support*: Dynamically update Feign client configurations while the application is running.

Some of the benefits of Spring Cloud OpenFeign are

- *Reduced development time*: Declarative approach and annotations simplify client development.

- *Improved maintainability*: Cleaner code with a clearer separation of concerns.

- *Increased reusability*: Interfaces promote code reuse and easier sharing.

- *Automatic Hystrix resilience*: Built-in fault tolerance for robust service communication.

- *Seamless Spring integration*: Leverage familiar Spring concepts and tools.

Spring Cloud OpenFeign helps developers build resilient, maintainable, and scalable RESTful clients for microservices architectures. If you want to know more about it, go to https://spring.io/projects/spring-cloud-openfeign.

We'll use Consul for My Retro App as well, and it needs a way to connect to Users App. For that purpose, we take advantage of the service discovery and load balancing features that OpenFeign and Consul provide. Keep in mind that there are two instances of the Users Service App up and running; My Retro App will connect to both of them.

Next, open/create the UserClient interface. See Listing 13-6.

Listing 13-6. src/main/kotlin/com/apress/myretro/client/UserClient.kt

```kotlin
package com.apress.myretro.client

import com.apress.myretro.client.model.User
import org.springframework.cloud.openfeign.FeignClient
import org.springframework.http.ResponseEntity
import org.springframework.web.bind.annotation.GetMapping
import org.springframework.web.bind.annotation.PathVariable

@FeignClient(name = "users-service")
interface UserClient {
    @get:GetMapping("/users")
    var allUsers: ResponseEntity<Iterable<User?>?>?

    @GetMapping("/users/{email}")
    fun getById(@PathVariable email: String?): ResponseEntity<User?>?
}
```

Let's review the annotations:

- @FeignClient: This annotation passes the name of the service, in this case users-service, the service registered in Consul.

- @GetMapping: You know this annotation, and as you can see, we are defining the same as in the UsersController. In this case, one method to get all users and the other method to find users by email.

Next, open/create the RetroBoardConfig class. See Listing 13-7.

Listing 13-7. src/main/kotlin/com/apress/myretro/config/RetroBoardConfig.kt

```kotlin
package com.apress.myretro.config

import com.apress.myretro.board.Card
import com.apress.myretro.board.CardType
import com.apress.myretro.board.RetroBoard
import com.apress.myretro.service.RetroBoardAndCardService
import org.springframework.boot.CommandLineRunner
import org.springframework.cloud.openfeign.EnableFeignClients
import org.springframework.context.annotation.Bean
import org.springframework.context.annotation.Configuration
import java.util.*

@EnableFeignClients(basePackages = ["com.apress.myretro.client"])
@Configuration
class RetroBoardConfig {
    @Bean
    fun init(service: RetroBoardAndCardService): CommandLineRunner {
        return CommandLineRunner { _: Array<String> ->
            val retroBoard = RetroBoard().apply {
                name = "Spring Boot 3 Retro"
                cards = listOf(
                    Card().apply {
                        comment = "Nice to meet everybody"
                        cardType = CardType.HAPPY
                    },
                    Card().apply {
                        comment = "When are we going to travel?"
                        cardType = CardType.MEH
                    },
                    Card().apply {
                        comment = "When are we going to travel?"
                        cardType = CardType.SAD
                    }
```

```
            )
        }
        service.saveOrUpdateRetroBoard(retroBoard)
    }
}
}
```

Listing 13-7 shows that the RetroBoardConfig class has a new annotation:
@EnableFeignClients(basePackages = "com.apress.myretro.client"). This
provides a way to tell the auto-configuration where all the clients are, and even though
there is only one client, this is how you set it, or you can use the clients parameter and
add the actual UserClient::class.java class as the value.

Next, we need to configure the UserClient interface to enable My Retro App to
communicate with Users App. Open/create the RetroBoardAndCardService class. See
Listing 13-8.

Listing 13-8. src/main/kotlin/com/apress/myretro/service/
RetroBoardAndCardService.kt

```
package com.apress.myretro.service

import com.apress.myretro.board.RetroBoard
import com.apress.myretro.client.UserClient
import com.apress.myretro.client.model.User
import com.apress.myretro.events.RetroBoardEvent
import com.apress.myretro.events.RetroBoardEventAction
import com.apress.myretro.exceptions.RetroBoardNotFoundException
import com.apress.myretro.persistence.RetroBoardRepository
import io.micrometer.core.instrument.Counter
import org.springframework.beans.factory.annotation.Autowired
import org.springframework.context.ApplicationEventPublisher
import org.springframework.stereotype.Service
import java.time.LocalDateTime
import java.util.*

@Service
class RetroBoardAndCardService {
    @Autowired
```

```kotlin
    private lateinit var retroBoardRepository: RetroBoardRepository
    @Autowired
    private lateinit var eventPublisher: ApplicationEventPublisher
    @Autowired
    private lateinit var retroBoardCounter: Counter
    @Autowired
    private lateinit var userClient: UserClient

    // Uncomment this to see the effect of the @Observed annotation
    // (Custom Observation))
    //@Observed(name = "retro-boards",contextualName = "allRetroBoards")
    fun allRetroBoards():List<RetroBoard> {
        return retroBoardRepository.findAll()
    }

    // Uncomment this to see the effect of the @Observed annotation
    // (Custom Observation))
    //@Observed(name = "retro-board-id",contextualName =
    "findRetroBoardById")
    fun findRetroBoardById(uuid: UUID): RetroBoard {
        return retroBoardRepository.findById(uuid)
            .orElseThrow{ RetroBoardNotFoundException() }
    }

    fun saveOrUpdateRetroBoard(retroBoard: RetroBoard): RetroBoard {
        val retroBoardResult: RetroBoard =
            retroBoardRepository.save<RetroBoard>(retroBoard)
        eventPublisher.publishEvent(
            RetroBoardEvent(
                retroBoardResult.retroBoardId,
                RetroBoardEventAction.CHANGED,
                LocalDateTime.now()
            )
        )
        retroBoardCounter.increment()
        return retroBoardResult
    }
}
```

```
fun deleteRetroBoardById(uuid: UUID) {
    retroBoardRepository.deleteById(uuid)
    eventPublisher.publishEvent(RetroBoardEvent(uuid,
        RetroBoardEventAction.DELETED, LocalDateTime.now()))
}

//@Observed(name = "users-service",contextualName = "getAllUsers")
fun allUsers() {
    userClient.allUsers!!.body!!.forEach{ x: User? -> println(x) }
}
}
```

The important piece in Listing 13-8 is that we are injecting the UserClient interface and using it in the allUsers method (we are just printing the values).

Next, open/create the RetroBoardController class. This is the accessor that exposes the /retros/users endpoint with the following code (no need to show everything):

```
@get:GetMapping("/users")
val allUsers: ResponseEntity<*>
    // External Call
    get() {
        retroBoardAndCardService.allUsers()
        return ResponseEntity.ok(
            Map.of(
                "status",
                200,
                "message",
                "Users retrieved. Should be in the console",
                "time",
                LocalDateTime.now()
            )
        )
    }
```

This code will call the service and print out the users in the console.

Next, open the application.properties file. See Listing 13-9.

Listing 13-9. src/main/resources/application.properties

```
## DataSource
spring.h2.console.enabled=true
spring.datasource.generate-unique-name=false
spring.datasource.name=test-db
spring.jpa.show-sql=true
## Server
server.port=${PORT:8080}
## Consul
spring.config.import=consul://
## Application
spring.application.name=my-retro-app
logging.pattern.correlation=[${spring.application.name:},%X{traceId:-
},%X{spanId:-}]
## Actuator Info
info.developer.name=Felipe
info.developer.email=felipe@email.com
info.api.version=1.0
management.endpoint.env.enabled=true
## Actuator
management.endpoints.web.exposure.include=health,info,metrics,prometheus
## Actuator Observations
management.observations.key-values.application=${spring.application.name}
## Actuator Metrics
management.metrics.distribution.percentiles-histogram.http.server.
requests=true
## Actuator Tracing
management.tracing.sampling.probability=1.0
## Actuator Prometheus
management.prometheus.metrics.export.enabled=true
management.metrics.use-global-registry=true
```

The important part in the application.properties file is to specify the name of the app, spring.application.name=my-retro-app, and the spring.config. import=consul:// that will use Consul as an external configuration (even though we haven't specified anything).

Running My Retro App

It's now time to run My Retro App. Make sure the Consul server and client are still up and running as well as the two instances of the Users Service App.

Set the PORT to 8081 (in case you need more than one instance). You can run it using your IDE (don't forget to set the PORT environment variable) or you can use this command line:

```
PORT=8081 ./gradlew bootRun
```

Once it is up and running, you can point the Consul UI to http://localhost:8500/ui/dc1/services. See Figure 13-10.

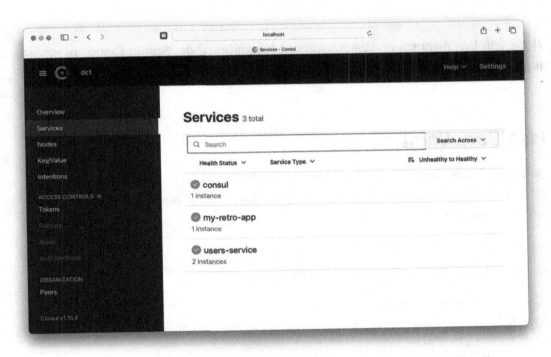

Figure 13-10. *Consul UI Services section showing my-retro-app and users-service*

Now my-retro-app is listed. If you call the /retros/users endpoint, you will see that the users have been printed out.

How does OpenFeign know where to locate users-service? If there are two instances of Users App, which one will be selected? This is the beauty of Spring Boot, Spring Cloud Consul, and Spring Cloud OpenFeign—the only thing you need to declare is the name of the service (`users-service`) that you want to consume, and Consul will do the service discovery and tell OpenFeign where to go. In this case, because there are two instances, OpenFeign will use a load balancer and round robin behind the scenes to reach these instances. This is so amazing! It requires minimal code—just let Spring Boot do the job!

HashiCorp Vault and Spring Cloud Vault

Next, let's look at HashiCorp Vault (`https://www.vaultproject.io/`) and Spring Cloud Vault and see how they can help us with this solution. First we'll review what HashiCorp Vault is, and then we'll use it in our two projects.

Note   In this discussion, "Vault" without "HashiCorp" or "Spring Cloud" preceding it always refers to HashiCorp Vault.

HashiCorp Vault

HashiCorp Vault is an identity-based secrets and encryption management system. It serves as a central repository for securely storing, accessing, and controlling access to sensitive data such as:

- API keys and passwords

- Certificates and encryption keys

- Database credentials

- Infrastructure credentials

Vault addresses various security challenges across diverse environments, including:

- *Microservices*: Securely store and manage service credentials, API keys, and database connections.

- *Cloud deployments*: Rotate and manage cloud platform credentials centrally across different providers.

- *Data encryption*: Encrypt data at rest and in transit using managed encryption keys.

- *Automated infrastructure*: Securely automate infrastructure provisioning and configuration with dynamic secrets.

- *Compliance and auditing*: Maintain auditable access logs and enforce granular access control for secrets.

Vault offers a rich set of features for secure secrets management:

- *Secure storage*: Utilizes encryption at rest and in transit to protect sensitive data.

- *Identity-based access control*: Enforces granular access control based on user identities and roles.

- *Dynamic secrets*: Generates and rotates secrets automatically based on predefined policies.

- *Secret leasing*: Issues temporary access to secrets with defined expiration times.

- *Audit logging*: Logs all access attempts and data revisions for auditing and compliance.

- *Integration with diverse tools*: Connects with popular DevOps and infrastructure platforms.

- *Multi-data center deployments*: Scales and replicates across multiple data centers for high availability.

Some of Vault's benefits are the following:

- *Enhanced security*: Provides centralized control and strong access control to mitigate security risks.

- *Operational efficiency*: Streamlines secrets management and automates workflows.

- *Improved compliance*: Provides simplified audit logging and access control enforcement.

- *Increased scalability*: Scales seamlessly to accommodate growing needs.

> **Caution**   Before continuing, *remove* the db.username and db.password
> properties from Consul.

Using HashiCorp Vault with Credentials Creation for PostgreSQL

Let's start with HashiCorp Vault. The idea is to have a special user role that can be created and rotate their credentials often (depending on our configuration), so we can make sure this service is secure and the credentials are not shared. Practically, Vault will rotate the credentials and Spring Cloud Vault will get the new credentials and use them accordingly. We are still using Consul, and we can configure Vault to use its storage and take advantage of the high availability that Consul provides.

Start the Vault server with the following command:

```
docker run --cap-add=IPC_LOCK -d --rm --name vault -p 8200:8200 \
-e 'VAULT_LOCAL_CONFIG={"backend": {"consul": {"address": "host.docker.
internal:8500","path":"vault/"}}}' \
-e 'VAULT_DEV_ROOT_TOKEN_ID=my-root-id' \
vault:1.13.3
```

This command starts Vault with Consul as storage. We also define a TOKEN_ID with the value my-root-id. This is just development, but normally you need to generate this key (TOKEN_ID) and its value and use them as an authentication mechanism. If you look at the Consul UI, you should see Vault listed as a service. See Figure 13-11.

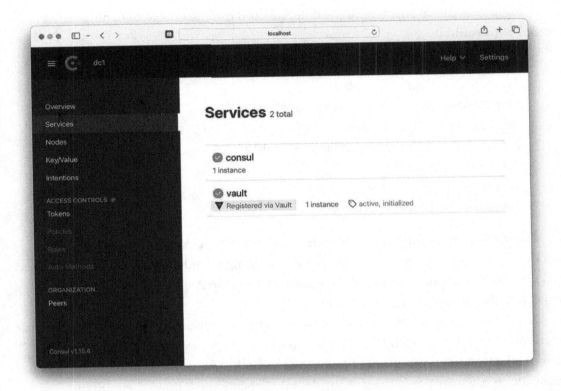

Figure 13-11. *Consul UI Service section showing Vault (http://localhost:8500/ui/ dc1/services)*

If you look at the Key/Value section in Consul, you should see the Vault key configurations.

Next, we need to configure Vault to use a database secret and rotate the credentials based on a default policy. To do this, you can use cURL to point to its REST API or use the vault CLI tool. You can install the CLI tool from `https://developer.hashicorp.com/vault/docs/install`. Then you can use the following command to log in to Vault:

```
vault login -address="http://127.0.0.1:8200"
```

The token will be `my-root-id`. This login is required to execute the next commands. Next, enable the Database Secrets engine with this:

```
vault secrets enable -address="http://127.0.0.1:8200" database
```

Next, create the connection to the database and use the PostgreSQL plugin that comes with Vault:

```
vault write -address="http://127.0.0.1:8200" \
    database/config/users_db \
    plugin_name=postgresql-database-plugin \
    connection_url="postgresql://{{username}}:{{password}}@host.docker.
    internal:5432/users_db?sslmode=disable" \
    allowed_roles="*" \
    username="admin" \
    password="mysecretpassword"
```

One of the main things to notice is that `connection_url` is pointing to the `host. docker.internal`, and this is because we are reaching outside the container, so we need to know the Docker host IP. It can't be localhost, because PostgreSQL has its IP but is exporting the access through port 5432.

Next, we need to create a role that will do all the operations in our database, and its credentials will be rotated by Vault based on its default policy (in this case, just a few minutes). Of course, you can change these defaults, but for now just to have a proof of concept here, we are going to leave the default. Execute the following command:

```
vault write -address="http://127.0.0.1:8200" \
    database/roles/users-role db_name=users_db \
    creation_statements="CREATE ROLE \"{{name}}\" WITH LOGIN PASSWORD
    '{{password}}' VALID UNTIL '{{expiration}}'; GRANT ALL PRIVILEGES ON
    DATABASE users_db TO \"{{name}}\"; GRANT USAGE ON SCHEMA public TO
    \"{{name}}\"; GRANT ALL PRIVILEGES ON ALL TABLES IN SCHEMA public TO
    \"{{name}}\"; ALTER DATABASE users_db OWNER TO \"{{name}}\";" \
    default_ttl="30s" \
    max_ttl="1m"
```

The preceding command basically says create a role (`users-role`) and enables it to operate on the `users_db`. We are using SQL statements to grant some privileges to this user role that will be created when needed.

Vault will rotate its credentials, meaning that the user will no longer be useful if you use its previous credentials. If you want to know about the users and their credentials, you can execute the following command:

```
vault read -address="http://127.0.0.1:8200" \
database/creds/users-role
Key                     Value
---                     -----
lease_id                database/creds/users-role/t8vRNfXvONqy15u41EQqqX3Q
lease_duration          30s
lease_renewable         true
password                ci8HZxkgJJn-KIvMRWoe
username                v-token-users-ro-2wtaGdop4qbR63NMsI1L-1707512396
```

In the output, a username and a password were created. You are all set.

You can access the Vault UI by going to http://localhost:8200. See Figure 13-12.

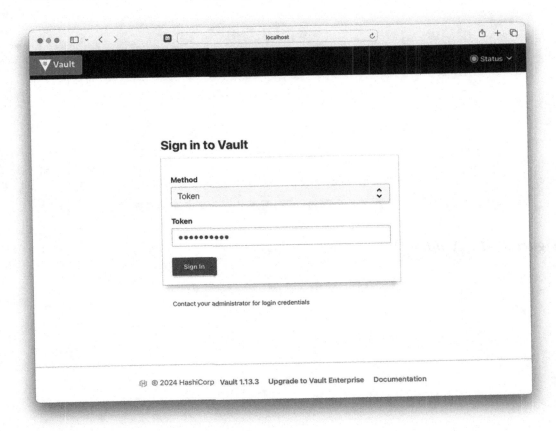

Figure 13-12. *Vault UI login page (http://localhost:8200 - token/my-root-id)*

The token is my-root-id. You can browse around and see the Secrets Engines (see Figure 13-13) and the Database Engine (see Figure 13-14).

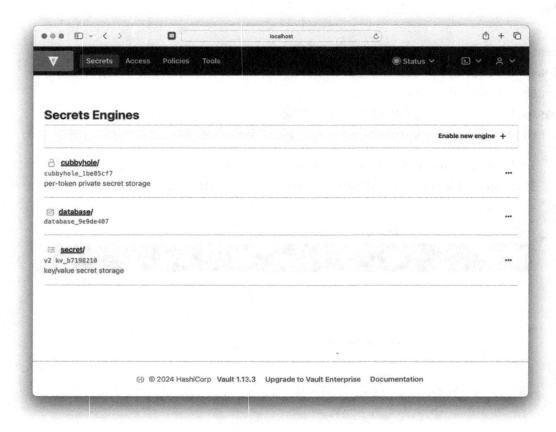

Figure 13-13. *Vault UI Secret Engines page*

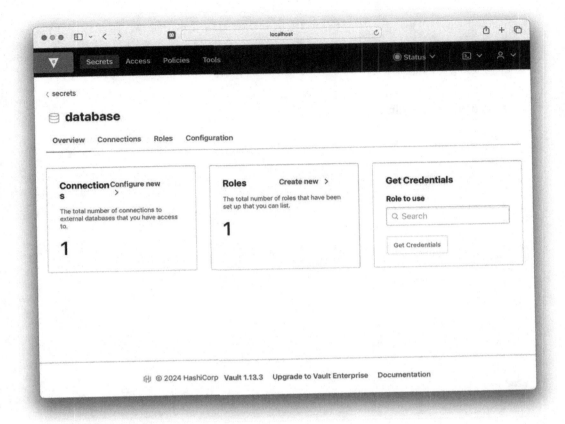

Figure 13-14. *Vault UI Database Engine page*

On the Secrets Engines page, click the Enable New Engine link to see what other Secrets Engines are available (see Figure 13-15). In this case, we use the standard database.

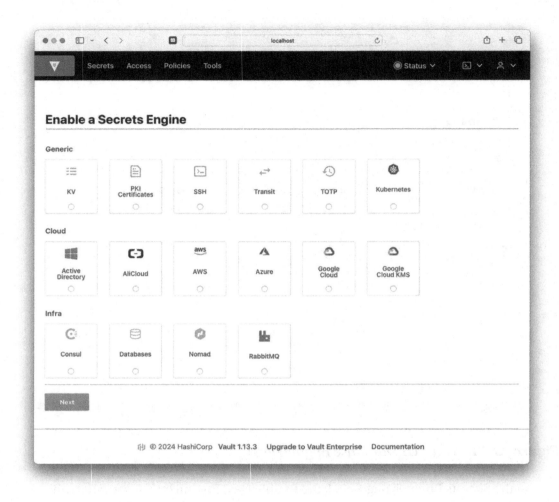

Figure 13-15. *Vault UI showing a list of available Secrets Engines*
(http://localhost:8200/ui/vault/settings/mount-secret-backend)

Spring Cloud Vault

Now that we have Vault up and running, let's review what Spring Cloud Vault is and how it can help with applications.

Spring Cloud Vault is a project that helps you integrate your Spring applications with HashiCorp Vault to manage secrets securely. Essentially, Spring Cloud Vault provides client-side support for externalized configuration using Vault as the central source. Let's dive into its benefits and features.

Spring Cloud Vault offers the following benefits (among others):

- *Improved security*: By storing sensitive information like passwords, API keys, and other credentials in Vault instead of in your application code, you significantly reduce the risk of exposure and potential breaches.

- *Centralized management*: Vault offers a single platform to manage secrets across all your applications and environments, simplifying operations and ensuring consistency.

- *Dynamic provisioning*: Spring Cloud Vault can dynamically generate credentials for various services like databases, cloud platforms, and more, ensuring they are always fresh and secure.

- *Reduced code complexity*: You don't need to embed secrets directly in your code, eliminating the need for hardcoding and improving code maintainability.

- *Enhanced configurability*: Easily manage configuration changes and rollbacks without impacting your application deployments.

Here are some of its features:

- *Secret retrieval*: Retrieves secrets from Vault and automatically refreshes them based on configured policies.

- *Environment initialization*: Initializes the Spring environment with remote property sources populated from Vault.

- *Secure communication*: Supports secured communication with Vault using SSL and various authentication mechanisms.

- *Credential generation*: Generates dynamic credentials for different services like MySQL, PostgreSQL, AWS, and others.

- *Multiple authentication methods*: Supports tokens, AppId, AppRole, Client Certificate, Cubbyhole, AWS EC2 & IAM, and Kubernetes authentication for secure access.

- *Cloud Foundry integration*: Enables integration with HashiCorp's Vault service broker through Spring Cloud Vault Connector.

Implementing Credential Generation on the Users Service App Using HashiCorp Vault

This section uses Users App with some modifications. Remember that you have access to the source code in the `13-cloud/users` folder so you can follow along.

The first thing we need to do is add the necessary dependencies to the `build.gradle` file. In this case, we add the `spring-cloud-vault-config-databases` and `spring-cloud-starter-vault-config` dependencies, as shown in Listing 13-10.

Listing 13-10. The build.gradle File

```
...

    // Vault
    implementation 'org.springframework.cloud:spring-cloud-vault-config-
    databases'
    implementation 'org.springframework.cloud:spring-cloud-starter-
vault-config'
...
```

Next, let's modify the `application.yaml` file. Add/replace the contents, as shown in Listing 13-11.

Listing 13-11. src/main/resources/application.yaml

```
spring:
  application:
    name: users-service
  config:
    import: consul://,vault://
  cloud:
    vault:
      authentication: TOKEN
      token: ${VAULT_TOKEN}  # my-root-id
      scheme: http
      database:
        enabled: true
        role: users-role
```

```yaml
    config:
      lifecycle:
        enabled: true
        min-renewal: 10s
        expiry-threshold: 1m
      fail-fast: true
  datasource:
    url: jdbc:postgresql://localhost:5432/users_db?sslmode=disable
  jpa:
    generate-ddl: true
    show-sql: true
    hibernate:
      ddl-auto: update
info:
  developer:
    name: Felipe
    email: felipe@email.com
  api:
    version: 1.0
management:
  endpoints:
    web:
     exposure:
        include: health,info,event-config,shutdown,configprops,beans
    endpoint:
      configprops:
        show-values: always
      health:
        show-details: always
        status:
          order: events-down, fatal, down, out-of-service, unknown, up
      shutdown:
        enabled: true
    info:
      env:
```

```
      enabled: true
logging:
  level:
     org.springframework.vault: ERROR
server:
  port: ${PORT:8080}
```

Let's review what is new and what changed in the `application.yaml` file:

- `spring.config.import`: Because we are using Vault, we need to get the credentials (set in the `spring.datasource.username` and `spring.datasource.password` properties) from `vault://` as well, and we are still using Consul for the other properties, so we can declare both, such as `consul://,vault://`.

- `spring.cloud.vault.*`: This section is for Vault. First, we need to tell Vault how we are going to authenticate, which in this case is using TOKEN and the token value that points to a `${VAULT_TOKEN}` environment variable that has the value `my-root-id`. Then, we have the `database.enabled` and `database.role` properties, which use the `users-role` we previously created using the command line. Some extra properties are also considered by default.

- `spring.datasource.url`: This URL only points to the `users_db` database, and if you look closely, there is no *username* or *password*, because Vault will generate the credentials and grant permissions to the user, and Spring Cloud Vault will gather these credentials and add them to the `spring.datasource.username` and `spring.datasource.password` properties automatically.

The other properties remain the same. And that's it. It was more configuration than code, right?

Running Users App with Vault

Before you run Users App, make sure to set the VAULT_TOKEN=`my-root-id` environment variable in your IDE (if you are running it from there) or by executing the following command:

```
PORT=8091 VAULT_TOKEN=my-root-id ./gradlew bootRun
```

Everything should work now! The credentials for the database were created by Vault and then Spring Cloud Vault set them in the applications. But wait! What happens if you execute a `curl` command or point your browser to `http://localhost:8091/users`?

After a few minutes, it will fail with an error like this:

```
org.postgresql.util.PSQLException: ERROR: permission denied for
table people
```

Do you know why? Vault has the credential rotation feature, so it has already changed it after a minute or two. This is based on a policy that you can change in Vault. How can we fix this issue?

Fixing Credential Rotation by Adding a Listener

One of the cool features of Vault and Spring Cloud Vault is that there are listeners that can send events about any change, and in this case, we can add one when a credential rotation happens. Spring Cloud Vault provides the `SecretLeaseContainer` class, which will help detect when Vault renews its lease/rotation.

Open/create the `UserConfiguration` class. See Listing 13-12.

Listing 13-12. src/main/kotlin/com/apress/users/config/UserConfiguration.kt

```
package com.apress.users.config

import com.apress.users.model.User
import com.apress.users.model.UserRole
import com.apress.users.service.UserService
import com.zaxxer.hikari.HikariDataSource
import jakarta.annotation.PostConstruct
import org.slf4j.LoggerFactory
import org.springframework.beans.factory.annotation.Autowired
import org.springframework.beans.factory.annotation.Value
import org.springframework.boot.CommandLineRunner
import org.springframework.boot.context.properties.
EnableConfigurationProperties
import org.springframework.context.annotation.Bean
import org.springframework.context.annotation.Configuration
import org.springframework.vault.core.lease.SecretLeaseContainer
```

```kotlin
import org.springframework.vault.core.lease.domain.RequestedSecret
import org.springframework.vault.core.lease.event.SecretLeaseCreatedEvent
import org.springframework.vault.core.lease.event.SecretLeaseExpiredEvent

// With Consul (Part 1)
@Configuration
@EnableConfigurationProperties(UserProperties::class)
class UserConfiguration {
    @Bean
    fun init(userService: UserService): CommandLineRunner {
        return CommandLineRunner { args: Array<String?>? ->
            userService.saveUpdateUser(
                User(
                    "ximena@email.com",
                    "Ximena",
                    "https://www.gravatar.com/avatar/23bb62a7d0ca63c9a80490
                    8e57bf6bd4?d=wavatar",
                    "aw2sOmeR!",
                    listOf(
                        UserRole.USER
                    ),
                    true
                )
            )
            userService.saveUpdateUser(
                User(
                    "norma@email.com",
                    "Norma",
                    "https://www.gravatar.com/avatar/f07f7e553264c9710105ed
                    ebe6c465e7?d=wavatar",
                    "aw2sOmeR!",
                    listOf(
                        UserRole.USER, UserRole.ADMIN
                    ),
                    false
                )
```

```kotlin
        )
    }
}

@Value("\${spring.cloud.vault.database.role}")
lateinit var databaseRoleName:String

@Autowired
lateinit var secretLeaseContainer:SecretLeaseContainer

@Autowired
lateinit var  hikariDataSource: HikariDataSource

@PostConstruct
fun postConstruct() {
    val vaultCredentialsPath = String.format("database/creds/%s",
    databaseRoleName)
    secretLeaseContainer.addLeaseListener{ event ->
        LOG.info("[SecretLeaseContainer]> Received event: {}", event);
        if (vaultCredentialsPath == event.source.path) {
            if (event is SecretLeaseExpiredEvent &&
                    event.getSource().mode == RequestedSecret.Mode.
                    RENEW) {
                LOG.info("[SecretLeaseContainer]> "+
                        "Let's replace the RENEWED lease by a
                        ROTATE one.")
                secretLeaseContainer.requestRotatingSecret(vaultCreden
                tialsPath)
            } else if (event is SecretLeaseCreatedEvent &&
                    event.getSource().mode == RequestedSecret.Mode.
                    ROTATE) {
                val username = event.secrets["username"].toString()
                val password = event.secrets["password"].toString()
                updateHikariDataSource(username, password)
            }
        }
    }
}
```

```
    private fun updateHikariDataSource(username: String, password:
    String) {
        LOG.info("[SecretLeaseContainer]> "+
                "Soft evict the current database connections");
        hikariDataSource.hikariPoolMXBean?.softEvictConnections()
        LOG.info("[SecretLeaseContainer]> "+
                "Update database credentials with the new ones.");
        val hikariConfigMXBean = hikariDataSource.hikariConfigMXBean
        hikariConfigMXBean.setUsername(username)
        hikariConfigMXBean.setPassword(password)
    }

    companion object {
        private val LOG = LoggerFactory.getLogger(UserConfiguration::c
        lass.java)
    }
}
```

The UserConfiguration class will help identify the renewed credentials and rotate them. Let's review it:

- @Value("\${spring.cloud.vault.database.role}"): This is used when we are getting the vault://database/creds/<role>; in this case, the value is the users-role defined in the application.yaml file and its content that we created with the vault CLI.

- SecretLeaseContainer: This class is an event-based container that requests secrets from Vault and renews the lease that is associated with the secret. We are adding a lease listener so that we get a notification from Vault every time there is a new/renewed lease. We need to ask for SecretLeaseExpiredEvent and the secret Mode (RENEW or ROTATE). If it's RENEW, we need to request the rotating secret, and if it's ROTATE, we need to get the new username and password and update DataSource.

- HikariDataSource/HikariPoolMXBean: By default, Spring Boot uses the HikariDataSource as DataSource, so we need to use HikariPoolMXBean to update the username and password.

744

If you run Users App again and wait for a minute or two, you will see the logs about receiving the `SecretLeaseContainer` event, and then the logic to renew the rotated credentials by updating it using the `DataSource` (`HikariDataSource`). This is so cool! You now know how to rotate credentials.

If you want to know more about the policies you can apply to Vault, look here: `https://developer.hashicorp.com/vault/docs/concepts/policies`.

It's time to finish the cloud architecture (shown previously in Figure 13-1) by adding an API gateway.

Using Spring Cloud Gateway

Spring Cloud Gateway is an API gateway built on top of the Spring ecosystem, and its purpose is to simplify API routing and add valuable features to your microservices architecture. We can define it as follows:

- A Java-based API gateway built on Spring Framework, Spring Boot, and Project Reactor

- Acts as a single entry point for your microservices, routing requests to the appropriate service based on various criteria

- Provides "cross-cutting concerns" like security, monitoring, and resiliency at the gateway level

Some of Spring Cloud Gateway's key features are

- *Routing*: Defines routes based on URL path, headers, methods, and more.

- *Predicates*: Controls which requests match specific routes using built-in or custom predicates.

- *Filters*: Adds preprocessing and post-processing logic to requests and responses.

- *Security*: Integrates with Spring Security for authentication and authorization.

- *Monitoring*: Tracks metrics and provides health checks for the gateway and downstream services.

- *Resiliency*: Integrates with *Spring Cloud Circuit Breaker* for fault tolerance and fallback mechanisms.

- *Discovery*: Integrates with Spring Cloud `DiscoveryClient` for automatic service discovery of your microservices.

- *Other features*: Includes rate limiting, path rewriting, Hystrix integration, and much more.

Some of the Spring Cloud Gateway use cases are

- *Single entry point*: Simplifies access to your microservices by providing a unified API endpoint.

- *Security*: Enforces centralized security for all API access.

- *Monitoring*: Provides insights into API traffic and health of your microservices.

- *Resiliency*: Protects against service failures and ensures high availability.

- *Load balancing*: Distributes traffic among multiple instances of your microservices.

- *API management*: Enables you to control access, rate limit requests, and collect usage data.

To summarize, Spring Cloud Gateway is a powerful tool for managing and enhancing your microservices architecture. It offers flexible routing, robust security, and valuable monitoring capabilities to streamline your API interactions.

Creating a My Retro Gateway

You can find this section's code in the `13-cloud/myretro-gateway` folder. If you want to start from scratch with Spring Initializr (`https://start.spring.io`), set the Group field to `com.apress` and the Artifact and Name fields to `myretro-gateway`. Add Actuator, Consul Configuration, Consul Discovery, Reactive Gateway, and Resilience4J Circuit Breaker as dependencies. Leave all other settings as their defaults. Then, generate and download the project, unzip it, and import it into your favorite IDE.

Let's review the `build.gradle` file. See Listing 13-13.

Listing 13-13. The build.gradle File

```
import org.jetbrains.kotlin.gradle.tasks.KotlinCompile
plugins {
    id 'java'
    id 'org.springframework.boot' version '3.2.3'
    id 'io.spring.dependency-management' version '1.1.4'
    id 'org.graalvm.buildtools.native' version '0.9.28'
    id 'org.jetbrains.kotlin.jvm' version '2.0.20-RC'
    id "org.jetbrains.kotlin.plugin.spring" version "2.0.20-RC"
    // <- simplifies spring proxying
}

group = 'com.apress'
version = '0.0.1-SNAPSHOT'

java {
    sourceCompatibility = '17'
}

repositories {
    mavenCentral()
}

ext {
    set('springCloudVersion', "2023.0.0")
}

dependencies {
    implementation "org.jetbrains.kotlin:kotlin-stdlib-jdk8"
    implementation "org.jetbrains.kotlin:kotlin-reflect"

    // Actuator
    implementation 'org.springframework.boot:spring-boot-starter-actuator'

    // Gateway
    implementation 'org.springframework.cloud:spring-cloud-starter-gateway'
    implementation 'org.springframework.cloud:'+
```

```
                         'spring-cloud-starter-circuitbreaker-reactor-
                         resilience4j'

    // Consul
    implementation 'org.springframework.cloud:spring-cloud-starter-
    consul-config'
    implementation 'org.springframework.cloud:spring-cloud-starter-consul-
    discovery'

    // Kubernetes
    implementation 'org.springframework.cloud:'+
                    'spring-cloud-starter-kubernetes-fabric8-all'

    testImplementation 'org.springframework.boot:spring-boot-starter-test'
    testImplementation 'io.projectreactor:reactor-test'
}

dependencyManagement {
    imports {
        mavenBom "org.springframework.cloud:"+
                    "spring-cloud-dependencies:${springCloudVersion}"
    }
}

tasks.named('test') {
    useJUnitPlatform()
}

tasks.named("bootBuildImage") {
    builder = "dashaun/builder:tiny"
    environment = ["BP_NATIVE_IMAGE" : "true"]
}

//    kotlin {
//        jvmToolchain(17)
//    }
tasks.withType(KotlinCompile).configureEach {
    kotlinOptions {
        freeCompilerArgs = ['-Xjsr305=strict']
```

```
    jvmTarget = '17'
  }
}
```

Listing 13-13 shows that we need to include the `spring-cloud-starter-gateway`, `spring-cloud-starter-circuitbreaker-reactor-resilience4j` (discussed a bit later in the chapter), and `spring-cloud-starter-kubernetes-fabric8-all` dependencies (which becomes relevant in the final section, "Using a Cloud Platform: Kubernetes"). We also added the Consul dependencies so that it gets registered into the Consul server automatically. One of the cool features of Spring Cloud Gateway is that if you are already using Consul, it can take advantage of local services without any programming.

Spring Cloud Gateway was created with WebFlux in mind, so basically you have the advantage of using this technology in a regular MVC or in a Reactive web application.

Next, open/create the `application.yaml` file. See Listing 13-14.

Listing 13-14. src/main/resources/application.yaml

```
spring:
  application:
    name: myretro-gateway
  config:
    import: optional:consul://
  cloud:
    gateway:
      routes:
        - id: users
          uri: lb://users-service
          predicates:
            - Path=/users/**
        - id: myretro
          uri: lb://my-retro-app
          predicates:
            - Path=/retros/**
  server:
    port: ${PORT:8080}
```

Let's review `application.yaml`:

- `spring.application.name`: Remember that you always need this property when you want to use service discovery, and because we are using Consul, this is a must. The `myretro-gateway` value is set and will automatically be registered in Consul with that name.

- `spring.config.import`: When adding the `spring-cloud-starter-consul-config` dependency, we need to specify this property even if we don't use it at all. In our example, we are not going to use Consul as an external configuration, so we can declare it as `optional:`, and that's why we added that to the beginning of its value.

- `spring.cloud.gateway.*`: This includes all the Gateway declaration configurations. In this case, we are defining two routes, one for the `/users` endpoint and the other for the `/retros` endpoint. The `uri` property for the user's route uses the name of the service (in this case, `users-service`), but with a prefix `lb://`, meaning that this is how we need to declare the usage of a load balancer. Remember that we have two Users Services apps instances running (on ports 8091 and 8092). We are declaring the `predicates.Path` with the `/users/**` and `/retros/**` values for each service. This means that when we access the Gateway with `/users`, it will redirect to `http://users-service/users` (`http://localhost:8091/users` or `http://localhost:8092/users`, depending on the load balancer, but normally this is a round-robin scenario).

Of course, there are more configuration options, but we've covered the minimal ones that involve service discovery and load balancing.

And that's it! No need of any programming or anything else.

Running the My Retro Gateway

Before running the My Retro Gateway, make sure you have all the services (`consul`, `vault`, `users-service`, and `my-retro-app`) up and running and visible in Consul.

To run My Retro Gateway, you can use your IDE or the following command:

```
./gradlew bootRun
```

By default, the app runs on port 8080. If you open the Consul UI (`http://localhost:8500`), you can see all the services. See Figure 13-16.

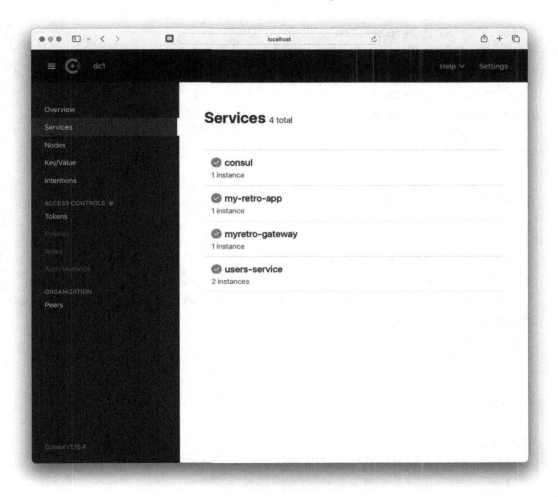

Figure 13-16. Consul UI Services section with a list of all services (http://localhost:8500/ui/dc1/services)

Now that you have the My Retro Gateway up and running, it's time to test it. You can use the browser or the terminal. If you are using the terminal, you can execute the following command to see the users:

```
curl -s http://localhost:8080/users | jq
[
  {
    "email": "ximena@email.com",
    "name": "Ximena",
    "gravatarUrl": "https://www.gravatar.com/avatar/23bb62a7d0ca63c9a80490
    8e57bf6bd4?d=wavatar",
    "password": "aw2s0meR!",
    "userRole": [
      "USER"
    ],
    "active": true
  },
  {
    "email": "norma@email.com",
    "name": "Norma",
    "gravatarUrl": "https://www.gravatar.com/avatar/f07f7e553264c9710105ede
    be6c465e7?d=wavatar",
    "password": "aw2s0meR!",
    "userRole": [
      "USER",
      "ADMIN"
    ],
    "active": false
  }
]
```

If you execute the following command, you will get the retros:

```
curl -s http://localhost:8080/retros | jq
[
  {
    "retroBoardId": "4efaf18e-2141-40c5-abff-0c0951d62938",
    "name": "Spring Boot 3 Retro",
    "cards": [
      {
```

```
      "cardId": "d9df505f-3564-4104-a339-415db9f4a29a",
      "comment": "Nice to meet everybody",
      "cardType": "HAPPY",
      "created": "2024-02-12 13:17:30",
      "modified": "2024-02-12 13:17:30"
    },
    {
      "cardId": "3906a3cb-69cc-412f-8965-42979ac91052",
      "comment": "When are we going to travel?",
      "cardType": "MEH",
      "created": "2024-02-12 13:17:30",
      "modified": "2024-02-12 13:17:30"
    },
    {
      "cardId": "fdbce1c8-f9ec-45fd-873b-b4ab43c2aff5",
      "comment": "When are we going to travel?",
      "cardType": "SAD",
      "created": "2024-02-12 13:17:30",
      "modified": "2024-02-12 13:17:30"
    }
  ],
  "created": "2024-02-12 13:17:30",
  "modified": "2024-02-12 13:17:30"
  }
]
```

But what happens if you turn off both users-service apps? To find out, turn them off and then execute the following:

```
curl -s http://localhost:8080/users | jq
{
  "timestamp": "2024-02-12T20:14:12.361+00:00",
  "path": "/users",
  "status": 503,
  "error": "Service Unavailable",
  "requestId": "2a02d2b8-2"
}
```

How can we add a default message or a dummy user in case of service disruption? Using the Circuit Breaker pattern, discussed in the following section.

More Gateway Features

Spring Cloud Gateway has many more features, such as predicates and filters. Examples of predicates include `After`, `Before`, `Between`, `Cookie`, `Header`, `Host`, `Method`, `Path`, `Query`, `ReadBody`, `RemoteAddr`, `XForwardedRemoteAddr`, `Weight`, `CloudFoundryRouteService`, and `custom`. The list of filters is long. The following is just a sample, presented in alphabetical order: `AddRequestHeader`, `AddRequestHeaderIfNotPresent`, `AddRequestParameter`, `AddResponseHeader`, `CircuitBreaker`, `CacheResponseBody`, `DedupeResponseHeader`, `FallbackHeaders`, `JsonToGrpc`. You can also create a custom filter if none of the filters provides the business logic that you need. Let's review some of these predicates and filters.

CircuitBreaker Filter

To understand the purpose of the `CircuitBreaker` filter, it's helpful to first understand the Circuit Breaker pattern. The Circuit Breaker pattern is a resilience mechanism that protects systems from cascading failures when a dependent service or resource becomes unavailable or overwhelmed. It acts like an automatic switch and can be in one of three states:

- *Closed*: Normal operation; requests are forwarded to the service.

- *Open*: Service failure threshold reached, requests are immediately short-circuited and directed to a fallback mechanism (e.g., cached response, alternative service).

- *Half-Open*: After a timeout, a single request probes the service. If it's successful, the circuit closes; if not, it stays open longer.

This pattern keeps the failing service from being further burdened and allows the system to continue functioning gracefully while the issue is resolved. The `CircuitBreaker` filter is based on the Circuit Breaker pattern.

Adding the CircuitBreaker Filter to the My Retro Gateway App

Let's add the CircuitBreaker filter to the application.yaml file in the My Retro Gateway app. Add the following snippet to the spring.cloud.gateway.routes users section:

```
filters:
  - name: CircuitBreaker
    args:
      name: users
      fallbackUri: forward:/fallback/users
```

We are defining the name of the filter to use CircuitBreaker, then we are declaring some of the arguments it requires, a name and fallbackUri, which indicates that if the /users endpoint is not reachable, it will default to the /fallback/users endpoint. The complete configuration is presented in Listing 13-15.

Listing 13-15. src/main/resources/application.yaml with CircuitBreaker

```
spring:
  application:
    name: myretro-gateway
  config:
    import: optional:consul://
  cloud:
    gateway:
      routes:
        - id: users
          uri: lb://users-service
          predicates:
            - Path=/users/**
          filters:
            - name: CircuitBreaker
              args:
                name: users
                fallbackUri: forward:/fallback/users
```

```
        - id: myretro
          uri: lb://my-retro-app
          predicates:
            - Path=/retros/**
          filters:
            - name: CircuitBreaker
              args:
                name: retros
                fallbackUri: forward:/fallback/retros
server:
  port: ${PORT:8080}
```

Listing 13-15 shows the final version of the application.yaml file. Talking about the fallbackUri, note that we are declaring a forward to a new route /fallback/users and /fallback/retros. This means that we need to implement these fallbacks. Open/create the MyRetroFallbackController class. See Listing 13-16.

Listing 13-16. src/main/kotlin/com/apress/myretrogateway/ MyRetroFallbackController.kt

```
package com.apress.myretrogateway

import org.springframework.http.ResponseEntity
import org.springframework.web.bind.annotation.GetMapping
import org.springframework.web.bind.annotation.RequestMapping
import org.springframework.web.bind.annotation.RestController
import java.time.LocalDateTime
import java.util.Map

@RestController
@RequestMapping("/fallback")
class MyRetroFallbackController {
    @GetMapping("/users")
    fun userFallback(): ResponseEntity<*> {
        return ResponseEntity.ok(
            Map.of(
                "status", "Service Down",
```

```
            "message", "/users endpoint is not available a this
            moment",
            "time", LocalDateTime.now(),
            "data", Map.of(
                "email", "dummy@email.com",
                "name", "Dummy",
                "password", "dummy",
                "active", false
            )
        )
    )
}

@GetMapping("/retros")
fun retroFallback(): ResponseEntity<*> {
    return ResponseEntity.ok(
        Map.of(
            "status",
            "Service Down",
            "message",
            "/retros endpoint is not available a this moment",
            "time",
            LocalDateTime.now()
        )
    )
}
}
```

Listing 13-16 shows the MyRetroFallbackController class. You have already seen this, so no need to explain. Practically, you are using a default response, which can be with a Map like we have it here. You can also reach out to a different service that you know is never down.

If you want to test this, you can shut down the two instances of the users-service app and rerun the My Retro Gateway with the new configuration. Execute the following command over the /users endpoint:

```
curl -s http://localhost:8080/users | jq
{
  "message": "/users endpoint is not available a this moment",
  "status": "Service Down",
  "data": {
    "active": false,
    "name": "Dummy",
    "email": "dummy@email.com",
    "password": "dummy"
  },
  "time": "2024-02-12T16:00:34.087459"
}
```

You can try to shut down the my-retro-app service, then call it with /retros and see the message from the controller.

Integrating the Cloud Environment into Docker Compose

So far, we have been dealing with every component in a separate way, so now let's work on everything in this single file. Let's use Docker Compose to set up the whole environment.

Let's first define the compose.yaml file. You can find this file in the 13-cloud/docker-compose folder. See Listing 13-17.

Listing 13-17. The compose.yaml File

```
services:
  ## HashiCorp Consul
  consul-server:
    hostname: consul-server
    container_name: consul-server
    image: consul:1.15.4
    restart: always
    networks:
      - cloud
```

```
    healthcheck:
      test: ["CMD", "curl", "-X", "GET", "localhost:8500/v1/status/leader"]
      interval: 1s
      timeout: 3s
      retries: 60
    command: "agent -server -ui -node=server-1 -bootstrap-expect=1
    -client=0.0.0.0"
consul-client:
  hostname: consul-client
  container_name: consul-client
  image: consul:1.15.4
  restart: always
  networks:
    - cloud
  command: "agent -node=client-1 -join=consul-server -retry-
  join=172.17.0.2"
consul-init:
  hostname: consul-init
  container_name: consul-init
  image: consul:1.15.4
  depends_on:
    consul-server:
      condition: service_healthy
  volumes:
    - ./consul-init.sh:/tmp/consul-init.sh
  networks:
    - cloud
  command: |
    sh -c "/tmp/consul-init.sh"
## PostgreSQL
postgres:
  hostname: postgres
  container_name: postgres
  image: postgres
  platform: linux/amd64
```

```yaml
      restart: always
      networks:
        - cloud
      environment:
        POSTGRES_PASSWORD: mysecretpassword
        POSTGRES_USER: admin
        POSTGRES_DB: users_db
      ports:
        - "5432:5432"
      healthcheck:
        test: pg_isready
        interval: 10s
        timeout: 5s
        retries: 5
    ## Users Service
users-service:
  image: users
    build:
      context: ../users
      dockerfile: Dockerfile
    restart: always
    environment:
      - SPRING_DATASOURCE_URL=jdbc:postgresql://postgres:5432/users_db
      - SPRING_CLOUD_CONSUL_HOST=consul-server
    networks:
      - cloud
    depends_on:
      consul-server:
        condition: service_healthy
      postgres:
        condition: service_healthy
    ## My Retro App
my-retro-app:
  image: myretro
    build:
```

```
      context: ../myretro
      dockerfile: Dockerfile
    environment:
      - SPRING_CLOUD_CONSUL_HOST=consul-server
    networks:
      - cloud
    depends_on:
      consul-server:
        condition: service_healthy
  ## Gateway
myretro-gateway:
  image: myretro-gateway
    build:
      context: ../myretro-gateway
      dockerfile: Dockerfile
    networks:
      - cloud
    environment:
      - SPRING_CLOUD_CONSUL_HOST=consul-server
    depends_on:
      consul-server:
        condition: service_healthy
    ports:
      - "8080:8080"
## Networks
networks:
  cloud:
    name: cloud
    #external: true
```

Listing 13-17 shows that we don't need to define an export port, just the gateway. Before continuing, review Listing 13-17 carefully and note that we need to add the SPRING_CLOUD_CONSUL_HOST environment variable to each Spring Boot service and the SPRING_DATASOURCE_URL for the users-service. There is also a consul-init service that will initialize the properties we need.

Now you can run the environment with this command:

```
docker compose up
```

The first time you run this command, it will take some time to complete because you are building every service. Subsequent runs should be very fast. After this is up and running, you can test it by trying to make some requests to the /users and /retros endpoints:

```
curl -s http://localhost:8080/users | jq
curl -s http://localhost:8080/retros | jq
```

To stop the services, you can open a new terminal and change to the directory where the compose.yaml is. Then execute this command:

```
docker compose down
```

In every project (users, myretro, and myretro-gateway), we created the following Dockerfile:

```
FROM eclipse-temurin:17-jdk-jammy AS build
WORKDIR /workspace/app
COPY . /workspace/app
RUN --mount=type=cache,target=/root/.gradle ./gradlew clean build -x test
RUN mkdir -p build/dependency && (cd build/dependency; jar -xf ../libs/*-
SNAPSHOT.jar)
FROM eclipse-temurin:17-jdk-jammy
VOLUME /tmp
ARG DEPENDENCY=/workspace/app/build/dependency
COPY --from=build ${DEPENDENCY}/BOOT-INF/lib /app/lib
COPY --from=build ${DEPENDENCY}/META-INF /app/META-INF
COPY --from=build ${DEPENDENCY}/BOOT-INF/classes /app
ENTRYPOINT ["java","-cp","app:app/lib/*","com.apress.users.
UsersApplication"]
```

This file is used by docker-compose to build the images. It will create each image in your local Docker registry. You can inspect with this command:

```
docker images | grep -E "retro|users"
```

If you don't get anything, you can build the images using the following commands (on each project folder):

```
# cd users
docker build -t users .
# cd myretro
docker build -t myretro .
# cd myretro-gateway
docker build -t myretro-gateway .
```

Creating Multi-Architecture Images

Docker with multi-architecture allows you to create a single Docker image that works seamlessly on different computer systems, like those with ARM or x86 processors. It's like having a universal remote that can control different TV brands—one image can run on various devices without needing separate versions. This is achieved by packaging multiple versions of your application (each compiled for a specific architecture) into a single image. Docker then automatically selects the right version for the device it's running on, making deployment simpler and more flexible. We are using an M3 Mac, so by default, some of the architecture layers are based on an ARM64. How could you do this on some multi-architecture, for example, on a Linux AMD64?

The newest versions of Docker come with the `--platform` parameter, which allows you to create a multi-architecture image. To create ARM64 and AMD64/Intel-based images, you can execute the following command:

```
docker build \
--push \
--platform linux/arm64,linux/amd64 \
--tag <your-username>/<your-image-name>:<your-tag> .
```

This command will not only create your image, but will also add the necessary OS architecture layers (ARM64/AMD64) and push the image to the Docker Hub registry (`--push`). This means that you need to log in to a Docker registry (we recommend creating an account at `https://hub.docker.com/`, which is free). Of course, you can remove the `--push`, but you are going to need it in the next section.

> **Note**   If you get an error, "`ERROR: Multi-platform build is not supported for the docker driver`," when executing the previous command, you need to enable the `containerd` feature. Check out this link: `https://docs.docker.com/desktop/containerd/#build-multi-platform-images`.

For the users project, execute the following:

```
docker build \
--push \
--platform linux/arm64,linux/amd64 \
--tag felipeg48/users:latest .
```

For the myretro project, execute the following:

```
docker build \
--push \
--platform linux/arm64,linux/amd64 \
--tag felipeg48/myretro:latest .
```

For the myretro-gateway project, execute the following:

```
docker build \
--push \
--platform linux/arm64,linux/amd64 \
--tag felipeg48/myretro-gateway:latest .
```

You can look at Docker Hub and review your images. For example, see Figure 13-17.

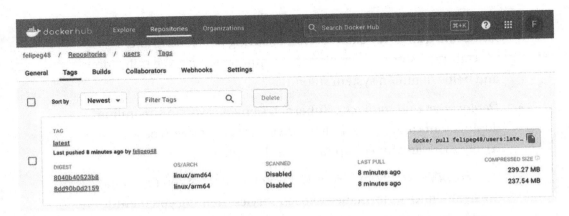

Figure 13-17. *Viewing images in Docker Hub (*`https://hub.docker.com/`
`repository/docker/felipeg48/users/tags`*)*

You are now ready to learn about using a cloud platform!

Using a Cloud Platform: Kubernetes

Kubernetes (`https://kubernetes.io/`), often abbreviated as K8s, is an open source
platform for managing containerized applications. Think of it as a conductor for an
orchestra, but instead of managing instruments, it manages containers across a cluster of
machines. Let's see how Kubernetes helps with microservices.

Benefits of using Kubernetes for microservices include the following:

- *Scalability*: Kubernetes enables you to easily scale individual services
  up or down based on demand, eliminating the need to provision
  entire servers. This lets you adapt quickly to changing traffic patterns
  and avoid wasting resources.

- *High availability*: Kubernetes keeps your services running even
  if a container or machine fails. It automatically restarts crashed
  containers and reschedules them on healthy nodes, ensuring your
  application remains available.

- *Decoupling and autonomy*: Kubernetes helps manage each
  microservice independently, allowing development teams to work
  autonomously and deploy updates faster without impacting other
  services.

- *Resource management*: Kubernetes enables you to define resource limits and quotas for each service, ensuring fair sharing and preventing resource starvation. This optimizes resource utilization and helps maintain system stability.

- *Deployment and rollbacks*: Kubernetes enables you to streamline deployments and rollbacks for individual services with ease. This reduces risk and makes updates less disruptive.

- *Observability and monitoring*: Kubernetes enables you to monitor the health and performance of each service, helping you identify and troubleshoot issues quickly.

The following are some key features of Kubernetes that aid microservices: .

- *Pods*: These are group-related containers that share resources and storage. Think of them as mini environments for your services.

- *Deployments*: You can define the desired state of your services and Kubernetes ensures they reach that state, handling scaling and updates automatically.

- *Services*: You can expose your microservices to other services or external clients and Kubernetes will handle load balancing and service discovery.

- *Namespaces*: Kubernetes enables you to isolate resources and configurations for different teams or environments, promoting security and organization.

Kubernetes provides a powerful platform for deploying and managing microservices, resulting in the following benefits:

- Increased agility and faster development cycles

- Improved scalability and high availability

- Efficient resource utilization and cost savings

- Simplified operations and management

Kubernetes isn't the only microservices platform, of course. Other popular microservices platforms include Docker Swarm (https://docs.docker.com/engine/swarm/), HashiCorp Nomad (https://www.nomadproject.io/), Marathon (https://

mesosphere.github.io/marathon/), Rancher (https://www.rancher.com/), Cattle (https://github.com/rancher/cattle), and Cloud Foundry (https://www. cloudfoundry.org/).

Kubernetes is a strong contender for orchestrating your containerized landscape. Kubernetes has a learning curve, but the benefits of using it to manage distributed systems, especially at scale, are significant.

Using Kubernetes

As previously described, Kubernetes offers service discovery, configuration, secrets, reliability, observability, high availability, and much more. Let's use Kubernetes as our cloud platform and see how we can deploy our apps.

This section uses Minikube as the Kubernetes cluster that you can test locally on your computer. You can use the same steps if you already have a Kubernetes cluster on Google Cloud, AWS, or Microsoft Azure.

If you are following along, you will find the files for this section in the 13-cloud/ k8s folder.

Prerequisites: Installation

The following are the prerequisites to run Minikube:

1. Install Minikube from https://minikube.sigs.k8s.io/ docs/start/.

2. Install the kubectl CLI from https://kubernetes.io/docs/ tasks/tools/. If you already have Docker Desktop installed, kubectl typically comes as part of the installation.

3. Optionally, install K9s from https://k9scli.io/. This is a text-based UI that can help visualize all the Kubernetes components without typing too much.

Starting Minikube

To start Minikube, make sure you have a minimum of 4GB of RAM. You can start the default configuration with this command:

```
minikube start
```

If you have more memory, you can use the `--memory` parameter. For example, if you have 8GB total in your computer, you can start `minikube` with this command:

```
minikube start --memory 4096
```

There are other parameters, such as `--cpu`, which allows you to specify how much CPU core to use. To learn more about the `minikube` CLI, check out the documentation here: `https://minikube.sigs.k8s.io/docs/`.

Creating the Postgres Deployment

Our Users App needs to use PostgreSQL as a database, so we need to start it using the declarations described next.

ConfigMap

We need to create the username and password. Kubernetes has a way to save them and use them when we need them. In this case, there is a component named `ConfigMap`, that's declared as follows:

```
apiVersion: v1
kind: ConfigMap
metadata:
  name: postgres-config
  labels:
    app: postgres
data:
  POSTGRES_DB: users_db
  POSTGRES_USER: admin
  POSTGRES_PASSWORD: mysecretpassword
```

PersistentVolume and PersistentVolumeClaim

We need to store the data correctly, and in Kubernetes, `PersistentVolume` (PV) is the actual storage space, like a hard drive, whereas `PersistentVolumeClaim` (PVC) is a user's request for a specific amount of that storage. Think of it as a parking lot (PV) where users request parking spaces (PVC). The `PersistentVolume` declaration is as follows:

```
kind: PersistentVolume
apiVersion: v1
metadata:
  name: postgres-pv-volume
  labels:
    type: local
    app: postgres
spec:
  storageClassName: manual
  capacity:
    storage: 5Gi
  accessModes:
    - ReadWriteMany
  hostPath:
    path: "/mnt/data"
```

The PersistentVolumeClaim declaration is as follows:

```
kind: PersistentVolumeClaim
apiVersion: v1
metadata:
  name: postgres-pv-claim
  labels:
    app: postgres
spec:
  storageClassName: manual
  accessModes:
    - ReadWriteMany
  resources:
    requests:
      storage: 1Gi
```

Deployment

Deployment in Kubernetes is your autopilot for pods, ensuring that a desired number of instances are running, updating smoothly, and rolling back if needed. The PostgreSQL deployment is as follows:

```yaml
apiVersion: apps/v1
kind: Deployment
metadata:
  name: postgres  # Sets Deployment name
spec:
  replicas: 1
  selector:
    matchLabels:
      app: postgres
  template:
    metadata:
      labels:
        app: postgres
    spec:
      containers:
        - name: postgres
          image: postgres
          imagePullPolicy: "IfNotPresent"
          ports:
            - containerPort: 5432  # Exposes container port
          envFrom:
            - configMapRef:
                name: postgres-config
          volumeMounts:
            - mountPath: /var/lib/postgresql/data
              name: postgredb
          resources:
            limits:
              cpu: "1"
              memory: "1Gi"
            requests:
              cpu: "0.5"
              memory: "512Mi"
      volumes:
        - name: postgredb
```

```
      persistentVolumeClaim:
        claimName: postgres-pv-claim
```

Before continuing, make sure you review this declaration carefully.

Service

A *service* in Kubernetes is a single entry point for reaching a group of pods, hiding their individual details, and ensuring high availability. The PostgreSQL service is as follows:

```
apiVersion: v1
kind: Service
metadata:
  name: postgres
  labels:
    app: postgres
spec:
  type: NodePort
  ports:
    - port: 5432
  selector:
    app: postgres
```

Installing the Declarations

All of these declarations are in a file named postgresql.yaml. To install them in your Kubernetes, you can execute the following command:

```
kubectl apply -f postgresql.yaml
```

Deploying Microservices in Kubernetes: Users App, My Retro App, and My Retro Gateway App Deployments

This section deploys all the microservices. Recall that we used in the My Retro APP and My Retro Gateway projects, respectively, the `spring-cloud-starter-kubernetes-client-all` and `spring-cloud-starter-kubernetes-fabric8-all` dependencies. With these dependencies, we can integrate our apps seamlessly within Kubernetes and take advantage of the Kubernetes features in our Spring Boot apps. We are going to talk about some of these features next.

ClusterRole and ClusterRoleBinding

`ClusterRole` defines cluster-wide permissions, whereas `ClusterRoleBinding` assigns them to users or groups across all namespaces. Think of it as setting access rules (`ClusterRole`) and then attaching them to users (`ClusterRoleBinding`).

We need to declare both because the Spring Cloud Kubernetes dependencies require access to *services*, *endpoints*, ConfigMap, *pods*, and more, to make this an easy integration without any code in the Spring Boot side. The `ClusterRole` declaration is as follows:

```
apiVersion: rbac.authorization.k8s.io/v1
kind: ClusterRole
metadata:
  name: cluster-read-role
rules:
- apiGroups:
  - ""
  resources:
  - endpoints
  - pods
  - services
  - configmaps
  verbs:
  - get
  - list
  - watch
```

The ClusterRoleBinding declaration is as follows:

```
apiVersion: rbac.authorization.k8s.io/v1
kind: ClusterRoleBinding
metadata:
  name: cluster-read-rolebinding
subjects:
- kind: ServiceAccount
  name: default
  namespace: default
roleRef:
  kind: ClusterRole
  name: cluster-read-role
  apiGroup: rbac.authorization.k8s.io
```

We these declarations, the Spring Boot apps that are using the Spring Cloud Kubernetes dependencies (My Retro App and My Retro Gateway) can use the integration features that we discuss next.

Users Deployment and Service

Let's start with the Users App Deployment declaration:

```
apiVersion: apps/v1
kind: Deployment
metadata:
  labels:
    app: users
  name: users
spec:
  replicas: 1
  selector:
    matchLabels:
      app: users
  template:
    metadata:
      labels:
```

```
      app: users
  spec:
    containers:
      - name: users
        image: felipeg48/users:latest
        ports:
        - containerPort: 8080
        env:
        - name: spring.cloud.consul.enabled
          value: "false"
        - name: spring.datasource.url
          value: "jdbc:postgresql://postgres.default.svc.cluster.
          local:5432/users_db"
        - name: spring.datasource.username
          valueFrom:
            configMapKeyRef:
              name: postgres-config
              key: POSTGRES_USER
        - name: spring.datasource.password
          valueFrom:
            configMapKeyRef:
              name: postgres-config
              key: POSTGRES_PASSWORD
        resources:
          limits:
            cpu: "0.5"
            memory: "768Mi"
        livenessProbe:
          httpGet:
            path: /actuator/health
            port: 8080
          initialDelaySeconds: 30
          periodSeconds: 10
          timeoutSeconds: 5
          failureThreshold: 6
```

Let's review this declaration:

- `felipeg48/users:latest`: We are using this image that we generated previously. You can switch to yours, but this image is publicly available.

- `spring.cloud.consul.enabled`: We are declaring environment variables in the env section. We are disabling Consul, because we are not going to use Consul for service discovery and configuration but instead use the Kubernetes defaults. We set this value to `false`.

- `spring.datasource.url`: This property holds the URL (yes, we are overwriting its value) using the standard way to locate services. The syntax is `<service-name>.<namespace>.svc.cluster.local`. We can just use `postgres`, but we want to show you the Kubernetes DNS use.

- `spring.datasource.username`/`spring.datasource.password`: We are also overwriting these properties. We are using the (`configMapKeyRef`) reference to the `ConfigMap` we defined earlier with `postgres-config`, by using the keys.

- `livenessProbe`: We are using this declaration to use the `/actuator/health` endpoint to make sure the app is healthy. We are also using some resource limits that help us minimize the overall use of our Kubernetes installation.

Next, let's check the Users App *service* declaration:

```
apiVersion: v1
kind: Service
metadata:
  labels:
    app: users
  name: users-service
spec:
  type: NodePort
  selector:
    app: users
  ports:
  - name: http
```

```
      protocol: TCP
      port: 80
      targetPort: 8080
```

Here we are defining a NodePort, and we are going to use port 80, which will redirect to the 8080 in the container.

My Retro Deployment and Service

Next, let's check out the My Retro deployment:

```
apiVersion: apps/v1
kind: Deployment
metadata:
  labels:
    app: myretro
  name: myretro
spec:
  replicas: 1
  selector:
    matchLabels:
      app: myretro
  template:
    metadata:
      labels:
        app: myretro
    spec:
      containers:
      - name: myretro
        image: felipeg48/myretro:latest
        ports:
        - containerPort: 8080
        env:
          - name: spring.cloud.consul.enabled
            value: "false"
        resources:
```

```
      limits:
        cpu: "0.5"
        memory: "768Mi"
    livenessProbe:
      httpGet:
        path: /actuator/health
        port: 8080
      initialDelaySeconds: 30
      periodSeconds: 10
      timeoutSeconds: 5
      failureThreshold: 6
```

We are using a specific image, but you are welcome to change to yours. We are also disabling the Consul configuration with the `spring.cloud.consul.enabled` property by setting the value to `false`.

Remember that this app uses `OpenFeign` to connect to the `users-service`, and because we used the Spring Cloud Kubernetes dependency, Kubernetes will handle the service discovery and load balancing behind the scenes by using/reaching to the service using something like `users-service.default.svc.cluster.local` as the host.

The Users Service declaration is as follows:

```
apiVersion: v1
kind: Service
metadata:
  labels:
    app: myretro
  name: my-retro-app
spec:
  type: NodePort
  selector:
      app: myretro
  ports:
  - name: http
    protocol: TCP
    port: 80
    targetPort: 8080
```

My Retro Gateway ConfigMap, Deployment, and Service

Next, let's look at the My Retro Gateway declaration. First, consider the ConfigMap:

```
apiVersion: v1
kind: ConfigMap
metadata:
  name: myretro-gateway
data:
  application.yaml: |-
    management:
      endpoint:
        gateway:
          enabled: true
      endpoints:
        web:
          exposure:
            include: "health,info,gateway,configprops,conditions,env,beans"
    spring:
      cloud:
        gateway:
          routes:
            - id: users
              uri: http://users-service
              predicates:
                - Path=/users/**
              filters:
                - name: CircuitBreaker
                  args:
                    name: users
                    fallbackUri: forward:/fallback/users
            - id: myretro
              uri: http://my-retro-app
              predicates:
                - Path=/retros/**
              filters:
```

```
    - name: CircuitBreaker
      args:
        name: retros
        fallbackUri: forward:/fallback/retros
```

Let's review it:

- `application.yaml`: In the data section of the `ConfigMap`, we are declaring a new `application.yaml` file. We are going to overwrite the `application.yaml` in the image. We are defining new properties, but the most important are next.

- `spring.cloud.gateway.routes.*`: We are redefining the `routes`, but the only change is the `uri` key, where instead of the `lb://` (load balancer) we are using just the `http://`. In this case, we are using the `http://` because the load balancing comes from the Kubernetes services, so there's no need to add this prefix (`lb://`). We are not using Consul anymore. We are using the Kubernetes defaults (service discovery and load balancing).

Next, the deployment declaration:

```
apiVersion: apps/v1
kind: Deployment
metadata:
  labels:
    app: myretro-gateway
  name: myretro-gateway
spec:
  replicas: 1
  selector:
    matchLabels:
      app: myretro-gateway
  template:
    metadata:
      labels:
        app: myretro-gateway
    spec:
```

```
containers:
- name: myretro-gateway
  image: felipeg48/myretro-gateway:latest
  ports:
  - containerPort: 8080
  env:
  - name: spring.config.import
    value: "kubernetes:"
  - name: spring.cloud.consul.enabled
    value: "false"
  resources:
    limits:
      cpu: "0.5"
      memory: "768Mi"
  livenessProbe:
    httpGet:
      path: /actuator/health
      port: 8080
    initialDelaySeconds: 30
    periodSeconds: 10
    timeoutSeconds: 5
    failureThreshold: 6
```

Here we are disabling the Consul (with spring.cloud.consul.enabled=false). We are also using a known property, the spring.config.import with the kubernetes:// value. Just by adding this, the Spring Cloud Kubernetes auto-configuration will look for a ConfigMap that matches the name of the application—in this case the myretro-gateway ConfigMap that we previously declared—and it will apply/overwrite the application. yaml file to the app with the new values. This is so cool! If you happen to have a different name for the ConfigMap, you can still use it, but you must follow some naming conventions. If you want to know more, go to: https://docs.spring.io/spring-cloud-kubernetes/reference/property-source-config/configmap-propertysource.html.

Next, let's review the service:

```
apiVersion: v1
kind: Service
metadata:
  labels:
    app: myretro-gateway
  name: myretro-gateway-service
spec:
  type: NodePort
  selector:
    app: myretro-gateway
  ports:
  - name: http
    protocol: TCP
    port: 8080
    targetPort: 8080
```

Here we are using port 8080.

In the source code 13-cloud/k8s folder, you can find a single myretro.yaml file that contains all the declarations we just reviewed. To apply this file, you can use the following command:

```
kubectl apply -f myretro.yaml
```

That's it. Now we can use the My Retro Gateway service to access our applications. You can check if the pods are up and running with the following commands:

```
kubectl get pods
kubectl get services
```

Keep in mind that we are showing you one alternative; you can use Consul as well, or some other component such as Istio or even a special *Spring Cloud Gateway for Kubernetes* that can be installed as Operator/Helm (with commercial support), and it's even better than using it alone. If you want to know more, look at https://docs.vmware.com/en/VMware-Spring-Cloud-Gateway-for-Kubernetes/index.html.

Access to My Retro Gateway: Using Port-Forward

Next, you can access the apps by using the Kubernetes `port-forward` and `myretro-gateway-service` commands. In a terminal, execute the following command:

```
kubectl port-forward svc/myretro-gateway-service 8080:8080
```

With this, you can go to your browser or use the following commands to reach the apps:

```
curl -s http://localhost:8080/users | jq
curl -s http://localhost:8080/retros | jq
curl -s http://localhost:8080/retros/users | j
```

If you want to look at some of the logs, first get the names of the pods with this command:

```
kubectl get pods
```

Then, you can look at the logs with this command:

```
kubectl logs <pod-name>
```

That's it! You now know how to deploy microservices in Kubernetes.

If you are interested in using Consul instead of the default Kubernetes service discovery, configuration, and load balancing, you can use Consul for Kubernetes, which makes it even easier to deploy microservices. Check out the documentation here:

```
https://developer.hashicorp.com/consul/docs/k8s.
```

Cleaning Up

The easiest way to shut down everything is by executing the following command, which removes the VM created for Kubernetes:

```
minikube delete --all --purge
```

If you want just to stop it, you can use this command:

```
minikube stop
```

I encourage you to continue experimenting with all the features that Spring Cloud offers, not only for Spring Cloud Consul and Spring Cloud Vault, but also for other projects.

Summary

This chapter reviewed Spring Cloud Consul for service discovery and configuration; Spring Cloud Vault for secrets and configuration; Spring Cloud Gateway for routing, filtering, and fallback by using the Circuit Breaker pattern; and some of the HashiCorp products, such as Consul and Vault.

It also looked at Docker Compose and Kubernetes and you saw how to use this cloud platform to have multiple instances, service discovery, high availability, and much more out of the box. Thanks to Spring Cloud Kubernetes, the integration is easier.

There are so many Spring Cloud technologies that we would need an entire second book to describe them. In the book *Spring Boot Messaging* (Apress, 2017), I (Felipe Gutierrez) cover Spring Cloud Stream, and in *Spring Cloud Data Flow* (Apress, 2020), I cover other technologies that complement your cloud journey.

CHAPTER 14

Extending Spring Boot

Felipe Gutierrez[a*]

ᵃ 4109 Rillcrest Grove Way Fuquay Varina, NC 27526-3562, Albuquerque, NM, USA

Benefits of a Custom Starter

The following are the potential benefits of creating a custom starter:

- *Increased development speed:*

    - *Reduced boilerplate*: By encapsulating common dependencies and configurations into a starter, you eliminate the need to manually include them in each project, saving time and effort.

    - *Consistent setup*: A starter ensures a consistent environment across all your projects, simplifying onboarding and maintenance for your team.

    - *Auto-configuration*: Spring Boot will automatically configure beans based on the dependencies included in your starter, further reducing manual work.

- *Improved code reusability:*

    - *Shareable code*: If your custom functionality might be valuable to others, you can publish your starter as a library for broader use.

    - *Modular design*: Starters promote modularity, making it easier to integrate specific features into different projects as needed.

    - *Dependency management*: You control the exact versions of dependencies included in your starter, avoiding conflicts and ensuring consistency.

© Peter Späth, Felipe Gutierrez 2025
P. Späth and F. Gutierrez, *Pro Spring Boot 3 with Kotlin*, https://doi.org/10.1007/979-8-8688-1131-9_14

- *Enhanced maintainability:*

  - *Centralized changes*: Updating a particular starter impacts all projects utilizing it, simplifying maintenance and upgrades.

  - *Reduced complexity*: Smaller projects with focused functionality generally lead to improved maintainability.

  - *Clear documentation*: Having well-documented starters clarifies expected behavior and simplifies troubleshooting.

Creating a custom Spring Boot starter can be beneficial for managing common configurations, promoting code reusability, and improving maintainability for projects with shared needs. However, it's crucial to weigh the benefits against the added complexity and ensure that the custom starter aligns with your specific project requirements.

Let's begin with a review of what we discussed in Chapter 1 regarding the Spring Boot internals and features, specifically how Spring Boot is doing the auto-configuration and how it uses certain annotations that can help determine which Spring Beans need to be created.

Revisiting @Conditional and @Enable

As you've seen throughout the previous chapters, the `@Conditional` annotation in Spring is a powerful tool for managing your application's configuration based on specific conditions. It allows you to control whether a bean, configuration class, or even an entire profile is included in the Spring application context, depending on various factors.

As a refresher, this is how the `@Conditional` annotation works:

- You annotate a bean, configuration class, or method with `@Conditional(MyCondition.class)`.

- `MyCondition` must implement the `Condition` interface and define a `matches` method.

- This `matches` method receives information about the bean and the application context and returns `true` if the condition is met and `false` otherwise.

- Spring checks the condition before creating the bean or loading the configuration.

Common uses of the @Conditional annotation include the following:

- *Environment-based configuration*: Load beans based on specific environment variables, like @ConditionalOnProperty("spring. profiles.active=dev").

- *Dependency checks*: Create beans only if certain libraries or classes are present in the classpath.

- *Testing*: Exclude beans that depend on external resources during unit tests.

- *Custom conditions*: Implement your own logic for specific needs (e.g., checking OS version).

The important part to remember when using this annotation is that @Conditional offers immense flexibility for conditional configuration in Spring Boot

In Spring and Spring Boot, the @Enable annotation serves as a convenient way to activate specific features or configurations within your application. It simplifies the process by taking care of various tasks under the hood, making your code concise and readable.

The @Enable annotation serves the following purposes:

- *Automatic configuration*: The primary function of @Enable annotations is to trigger auto-configuration based on provided classes or conditions. This saves you from manually writing boilerplate code and leverages Spring's built-in capabilities.

- *Declarative approach*: Instead of explicitly configuring every aspect of a feature, you use the @Enable annotation to declare your intent, and Spring handles the specifics. This leads to cleaner and more maintainable code.

Here are some common use cases of @Enable annotations:

- *Enabling features*: Some examples are
  - @EnableWebMvc: Enables Spring MVC web application support.
  - @EnableAsync: Allows asynchronous method execution using @Async.
  - @EnableJpaRepositories: Enables automatic scanning for JPA repositories.
  - @EnableCaching: Activates Spring's caching framework.

> **Note**   All the preceding annotations (except for @EnableAsync) are enabled by default in a Spring Boot app when the auto-configuration starts and the dependency is in the classpath. But you already knew that!

- *Customizing features:*

  - Many @Enable annotations accept configuration attributes to tailor their behavior.

  - @EnableScheduling(fixedRate = 1000): Schedules tasks with a fixed rate of one second.

  - @EnableJpaRepositories(basePackages = "com.apress.myretro.repository"): Scans for repositories only in the specified package.

- *Creating custom starters:*

  - You can develop your own @Enable annotations within custom Spring Boot starters.

  - This allows you to package reusable configurations and simplify feature activation across projects.

By effectively using @Enable annotations, you can streamline configuration, promote code reusability, and leverage Spring's powerful features efficiently.

Having reviewed the annotations, it's time to identify the requirements of our own custom Spring Boot starter.

Requirements of the Custom Spring Boot Starter

As you know from Chapter 10, both projects (Users App and My Retro App) have events that use the Spring Events mechanism to log what is happening in the services or in any other part of the system. Right now, it is an adequate solution, but imagine that you need this kind of event or audit in more modules that will be built in the next release, so you will be duplicating and doing the same process (copy/paste) again.

The solution is to modularize, and the best way to implement that solution is to create a custom Spring Boot starter that can do the following:

- Create a generic event that contains a timestamp of when the event occurred, the method that was called, the arguments of the method with values, a result if that method returns something, and a message that allows you to see what happened.

- Add a configurable way to log the events before, after, or both.

- Add a configurable way to log the events in plain text or JSON format.

- Add a configurable way to do a pretty print when printing to the console, such as the JSON format.

- Add a configurable way to persist into a database the events, or just the console.

- Add a configurable property to add a prefix to the event.

- Add a configurable way to generate logs or standard output.

Tip   As a suggestion, you can use the @Enable* annotation, a custom annotation, and the ability to add properties and override them if necessary.

With these requirements, we can create a custom starter that allows us to share the same practices and modules with other developers. In other words, after we create our custom starter, any new developer who wants to use the starter's functionality in their own project will simply have to add the dependency and use the required annotations in the program to create an event or audit. In their build.gradle file, they would have something like this:

```
implementation 'com.apress:myretro-spring-boot-starter:0.0.1'
```

Rules and Guidelines for a Custom Spring Boot Starter

When creating a custom Spring Boot starter, you need to follow certain rules:

- *Structure*: Divide your project into two modules:

  - *Autoconfigure module*: Contains auto-configuration classes and properties classes.

  - *Starter module*: Includes the autoconfigure module as a dependency, along with the library your starter supports and any additional dependencies.

In this case, we will have only one project, to make things simpler, so we are going to create only one project that holds the auto-configuration and the starter module.

- *Auto-configuration class*: Use the @EnableAutoConfiguration annotation on your main auto-configuration class:

  - Extend the SpringBootApplication class (optional, especially for complex configurations).

  - Use conditional checks and bean factory methods to create beans conditionally based on classpath presence and properties.

  - Consider @ConfigurationProperties for custom configuration options.

- *Properties class:*

  - Define a class annotated with @ConfigurationProperties to hold configurable properties for your library.

  - Use descriptive names and consider sensible defaults.

- *Starter pom:*

  - In the starter pom, define your project's groupId, artifactId, and version.

  - Add dependencies for the autoconfigure module, the supported library, and any additional dependencies.

- *Enable auto-configuration:*

  - Define your auto-configuration classpath in the `META-INF/spring/org.springframework.boot.autoconfigure.AutoConfiguration.imports` file in your starter module.

  - Use the following format: `[package].YourAutoConfigurationClass`

- *Additional considerations:*

  - Use Spring Boot best practices for code style and documentation.

  - Test your starter thoroughly under various configurations.

  - Consider providing examples and documentation for users.

- *Gradle-specific considerations:*

  - Use appropriate Gradle plugins for build management and testing.

  - Leverage Gradle features like multi-project builds and tasks customization.

- *Follow the naming convention:*

  - Your module should never start with `spring-boot`; this is a specific rule from the Spring Team that is intended to avoid any conflicts with the Spring and Spring Boot packages.

  - This project is `myretro`, so we will name the module `myretro-spring-boot-starter`.

Creating My Retro Spring Boot Starter

You can locate the source code for the projects in the `14-extending/` folder. You can import the `myretro-spring-boot-starter` project into your favorite IDE. If you want to start from scratch with the Spring Initializr (`https://start.spring.io`), set the Group field to `com.apress`, the Artifact and Name fields to `myretro-spring-boot-starter`, and the Package field to `com.apress.myretro`. Add Web, JPA, Processor, and H2 as dependencies. Generate and download the project, unzip it, and import it into your favorite IDE.

Let's start with the `build.gradle` file. See Listing 14-1.

Listing 14-1. The build.gradle File

```
import org.jetbrains.kotlin.gradle.tasks.KotlinCompile
plugins {
    id 'org.springframework.boot' version '3.2.3' apply false
    id 'io.spring.dependency-management' version '1.1.4'
    id 'org.jetbrains.kotlin.jvm' version '2.0.20-RC'
    id "org.jetbrains.kotlin.plugin.spring" version "2.0.20-RC"
    // <- simplifies spring proxying
}

group = 'com.apress'
version = '0.0.1'

java {
    sourceCompatibility = '17'
}

configurations {
    compileOnly {
        extendsFrom annotationProcessor
    }
}

tasks.named('compileKotlin') {
    inputs.files(tasks.named('processResources'))
}

repositories {
    mavenCentral()
}

dependencyManagement {
    imports {
        mavenBom org.springframework.boot.gradle.plugin.SpringBootPlugin.
        BOM_COORDINATES
    }
}
```

```
dependencies {
    implementation "org.jetbrains.kotlin:kotlin-stdlib-jdk8"
    implementation "org.jetbrains.kotlin:kotlin-reflect"

    implementation 'org.springframework.boot:spring-boot-starter-web'
    implementation 'org.springframework.boot:spring-boot-starter-aop'
    implementation 'org.springframework.boot:spring-boot-starter-data-jpa'
    implementation 'com.fasterxml.jackson.datatype:jackson-datatype-jsr310'

    runtimeOnly 'com.h2database:h2'

    annotationProcessor 'org.springframework.boot:spring-boot-
    configuration-processor'

    testImplementation 'org.springframework.boot:spring-boot-starter-test'
}

tasks.named('test') {
    useJUnitPlatform()
}

//    kotlin {
//        jvmToolchain(17)
//    }
tasks.withType(KotlinCompile).configureEach {
    kotlinOptions {
        freeCompilerArgs = ['-Xjsr305=strict']
        jvmTarget = '17'
    }
}
```

Let's review the build.gradle file:

- plugins: Note that the id org.springframework.boot is using the apply false statement. This means that this specific plugin will not be applied to the current build. While it's declared and available, its functionalities won't be accessible during this build. These are the common reasons for using the apply false statement:

- *Conditional application*: You might have a build property that determines whether to apply the plugin based on specific conditions.

- *Conflict avoidance*: If another plugin provides similar functionality and might cause conflicts, using `apply false` can prevent issues.

- *Build simplification*: For builds that don't need specific functionalities, excluding unnecessary plugins can keep the configuration cleaner.

But why is this necessary? Well, remember that the custom starter will be a library and not an application, so we need just to build it, not run it.

- `tasks.named('compileKotlin')`: This refers to the `compileKotlin` task, responsible for compiling Kotlin source code in the project. `inputs.files(tasks.named('processResources'))` instructs the `compileKotlin` task to consider the files produced by the `processResources` task as part of its inputs. We need this task because we are going to create custom properties to configure the output prefix, and the usage of a Logger for the console output; and we are going to provide some metadata that allows other IDEs to get hints about what our properties mean.

- `dependencyManagement`: This section serves as a central location for declaring dependencies and their versions without including them in the project. Think of it as a template for dependencies.

  - `imports { }`: We are importing dependencies defined elsewhere.

  - `mavenBom org.springframework.boot.gradle.plugin. SpringBootPlugin.BOM_COORDINATES`: This specific line imports a bill of materials (BOM) from the Spring Boot Gradle plugin. A BOM is a compressed list of dependencies with specific versions, ensuring consistency and compatibility across projects.

Next, let's check/define the model that we will use as an event. In the end, this event will be persistent in a database. Listing 14-2 shows the `MyRetroAuditEvent` class.

Listing 14-2. src/main/kotlin/com/apress/myretro/model/
MyRetroAuditEvent.kt

```kotlin
package com.apress.myretro.model

import com.fasterxml.jackson.annotation.JsonFormat
import jakarta.persistence.Entity
import jakarta.persistence.GeneratedValue
import jakarta.persistence.GenerationType
import jakarta.persistence.Id
import java.time.LocalDateTime

@Entity
data class MyRetroAuditEvent(
    @Id
    @GeneratedValue(strategy = GenerationType.AUTO)
    var id: Long? = null,

    @JsonFormat(pattern = "yyyy-MM-dd HH:mm:ss")
    var timestamp: LocalDateTime = LocalDateTime.now(),

    var interceptor: String? = null,
    var method: String? = null,
    var args: String? = null,
    var result: String? = null,
    var message: String? = null
)
```

The MyRetroAuditEvent class will be our main event with the fields we need, the
timestamp (when the event occurred), a method (the method being executed), args
(any arguments passed to the method), a result (if the method returns something),
a message (text that can be used to identify the event), and an interceptor (the name
of what action happens, a BEFORE, AFTER, or AROUND). And, of course, this class will be
persistent in a database, so we need to use the @Entity and @Id annotations. The @Id
annotation is an auto-increment feature.

Next, check/define the repository pattern we use. Listing 14-3 shows the
MyRetroAuditEventRepository interface.

Listing 14-3. src/main/kotlin/com/apress/myretro/model/
MyRetroAuditEventRepository.kt

```
package com.apress.myretro.model

import org.springframework.data.repository.CrudRepository

interface MyRetroAuditEventRepository : CrudRepository<MyRetroAuditEvent, Long>
```

The `MyRetroAuditEventRepository` interface will be the JPA repository model that will be persistent in the database.

Now that you have set the model and repository, you can open/create the `MyRetroAudit` annotation. See Listing 14-4.

Listing 14-4. src/main/kotlin/com/apress/myretro/annotations/
MyRetroAudit.kt

```
package com.apress.myretro.annotations

@Retention(AnnotationRetention.RUNTIME)
@Target(
    AnnotationTarget.FUNCTION,
    AnnotationTarget.PROPERTY_GETTER,
    AnnotationTarget.PROPERTY_SETTER,
    AnnotationTarget.CLASS
)
annotation class MyRetroAudit(
    val showArgs: Boolean = false,
    val format: MyRetroAuditOutputFormat = MyRetroAuditOutputFormat.TXT,
    val intercept: MyRetroAuditIntercept = MyRetroAuditIntercept.BEFORE,
    val message: String = "",
    val prettyPrint: Boolean = false
)
```

Listing 14-4 shows the `MyRetroAudit` custom annotation that will be used in any method we want to emit the audit/event. Let's review the parameters it's using:

- `showArgs`: This parameter will be a Boolean, meaning that if it's set to `true`, the event will show the arguments passed to the method being audited as part of the event; `false` will be otherwise. The default value is set to `false`.

- `format`: This is an enum value (from `MyRetroAuditOutputFormat` enum) that has only JSON or TXT values. The default value is set to `MyRetroAuditOutputFormat.TXT`.

- `intercept`: This is an enum value (from `MyRetroAuditIntercept` enum); this enum has the `BEFORE`, `AFTER`, and `AROUND` values. This parameter will set the event behavior if the audited method is called and will generate the event before, after, or during its execution. The default value is set to `MyRetroAuditIntercept.BEFORE`.

- `message`: This is an arbitrary message that can be set as part of the event. We can use it to enable some convention for future reference, perhaps in a logging system (such as Splunk or PaperTrail) to find events and group them quickly. The default value is set to an empty string.

- `prettyPrint`: This is a Boolean value that will set the way it prints the event in the console. Normally, if the output is a JSON string, you will want it to be in a pretty form and not in a single line. The default value is set to `false`.

Listings 14-5 and 14-6 show the `MyRetroAuditOutputFormat` and `MyRetroAuditIntercept` enums.

Listing 14-5. src/main/kotlin/com/apress/myretro/annotations/ MyRetroAuditOutputFormat.kt

```kotlin
package com.apress.myretro.formats
enum class MyRetroAuditOutputFormat {
    JSON, TXT
}
```

Listing 14-6. src/main/kotlin/com/apress/myretro/annotations/
MyRetroAuditIntercept.kt

```
package com.apress.myretro.annotations
enum class MyRetroAuditIntercept {
    BEFORE, AFTER, AROUND
}
```

Next, open/create the EnableMyRetroAudit annotation. See Listing 14-7.

Listing 14-7. src/main/kotlin/com/apress/myretro/annotations/
EnableMyRetroAudit.kt

```
package com.apress.myretro.annotations

import com.apress.myretro.configuration.MyRetroAuditConfiguration
import org.springframework.context.annotation.Import

@Retention(AnnotationRetention.RUNTIME)
@Target(AnnotationTarget.CLASS)
@Import(
    MyRetroAuditConfiguration::class
)
annotation class EnableMyRetroAudit(
    val storage: MyRetroAuditStorage = MyRetroAuditStorage.DATABASE)
```

The EnableMyRetroAudit annotation will be required to configure the @
MyRetroAudit annotation. It is our @Enable* feature! The parameter we are using is the
storage, which is a MyRetroAuditStorage enum with the CONSOLE, DATABASE, and FILE
values. This will persist the event (DATABASE), to console (CONSOLE, not persistent) or in
a file (FILE). The default value is set to MyRetroAuditStorage.DATABASE. Listing 14-8
shows the MyRetroAuditStorage enum.

Listing 14-8. src/main/kotlin/com/apress/myretro/annotations/
MyRetroAuditStorage.kt

```
package com.apress.myretro.annotations
enum class MyRetroAuditStorage {
    CONSOLE, DATABASE, FILE
}
```

Next, to be able to know at runtime what `storage` value was set in the @ EnableMyRetroAudit annotation, we need to determine the value at runtime. There are many ways to do this in Spring; we demonstrate only one of them.

Open/create the EnableMyRetroAuditValueProvider class. See Listing 14-9.

Listing 14-9. src/main/kotlin/com/apress/myretro/annotations/ EnableMyRetroAuditValueProvider.kt

```kotlin
package com.apress.myretro.annotations

import org.springframework.beans.BeansException
import org.springframework.beans.factory.config.BeanFactoryPostProcessor
import org.springframework.beans.factory.config.
ConfigurableListableBeanFactory
import org.springframework.stereotype.Component
import java.util.*

@Component
class EnableMyRetroAuditValueProvider : BeanFactoryPostProcessor {
    @Throws(BeansException::class)
    override fun postProcessBeanFactory(beanFactory:
    ConfigurableListableBeanFactory) {
        val beanName = beanFactory.getBeanNamesForAnnotation(
            EnableMyRetroAudit::class.java
        ).firstOrNull()
        if (beanName != null) {
            storage = beanFactory
                .findAnnotationOnBean(beanName, EnableMyRetroAudit::
                class.java)!!.storage
        }
    }

    companion object {
        var storage = MyRetroAuditStorage.DATABASE
            private set
    }
}
```

Let's review the `EnableMyRetroAuditValueProvider` class:

- `BeanFactoryPostProcessor`: The `BeanFactoryPostProcessor` shines in Spring for customizing Spring Bean definitions before they're instantiated. Think of it as a handy tool for fine-tuning your application's configuration after Spring reads initial settings. It's great for the following:

    - *Dynamic configuration*: Adapt bean definitions based on environment variables, external files, or runtime conditions.

    - *Centralized property handling*: Inject shared properties into multiple beans without repetitive configuration.

    - *Conditional bean registration*: Create beans only if specific conditions are met, making your application flexible.

    - *Custom bean modification*: Add custom logic or modify bean definitions before bean creation, tailoring behavior to your needs.

- `postProcessBeanFactory (ConfigurableListableBeanFactory beanFactory)`: This is the method to implement. Note that with the `ConfigurableListableBeanFactory;` we can find the annotations declared in Spring Beans. We are using `EnableMyRetroAudit` to be found in all beans, then if the auto-configuration finds this annotation (`@EnableMyRetroAudit`), we can get the value used in the `storage` parameter. If it's not found, it will use the default value, the `MyRetroAuditStorage.DATABASE`.

Also notice that this class is marked using the `@Component` annotation, so it will be picked up during the Spring Bean lifecycle and initialization. At any time, we can use the following code to retrieve the value set:

`EnableMyRetroAuditValueProvider.getStorage()`

Next, let's talk about the formats we are going to use. Recall that `@MyRetroAudit` can use the `format` parameter. Let's create a strategy that can help with the format (pretty print or not) of the received event, which will be easy to use and extend if necessary.

Open/create the `MyRetroAuditFormatStrategy` interface. See Listing 14-10.

Listing 14-10. src/main/kotlin/com/apress/myretro/formats/
MyRetroAuditFormatStrategy.kt

```
package com.apress.myretro.formats

import com.apress.myretro.model.MyRetroAuditEvent

interface MyRetroAuditFormatStrategy {
    fun format(event: MyRetroAuditEvent): String
    fun prettyFormat(event: MyRetroAuditEvent): String
}
```

We are defining two methods in the MyRetroAuditFormatStrategy interface, format and prettyFormat. They accept MyRetroAuditEvent and return a String type.

Next, open/create the MyRetroAuditFormatStrategyFactory class, which, as the name implies, will help us create the strategy we need based on the MyRetroAuditOutputFormat enum. See Listing 14-11.

Listing 14-11. src/main/kotlin/com/apress/myretro/formats/
MyRetroAuditFormatStrategyFactory.kt

```
package com.apress.myretro.formats

import com.apress.myretro.annotations.MyRetroAuditOutputFormat

object MyRetroAuditFormatStrategyFactory {
    fun getStrategy(outputFormat: MyRetroAuditOutputFormat?):
            MyRetroAuditFormatStrategy =
            when (outputFormat) {
            MyRetroAuditOutputFormat.JSON -> JsonOutputFormatStrategy()
            MyRetroAuditOutputFormat.TXT -> TextOutputFormatStrategy()
            else -> TextOutputFormatStrategy()
        }
}
```

As you can see, this is a very simple Factory implementation. Next, let's check the two strategy implementations. Open/create the JsonOutputFormatStrategy and TextOutputFormatStrategy classes that will implement the strategy MyRetroAuditFormatStrategy interface. See Listings 14-12 and 14-13.

Listing 14-12. src/main/kotlin/com/apress/myretro/formats/
JsonOutputFormatStrategy.kt

```kotlin
package com.apress.myretro.formats

import com.apress.myretro.model.MyRetroAuditEvent
import com.fasterxml.jackson.databind.ObjectMapper
import com.fasterxml.jackson.datatype.jsr310.JavaTimeModule

class JsonOutputFormatStrategy : MyRetroAuditFormatStrategy {
    private val objectMapper = ObjectMapper().apply {
        registerModule(JavaTimeModule())
    }

    override fun format(event: MyRetroAuditEvent): String =
        objectMapper.writeValueAsString(event)

    override fun prettyFormat(event: MyRetroAuditEvent): String =
        "\n\n" + objectMapper
            .writerWithDefaultPrettyPrinter()
            .writeValueAsString(event) + "\n"
}
```

Listing 14-13. src/main/kotlin/com/apress/myretro/formats/
TextOutputFormatStrategy.kt

```kotlin
package com.apress.myretro.formats

import com.apress.myretro.model.MyRetroAuditEvent

class TextOutputFormatStrategy : MyRetroAuditFormatStrategy {
    override fun format(event: MyRetroAuditEvent): String =
        event.toString()

    override fun prettyFormat(event: MyRetroAuditEvent): String =
        """

        $event

        """.trimIndent()
}
```

As you can see, these classes are very straightforward, but you should still review them before continuing.

Next, open/create the MyRetroAuditAspect class, shown in Listing 14-14. This class, as the name says, will implement an AOP Aspect which allows us to intercept calls and do much more, and in this case, it will do all the logic based on the requirements.

Listing 14-14. src/main/kotlin/com/apress/myretro/aop/
MyRetroAuditAspect.kt

```kotlin
package com.apress.myretro.aop

import com.apress.myretro.annotations.MyRetroAudit
import com.apress.myretro.annotations.MyRetroAuditIntercept
import com.apress.myretro.annotations.MyRetroAuditStorage
import com.apress.myretro.configuration.MyRetroAuditProperties
import com.apress.myretro.formats.MyRetroAuditFormatStrategy
import com.apress.myretro.formats.MyRetroAuditFormatStrategyFactory
import com.apress.myretro.model.MyRetroAuditEvent
import com.apress.myretro.model.MyRetroAuditEventRepository
import org.aspectj.lang.ProceedingJoinPoint
import org.aspectj.lang.annotation.Around
import org.aspectj.lang.annotation.Aspect
import org.slf4j.LoggerFactory
import org.springframework.beans.factory.annotation.Autowired

@Aspect
class MyRetroAuditAspect(
    private var eventRepository: MyRetroAuditEventRepository,
    private var properties: MyRetroAuditProperties,
    private var storage: MyRetroAuditStorage) {

    @Around("@annotation(audit)")
    @Throws(Throwable::class)
    fun auditAround(joinPoint: ProceedingJoinPoint, audit:
    MyRetroAudit): Any {
        var myRetroEvent = MyRetroAuditEvent().apply {
            method = joinPoint.signature.name
```

```
            args = if (audit.showArgs) joinPoint.args.contentToString()
            else null
            message = audit.message
            if (audit.intercept == MyRetroAuditIntercept.BEFORE) {
                interceptor = MyRetroAuditIntercept.BEFORE.name
            } else if (audit.intercept == MyRetroAuditIntercept.AROUND) {
                interceptor = MyRetroAuditIntercept.AROUND.name
            }
        }

        val result: Any = joinPoint.proceed(joinPoint.args)

        myRetroEvent.result = result.toString()
        if (audit.intercept == MyRetroAuditIntercept.AFTER) {
            myRetroEvent.interceptor = MyRetroAuditIntercept.AFTER.name
        }

        // Database, Console or File
        if (storage == MyRetroAuditStorage.DATABASE) {
            myRetroEvent = eventRepository.save<MyRetroAuditEvent>(myR
            etroEvent)
        }

        // Logger or Console
        val formattedEvent = formatEvent(audit, myRetroEvent)
        if (properties.useLogger) {
            LOG.info("{}{}", properties.prefix, formattedEvent)
        } else {
            println(properties.prefix + formattedEvent)
        }
        return result
    }

    private fun formatEvent(audit: MyRetroAudit, myRetroEvent:
    MyRetroAuditEvent):
            String {
        val strategy: MyRetroAuditFormatStrategy =
```

```
        MyRetroAuditFormatStrategyFactory.getStrategy(audit.format)
    return if (audit.prettyPrint) strategy.
    prettyFormat(myRetroEvent) else
        strategy.format(myRetroEvent)
}

companion object {
    private val LOG = LoggerFactory.getLogger(MyRetroAuditAspect::c
    lass.java)
}
}
```

In the MyRetroAuditAspect class, we are using MyRetroAuditEventRepository, MyRetroAuditProperties, and MyRetroAuditStorage as fields that are required when this class is constructed. MyRetroAuditEventRepository will help persist the event in the database; MyRetroAuditProperties will be used to get the properties' values from the prefix, file, and useLogger fields from this class; and MyRetroAuditStorage will get the value from the EnableMyRetroAuditValueProvider class. Let's review this more in detail:

- @Aspect: This annotation indicates that this class is an AOP Aspect, and there are some configurations that need to be set.

- @Around("@annotation(audit)"): This annotation is an AROUND advice that will be executed when the @MyRetroAudit annotation is found. With the AROUND advice, we have control over what to call, what to send to the actual method call, and how to respond. (Use this carefully; with this, you could become a hacker!)

- auditAround(ProceedingJoinPoint, MyRetroAudit): This method is the *pointcut* that will be executed when the method is about to be called. For an AROUND advice, this will always require the ProceedingJoinPoint, and in this case, the @MyRetroAudit annotation. This is because we need its parameter values, if any; if not, we are using the defaults.

Before continuing, review this class and see the sections of the Database and the logger.

Next, open/create the MyRetroAuditProperties class. See Listing 14-15.

Listing 14-15. src/main/kotlin/com/apress/myretro/configuration/
MyRetroAuditProperties.kt

```kotlin
package com.apress.myretro.configuration

import org.springframework.boot.context.properties.ConfigurationProperties

@ConfigurationProperties(prefix = "myretro.audit")
data class MyRetroAuditProperties(
    /**
     * The prefix to use for all audit messages.
     */
    var prefix:String = "[AUDIT] ",

    /**
     * The file to use for audit messages.
     */
    var file:String = "myretro.events",

    /*
     * User logger instead of standard print out.
     */
    var useLogger:Boolean = false
)
```

Listing 14-15 shows that, in the @ConfigurationProperties annotation, we are defining the configurable properties that will be exposed as myretro.audit.* (prefix, file, useLogger). We are creating some comments/documentation on each field, because we want these to be used as hints/descriptions when other developers use this custom starter. (We are going to talk more about these hints in the following sections; we need to ensure that these hints are processed so they can be used by editors.)

Next, open/create the MyRetroAuditConfiguration class. This will be the magic behind the custom starter; this is when the auto-configuration happens. See Listing 14-16.

Listing 14-16. src/main/kotlin/com/apress/myretro/configuration/
MyRetroAuditConfiguration.kt

```kotlin
package com.apress.myretro.configuration

import com.apress.myretro.annotations.EnableMyRetroAuditValueProvider
import com.apress.myretro.aop.MyRetroAuditAspect
import com.apress.myretro.listener.MyRetroAuditListener
import com.apress.myretro.model.MyRetroAuditEventRepository
import org.springframework.boot.autoconfigure.AutoConfiguration
import org.springframework.boot.autoconfigure.domain.EntityScan
import org.springframework.boot.context.properties.EnableConfigurationProperties
import org.springframework.context.annotation.Bean
import org.springframework.context.annotation.ComponentScan
import org.springframework.context.annotation.Conditional
import org.springframework.data.jpa.repository.config.EnableJpaRepositories

@EnableConfigurationProperties(MyRetroAuditProperties::class)
@Conditional(
    MyRetroAuditCondition::class
)
@EnableJpaRepositories(basePackages = ["com.apress"])
@ComponentScan(basePackages = ["com.apress"])
@EntityScan(basePackages = ["com.apress"])
@AutoConfiguration
class MyRetroAuditConfiguration {
    @Bean
    fun myRetroListener(): MyRetroAuditListener =
        MyRetroAuditListener()

    @Bean
    fun myRetroAuditAspect(
        myRetroAuditEventRepository: MyRetroAuditEventRepository,
        properties: MyRetroAuditProperties
    ): MyRetroAuditAspect =
        MyRetroAuditAspect(myRetroAuditEventRepository,
                properties, EnableMyRetroAuditValueProvider.storage)
}
```

Again, the MyRetroAuditConfiguration class is the magic that we are providing to developers who will be using this custom starter. The key piece here is the @Conditional annotation, which checks out if a condition is met, and in this case, that condition is from the MyRetroAuditCondition class (discussed shortly). If this condition is not met, any declaration from this class is omitted/skipped.

The other annotations are standard to our custom starter. The @AutoConfiguration annotation indicates that a class provides configuration that Spring Boot can automatically apply. This annotation is a subclass (or composed annotation) of @Configuration, and it has the proxyBeanMethods parameter set to false.

Spring creates proxies for @Bean methods in configuration classes. These proxies ensure consistent bean lifecycle management and enforce singleton behavior even if you call the @Bean method directly. However, using proxyBeanMethods = false disables this behavior. With the proxyBeanMethods = false:

- No proxies are created for @Bean methods.

- Calling a @Bean method directly creates a new instance of the bean. This can improve performance, as proxy creation and invocation have some overhead. However, singleton behavior is not enforced if you call the method directly.

And this is what we want, because we are creating the @Bean MyRetroAuditAspect! In Listing 14-16, we are creating a new instance and passing the necessary fields—MyRetroAuditEventRepository, MyRetroAuditProperties, and the value of the EnableMyRetroAuditValueProvider.getStorage().

Again, we are providing the magic behind using the @EnableMyRetroAudit annotation when it's declared. Open/create the MyRetroAuditCondition class. See Listing 14-17.

Listing 14-17. src/main/kotlin/com/apress/myretro/configuration/ MyRetroAuditCondition.kt

```
package com.apress.myretro.configuration

import com.apress.myretro.annotations.EnableMyRetroAudit
import org.springframework.context.annotation.Condition
import org.springframework.context.annotation.ConditionContext
import org.springframework.core.type.AnnotatedTypeMetadata
```

```kotlin
class MyRetroAuditCondition : Condition {
    override fun matches(context: ConditionContext,
            metadata: AnnotatedTypeMetadata): Boolean =
        context.beanFactory!!.getBeansWithAnnotation(EnableMyRetroAudit::
        class.java)
            .isNotEmpty()

}
```

In the MyRetroAuditCondition class, if the call of this condition (which checks for the @EnableMyRetroAudit being declared) is false, then the auto-configuration skips it and doesn't continue with the rest of the configuration. It goes to the next auto-configuration. But if the call returns true, the logic or statements of the auto-configuration continue.

Note that the MyRetroAuditCondition.matches queries context.getBeanFactory().getBeansWithAnnotation to see if it's in the Spring registry map.

Next, we already defined our auto-configuration, and per the rules of creating a custom starter, we need to tell Spring Boot where to get this auto-configuration. We need to create the org.springframework.boot.autoconfigure.AutoConfiguration.imports file in the META-INF/spring folder with the name of our auto-configuration class. See Listing 14-18.

Listing 14-18. src/main/resources/META-INF/spring/org.springframework. boot.autoconfigure.AutoConfiguration.imports

```
com.apress.myretro.configuration.MyRetroAuditConfiguration
```

We are defining the complete name (package.name) of the auto-configuration class. Automatically, Spring Boot will see that we defined this org.springframework.boot.autoconfigure.AutoConfiguration.imports file, and it will execute any logic behind this auto-configuration class. You can add multiple classes; each class has to be on its own line (with a carriage return). If you need to, you can take a peek at the spring-boot-autoconfigure JAR and see this file.

As a final step, we need to give our developers hints about using the custom starter properties. Open/create the META-INF/additional-spring-configuration-metadata.json file. See Listing 14-19.

Listing 14-19. src/main/resources/META-INF/additional-spring-configuration-metadata.json

```json
{
  "groups": [
    {
      "name": "myretro.audit",
      "type": "com.apress.myretro.configuration.MyRetroAuditProperties",
      "sourceType": "com.apress.myretro.configuration.
      MyRetroAuditProperties"
    }
  ],
  "properties": [
    {
      "name": "myretro.audit.prefix",
      "type": "java.lang.String",
      "sourceType": "com.apress.myretro.configuration.
      MyRetroAuditProperties",
      "defaultValue": "[AUDIT] ",
      "description": "Prefix for audit messages"
    },
    {
      "name": "myretro.audit.file",
      "type": "java.lang.String",
      "sourceType": "com.apress.myretro.configuration.
      MyRetroAuditProperties",
      "defaultValue": "myretro.events",
      "description": "File to write audit messages to"
    },
    {
      "name": "myretro.audit.useLogger",
      "type": "java.lang.Boolean",
      "sourceType": "com.apress.myretro.configuration.
      MyRetroAuditProperties",
      "defaultValue": "false",
      "description": "Enable audit logging"
```

```
    }
  ],
  "hints": [
    {
      "name": "myretro.audit.prefix",
      "values": [
        {
          "value": "[AUDIT] ",
          "description": "Prefix for audit messages"
        },
        {
          "value": ">>> ",
          "description": "Prefix for audit messages"
        }
      ]
    },
    {
      "name": "myretro.audit.file",
      "values": [
        {
          "value": "myretro.events",
          "description": "File to write audit messages to"
        },
        {
          "value": "myretro.log",
          "description": "File to write audit messages to"
        }
      ]
    },
    {
      "name": "myretro.audit.useLogger",
      "values": [
        {
          "value": "true",
          "description": "Enable audit logging"
```

```
      },
      {
        "value": "false",
        "description": "Disable audit logging, just print out console"
      }
    ]
  }
 ]
}
```

This JSON file is very straightforward; we just define some values and descriptions for our properties (prefix, file, useLogger). When we compile our project automatically, the configuration-processor will generate the necessary metadata for editors. This is very helpful for developers when they have to know what those properties mean and which values they can be set to.

Building the myretro-spring-boot-starter Custom Starter

Let's compile the custom starter now. If everything went smoothly in the previous sections, you can build the custom starter with the following command:

```
./gradlew build
```

This command generates the myretro-spring-boot-starter-0.0.1.jar file in the build/libs folder, ready to be used! If you want to skip the following section of publishing the JAR to a Maven repository, you can do so and use just this JAR in the following form in your client (Users) App project (in your build.gradle file):

```
//...
dependencies {
    //...
    implementation files('../myretro-spring-boot-starter/build/libs/
    myretro-spring-boot-starter-0.0.1.jar')
    //...
}
```

This declaration assumes that you have the `myretro-spring-boot-starter` project one level below. If you want every developer to have access to it, you need to publish it to a Maven repository.

Publishing the Custom Starter in GitHub as a Maven Artifact

To publish the starter, you can use GitHub as a Maven artifact repository. The good part is that GitHub gives you publishing features, not only for Maven but also for Docker images.

To publish a Maven artifact, you need to do three things:

1. Create a GitHub token that allows you to write/publish to your repositories. Consult this documentation to create your personal token: `https://docs.github.com/en/authentication/keeping-your-account-and-data-secure/managing-your-personal-access-tokens`.

2. Create a new empty repository in GitHub as a regular project. In this case, we created a new repo: `https://github.com/felipeg48/myretro-spring-boot-starter`.

3. Add the necessary declarations to the `build.gradle` file to publish the artifact.

To start, let's modify the `build.gradle` file. See Listing 14-20.

Listing 14-20. The build.gradle File

```
import org.jetbrains.kotlin.gradle.tasks.KotlinCompile
plugins {
    id 'org.springframework.boot' version '3.2.3' apply false
    id 'io.spring.dependency-management' version '1.1.4'
    id 'maven-publish'
    id 'org.jetbrains.kotlin.jvm' version '2.0.20-RC'
    id "org.jetbrains.kotlin.plugin.spring" version "2.0.20-RC"
    // <- simplifies spring proxying
}
```

```
group = 'com.apress'
version = '0.0.1'

java {
    sourceCompatibility = '17'
}

configurations {
    compileOnly {
        extendsFrom annotationProcessor
    }
}

tasks.named('compileKotlin') {
    inputs.files(tasks.named('processResources'))
}

repositories {
    mavenCentral()
}

dependencyManagement {
    imports {
        mavenBom org.springframework.boot.gradle.plugin.SpringBootPlugin.
        BOM_COORDINATES
    }
}

dependencies {
    implementation "org.jetbrains.kotlin:kotlin-stdlib-jdk8"
    implementation "org.jetbrains.kotlin:kotlin-reflect"

    implementation 'org.springframework.boot:spring-boot-starter-web'
    implementation 'org.springframework.boot:spring-boot-starter-aop'
    implementation 'org.springframework.boot:spring-boot-starter-data-jpa'
    implementation 'com.fasterxml.jackson.datatype:jackson-datatype-jsr310'

    runtimeOnly 'com.h2database:h2'
```

```
    annotationProcessor 'org.springframework.boot:spring-boot-
    configuration-processor'

    testImplementation 'org.springframework.boot:spring-boot-starter-test'
}
tasks.named('test') {
    useJUnitPlatform()
}

publishing {
    publications {
        mavenJava(MavenPublication) {
            from components.java
            artifactId = 'myretro-spring-boot-starter'

            versionMapping {
                usage('java-api') {
                    fromResolutionOf('runtimeClasspath')
                }
                usage('java-runtime') {
                    fromResolutionResult()
                }
            }

            pom {
                name = 'My Retro Starter'
                description = 'A spring-boot-starter library example'

                licenses {
                    license {
                        name = 'The Apache License, Version 2.0'
                        url = 'http://www.apache.org/licenses/
                        LICENSE-2.0.txt'
                    }
                }
                developers {
                    developer {
```

```
                            id = 'felipeg48'
                            name = 'Felipe'
                            email = ''
                        }
                    }
                    scm {
                        connection = 'scm:git:git://github.com/felipeg48/
                        myretro-spring-boot-starter.git'
                        developerConnection = 'scm:git:ssh://github.com/
                        felipeg48/myretro-spring-boot-starter.git'
                        url = 'https://github.com/felipeg48/myretro-spring-
                        boot-starter'
                    }
                }
            }
        }
    repositories {
        maven {
            name = "GitHubPackages"
            url = uri("https://maven.pkg.github.com/felipeg48/myretro-
            spring-boot-starter")
            credentials {
                username = project.findProperty("GITHUB_USERNAME") ?:
                System.getenv("GITHUB_USERNAME")
                password = project.findProperty("GITHUB_TOKEN") ?:
                System.getenv("GITHUB_TOKEN")
            }
        }
    }
}

//    kotlin {
//        jvmToolchain(17)
//    }
tasks.withType(KotlinCompile).configureEach {
    kotlinOptions {
```

```
    freeCompilerArgs = ['-Xjsr305=strict']
    jvmTarget = '17'
  }
}
```

Let's review the modified `build.gradle` file per section:

- `plugins`: Here, we added the `maven-publish` plugin, which has the logic to publish the artifact to a Maven repository.

- `publishing`: This section helps define the metadata necessary for the Maven repository; it also identifies how to sign in if the repository is private or if it requires credentials or some authentication mechanism.

- `publishing.publications`. Here, we are defining the metadata that the artifact needs to be registered in the Maven repository. Reviewing it is very straightforward.

- `publishing.repositories`: This section defines where the repository is located. We have a special URL, `https://maven.pkg.github.com/felipeg48/myretro-spring-boot-starter`. This URL is a declaration and it is used to find the packages. It also defines any credentials, and in this case, we are looking for the username and password using the `GITHUB_USERNAME` and `GITHUB_TOKEN` variables (which can be set in the `$HOME/.gradle/gradle.properties` file or with environment variables).

Now that everything is in place, let's publish the artifact. Remember that you need to create an empty repository; in this case, we created the `myretro-spring-boot-starter` in GitHub (as a project). Execute the following command to publish the artifact in your repo (see Figure 14-1):

```
./gradlew publish
```

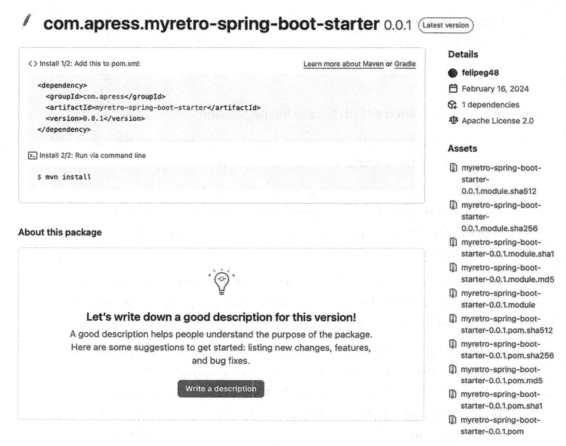

Figure 14-1. *Package in GitHub (https://github.com/felipeg48/myretro-spring-boot-starter/packages)*

As you can see, the package was deployed successfully. It's time to use it.

Using the myretro-spring-boot-starter Custom Starter

Let's open the Users App project; you can import it into your favorite IDE from the 14-extending/users directory. Or if you want to start from scratch with the Spring Initializr (https://start.spring.io), set the Group field to com.apress and the Artifact and Name fields to users. Add Web, JPA, Processor, Validation, Actuator, and H2 as dependencies. Generate and download the project, unzip it, and import it into your favorite IDE.

Next, open the build.gradle file. See Listing 14-21.

Listing 14-21. The build.gradle File

```
import org.jetbrains.kotlin.gradle.tasks.KotlinCompile
plugins {
    id 'java'
    id 'org.springframework.boot' version '3.2.3'
    id 'io.spring.dependency-management' version '1.1.4'
    id 'org.hibernate.orm' version '6.4.1.Final'
    id 'org.jetbrains.kotlin.jvm' version '2.0.20-RC'
    id "org.jetbrains.kotlin.plugin.spring" version "2.0.20-RC"
    // <- simplifies spring proxying
}

group = 'com.apress'
version = '0.0.1-SNAPSHOT'

java {
    sourceCompatibility = '17'
}

configurations {
    compileOnly {
        extendsFrom annotationProcessor
    }
}

repositories {
    mavenCentral()
    maven {
        url 'https://maven.pkg.github.com/felipeg48/myretro-spring-
        boot-starter'
        credentials {
            username =
project.findProperty("GITHUB_USERNAME") ?: System.getenv("GITHUB_
USERNAME")
            password =
```

```
    project.findProperty("GITHUB_TOKEN") ?: System.getenv("GITHUB_TOKEN")
        }
    }
}

dependencies {
    implementation "org.jetbrains.kotlin:kotlin-stdlib-jdk8"
    implementation "org.jetbrains.kotlin:kotlin-reflect"

    implementation 'org.springframework.boot:spring-boot-starter-web'
    implementation 'org.springframework.boot:spring-boot-starter-
    validation'
    implementation 'org.springframework.boot:spring-boot-starter-data-jpa'
    implementation 'org.springframework.boot:spring-boot-starter-actuator'

    // H2 runtime only
    runtimeOnly 'com.h2database:h2'

    // My Retro Starter
    //implementation files('../myretro-spring-boot-starter/build/libs/
    myretro-spring-boot-starter-0.0.1.jar')
    implementation 'com.apress:myretro-spring-boot-starter:0.0.1'

    annotationProcessor 'org.springframework.boot:spring-boot-
    configuration-processor'

    // Web
    implementation 'org.webjars:bootstrap:5.2.3'

    // Test
    testImplementation 'org.springframework.boot:spring-boot-starter-test'
}

tasks.named('test') {
    useJUnitPlatform()
}

//    kotlin {
//        jvmToolchain(17)
//    }
```

```
tasks.withType(KotlinCompile).configureEach {
    kotlinOptions {
        freeCompilerArgs = ['-Xjsr305=strict']
        jvmTarget = '17'
    }
}
```

Let's review the build.gradle file:

- repositories.maven: In this statement, we are using the url that we set to https://maven.pkg.github.com/felipeg48/myretro-spring-boot-starter, and then in the credentials section we are looking at the GITHUB_USERNAME and GITHUB_TOKEN variables (which can be set in the $HOME/.gradle/gradle.properties file or with environment variables). If your repository is public, you can omit the credentials section.

- implementation 'com.apress:myretro-spring-boot-starter:0.0.1': Here we are using the artifact that we just published! Remember that if you need to test the JAR alone, you can use the following (assuming you have the projects in the same folder):

  implementation files('../myretro-spring-boot-starter/build/libs/myretro-spring-boot-starter-0.0.1.jar')

If you are using the source code from 14-extending/users, you can continue following along, but if you are creating this from scratch, you can use the code from the JPA chapter by removing the events package and fixing the UserService where we are using/publishing the events. This will change now.

Next, open/create the UserService class. See Listing 14-22.

Listing 14-22. src/main/kotlin/com/apress/users/UserService.kt

```kotlin
package com.apress.users.service

import com.apress.myretro.annotations.MyRetroAudit
import com.apress.myretro.annotations.MyRetroAuditOutputFormat
import com.apress.users.actuator.LogEventEndpoint
import com.apress.users.model.User
import com.apress.users.repository.UserRepository
import org.springframework.beans.factory.annotation.Autowired
import org.springframework.context.ApplicationEventPublisher
import org.springframework.stereotype.Service
import java.util.*

@Service
class UserService {
    @Autowired
    private lateinit var userRepository: UserRepository
    @Autowired
    private lateinit var publisher: ApplicationEventPublisher
    @Autowired
    private lateinit var logEventsEndpoint: LogEventEndpoint

    val allUsers: Iterable<User>
        get() = userRepository.findAll()

    fun findUserByEmail(email: String): Optional<User> =
        userRepository.findById(email)

    @MyRetroAudit(
        showArgs = true,
        message = "Saving or updating user",
        format = MyRetroAuditOutputFormat.JSON,
        prettyPrint = true
    )
    fun saveUpdateUser(user: User): User =
        userRepository.save<User>(user)
```

```kotlin
    fun removeUserByEmail(email: String) =
        userRepository.deleteById(email)
}
```

Listing 14-22 shows that we are using the @MyRetroAudit annotation, and we are using some parameters there.

If you try to run the application now (with ./gradlew bootRun), nothing will happen. There are no logs; there are no records of the events in the database. We are missing the @EnableMyRetroAudit annotation. Let's add it. Open/create the UserConfiguration class. See Listing 14-23.

Listing 14-23. src/main/kotlin/com/apress/users/config/UserConfiguration.kt

```kotlin
package com.apress.users.config

import com.apress.myretro.annotations.EnableMyRetroAudit
import com.apress.users.model.User
import com.apress.users.model.UserRole
import com.apress.users.service.UserService
import org.springframework.boot.CommandLineRunner
import org.springframework.boot.context.properties.
EnableConfigurationProperties
import org.springframework.context.annotation.Bean
import org.springframework.context.annotation.Configuration
import java.util.List

@EnableMyRetroAudit
@Configuration
@EnableConfigurationProperties(
    UserProperties::class
)
class UserConfiguration {
    @Bean
    fun init(userService: UserService): CommandLineRunner {
        return CommandLineRunner { _: Array<String> ->
            userService.saveUpdateUser(
                User(
                    "ximena@email.com",
```

```
                    "Ximena",
                    "https://www.gravatar.com/avatar/23bb62a7d0ca63c9a80490
                    8e57bf6bd4?d=wavatar",
                    "aw2s0meR!",
                    listOf(UserRole.USER),
                    true
                )
            )
            userService.saveUpdateUser(
                User(
                    "norma@email.com",
                    "Norma",
                    "https://www.gravatar.com/avatar/f07f7e553264c9710105ed
                    ebe6c465e7?d=wavatar",
                    "aw2s0meR!",
                    listOf(UserRole.USER, UserRole.ADMIN),
                    false
                )
            )
        }
    }
}
```

Listing 14-23 shows that now we are using the @EnableMyRetroAudit annotation (with no parameters, meaning that it will take the default value).

Before we run it, let's add some properties to the application.yaml file. See Listing 14-24.

Listing 14-24. src/main/resources/application.yaml

```
spring:
  application:
    name: users-service
  h2:
    console:
      enabled: true
  jpa:
```

```yaml
      generate-ddl: true
      show-sql: true
      hibernate:
        ddl-auto: update
    datasource:
      url: jdbc:h2:mem:users_db
info:
  developer:
    name: Felipe
    email: felipe@email.com
  api:
    version: 1.0
management:
  endpoints:
    web:
      exposure:
        include: health,info,event-config,shutdown,configprops,beans
    endpoint:
      configprops:
        show-values: always
      health:
        show-details: always
        status:
          order: events-down, fatal, down, out-of-service, unknown, up
      shutdown:
        enabled: true
    info:
      env:
        enabled: true
  server:
    port: ${PORT:8091}
  myretro:
    audit:
      useLogger: true
      prefix: '>>> '
```

Listing 14-24 shows that we are using the `myretro.audit.*` properties to set `useLogger` and `prefix`. If you play around with the properties in an IDE, you should see the help, description, and hints that we added to the `additional-spring-configuration-metadata.json` file.

Now we are ready to run the app.

Running Users App with myretro-spring-boot-starter

To run Users App, you can use your IDE or the following command:

`./gradle bootRun`

In the `UserConfiguration#init` method, we are using `UserService` to save two users. So when you run the project, you should see the following output in your console:

```
...
...
INFO 19475 --- [users-service] [main] MyRetroAudit: >>>
{"id":1,"timestamp":"2024-02-20 18:34:38","interceptor":"BEFORE","method":
"saveUpdateUser","args":"[User(email=ximena@email.com, name=Ximena,
gravatarUrl=https://www.gravatar.com/avatar/23bb62a7d0ca63c9a804908e57bf6bd
4?d=wavatar, password=aw2s0meR!, userRole=[USER], active=true)]","result":
"User(email=ximena@email.com, name=Ximena, gravatarUrl=https://www.gravatar.
com/avatar/23bb62a7d0ca63c9a804908e57bf6bd4?d=wavatar, password=aw2s0meR!,
userRole=[USER], active=true)","message":"Saving or updating user"}
....
....
INFO 19475 --- [users-service] [main] MyRetroAudit: >>>
{"id":2,"timestamp":"2024-02-20 18:34:38","interceptor":"BEFORE",
"method":"saveUpdateUser","args":"[User(email=norma@email.com, name=Norma,
gravatarUrl=https://www.gravatar.com/avatar/f07f7e553264c9710105edebe6c46
5e7?d=wavatar, password=aw2s0meR!, userRole=[USER, ADMIN], active=false)]",
"result":"User(email=norma@email.com, name=Norma, gravatarUrl=https://
www.gravatar.com/avatar/f07f7e553264c9710105edebe6c465e7?d=wavatar,
password=aw2s0meR!, userRole=[USER, ADMIN], active=false)","message":
"Saving or updating user"}
....
....
```

Yeah! We have our custom starter using the logger and the JSON format.

Let's see if the events were persisted in the database. In the `application.yaml` file, we enabled the H2 console (with `spring.h2.console.enabled=true`). Open your browser and go to `http://localhost:8091/h2-console`. In the `url` field, enter `jdbc:h2:mem:users_db`, and then click Connect. You will see two tables, `PEOPLE` and `MY_RETRO_AUDIT_EVENT`. Select the `MY_RETRO_AUDIT_EVENT` table and run the following SQL statement:

```
SELECT * FROM MY_RETRO_AUDIT_EVENT
```

You should see two rows listed, as shown in Figure 14-2.

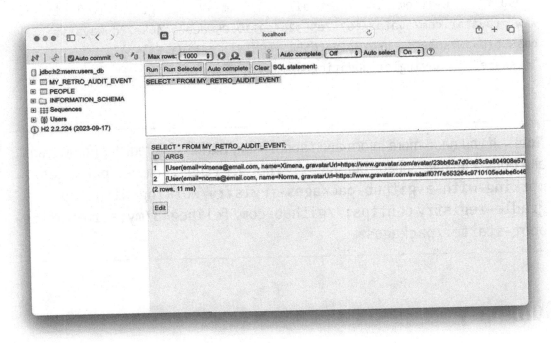

Figure 14-2. *http://localhost:8091/h2-console*

Congrats! You have just created your Spring Boot starter!

You can experiment with all the settings we added; for example, if you change `prettyPrint` to `true` and rerun the app, you should see something like the following (in a pretty JSON format!):

```
2024-02-20T18:45:26.405-05:00  INFO 20644 --- [users-service] [       main]
MyRetroAudit                              : >>>
{
  "id" : 2,
  "timestamp" : "2024-02-20 18:45:26",
  "interceptor" : "BEFORE",
  "method" : "saveUpdateUser",
  "args" : "[User(email=norma@email.com, name=Norma, gravatarUrl=https://
  www.gravatar.com/avatar/f07f7e553264c9710105edebe6c465e7?d=wavatar,
  password=aw2sOmeR!, userRole=[USER, ADMIN], active=false)]",
  "result" : "User(email=norma@email.com, name=Norma, gravatarUrl=https://
  www.gravatar.com/avatar/f07f7e553264c9710105edebe6c465e7?d=wavatar,
  password=aw2sOmeR!, userRole=[USER, ADMIN], active=false)",
  "message" : "Saving or updating user"
}
```

Note   If you need more information about using GitHub as a registry (for Maven
and Docker images), check out https://docs.github.com/en/packages/
working-with-a-github-packages-registry/working-with-the-
gradle-registry or https://github.com/felipeg48/myretro-spring-
boot-starter/packages.

Summary

In this chapter, you learned how to create your own Spring Boot starter. You also learned
more about the @Conditional*, @Enable*, and @AutoConfiguration annotations, which
perform the magic behind the scenes to create what you need.

You learned about the Condition interface and how you can modify it to go through
even more configuration and logic to create your own beans or skip to the next auto-
configuration.

You learned that you need to declare your auto-configuration classes in `META-INF/spring/org.springframework.boot.autoconfigure.AutoConfiguration.imports`. You also learned more about `BeanFactoryPostProcessor` and how to use it to initialize your beans or find information like you did in your `@EnableMyRetroAudit` annotation.

Now that you have a clearer understanding of how Spring Boot works and what you can do with it, Chapter 15 reviews two new Spring projects: Spring Modulith and Spring AI.

CHAPTER 15

Spring Boot New Projects

Felipe Gutierrez[a*]

  [a] 4109 Rillcrest Grove Way Fuquay Varina, NC 27526-3562, Albuquerque, NM, USA

Spring Modulith

Imagine building a complex city, not brick by brick, but by assembling predesigned districts, each with its own function and character. This is the essence of Spring Modulith (`https://spring.io/projects/spring-modulith`) for building software. Just as Spring Boot is an opinionated runtime (as discussed in Chapter 1), Spring Modulith is an opinionated set of tools with which to organize your application, not just technically but also functionally.

Just as Spring Boot provides a blueprint for the technical foundation, Spring Modulith guides you in structuring your app's core functionalities as distinct, interacting modules. This approach makes your application more modular and adaptable, allowing you to easily swap or update individual modules as your business needs evolve.

In short, Spring Modulith helps you build software that's easier to change and grow with your business, just like a city adapts to its residents' needs.

Comparing Spring Modulith with Microservices

Spring Modulith and microservices both aim to build complex applications efficiently, but they take different approaches. To understand the differences, consider the analogy of constructing a metropolis.

The Spring Modulith approach resembles building well-defined districts within a single city. Each district has its own function (e.g., shopping, residential, industrial) and interacts with other districts through defined channels (roads, bridges). In Spring Modulith, each module has its own function and interacts with other modules through defined channels. The benefits of this approach include

831

P. Späth and F. Gutierrez, *Pro Spring Boot 3 with Kotlin*, https://doi.org/10.1007/979-8-8688-1131-9_15

- *Easier development and deployment*: You build and deploy the application, simplifying initial setup and maintenance.

- *Reduced complexity*: Communication between modules happens internally, avoiding the overhead of network calls in microservices.

- *Faster iteration*: Updates can be made within modules without affecting the entire system, allowing quicker changes.

By comparison, the microservices approach resembles building entirely independent cities. Each city (microservice) is self-sufficient and interacts with other cities (microservices) through the equivalent of APIs for interaction between cities (APIs). Benefits of this approach include the following:

- *High scalability*: Each service can scale independently based on its needs, making the overall system more flexible.

- *Technology independence*: Different services can use different technologies, fostering innovation and flexibility.

- *Resilience*: Failure in one service doesn't bring down the entire system, improving fault tolerance.

However, microservices also come with the following drawbacks:

- *Increased complexity*: Development, deployment, and communication between services are more involved.

- *Performance overhead*: Network calls between services can add latency and complexity.

- *Distributed complexity*: Debugging and monitoring become more challenging across multiple services.

Choosing the Right Approach

The best approach depends on your specific needs. Spring Modulith is ideal for:

- *Smaller applications or initial stages of development*: Its simplicity and faster iteration make it great for starting projects.

- *Applications with tightly coupled functionalities*: When modules rely heavily on each other, Spring Modulith's internal communication can be more efficient.

- *Limited technical resources*: Spring Modulith's centralized deployment and configuration are easier to manage with smaller teams.

Microservices are better suited for:

- *Large, complex applications with independent functionalities*: When each service can operate independently, microservices offer better scalability and resilience.

- *Teams with diverse technical expertise*: Microservices allow different technologies for different services, leveraging team strengths.

- *Need for high availability and fault tolerance*: The distributed architecture of microservices minimizes the impact of failures in individual services.

Ultimately, the best approach depends on your project's needs and constraints. Consider the trade-offs between simplicity and flexibility before building your software metropolis!

Fundamentals

To use Spring Modulith in your projects, you must add the following to your build. gradle file and declare some of the Spring Modulith libraries you will be using:

```
dependencyManagement {
    imports {
        mavenBom 'org.springframework.modulith:spring-modulith-bom:1.1.2'
    }
}
dependencies {
//...
implementation 'org.springframework.modulith:spring-modulith-starter-core'
implementation 'org.springframework.modulith:spring-modulith-starter-jpa'
```

```
testImplementation 'org.springframework.modulith:spring-modulith-
starter-test'
//...
}
```

Spring Modulith helps developers organize Spring Boot applications into logical building blocks called *modules*. It provides tools to:

- *Validate the structure*: Ensure the modules are well-organized and adhere to best practices.

- *Document the arrangement*: Create clear documentation of how the modules interact.

- *Test modules independently*: Conduct integration tests on individual modules without relying on the entire application.

- *Monitor module interactions*: Observe how modules communicate and behave during runtime.

- *Promote loose coupling*: Encourage interactions between modules that avoid tight dependencies.

Spring Boot applications can be organized into modules, each focused on a specific function. These modules have three key parts:

- *Public interfaces*: This is like a service menu, offering functionalities (implemented as Spring Beans) and events that other modules can access.

- *Internal workings*: This is the "kitchen" where the module's magic happens, hidden from other modules.

- *Dependencies*: Like ingredients needed for a recipe, modules rely on functionalities (beans), events, and configuration settings provided by other modules.

Spring Modulith offers various ways to build these modules with different levels of complexity. This lets developers start simple and gradually add more advanced features as needed.

Understanding Module Packages in Spring Boot

Let's review how Spring Modulith structures your code packages:

- *Main package*: This is where your main application class lives, usually annotated with @SpringBootApplication and containing the main method that starts the application.

- *Sub-packages*: Any package directly under the main package is considered an *application module package*. If there are no sub-packages, the main package itself becomes the module.

- *Code visibility*: Using Java's package scope, inherited by Kotlin, code within a module package is hidden from other packages. This means classes cannot be directly injected into other modules, which promotes loose coupling.

- *Module API*: By default, the public classes in a module package form its API, accessible to other modules. This API defines how the module can be interacted with.

As an example, consider the Users App structure:

```
Users
└   src/main/kotlin
    ├── com.apress.users
    │   └── UsersApplication.kt
    └── com.apress.users.model
        ├── User.kt
        └── UserRole.kt
```

Spring Modulith will take the com.apress.users.* as an application module called users.

Let's continue with the complete solution to see Spring Modulith in action.

Using Spring Modulith in the My Retro Solution

Throughout the book, we have been working on two packages—Users App and My Retro App. Now it's time to create a Modulith with them and see how Spring Modulith can help us create a robust modular single application.

This My Retro App solution will consist of merging both projects into one. The complete source code is available in the `15-new-techs/myretro-modulith` folder, and you can import it into your favorite IDE.

If you want to start from scratch, you must create a folder named `myretro-modulith`, copy the `myretro` and `users` packages into the same `src/` folder, and move/create the `MyretroApplication` class in the `com.apress` package level. Remove any other classes that contain the `@SpringBootApplication` annotation (such as `UsersApplication`). You should end up with a structure like that shown in Figure 15-1.

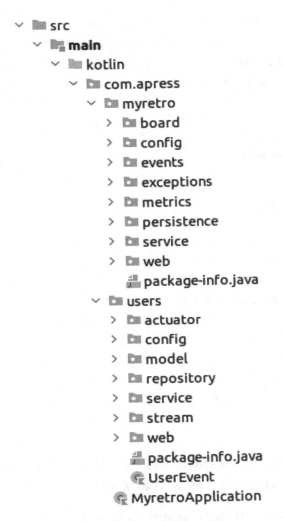

Figure 15-1. Structure of myretro-modulith solution

Figure 15-1 shows the final structure we are going to use. Open/create the build. gradle file. See Listing 15-1.

Listing 15-1. The build.gradle File

```
import org.jetbrains.kotlin.gradle.tasks.KotlinCompile
plugins {
    id 'java'
    id 'org.springframework.boot' version '3.2.3'
    id 'io.spring.dependency-management' version '1.1.4'
```

```
        id 'org.hibernate.orm' version '6.4.1.Final'
        id 'org.jetbrains.kotlin.jvm' version '2.0.20-RC'
        id "org.jetbrains.kotlin.plugin.spring" version "2.0.20-RC"
        // <- simplifies spring proxying
    }

    group = 'com.apress'
    version = '0.0.1-SNAPSHOT'

    java {
        sourceCompatibility = '17'
    }

    configurations {
        compileOnly {
            extendsFrom annotationProcessor
        }
    }

    repositories {
        mavenCentral()
    }

    dependencies {
        implementation "org.jetbrains.kotlin:kotlin-stdlib-jdk8"
        implementation "org.jetbrains.kotlin:kotlin-reflect"

        implementation 'org.springframework.boot:spring-boot-starter-web'
        implementation 'org.springframework.boot:spring-boot-starter-
        validation'
        implementation 'org.springframework.boot:spring-boot-starter-data-jpa'
        implementation 'org.springframework.boot:spring-boot-starter-actuator'

        // H2 runtime only
        runtimeOnly 'com.h2database:h2'

        // Modulith
        implementation 'org.springframework.modulith:spring-modulith-
        starter-core'
```

```
    implementation 'org.springframework.modulith:spring-modulith-
    starter-jpa'

    annotationProcessor 'org.springframework.boot:spring-boot-
    configuration-processor'

    // Web
    implementation 'org.webjars:bootstrap:5.2.3'

    // Test
    testImplementation 'org.springframework.boot:spring-boot-starter-test'
    testImplementation 'org.springframework.modulith:spring-modulith-
    starter-test'
}

dependencyManagement {
    imports {
        mavenBom 'org.springframework.modulith:spring-modulith-bom:1.1.2'
    }
}

tasks.named('test') {
    useJUnitPlatform()
}

test {
    testLogging {
        events "passed", "skipped", "failed" //, "standardOut",
        "standardError"

        showExceptions true
        exceptionFormat "full"
        showCauses true
        showStackTraces true

        // Change to `true` for more verbose test output
        showStandardStreams = true
    }
}
```

```
//    kotlin {
//        jvmToolchain(17)
//    }
tasks.withType(KotlinCompile).configureEach {
    kotlinOptions {
        freeCompilerArgs = ['-Xjsr305=strict']
        jvmTarget = '17'
    }
}
```

Listing 15-1 shows that we are using the dependencyManagement section, and we are declaring the spring-modulith-starter-core, spring-modulith-starter-jpa, and spring-modulith-starter-test dependencies, which will ensure that our application follows the modular structure we need.

Reviewing Figure 15-1, note the package-info.java file at the top of the com.apress. myretro and com.apress.users packages. This is useful information that can be used, based on Java 9 modularity, as part of your modular application. See Listings 15-2 and 15-3.

Listing 15-2. src/main/kotlin/com/apress/myretro/package-info.java

```
@org.springframework.lang.NonNullApi
package com.apress.myretro;
```

Listing 15-3. src/main/kotlin/com/apress/users/package-info.java

```
@org.springframework.lang.NonNullApi
package com.apress.users;
```

Normally, package-info.java can help specify package-level visibility modifiers or declare custom annotations for your own framework or library, as well as set default annotations for tools like FindBugs, Lombok, Spring Security, and Spring Modulith.

One of the benefits of using Spring Modulith in your Spring Boot app is that it provides module validation tests. Let's look at this. Create/open the ModularityTests class. See Listing 15-4.

Listing 15-4. src/test/kotlin/com/apress/ModularityTests.kt

```kotlin
package com.apress

import com.apress.myretro.MyretroApplication
import org.junit.jupiter.api.Test
import org.springframework.modulith.core.ApplicationModule
import org.springframework.modulith.core.ApplicationModules
import org.springframework.modulith.docs.Documenter
import java.util.function.Consumer

class ModularityTests {
    private var modules = ApplicationModules.of(MyretroApplication::
    class.java)

    @Test
    fun verifiesModularStructure() {
        try {
            modules.verify()
        }catch (e:Exception){
            // leave me alone - this is just a recommendation...
            when{
                e.toString().contains("Prefer constructor injection
                instead") -> {}
                else -> throw e
            }
        }
    }

    @Test
    fun createApplicationModuleModel() {
        val modules = ApplicationModules.of(MyretroApplication::class.java)
        modules.forEach(Consumer { x: ApplicationModule? -> println(x) })
    }

    @Test
    fun createModuleDocumentation() {
```

```
        Documenter(modules).writeDocumentation()
    }
}
```

The first thing to review in Listing 15-4 is the ApplicationModules class, which will set up everything that we need to know about our apps and how modular our app is. We need to pass the name of our main app, in this case, the MyretroApplication class (where the @SpringBootApplication is declared).

Let's run the tests, one by one, and look at the results. Let's start with the verifiesModularStructure test:

```
./gradlew test --tests ModularityTests.verifiesModularStructure
> Task :test
ModularityTests > verifiesModularStructure() PASSED
BUILD SUCCESSFUL in 2s
5 actionable tasks: 5 executed
```

Recall that, normally, we can communicate from My Retro App to Users App by requesting the getAllUsers, which we do by reaching out to the /users endpoint. Well, we can certainly still communicate from My Retro App to Users App, but now we can do it directly, without the help of the /users endpoint. The question is, is this okay?

Let's imagine that for every new user (saved into the database), we emit an event that a user was saved with the actual use, right?

In the saveUpdateUser method of the com.apress.users.service.UserService class, use the following code:

```
@Autowired
private lateinit var ApplicationEventPublisher events
@Transactional
fun saveUpdateUser(user:User):User {
    var userResult = this.userRepository.save(user)
    // Only when the user is saved do we publish the event
    events.publishEvent(user)
    return userResult
}
```

You already know about the ApplicationEventPublisher class and how to publish an event, and in this case, we are just publishing the user.

Then, in the com.apress.myretro.service.RetroBoardAndCardService class, add the following code:

```
@Async
@EventListener
fun newSavedUser(user:User){
    LOG.info("New user saved: {} {}",user.email, LocalDateTime.now())
}
```

You already know how to use the EventListener. If we run the tests again, we will have the following output:

```
./gradlew tests --tests ModularityTests.verifiesModularStructure
> ...
> Task :test FAILED
ModularityTests > verifiesModularStructure() FAILED
    org.springframework.modulith.core.Violations: - Module 'myretro'
    depends on non-exposed type com.apress.users.model.User within module
    'users'!
    User declares parameter User.newSavedRetroBoard(User) in
    (RetroBoardAndCardService.kt:0)
    - Module 'myretro' depends on non-exposed type com.apress.users.model.
    User within module 'users'!
    Method <com.apress.myretro.service.RetroBoardAndCardService.
    newSavedRetroBoard(com.apress.users.model.User)> calls method <com.
    apress.users.model.User.getEmail()> in (RetroBoardAndCardService.kt:64)
    - Module 'myretro' depends on non-exposed type com.apress.users.model.
    User within module 'users'!
    Method <com.apress.myretro.service.RetroBoardAndCardService.
    newSavedRetroBoard(com.apress.users.model.User)> has parameter of type
    <com.apress.users.model.User> in (RetroBoardAndCardService.kt:0)
```

There is a failure due to the following violation: Module 'myretro' depends on non-exposed type com.apress.users.model.User within module 'users'!

We are in a modular error because the user lives in an internal and private package that shouldn't be a dependency of any other class. How can we fix this? There are different ways to avoid these conflicts, and you can use Spring Modulith to help with all of this.

843

First, let's create a UserEvent class that will hold some important information. After all, we don't want to pass all the user's info (password, gravatar, active, etc.), right? See Listing 15-5.

Listing 15-5. src/main/kotlin/com/apress/users/UsersEvent.kt

```
package com.apress.users

data class UserEvent(
    var email: String? = null,
    var action: String? = null
)
```

Listing 15-5 shows that we are creating the UserEvent class in the com.apress.users package level. We are making sure that all other sublevels are kept private.

Next, in the UsersService#saveUpdateUser, we change the event so that instead of sending a User, we send a UserEvent:

```
events.publishEvent(UserEvent(user.email, "save"))
```

In the RetroBoardAndCardService#newSavedUser, we change this using the following code:

```
@Async
@TransactionalEventListener
fun newSavedUser(userEvent:UserEvent){
  LOG.info("New user saved: {} {} {}",userEvent.email, userEvent.action,
  LocalDateTime.now())
}
```

We are now using a Spring Modulith annotation, @TransactionalEventListener. This is an annotation that inherits from @EventListner, and it has more logic within Spring Modulith that allows us to persist the event into the database if the dependency is added.

Now that the changes have been made, let's rerun the test:

```
./gradlew clean test --tests ModularityTests.verifiesModularStructure
> ...
> Task :test
ModularityTests > verifiesModularStructure() PASSED
```

```
BUILD SUCCESSFUL in 2s
5 actionable tasks: 5 executed
```

Yes, this solution is modular! What happens if we have some heavy dependencies that we cannot avoid? We can do the following in package-info.java:

```
@org.springframework.lang.NonNullApi
@org.springframework.modulith.ApplicationModule(
  allowedDependencies = "users"
)
package com.apress.myretro;
```

In this case, code in the myretro module was only allowed to refer to code in the users module (not code assigned to any module in the first place).

Spring Modulith can print out your modules and dependencies, and not only that, you can generate documentation as well. Next, run the ModularityTests#createApplic ationModuleModel test:

```
./gradlew clean test --tests ModularityTests.createApplicationModuleModel
> ...
> Task :test
ModularityTests STANDARD_OUT
    15:07:18.494 [Test worker] INFO com.tngtech.archunit.core.PluginLoader
    -- Detected Java version 17.0.9
ModularityTests > createApplicationModuleModel() STANDARD_OUT
    # Myretro
    > Logical name: myretro
    > Base package: com.apress.myretro
    > Spring beans:
      o ....config.RetroBoardConfig
      o ....events.RetroBoardLog
      o ....metrics.RetroBoardMetrics
      o ....persistence.RetroBoardRepository
      o ....service.RetroBoardAndCardService
      o ....web.RetroBoardController
      o io.micrometer.core.instrument.Counter
      o io.micrometer.observation.aop.ObservedAspect
```

  o org.springframework.boot.CommandLineRunner

  o org.springframework.web.servlet.handler.MappedInterceptor

 # Users

 > Logical name: users

 > Base package: com.apress.users

 > Spring beans:

  o ....actuator.EventsHealthIndicator

  o ....actuator.LogEventEndpoint

  o ....config.UserConfiguration

  o ....config.UserProperties

  o ....repository.UserRepository

  o ....service.UserService

  o ....stream.UserProcessor

  o ....stream.UserSource

  o ....web.UsersController

  o java.util.function.Function

  o java.util.function.Supplier

  o org.springframework.boot.CommandLineRunner

```
ModularityTests > createApplicationModuleModel() PASSED
BUILD SUCCESSFUL in 1s
5 actionable tasks: 5 executed
```

The output shows you the modules and its submodules. With this output, you can better understand what to do when a dependency is needed.

Next, let's run the ModularityTests#createModuleDocumentation test:

```
./gradlew clean test --tests ModularityTests.createModuleDocumentation
> ...
> Task :test
ModularityTests STANDARD_OUT
    15:09:46.442 [Test worker] INFO com.tngtech.archunit.core.PluginLoader
    -- Detected Java version 17.0.9
ModularityTests > createModuleDocumentation() PASSED
BUILD SUCCESSFUL in 1s
5 actionable tasks: 5 executed
```

This test generates the documentation in AsciiDoc format (https://asciidoctor.org/), similar to a markdown language. It will generate a PlantUML (https://plantuml.com/) code so that you can generate the graph of your modules. The generated docs and code are in the build/spring-modulith-docs folder. See Figure 15-2.

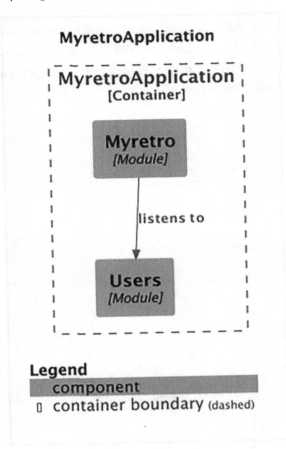

Figure 15-2. *Spring Modulith docs*

Note   In JetBrains IntelliJ IDEA, there is a plugin for AsciiDoc and PlantUML. You also need to install GraphViz (https://plantuml.com/graphviz-dot) so that you can visualize the graphs.

Running the My Retro Solution

Run the application either using your IDE or the following command:

```
./gradlew bootRun
```

Now check the /h2-console endpoint. Use the jdbc:h2:mem:myretro_db URL and click Connect, and you will see not only the PEOPLE, CARD, and RETRO_BOARD tables but also the EVENT_PUBLICATION table, which includes everything that Spring Modulith does when there is an event. See Figure 15-3.

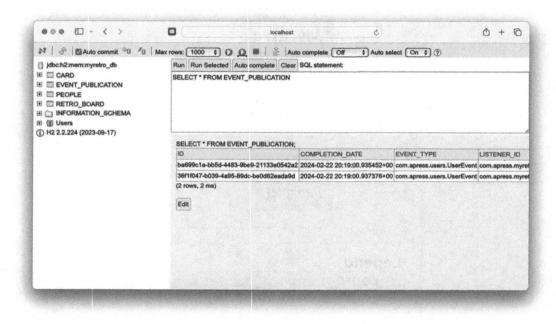

Figure 15-3. `http://localhost:8080/h2-console; URL`
`jdbc:h2:mem:myretro_db`

This section has provided a sneak peek of Spring Modulith and how it can help you create a modular application with Spring Boot. Spring Modulith is in General Availability (GA), and at the time of this writing the version is 1.1.2. If you want to learn more about Spring Modulith, visit https://docs.spring.io/spring-modulith/reference/index.html.

Spring AI

Spring AI (`https://spring.io/projects/spring-ai`) helps developers build AI-powered applications without getting bogged down in complexity. Inspired by Python projects like LangChain and LlamaIndex, Spring AI is specifically designed for developers using various programming languages, not just Python.

At its core, Spring AI provides building blocks (abstractions) for different AI tasks. These blocks can be easily swapped out, allowing you to switch between different tools (like OpenAI, Azure OpenAI, Hugging Face, etc.) with minimal code changes. This makes your applications flexible and adaptable.

Beyond basic blocks, Spring AI offers prebuilt solutions for common tasks. Imagine asking your own documentation questions or having a chatbot powered by your documentation! As your needs grow, Spring AI integrates with other Spring tools (such as Spring Integration and Spring Data) to handle complex workflows.

Spring AI focuses on AI models that process language input and provide language output. Some of the models Spring AI uses are GPT-3.5, GPT-4, and much more.

At the time of writing, this project is still in the early phases and is in version 0.9.0-SNAPSHOT, but it's mature enough to try.

AI Concepts

This section provides a brief overview of some of the AI concepts that Spring AI incorporates.

Models

Think of AI models as powerful tools that learn from tons of data. They analyze information, identify patterns, and even mimic how we think. This enables them to create things like text, images, and predictions, helping humans in many ways across different fields.

There are many types of AI models, each with its own specialty. Think of ChatGPT, which generates text based on what you type. But there are also models that turn text into images, like Midjourney and Stable Diffusion!

Spring AI currently focuses on models that understand and respond to language. Think of it like talking to a friend who's super good at understanding and replying. We're starting with OpenAI and Azure OpenAI, but there's more to come!

What makes models like ChatGPT special? They're pretrained, so you have a head start in learning. This makes them easier to use, even if you're not an AI expert!

Prompts

Imagine talking to a super smart friend, but they need specific instructions to understand you. That's where *prompts* come in! They tell AI models like ChatGPT what to do with your words.

- *More than just text*: Unlike asking, "Hey Google, what's the capital of France?", prompts in ChatGPT can have different parts like "Tell me a story" (user role) and "Once upon a time..." (system role) to set the scene.

- *Crafting prompts is an art*: It's not just about typing. Like talking to a friend, you must be clear and guide the AI model in the right direction.

- *Learning to speak "AI"*: Since interacting with AI models is different from asking questions, like in SQL, experts are learning how to best talk to AI models. This is called *prompt engineering*, and it's helping us get better results.

- *Sharing tips and tricks*: People are even sharing their best prompts, and researchers are studying how to make them even more effective.

- *It's not always easy*: Just like learning a new language, it takes practice to master prompts. Even the best models like ChatGPT 3.5 might not understand us perfectly, but it's improving daily.

- *Remember*: Prompts are the key to unlocking the full potential of AI models. By understanding them better, we can build even more amazing things together!

Prompt Templates

Crafting good prompts for AI models is like setting the stage for a play. You need to

1. *Set the scene*: Explain what you want the AI model to do by providing context.

2. *Fill in the blanks*: Replace parts of your request with specific details from the user's input.

   - *Think of templates like scripts*: We use a tool called `StringTemplate` to create templates with placeholders for those details.

     Example: Imagine a template that says, "Tell me a {funny} joke about {cats}." When someone asks for a joke, we replace the placeholders with their input (e.g., "Tell me a silly joke about puppies").

   - *Templates are like views in apps*: They provide a structure, and we fill it with data (like a map) to create the final prompt for the AI model.

   - *Prompts are getting more complex*: They used to be simple text, but now they can have multiple parts with different roles for the AI model.

Embeddings

Imagine you're a Java/Kotlin developer and you want to add AI features to your app. You might come across the term "embeddings," which sounds complex. But worry not! You don't need to be a math genius to use embeddings.

Here's the gist: Embeddings take text (like sentences) and turn it into numbers (like arrays). This helps AI models "understand" the meaning of the text. Think of it like translating words into a language the AI model speaks.

This transformation is particularly useful for tasks like these:

- *Finding similar things*: Imagine you have a product recommendation system. Embeddings can help the AI model group similar products together based on their "meaning" in the text descriptions.

- *Classifying text*: Do you want to automatically categorize emails as either spam or important? Embeddings can help the AI model understand the meaning of the email content and classify it correctly.

Think of it like a map: Instead of words, the AI model uses these numbers (embeddings) to navigate a map of meaning. Similar words and sentences are closer to each other, making it easier for the AI model to identify connections and relationships.

While the "how" behind embeddings is complex, understanding their "what" and "why" is crucial for using them effectively in your applications. They can be powerful tools for adding intelligence and functionality to your projects.

Tokens

AI models are somewhat like word processors:

- *Input*: The AI model breaks down sentences into smaller units called *tokens*, similar to words. One token is roughly 3/4 of a word.

- *Processing*: Internally, the AI model uses these tokens to understand the meaning of your text.

- *Output*: Finally, it converts the tokens back into words to give you the answer.

Think of tokens as the "currency" for AI models:

- You pay for using AI models based on the number of tokens you use, both for input and output.

- Each model has a limit on how many tokens it can handle at once, called the *context window*. Imagine it as being like a short message box.

- Different models have different limits: ChatGPT3 has a 4,000-token limit, while others offer options like 8,000 or even 100,000!

- This token limit means that if you want to analyze massive amounts of text, like Shakespeare's works, you need to break it down into smaller chunks to fit within the model's limit.

- Spring AI helps you with this. It provides tools to chop up your data and present it to the model in the right way, maximizing efficiency and avoiding hitting those limits.

Teaching AI New Tricks: Beyond the Training Dataset

Imagine you have an AI model trained on a massive dataset, like GPT-3.5/4.0. The model is great, but its knowledge stops in September 2021. What if you need answers about newer events? Here are your options to "equip" the model with beyond-the-training data:

- *Fine-tuning (expert mode)*: Think of this as rewiring the AI model's brain. You feed it your specific data and adjust its internal workings. This is powerful but complex, requiring machine learning expertise and many resources, especially for large models like GPT. Plus, not all models offer this option.

- *Prompt stuffing (more practical)*: This is like whispering hints to the AI model. Instead of rewiring it, you embed your data within the question or prompt you give it. But there's a catch: the AI model has limited attention (like a short message box). Techniques are needed to fit your data within the model's context window. Think of it as "stuffing the prompt" with relevant info.

- *Spring AI to the rescue*: Don't worry about the stuffing techniques! Spring AI provides tools to help you present your data effectively within the context window, maximizing what the AI model can learn from your prompts. It's like having a helper to whisper the right information at the right time.

There are more AI concepts that Spring AI uses, but for now, this is enough to continue with the following example.

Creating a Chat GPT Client

Spring AI is still in progress, not yet GA, but it is mature enough to do a lot of AI applications. One of the easy and out-of-the-box solutions is that Spring AI has a ChatGPT client ready to use. Let's start with that.

There is no Spring Initializr yet to create or include a Spring AI. The Spring AI team relies on the *Spring CLI* (`https://spring.io/projects/spring-cli`) project (also pre-release), which supports creating different Spring Boot apps with ease. Let's start with these simple steps:

1. Install the Spring CLI:

    If you are on a Mac, you can install the Spring CLI with

    ```
    brew tap spring-cli-projects/spring-cli
    brew install spring-cli
    ```

    If you are on Windows, visit this link: `https://github.com/spring-projects/spring-cli/releases/tag/early-access`. Be sure to do so something like this to execute the Spring CLI: `java -jar <YOUR-INSTALLATION>/spring-cli-0.8.1.jar'`
    On Windows, you can create a `spring.cmd` that executes the JAR. The idea is to have the `spring` command.

2. Create the Spring AI app with the following command:

    ```
    spring boot new --from ai --name myretro-ai
    ```

This will generate the `myretro-ai` folder structure with Maven as a build tool by default. You can now import your project in your favorite IDE.

Note   At the time of writing, the Spring CLI supports only single-module Maven projects. Support for single-module Gradle projects is planned for the 1.0 release. No timeline is defined for supporting multi-module projects.

By default, the `spring boot new` command will generate multiple files. First look at the `README.md` file, which includes all the instructions on how to run it. It will also create a package called `org.springframework.ai.openai.samples.helloworld`. It will generate the `Application` and `SimpleAiController` classes. You can open the `SimpleAiController` class, as shown in Listing 15-6.

Listing 15-6. src/main/java/org/springframework/ai/openai/samples/
helloworld/simple/SimpleAiController.java

```java
package org.springframework.ai.openai.samples.helloworld.simple;
import org.springframework.ai.chat.ChatClient;
import org.springframework.beans.factory.annotation.Autowired;
import org.springframework.web.bind.annotation.GetMapping;
import org.springframework.web.bind.annotation.RequestParam;
import org.springframework.web.bind.annotation.RestController;
import java.util.Map;
@RestController
public class SimpleAiController {
    private final ChatClient chatClient;
    @Autowired
    public SimpleAiController(ChatClient chatClient) {
        this.chatClient = chatClient;
    }
    @GetMapping("/ai/simple")
    public Map<String, String> completion(@RequestParam(value = "message",
    defaultValue = "Tell me a joke") String message) {
        return Map.of("generation", chatClient.call(message));
    }
}
```

The only important part to note in the SimpleAiController class is that we are using
a ChatClient class. This class has all the logic to call to ChatGPT.

The Kotlin transcription is shown in Listing 15-7.

Listing 15-7. src/main/kotlin/com/apress/myretro/SimpleAiController.kt

```kotlin
package com.apress.myretro

import org.springframework.ai.chat.ChatClient
import org.springframework.beans.factory.annotation.Autowired
import org.springframework.web.bind.annotation.GetMapping
import org.springframework.web.bind.annotation.RequestParam
import org.springframework.web.bind.annotation.RestController
```

```kotlin
@RestController
class SimpleAiController @Autowired constructor(private val chatClient:
ChatClient) {
    @GetMapping("/ai/simple")
    fun completion(
        @RequestParam(
            value = "message",
            defaultValue = "Tell me a joke"
        ) message: String?
    ): Map<String, String> {
        return mapOf("generation" to chatClient.call(message))
    }
}
```

Running the App

To run the app, it is important to set the SPRING_AI_OPENAI_API_KEY with your key. You can get it from https://platform.openai.com/api-keys (after you sign up, of course). Then you can run it with the following:

```
SPRING_AI_OPENAI_API_KEY=<yourkey> ./gradlew bootRun
```

You can execute a cURL command to get the result of using ChatGPT in a Spring Boot app with this command:

```
curl localhost:8080/ai/simple
Why did the cow go to space?
Because it wanted to see the mooooon!
```

Congrats! You just created a simple ChatGPT app!

Summary

This chapter reviewed two of the most anticipated technologies from the Spring team—Spring Modulith and Spring AI. Spring Modulith enables you to create modular applications with Spring Boot and ensure that your architecture is good and in the right place. Spring AI helps you create an out-of-the-box interface with OpenAI/ChatGPT.

Spring Boot Migration

If you need to migrate Spring Boot 2.x apps into the most recent version of Spring Boot 3.x, this appendix shows you how to do so. We work on code snippets and not complete solutions here, but this will give you an idea of what you need to prepare for a migration. We present the code snippets in a From/To format for easy comparison and understanding.

Let's start with Spring Security.

Migrating Spring Security

It's important to know that, since Spring Security 5.7, `WebSecurityConfigurerAdapter` has been deprecated. So, you need to do the following when replacing the extends of this class.

Using HttpSecurity

In Spring Security 5.4, the Spring Security team introduced a way to configure the `HttpSecurity` class by creating a `SecurityFilterChain` bean. For example:

From:

```kotlin
@Configuration
class UserSecurityConfig : WebSecurityConfigurerAdapter() {
    override
    fun configure(http:HttpSecurity) {
        http
            .authorizeHttpRequests{ auth -> auth
                .anyRequest().authenticated()
            }
```

857

© Peter Späth, Felipe Gutierrez 2025
P. Späth and F. Gutierrez, *Pro Spring Boot 3 with Kotlin*, https://doi.org/10.1007/979-8-8688-1131-9

```
            .httpBasic(withDefaults())
    }
}
```

To:

```
@Configuration
class UserSecurityConfig {
    @Bean
    fun filterChain(http:HttpSecurity): SecurityFilterChain {
        http
                .authorizeHttpRequests{ auth -> auth.anyRequest().
                authenticated() }
                .httpBasic(Customizer.withDefaults())
        return http.build()
    }
}
```

WebSecurity Configuration

Spring Security 5.4 also introduced WebSecurityCustomizer. This is a callback interface for customizing WebSecurity. Beans of this type will automatically be used by WebSecurityConfiguration to customize WebSecurity.

From:

```
@Configuration
class UserSecurityConfig : WebSecurityConfigurerAdapter(){
    override
    fun configure(web:WebSecurity) {
        web.ignoring().antMatchers("/about", "/docs")
    }
}
```

To:

```
@Configuration
class UserSecurityConfig {
    @Bean
```

```
    fun webSecurityCustomizer(): WebSecurityCustomizer {
        return {web -> web.ignoring().antMatchers("/about", "/docs") }
    }
}
```

LDAP Authentication

Spring Security 5.7 introduced the EmbeddedLdapServerContextSourceFactoryBean,
LdapBindAuthenticationManagerFactory, and
LdapPasswordComparisonAuthenticationManagerFactory classes. These classes
can help create an embedded LDAP server instead of the hassle of using one and
configuring it (which presents a lot of issues, in our experience), and then using
AuthenticationManager to perform the LDAP authentication.

From:

```
@Configuration
class UserSecurityConfig : WebSecurityConfigurerAdapter() {
    override
    fun configure(auth:AuthenticationManagerBuilder) {
        auth
            .ldapAuthentication()
            .userDetailsContextMapper(PersonContextMapper())
            .userDnPatterns("uid={0},ou=people")
            .contextSource()
            .port(0)
    }
}
```

To:

```
@Configuration
class UserSecurityConfig {
    @Bean
    fun contextSourceFactoryBean(): EmbeddedLdapServerContextSource
    FactoryBean {
        val contextSourceFactoryBean =
```

```
                EmbeddedLdapServerContextSourceFactoryBean.fromEmbeddedLdap
                Server()
        contextSourceFactoryBean.setPort(0)
        return contextSourceFactoryBean
    }
    @Bean
    fun ldapAuthenticationManager(
            contextSource:BaseLdapPathContextSource): Authentication
            Manager {
        val factory =
            LdapBindAuthenticationManagerFactory(contextSource);
        factory.setUserDnPatterns("uid={0},ou=people")
        factory.setUserDetailsContextMapper(PersonContextMapper())
        return factory.createAuthenticationManager()
    }
}
```

In-Memory Authentication

As of Spring Security 5.X, configuring in-memory authentication is easier than ever.

From:

```
@Configuration
class UserSecurityConfig : WebSecurityConfigurerAdapter() {
    override
    fun configure(auth:AuthenticationManagerBuilder) Exception {
        val user = User.withDefaultPasswordEncoder()
            .username("admin")
            .password("admin")
            .roles("ADMIN")
            .build()
        auth.inMemoryAuthentication()
            .withUser(user)
    }
}
```

To:

```
@Configuration
class UserSecurityConfig {
    @Bean
    fun userDetailsService(): InMemoryUserDetailsManager {
        val admin = User
                .builder()
                .username("admin")
                .password(passwordEncoder.encode("admin"))
                .roles("ADMIN", "USER")
                .build()
        return InMemoryUserDetailsManager(admin)
    }
    @Bean
    fun passwordEncoder():PasswordEncoder {
        return BCryptPasswordEncoder()
    }
}
```

JDBC Authentication

From:

```
@Configuration
class UserSecurityConfig : WebSecurityConfigurerAdapter() {
    @Bean
    fun dataSource(): DataSource {
        return EmbeddedDatabaseBuilder()
            .setType(EmbeddedDatabaseType.H2)
            .build()
    }
    override
    fun configure(auth:AuthenticationManagerBuilder) {
        val user = User.withDefaultPasswordEncoder()
            .username("admin")
            .password("admin")
```

```
                .roles("ADMIN")
                .build()
          auth.jdbcAuthentication()
                .withDefaultSchema()
                .dataSource(dataSource())
                .withUser(user)
      }
}
```

To:

```
@Configuration
class SecurityConfiguration {
    @Bean
    fun dataSource(): DataSource {
        return EmbeddedDatabaseBuilder()
            .setType(EmbeddedDatabaseType.H2)
            .addScript(JdbcDaoImpl.DEFAULT_USER_SCHEMA_DDL_LOCATION)
            .build()
    }
    @Bean
    fun users(DataSource dataSource): UserDetailsManager {
        val admin = User
                .builder()
                .username("admin")
                .password(passwordEncoder.encode("admin"))
                .roles("ADMIN", "USER")
                .build()
        val users = JdbcUserDetailsManager(dataSource)
        users.createUser(admin)
        return users
    }
    @Bean
    fun passwordEncoder():PasswordEncoder {
        return new BCryptPasswordEncoder()
    }
}
```

Upgrading to Spring Boot 3

This section enumerates what is new in Spring Boot 3 and what you need to do to migrate from the previous version of Spring Boot. Remember, these are just snippets and include a bit of explanation when necessary.

- Java 17 baseline and Java 19 support: Spring Boot 3.0 requires Java 17 as a minimum version.

- Spring Boot requires GraalVM 22.3 (`https://www.graalvm.org/`) or later for native development and Native Build Tools Plugin 0.9.17 or later.

- Spring Framework 6:

  - The entire framework codebase is based on Java 17 source code level now.

  - Migration from `javax` to `jakarta` namespace for Servlet, JPA, and so on.

  - Runtime compatibility with Jakarta EE 9 as well as Jakarta EE 10 APIs.

  - Compatible with latest web servers: Tomcat 10.1, Jetty 11, and Undertow 2.3.

  - Early compatibility with virtual threads (in preview as of JDK 19).

  - Upgrade to ASM 9.4 and Kotlin 1.7.

  - Complete CGLIB fork with support for capturing CGLIB-generated classes.

  - Comprehensive foundation for Ahead Of Time (AOT) transformations.

  - First-class support for GraalVM native images.

  - `RSocket` interface client based on `@RSocketExchange` service interfaces.

  - Early support for Reactor Netty 2 based on Netty 5 alpha.

  - Support for Jakarta WebSockets 2.1 and its standard `WebSocket` protocol upgrade mechanism.

  - HTTP interface client based on `@HttpExchange` service interfaces.

  - Support for RFC 7807 problem details.

- Unified HTTP status code handling.

- Support for Jackson 2.14.

- Alignment with Servlet 6.0 (while retaining runtime compatibility with Servlet 5.0).

- Improved `@ConstructorBinding` detection.

- Micrometer updates:

  - The new `ObservationRegistry` interface can be used to create observations, which provides a single API for metrics and traces.

  - Spring Boot now auto-configures *micrometer tracing* for you.

  - When there is a micrometer tracing `Tracer` bean, and Prometheus is on the classpath, `SpanContextSupplier` is now auto-configured.

- More flexible auto-configuration for Spring Data JDBC.

- Enabling ASYNC ACKs with Apache Kafka: A new property, `spring.kafka.listener.async-acks`, has been added for this purpose.

- ElasticSearch Java client: Auto-configuration for the new ElasticSearch Java client has been introduced. It can be configured using the existing `spring.elasticsearch.*` configuration properties.

- Auto-configuration of `JdkClientHttpConnector`.

- `@SpringBootTest` with main methods: The `@SpringBootTest` annotation can now use the main method of any discovered `@SpringBootConfiguration` class if it's available. This means that tests can now pick up any custom `SpringApplication` configuration performed by your main method.

- Testcontainers: There is now support for using Testcontainers to manage external services at development time.

- Docker Compose:

  - A new module, `spring-boot-docker-compose`, provides integration with Docker Compose. When your app starts up, the Docker Compose integration will look for a configuration file in the current working directory: `compose.yaml`, `compose.yml`, `docker-compose.yaml`, and `docker-compose.yml` are supported.

  - To use a non-standard file, set the `spring.docker.compose.file` property.

- Auto-configuration for Spring Authorization Server: Support has been added for the Spring Authorization Server project along with a new `spring-boot-starter-oauth2-authorization-server` starter.

- Docker image building: The `spring-boot:build-image` Maven goal and `bootBuildImage` Gradle task are available.

- `RestClient` support: Spring Boot 3.2 supports the new `RestClient` interface introduced in Spring Framework 6.1. This interface provides a functional-style blocking HTTP API with a design similar to `WebClient`.

- Support for `JdbcClient`: Auto-configuration for `JdbcClient` has been added based on the presence of a `NamedParameterJdbcTemplate`. If the latter is auto-configured, properties of `spring.jdbc.template.*` are considered.

- Support for virtual threads:

  - Spring Boot 3.2 ships support for virtual threads. To use virtual threads, you must run on Java 21 and set the `spring.threads.virtual.enabled` property to `true`.

  - When virtual threads are enabled, Tomcat and Jetty will use virtual threads for request processing.

  - Spring WebFlux's support for block execution is auto-configured to use the `applicationTaskExecutor` bean when it is an `AsyncTaskExecutor`.

  - When virtual threads are enabled, the `applicationTaskExecutor` bean will be a `SimpleAsyncTaskExecutor` that's configured to use virtual threads.

- When virtual threads are enabled, the `taskScheduler` bean will be a `SimpleAsyncTaskScheduler` that's configured to use virtual threads. The `spring.task.scheduling.thread-name-prefix` and `spring.task.scheduling.simple.*` properties are applied. Other `spring.task.scheduling.*` properties are ignored, as they are specific to a pool-based scheduler.

As you can see, there are a lot of updates and improvements to consider when migration is a must.

Using Configuration Properties Migration

With all these changes introduced in Spring Boot 3.0, it should include a tool or library that can help you migrate, right? You need to change a few configuration properties that have been renamed or removed, so your trusty `application.properties` or `application.yml` needs an update.

But don't worry; Spring Boot has your back with the new `spring-boot-properties-migrator` module. Add it to your project, and it will:

- *Scan your environment*: Like a detective, it sniffs out all your properties.

- *Print helpful messages*: It tells you exactly which properties need attention.

- *Temporarily fix things*: No need for immediate code changes! It automatically adjusts your properties at runtime for a smooth transition.

If you are using Maven, this is what you need to include in your `pom.xml`:

```
<dependency>
    <groupId>org.springframework.boot</groupId>
    <artifactId>spring-boot-properties-migrator</artifactId>
    <scope>runtime</scope>
</dependency>
```

If you are using Gradle, include this:

```
runtime("org.springframework.boot:spring-boot-properties-migrator")
```

That's it. Run the app, and these properties will analyze things and then tell you what to change and what to do.

Using the `spring-boot-properties-migrator` module, you can migrate more easily and keep your Spring Boot application running smoothly!

Spring Boot Migrator

Even though there is the Configuration Properties Migration library, this is only for your properties. Is there anything better? Yes, there is! It's called Spring Boot Migrator, which you can find here: `https://github.com/spring-projects-experimental/spring-boot-migrator`.

If you have a very *old* Java app (not Spring) and Spring Boot version 2.x or earlier, the Spring Boot Migrator can help you with the migration.

Summary

In this appendix, you learned the basics of migrating to the latest version of Spring Boot 3. You saw some of the new features and changes and discovered that there are tools that can help you with your migration, such as Configuration Properties Migrator and the Spring Boot Migrator project.

APPENDIX B

Spring Boot GraphQL

This appendix introduces GraphQL and describes how you can use it with Spring Boot. The appendix begins with some basic concepts of what GraphQL is and how it can help in some use cases. You then see how easy it is to implement logic around GraphQL using Spring Boot.

What Is GraphQL?

GraphQL (https://graphql.org/) is an open source query language and server-side runtime for APIs. It allows clients to request exactly the data they need, unlike REST APIs, which often return entire datasets. Using GraphQL leads to a more efficient and flexible experience for developers and users.

The following are some use cases for GraphQL:

- *Mobile apps*: With limited bandwidth and resources, GraphQL's ability to fetch only necessary data shines.

- *Single-page applications (SPAs)*: SPAs often need dynamic data fetching, and GraphQL's flexibility makes it a good fit.

- *Complex data structures*: When dealing with interconnected data, GraphQL's ability to traverse relationships easily is helpful.

- *Content management systems (CMSs)*: GraphQL empowers content editors to retrieve specific content sections efficiently.

© Peter Späth, Felipe Gutierrez 2025
P. Späth and F. Gutierrez, *Pro Spring Boot 3 with Kotlin*, https://doi.org/10.1007/979-8-8688-1131-9

GraphQL offers the following performance benefits:

- *Reduced data transfer*: GraphQL sends only requested data, minimizing network traffic and improving load times.

- *Client-side caching*: Clients can cache specific queries, reducing server calls and improving responsiveness.

- *Batching*: Multiple queries can be combined into a single request, further boosting performance.

Table B-1 provides a comparison of REST and GraphQL.

Table B-1. *REST vs. GraphQL*

Feature	REST	GraphQL
Data fetching	Predefined endpoints	Client-specific queries
Data granularity	Entire datasets returned	Only requested data returned
Flexibility	Limited	Highly flexible
Performance	Can be inefficient	Can be more performant

Consider the following recommendations for using GraphQL:

- *Start with a good use case*: GraphQL isn't a silver bullet. Choose it when its benefits align with your project's needs.

- *Design a clear schema*: Define your data structure clearly for efficient client queries.

- *Use a GraphQL client library*: Simplify data fetching and error handling on the client side.

- *Consider security*: Implement proper authentication and authorization mechanisms.

- *Monitor performance*: Track query response times and optimize as needed.

Remember that GraphQL is a powerful tool, but it's not always the right choice. Evaluate your project's needs and weigh the pros and cons before diving in.

Spring for GraphQL

Spring for GraphQL (`https://spring.io/projects/spring-graphql`) is a library that brings a bunch of advantages to developers building GraphQL APIs on the Spring platform. Here's what it offers:

- *Simplified development:*

  - *Annotation-based approach*: Instead of manual configuration, you define data-fetching methods using annotations like `@QueryMapping` and `@MutationMapping`, making the code cleaner and more readable.

  - *Leverages the Spring ecosystem*: Integrates seamlessly with other Spring libraries you're already familiar with, like Spring Security and Spring Data, therefore reducing development time.

  - *Built-in features*: Offers automatic schema generation, data validation, and error handling, freeing you from boilerplate code.

- *Enhanced performance:*

  - *Efficient data fetching*: Optimizes data retrieval by leveraging Spring's caching and data access capabilities, improving API performance.

  - *Batching*: Combines multiple queries into one request, reducing roundtrips and boosting speed.

  - *Data loaders*: Allows you to prefetch related data, further minimizing database calls and improving response times.

- *Improved maintainability:*

  - *Modular design*: Separates schema definition from data fetching logic, making code easier to understand and maintain.

  - *Testing tools*: Provides built-in tools for testing GraphQL resolvers and mutations, ensuring code quality and stability.

  - *Reactive support*: Offers reactive programming capabilities for building scalable and responsive APIs.

- *Additional benefits:*

  - *Community support*: Backed by a large and active community, providing resources, tutorials, and help when needed.

  - *Regular updates*: Continuously updated with new features and improvements, keeping your API modern and secure.

Spring for GraphQL and Spring Boot: A Match Made in Developer Heaven

Spring for GraphQL and Spring Boot are both built on the Spring platform, making them perfectly compatible and complementary. Here's how they play together:

- *Seamless integration:*

  - *Spring Boot Starter*: Spring for GraphQL offers a Spring Boot Starter (`spring-boot-starter-graphql`) that simplifies setup and configuration. Just add the starter dependency to your Spring Boot project, and you're ready to go.

  - *Auto-configuration*: Spring Boot's auto-configuration magic applies to Spring for GraphQL as well, automatically detecting and configuring beans based on your project setup.

  - *Existing Spring components*: You can reuse existing Spring components like Spring Data and Spring Security with Spring for GraphQL, leveraging their features and expertise.

- *Enhanced development experience:*

  - *Developer-friendly*: Spring Boot and Spring for GraphQL are both known for their developer-friendly approach, simplifying complex tasks and offering clear documentation.

  - *Rapid prototyping*: Spring Boot's fast startup time and opinionated conventions make it ideal for rapid prototyping of GraphQL APIs.

  - *Production-ready*: Once you're ready for production, Spring Boot and Spring for GraphQL provide robust features and security for reliable deployments.

Using GraphQL in Users App

You have access to this code in the appendix-b-graphql/users folder. But if you want to start from scratch with the Spring Initializr (https://start.spring.io), set the Group field to com.apress and the Artifact and Name fields to users. Also add the following dependencies: Web, GraphQL, JPA, Validation, H2, and PostgreSQL. Finally, click Generate and download the project, unzip it, and import it into your favorite IDE.

Let's start by reviewing the build.gradle file. See Listing B-1.

Listing B-1. The build.gradle File

```
import org.jetbrains.kotlin.gradle.tasks.KotlinCompile
plugins {
    id 'org.springframework.boot' version '3.2.3'
    id 'io.spring.dependency-management' version '1.1.4'
    id 'org.jetbrains.kotlin.jvm' version '2.0.20-RC'
    id "org.jetbrains.kotlin.plugin.spring" version "2.0.20-RC"
    // <- simplifies spring proxying
}

group = 'com.apress'
version = '0.0.1-SNAPSHOT'
sourceCompatibility = '17'

repositories {
    mavenCentral()
}

dependencies {
    implementation "org.jetbrains.kotlin:kotlin-stdlib-jdk8"
    implementation "org.jetbrains.kotlin:kotlin-reflect"

    implementation 'org.springframework.boot:spring-boot-starter-web'
    implementation 'org.springframework.boot:spring-boot-starter-
    validation'
    implementation 'org.springframework.boot:spring-boot-starter-graphql'

    implementation 'org.springframework.boot:spring-boot-starter-data-jpa'
```

```
    runtimeOnly 'com.h2database:h2'
    runtimeOnly 'org.postgresql:postgresql'

    // Web
    implementation 'org.webjars:bootstrap:5.2.3'

    testImplementation 'org.springframework.boot:spring-boot-starter-test'
    testImplementation 'org.springframework.graphql:spring-graphql-test'
}

tasks.named('test') {
    useJUnitPlatform()
}

//      kotlin {
//          jvmToolchain(17)
//      }
tasks.withType(KotlinCompile).configureEach {
    kotlinOptions {
        freeCompilerArgs = ['-Xjsr305=strict']
        jvmTarget = '17'
    }
}
```

Listing B-1 shows that we are adding the spring-boot-starter-graphql dependency to build.gradle. Spring Boot will auto-configure all the necessary beans for GraphQL and set up the GraphiQL app (https://github.com/graphql/graphiql). You will have access using the /graphics endpoint.

Next, open/create and review the User class. See Listing B-2.

Listing B-2. src/main/kotlin/com/apress/users/User.kt

```
package com.apress.users

import jakarta.persistence.Entity
import jakarta.persistence.Id
import jakarta.persistence.PrePersist
import jakarta.validation.constraints.NotBlank
import jakarta.validation.constraints.Pattern
```

```kotlin
@Entity(name = "USERS")
data class User(
    @Id
    @get:NotBlank(message = "Email cannot be empty")
    var email:  String? = null,

    @get:NotBlank(message = "Name cannot be empty")
    var name: String? = null,

    var gravatarUrl: String? = null,

    @get:Pattern(
        message = "Password must be at least 8 characters long and contain
        at least one number, one uppercase, one lowercase and one special
        character",
        regexp = "^(?=.*[0-9])(?=.*[a-z])(?=.*[A-Z])(?=.*[@#$%^&+=!])
        (?=\\S+$).{8,}$"
    )
    var password:String? = null,

    var userRole: List<UserRole>? = null,

    var active:Boolean = false
){
    @PrePersist
    private fun prePersist() {
        gravatarUrl = gravatarUrl ?: UserGravatar.getGravatarUrlFromEmail
        (email!!)
        userRole = userRole ?: listOf(UserRole.INFO)
    }
}
```

As you know, you need to add the @Entity and @Id annotations to make the User class persistent in the database. We also added some validation annotations. Next, open/create and check the UserRole enum. See Listing B-3.

Listing B-3. src/main/kotlin/com/apress/users/UserRole.kt

```kotlin
package com.apress.users
enum class UserRole {
    USER, ADMIN, INFO
}
```

Next, open/create and review the UserRepository interface. See Listing B-4.

Listing B-4. src/main/kotlin/com/apress/users/UserRepository.kt

```kotlin
package com.apress.users
import org.springframework.data.jpa.repository.JpaRepository
import org.springframework.data.repository.CrudRepository
interface UserRepository : JpaRepository<User,String>
```

Next, let's add some users. Open/create and review the UserConfiguration class. See Listing B-5.

Listing B-5. src/main/kotlin/com/apress/users/UserConfiguration.kt

```kotlin
package com.apress.users

import org.springframework.boot.CommandLineRunner
import org.springframework.context.annotation.Bean
import org.springframework.context.annotation.Configuration
import org.springframework.context.annotation.Profile
import java.util.*

@Configuration
class UserConfiguration {
    @Bean
    @Profile("default")
    fun init(userRepository: UserRepository): CommandLineRunner {
        return CommandLineRunner { _: Array<String> ->
            userRepository.save(
                User(
                    "ximena@email.com",
                    "Ximena",
```

```
                "https://www.gravatar.com/avatar/23bb62a7d0ca63c9a80490
                8e57bf6bd4?d=wavatar",
                "aw2s0me!X",
                mutableListOf(UserRole.USER),
                true
            )
        )
        userRepository.save(
            User(
                "norma@email.com",
                "Norma",
                "https://www.gravatar.com/avatar/f07f7e553264c9710105ed
                ebe6c465e7?d=wavatar",
                "aw2s0me!X",
                mutableListOf(UserRole.USER, UserRole.ADMIN),
                true
            )
        )
    }
}
}
```

Next, open/create and review the UserGravatar class, which helps collect the Gravatar for the user based on their email address. See Listing B-6.

Listing B-6. src/main/kotlin/com/apress/users/UserGravatar.kt

```
package com.apress.users

import java.security.MessageDigest

object UserGravatar {
    @OptIn(ExperimentalStdlibApi::class)
    fun getGravatarUrlFromEmail(email: String) =
        String.format("https://www.gravatar.com/avatar/%s?d=wavatar",
        md5Hex(email))

    @kotlin.ExperimentalStdlibApi
```

```
    private fun md5Hex(message: String) =
        MessageDigest.getInstance("MD5")
            .digest(message.toByteArray(charset("CP1252"))).toHexString()
}
```

All these classes are part of the JPA persistence package introduced in Chapter 5. The next section is where GraphQL will shine!

The Users GraphQL Controller

Next, open/create and review the UsersController class. See Listing B-7.

Listing B-7. src/main/kotlin/com/apress/users/UsersController.kt

```
package com.apress.users

import jakarta.validation.Valid
import org.springframework.beans.factory.annotation.Autowired
import org.springframework.graphql.data.method.annotation.Argument
import org.springframework.graphql.data.method.annotation.MutationMapping
import org.springframework.graphql.data.method.annotation.QueryMapping
import org.springframework.http.HttpStatus
import org.springframework.stereotype.Controller
import org.springframework.validation.FieldError
import org.springframework.validation.ObjectError
import org.springframework.web.bind.MethodArgumentNotValidException
import org.springframework.web.bind.annotation.ExceptionHandler
import org.springframework.web.bind.annotation.ResponseStatus
import java.time.LocalDateTime
import java.time.format.DateTimeFormatter

@Controller
class UsersController {
    @Autowired
    private lateinit var userRepository: UserRepository

    @QueryMapping
    fun users(): Iterable<User> =
```

```kotlin
    userRepository.findAll()

@QueryMapping
@Throws(Throwable::class)
fun user(@Argument email: String): User =
    userRepository.findById(email).orElseThrow {
        RuntimeException("User not found") }!!

@MutationMapping
fun createUser(@Argument @Valid user: User): User {
    user.gravatarUrl = UserGravatar.getGravatarUrlFromEmail
    (user.email!!)
    return userRepository.save(user)
}

@MutationMapping
fun updateUser(@Argument  @Valid user: User): User {
    val userToUpdate = userRepository.findById(user.email!!)
        .orElseThrow { RuntimeException("User not found") }!!.apply {
            name = user.name
            password = user.password
            userRole = user.userRole
            active = user.active
        }
    return userRepository.save(userToUpdate)
}

@MutationMapping
fun deleteUser(@Argument email: String): Boolean {
    userRepository.deleteById(email)
    return true
}

@ExceptionHandler(MethodArgumentNotValidException::class)
@ResponseStatus(HttpStatus.BAD_REQUEST)
fun handleValidationExceptions(ex: MethodArgumentNotValidException):
        Map<String, Any> {
    val response: MutableMap<String, Any> = mutableMapOf()
```

```
            response["msg"] = "There is an error"
            response["code"] = HttpStatus.BAD_REQUEST.value()
            response["time"] =
                LocalDateTime.now()
                .format(DateTimeFormatter.ofPattern("yyyy-MM-dd HH:mm:ss"))
            val errors: MutableMap<String, String> = mutableMapOf()
            ex.bindingResult.allErrors.forEach{ error: ObjectError ->
                val fieldName: String = (error as FieldError).field
                val errorMessage: String = error.getDefaultMessage() ?: "undef"
                errors[fieldName] = errorMessage
            }
            response["errors"] = errors
            return response
        }
}
```

The UsersController class includes the following annotations:

- @Controller: Like in Spring MVC, we are using the @Controller
  annotation (we are no longer in REST city!) to mark the class as a
  bean for Spring management, but instead of handling HTTP requests,
  it identifies methods that fetch data for GraphQL fields. These
  methods are annotated with @QueryMapping or @MutationMapping.
  This means there is no view rendering; Spring for GraphQL is not
  designed for view rendering. The data returned from the methods
  annotated with @QueryMapping and @MutationMapping is part of the
  GraphQL response directly.

- @MutationMapping: This annotation defines methods that handle
  mutations in a GraphQL schema. Mutations represent actions
  that modify data on the server, like creating, updating, or deleting
  data. Methods annotated with @MutationMapping typically return
  the newly created object or the updated object after the data
  modification.

- `@QueryMapping`: This annotation marks methods that handle queries in the GraphQL schema. Queries represent requests for data from the server. Methods annotated with `@QueryMapping` typically return the requested data, either a single object or a collection of objects. The method name often corresponds to the field name in the schema, but the name can be explicitly specified in the annotation.

- `@Argument`: This annotation is used on method parameters to bind them to arguments in a GraphQL field definition. It specifies which parameter receives the value corresponding to a specific argument in the GraphQL query. By default, the argument name and the parameter name match, but you can specify the argument name explicitly in the annotation.

Other annotations used with Spring for GraphQL include the following:

- `@SchemaDirective`: Used to define custom directives that modify the behavior of the schema.

- `@DataFetcher`: An alternative to `@QueryMapping` and `@MutationMapping` that allows you to define a `DataFetcher` directly on a field in the schema.

- `@SubscriptionMapping`: Used to define methods that handle subscriptions, a real-time data stream feature in GraphQL.

- `@PathVariable`: Like `@Argument` but used with path variables in the URL that map to method parameters.

The Users GraphQL Schema

Next, you need to declare a GraphQL schema. This is the key for Spring for GraphQL to work, because the GraphQL schema does the following:

1. Defines a contract between the client and server:

   - The schema acts as a contract by outlining the available data types, fields, queries, and mutations within your API.

   - It explicitly specifies what data the client can access and how they can request it, ensuring consistency and clarity.

2. Enables introspection and validation:

- Clients can use the schema to introspect your API, dynamically discovering available fields and their types.

- This allows the client to build self-documenting interfaces and validate their queries against the schema before sending them to the server.

3. Facilitates efficient data fetching:

- Spring for GraphQL leverages the schema to optimize data fetching.

- It knows what data each query requests based on the schema, allowing it to efficiently fetch only the necessary information.

4. Improves developer experience:

- A well-defined schema improves code readability and maintainability.

- Developers can easily understand the available data and how to access it, making code navigation and updates smoother.

5. Encourages consistent API design:

- By having a centralized schema, you can ensure consistency and predictability in your API design.

- This helps maintain a consistent experience for client applications interacting with your API.

While Spring for GraphQL allows automatic schema generation from code, it's generally recommended to explicitly define your schema for clarity and maintainability. You can use schema definition tools like GraphQL Schema Language (SDL) or dedicated libraries to define your schema in a structured way.

To create a GraphQL schema, you need to do the following:

1. Define data types:

- Use types like `Int`, `String`, and `Boolean` for basic data.

- Define custom types (objects) to represent your domain entities (e.g., `User`, `UserRole`).

2. Specify fields in types:

- Define fields for each custom type, representing the data they contain (e.g., name and email for User).

- Specify the field's type.

- Optionally, use arguments to provide additional filtering or sorting options for queries.

3. Define queries and mutations:

- Define the @QueryMapping and @MutationMapping annotated methods to handle data fetching and manipulation requests.

- These methods return the requested data or a response for mutations.

Next, open/create and review the schema.graphqls file, which is mandatory. This file must be in the resources/graphql folder. See Listing B-8.

Listing B-8. src/main/resources/graphql/schema.graphqls

```
type Query {
    users: [User]
    user(email: String): User
}
type Mutation {
    createUser(user: UserInput!): User
    updateUser(user: UserInput!): User
    deleteUser(email: String!): Boolean
}
type User {
    email: String!
    name: String!
    gravatarUrl: String
    password: String!
    userRole: [UserRole]!
    active: Boolean!
}
```

```
input UserInput {
    email: String!
    name: String!
    password: String!
    userRole: [UserRole]!
    active: Boolean!
}
enum UserRole {
    USER
    ADMIN
    INFO
}
```

Listing B-8 shows that the schema.graphqls file includes the following data types, queries, and mutations:

- *Data types:*

  - User: Represents individual users with fields for email, name, gravatarUrl, password, userRole (an array representing roles), and active status.

  - UserInput: Used for inputting user data during creation and updates.

  - UserRole (Enum): Defines possible user roles: USER, ADMIN, and INFO.

- *Queries:*

  - users: Retrieves a list of all users.

  - user(email: String): Fetches a specific user based on their email address.

- *Mutations:*

  - createUser(user: UserInput!): Creates a new user with the provided input.

  - updateUser(user: UserInput!): Updates an existing user's information based on the input.

  - deleteUser(email: String!): Deletes a user with the specified email address.

The ! in the mutations means that the field is non-nullable. In other words, the field must always have a value and cannot be empty.

Next, let's add a particular property that will allow us to use the GraphiQL app. Listing B-9 shows the `application.properties` property.

Listing B-9. src/main/resources/application.properties

```
spring.h2.console.enabled=true
spring.datasource.generate-unique-name=false
spring.datasource.name=test-db
spring.graphql.graphiql.enabled=true
```

Setting the `spring.graphql.graphiql.enabled` property to `true` activates the / graphiql endpoint.

Running Users App

You can run the Users App project in your IDE or use the following command:

```
./gradlew bootRun
```

Once Users App is up and running, direct your browser to `http://localhost:8080/` graphiql and you will see the GraphiQL app. Enter the following query and click the Run button. See Figure B-1.

```
query {
    users {
        email
        name
        userRole
        active
    }
}
```

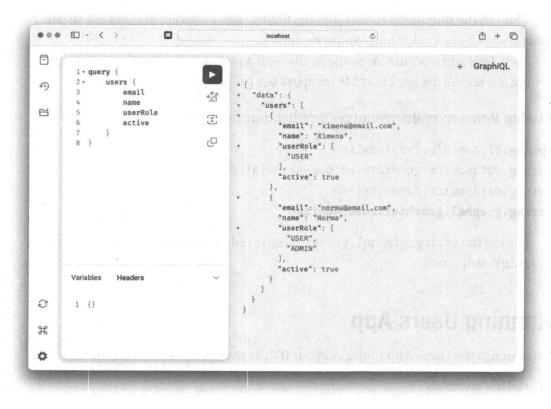

Figure B-1. *Running Users App in the GraphiQL app (http://localhost:8080/ graphiql)*

Figure B-1 shows the /graphiql endpoint where you can add your queries and mutations. We are using the query { } keyword and adding the model with the fields we need, so you can use the following:

```
query {
    users {
        email
        name
    }
}
```

You should get the following:

```
{
  "data": {
    "users": [
      {
        "email": "ximena@email.com",
        "name": "Ximena"
      },
      {
        "email": "norma@email.com",
        "name": "Norma"
      }
    ]
  }
}
```

Next, try to run the queries and mutations. Query the user(@Argument String email) method with this:

```
query {
    user(email: "ximena@email.com") {
        email
        name
        userRole
        active
    }
}
```

You will get this:

```
{
  "data": {
    "user": {
      "email": "ximena@email.com",
      "name": "Ximena",
      "userRole": [
        "USER"
```

```
        ],
        "active": true
    }
  }
}
```

Use the `User createUser(@Argument @Valid User user)` mutation with this code:

```
mutation {
    createUser(user: {
        email: "dummy@email.com"
        name: "Dummy"
        password: "awesome!R2D2"
        userRole: [USER]
        active: true
    }) {
        email
        name
        gravatarUrl
        userRole
        active
    }
}
```

Remember that a mutation regularly returns something, so you need to specify what field you want back from the created user. The previous mutation will give you:

```
{
  "data": {
    "createUser": {
      "email": "dummy@email.com",
      "name": "Dummy",
      "gravatarUrl": "https://www.gravatar.com/avatar/fb651279f4712e20999
      1e05610dfb03a?d=wavatar",
      "userRole": [
        "USER"
      ],
```

```
    "active": true
    }
  }
}
```

You can test the `User updateUser(@Argument @Valid User user)` mutation with this:

```
mutation {
    updateUser(user: {
        email: "dummy@email.com"
        name: "Dummy"
        password: "awesome!C3PO"
        userRole: [USER, ADMIN]
        active: true
    }) {
        email
        name
        gravatarUrl
        userRole
        active
    }
}
```

You will get this:

```
{
  "data": {
    "updateUser": {
      "email": "dummy@email.com",
      "name": "Dummy",
      "gravatarUrl": "https://www.gravatar.com/avatar/fb651279f4712e20999
      1e05610dfb03a?d=wavatar",
      "userRole": [
        "USER",
        "ADMIN"
      ],
```

```
        "active": true
      }
    }
}
```

Finally, you can test the deleteUser(@Argument String email) mutation with this:

```
mutation {
    deleteUser(email: "dummy@email.com")
}
```

and you will get back:

```
{
  "data": {
    "deleteUser": true
  }
}
```

Congrats! You now know how GraphQL and Spring for GraphQL work!

Using GraphQL in My Retro App

Using GraphQL in the My Retro App project is basically the same idea as using it in Users App. You can get any of the other chapter projects and use the spring-boot-starter-graphql dependency to activate GraphQL. But if you have already downloaded the code, you can import it from the appendix-b-graphql/myretro folder.

This section shows you the My Retro App controller (Listing B-10), the GraphQL schema (Listing B-11), and the queries and mutations you can run (Listing B-12).

Listing B-10. src/main/kotlin/com/apress/myretro/web/
RetroBoardController.kt

```
package com.apress.myretro.web

import com.apress.myretro.board.Card
import com.apress.myretro.board.RetroBoard
import com.apress.myretro.service.RetroBoardService
import jakarta.validation.Valid
```

```kotlin
import org.springframework.beans.factory.annotation.Autowired
import org.springframework.graphql.data.method.annotation.Argument
import org.springframework.graphql.data.method.annotation.MutationMapping
import org.springframework.graphql.data.method.annotation.QueryMapping
import org.springframework.http.HttpStatus
import org.springframework.stereotype.Controller
import org.springframework.validation.FieldError
import org.springframework.validation.ObjectError
import org.springframework.web.bind.MethodArgumentNotValidException
import org.springframework.web.bind.annotation.ExceptionHandler
import org.springframework.web.bind.annotation.ResponseStatus
import java.time.LocalDateTime
import java.time.format.DateTimeFormatter
import java.util.*

@Controller
class RetroBoardController {
    @Autowired
    private lateinit var retroBoardService: RetroBoardService

    @QueryMapping
    fun retros(): Iterable<RetroBoard> =
        retroBoardService.findAll()

    @MutationMapping
    fun createRetro(@Argument name: String?): RetroBoard {
        return retroBoardService.save(RetroBoard(id = UUID.randomUUID(),
        name=name))
    }

    @QueryMapping
    fun retro(@Argument retroId: UUID): RetroBoard =
        retroBoardService.findById(retroId)

    @QueryMapping
    fun cards(@Argument retroId: UUID): Iterable<Card> =
        retroBoardService.findAllCardsFromRetroBoard(retroId)
```

```kotlin
@MutationMapping
fun createCard(@Argument retroId: UUID, @Argument @Valid card: Card):
Card {
    return retroBoardService.addCardToRetroBoard(retroId, card)
}

@QueryMapping
fun card(@Argument cardId: UUID): Card =
    retroBoardService.findCardByUUID(cardId)

@MutationMapping
fun updateCard(@Argument cardId: UUID, @Argument @Valid card: Card):
Card {
    val result: Card = retroBoardService.findCardByUUID(cardId)
    result.comment = card.comment
    return retroBoardService.saveCard(result)
}

@MutationMapping
fun deleteCard(@Argument cardId: UUID): Boolean {
    retroBoardService.removeCardByUUID(cardId)
    return true
}

@ExceptionHandler(MethodArgumentNotValidException::class)
@ResponseStatus(HttpStatus.BAD_REQUEST)
fun handleValidationExceptions(ex: MethodArgumentNotValidException):
        Map<String, Any> {
    val response: MutableMap<String, Any> = mutableMapOf()
    response["msg"] = "There is an error"
    response["code"] = HttpStatus.BAD_REQUEST.value()
    response["time"] =
        LocalDateTime.now()
        .format(DateTimeFormatter.ofPattern("yyyy-MM-dd HH:mm:ss"))
    val errors: MutableMap<String, String> = HashMap()
    ex.bindingResult.allErrors.forEach{ error: ObjectError ->
        val fieldName: String = (error as FieldError).field
```

```
        val errorMessage: String = error.getDefaultMessage() ?: "undef"
        errors[fieldName] = errorMessage
    }
    response["errors"] = errors
    return response
}
```
}

Listing B-11. src/main/resources/graphql/schema.graphqls

```
type Query {
    retros: [RetroBoard]
    retro(retroId: ID!): RetroBoard
    cards(retroId: ID!): [Card]
    card(cardId: ID!): Card
}
type Mutation {
    createRetro(name: String!): RetroBoard
    createCard(retroId: ID!, card: CardInput!): Card
    updateCard(cardId: ID!, card: CardInput!): Card
    deleteCard(cardId: ID!): Boolean
}
type RetroBoard {
    id: ID!
    name: String!
    cards: [Card]
}
type Card {
    id: ID!
    comment: String!
    cardType: CardType!
}
enum CardType {
    HAPPY
    MEH
```

```
        SAD
}
input CardInput {
    comment: String!
    cardType: CardType!
}
```

Listing B-12. Queries and Mutations

Queries

```
query {
  retros {
    id
    name
    cards {
      id
      comment
      cardType
    }
  }
}
query {
  retro(retroId: "1") {
    id
    name
    cards {
      id
      comment
      cardType
    }
  }
}
query {
  cards(retroId: "1") {
    id
    comment
```

```
    cardType
  }
}
query {
  card(cardId: "1") {
    id
    comment
    cardType
  }
}
```

Mutations

```
mutation {
  createRetro(name: "Retro 1") {
    id
    name
  }
}
mutation {
  createCard(retroId: "1", card: {comment: "Great job team!", cardType: HAPPY}) {
    id
    comment
    cardType
  }
}
mutation {
  updateCard(cardId: "1", card: {comment: "Great job team!", cardType: HAPPY}) {
    id
    comment
    cardType
  }
}
  mutation {
    deleteCard(cardId: "1")
  }
```

Happy GraphQL!

Summary

In this appendix, you learned about GraphQL and how to use it with Spring for GraphQL and Spring Boot. You learned how to create queries and mutations. You also learned about the @QueryMapoping and @Muttation mapping annotations and how to create your GraphQL schema.

Index

E

F

G

T

U

Printed in the United States
by Baker & Taylor Publisher Services